FANNY STEVENSON
A Romance of Destiny

Alexandra Lapierre

FANNY STEVENSON

A Romance of Destiny

Translated from the French by Carol Cosman

Carroll & Graf Publishers, Inc.
New York

Originally published by Editions Robert Laffont, Paris

First Carroll & Graf edition 1995

Carroll & Graf Publishers, Inc.
260 Fifth Avenue
New York, NY 10001

Library of Congress Cataloging-in-Publication Data

Lapierre, Alexandra.
    [Fanny Stevenson. English]
    Fanny Stevenson : a romance of destiny / Alexandra Lapierre ;
translated by Carol Cosman. — 1st Carroll & Graf ed.
        p.   cm.
    Includes bibliographical references and index.
    ISBN 0-7867-0127-7 : $26.00 ($36.00 Can.)
    1. Stevenson, Fanny Van de Grift, 1840–1914.   2. Stevenson, Robert
Louis, 1850–1894—Marriage.   3. Women artists—United States—
Biography.   4. Authors' spouses—Scotland—Biography.
5. Americans—Europe—Biography.   I. Title.
PR5499.S1Z6713   1995
828'.809—dc20
    [B]   94-22424
                                                                         CIP

Text design by Terry McCabe

Manufactured in the United States of America

To J. C. F.

Acknowledgments

Unfortunately, I cannot thank all the people who helped me through this long, adventurous project. Without the emotional support of my family and my friends, without the collaboration of many correspondents, this book would never have been written.

I would like to express my gratitude especially to Danielle Guigonis, whose patience and quotidian competence sustained me in moments of doubt. Rina and Takis Anoussis and Colette Goujon in New York, Tony Guigonis and Emilia Rosa in Paris, Anna Rossi and Colin Smith in Rome, and Georges Tuiletufuga in Upolu must know how much I appreciated their help and kindness.

For their great patience and kindness I thank Paul and Manuela Andreota, Carole Hardouin, Sophie Lajeunesse, and Mathieu Meyer, who spent long hours correcting the original manuscript, and Carlos and Xavier Moro who accompanied me on my most arduous travels.

My warmest gratitude goes to the author of a remarkable biography of Robert Louis Stevenson, Mr. J. C. Furnas, who has been consistently supportive with his encouragement and his invaluable advice. I would also like to thank the "Stevensonians" of the world, who did not hesitate to take time out of their own work to answer my incessant questions. Heartfelt thanks go to Mr. Ernest Mehew in England; Mrs. Jenni Calder, Mr. David Daiches, Mr. Robin Hill in Scotland; Mr. Francis Lacassin in France; Mrs. Betty Lane, Mr. Barry Menikoff, Mr. Roger Swearingen, Mr. Robert E. Van Dyke, Mr. Dan Wakefield and Mr. Jim Winegar in the United States. And to the curators of two very important libraries with collections devoted to Robert Louis Stevenson, Mr. Vincent Giroud of the Beinecke Rare Book and Manuscript Library at Yale University, and the late Miss Ellen Shaffer of the Silverado Museum in St. Helena, who both showed me untiring generosity; without them, this book would not exist.

Many thanks go to the various libraries I used for being so accomodating, notably the Beinecke Rare Book and Manuscript Library, Yale University; the Silverado Museum, St. Helena, California; and the Bancroft Library, University of California, Berkeley, for generously allowing me to cite unpublished letters in their collections from Dora Williams, Fanny Stevenson, and Timothy Rearden. All my thanks go as well to the Archives of Hawaii, the Auckland Public Library, the Bishop Museum of Honolulu, the British Museum, the California Historical Society, the California State Library, the Danville Public Library, the Indiana State Historical Society Library, the Indiana State Library, Lady Stair's House, the Library of Congress, the Lily Library, the Monterey State Historic Park, the National Library of Australia, the National Library of Scotland, the Nevada State Historical Society, the Nevada State Museum, the New York Historical Library, the New York Public Library, the Oakland Public Library, the Pierpont Morgan Library, Princeton University Library, the Public Library of Western Samoa, the Robert Louis Stevenson Club of Scotland, the Sacramento History Center, the University of Hawaii at Manoa. And the embassy of Western Samoa in Brussels.

In citing passages from *This Life I've Loved* by Isobel Field (1937), I am grateful to Longman's Green & Co.; I would also like to thank Charles Scribner & Sons for permission to quote from *An Intimate Portrait of R. L. S.* by Lloyd Osbourne (1924), and Yale University Press for permission to use material from *Stevenson's Letters to Charles Baxter* (1956).

I want to thank my translator Carol Cosman for her great patience and her dedication to the task of putting this epic back in the language of Fanny Stevenson. I would also like to express my gratitude to my agent, Al Zuckerman.

Finally, my admiration and special affection go to my publisher Robert Laffont, to Bernard Fixot, Kent Carroll and their collaborators.

TABLE OF CONTENTS

Warning to the Reader

I lived with Fanny for five years, following her across the world, tracking her more than 60,000 miles. I visited all the places she had lived, except Davos, Bournemouth, and certain islands in the Pacific.

Many of the letters reproduced here are still unpublished. Some of them are a montage of two letters from the same period. The reader can be sure, however, that the facts conveyed here are strictly true, and will find indicated in the Notes the reasons for the few guesses I had to make when I could not be certain of what happened, as well as an explanation of my hypotheses and my choices.

My Wife

Trusty, dusky, vivid, true
With eyes of gold and bramble-dew,
Steel-true and blade-straight
The great artificer
Made my mate.

Honour, anger, valour, fire;
A love that life could never tire,
Death quench or evil stir,
The mighty master
Gave to her.

Teacher, tender comrade, wife,
A fellow-farer true through life,
Heart-whole and soul-free
The august father
Gave to me.

—Robert Louis Stevenson

FANNY STEVENSON
A Romance of Destiny

Prologue

Our Voices Mingled

*She was the only
woman in the world
worth dying for.*

Paris—1988

R.L.S.—it all began with those three initials: Robert Louis Stevenson.

I did not discover his most famous works in adolescence but long afterwards, when I found myself devouring, almost by chance, novels I would have loved to write myself, adventures I would have wanted to live. I buried myself in the work, avid and fascinated, as I compared notes and variants, and examined prefaces.

I quickly found the keys I was looking for. In every edition over the decades, whether in France, the United States, or Great Britain, it was always the same image of Stevenson: a writer of children's books, a courageous adventurer, an exemplary man. The fixed quality of this figure and its coherence invited me to explore further. Beyond the writer's loyalty to his friends, all the prefaces mentioned the presence of a woman at his side, only one, his wife. But here, the accounts diverged. Depending on the view, the great man's companion was a muse and a madonna, or a shrew and a virago; an adventuress or a petty bourgeois; an illiterate or a hussy; a blue-stocking or a profligate; demon or martyr. The passion spent in denouncing the influence of this woman amused me. The final dedication of the work Stevenson wrote the year of his death, in 1894, intrigued me:

To Fanny,
—Take thou the writing; thine it is. For who
Burnished the sword, blew on the drowsy coal,
Held still the target higher, chary of praise
And prodigal of counsel—who but thou?
So now, in the end, if this the least be good,

3

If any deed be done, if any fire
Burn in the imperfect page, the praise is thine.

What sort of woman deserved such praise from this writer? Our
encounter took five years of my life. I got off easily. All those
who knew Fanny Vandegrift spent their whole lives with her. More
barbaric, more baroque than anything I could have imagined, more
humane and more monstrous, this American woman embodies a
myth and a world in herself. If her intimacy with Robert Louis
Stevenson gives her a rightful place in his legend, her story goes
beyond the frame of a marriage to a celebrated man. She had lived
before she met him, and she continued to live after him. Witness
the memories of her last companion, the man who would close her
eyes the morning of her death, the young lover who would spend
the rest of his days in her shadow.

San Francisco—February 1914

Narrative by Ned Field (Edward Salisbury Field), illustrator, dramatist, and future screen writer of George Cukor's production of
Little Women.

She was the only woman in the world worth dying for.
The first time I saw her was eleven years ago, in January 1903,
in the shop of William Doxey, the avant-garde bookstore owner of
San Francisco. As I did every last Wednesday of the month, I was
there for my meeting with the layout editor and publishers of the
famous Overland Monthly. *The newspaper had offices on the second*
floor of the same building as Doxey on Market Street, and I was
worrying that my illustrations, caricatures, and comic strips would
once more be rejected as I stood leafing through some artistic mani-
festos. If the atmosphere of the offices of the Overland *newspaper*
still impressed me, the fin de siècle poses of the intellectuals who
frequented Doxey's left me cold. I was twenty-three years old, I
had just spent six months in Paris, and I thought I knew all the
excesses of bohemian life.
When the entrance bell of the shop rang, I did not deign to raise
my head. But from under my book I glimpsed a tiny foot shod in
a red ballet slipper agilely descending the three shaky stairs. Some-

thing quite coquettish in the twist of ribbons around the ankles, in the fall of lace and silk on the leg excited me enormously. My God, it was the most impertinent foot I'd seen since the little boots of the ladies at the Moulin Rouge.

As a young woman she must have been pretty, by this time she was beautiful.

With her ample, stiff dress, without waist or corset, her barbarous jewelry, her extraordinary crown of wiry, gray curls cut short, and her heavy, fixed gaze, she was reminiscent of a tropical plant, a world of lilies, of vines and flowers—intense and vivacious, ageless and nameless.

Despite her somewhat precious manners, her slight plumpness and small size—she stood barely five feet tall—this woman exuded a scent of savagery, and I remember telling myself that the creature must have had mysterious powers that ought not to be toyed with. Furthermore, she was infinitely modest and feminine in her way of greeting Doxey, who fell all over himself to welcome her, while she implored him in a low, uninflected voice not to trouble himself, to stop drawing attention to her, to take her to the back office. She put the graceful hand of a little boy on the bookseller's sleeve. They crossed the shop, and I saw passing beneath the whimsical plumes of her hat an amber, Napoleonic profile, with no hint of a smile. The door closed behind them. An emptiness, a silence descended over the shop. A long moment of stupor.

"Good Lord!" exclaimed a customer. "Who was that?"

The double impression of extravagance and timidity, the mixture of modesty, which seemed almost excessive in this woman, and the dramatic intensity of her self-presentation, the insistence, the near violence of her gaze, that vital force which emanated from her, raw and disordered, both distressed and intrigued us all, and the men's eyes remained riveted to the office door. In twenty years, allowing that she was still in this world in twenty years, I knew that I would be able to recognize this woman from the back, at night, in near darkness.

"Excuse me," I pressed the cashier, "but who was that?"

"My mother," a singing voice answered behind me which I recognized as that of Belle Strong.

This woman, to whom I had occasionally spoken, worked periodically for Doxey, crossing the world in search of first editions of American authors. Cosmopolitan and divorced, she had seemed to *me rather piquant, and I was charmed by the spontaneity of her talk, her flirtatious glances, her swaying walk, her quick and bounding laughter—very much a "bird of the islands." But someplace in Hawaii or Australia, Belle Strong had a son who, like me, was seeking to make a name for himself, a son my own age—in short, Belle must have been in her mid-forties.*

"My mother," she repeated, without concealing her pride, "Mrs. Stevenson." And as I did not react, she emphasized: The Strange Case of Dr. Jekyll and Mr. Hyde *. . . R. L. S."*

"His wife?"

"His widow."

The surprising thing is that I had kept the address of Mrs. Robert Louis Stevenson in my wallet for six months now, and had not spent a day in San Francisco without hearing about her. Her many adventures, her voyages, her scandals, her relationship with one of the most admired writers of her generation provided material for endless articles, literary gossip, vulgar tattle, and I had always had difficulty reconciling on the same canvas, in the same portrait, the lines of these thousand figures projected in my imagination. None conformed to the one I had just glimpsed.

I had come across the rude pioneer of the Far West, the gold seeker of American legend. Perched on her wagon in the Nevada deserts, her Winchester on her knees, her man's gold nuggets in her pockets . . . It was difficult, however, very difficult to visualize the subtle and flamboyant person at Doxey's in a dusty cotton coat and calico skirt, flinging herself, along with a whole convoy of prospectors, into the mines of Virginia City. I had also encountered descriptions of an artist painter of the Barbizon School during the torched Paris of the Commune, penniless rival of Corot, student with Marie Bashkirtseff at the Academie Julian. And I had been told the story of a cacao planter on a Samoan island, who had dared to support the rights of the natives against the interests of the Whites . . .

And all these figures, all these faces were scrambled in my mind with the names of all those whom the wife of Robert Louis Stevenson had loved: her husbands, her children, her friends—the king of Hawaii, the poor cook in Monterey, Henry James; as well as with the names, equally celebrated and obscure, of those Mrs. Stevenson had hated. In order to complete the confusion of my images, she was an old classmate of my mother and the only person from

Indianapolis who might further my interests in the world. When I had left Los Angeles, where my family had settled, to live in San Francisco, my parents had strongly advised me to pay her a visit. Although they had lost sight of her forty years before, they had written to announce my arrival and begged her to look after me. Out of shyness or a refusal to visit any Indiana natives when in California, I had put off my visit from one day to the next.

But the following day, March 8, 1903, found me at ten o'clock on the top of Telegraph Hill, at the corner of Hyde and Lombard streets, before an enormous house with a rough, white exterior built like a fortress overlooking the Pacific.

I hadn't any presentiment, any suspicion, nothing. Not the slightest intuition that in slipping behind the curtain of trees that completely concealed the stairway from the sight of the street, I was toying with my fate. However, I was moved—and I had reason to be. Entering here, I was penetrating into the sanctuary of the hero of my youth. Robert Louis Stevenson, the master of Treasure Island, the adventurer who had lived his dreams and had built a realm somewhere in the South Seas. I was going to meet the beloved woman he had pursued across a continent, the wife for whom he had risked everything—scandal, poverty, and illness. His friend, his muse, his judge: this was the formidable siren from Doxey's ... There was something in this to exalt the most blasé Lothario of twenty-three. But to imagine that after going through this door I would never leave this woman's side, for even a single day, for the next eleven years, that every moment near her would always be the most intense, often the most amusing of my existence, and that together we would roam through Europe, explore Mexico, build three houses, plant parks—impossible!

On that day in March 1903, on the platform that then served as the front steps to Fanny Stevenson's fortress, I remember facing away from the house a moment. Below me, at the end of the straight street that descended sharply to the sea, a schooner appeared. Its sails silently skirted the red rocks of Alcatraz Island, the horizon rose up, round, heavy and oily, and I contemplated the ocean with an astonished gladness, as if I were looking at the Pacific for the first time.

"My life," she would tell me that morning, not without humor, "my life, young man, resembles a wild ride on the crest of a wave that rolls on and never breaks."

How can I accept that today, Wednesday, February 18, 1914, I closed her eyes for the last time? She was seventy-four years old, and I thought she was immortal. Let us be clear, I am neither a dreamer nor an innocent. Nor, contrary to slanderous comments, a sponger. And, with all deference to Mrs. Stevenson's heirs, I am not a gigolo either.

For someone who refuses mediocrity, Fanny was simply the only woman in the world. To have known her, to have loved her, would have given meaning enough to a man's life. But to have been loved by her!

*
**

Here Ned Field's narration ends. Are these three pages a sketch for an obituary? The beginning of a biography?

When I, too, fell in love with Robert Louis Stevenson's work and set out to find "Fanny," the wife cited in all the prefaces to all the editions since 1901, and found in California the archives of the man who had been her secretary, and to all appearances her last lover, I was overwhelmed. Here was material for an exhaustive inquiry, the work of a lifetime, the work that Ned Field never wrote. Interviews with Fanny Stevenson's family and friends, piles of correspondence, press clippings, photographs—he had assembled everything.

His notebooks, my notes, his readings, my travels mingled together in the end. In pursuing Fanny, we were on the same quest. We shared the same vision. To evoke today this woman whom he had so deeply loved, I can only borrow Ned's eyes and voice. He had preferred to remain silent. I choose to tell. But was there a special reason for his silence? On August 29, 1914, six months after Mrs. Stevenson's death, Ned Field bound himself as tightly as possible to her memory. He married her double—her daughter—the Mrs. Belle Strong he mentions at Doxey's bookstore.

Belle was then fifty-six years old. He was thirty-four. She resembled Fanny feature for feature. Half a century younger than the one, several decades younger than the other, Ned Field would find happiness with both generations.

His extraordinary adventure does not end there.

Ned had previously advised Mrs. Stevenson to invest her deceased husband's royalties in property, and made her buy several parcels of land around Los Angeles. Belle inherited these properties. In 1921, oil was discovered on them. Belle and Ned became millionaires, and one of the strangest—and richest—couples in the Hollywood of the Roaring Twenties. That is, until Ned's death on the evening of Belle's seventy-eighth birthday. Mrs. Field survived her young husband by another fifteen years, just as Fanny had survived Stevenson.

These two women exercised strange powers over the same men, and we find mysterious echoes from one life to the other. Repetitions, coincidences.

Mother and daughter were married a first time, divorced, and lost their younger sons, who bore the same name. They had studied painting with the same teachers, shared the same friends, sailed through the same tropics. They had both fervently loved and understood the Polynesia they had to leave together.

Here ends an intriguing communion.

Belle had lived her life through her mother. But Fanny had lived hers through her lover, Robert Louis Stevenson.

For him, to save him from the death that stalked him, she defied fate for fifteen years. Belle would never have suspected Fanny's constancy, her violence, the extent of her contradictions and her despair.

"Heart-whole and soul-free," Robert Louis Stevenson wrote, speaking of his wife. With a free soul and wholeheartedly, Fanny sacrificed her tastes to Stevenson, her needs, even her own health. But she renounced nothing. Not for a moment did she lose sight of herself. She worked without respite for the realization of her most intimate need.

"No man is of any use till he has dared everything," Stevenson notes in setting off to pursue her across a whole continent.

To surpass her own limits, to drown herself in the love of another, to travel far away and to the very ends of her own being—Fanny embraced that adventure. In her, hope had conquered fear.

She remains, in the eyes of those who loved her, the woman who dared.

Part One

The Sphinx
1864–1875

I

Jacob's Daughter

A mine is a hole in the ground
that belongs to a liar.

—Mark Twain

Indianapolis, May 1864

When I think of the twenty-three-year-old Fanny leaving in silence a family she adored to cross the world with little hope of return, I feel a rush of pity, a pity all the more surprising because as an old woman she no longer elicited such sentiments. She was too secretive and too dignified. In ten years, I do not think Ned heard her complain a single time, or express any regret for the past. She pronounced no final judgments, either on the circumstances of her life or on the motives for her actions. It was impossible to get her to talk about herself.

Ned wrote in his notes that if he happened to question her about herself, her appearance, her state of mind, her dreams at the age of twenty, Fanny would shrug her shoulders . . . Or she would be evasive and dwell on the scenery of her travels. But from all the worlds she carried within her, Fanny remained resolutely absent. She knew how to portray her relations with others vividly in a word—a harsh, sarcastic, or tender word; and she could remember the most insignificant creature who had crossed her path. She conveyed such violent affection and antipathy for those long gone that Ned, without having known them, ended by taking sides. But about "Fanny," nothing, not a word. She was stony, mute, as she'd had to be in her youth. What did she feel, leaving Indiana for the first time? Fear? Anger? Regret? Or was she impatient and eager for adventure? What was she looking for at the other end of the continent? A vague, sphinxlike smile floated on her closed lips. Not a gesture, not a word: was this modesty or humility? Did she even know what she was feeling? Yet Fanny had believed only in feelings. No one had ever surrendered to her emotions with less restraint. No one had followed her instincts more impudently, more impulsively, to the very end, yet it seemed impossible for her to tell her own story. Immersed in living her vividly felt life, Fanny had probably forgotten all about herself. Fortunately, others kept engraved in their memories the image of the young girl in a yellow cape saying good-bye to a happy childhood on the platform of the Indianapolis railroad station.

I see her that day in May 1864, tiny and fragile in her short, ruffled "walking skirt," worn over a mustard-colored underskirt and ankle boots, her hat ribbons tied under her chin, her purse gripped tightly in her fist.

"It's so hard to leave you . . ." she had murmured, looking up at her father. "So hard that I'm afraid I won't be able to go."

He had pulled her against him without answering.

Indifferent to the travelers hurrying along the platform, to the dogs sniffing at the trunks, to the poultry quacking and clucking in their baskets, they stood embracing in the sunshine, at the foot of the water tank.

Standing at some distance, under the roof of the train shed, Mrs. Vandegrift, Fanny's mother, watched them. Her lips trembling, her small person crushed by the heap of bundles, she was waiting for their good-byes to end, holding the hand of a little girl of six who was straining to run down the track. Along the length of the train stood Fanny's four sisters, her young brother Jake, and her childhood friends. They were escorting the trunks to the baggage car, tramping down the corridors of the train cars, depositing the hatbox, the toy bag, the picnic basket, the bouquet of tiger lilies on Fanny's seat. They came and went, passing Fanny without a word, without looking at her, without signaling their affection. Each of them accepted the privileged intimacy of father and daughter. There was total understanding between them. Jacob Vandegrift's educational principles had won his children's warm affection, as well as the comments of his neighbors. Firmly believing that a good nature remains good, and that a bad one remains bad, he had chosen not to intervene in the children's development. He allowed instinct to rule them.

Yet this was the era of strict child rearing: "Spare the rod and spoil the child." Some claimed that Jacob's five daughters were proud, insolent, their heads in the clouds, and poor housekeepers besides. In a word, unmarriageable. Others observed that the sisters' demeanor seemed to attract all the young men in the county, that the two older sisters had married at sixteen; that the sons-in-law—very suitable—had set up housekeeping with their in-laws; that despite the Civil War, or perhaps because of it, the boys of Danville, Clayton, and Indianapolis continued to visit. The Vandegrifts' door was always open, and a visitor could stay for one day or fifteen; their parlor even served as a meeting place for the Universalists, who had not finished building their church. At Christmas, at Thanksgiving, on neighbors' birthdays, on cousins' betrothals, the long oak table was laden with cream, cider, and hot apple pies, and they danced all night to Jake's violin. In summer, at the first light of dawn, they ate a breakfast of waffles and maple syrup on the sloping lawn. In winter, they raced their sleds between the trees of the little wood that reached down to the turn in the road. Those who took a spill at the foot of the trees could see the names of the boys who had fallen before them, Alex, Tom, Dan, with hearts carved in the bark, and the initials F.V., Fanny Vandegrift, the oldest of Jacob's daughters.

Besieged by so many admirers, she was now married and the mother of a little girl. She was twenty-three years old. She looked fifteen.

With her amber skin, her hair twisted into a braid, the frizzy tendrils, damp with humidity, escaping everywhere on her forehead, her temples, her neck, her eyes the color of blackberries and her gold earrings, she looked like a gypsy. For a long time she had thought she was ugly. According to Victorian standards of fashion, a pretty girl had to have fair skin and straight blond hair. In the futile hope of protecting herself from the sun, Fanny had worn bonnets glued to her head until the age of twelve, and every day she had rubbed her hands, her face, and her neck with a disgusting concoction that smelled so bad she wanted to vomit. But today she took revenge by defying all the rules. Since her marriage she wore only bright colors, blood red, mustard, and bold blue that set off her dark skin. She preferred colorful glass beads and scoffed at hats.

Jacob's education had had the clearest consequences on the temperament of his oldest daughter. Having never been contradicted or even vaguely directed, she had developed in all directions, disorderly and richly layered, like a wild plant, sure of herself, spontaneous, dominating, incapable of the slightest calculation, and also incapable of self-scrutiny. Introspection and study were not her strength, school had scarcely had any place in her life.

Yet Fanny had been one of those children whom teachers and schoolmates would always remember. She did what she liked with more passion than the others—she loved to paint and tell stories, and her utterly unbridled imagination enjoyed the bizarre and the tragic; she had a sense of humor, and her caricatures, her anecdotal drawings, and compositions delighted the whole class. She knew how to dramatize daily life and to make a good story out of a dull subject for composition. Facts and dates meant little to her. A passerby became a conspirator, all her princesses were ghosts. She aimed at effect, was not stingy with superlatives, and the other students begged her to read her homework aloud. She did it without affectation. She loved to scare herself. She loved to make a strong impression. Otherwise, Fanny spoke very little. She had inherited from her mother a taste for silence and secrecy.

Instinctively she felt part of the earth. She knew the names of trees, flowers, wild fruit; she planted, groomed and rode horses, trained dogs better than anyone. Perfectly at ease in the material world, Fanny was not satisfied. In this she differed from her father.

He had bequeathed her his violence and his generosity, a fundamentally quarrelsome temperament, and a clear penchant for lost causes, for championing the weak and the oppressed. This "protective" side of their common nature concealed a certain internal fragility. Beneath Jacob's massive shoulders and intense blue eyes Fanny perceived a weakness that touched her deeply. She revered her father. It was she who acted as manager of the family property. The farm was not profitable, but it was self-sufficient: Fanny's vegetables, her trees, her sheep, her poultry fed, clothed, and provided furnishings for the eight Vandegrifts. There were few luxuries but little want. Jacob was not a peasant and hardly worried about selling his crops. He owned a lumber company in town that provided wood for housing and fuel for the trains of the Vandalia Railroad through Indiana.

The steam engine began to snort. The water tank hose was being pulled back up. Time was running out.

"I have given your name to all the stationmasters," he murmured in her ear without letting her go. "You ought to travel comfortably at least as far as New York. Afterwards . . ."

Afterwards, Jacob knew, he would lose all control over Fanny's well-being and survival. She was going to set off with her little girl on a journey down the Atlantic by ship to Aspinwall, Panama, overland across the isthmus, then through the Pacific to San Francisco and into the back country bloodied by the Indian wars. The East-West railroad would not be completed until 1869, five years hence, so the two American coasts had not yet been brought together. To reach California without going by covered wagon or stagecoach across a whole continent of mountains, plains, and deserts, the "Panama route" was the alternative. Everyone preferred to forget that two ships running bodies and goods had just been lost at sea, that dysentery, yellow fever, and cholera usually killed off more than a quarter of the passengers, and that children had almost no resistance to the "Panama fevers."

Jacob looked anxiously at little Belle who was shouting with joy at being passed from arm to arm under the station roof. The family had regrouped around the mother, Mrs. Vandegrift, and Fanny's sisters were playing with their niece a last time.

"Are you sure you have enough money?"

"Oh yes! Don't worry, I've got quite enough."

To undertake this trip, Fanny had sold all her belongings. She had sold the house her father had given her as a marriage gift, she had cashed in her dowry by ceding her part of the inheritance to her sisters. Jacob did not know, however, that while his daughter had no more possessions in Indiana, she had no cash at her disposal either. As requested by Sam, she had sent everything out West, where he had already spent it. She was leaving for the end of the world short of funds.

"It's time, my dear, go kiss your mother."

*

Half leaning out the window, she had watched their familiar figures disappear at the end of the platform.

Anguish caught in her throat, weighed on her chest. She was so heartsick she could not cry. So heartsick and so afraid. How would she live without them, without her mother's gentleness, without Betty, without Cora, without Jake, without Nellie? How would she live without Jo, her constant companion, her junior by two years, pregnant and widowed now, who needed her so? The images of her lost happiness passed before her dry eyes. In the flat plain, along the iron track, she saw Jo again at thirteen on her old pony, as she galloped ahead with George Marshall. Jo was probably in love with George even then, just as George was with Fanny, and Fanny with Sam Osbourne. Family legend had it that Sam and Fanny had fallen in love at first sight.

Originally from Kentucky, Sam Osbourne had done some legal studies and then served as personal secretary to the governor of Indiana. As soon as he arrived in town, he had come to present himself to the Vandegrifts, whose lumber business was across a square from the house. Jo liked to describe how Fanny, always a tomboy, was ambling around the garden on stilts when Lieutenant Osbourne, buttoned up tight in his uniform, had pushed open the gate. She had observed him with that intense stare of hers that seemed, like Jacob's, to pin you to the wall. "Jo," she had announced, in her grand manner, "you can have Marshall, I'll take Osbourne." She was sixteen, he was eighteen. They were married on Christmas Eve 1857. It was a child marriage, and a happy one— until the Civil War.

Carried away by the patriotic zeal that moved the North against the secessionist states, Sam Osbourne and George Marshall volunteered to defend the Union. For two years they fought on the Yankee side, in the same company. The two boys came home captains. Fanny could have had no idea of their sufferings.

On January 15, 1863, five years after Sam and Fanny's marriage, George married Jo. But the two homes were not happy now. In the Union Army George had contracted tuberculosis. Indiana's rains made it worse. Only the California climate could save him. Sam, emotionally inaccessible since the war, had borrowed 1,200 dollars to take his brother-in-law to San Francisco, settle him in a mild climate, and come home. On January 20, a stormy day, the two friends had embarked on the *Ocean Queen*. The exhausting crossing, scurvy, and fevers finished what the dampness of the army encampments had begun: George Marshall died on the 23rd. He was buried in one of the numerous cemeteries on the Isthmus of Panama.

Then Fanny received the letter telling her that Sam would not be coming home. He asked her to dissolve all their assets, to leave her parents, embark with their little girl, and follow him. She had obeyed, despairing, but without a moment's hesitation. If the eldest of the Vandegrift's daughters revered her father, she worshipped her husband. The war in which he had volunteered to fight, his decision to accompany George to California after such a prolonged absence, had not diminished Fanny's devotion. She loved Sam as she loved Jacob, with a violent and passionate loyalty, a trust in whose name she unconditionally accepted any sacrifice, even her own happiness.

She was going to join him.

Never mind that Sam Osbourne had spent his wife's dowry and all their savings to buy a hole in the ground somewhere in the Sierra Nevada. With the touching faith of a prospector's wife, Fanny called this hole a "silver mine."

New York, Reunion House on 10 West Street, April 1864

My dearest Jo,

It was impossible to write you in the train: for five days we were shaken, shoved and kneaded like a bunch of bones in a sack. By the time you receive this letter, around the 21st of this month, we will, I hope, be grilling under the Panama sun. A triumphal journey to New York—except that the ticket collector did not accept the free pass Papa obtained for me from the directors of the Vandalia. That nasty brute made me pay for my seat, plus a fine! Wait, that's not all. At Dayton, a change of trains, a change of ticket collector. I answer (politely) to the new brute who demands the price of my passage that his predecessor relieved me of thirteen dollars, and kept my ticket.

"No ticket, no journey."

I explode. He throws my baggage on the track. I ask everyone in the wagon to witness. The passengers stand. There is a riot.

"Inadmissible!" shouts my neighbor, a certain Mr. Hill (I will tell you about him). I saw this young lady pay for her ticket. Everyone saw it . . ."

"That is not my concern, she pays or I throw her out."

And he dragged me to the platform!

The next train comes through on Monday, I caught myself and changed tactics:

"Twenty-six dollars? Oh, Mr. Ticket Collector, that is more than half my budget for the entire trip. And I am going to California, on the way through Panama!"

"That is not my concern. People should not travel without money in their pockets. Especially women . . ."

Up there he looks at Belle, who was clinging to my skirt, repeating: "Slave driver—tyrant—Confederate . . ."

"Madam, that child speaks too well for her age. She must be older than five. You are going to pay me thirteen dollars for you, and thirteen dollars for her."

In short, Jo, Papa's Railroad swindled me out of thirty-nine dollars . . . But don't panic, I got back fifteen of them. Mr. Hill organized a little collection for me amongst the passengers. And believe me, I was quite proper: I began by refusing. Do not tell this to our folks. It's useless to worry them. Poor dear Papa. In the envelope he gave me as we parted, I found Uncle Knodle's wonderful pistol, the pocket derringer with the ivory cross, and the most moving letter: "Watch out for the riff-raff, my dear. The Far West is a promising country, but dangerous. I fear that you will find life there very different from what you have known. You are going to encounter the best and the worst. I know you are courageous, Fanny. Be careful!" Perhaps, Jo, we are going to return to you very rich! Sam said that the Nevada veins had provided gold for all the Union Army. Millions and millions of dollars. Sam said that it was only thanks to the richness of the mines that the North had been able to pay for the war, thanks to them that we are going to conquer the confederates. He said that in San Francisco, the prospectors have diamond buttons on their shirts, that their women take baths in champagne, that their houses in white marble are like pieces of sculpture. If our mine yields a hundred thousand dollars a month, like those of Sam's friends, we will visit Europe all together, what do you say to that? . . . I am letting myself go, my dear Jo, it is my stupid way of overcoming my sadness. Take good care of yourself and the baby, I would have so liked to be with you for the birth! Take good care of Papa. I miss you all so much! I feel like I've been gone forever. You will tell me if the tulips have taken. I hope that the begonias are going to do something. I would love to know how the huckleberries I planted are coming along.

This idea of huckleberries makes my mouth water. I am stuffing Belle with pine nuts we bought from the Indians at the stations, but she woke up three times this night, repeating: "I am hungry, Mama." I don't dare spend anything more until Panama. They are going to ask for eighty dollars, and twenty-five cents per pound of luggage for crossing the Isthmus. We absolutely have to economize—because "my girl," as Papa would say, "my girl, we are not there yet!"

With her nerve and her modesty, with that magnificent youthful intrepidness that her enemies would one day call a "schoolgirl's blitheness," what Fanny did not say was that she had not eaten in three days, that she was writing from a room overrun with rats, and that a storm had been ravaging the port of New York for two days.

The steamer had waited long enough: With 730 passengers, including forty women and sixty children, the *Iroquois* would get underway the next day on rough seas.

Aspinwall, Panama—May 1864

"Mama, I'm hot."

Not a breath of air stirred, and the steam rising from the swamp shrouded the port in a gray, nauseating cloud.

"I'm hot," Belle repeated.

Fanny lifted the fretful child's damp cheek from her chest. Squeezed together in the same hammock, they were vainly trying to get some sleep somewhere in the vague area that served as the backyard of the Union Hotel. All around them posts bristled in the night like a forest of burnt stumps, and huge chrysalis shapes swung moaning between the posts, covered by waves of mosquitos. These were the hundred hammocks in which the other passengers from the *Iroquois* tossed and turned after their arrival that morning. The first-class travelers who had managed to find a bed were resting in shaded quarters behind the balconies on the first floor.

For fifteen years now, since the time of the Gold Rush, the New

York shipping companies had continued their runs to the Isthmus of Panama's Atlantic coast, where they unceremoniously discharged an average of a thousand people per week and promptly returned for more. Ordinarily the travelers never spent more than one night in Aspinwall. At dawn they would pile into a local train that took six to eight hours to cross the Isthmus. After they arrived in Panama City, they could embark the following day on the slow journey to California. The voyage through the Pacific from Panama City to San Francisco then took fifteen days. But this time, God only knew if they would ever sail. The *Saint Louis* had not arrived on the other side of the Isthmus. Furthermore, the railroad company was taking advantage of the panic among the travelers by charging five times the price of passage overland to Panama City. No money, no train ticket. Those who could not pay the exorbitant price would be stranded on the Atlantic coast, crowded by the thousands in this sinkhole where they were rotting away in the tropical filth.

Fanny's brother-in-law and childhood friend George Marshall had died here, she was sure of it when she saw the bay. Yet there was nothing oppressive in those wooded, greenish-yellow, mossy hills that sloped gently down to the breakers. A flotilla of native fishing boats flecked a lagoon that lay golden in the burning sun. The masts of three American sailing ships pitched at the far ends of three breakwaters that barred the slack sea in long, parallel lines. Perpendicular to the jetties ran the railroad tracks. From the piers to the depots, from the depots to the station, from the station to the sailing ships, two lines of stevedores with backs bent, only their hats and white trousers visible, carried, pushed, and pulled huge red cargo bales on hand carts or blue wheelbarrows.

During the last six days of the crossing, the mood on the *Iroquois* had swung between a narrow stiffness and an almost promiscuous excitement. After passing Santo Domingo, something unheard of had happened: gentlemen traveling in first class played cards with men from second class, and immigrants from steerage appeared half naked in the sun between-decks. The heat grew more intense by the hour, and soon gloves, underskirts, crinolines, and corsets were shed and packed away. Fashion and convention went out the window as they arrived in the tropics. However, the first consideration was decency and conformity, propriety and precedence. Unlike the men, the forty female passengers did not mingle between decks. Their modesty, their affectation, their snobbery were their last

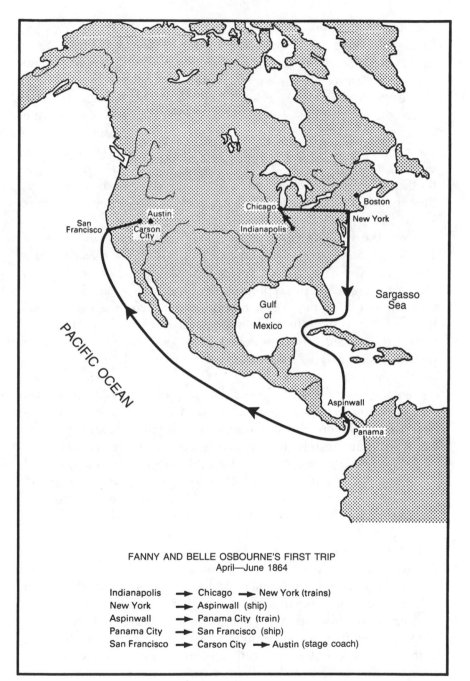

FANNY AND BELLE OSBOURNE'S FIRST TRIP
April—June 1864

Indianapolis ➡ Chicago ➡ New York (trains)
New York ➡ Aspinwall (ship)
Aspinwall ➡ Panama City (train)
Panama City ➡ San Francisco (ship)
San Francisco ➡ Carson City ➡ Austin (stage coach)

anchors in this sea of shifting values. They tried to regroup, furiously seeking out the company of their equals, but this was not an easy task, made all the more difficult as they themselves came from many social classes and their signposts were now confused. Bourgeois or peasants, Americans by birth or new immigrants, they shared the same dream—to make their fortune—and all of them were following a man in the grip of gold fever. Like Fanny, they were young, mostly married, mothers with one or two children. The difference was that they were not crossing the world unescorted. A brother, a cousin, an older son, a lover, usually a husband acted as their guardian, at least as far as California. Once there, the rules would change.

From the first, the absence of a male escort had conferred on Fanny and her daughter a unique status, so unique that despite a storm in New York Harbor the crossing had seemed like a marvelous cruise. With no prompting, the cabin steward had raised them to first class, the doctor had cared for them, the captain had invited them to share his table nearly every evening. Mr. Hill, their traveling companion, had watched over their every comfort with paternal zeal, and all these gentlemen vied with each other to amuse and protect them.

Fanny's freshness, her silences, her lack of affectation often had this effect on men. All they had to do was look at her, tiny and very straight before the vast ocean, her daughter laughing in her arms, and immediately they wanted to act as a buffer between her and the world. She knew it. She took advantage of it. She accepted all invitations, all gifts, all help with grace and simplicity—no greed, no tricks, and not an ounce of naiveté. If someone wanted to help her, fine! What could be better? But she expected nothing from Mr. Hill or anyone else, and indeed she wouldn't have thought to ask. Yet she was happy to adapt herself to their image of her. Because she was secretive, silent, and something of a chameleon, she seemed like a helpless child. In her presence most of the men felt an emotion tinged with admiration that Mr. Hill always translated into the remark: "There goes a brave little woman!" Unprejudiced by class or fortune, she paced all the decks, shot dice with the sailors, fraternized with the crew. Her seductive powers never ceased to amaze the ladies, whatever their class. They saw nothing touching in that dark profile; nothing vulnerable in her steady, self-containment; nothing very feminine in that graceful body, which was slim perhaps, but too nervous and too firm. Fanny's charm never would be obvious to other women. A certain reciprocated antipathy would always characterize her relations with her female peers. With the exception of her mother and sisters, whom she admired, Jacob's daughter was indifferent to other women. But not so indifferent that she would endure their slights or assaults. Fanny had an avenging arm, and in the family she had the reputation of bearing a savage grudge. She could hate as faithfully as she loved.

She had no sooner disembarked at Aspinwall than she set out to find the cemetery where she imagined George Marshall was buried. Without worrying about her trunks, which had been piled on top of each other at random, without haggling over a high-priced room, Fanny set off down the main street, threading her way, her daughter in tow, between the slums and brothels, the billiard parlors and gambling dens. Then she crossed the iron track along the seafront and the sheds where rows of bananas, coconuts, heaps of coral, and vegetable ivory awaited shipment to New York, baking under roofs of corrugated metal. In this way she reached the second main street of the town. Cabins built on pilings to escape the snakes were lined up one after the other, each with its rows of balconies. The ground floors, open to the weather, served as storerooms for the heaps of baggage the travelers hoped to transport across the Isthmus; the first floors served as hotels. There, in the heart of the village, stood two stagnant ponds, former tide pools that had been cut off from the sea with the construction of the railroad. All sorts of refuse floated in them, rags, coconut leaves, dead fish and monkeys, even pack mules decomposing in a suffocating odor of rotting flesh.

The vapors from these ponds killed off several native families every week. You did not have to succumb on the spot. Four of the travelers from the *Iroquois* who had already visited Panama had died at sea as they approached the tropics. Even the lucky ones, who thought they had escaped the famous "Aspinwall fevers," would have bouts of malaria all their lives.

Gagging on the stench, Belle had begun to cry. Just in front of them, at the entrance of the Union Hotel, three vultures were tearing apart a sea turtle. The hem of the child's little lace panties was soaked in a greenish liquid. Fanny had seized her daughter around the waist and continued quickly toward the interior of the village. With her free hand she had raised the hoop of her ample red skirt up to her knees, revealing her white stockings and the tops of her ankle boots. Her train dragged in the mud. Newly gloved, corseted, and hatted for the landing, like all the female passengers, she presented a powerful contrast to the Indian women crouched on their doorsteps, their dresses rolled up to their hips who watched her pass while kneading pastel muslin in iron buckets. Under the black mesh of her short veil, Fanny's eyes lingered, leapt away and returned to those pendulous breasts, naked and glistening.

She came to the end of the street. There, at the edge of the equatorial forest, lay the cemetery. It was an enormous white graveyard, where tombs and crosses were laid out in an orderly fashion between four walls. Alas, the nauseating odor persisted in this necropolis solidified by the heat and laced with filth, with the noise and ferment of the port. Yet a peace such as Fanny had never known settled over the dead.

She set her daughter down and walked through the transverse row without taking her eyes off the trees of the surrounding forest, whose hairy vines clung to the walls and took root in the graves. She felt someone's eyes were watching her. Belle must have shared this impression because she followed her mother carefully, keeping her face under her big straw hat raised toward the fleecy sky.

The piercing cry of a parrot rent the silence. The child grabbed her mother's hand. And then from every side came a tide of insults, the cries of thousands of monkeys washed over them, a piercing, menacing clamor that nailed them among the gravestones, tiny red dots in the midst of this white vastness. Peace descended once again, even more oppressive.

They had no trouble finding what they were looking for. Fanny's husband Sam had forgotten to specify the name and place of the cemetery, but his letter provided topographical clues for finding the grave: off the central path, third to the right, last cross. It was there. Fanny's intuition had not misled her. CAPTAIN GEORGE MARSHALL. 1836–1864.

The plaster was already crumbling, weeds pushing up through the cracks. The grave, raised by tropical vines, covered with ivy, was disappearing.

"Say a prayer, Belle."

Without much feeling for this uncle she'd hardly known, the little girl put her hands together and kept her head down for some time. When she rose, she was surprised to see her mother's face wet with tears. This was the first time Belle had seen Fanny weep.

She was weeping with pity, with regret for her playmate, her first flirtation. She was weeping for Sam, who had buried his beloved friend here, alone. She was weeping for her sister Jo, whose life was shattered by this grave. She was weeping for their youth.

When she had married, Fanny was still a child. She had not yet grown up when she brought Belle into the world, or even when she parted from her father under the water tank at the Indianapolis train station. It was here and now that she was putting her childhood behind her, and she knew it.

*
**

"We'll all die here, we'll never get to California."

These words, whispered among the travelers as they tried in vain to light a campfire, spread like wildfire from one hammock to another. "We'll all die here." An icy rain had fallen that evening. The wood did not catch. Clothing stuck to their skin. Despite the heat, or because of it, they could not get dry. They were cold, they were stifling. Panic was rising. No one had been able to sleep for four nights. They could hear the fever victims chattering, moaning and delirious in their hammocks. The woman next to Fanny was sobbing. From the hovels on the beach came the cries of men playing cards and drinking. Fanny had stopped her daughter from quenching her thirst with the dirty water distributed among the travelers each evening at sundown. In his letter, Sam had strongly advised them not to touch the water. She was following his instructions to the letter, buying Belle boiled drinks, tea or coffee, which excited the child without quenching her thirst. For herself, Fanny purchased a cup of coconut liquor, the local rotgut. It was less expensive, much less expensive, than a meal, but she was always slightly drunk and had been like this since her visit to the cemetery nearly a week ago. Even if the price of the ticket across the Isthmus were lowered, she no longer had the necessary twenty-four dollars. Between renting a hammock and procuring food, her money had dwindled away. Food? Hardly! Aspinwall could not meet the needs of all these visitors facing the prolonged wait. Other passengers might disembark from New York at any moment. And while the natives made raids on the baggage and the Yankee merchants raised their already steep tariffs, the passengers of the *Iroquois* ate iguana, raw monkey, and peeled fruit at the warehouses, which gave them diarrhea. All they could think of was getting out of there, at any price. But how? Fanny could no longer count on the help of her admirers. The "rich," who had agreed to spend all their liquid assets at once, had embarked on the first and only train running the forty-seven miles from East to West. The others, those who couldn't pay, like Fanny, ran the risk of missing the boat. Providing it ever arrived, the *Saint Louis* could take on only 1,200 persons; there were already 2,000 waiting in Panama City. Surely Jacob Vandegrift had booked a cabin, he had certainly cabled the 600 dollars for the crossing to the California company. But what good were his dollars if Fanny was not at the port, ready to take the steamer?

For the hundredth time she left the Union Hotel, skirted the ponds, walked along the railroad tracks, and went into the shed that served as a station. Belle tottered after her. It must have been midnight, perhaps later. Here the hours became confused. They slept in the afternoon and wandered about at night. "Papa," moaned the child, half asleep, "Papa." Like Belle, Fanny craved Sam. Only the idea of being with him at last allowed her to conquer her daily fear of dying in Aspinwall. She had decided to find the stationmaster this evening. She was going to coax him, seduce him, force him to charter a train to Panama, just for her.

She knew these places. She had cooled her heels for two days right under the metal roof of this red hot "waiting room." There was no one to give her any information, and not a bench or chair to sit on. But at night the room seemed less barren, less filthy, and Belle curled up in a corner. Fanny looked worriedly at her child settled there on the floor. She searched for the coiled snake, the tarantula lurking in the shadows. People did not sleep on the ground here, for fear of never waking. "No, Belle, no, no." She always stopped her daughter from drinking, from eating, from following her to the edge of the ponds; she hadn't the heart to stop her from sleeping. After prowling around the little girl several times, she approached the ticket window. Behind the grillwork glowed the end of a cigar. Occasional puffs of smoke floated through the small window. Finally, someone was there! She leaned over. A man, sitting in the dark, was rocking as he carved a piece of wood.

"Are you the stationmaster?"

He didn't answer. Perhaps he didn't understand English. She couldn't see him very clearly. He appeared to have a beard, his Panama hat angled over his eyes. His boots were on the table next to the telegraph equipment.

"*Quiero ver,*" she tried in Spanish, the only two words she had learned during a week in Aspinwall.

"Don't bother."

He was American.

"When does the next train leave for Panama City?" No answer. "What are you doing behind the ticket window?"

"Waiting."

"What are you waiting for?"

He chuckled.

"The next train."

"When?"

"Ah, that . . ." he laughed again. "For that, my little lady, you have to ask the stationmaster."

She gave him a dirty look and went to make sure that Belle was in no immediate danger. Then she headed toward the open door leading to the platform, and leaned against the frame. She was looking for a railroad employee, a switchman, a conductor, anyone capable of taking her across the Isthmus. She would offer them her wedding ring.

"I have been in your situation more than once," breathed the man, who became talkative. "If you're hoping to sell your ring, I don't think that will interest them."

She saw rats running along the railroad track, human silhouettes in the distance passing from one waterfront bar to another, and the black ocean, glistening, the waves breaking on the beach between the shacks.

"No, I really don't think that will interest them," he repeated.

She heard him push back his chair and rise. She was thinking how Sam would worry if he did not find her on the quay in San Francisco among the passengers of the *Saint Louis,* and of the horror of spending one more day in Aspinwall.

"But I'll take what you have to sell," the man whispered in her ear. "I'll pay your place if you'll share my hammock."

Fanny's astonishment froze her. No man had ever insulted her like this. She did not even know what he meant. Taking her silence for acquiescence, the man put his arms around her and pressed her against the door frame. He had no sooner touched her than the barrel of the derringer was against his throat. Raising her arm, she aimed the gun right at him. He retreated. She advanced, without loosening her grip.

"Do I look like that kind of woman?"

The man thought he could joke with her:

"Well, not exactly, lady, but you don't have a penny."

Pushing him back against the wall, she sank her gun into his throat.

"I have this."

"That won't get you very far," he gasped.

He saw her index finger tighten around the trigger. He thought she was going to pull it. She thought so, too. Her finger was already closing, she was going to fire. He closed his eyes.

"Clear out!" she growled.

Without further comment, he slipped away. She remained standing there, her arm held out, dumbfounded.

It was not fear but anger, the brutality of her hatred, that overwhelmed her. She remained frozen there, her face impenetrable, staring after him. She lowered her arm alongside her skirt, faded from sun and perspiration. She kept the pistol glued against her thigh. Finally, she began trembling.

Then she saw Belle. An animal caught in a trap, half risen in the corner, the child had followed the scene not daring to move. A wave of pity shook Fanny. With a slight flip of the thumb she uncocked the gun, nonchalantly put it back in her pocket, and tried to smile at her daughter.

"Well, now," she joked, "it wouldn't have taken much. Your mother almost killed a man." She held out her hand. "Come along."

*

"Cross the Isthmus on foot? You're joking, my girl!"

She had gone to wake Mr. Hill, who was resting with the first-class passengers in the dormitories on the hotel balconies. Here the men and women were sleeping separately, and her presence at this hour in the men's section was already provoking comments.

"Come on—surely you're joking! Forty-seven miles on foot, with the fevers and the heat? And how do you cross the river, there's no bridge!"

Imperturbable, she swept away his argument:

"There must be a bridge, Mr. Hill."

"And what about the mountains," he chattered, "the tropical forest, the swamps—forty miles of swamps. My girl, you'll get lost!"

"We will follow the railroad tracks."

"You will be crushed! There are nothing but winding mountain passes and steep cliffs. No shoulder to the right or to the left of the tracks. What if a train comes?"

"There is no train."

"It will come soon, patience."

"Be quiet. Get dressed. Meet me downstairs."

It was her tone of voice. He didn't bother to take offense and got up. She made her way along the outside corridor and went down the stairs, always followed by little Belle, so small she didn't even reach the bannister. Standing in the ever-present mud under the pilings of the Union Hotel, Fanny waited for him while she forged a plan. She had not reflected on it, even for a minute.

It had to be possible. Others before her had crossed the Isthmus on foot. Before the railroad was built, travelers had no choice. Yes, it was possible, it was feasible. It would have to be, for she was not willing to take the risk of missing the boat. She was counting on this argument to convince Mr. Hill, who had made the mistake of not taking the first train when he had the means to do so.

At fifty, Mr. Hill believed in reason. He also believed in the greatness of the United States and the obligation of its citizens to help a stranger. In this, Mr. Hill was a man of the eighteenth century and a poet. He was on his way to San Francisco via Panama in order to choose seeds and tropical plants for cultivation in his greenhouses in Indiana. This passion for horticulture had appealed to Fanny. She had listened to him with interest as he discoursed on the selection of orchids. The lessons in gardening had continued even here, until this evening. During the passage Fanny had learned that he belonged to the same Masonic lodge as her father, a weighty argument in the discussion they were about to have.

She only hoped that Aspinwall's prohibitive prices had not completely cleaned out Mr. Hill's supply of cash, that he still had enough money to buy the provisions and mules they would need. Four mules to transport Belle and their baggage.

"We can always sell them again in Panama City," she whispered when he had joined her under the balcony of the Union Hotel. "We should be there in three days."

"The chief thing," he sighed, "is to get there."

"If you know how to be quiet, Mr. Hill, I will get you there."

The surprising thing is that he was beginning to believe her. She wasn't even half his age, had no idea of life, no experience of the tropics. But he was seduced by the solidity of this little woman, by her common sense, and above all by her prodigious self-confidence. Fanny's strength of will, that determination that brooked no doubt or failure, surprised and subdued him. Mr. Hill was losing ground. She could feel it.

Lowering her voice, nearly inaudible, she went on:

"Not a word to the others . . . If all the passengers take it into their heads to leave on foot, the natives will sell their animals for the price of gold. So, mum's the word until I've found our mules. How much do you have?"

"A hundred dollars."

"Give it to me. You get busy gathering your trunks and bring them to the cemetery. I will be there at dawn. We'll leave immediately."

This was the first time she had spoken more than five words in a row to him. Struck by her tone of authority, Mr. Hill was inspired by Fanny's youthful energy. Her taste for action, for secretiveness and drama, was contagious. With her conspiratorial air, she moved him enormously.

"In three hours, I will have a guide, provisions and mules . . . Come to the cemetery, Mr. Hill. And in three days, we will be in Panama City."

"And in fifteen," she added to herself, "Sam!"

With her daughter at her side, she disappeared along the ponds, toward the ocean.

*
**

Neither Fanny nor Belle would tell the story of their tramp across the Isthmus. Not a word about their excursion with Mr. Hill. Not even a line in their correspondence. Were some other letters to their family lost en route? Or had Fanny erased this painful episode from her memory? To be silent about something disturbing was just her style.

She would not, however, forget the horrors of Aspinwall. The stench of the ponds would remain in her nostrils. And the fear of dying of the "fevers" in the hammock at the Union Hotel, of abandoning Belle on the Isthmus, the terror of never seeing Sam again would fill her nightmares for many months to come.

Most likely she did not cover the entire route on foot. Between Matachin and Panama she must have caught a train, for Belle, in evoking the adventures of her childhood in her autobiography, mentions the window of a train car from which she watched "monkeys and parrots; an entire mysterious jungle, hot and noisy." But was this the same trip? Belle was not even six years old. At ten, she would pass through the tropics again.

Not a word, either, on their stay in the port of Panama.

Nothing about the voyage on the *Moses Taylor*, the steamer that finally took them to San Francisco. As for Mr. Hill, his name does not figure on the passenger list. Did he manage to get to Panama alive?

Fanny, who was incapable of indifference, claimed to have no idea of what happened, no memory. And she left no record of her very first impressions of the Pacific, nothing about San Francisco.

After forty-seven days of traveling, on Wednesday, June 20, 1864, she docked at the city by the Golden Gate.

Sam was no longer waiting for her.

They had missed each other by less than twenty-four hours.

Despite Belle's memories of resting several days before departing for Nevada with her father, she and Fanny set out the following day, June 21, on the stagecoach of the Pioneer Line. Direction Placerville, again alone.

Yet Sam had come down from the Sierras to collect his wife and daughter at the port. He had ridden a whole week through the heat of the deserts that lay between his camp and the ocean. Impatient, feverish, he had watched for the ships entering the bay, always hoping to see Fanny's silhouette leaning on the rail. But day after day, the much awaited *Saint Louis* did not appear. And on the 19th, a catastrophic telegram from his partner had called him back to camp.

No prospector, even a legal owner of the land, could take the risk of leaving his mine unexploited, and even less of leaving it unattended. "Finders keepers, losers weepers" was the custom, and other gold hunters were only too happy to find shafts and tunnels already dug, and to set to work extracting the minerals. This activity was called "jumping a claim." So Sam, unprotected by the law, had lost his mine. Only the law of force prevailed—the law of the Colt 45.

Occidental Hotel—June 21, 1864

My dear parents,
A quick word from San Francisco. Sam is waiting for us at Austin, just beyond Placerville and Carson City. We will leave in one hour—and in 10,988 minutes, we will be with him! Even from a distance he enfolds us, Belle and me, he wraps us in his thoughts. On the platform, at midnight, we found one of his friends whom he had entrusted with waiting for all the boats. Laden with a bouquet of my tiger lilies, this gentleman, Atchinson, drove us in a buggy to the Occidental Hotel, where Sam had reserved the prettiest room for us. The proprietors were extremely gracious to us, for they love Sam like their own son. You cannot imagine how popular he is, how in six months he knows everyone in San Francisco. Nearly the whole town came in his name to greet us this morning. Yes, I am exaggerating . . . But at the hotel, the men talk about him all the time, about his generosity, about his bravery—and gold. Little sacks of dust are passed from table to table, and Mr. Atchinson has shown me a "nugget" from our mine. It is greenish. It looks like the most ordinary stone, and you would never suspect that with this bit of quartz Sam is going to settle us in Paradise!

There is the same light tone at the end of the letter: no complaint, no hint of the terrible disappointment she must have felt at not finding Sam at the end of the line, only her impatience to join him.

Impervious to the pleasures of San Francisco, Fanny was off to bury herself in the most isolated, arid region in the entire American West: 450 miles by stagecoach, almost 200 across the dizzying peaks of the Sierras and 250 through the desert. This was the famous route of the Pony Express.

Nevada—June 1864

"How long until Austin?"

"Dearie, you'd better have a good, stiff drink before Devil's Gate! It's no picnic going through the Sierras at night. Get down. You're in my way."

On the outside seat of the stagecoach, Fanny clung to the straps, her face between her knees, bent over so the driver could rest the barrel of his gun against her back.

In the canyons, he drove with one hand; with the other, perpendicular to his hip, he brandished his weapon; his eyes swept to the right, watching out for the horses and the sheer drop, and to the left, searching the overhanging rocks. That's where the bandits would come from, on Fanny's side. In case of attack, she would be right in his line of fire.

"Lie down, for God's sake!"

At the coach inn in Placerville where they changed horses, she had convinced him to let her ride lookout. Ordinarily, he could tolerate only the Wells Fargo employee, his strongbox, and his rifle. But in the Sierras, with an ambush likely, no one wanted this seat, and the bank had disguised its agent, with his gold, among the passengers. So the bandits were now given to rushing them and, if in doubt, assaulting everyone. In twenty years of stagecoach attacks, no traveler had ever been robbed before the men transporting bank funds had begun to disguise themselves as miners.

Inside the coach they all looked alike: the Colt in their belt, the flask of whiskey slung over their shoulder, no collar or tie, but the three buttons of their red flannel shirt buttoned up to their stubble, and a soft brown felt hat pulled low over their eyes. The men, a dozen in all, had the banal look of prospectors down on their luck and determined to pursue it through the mountains. With downcast eyes, they stared at one another, squeezed, shaken, tossed around, wondering which of these shabby travelers was carrying the Wells Fargo money in his well-worn boots or frock coat. And all of them, in small gulps, were silently getting drunk. They were afraid of Indians, afraid of the hairpin turns the driver took without slowing down, and afraid of the stagecoach overturning, thrown down a steep ravine by the galloping horses whose jingling bells could no longer be heard through the howling of the wind in the pines.

There was scarcely a yard between one turn and the next, with the rocks above, the void below.

Fanny, her head lowered on the seat, spied the bleached skeletons of crushed animals at the bottom of the ravines, as well as wheels and axles caught in the trees. Belle was fortunately asleep inside, between the boots of the passengers whom the alcohol had begun to warm. The driver, too, was brave enough, but his eyes swept the landscape, reins in one hand, rifle in the other, his weapon resting on his passenger's back—the barrel moving, pointed above her toward the overhanging rocks.

"How long," she muttered against her skirt in gulps, "before we arrive?"

"If you move," he muttered, now pushing her down, "it's your head'll get there first. You ought to have had a stiff drink!"

"Thank you, but I don't drink."

"I see. Warm water, huh?"

"Yes, warm water,"

"Have you been in the West long?"

"Since yesterday."

"Just what I thought. The ladies here don't make a fuss about getting drunk. Best thing for the jitters. You'll come to it yet!"

Idiot! What did she need a stimulant for? She felt no fear, cold, or nerves. She did not even feel the discomfort of her position. Bravely, she sat up. But in the ferocity of her look there was not a trace of courage, none of that famous "pluck" that had seduced Mr. Hill, but something obsessive, haggard, and overexcited.

"Get down!"

She struggled with all her strength against the pressure of the gunstock he applied between her shoulder blades.

"You want your face smashed in?"

The idea that she could fall never even occurred to her. He finally released her.

"Your tough luck."

She sat up again, very straight, her head directly in the line of fire of the driver's rifle, which he kept pointed at the mountain.

This was probably the first of those attacks that Fanny would call, somewhat jokingly, "my little bouts of brain fever."

Since their departure from Sacramento, when the horses went into a gallop she would start to tremble. Was it fatigue? Impatience? At the coach inn at Placerville, Belle had seen her buzzing like a gadfly around the animals as they were being readied, gesticulating, talking to herself. Too near and too far from the goal—she couldn't wait anymore. Everything in her was exploding. The time was past when the memory of Sam, the thought of seeing him again, of being close to him for the rest of her days soothed her anguish. She could not even imagine him now, their reunion, their future life together. She could think of nothing. But heading toward "Austin" she held on with all her might, all her nerves. She could almost feel every lash of the whip on her own flesh. Her mind, haunted by the obsession of arrival, raced down the steep slopes before the horses did. She perceived everything, the contractions of the six haunches, the clatter of the hooves, the hard breathing at the bottom of the vale as the wheels barely skimmed the shoulder of the road. After a night and a day, the stagecoach careened into the desert.

The road was a pale yellowish line through the heart of a brown vastness that reached into the distance until it was lost from sight in the new range of the Toiyabes that enclosed this infinite space. And somewhere in these mountains was Austin, but so far away that the black ridge seemed to graze the rosy line of the horizon. And behind, stretched like a vast and empty canvas, was the sky, a cloudless, sunless blue. It was dusk: no moon yet, no mist or fog, not even dust. The galloping horses left nothing in their wake, just an impression of emptiness. Not a tree, not a rock, not a shape to catch the eye, blurred by the speed of the horses into a sepia flatness, the gray stones and the silvery tufts of sage mingled with the carcasses strewn along the way. Overturned carts, barrows, abandoned bundles, pickaxes, rusty shovels, the rubble of a former gold rush sunk in the dryness of the desert.

You have to see this part of Nevada to appreciate the desolation to which Sam was bringing his wife and daughter. When I finally set foot in Austin, following Fanny's trail, I had only one idea, to get out of there fast! Stones, sand, thorn bushes, alkali dust that burns the eyes, cracks the lips, pollutes the water: On this plateau, as in the desert, nothing grows. There is no smell or color, only roofless, windowless shacks squeezed into the canyons or set askew on the hillsides. Steep paths score the slopes like the fingers of an open hand. And they stop suddenly, as if amputated. One hundred and ten degrees in summer, freezing in winter, with blizzards and avalanches. Somewhere there is a river.

Was this the site of the camp? The cloak of darkness that fell in the afternoon, the pyramids of gravel, the gaping shafts, the rails—all that sadness common to mining regions. The place depressed me so much that I thought seriously of returning to the desert. Or was it the certainty that this wretched hole so closely resembled the Austin that Fanny had found at end of her journey? This camp was not a ghost town, there was nothing to reconstruct in imagination, no possible food for nostalgia.

Everything here had begun only four years before her arrival. Until then there was nothing, not even the trail in. Rather than cross a series of mountain ranges, the wagons coming from the East had preferred the longer but less arduous route to the North, along the Humboldt River. Even the forty-niners had not ventured into this godforsaken country.

Two events, however, had transformed this vast, empty terrain into a swarming hive of activity: the Pony Express and the telegraph. Two inventions that were the result of the impatience of Californians to communicate quickly with the East, more quickly than they could via Panama.

Seeking young men: thin, sturdy, tough. Exp. horsemen, max. 18 years. Ready to die. Orphans preferred.

With this little advertisement posted in all the banks throughout the West, in train stations and saloons, the Pony Express was offering twenty-five dollars a week to suicidal orphans ready to ride the relay on the Overland trail between Missouri and California in eight days. This meant 2,000 miles in a straight line over the most difficult terrain, braving Indian arrows, riding in relay as much as 200 miles a day.

A feat of short duration. Several months after the Pony Express riders had pounded through the quiet of the deserts for the first time, telegraph poles were raised along the same route. This made communicating with the East even faster, and the Pony Express had no more reason to stay in business. Now only the crackling of the telegraph lines mingled with the moaning of the pine trees in the Sierras. No paleface was to be found for 250 miles, except for the old riders. Set adrift, they continued to hang around the abandoned relay posts.

And so it was that a former Pony Express rider, a certain Talcott, had reported in 1862 at "Jacob Station," the last relay post before the mountain, a stone of greenish color that had intrigued him.

Greenish like the veins of silver in quartz. The news traveled from one relay station to the next.

In October 1862, there were ten or so men digging in the frozen earth, with no provisions, no heat, in tents or shacks. It was below freezing at night.

In December, the samples sent to the assay office in Virginia City had revealed a vein containing an exceptional quantity of silver. The miracle had happened.

In January, fifty prospectors were camped between Jacob Station and the Reese River, a meager stream at the foot of the mountain. In February, they baptized their hillside village "Austin," in memory of the capital of their native Texas. In March, two brothels, two hotels, five saloons, and a newspaper were established in the area of Pony Canyon. There was a total of fifty buildings. By July there were 279 and by October, 366. Along with 1,300 mining companies and 4,000 people.

In the desert, along the old, straight, endless trail of the Pony Express, convoys laden with hay, wood, equipment for drilling, crushing, and sifting, twenty-mule teams, covered wagons, carts, riders, pedestrians, and stagecoaches followed each other single file. If a stagecoach happened to fall out of line, it would take an hour's wait in the snows of this October of 1863 before it could reenter the line of traffic between two convoys.

The gold rush had lasted one year. In December, it was all over. No one dared to leave. But instead of a hundred prospectors arriving daily in Austin, there were only twenty. Then ten. Then, in April 1864, only five. Among them, Sam Osbourne. He was one of the last adventurers to dream of making a fortune on the banks of the Reese River.

For three months, news had been traveling fast that the lodes were worthless, that the veins, if there were veins, were too expensive to exploit, that the craze for the region was due to the plotting of speculators. Whether these rumors were true or false, as Fanny continued her journey among the rubble of the gold rush, the Stock Exchange in San Francisco was plummeting.

Austin—end of June 1864

Midnight. Beneath the sash windows of the International Hotel, at the entrance to the saloon, fifty or so miners were waiting. The same dirty felt hat over the eyes, the same flannel shirt, the same brown canvas pants—one leg forward, the other back, in the same square-toed boots—the same briar pipe clenched between the teeth, the same double-barrel shotgun, terror of the buzzards, held by the same shoulder strap under the right arm. All of them bearded and unkempt, ragged and patched, they exuded the same sour odor of perspiration and chewing tobacco, and the explosives they used to hollow out their tunnels. And all of them concealed in their sagging pockets the same stones, which they fingered with the same nervous gestures.

The overexcitement of these ageless young men, nearly identical and interchangeable, was unlike anything else. Imagine an army of beggars, each of whom thought he was Creosus. None of them had anything to go home to, but each one thought he was the richest man in the world, and acted like it. Beggars and millionaires.

"Look here," they muttered to each other, taking from a pocket a stone as big as a nut. "You see, there, the flecks of gold? And the veins of silver? That comes from my mine, the Queen of the Mountains. And that's just from the surface! Turned up with just a few blows of the pickax. The thing's loaded with silver. And because you're my friend, I am giving you six feet of it if you invite me for supper. What's six feet more or less to me? The Queen of the Mountains is so rich, what difference does it make? But for you! Look at the report . . . I'm not asking you to believe me without looking at the report. Look . . ."

One or the other of them would then brandish a piece of greasy paper certifying that the rock analyzed contained a proportion of silver worth thousands of dollars per ton. It was on the strength of these reports that described the stone as characteristic of the mine—when the prospector had obviously sent for analysis only the richest sample, one small stone out of a ton of rubble that contained a mere particle of precious metal—it was on the strength of these "reports" that the whole country had gone mad.

And these dreamers were living like dogs and working like convicts. They had freely chosen the most exhausting, dangerous, and thankless labor. Under the earth, gas explosions, fires, and cave-ins claimed endless victims. Those whom accidents, exhaustion, scurvy, brawling, and whiskey didn't kill would die of the famous "miner's sickness," silicosis, a lung disease caused by the deposits of rock dust produced by the "widow makers," the first compressed air drilling machines. Little did they care, they persisted in using them and thinking that money, their money, was to be found on the surface of the soil. Another mistake. For all they knew, their lode, if there was one, might just as easily run 500 yards deep. So they had a choice: either sink a shaft vertically into the rock containing the vein, or go down to the desert and tunnel into the mountain to reach their vein from below. If they ever did reach the rock containing the mineral, they would need to extract it and convey thousands of tons of rock to the refining equipment in order to obtain a few grams of silver. If you consider that simply separating mineral from dross was costing the miners a hundred dollars per ton, their ingots were decidedly light-years away. This idea, however, did not occur to them. Euphorically they dug their tunnels, and every Saturday night they came down from their distant claims to Austin, crossing twelve miles through the mountains so as not to miss the great entertainment, the arrival of the stagecoach.

It was always the same ritual. They drank, played cards, bought and sold parts of their mines until the uncertain hour when, beyond the rampart of rocks that tumbled down to the desert, someone spied the lanterns of the stagecoach.

Instantly the bellowing of drunks and clinking of player pianos stopped, and with the muffled sound of boots on the wooden sidewalks, the whole camp hurried toward the International Hotel.

At the jingle of bells muted by the turnings of the road, all these men began to dream again. But what they hoped for was not their mail, the newspapers, the news conveyed by the passengers, the price of silver in San Francisco, of gold in New York, the state of the mines in other camps—what they hoped for was "the sight of a woman."

Ah, the ruffled dress that might appear from the coach, the perfumed hair, the flat sound of the little boot on the wooden sidewalk, the glimpse of an ankle or lace underskirt—who knows, maybe even a stocking? They imagined themselves making a gallant compliment, offering the owner of that little boot a gift.

Strangely enough, the men of the West had the mentality of schoolgirls. Their thoughts were not of hasty seductions but of marriage.

It was the women in the mining camps who chose their husbands. They could divorce, remarry, and divorce at their whim. They cheated on their men with impunity, and stole from them, murdered them—a Nevada court had never yet condemned a female. Provided the lady was of the white race, she would emerge with her reputation untarnished, with shabby excuses from the jury.

This clemency, this respect, and in many cases this authentic chivalry practiced by the men of the West was the result of the terrible dearth of women. Around the Reese River, in the entire district, there were only fifty-seven women for 4,000 men. And among them, a dozen were lower-class prostitutes and five were less than ten years old. Even the older ones who had reached thirty found as many opportunities as concessions in the mountains. So the men had to move fast, and catch the lady as she stepped off the stagecoach. At this point, the ceremony would last as long as the courtship—about sixty seconds.

"Do you take him?"

"Yes."

"Do you take her?"

"Yes."

"That's it, then. One dollar, please."

When Fanny jumped down from the stagecoach, her lips cracked by the wind, her eyes red, her hair tangled, a quasi-religious silence fell over Austin—not a joke, not even the sound of chewing. Motionless and mute, the crowd of miners leaning on the wheels that served as a fence around the International Hotel watched her open the door and take her child in her arms. They stood in the middle of the street. The pale light of the moon wrapped the two in the same glow. There was not a breath of air—an oppressive night. They were alone. The other travelers had taken the road into the camps. Fanny hesitated a moment, and they surged forward all together, encircling her, unaggressively but hungrily. She did not move. They took advantage of this to squeeze closer, touching her, pressing against her, pushing her. She scarcely felt them. Motionless herself, she looked into their faces, and in their feverish eyes she saw the same haste, the same desire. She grabbed one after the other, greedily searching under all those hats, behind all that stringy hair, all those ragged beards for Sam's eyes, Sam's mouth. Sam's body.

Finally the jostling crowd caught her off balance, and she took one step, like a hesitant butterfly, toward the light of the hotel. The ranks opened before her, respectfully. She passed through. Then a tall figure appeared, framed in the lighted doorway with arms outspread, pushing open the swinging doors of the saloon. Belle was the first to recognize him.

"Papa!"

They fell against him and he held them tight in the same embrace.

They didn't speak.

He did not ask about her journey, she told him nothing. Not a word was spoken of their fervor to see each other again, how much they had missed each other.

Huddling against him, she kept her eyes closed, her forehead raised, her lips against the neck of the man she loved. She breathed in the special softness of this place, of Sam's flesh, the wonderfully silky, warm skin, the regular pulsing of blood in the veins, the leather and honey of his tobacco, Sam's special smell. Then, under the unfamiliar beard, she felt Sam's lips brush hers: a furtive kiss like a warm wave washing over her.

He gently detached her and, swinging Belle onto his shoulders, led them away.

"That was Osbourne's wife," one miner commented.

The melancholy crowd lingered, watching their silhouettes climb the path toward the heights of Austin, and then dispersed.

*
**

Contrary to all logic, they were neither surprised nor disappointed in one another. Their reunion brought them the great happiness they had longed for.

The adventures Sam had lived through without her, Fanny's eventful journey, the nostalgia for her family, for comfort and security, none of this came between them. She did not feel the infinite sadness of the camp, she did not suffer from their poverty, from their increasing solitude.

They were just as close, perhaps closer, than they had been before. Sam's personality, his presence, gave her exactly what she wanted from life. It all happened as Fanny had dreamed.

II

Sam's Wife

Nothing that glitters is gold.

—Prospector's saying.

Austin—July 1864–March 1865

He had blond hair, parted on the side, prominent cheekbones, and sensual lips. His light eyes—probably an intense blue, and almond shaped—had a gentle, dreamy expression. In the few photos I have seen, Sam Osbourne looks like a very handsome man.

What also strikes me about him is that interesting, rather touching combination of virility and childishness, strength and absence.

The memories he left behind in Indiana, his reputation at the Bohemian Club of San Francisco, the quality of his friends, their loyalty to his memory made me sympathetic to him. And his daughter obviously adored him. Belle, who was always sensitive to aesthetic matters, does not hesitate to eulogize her father's physical and moral beauty. Forty years after their reunion in Austin, she still describes him as he appeared to her then, as strong, as tall as her mother was small, as blond as she was dark, as playful and tender as Fanny was intense.

To the best of my knowledge, the word that probably sums up Sam Osbourne would be "charm." He was charming because he

44

was open, expansive, without a trace of meanness or fanaticism. And charming because he was elusive.

Unlike the other prospectors, most of them first-generation immigrants with no property or place to call home, poor devils who had everything to gain in the mines—deserters from the army, murderers fleeing from justice into the depths of this isolated region—Sam Osbourne was an officer, a law school graduate, and son of a respectable family. He could have prospered quite pleasantly in Indiana. His position with the State Supreme Court, his good relations with his in-laws, his marital happiness had satisfied him completely, until the Civil War. Like many soldiers, he had come home "changed," incapable of fitting back into the daily routine, incapable, some would say, of "settling down."

He was probably emotionally unstable. Even Belle could not deny that there were obscure currents, morbid and painful obsessions hidden beneath her father's apparent health and simplicity. I suspect that it was these forces that seduced Fanny.

No, nothing compelled Sam to exile himself to the end of the world. Gold in itself did not interest him. And if the thought of making a fortune intoxicated him, if he dreamed of the thousand ways he would spend his money, the success or failure of his enterprises left him, at bottom, rather indifferent. Why, then, sink all he owned into it? Why risk his life, and the lives of the two human beings he adored, in that gloomy canyon? Nothing made him do it, except perhaps a taste for danger, a taste for wandering and dreaming.

Fanny's husband was probably one of the only authentic adventurers in Austin.

She would say little about him—he meant too much to her. She remained silent, as always, about her own feelings. But when Ned Field met her, Mrs. Stevenson was very critical of her first husband. The young Ned would clearly remember her saying that neither good conscience nor comfort nor money had ever appealed to her in a man. Even security—so she said at the age of seventy—did not interest her. By instinct she loved vagabonds, gamblers, and idealists, all men who were chasing a dream, men like Sam Osbourne—and like Robert Louis Stevenson—who were looking for adventure for adventure's sake. And to some degree, like Ned Field, who at the age of twenty-three would become the companion of a woman half a century older than he.

In his notes, Ned does not emphasize that it was precisely the precariousness and irregularity of his situation, the spontaneity, the courage, the touch of madness that made him appealing to Mrs. Stevenson. This last attachment of Fanny's had more than one thing in common with the first, similarities that Ned preferred to gloss over—he would lose too much by the comparison.

Feelings ran deep between Fanny Vandegrift and Sam Osbourne. There was nothing fleeting in their relationship, which long outweighed adverse circumstance. She loved him passionately, he loved her as his wife.

*
**

In the dry heat of midday, everything was utterly still. No one was on the paths, no dogs or cats, not even mules in the barns, not a soul living in the shacks. Here and there, however, lay the remains of a breakfast, a shirt on the ground, fossilized. Only the hundreds of stakes that dotted the mountains, shovels stuck straight up in the old works, and little pyramids of sand that seemed to vibrate in the July heat. But on the platforms around the shafts, nothing. Men and animals were working in the tunnels. From sunrise to sunset, every day of the year, the camp was shrouded in utter silence. If you listened carefully, you could hear the muffled and intermittent hammer blows rising from the river.

Kneeling on a rock, Fanny was scrubbing her laundry. The river bed was dry, but between the stones stood yellowish puddles. With her throat and arms bare, perspiring, her hair piled up in Sam's old felt hat, she scrubbed, rinsed, and began again. The water, full of alkali, was not good for washing.

There was little drinking water, and almost no bread, sugar, or coffee. Too far away from the markets, Austin was bereft of everything, and the Osbourne family's subsistence, the organization of their life was exclusively dependent on Fanny's ingenuity. She created the taste of sugar, made leavening with bicarbonate of soda (soda bread), coffee out of bran, soap from lard; these concoctions took days, sometimes weeks to prepare. And then she had to deal with Belle's cough or stomachache or infected cut. In her isolation she observed the Indians, their way of using plants and roots.

The miners managed to get along with the Indians without really seeing them, but Fanny felt as though she were living among them.

As soon as Sam went down into his mine, the Piutes appeared at her window with their tattooed chins, their nostrils striped with red lines to the temples, heads and torsos naked, no feathers or necklaces, but armed. Knives at their belts, rifles on their backs.

Men, women, and children congregated at the window. They watched her attend to her chores. For hours at a time they would follow her slightest movements, commenting quietly on her gestures. She thought of chasing them off, but she didn't dare. She knew they were fierce, and she was afraid of them.

Perhaps they thought she was one of their own race, with her dark skin, her black eyes, her hair, which she often wore braided down her back. Sam, half-seriously, feared a kidnapping. Perhaps they were only coming for the "coffee" she always served them at the window. She held it out to them one cup at a time. She offered them a drink with the same reserve and timidity the Piute Indians showed in accepting it. There was no smile or graciousness on either side. Yet Fanny was the only person in Austin who was interested in their practices, the only person, along with Sam, who felt no condescension toward them.

As soon as they had drunk their coffee, they disappeared. Ordinarily, this disappearance was a relief. But the prolonged absence of the Indians could mean preparation for war and a massacre of the Whites. A week had gone by since she'd last seen them. Even the Shoshones, whom she usually met at the river, had not shown up.

Lifting her laundry paddle, she suddenly froze. She had just heard something behind her, like a trickle of gravel.

Slipping toward her between the rocks was a rattlesnake. With her hands on her laundry, her head down, body tensed, she waited. It approached, she felt it less than a yard away from her ankle. It was going to bite her. Whistling like a top, the snake rose up.

With incredible speed, she turned, aimed, and fired. The reptile's head exploded, stopped in its tracks, while its body continued its furious twisting between Fanny's legs.

The recoil had knocked her against the rocks. Her back was scraped and bloody. But she was exultant. She was as skillful with the Navy Colt, the deadliest of pistols, as she was with her pocket derringer! She looked triumphantly up toward the overhanging mines. What was she waiting for, an ovation? No one, no miner had come out of his tunnel. Not even Sam, assuming that he could hear the shot, would emerge to discover her fate. This was the life of a pioneer woman among gold seekers, a hard, wearying life. And above all, a horribly solitary life.

The idea of reproaching Sam did not cross her mind. Never a word, never a look or sigh expressing the slightest regret for the good life of former times.

Since she had joined him, Fanny thought of only one thing: making a comfortable home for him. Everything was for Sam's comfort, Sam's peace of mind. She had exerted herself with canvas and paper, transforming the shack where he had settled her—really a lair, with no stove, furniture, or window—into a little home which, even in that arid countryside, boasted a kitchen garden! She had made a table, chairs, and beds all with her own hands. Capable and secretive, she had set to work.

This "industrious" and nurturing side made Fanny extremely attractive to men. Sam Osbourne, like Stevenson and Ned Field, was the sort of virile young man who liked someone to fuss over him. She was one of those women, at once mysterious and earthy, who would spin a cocoon around those they loved, a cocoon that Stevenson and all her other lovers would find very safe; a cocoon that her detractors would one day describe as stifling. Clearly, they had not felt its enchantment.

She casually left her mark. Three months after her arrival, she had turned everything in the life of the camp upside down with the exclusive purpose of pleasing Sam. Seven summers after their first meeting, he continued to be the only man in the world for her, the lover. For him she was the wife, the admired and respected wife who made concrete the treasured image of family and home. Belle, however, had come between them. Fanny tended to exclude her child from her relations with her man, while Sam entirely included his daughter in the tenderness he felt for his wife.

"Osbourne's wife," with her sphinxlike smile, her way of listening quietly, her prodigious competence in a world where only determination could change or save a life, with her practical sense and her whimsy, was the kind of woman men put on a pedestal. And while the few women of the region had found her proud, the miners themselves thought her "ideal."

To Sam's great joy—since the war he had liked nothing so much

as the company of other men, friends, buddies, partners—all of
Austin flocked to his home. His house became the center of social
life, a haven where they savored the dishes the mistress of the
house managed to concoct, where they discussed the state of the
mines, where they played monte and charades, where the homesick
miners sang their native songs. Nothing intellectual, nothing artistic.
But for these men who rarely had the amusement of a theater troupe
or the comfort of gentle living, the arrival of "Osbourne's wife"
changed their existence. She embodied the dream which, in their
solitude, they could only imagine. And as she liked to be loved, she
welcomed them all, combining the roles of confidante, advisor, and
goddess. In this primitive camp at the far end of the desert, hundreds
of miles from the nearest city, Sam was enjoying the refinements of
civilization, of what in other places and in other times he would
resolutely call his "club," and what she would one day call a "salon."

*
**

"You're a honeymoon child, Belle," he murmured in his daughter's
ear, "That's why you're so pretty . . ."
Leaning over a table at some distance, Fanny, who was cutting
up one of her dresses to make curtains, raised her black eyes.
Suddenly she was flooded with the certainty that she could never
be happier in this world.
Sam had just finished reading aloud *Beauty and the Beast*, their
favorite story. The September night was falling hot and late. He was
gently rocking, holding their child against him, that little girl who was
so like Fanny, dark like her, tiny for her age, flirtatious and smart.
"That's why," he went on, "you're so pretty and so gay. Because
your mama and I wanted you during our honeymoon."
Sam's twinkling eyes slipped from Belle and caught Fanny's gaze.
He smiled at her. Affection, understanding, desire: she recognized
what she was feeling in the warmth of that smile. She tried to
return it, but unable to bear the violence of her emotion, she
abruptly lowered her head. In her agitation she was looking at the
half-cut calico on the table without really seeing it. She was
conscious only of Sam's presence. He got up and gently carried the
already sleeping child to the little mattress on the ground. It did

not matter that behind him, through their only window for which she was making the curtains, Fanny could glimpse a dozen little fires in the night, and clouds of smoke that rose in puffs toward the starry sky. Smoke signals were everywhere through the mountains. It did not matter that the Shoshones had allied themselves with the more warlike Piutes, with the aim, it was said, of attacking all the camps around the Reese River. The miners of Hangtown, twenty kilometers to the north, had been massacred the night before. There were no survivors.

When he had put his daughter to bed, he took down his rifle and loaded it. He also loaded the two pistols in his gun belt. Then he buckled the belt around Fanny's hips, and they began the long, terrible vigil of pioneers in Indian country.

She had already learned to live with death. She had walked through the Austin graveyard, read the dates and epitaphs on the gravestones, and seen that none of their occupants had reached the age of twenty-five. That they had all ended badly. But what haunted Fanny's dreams was the story the women of the region told. During their first and only visit, they had regaled her with the details of tortures inflicted by the Piutes on one of their neighbors, that poor Mrs. Patterson, raped by the whole tribe and tattooed with a red and black paste that permanently marked her chin like a bloody beard. Her nose had been burned to the bone.

Sam knew the fate that awaited his wife and daughter. He knew, of course, that at the first war cry, the first hail of arrows or bullets, their shack would collapse.

Yet he would remember this night as his best evening in Nevada.

Around eleven o'clock, the war cries and poundings on the wall had him frozen with terror. Fanny, suddenly losing her composure, had fired her two pistols—a dozen bullets into the door.

At the final blast, the whole window, frame and all, fell out and rolled off into the night. Unarmed, Fanny found herself facing a group of Indians flattened on the ground. "To Lloyd's!" shouted Sam, pushing her down the slope. She plunged off. He grabbed Belle. Rolling, stumbling, they ran like hell to the neighboring cabin. The violence of their intrusion did not seem to surprise or disturb the two men at the table playing monte.

"Indians!" croaked Fanny, in a fit of hysteria.

"I have two aces."

Sam barricaded the door, swept the cards off the table and used it to block the entrance. No reaction from the players.

"Sacks," he ordered, "for the windows!"

Nothing. Standing a little aside, their hosts watched them passively. Fanny hid her daughter under the straw mattress.

"Be quiet, even if you hear me scream, don't move!"

She covered the bed with all the rocks lining the steps, then turning toward the youngest man, a blond fellow named John Lloyd, she hurriedly grabbed his Colt. Seeing her do this, the other miner bent over and put his hand to his mouth, hiccuping. She thought he was going to vomit. Outside the cries and banging began again. The Indians circled the hut. Finally the boy she had disarmed made a decision. With a single stride, he crossed the room, moved the table, and opened the door:

"Shut up!" Sudden silence. "That's enough. Get in here!"

Belle could not see Fanny's expression, but she would always remember the enormous burst of laughter that greeted the apparition of ten or so miners feathered and smeared with dirt.

"It's . . ." they hiccuped between bouts of laughter, "it's a joke! You fell for it like greenhorns!"

"Bunch of bastards!"

Sam gasped, looking at them with his eyes popping out.

He caught his breath, inhaled deeply, chuckled, guffawed. "You nailed me!" He laughed so hard it brought tears to his eyes. "Damn . . . I fell for it!"

Not a moment's hesitation, not a protest. This comradely prank was too much of a relief for him not to share his friends' euphoria in all sincerity.

"When the wall fell down . . . for God's sake, I thought that was it!" he shouted gleefully, "I saw my wife's scalp swinging in the night!"

Their screams of laughter ended in a formidable drinking bout. Sam was quite used to this sort of amusement, and he appreciated the humor of it.

Disguising themselves as bandits, robbing their partners, terrorizing someone for a brief half-hour were traditional entertainments in the camps of the Sierra Nevada. The miners amused themselves as best they could, and there was no place among them for the fainthearted or poor sports. Statistically, two-thirds of the holdups were hoaxes instigated by the best friends of the victim.

Fanny was no angrier than Sam. She kept quiet.

Once the shock was over, she helped Belle out of her hiding place, laid her on the bed, and rocked her. And when despite the ruckus the child fell asleep, Sam's wife withdrew into a corner and waited for the drinking to end.

I am surprised, all the same, that she didn't react, that given the circumstances she did not express some indignation. As Stevenson's wife she was quick to denounce anything she thought stupid or dangerous. Sam Osbourne's wife, however, seemed capable of putting up with it and holding it all in, joy as well as anger. Fanny stored everything up and forgot nothing.

There seems to be such a distance between the Fanny of Austin, who dreamed only Sam's dreams, had no inner life, ambition, or ideas except her husband's, and the exotic, ageless siren Ned would meet in San Francisco, that I sometimes ask myself how one became the other, and if I can claim to know either of them.

Several years ago, rereading what Robert Louis Stevenson had written about his wife, I came upon a statement about Fanny that more or less answers my questions. *The most masculine and direct of women,* he observed, *will some day, to your dire surprise, draw out like a telescope into successive lengths of personation.*

Fanny's incarnations were the least of it. And I'm afraid that Sam either did not sense—or sensed too late—the depths that Fanny's silences concealed.

Because she'd just had the fright of her life and continued to dread an Indian attack, and because he had participated despite himself in such a heavy-handed joke, John Lloyd withdrew along with Fanny, and wrapped himself, with her, in the same reserve. That evening, their silence in the midst of the uproar, their consciousness of danger and their passivity sealed the bonds of a friendship that lasted twenty years.

With his ruddy complexion and very blond curls, his long nose and spindly legs, John Lloyd suffered from what he thought was his ugliness. His small stature obsessed him. So he kept his distance from the world, a half-coy, half-stilted distance that heightened the ostentatious regularity of his habits.

Certainly he drank; but always to the "health of the Queen!" On Her Majesty's birthday, he would busy himself with the confection of a sort of pudding, which he would share with an English miner.

He was a Welshman himself, from what sort of background it was hard to say. Certainly not the navy or the peasantry. Nor was he the son of a respectable family in quest of adventure; John Lloyd detested "adventure." He liked order and tradition. And if he thirsted for money, it was out of social ambition. He was probably the child of shopkeepers and had not pursued his studies to university level before necessity forced him to emigrate. Fanny knew no more about him.

Their relative education, among men who surely did not know how to read or write, drew Lloyd and Osbourne together. Ideologically they were in opposite camps: Sam was a former volunteer in the Union Army, Lloyd fancied himself a partisan of slavery and the secessionist South. But this mattered very little in Austin, which was far from the world and a place where politics were only a pretext for drinking. Over a bottle, the two men understood each other perfectly.

His rather mistrustful and jealous fascination with his best friend's wife would make John Lloyd incapable of marrying until the age of fifty. And when he finally did, having become a respectable banker, he simply broke off relations with this couple of vagabonds whom he had perhaps loved too much. Neither Fanny nor Sam would ever allude to Lloyd's complicated feelings, but they gave their first son his name.

*
**

We the undersigned, John Lloyd and Sam Osbourne, claim 300 feet on this silver vein beginning at this stake and running north to south, with all its branches, angles, and windings. And 150 feet of ground of each side of the vein, for exploitation.

This bit of cardboard, half burned by the snow and winds in front of a cave entrance, constituted the only vestige of Sam's mining efforts.

"Ultimately," he concluded by the winter of 1865, "I am not suited for manual labor."

The Piutes had not massacred his family, but Fanny's dowry, the loans from the San Francisco banks, the hundreds of dollars lent many times over by Jacob Vandegrift and Jo, George Marshall's widow, had all been swallowed by his mine. A bottomless pit. At the

end of a year of privation in this godforsaken place, the Osbournes
owed money in three different states, Indiana, California, and Nevada,
with a grocery bill longer than their tunnels.

That Wednesday, Sam and his partner emerged from their shaft
at lunchtime. They sat down side by side on the platform and,
leaning against the handcart, warmed themselves in the March sun.

"Do you want me to tell you," Sam began, lighting his pipe, "the
real secret of success in the silver mines? It's not to work them!"

"Right. Just do nothing," Lloyd agreed.

"You leave peacefully to go prospecting in the mountains, you
enjoy the countryside, you break a few rocks while sipping a beer,
you find a vein loaded with silver, and you sell the lode to slaves
of manual labor who will die exploiting it."

Sam smiled at the memory of the foolish miners who had jumped
his claim when he went to San Francisco. They had broken their
backs and their teeth. It had been worthless. The worst of it was
that his second tunnel, the one he'd been digging for six months
with Lloyd, seemed profitable only for Belle.

Shouldering her pick, the child went underground every
morning. Settled next to her father, she would dig her little hole,
and in the evenings, miraculously, she struck metal. There, between
two stones—already minted—she found a penny!

"What the hell, pal, neither of us is a beast of burden."

"Shareholders, yes!" Lloyd interrupted. "prospectors, no. And no
more selling to independents, only buying shares in a big operation,
a really big operation that has the dough to bring the best geologists
from Europe to trace the vein into the center of the earth, going
down with hundreds of men . . ."

He fell silent, and the two men sat thinking.

"The silver mines are probably too expensive to exploit," Sam
conceded. "Too expensive for independent miners, even too
expensive for mining companies."

"Who's talking about miners? Miners have nothing to do with the
dough. They work for the outfits that pay them, that's all . . . the
outfits with stockholders from the East."

Lloyd didn't like to explain things. With a stubborn look in his
eye, he stopped. Silence. With a pipe clenched in his teeth, Sam
gave him a shove.

"Go on, I'm listening."

"When the war is over, the Eastern industrialists who are using their dough to finance it will turn to the West. And by God I'm going to be there to greet them!"

Sam shrugged his shoulders:

"The fellows you're talking about don't need us . . . You'll never make a fortune with them."

"And what do you suggest?"

Their gaze strayed slowly over the barren slopes, the tents below, the pitiful shacks with their whiskey barrels for chimneys, the mounds, the holes. They lingered over the shafts that gaped to their right. The idea of going back down, of digging all day, of placing sticks of explosives, of risking their lives . . .

"You're right," muttered Sam, "I'm sick of this. This is a dead end." He jumped to his feet, knocked the dust from his hat against his thigh, emptied the barrel of his pipe, and concluded: "Come on, let's pull out! I need a good bath and a good meal in town. Let's get back to civilization!"

In a moment they junked six months' worth of effort. They abandoned their mine, the tons of minerals they had taken out of the ground, the carts, the untransportable tools, and they returned to camp. This conversation, the first of its kind between the two friends, was begun on March 2 at midday. At dawn on the 3rd, the door of the little house that had sheltered Fanny's happiness hung open, banging in the wind.

If she imagined, while packing, that this sudden collapse meant a "return home," then she had not understood the mentality of these men. No miner would go home before making a fortune. It was a question of self-respect and morale. They had sacrificed too much to renounce it: those who did not capitulate the first week, never would. And the longer they stayed, the more they failed, the less they could go back. "Not now! Not so near the goal." So neither Sam nor Fanny would soon see the solid family house on the greening route to Danville. On the other hand, they were no strangers to stones and sagebrush.

That morning in March, the Piutes waited in vain for their cup of coffee. They ended by helping themselves. By evening, the table, chairs, beds, the objects Fanny had fashioned, the plants Fanny had cultivated, everything had disappeared into the mountains. As for the rest, the shovels, the axes, the dishes and the few trunks saved from the raids in Aspinwall, these had been used the evening before to pay the most egregious grocery bills. Just a few personal belongings and toys rattled on the roof of the stagecoach. Twelve hours after their departure, no trace of the Osbournes remained in Austin.

Nothing was left behind, nothing lay before them, they had no regrets, no projects; and reversing their journey across the Pony Express route, they were back to square one.

Virginia City, Nevada—March 1865–December 1866

Seven cemeteries full of murdered men, seven empty prisons, 120 saloons, 800 prostitutes, and 16,000 quarts of whiskey consumed each week—it was here in this hive of industry and lair of cutthroats that the drama took place. Virginia City was the most brutal town in the American West, the biggest community of alcoholics in the world, with one of the richest subsoils in history.

The Comstock Lode, the greatest silver-mining center in the U.S. during the 1800's, was reported by the United States Commissioner of Mines and Mining to have yielded over 14,000,000 dollars in the year 1866 alone, and that number would rise hundreds of millions in the following decade.

They ate truffles, caviar, and lobsters here in the middle of the desert, thousands of miles from Napoleon III's Paris, and imported Mercier champagne, Boucheron rubies, Worth gowns.

Adah Menken, the future mistress of Alexandre Dumas, was installed in a suite at the International Hotel; Modjeska, the celebrated actress, performed at Piper's Opera House; and Mark Twain was one of the editors of the *Territorial Enterprise*. In short, Virginia City was the Mecca of artists, the Athens of the West, the Eldorado of option hunters, professional card players, and sleazy lawyers—a beacon between sky and stone.

Visible everywhere in the heart of the gray vastness were tall brick buildings, the smokestacks of factories. Redwood houses, banks, stock exchanges, brothels, storefronts hung over the void.

At an altitude of over seven thousand feet, it glowed like a torch.

In the distance, set against a pristine blue veil, stood the eternal snows. In the foothills lay a vast region covered with shining lakes like fallen moons, air so thin, so light it made the heart beat fast and the ears ring, like a vibration of crystal.

Fanfares, firemen, revolvers, soldiers, spurs, and swords formed an incandescent flow along the sloping checkerboard of streets and avenues. Eighteen thousand people inhabited a space less than a few thousand acres situated above eight levels of underground tunnels, a thirty-mile maze running 1,500 feet into the earth.

The miners of Austin had never seen anything like it.

Here the smallest mine on the Comstock Lode, the main vein, employed 600 men working round the clock in three shifts. Day and night, like the hands of the clock, the axes struck, the heavy gunpowder exploded, and death took its toll.

At 8:00 A.M., 4:00 P.M., and midnight, the miners of Virginia City, with their lanterns and dinner pails in hand, and lights on their helmets, with red flannels below the waist and torsos stripped, gathered by twos or threes on the platforms that lowered them down vertically for what seemed an eternity, more than half a mile into the earth.

There were fumes, gas, suffocation. The farther down they went, the hotter it became. If by chance their elbows touched the walls of the shaft, they got third-degree burns.

At the lowest level the thermometer might rise to 115 degrees Fahrenheit. They had to survive this hell for eight hours, often far from ventilation shafts. At the end of half an hour in this furnace, their hearts were giving out. So they took a break every thirty minutes and hurried into the "cold room," where huge blocks of ice had been placed. They rubbed themselves against the ice, rolled around in the melting cubes, licked it, sucked it, and finally emptied bags of it into their pants. This took a hundred pounds of ice per man per day. Two cold rooms per tunnel. But a miner always fainted somewhere. If he lost consciousness on the platform bringing him to the surface, he simply fell into the void.

"I am not suited for manual labor." This time, Osbourne and Lloyd stuck to their words.

Returning to his first profession, Sam found a job as a stenographer at the courthouse, which held five or six sessions a day. If justice in Virginia City was sold, it was honestly paid for.

My Dear Father,
Sam wrote to Jacob Vandegrift,
"Manners first and pleasure afterward," as Richard the Third said

*when he shaved himself previous to smothering the babes in the Tower
. . . Joe Plumb, one of my men, wrote me from New York . . . eight
pages about Jesus and Deuteronomy and all the other Apostles, and
in his letter asked me for a discharge, which he sent me from New
Orleans to keep. I put it with other papers on my secretary . . .
please have Jo hunt it up and send it to Captain Plumb . . .*

*I still have all of George's papers, among others, his commission
on parchment signed by Mr. Lincoln. It is too precious to mail. I
shall keep it till Fanny brings it home with her.*

*I want Fanny and Belle to return home this fall, and shall send
them if I get . . . a berth as an amalgamator in a big mill—nothing
to do with squaws or negroes at all . . . It is a process of quicksilver,
used in the mill to extract the silver from the ore . . . it would give
an opportunity for securing the superintendence of a mill sometime,
and they generally get $500 a month.*

*If I do not get this place, I will be out of a situation in January,
and will have to "rustle." Fanny is doing splendidly. She goes to
sew every day at the town notables, and the rich children of Nevada
are all clothed by madam. The mothers, who go out every evening,
are eager for her to stay with their progeny at home, in short, she
is making four dollars per evening, a day's earnings for a miner.
Add to that, she is playing monte like a professional. She won forty
dollars yesterday. You ought to have seen her . . . dealing the
Spanish cards and raking in the persimmons! I tell her that this
shall be her last gambling . . . she has a fine talent in that line—is
bold and fearless and it is better to "stop winner" than to keep on.*

*I never was more glad in my lifetime when I received your last
letter. Most people in your fix would have blown a youngster up
sky high who had filched a thousand dollars of their money into
the sea. You can bet high, however, that I will see this money
refunded, or I will remain here till Doomsday, trying to get it back.
I will not overload you with my thanks for your kindness, but will
try to show that I am sensible of, and grateful for it. If I come
home I can square up all my debts in a jiffy.*

*I am still a clerk for Squire Mills. I mean . . . lawyer, and don't
make more than one hundred and fifty or two hundred a month.
But if I get another place as clerk of Judge Murray's court, that
will pay almost $200 a month or more.*

*Take it all together I don't think I can afford to return home yet
awhile. But Fanny is now making up clothing in anticipation of*

her going this fall. I hope Betty won't marry anybody before Fan comes home! You cannot imagine how happy she is at the thought of being with you all for the wedding.

What kind of colt are you keeping for Belle? She was a little ill. Fanny took her for a week to recuperate in the valley and now everything is fine! But how we miss the farm out here!

Jake you rascal why don't you write? And little Cora and Nell. I have written to you all, and you never answered my letters. Maybe the Shoshones, the Piutes, or the Arrapahoes got my letters for they have disturbed the mail considerably lately.

I wish I were out on the porch with you today, taking a friendly smoke with the grape vine overhead, the chickens pecking on the porch, the dogs revolving around on their axis and dinner just getting ready. Never mind . . . we will be with you again or at least some of us will. Our best to all . . . and believe us most truly affectionately,

Your son & daughter.

Not a word from Fanny. Not even a postscript, a hello, or a signature. This letter was typical of Sam's relations with his in-laws: affection and complaints, requests for money and promises, no details about their real life in Virginia City.

He does, however, speak of health problems. He mentions a trip Fanny and Belle took to San Francisco, saying nothing of what transpired in their absence or what happened after their return.

*
**

Around three weeks after the Osbournes had settled in Virginia City, an epidemic of scarlet fever broke out.

Sam and his family were living in a small white wooden cabin, one of the hundreds of prefabricated cabins that crowded the periphery of Virginia City. It was perhaps 250 square feet, including the land enclosed by a little gate, and boasted a porch, two rooms, and a kitchen in the little garden. Fanny had once again hunted up some boards, barrels, and nails, dug, planted, cut, sewn, and made a "home sweet home" complete with flowered curtains and rocking chairs, a new nest where their friend Lloyd came to enjoy himself each evening.

This morning, just as she was leaving to sew for one of her customers, she noticed that Belle was pushing away her breakfast.

"Aren't you hungry?"

"Yes, Mama."

She studied the child's congested face.

"Are you sick?"

"No . . ."

Uneasy, Fanny nonetheless took her along as she always did when she went to work outside the house. But the little girl just lay prostrate at her feet. At one o'clock she took her home. By evening, Belle was delirious.

"I'm going for a doctor!" exclaimed Lloyd, coming in for dinner with Sam who, with a sudden gesture, grabbed his sleeve.

"Hold on! No quack is going to come near my daughter . . ."

Having been a medical aid during the war at bleedings and amputations, Sam had blatant and utter contempt for the medical profession. This was his only prejudice.

"Fanny is the one who knows Belle's constitution . . . If anyone can save her, Fanny can. And only Fanny!"

"We need a doctor," insisted Lloyd. "Children are dying everywhere."

"Precisely!" Fanny retorted.

Leaning over her daughter, anticipating her slightest breath, she watched over her and cared for her. She did not sleep and hardly ate. The men tried to relieve her, but they always dozed off. By the end of the second week, when she pressed a drop of grape juice onto the child's poor swollen tongue, Fanny heard her murmur: "More, Mama." The first words she'd spoken since her illness. When Fanny had squeezed the whole grape in her mouth, the child seemed satisfied. She rested calmly. The fever broke that night. Belle was saved. And now Fanny succumbed.

Exhausted, she let Sam send them both to the seaside to convalesce with the family of one of their many friends. He saw them off at dawn on April 8, 1865, on the stagecoach to San Francisco. They were leaving only under duress.

"You both need a good rest," he murmured, squeezing their little hands.

The fervor on their pinched faces, their fixed gaze, their distress were heart-wrenching.

It crossed his mind that he was seeing the last of his happiness. He did not want to dwell on his intuition that this separation perhaps signaled the end of an era, that this departure would be definitive. The horses, keyed up from the long wait, pulled away violently. Sam saw Belle and Fanny thrown to the back of the stagecoach. It was already on its way down C Street and, passing through the sleeping city, turned the corner and set off into the desert. They had not even had time to say good-bye.

Dazed, empty, Sam remained standing in the middle of the street. Belle's illness, Fanny's exhaustion, the sadness, the tension of the last weeks had taken its toll on him as well.

A sudden flush of joy rose up in him: It was all over! Belle was doing beautifully, and Fanny would recuperate. Life would go on, and he loved life so. He could laugh again, and have fun. During the war, having fun meant drinking with his pals and going to whores. There was no dearth of whores in Virginia City. For a moment, the thought of going to a brothel at this hour cheered him up. But he bravely resisted and went off to work instead.

On the way, among the few people out and about that early in the morning, he was surprised to recognize the pretty face of Mrs. Betty Beaumont Kelly, a charming young widow he had met on the steamer between New York and Aspinwall.

"What a surprise!"

Mrs. Kelly had helped care for George Marshall in his last moments. Sam was grateful to her. She had been very good to George, and very good to him, too, after George had died. They had lost track of each other in Panama, but met again at the Occidental Hotel in San Francisco. They had spent only one night together; both remembered it fondly.

"What are you doing in this dump?"

Betty told him she was running a boarding house for miners, yes, right here on C Street. She was just getting started. She had done things in a big way and ordered furnishings in San Francisco. But it was a disaster, her things hadn't arrived! So her parlor was completely bare, the rooms had no pitchers or wash basins. Her customers were complaining, and she was going out of business even before she had time to recover her expenses. Quite naturally, Sam proposed to lend her his own things. She could bring over all the chairs, dishes, even the curtains: His wife and daughter were gone, and he didn't need anything for himself. This would give her some time until her boxes were delivered. Mrs. Kelly accepted, and so as not to inconvenience him, she offered to put him up as well.

What happened next Sam would hardly remember. At least, hardly more than the other 20,000 or so inhabitants of Virginia City. He could only say that on April 10, during a rather foggy morning, he had heard church bells ringing throughout the city. The military governor's cannons, hundreds of rifles, thousands of revolvers, tons of explosives—anything that could be was exploded on C Street. People ran through the streets in a mob, yelling and shouting. The extraordinary news, the surrender of General Lee and the entire Confederate Army, had reached the telegraph office. The most murderous conflict in American history—more murderous for the United States than the world wars of the following century—was over. And Sam's party, the party of most of Virginia City, had won.

All the mines and businesses closed, all except for 120 saloons. An ocean of whiskey submerged the city. This was the most formidable binge of the Old West. Twenty thousand people dead drunk for five days and five nights.

On the morning of the sixth day, when the gutters were strewn with accumulated, swelling bodies, a second telegram arrived at the Western Union Office: *His Excellency President Lincoln was assassinated at the theater tonight.*

Then, one after the other, two dispatches:

President Lincoln died at 8:30 this morning and Secretary Stewart a few minutes past 9. Reports are contradictory.

It is reported that President died at 7:22.

Then nothing, no news for forty-eight hours. In its stupefied state, Virginia City had ceased to communicate with the outside world.

Riots had broken out in San Francisco. The crowd had ransacked the newspapers suspected of Southern sympathies. A state of emergency was declared. In the panic, the telegraph wires had been cut.

And so Fanny, stunned by these recent events, came home unexpectedly. After less than a week away, she was in for a big surprise.

*
**

Coming into the house, she was taken aback. It was empty—not a stick of furniture, nothing. Even the wood-burning stove had disappeared; the stovepipe was hanging from the roof and there was a big soot mark on the floor. And no trace of Sam.

She went out again, circled twice around the house like a disoriented animal, came back in and stood in the middle of the room that had been her parlor.

Quite still, covered with dust, her carpet bag at her feet, her daughter pressed against her skirt, she was looking on the walls, on the door, for a piece of paper—anything that might be a message.

"They even took my drawings," whimpered Belle.

As astonished as Fanny, and much angrier, the child noticed that her tea set, her dolls, and her books were missing, too. "Where is Papa?" The child began to cry.

Her daughter's distress shook Fanny out of her stupor. She grabbed her by the hand and left to find her neighbors.

They knew nothing. Yes, they had seen Mr. Osbourne move out. He was driving a wagon, heading toward C Street. No, he didn't seem to be ill. A lady was with him.

"Who?"

They didn't know. They might be able to describe her, Fanny might know her, she was exactly her opposite: "Fair, beautiful, blond. Long jade earrings. A stylish batiste collar, a black silk skirt . . ."

Stung by each detail, Fanny stiffened. She was not suffering, this was just a vague irritation, an annoyance. Very clearly, an annoyance.

". . . She looked very friendly, very agreeable. A widow, maybe? Certainly rich!"

Fanny searched her memory for an image, a name. She did not see . . . she did not see any connection between the widow, her furniture, and Sam.

Quite by chance the neighbor gave her the address on C Street of a family boardinghouse where Fanny could wait for news of her husband. Something in the woman's tone of voice made her stomach contract. This time, she was ill. She was also very frightened.

She reacted as she always did to threat or danger, she swooped down on what terrified her.

Her hat askew, her boots stamping angrily, her skirt furiously sweeping aside the empty bottles, she dragged her daughter toward C Street.

What did she imagine? What scenes, what voices, what faces? What was the connection between this widow and Sam? When she arrived at number 330, Fanny began to sob.

Her daughter would describe her in a way that she had never seen before: a little woman sobbing at the gate of a well-appointed cottage. What was she afraid of? I am not sure she knew herself. But it was the first time, feeling so sad, that she could not call upon Sam to rescue her.

Remembering their understanding of each other, that union she had counted on for eight years, had become painful to her. Worse, the impossibility of calling on Sam left Fanny quite bereft, rootless, hollow. It was this emptiness that was taking its toll. Or perhaps it was the atmosphere of the city, the flags at half-mast on all the columns, the funeral hangings draped from balustrades to balconies on huge, dirty signs that set off the red brick of the facades; or the cries of a prophet who threatened Virginia City with destruction. Perhaps it was the silence of the miners in front of the banks and saloons, the continuous murmur of prayers rising from the churches, and black everywhere. And the service for the dead.

Reading the sign, B. B. KELLY, LODGINGS, Fanny clutched desperately at her daughter's hand, her eyes brimming with tears.

Her first reflex, however, was to keep Belle out of it.

"Stay in the garden."

The child stopped in the middle of the walk. Fanny kept going. On the porch, about to ring the bell, she drew in her breath and looked in the window. How surprised she must have been to recognize, pinned to red and gold wallpaper, the fashion engravings she had cut out of her *Harper's Weekly*. And the buffet, the armchairs, and the table she had made with her own hands.

She did not ring. She walked right in.

In the ruckus that followed, I recognize her as the woman Ned Field knew. Falling on the fair, blond proprietress, she gave her a good dressing down. Her shouts of "thief" were heard from one end of town to the other. In normal times, her insults would not have disturbed anyone. But on the day of Lincoln's funeral, in the midst of this unusual moment of meditation, it became a scandal that kept the tongues of Virginia City wagging for months.

Terrified by the uproar, the widow Kelly tried to quiet her down by immediately restoring all her effects. This was a big mistake. The comings and goings of the move, orchestrated by Fanny's resounding orders to the porters, attracted still more attention. A crowd gathered, and the sheriff showed up as well. Fanny explained the case. Never had Belle heard her explain herself so clearly:

"My furniture!"

Not a word about Sam. She did not utter his name or mention

his disappearance. She was reclaiming "her furniture." For someone who would eventually spread her things far and wide, she put tremendous energy into recovering them this time.

By evening the Osbourne ladies had refurbished their sitting room; wood-burning stove, drawings, engravings, tea set, not a pin was missing from the sewing box.

Sam, hearing the scene outside from his mistress's bed, thought it prudent to lie low. But if he believed that Fanny was so obsessed with her furniture that she had not suspected his infidelity, he took her for more naive than she was.

The look that met him at the end of the day gave him no inkling of the turmoil in store for him.

Relieved that Fanny did not make a scene, Sam did not explain. By minimizing this incident, which he always persisted in calling "that stupid furniture business," he thought that she would quickly forget it. And just as he was reassuring himself, and even thinking of introducing the widow Kelly to his wife, she attacked him.

Sam was unaware of it, but Fanny's whole world had collapsed. For eight years their life had been trickery and shoddy goods. She had suddenly realized that her "ideal" husband and happy marriage were based on nothing. Sam loved her, yes, he liked her a little more, he loved her a little less, yet he had probably never stopped running around, and this was not the worst of it.

The worst thing was that he had made her perfectly content, that she had gotten from him and from life in general just what she had expected. And that was worthless, a sham.

From now on Fanny would not know how to invest her formidable energy. Except in rebellion.

They often said, at least in the Osbourne family, that it was Fanny's intransigence that pushed her husband to infidelity. Sam's escapades, his taste for women, cards, speculation, repeated financial ruin, were all Fanny's doing. They may have been right. This wife who was so loyal in adversity, so discreet or submissive, would let loose a flood of reproaches, enough to drive away even the best of husbands. Deliberately, in eight days, Fanny was ready to destroy eight years of harmony.

For this intuitive woman, the questioning of everything she had ever felt and wanted sent her spinning. The abyss of doubts about herself was so complete that Sam could probably do nothing to save them.

The evening before the first of these scenes, which she would later describe as "shamefully common," they had made love.

Closer, more bound to each other than ever, this was their swan song. Sam remembered it as a particularly sweet and perfect communion. Had he been less spontaneous, he would have seen how savagely Fanny watched him revel in his pleasure while she held herself back, the brutality of her joy in bringing him, drowning him in pleasure while she remained on the brink.

In the morning he was cheerfully shaving when, lying in bed behind him, she said: "Let's separate."

Without gashing himself, Sam's arm fell. He turned around. "Why?"

"I do not want to live with a man I don't respect."

She spoke in a monotone, her hands on the sheet, her back against a pillow. At this moment of total immobility, with her crown of black curls, her pupils staring at nothing, her heavy naked breasts, and the necklaces of colored glass glittering between them, she resembled some primitive and dangerous idol.

Wiping the soap that still covered his beard above his cheeks, Sam came toward her. "What's the matter with you? Is it that stupid furniture business again?"

"I think I don't trust you anymore."

"Oh Fanny, you're always dramatizing!"

She did not answer. With an exasperated gesture, he slapped the towel against the bed. "Come now, what have I done that's so terrible? Mrs. Kelly was a friend of George's, she was having problems, I wanted to help her, I didn't think you would be so upset . . . Neither your sister nor you were there to nurse George. The last night he was alive, it was Mrs. Kelly who stayed with him, he died in her arms! And to say that you would ruin our lives over some stupid furniture business!"

Fanny lowered her head. Had her instinct betrayed her once again? Was it really just a matter of furniture? Was she mistaken? Yet Fanny was not inventing her suffering, it existed, and her disgust at the name of the widow Kelly, this fear. Was she crazy? Was she so weak-minded that this "stupid furniture business" could plunge her into paranoia? By making her doubt everything, herself, her feelings, the legitimacy of her anger, Sam managed to push her into that gaping hole that terrified her. Fanny lashed out again, at random.

"You gave her Belle's drawings."

"I did not 'give' her anything. I lent her the house while she was waiting for her things."

" 'My' house."

"Our house! . . . for God's sake, Fanny, I never knew you were so jealous, jealous of everything and of the whole world!"

He went out. She stayed there, naked and still.

Sam was going to endure a fire that had been stoked for six months. And the more he tried to slip away, the more tenacious she became.

In public, Fanny kept quiet as usual. In front of Lloyd, in front of Belle, not a word of reproach. The child never heard any shouts behind the thin partition. And if Belle perceived any change, she found it to her advantage: Her mother was finally paying attention to her. As for Sam, he grew closer to his daughter each day, and showed her how he felt. Fanny showed nothing.

But when her gaze rested on Sam's blue eyes, on his blond beard, on his lips, a crazed light came into the beautiful Mrs. Osbourne's eyes that could give you gooseflesh; even John Lloyd noticed it. "She's carrying this too far," he thought. Sam was in complete agreement.

His affair with Betty Kelly was no longer enough, he surrounded himself with an entourage of whores and played cards with the owners of gambling dens and saloons, with miners and brokers, making himself popular with the charm Fanny knew only too well.

Christmas 1865 was pure hell.

She had not been able to return to her parents' house that autumn, as Sam had promised in his letter to the Vandegrifts. She had spent two years far from the family home, far from Jo and from her father. So what? Sam, penniless once again, believed he was a millionaire. He owned nearly 30,000 "feet" in all the unexploited mines of Virginia City. Convinced that every foot was worth five or ten thousand dollars, he continued to borrow, to buy and sell and speculate. He was in the grip of gold fever and couldn't shake it.

And when one of his numerous partners proposed to go off prospecting, he jumped at the chance.

He would go into the mountains of Montana for one month. It

was the moment to make a fortune in this region where they had just discovered fabulous mineral deposits. Fanny and Belle would wait for him in Virginia City.

The little girl watched alone as the convoy, the mule train, eight wagons, and forty prospectors on horseback set off into the dusty desert on the morning of March 28, 1866.

This was the first exodus from Virginia City. It would become the worst massacre of Whites for the year of 1866.

*
**

Do you know, my dear Betty, Fanny wrote to her second sister, who was about to be married, *I feel assured that you have before you a future of comfortable happiness? That is a great deal for anyone to look forward to . . . your own home, no anxious pondering over tomorrow, a husband whom you can respect and believe in completely, and who loves you.* Everything she had lost, she felt, through her own doing.

The spring and summer passed without news of Sam. Not a word, not a message: total silence.

She dreamed about him every night, always the same nightmare. She saw herself sitting on a bench, in an empty, closed room. Shapes were grasping at Sam and she could do nothing. They clung to him and dragged him to the end of a corridor. Fanny stood there waiting for him. Finally the door opened. They threw Sam at her feet. He was unrecognizable. He was bleeding, his beard was burned off, his fingernails pulled out, his eyes hollow. She would scream and wake up. She was guilty for not being tortured in his place, and this feeling lingered.

It was because of her that he was not coming back. It was her intransigence that had driven him away from Virginia City. Perhaps she had sent him off to be killed. If he was dead . . .

She didn't dare go out to work anymore. She was afraid that if he found the house empty, he would not return to her. And so she did her sewing at home and spoke to Sam in her head.

She would have so much wanted to tell him that she forgave him, that she was the one who should ask forgiveness, a painful monologue that went on and on.

At dawn, awakened by her nightmare, she would post herself at the window. Every moment she would hear the gate open. The November blizzard shook the floorboards, rolled bales of hay through the street, pushed barrels and tanks down the slopes.

When she went to town, she thought she recognized Sam's bay mare everywhere, and under a rider's hat, Sam's beard, under the long coat, Sam's boots and spurs. She would breathlessly pursue the man to the edge of the desert, slipping on the tobacco juice that collected on the wooden sidewalks, or falling headlong in the snow.

That winter, the line of thirty telegraph posts, the pillars and pylons that bordered C Street, half disappeared under the powdery snow. The red porches, balustrades, and balconies, made pink by the frost, bowed under the weight of stalactites.

Around the mines, the pyramids of mining debris that bristled on the bland uniformity of the terrain were reminiscent of lunar volcanoes. With their covers of ice, the shafts looked like craters. In the whiteness of the tunnels, long trains of mules, horses, and donkeys breathed and smoked, and among them the idle men gesticulated, stamping their heels.

With the cold, the recession that had emptied the Austin Camp had just hit Virginia City.

For some time now, the wealth of the mother lode had seemed exhausted. The refining factories functioned at one-third capacity. This was a crisis—but not ruin. Everyone still had faith in the richness of the subsoil. They just had to dig deeper.

In order to hold on until the discovery of new veins, the companies without shareholders borrowed from the banks, which advanced enormous loans. Two million dollars was advanced in one year to small landowners. John Lloyd's predictions had been right on this point: At the end of the war, the big Eastern capitalists had turned toward Virginia City. To such an extent that this winter of 1866, the refining factories, mortgaged estates, insolvent transport companies, and most of the mines of the Comstock Lode had just fallen into the hands of the bankers. Now it was time for individual owners to fold up their tents.

"Sam was right!" exclaimed Lloyd, who appeared in Fanny's sitting room on the morning of December 3. "The big boys are getting rich all by themselves, they don't need us!"

He plunged his baby face into the steam rising from his cup.

What he had come to say embarrassed him, and the heat from the coffee was making his face even redder.

"People are leaving town, the small owners, I hear. The ones who've gone broke. They're going back to San Francisco."

Lloyd hesitated and, taking advantage of the moment when Fanny turned around to put the coffeepot on the stove, he admitted: "I'm going, too."

She paled under her tan. With Lloyd going away, her last link to reality would be gone as well. Leaning on the back of the chair, she looked for a moment at this head of cropped curls, the reddish neck covered with freckles, the short, gnarled finger that kept scratching at an imaginary spot on the square cloth. She clung to Lloyd. She clung to him as much as he clung to her, but for other reasons.

Embarrassed by their silence, he went on: "You should do the same, Mrs. Osbourne!"

"And Sam?" she asked.

"Sam will always make out. But you, a week from now, you won't be able to get through. The route from Reno is already closed. The rivers are flooding. There are avalanches everywhere. You are going to be stuck here all winter. You'd better hurry—the stagecoaches are crammed. I had to reserve my seat two weeks in advance."

She made an effort to appear calm, and sat down. "When do you leave?"

Again, Lloyd hesitated. "This evening."

She nodded her head, thoughtfully: "Of course."

"You should do the same," he insisted.

"What if Sam comes back and finds us gone?"

"Be reasonable, Mrs. Osbourne! All your customers are going down to spend the winter in the valley. How will you survive? Sam would never have left you and Belle here to freeze to death! In San Francisco you will easily find work. You could wait for him there."

"How will he find us there?"

"He'll find you."

Made anxious by the responsibility he was taking for a woman who should have been nothing to him, Lloyd again began to clean the tablecloth. This was the first time in eight months of daily visits that he was speaking to Fanny in such a direct way. Ordinarily, their conversations were much more circumspect, they understood each other without coming to the point. In any case, Lloyd usually stayed only a few moments. Fanny did not keep him, and when they said good-bye, they generally did not mention Sam, though the thought of him obsessed them both. Lloyd also felt a vivid sense of guilt toward Sam. He loved his friend's wife, but he loved her with a tormented passion in which attraction and repulsion figured equally.

The confusion of his two desires—to flee from Mrs. Osbourne, who rather frightened him, and to protect and possess her—was expressed in attacks of aggressiveness and silence. Neither of them knew why, but Lloyd could sulk with Fanny for a whole week. He sulked with her, but he came. Not a day passed that he did not come to take his coffee with her. And that fidelity was what attached Fanny to John Lloyd.

"Don't go. Not this evening! I will go with you in one week. Let me wait for him just one more week."

They waited in vain.

On Christmas Eve the neighbors saw Mrs. Osbourne, armed with a bucket and a brush, furiously covering her house with red graffiti.

Half an hour later, she left her famous furniture behind and set out with Belle on the last stagecoach to cross the Sierras before spring.

The looters and squatters who carved up the remains of the cabin read on every wall the same bloody message: *In San Francisco. The hotel where you put us up. We are waiting for you. Come!*

San Francisco—Occidental Hotel—1867

"You're wanted at the bar."

Half turned toward the bellboy, Fanny sat still in her armchair, but in the dim light the boy could divine the question that trembled on her lips: "Who?"

"Don't know," he confessed. "But a man."

This woman's deep emotion embarrassed the young fellow so that he could neither press her nor withdraw. So he stood there in the doorway of suite 11, waiting for the guest to find the strength to rise and come downstairs. With her questioning, apparently terrified gaze fixed on some invisible point, she did not move.

Behind her, the edges of the drapes fluttered in the ocean breeze like a wall of foam. The window framed the white sun, the hard and crystalline sky of a magnificent day in San Francisco. The air of the room smelled of the sea, of tobacco, strawberries, and pineapple. A basket of fruit was ripening between the candlesticks on the mantel, which held an ashtray full of cigarette butts as well.

She was alone, as she was every afternoon. Her little girl was out walking, without a chaperone, while she stayed in, sewing and rolling her cigarettes near the window. This was Fanny—industrious and passive.

Her brown curls were neatly gathered at the nape of her neck. She wore no earrings or ornaments. A white collar, a puce-green skirt, a cropped jacket of Scottish wool. The simplicity, not to say austerity of her clothing, plus the eccentricity of some of her habits, surprised the staff. Did this woman confuse the Occidental Hotel with some wretched boardinghouse for miners? She darned her own stockings, washed her linen, made her bed, picnicked on the carpet with cold meals she herself prepared. Was she simply economical or was she shy? Yet she did not seem overwhelmed by the fine crowd in the dining room, or even impressed by the luxury of the hotel. She made her way among the hanging tapestries, settled into the velvet upholstery, curled up on the silk of her bedspread in the most natural way, as if she had lived in palaces all her life. She also knew how to distribute tips and give orders. But she allowed no one to oversee her personal affairs.

In short, Mrs. Osbourne was different from the other guests at the Occidental.

She had appeared at the hotel at least a week earlier, on a Saturday, around five o'clock: the moment when wives, newly rich from their husbands' mining speculations, were enjoying a platter of oysters after shopping on Montgomery Street. This was the first snobbery of the San Francisco wealthy, almost a tradition.

Jumping from the coach the evening of their arrival, while Fanny and Belle dusted themselves off, John Lloyd had counted the banks. Eight banks in a single block of buildings. Eight gas-lit banks, whose advertising consisted of a patchwork of banknotes from all over the world covering the windows from the ground to the firm's name plate.

"So much money!"

As they walked to the Occidental, Lloyd, half fascinated, half shocked, had also wanted to count the restaurants. So many and all crammed full. He had observed their two entrances, one on the street for "families," the other in the alley, in the shadows, for

"private parties." And the five floors of rooms were always organized according to the same system: on the ground floor, a common
room reserved for pseudo-legitimate couples, for women alone and
children who were taking their meals in town; on the first floor,
salons reserved for Masonic gatherings, for clubs, and banquets;
finally, on the three upper levels, the "P.C." reserved for romantic
dining. P.C., Private Cooking, was a translation of the initials, of
those *Cabinets Particuliers* of the illustrious Parisian restaurants.
La Maison Dorée, Le Café Riche, Tortoni, the same names were
found on the signs in San Francisco, and the same decor. Hallways,
low doorways, red banquettes, beveled mirrors, bell cords to ring
for the waiters, and small locks on the doors. But in California one
expected *"towels and soap upstairs," "showers and cloakrooms at
the end of the hall."* Quite a difference.

"So much money!" Lloyd had repeated with a deep sigh that
expressed a mixture of envy, pleasure, and disdain. "Are you sure
you want to go to the Occidental?"
"The owners are friends of Sam."
An explanation that sufficed in Fanny's eyes to justify all extravagance: Without a penny in her pocket, she had settled into the
most expensive hotel in the city.
"She must be much, much richer than I thought," Lloyd said to
himself as he handed her bag over to her at the coach entrance.
There was an awkward moment when neither of them had known
quite what to say or how to take leave of each other.
"When I have found a place, Mrs. Osbourne, I will come to find
out how you are. Good luck."
"I'll expect your visit. Don't forget me, John!"
They had parted abruptly. She had watched his short figure disappear in the fog, vanishing over the rise of the road toward the
Bay. Then, turning around, she had entered the hotel.
What an effervescent swarm of people! In the hubbub among
the watered silks, the grosgrain, the shantung, she did hot hesitate
but went straight to the reception desk.
Her hair covered with alkali dust, carrying a single threadbare
saddlebag, her ragamuffin child in her wake, Fanny Osbourne had
made quite a sensation. This was probably the first of her formidable entrances into the lobbies of hotels, shacks, or palaces across
the world that Ned Field witnessed in the last ten years of her life.

But during the period when Ned served as her secretary, when clients and domestics would pursue him to the elevators with their eternal questions, "Who is that?" "What is that person's name?", the barbarity of Mrs. Robert Louis Stevenson's attire, her baroque hats, her stiff dresses, her tribal jewelry, were enough to explain the curiosity of the passersby. She never noticed anything: "My God, how friendly these people are!" She would be astonished when all the doormen would vie with each other for the pleasure of opening a door for her, all the chambermaids for the honor of serving her. She was too natural, too instinctive, and too humble as well to imagine for a moment that such compliments or reproaches could be meant for her. "Me? But who would be interested in my little manias?" She truly believed she was invisible, "ordinary," as ordinary as she was at the age of twenty-five, crossing the lobby of the Occidental Hotel. Yet she nearly got herself lynched there. With her imperious manner, her chin up, a determined look in her black eyes, she had forced her way through the mob of seated women, her elbows knocking the birds stuck in their chignons, her bag catching the decorative fruit on their hats, shaking the bells of the "follow me, young man," the long ribbons worn by the elegant women of the time.

Disheveled, rumpled, their wigs askew, false hummingbirds over their eyes, these ladies showed their fangs. Fanny, unconscious of the carnage, went on her way. She was already ringing the bell at the reception desk when an urgent but quiet, almost inaudible voice demanded the client's name:

"Sam's wife."

"Mrs. Osbourne?"

To the great surprise of the staff, the manager had fallen all over himself:

"Mrs. Osbourne! What good news! You're very welcome, my little lady . . . Number 11 for Mrs. Sam!"

Eddies of surprise, a vibration of revolt through the lobby: Hadn't suite 11 been occupied a month earlier by Queen Emma of Hawaii?

"That's the room Sam reserved for your arrival, do you remember?" Yes, Fanny remembered! "We have to straighten up, but I believe it will be worth waiting for . . ."

The red and gold door closed behind her, Fanny had thrown herself on the bed in relief. Secure at last!

It wasn't the luxuriousness of the room, the thickness of the walls or the solidity of the furniture. It was the place Sam had chosen

for welcoming her. He had been loved, admired, doted on here.
Here she had become Mrs. Osbourne again, "Sam's wife." Here
he would look for her, and find her.

*

"Someone's at the bar," the boy insisted at last. "A man is waiting
for you downstairs."

Drunk with joy, the hoops of her skirt raised to her chin, Fanny
ran down the halls, hurtled down the stairs and across the lobby.
Her nightmare was over!

"Mrs. Osbourne?"

Standing at the bar, on the side that connected with the hotel,
was a stranger.

Dressed in a red-checked shirt, trousers tucked into his boots,
he wore the prospector's familiar uniform, but he smelled of soap
and lavender, and was clean-shaven for the occasion.

"Mrs. Osbourne?"

She could not answer. She could hardly speak. She stood like a
statue in the doorway.

Finding her so small, already looking so hurt, the man's face
hardened. He put down his glass, removed his hat, and repeated:

"Are you really Mrs. Samuel Osbourne?"

"Yes," she whispered.

He hesitated. Fanny's blood drained from her cheeks and flooded
her beating heart.

Both paled as they looked at each other. The stranger lowered
his eyes. He asked quickly: "Did your husband leave Virginia City
on the 26th of last March with the Atchinson convoy?"

"Yes."

"I have bad news for you."

This time she staggered. Her mouth went dry and she had difficulty breathing.

The man hurried: "It happened in July. North of Hangtown, a
few miles away, the Indians attacked, early in the morning. About
twenty of them. Your husband was wounded."

Fanny felt a rush of joy: Sam was only wounded!

The man read the relief in her eyes, but said nothing. She understood then the worst was yet to come.

"He's not . . . ?"

The man nodded his head in the affirmative. Then, as if to mitigate the horror of the news, he concluded: "There were no survivors."

She did not faint. She made no sound, no cry, no complaint, no sobs or moans. What she had dreaded day and night for eight months had come to pass. She thanked the man for having taken the trouble to tell her. Slowly she returned to her room. Once alone, she swayed but did not fall.

Henceforth Fanny Osbourne would refuse herself even the relief of regret and remorse. She refused even to give herself permission to admit her sorrow and grieve.

Sam was dead. She had killed him. She was not his widow, she was his murderer. Unworthy of tears, she denied herself the right to weep, the right to sorrow and mourning.

*
**

"Now you'll return home," murmured John Lloyd, watching her pack her luggage.

"No."

This answer surprised him, but fearing an indiscretion, he kept quiet.

Indifferent to what people would say, Fanny received John Lloyd in her room. He was sitting delicately on the bed beside the carpet bag she was buckling.

"I cannot afford the return trip for Belle and me."

"Your family would wire you the money . . . or they would send you the ticket."

"I don't think so."

Lloyd hesitated. He shifted uncomfortably from one buttock to the other. Finally, he asked timidly: "Have you written to them?"

"No."

"You haven't written them!"

Flabbergasted, he jumped to his feet. "You haven't told them anything about Sam? They don't know that Sam is deceased?"

She did not answer and shut her bag with a click of the two clasps. He watched her grab the handle, lift it, and set it on the floor.

"And you're figuring on staying here?"

"Yes."

"All alone?"

"Yes."

"But why?"

Again, she did not answer. Her gaze, ordinarily so direct, was evasive. She bent down and reopened her bag.

"What are you going to do in San Francisco, all alone with your girl?"

"I will work."

He paced the room with his quick steps. He didn't understand. "But you so much wanted to go home! You used to talk to me constantly about your family. You told me that you missed your sisters. You used to tell me that you and your father . . ."

She got up. Their eyes met. Lloyd sensed that he was torturing her. The despair of this woman frightened him so that he dropped the subject.

"All right," he conceded, "obviously, if you insist, I suppose you could rent a room in the boardinghouse where I'm living. The neighborhood isn't very lively, but the place is clean. And the lady who runs the place gives credit."

Unable to speak, Fanny acquiesced. She took Belle by the hand. John Lloyd lifted the bag and they went downstairs.

In the long upholstered hallways on the red steps of the stairs, she seemed to be drowning deep in the flowered velvet wallpaper. She already wore clothes that seemed to make her shrink even more, a pitiful little figure in black.

"At home," Lloyd insisted, "at home with your family, Mrs. Osbourne, your sorrow wouldn't be so hard to bear."

"Exactly," she murmured.

He shrugged his shoulders. Then, suddenly anxious as they passed the cashier, he blurted out: "And may I ask how you are going to pay your hotel bill?"

She did not look at him, but said: "I will pay it."

*
**

Indeed, she paid, and even largely settled her debt. Knowing Fanny's moral inclinations, I have good reason to think that she was seeking to expiate her sins.

I am sorry that Ned did not question her more about this period.

She constantly repeated that she had no memory of it. He knew that she could describe the floor of her room inch by inch, the color of the walls, the smell of the boardinghouse; he knew that she kept stored in her memory the most infinitesimal details of the winter of 1867. And Ned got nothing out of her, not even an impression.

Was Fanny silent to combat the ghastliness of certain memories, of certain emotions that continued to haunt her? Or was she defending herself against the intolerable idea that she had been torturing herself for nothing, by accident, out of someone else's boredom and indifference?

Perhaps, too, she was suffering from a vague and deep-seated feeling of guilt toward Belle. A guilt she immediately denied but that tore her apart. What right did she have to refuse her daughter the return to the solid family home, the consolations and support of Jacob Vandegrift? What right did Fanny have to keep her child in San Francisco in this state of near material and moral destitution?

*
**

She had known isolation in a world of men, the struggle for survival in the wide open spaces; she had discovered the wretchedness and solitude of a swarming city. Now she was a widow with a child, with no friends or resources, cut off from her family by the entire continent. And she was sad, so deeply sad that for the rest of her life Fanny Osbourne would not be able to cry. Yet she would rebuild her world.

She quickly found employment as a finisher in a dress shop. Something different, mysterious in her ways, her smallness, or perhaps her dexterity with the needle allowed her to pass for a Frenchwoman in exile. "French"—that was so much more elegant in the fashion business! She even presented herself officially as a seamstress from Paris. Never mind that she didn't speak the language, that she hadn't the faintest notion of the geography or government of her putative country, she bluffed shamelessly.

Afterwards, like it or not, Fanny would always pass for a foreigner, even at home. From the plains of Indiana to the Pacific islands, from San Francisco to Grez-sur-Loing, from Edinburgh to Sidney, she was always from somewhere else. This is a curious paradox. For there was no one better able to blend into the background, no one more adaptable to circumstances.

The "Frenchwoman" labored from dawn to dusk in the back room of Singer's. Not a word of complaint about the work. On the contrary, she asked for more. In the evenings, she carried it home with her to the boardinghouse and continued, beside her sleeping daughter, to hem the bottoms of skirts with long twists of dried lavender that would perfume the balls of San Francisco.

For her, the spinning waltzes, the Scottish dances and quadrilles, were over. Over, too, the galloping rides on horseback, the nature walks, tramping the earth. She denied herself the right to any respite or pleasure. Even on Sundays, at the call of the seagulls, when Belle and John Lloyd would leave to explore the wharfs, Fanny remained shut in. In addition to the orders for Singer's, she embroidered layettes, tablecloths, and cushions which she sold on Market Street through the Women's Exchange. During all those months she saw neither the sea nor the masts that swayed at the end of the street. But in September, she knew that she would be able to feed, clothe, and educate her child without appealing to the Vandegrifts, whose support she felt she no longer deserved. Only then did she write to them of her husband's death. That evening she prepared to celebrate Belle's ninth birthday.

My mother, Belle would write, (*at the cost of I dare not think how many stitches) bought the head of a china doll, and made the body herself, stuffing it with rags. Whatever little Matilda (that was her name) lacked in grace of body she made up in beauty of feature and magnificence of apparel. Out of silk and satin and other bits left over from her dressmaking, my mother made for the little doll a marvelous wardrobe—clothes that could be put on and off and most elegant underwear trimmed with lace and perfect in every detail, even to the tiny buttons and buttonholes. John bought a set of toy tin dishes complete with teapot and cups and saucers. With some cigar boxes he had made a table and two chairs to match.*

My birthday was charming. John, my mother and I sat on the floor around the little table with Matilda in one of the new chairs presiding. My birthday cake was a cup cake which I cut with John's penknife . . . My mother, in her black dress, did her best to smile and when I asked her age she said that in a few years she would be a quarter of a century old! John was very gay and looked happy

*and boyish with his pink cheeks, and crisp curly hair. I imagine
he was working as hard to distract my mother's attention as he
was to entertain me . . .*

John Lloyd sometimes did manage to distract Fanny, but neither
he nor she had time for amusement.

He loved her, certainly. He loved her all the more, he loved her
all the better as she seemed unable to love him. If she had thrown
off her widow's weeds, he would have fled. She knew it, and he
did too. John worked by day as a messenger in a bank; at night,
with books borrowed from the public library, he studied law. It
was a hard-working life for both of them, a life without luxury and
little hope, a life that she had almost come to accept without rebellion. And then, in the first days of October, the miracle happened.

*
**

The morning routine. The boardinghouse reeked with the acidic,
almost oppressive odor of cabbage and gas. In the distance bells
were ringing: a fire somewhere. Fanny, bent over the door she was
trying to close, raised her head. She listened, counting. Five alarms?
The fire was in this neighborhood. Six alarms? Disaster struck in
another part of town. Outside, she heard the clopping of horseshoes
on the wooden streets. On horseback, on foot, in bed, everywhere
the inhabitants of San Francisco were counting. Some hurried
home, others hurried out. In summer, the bell sent them into motion several times a day. The fire alarms were the distinctive song
of San Francisco. Today it was raining. Along with the fire bells,
the drops of rain that pattered on the street corners were vibrating
the tassels and trimmings in the hallway. Nine alarms: the danger
was far away. Fanny finished closing her door. Brown curls over
her eyes, her purse clasped in her hand, she pulled the door shut,
lifted the handle, and turned the key. This wasn't easy; the lock
was stuck. Their room was over the stairwell. A few steps away,
Belle daydreamed as she waited.

Downstairs, the doorbell rang. With his Stetson over his eye, a man
entered in a long, dripping coat. He wore boots with worn-down heels,
and a powder horn. Belle, ever the coquette, admired his pointed

boots. She loved cowboy boots, but clean ones. Fanny had replaced the key in her purse, put on her gloves, and rearranged her veil. She was ready to go downstairs. Her skirt rustled against the railing. The man raised his head. A shout cut through the air.

"My little girl!"

"Papa!"

Belle flew into his arms. Fanny paled. She felt a happiness so violent it was close to pain. Sam was alive. How many times in the last two years had she dreamed of Sam alive, Sam's return. She faltered. A wave washed over her, and she drowned. Sam was suffocating her, hugging her. Fanny was passive, dead inside.

*
**

"And so?"

"And so, on the same day I nearly died four times! First, Sam Orr and I—Sam's my new partner—we found ourselves all alone in the middle of the desert. Don't ask me how we did it, we never did figure it out. Orr claims that we were sleeping as we rode! Possible. Ahead of us, no more convoys! The wagons had disappeared. We called, we shouted, we went after them. Wasted effort. We were wandering through the desert. And that's how we escaped death again. Indians attacked the others a few miles away. But we heard nothing. And remember, we had no water, no provisions— even the compasses and maps were in the wagons. A burning sun, rocks everywhere, not even a line of horizon to fix our eyes on. Just a white expanse, boiling hot. The horses were dead from thirst the next day, and I had to put Myra down. We continued on foot. The sun and thirst drove us crazy. As we walked we shed our garments one by one, probably thinking that we wouldn't be so hot naked. In the end, I had thrown everything away, except for one thing. You know what it is, Belle? No, you don't know?"

The child shook her head and burrowed into the hollow of her father's arm. With delight she found again the sweet odor of his tobacco, the warmth of that body, of that voice. A serious, lively voice, a bit lilting, with its Kentucky accent. He was a "gentleman," her father. Despite his overgrown beard, his long hair streaked by the wind, Sam was still supremely elegant. His gestures had such distinction, as Fanny well knew. He removed a little canvas book from his shirt.

"Do you recognize it? Here, I've brought it back to you."

The little girl grabbed it. Of course she recognized it! It was her favorite story, *Beauty and the Beast,* which she had given as a gift to her father on the day of his departure. "Here, I've brought it back to you." All of Sam was contained in this gesture. Sentimental, gallant, charming. In one sentence, he had erased two years' absence.

"And so?"

"So, so, we thought we were dead. I was imagining the two of you, my dears, on Grandfather Vandegrift's green lawn, when suddenly, between two rocks, a pool. Small, but a pool! Water! We dragged ourselves to it. I got there first. I'm dunking my head in when behind me, Orr growls: "Don't move!" I turn around. There, two fingers from my face, a rattlesnake! Orr fires. He kills the snake. The bullet ricochets off a stone and hits me in the forehead. I lose consciousness. Saved! Saved a fourth time! If I had drunk a single drop of that water, I would have been a goner. That's what the prospectors told us who were attracted by the gunshot. The pool was poisoned by alkali. A lucky day—Indians, thirst, snake, water. Death really didn't want anything to do with me. The prospectors welcomed us, we went off with them, and here I am."

The rest of his adventures were lost in a chaos of memories: long marches, barber shops, saloons, long marches. Why hadn't he written?

"My letters must have been lost."

What had he done, day after day, month after month? According to him, he had been lost in other deserts.

She did not question him further. Sam was here, against her. Sam was reading aloud a Christmas story. Sam was putting Belle to sleep. Christmas morning, Sam and Fanny hid together behind the bed and watched their child discover the pile of presents.

They were a joyful family, just as before.

*
**

They did not discuss the months prior to Sam's departure. The widow Kelly was a thing of the past. They took up the thread of their life as they had left it in the camp at Austin, an understanding and happiness unaffected by the harshness of their circumstances.

Material life was considerably improved with Sam's return. His ease, his ingratiating manners and education quickly earned him the acquaintance of the intellectuals and adventurers of San Francisco, and the city was not lacking in this respect.

In fifteen days, thanks to his numerous friendships, he found employment as a court stenographer, took his family out of the gloomy boarding-house, and moved them to a little house on 5th Street. And as before, John Lloyd came to supper every night. Sam's return eased his existence as well. No more hesitations, no more anguish: "Do I dare or not?" The wife of his best friend, Fanny Osbourne once more became the impossible love, the sorrow and comfort of his life.

*
**

Everything was as before. Fanny was jubilant, Sam was tender. Sam was in love, as before. The Osbournes hosted the young lions of the city. Lawyers without cases, painters without commissions, bankers without funds—a sort of bohemia. They discussed art, politics, and mining speculation. They made music on flute and guitar, and the pretty mistress of the house cooked, listened, and kept quiet.

But her muteness had a different meaning now. She listened quietly, but with an alertness that Lloyd had never seen before. She was learning.

I take watercolor lessons, she confides to her sister. *I want to learn to color and retouch photographs. If I ever be in necessity, it will stand me in good stead, for it is very showy, cheap, and can be done in a short time . . .*

The idea had come to her that she should be able to survive without Sam. In her letters to her sisters she is still silent about their concerns, hers and Sam's, in this month of February 1868. She is expecting a baby, but no one in Indiana knows about it. She doesn't say a word in her letters about this new pregnancy. On the other hand, she never stops singing John Lloyd's praises.

As I write you, Pa's picture is looking down upon me. I have never had a frame for it and the other day John carried it away secretly and brought it back in an elegant frame. Wasn't that

*thoughtful and kind? ... I mean to have John's picture taken too.
He imagines himself to be so very ugly that he thinks any references
to looks or pictures are something personal. He is not good looking
to be sure, but then he is not ugly either and the more one knows
him and how reliable and straight forward he is ... the more you
like him, and the better looking you think he is.*

Not a word about "handsome Sam."

*
**

As before. Yes everything was as before—at the time of the widow
Kelly. During his wife's pregnancy, Sam once again began chasing
women. This time, Fanny sensed it immediately. His odor, something
nervous and evasive in his look. She sniffed it out. This was jealousy,
base jealousy with its nights of insomnia and suspicious fury.

Now Sam slept elsewhere, he had a mistress, a divorcée whom
he supported with the household money. It didn't mean a thing,
he said, just a passing fancy, it's nothing, Fanny, be patient. She
imagined him holding this other woman in his arms, repeating the
same words to her.

"It's either her or me!" the wife threatened, taking a chance.

"But of course it's you."

Fanny grew heavier, and Sam did not break off with his mistress.

This time it was clear: Fanny was afraid, her heart was filled
with an abiding anguish. Again, she was afraid of life without him
and afraid of living with this threat. When she thought of the horror
of those two years of abandonment, she told herself, "Never again."
She was obsessed with the terror of being left again.

On April 28, 1868, in the Osbourne's little house, a boy was born.

One month later, scarcely recovered from childbirth, Fanny
packed her bags. She was leaving Sam. She fled. It was over, the
illusion of happiness, the illusion of love. She returned to Indiana.

With a newborn at her breast, a girl of ten holding her hand, she
traveled third class to Panama. The fevers of Aspinwall, its poisonous
ponds, its hammocks and horrors were experienced all over again. But
this time Fanny Osbourne had nothing to look forward to.

During the voyage, she baptized her son Samuel Lloyd, in memory of
the two men she'd left behind, the one who loved her and the one who

had loved her. Two persons from the past. Out of a total of ten years, nothing remained. The child would survive, but his father's name eventually vanished and everyone called him Lloyd.

She would spend a whole year on the other side of the continent, far from Sam.

Clayton, Indiana—May 1868–June 1869

I must have been half starved, she admitted at the end of her life, *to have kept such a memory of food in Indiana!*

No one who hasn't been to the Vandegrift house can imagine the sweetness of life there. It is an axle, an anchor, the destination of all travels. Built on a curve in the road, it seems to reach out in both directions, a solid building of red brick blocking the horizon. But it does not feel encased or enclosed. The farm is hidden by a vast lawn that slopes toward a wood. Apple trees line the gently undulating prairie grass that froths between the groves of nut trees, soft and bucolic. An anti-Nevada. Behind a thick hedge hides a wooden porch, three white steps, large sash windows. And there are tiger lilies, Fanny's fetish flower.

The fragrance of the Vandegrift house was female, a combination of beeswax (the woodwork, the parquet floor, the stairway were polished every day), apples ripening in the fruit bins, and spice breads baking in the huge wood stove. The buzzing of seven women filled the house, their scissors and needles clicking. There was something sweet in the air, humming, rustling, singing softly. This was a far cry from the tensions of Virginia City. The garden rang with the laughter of children following their little grandmother to the cellar. Every evening, Esther Vandegrift led her flock between the barrels of cider, the jars of jams and preserves, the strings of onions and dried thyme hanging from the ceiling. *This was the little snack our grandmother handed out to each one of us,* Belle would recount, marveling. *A large thick slice of homemade bread (in my memory about a foot across) and on that lumps of fresh butter too cold to spread, on that a layer of jam topped by a slab of cheese; taking this, an apple a and pickle, we trooped up to bed.* [There was] *Cora, Nellie, my cousin George,* [the son of Josephine and the deceased George Marshall], *and myself.*

Nellie, Cora and I slept in the same room . . . We all wore night-

gowns of pink dotted calico of the same pattern . . . so long we had to hold them up in front when we walked.

Leaning on a column, Fanny was watching Jacob Vandegrift's profile. The cropped gray hair, the curved nose, the sensual lips. Every movement of the rocking chair plunged this beloved head into darkness. It reappeared dark and powerful, wreathed in smoke. The odor of his tobacco made her think of Sam, and so did the half-smiling expression around his mouth. Jacob enjoyed these summer nights when his wife, his daughters, his son, and his grandchildren gathered around him. Jo had just remarried a neighbor they had known for a long time.

And they were all so young! None had reached the age of thirty. Fanny, the oldest, was twenty-eight. The others were twenty-six, twenty-two, twenty, sixteen. Lively young people. At meals, having a coffee or beer, they planned a project, a picnic, reminisced about their childhood.

"Do you remember, Fanny, when we tied Jake to the tree and he. . . ." Jo asks, clearing the table.

Fanny remembered, of course! But now there was a gulf between Jo and Fanny, they had nothing to say to each other. Jo, her old companion, wasn't even conscious that they were separated by a century, a continent.

Sometimes I have a presentiment that I will never see you again, Fanny had written from San Francisco. *That it would seem too great a happiness for me.*

Now this feeling of isolation among those she thought so close was making her terribly sad. For four years she had thought of nothing but the joy of seeing them again. Yet now she felt no joy, no pleasure—nothing, not even boredom. And yet, they had not changed. They were just the same: lighthearted, kind, easy. But she still had the taste of alkali dust in her mouth, and the taste of ashes. The summer passed. Evening after evening, they grew more distant. She did not know how to reach them. She would have liked to share her experience with them and tried to tell them, to describe it to them—the landscapes, the frenzy of the miners, the customs of the Indians. They listened, they were interested. But Fanny would lose the thread of her talk. Her talent for storytelling had deserted her, and she clung to the concrete, practical details, raw material: the price of a Winchester in Virginia City, an axe in Austin, the price of rope. She explained to the girls the recipe for Chinese rice and spring rolls from San Francisco. But the miracle did not happen. Even with Belle, there was a rupture. Coddled, cosseted, the little girl adapted and grew closer to her young aunts than to Fanny.

"Did you have good news from Sam this morning?" Jacob murmured, puffing on his pipe.

She did not think of Sam anymore, or of her former life. She felt no nostalgia or even pain for that other life that did not seem to concern her, or very little. Her widowhood in San Francisco, her work as a seamstress, Sam's miraculous resurrection—that was in another time, another place. Jacob casually persisted.

"His business is going well?"

The only feeling she retained, thinking about Sam, was the pain of the last months, like a vise constricting her throat, strangling her: Sam smitten with another woman, Sam, thinking, speaking, smelling like that other woman. Fanny could still see his silhouette from a distance, wreathed in that new perfume and new promises, disappearing over the rise in the road, heading toward the Bay. "This evening, or tomorrow morning, or ten days, or ten years from now he will not come home." Certain that she was no longer loved, she was afraid of being left all over again.

In the big Vandegrift house Fanny had nothing left but this fear. She exorcised it by clinging to her most distant memories. This was wasted effort. The happy times? Wasted effort, too. She drove the buggy to Indianapolis, stood in front of the little house where her roses once climbed. But she could feel nothing. The new owners had just added an upper floor, they talked of tearing it down and rebuilding elsewhere, but it hardly mattered to her. Embarrassed, ashamed of her indifference, she tried to rekindle the flame, leafing through the family album, finding the account of her marriage in the *Indianapolis Star* of December 28, 1857. "In the presence of a large and joyful assembly, in the presence of the Governor and his entire cabinet, on the twenty-fourth of this month were married, by the Reverend Foster, Samuel Osbourne, Esq. and Miss Fanny Vandegrift, daughter of Jacob Vandegrift of this city. May our wishes come true: May they find conjugal happiness in their journey through life, the only happiness left to us from paradise lost. Conjugal Happiness, the sole felicity to survive the Fall."

She sighed, feeling no anger or regret. She could no longer conjure up Sam's image—his saber at his side, the polished buttons of his tunic, standing so straight in his lavender blue uniform. There was nothing left but the words: "Saber at his side, polished buttons." And then, sometimes, too, she experienced a kind of dizziness, the physical sensation of losing her footing. Any moment, anywhere, in the kitchen, in a field, the ground would suddenly give way, the earth come toward her, the trees converge, the sky descend and crush her; the air vibrated, the distant booming of a double bass filled her head, invaded her limbs, agitated her body, which seemed to be swinging above the void. She would lose her breath, struggle, clutch at something nearby, and suddenly swoon. She would fall straight down an interminable shaft, half bowel, half tunnel, that led to death. At the very bottom, black water trembled with the image of Sam's face. Was he her savior or her executioner? His sensual mouth came near, supplicating and charming. It was about to open up, to absorb her, to take her back.

"A woman's place, Fanny, is at her husband's side."

It was Jacob who launched this attack. Behind them, the little gang was hurrying to clear the table. Jo carried out the last bottles, the mother disappeared and replaced the mosquito netting. Father and daughter were left alone. Slightly in retreat, Fanny rolled a cigarette, a habit she had taken up in the mining camps; Jacob continued to swing, his lips closed around his pipe, his eyes fixed on the black expanse.

"Whatever happened between you and Sam, Fanny, you must go back . . ."

"Where?"

"Home."

"But I am home!"

"You know that's not so . . ."

Still neutral, their voices echoed in the night. Fanny crushed her cigarette butt under her little boot. Jacob puffed on his pipe.

"Home is in San Francisco with your husband."

"I will not go back to him."

"He still loves you, he wrote to me . . ."

"He wants to see Belle and Samuel Lloyd, not me!"

"He loves you, Fanny."

"If he loves me, let him come here."

Jacob got up and faced her. With his blue gaze as intense as his daughter's, he pinned her down: "It is certainly true that Sam has behaved badly toward you. But you, my girl, you are not easy to live with either! He is a fine boy. The way he behaved at George's death proved it. He has sent me his accounts. He's not making out so badly. He has bought a little house on the other side of the Bay, just opposite San Francisco, a house for you, Fanny, with a garden, a kitchen . . ."

"And are you the one to be telling me this?"

Wounded, she took his measure. Her father, that indomitable man who only believed in instinct, in emotions, in feelings.

"Are you the one to talk to me about kitchens and property, about spending the rest of my life with a man who couldn't care less about me and cheats on me?"

Either Jacob had aged, or Fanny had never understood what she had the right to ask of life and of herself.

*
**

Even as an old woman, when the first movement for women's liberation became fashionable in the United States, Fanny was not a feminist or suffragette. She would shrug her shoulders at "the equality of the sexes" and smile at the "vote for women." In 1910, she was a skeptical attendant at the round of meetings Belle held as a militant in the ranks of the first feminist movement. *With the cry "Emancipation!" my daughter galvanizes the female crowd, what talent, what stupidity!* notes this outrageous old lady, who for seven years played a political role in all the internal struggles of Samoa, who was living at the time with a young man half a century her junior. *As for me, these theories bore me. True, I must be senile: Belle and her friends' demands put me to sleep.* An astonishing misunderstanding of herself that typifies her to perfection. For no one had ever so urgently demanded the right to be free, and to be a woman. Her life had really been one long, untiring quest for autonomy.

*
**

Yet the thirty-year-old Fanny would play by the rules. She would obey her father and reassure her family; she would go back to her husband and make a home for her children. But what precipitated

her out of Indiana in May 1869 was not parental pressure or the
desire to please, or even Belle's tears and the cries of her little son who
needed a father. It was the letter from Sam that arrived one morning:

*Try me. Try us. What have you got to lose? There is something
basic between us. I am expecting you. Together, let us rebuild.*

Rebuild? For nearly a year, her feet and hands in the earth, she had
planted, sown, pruned, watered, cultivated. The kitchen garden had
never produced so many tomatoes. The garden was a profusion of flowers, the vine was growing to the roof. Rebuild—if only it were possible.

Suddenly, Fanny packed up her trunks and made the return
journey, a girl of eleven beside her and a baby in her arms. Once
again she traveled thousands of miles to rejoin Sam, but this time
not by way of Panama. The fevers of Aspinwall were behind her.

On May 10, 1869, three weeks before Fanny's trip, the rails
connecting the East and West coasts of the United States were
joined midway in the mountains of Utah. The transcontinental railroad was in business, a titanic enterprise that took six years of
financial battles, accidents, murders, and the labor of more than a
million men, 10,000 of them six feet under. The shorter route between the Atlantic and the Pacific involved 200 stops, about thirty
train changes, and ten days of travel.

Upon arrival, Fanny kept forever impressed in her mind the
image of a riotous, virgin nature, the sense of a civilization in the
making, the revelation of a world. This ecstasy of unfettered force
mirrored her own.

Six years later, Robert Louis Stevenson would recognize this embodiment of a foreign world in Mrs. Osbourne. As soon as he met
her in the heart of old Europe he would describe her to his friends
as the incarnation of a new feminine ideal: *"the American girl."*
And it was with that sense of freedom, with the savagery of the
Great Plains, that he fell in love.

*

In June 1869, the wife that Sam Osbourne welcomed at the train
in Sacramento bore scarcely any resemblance to the romantic
spouse of Austin. This new person was even younger, a Fanny
before maternity, before marriage, before love, a person hungry to
learn, eager to exist on her own and absorb everything.

III

Rearden's Friend

In San Francisco, the law is vile:
when a man does not treat his wife
as she would like, she divorces him
and finds another husband!

—Timothy Rearden, judge.

East Oakland—1869–1875

A grid of white gates, barns with sloping roofs, tree-lined squares, and dusty paths were flanked by an ocean of greenery that rolled its tide of grasses to the Pacific, a harsh, blinding sea that swallowed the dying smoke of the ferries crossing the Bay. Far off, a jumble of yellowish squares bobbed on bristling swells, where the straight lines of black masts seemed to shoot up from the boats. This was San Francisco seen from Fanny's house. Inseparable from the garden and the sea, this prefabricated house had arrived in pieces in the belly of a ship, a little white wooden house that had made the crossing around Cape Horn before disappearing between the blond palm trees and brick colored laburnum, beneath a mass of fiery roses.

When the two enormous bushes leaning against the veranda blazed together, the effect was striking, Belle would write. *Straw yellow and blood red, their entwined branches choked the frail columns of the porch, zigzagging like sparks up a flue, catching the whole roof on fire, flinging themselves toward the chimney where*

91

golden flares seemed to burst forth, the sea breeze making them rattle against the three, green-shuttered windows of the upper floor. A slow, copper-colored shower of petals came, then, to stain the patches of sunlight between the flowering shrubs of the lawn.

In the Oakland garden, as in all of Fanny's gardens, the space was not divided along any axis; there were no right angles, no clear borders or trimmed hedges, no maze or enclosure. Rather it was a vast space punctuated by sheaves of color where all the botanical forms, textures, and odors intermingled. *In the shadow of one of these shrubs, mysterious paths began,* Belle goes on: *They meandered and disappeared down the slopes. Behind other trees and bushes were hidden my mother's stable, her shooting range, her photography studio, a whole world one wouldn't have suspected looking from the house.*

Three years after returning to Sam, Fanny spent the summer in perpetual motion. On horseback at dawn, she galloped over the dusty roads, stuffed her squash, pruned her roses, picked the heavy peaches, which she covered with vanilla and sprinkled with crystallized petals. In the kitchen, at the office, in the garden, not an hour of the day was unoccupied. At night, she made her own dresses, very freely copied from Parisian fashion magazines. Knots, frog fastenings, feathers, velours, flounces—she aimed for effect. Not that Fanny had outright bad taste, just a tendency to excess. On the boulevards of Paris, she would no doubt have been taken for a provincial woman—or an American! In Oakland, her children's elegance—Belle in lace trousers, Lloyd in a sailor suit—gained her the admiration of all the county mothers. Mrs. Osbourne passed for a sophisticated woman, and she took pride in this reputation.

A good cook, a good housekeeper, economical, and cleanly: This is still one of Fanny's contradictions, that this woman in search of herself was above all a consummate housewife. She thought in terms of recipes, patterns, and cooking. She adored her curtains, her knickknacks and trinkets. She trailed an odor of beeswax and cinnamon, and her sounds were the clicking of kitchen utensils, the hum of the sewing machine.

In describing Fanny's many travels, her very modern aspirations, I must make an effort to remember that every morning she squeezed herself into a corset, buckled a padded bustle around her hips, piled on camisoles and skirts, hooked up the fifty eyelets of a bustier, and trimmed herself out with a bustle and a train.

Mrs. Osbourne truly belonged to the Victorian era. "She also belonged to the prehistoric age!" her future detractors would one day grumble.

*
**

She had short nails, slender fingers, with flexible thumbs bent outward, and wrists so delicate they might break. Holding a ball of clay, of wool, or wholewheat flour, Fanny's hands kneaded the dough. Tirelessly they rolled, punched, molded. These were the hands of an industrious squaw, the hands of a very young boy. These were Fanny's hands: dark, supple, capable; and each one so different they seemed to belong to different people.

The right hand, squarish with almost knotty fingers, would plunge into the dough, squeezing it, slapping it, while the left hand, oval and smooth like an ivory shell, would roll it under its palm, twisting it with snakelike motions, polishing it like water on a rock.

A last press of the thumb, a final pat, together, this time with the same gesture, the hands would grab their work, put it on a platter to bake in the oven, and move on to a new task.

But soon the nosey neighbor woman, always angling for Fanny's secrets, would open the oven and give a terrified scream. There amidst the flames laughed a gaping mouth and dead eyes: a Gorgon's head rather similar to the antique coins Fanny had never seen.

"Is it a sculpture?" Belle would ask, frightened.

"Silly," her brother Samuel Lloyd would reply, "it's bread for supper."

Sam was enchanted by the monsters, the fear, these games so dear to Fanny's imagination.

He watched her in fascination as she swooped down on this modest piece of land and frenziedly transformed it into a paradise full of flowers, fruit, smells his children adored. He rejoiced in her accomplishment with not an ounce of male chauvinism, and after fifteen years of marriage, Fanny's energy continued to amaze him. He approved of her projects, encouraged what others took for fads. Her interest in daguerreotype, for instance: When Fanny aspired to something more than embroidering flowers on silk and decided to fix her bouquets on plates of acid, developing her negatives at night in a black and smelly place in the garden she pompously called her "laboratory," he was the only one of family and friends not to scoff. Developing photographs was an avant-garde passion in 1870, an unfashionable exploit.

"But who knows if this won't be of some use to you in hard times? A woman must be able to make out alone."

Quite a liberal for his time, Sam had already put this principle into practice by disappearing for a good while without leaving any address. Fanny may have thought she'd forgiven him, but she hadn't forgotten.

He, on the other hand, had quickly erased all memory of the bad years. "Everything's fine," he thought lightly. The children had come back to him, the house was bustling: They were preparing for a wedding. Fanny had brought her younger sister, Cora, out with her from Indiana. The adolescent had just reached an understanding with Sam Orr, Sam's companion in hardship with whom he so narrowly escaped the Indian massacre. The lovers were flirting under the arbor, the dogs burrowing in the lawn; Belle was becoming a charming adolescent whom her father sometimes took out for a private supper, just the two of them.

I cannot remember ever hearing a cross word from my father, she reports. *If he would ask me to sew a button, or darn some socks, and it was not done, instead of scolding, like most fathers, he'd stick a notice on my mirror: "Miss Handsome's attention is directed to her papa's socks," or "Miss Osbourne's papa is now buttonless." Naturally I ran to find my needle, giving him a hug in passing.*

Belle increasingly resembled Fanny, at least physically. Small like her, amber skinned, she shared her mother's consciousness of appearance, her skill with the needle, and a passion for her father. Jacob Vandegrift and Sam Osbourne gave their children a similar education: "Learn to enjoy the moment," Sam told his daughter. "Life is so short! Yesterday is already gone, and tomorrow has not come." Sam left the "tomorrows" to Fanny.

As tireless as her horses and dogs, she did not shrink from the task. She hardly slept now. She was probably afraid of that strange anxiety throbbing in her veins, the vague but constant feeling that she was about to miss something or had an urgent task to accomplish, though she didn't know what or why.

During the long golden days and endless nights, she was plagued by inarticulate longings, vague hopes and dreams like those she'd had at fifteen in the woods of Indianapolis. Were these desires for love? But she loved Sam, at least she liked him, though less than she had. He was no longer the center of her life, which was neither her passion for a man nor her love for Belle and Samuel Lloyd. And yet in the month of June 1871, Fanny was about to give birth to her third child. She had never had such an easy pregnancy. Without slowing down her activities, without giving up her riding, she waited for this baby with a sense of the fullness of her life. What she had loved in her daughter's arrival was Sam's child, with the birth of her son, the promise of a new conjugal happiness. But with this child she was feeling all the tenderness in the world, the certainty that together they would be invulnerable, the utter confidence of maternal love.

*
**

"Are you happy?" Sam asked, handing her the newborn.

She took him avidly, held him against her, bent her brown curls over the baby's blond down, and lost herself in contemplation.

Yellow roses bloomed on the night table. A warm and uneven ray of light was falling from the ceiling lamp, two globes of cut glass that almost touched the foot of the bed, a big four-poster of dark wood flanked by tall, carved columns. Holding one of them, Sam was watching his wife and his son.

"He looks like me!" he said. "It's striking!"

Fanny raised a blind eye to him. Her lips, naturally pouting, curled into an enigmatic smile. Her forehead glistened impassively in the shadow.

"I don't think so," she murmured.

Her voice, her hair, her head floating on the whiteness of the large lace pillows, the fatigue that pulled at her features and effaced her dimples refined the lines of her nose, perfected the oval of her face. Her immobility reminded Sam of something unpleasant: the idol's mask of Virginia City, the dreadful statue she had become during their first domestic argument, the woman who ended a night of love with the words, "I no longer want to live with a man I do not respect!" This time there was no trace of aggression in Fanny's tone.

"What shall we call him?" he asked.

"Hervey."

"Hervey? What a funny name!"

"Hervey," she repeated in a cool voice.

"If you wish," he conceded prudently.

She had an angelic smile on her face, which he had never seen before, as she slowly unbuttoned her gown with one hand and picked up the infant. Her neck, her arms, her heavy breasts, exuded a joy that touched Sam and embarrassed him. At the age of thirty-one, Fanny seemed to become a mother for the first time. Feeling helpless, he left.

Sam would soon leave all the rooms she inhabited without her noticing. From one day to the next, she seemed to forget the existence of her children's father.

The birth of Hervey made her languid, slowed her down. At this autumn's end her figure had a new grace, something rounded and fuller in the shoulders and hips. John Lloyd, in love with her as always, crossing the Bay every Sunday to lunch with them, mistrusted this softness. The beautiful Mrs. Osbourne was vibrating alone with sensual joys and secret pleasures from which he, like the others, was excluded.

Our mother had never been a sort of mother hen, Belle and Samuel Lloyd recall. *She loved children, but did not fuss over them. Babies left her rather cold. Because of the harshness of the circumstances, she had hardly been able to play with us when we were little . . . With Hervey, everything changed! We heard her cooing from one end of the garden to the other, and laughing, laughing! We had never really heard her burst out laughing. For us, this explosion of gaiety was mysterious and wonderful.*

"I'm sorry, Sam," she murmured, pushing to the edge of the bed. "I'm sorry, I . . ."

She rolled still farther away, suspended above the floor between the mattress and the covers. She remained there, cornered, hoping Sam would fall asleep.

"Don't you want to?" he asked in her ear.

She disengaged herself.

"I cannot."

"What do you mean, you cannot?"

She was quiet. She was listening to Hervey rustling in the next room.

"I cannot," she sighed, feeling him caress her again. And suddenly, vehemently: "It's true," she repeated, "I cannot!"

Repulsion? Revenge? Sam left her cold. She was so preoccupied with herself, with her physical involvement in her little son, that no other tenderness could touch her, only devouring her child's cheeks with kisses, breathing in the sweet perfume of his skin, feeling her arms full with his plump body, admiring the grace of his curving neck.

Sam let himself be repulsed without another word and went to sleep. He could not deal with states of the soul, explanations, complications. And then, he pleased too many women to be tempted by the idea of raping his own wife.

He waited patiently for a month. Then he acted. He rented an apartment in San Francisco where he installed a mistress who adored him, and he spent nights with her, with no attempt to hide the fact. His friends knew about the two homes he supported on his meager earnings, one in town near the courthouse where he worked, the other in East Oakland, where he spent his weekends.

This new infidelity awakened Fanny's demons. Very quickly she recognized, unchanged, the old suffering that knotted her stomach and choked her to the point of nausea. Absent to herself, she lived for several months as she had before, waiting for Sam. Was this the final throes of a moribund love or an inability to rid herself of something she had made her own? When, spruced up and lively, Sam would arrive on Friday evenings at the house full of roses, when he ostentatiously embraced her in front of the children, spent his weekends busy with them, listening to their stories, telling them about his adventures—the good father, the good husband—Fanny became a pillar of salt, full of violent hatreds.

During her nights alone, she saw herself, with Sam and the children, on a stormy sea, on the edge of a sailing ship with broken masts. A wave swept Sam away, the current dragged him down and he let himself go. Fanny plunged in to rescue him, struggling against the current only to find that he was fastened to a bouy, that he was floating pleasantly on the water, babbling and smiling. Behind her, the boat was drifting toward the reefs, the children were about to be crushed. And Fanny went shouting and swimming after them.

In the spring, she exchanged her three ponies for a thoroughbred, her lady's derringer for a Winchester, and her frilly layette for the good old gray miner's tobacco, and she got back to the saddle and the kitchen.

With a cigarette between her lips, her sleeves rolled up, a battery of casseroles in progress, she lit up her ovens. Alchemist or magician, this time her bisques, her sauces and roasts reached perfection. She no longer improvised recipes but was inspired by the cookbooks she received from France and laboriously translated, with much reliance on dictionaries. She corresponded with three chefs from Louisiana, comparing their techniques, their utensils, their ingredients. Another aspect of Fanny's originality, and one particularly unusual in the nineteenth century, was her interest in international cuisine. She was a passionate admirer of Asian cooking, and shopped in the swarming markets of Chinatown where no white woman dared set foot. She jotted down her research, her experiments, her failures, despaired of her groping efforts, aimed at excellence, and, without being in the least conscious of it, struggled to turn her culinary gifts into an art.

She had at last found an outlet for her anxieties, her restlessness, her dreams.

Closer to a wizard's book of spells than a cookbook, Fanny's notebook takes the form of a thick volume bound in red Moroccan leather, with gilt-edged pages that crackle as they turn. Through these overloaded, scratched-out pages smelling of vanilla and chocolate, a whole world takes shape riotous with taste and smell, word and line.

Between spots of sugar or fruit, columns of numbers, measurements, and cooking times, she sketched the phantoms that peopled her nightmares of suicides and shipwrecks, she wrote fragments of moral tales, fables about animals and flowers, childish allegories that helped her live. About herself or her loved ones, Fanny said nothing. This book of spells is never in danger of becoming a private journal. Rather it is a loom, a canvas of woven threads striped with blue or black ink. The margins, the backs of pages, are overlaid with pastels and watercolors, colorful forms. Fanny draws, doodles, and caricatures. Here the bulging silhouette of a sifter; there the gaudy kaleidoscope of a dish of sherbet; further on the horrified profile of her guests before a plate of pigs' knuckles. Her drawings are amusing, sometimes macabre. Only sound is missing, no score to accompany this celebration.

In the afternoons, however, the garden always vibrated to the sound of Belle's piano. Fanny herself tried to play the guitar. Ready to absorb everything, she also belonged to a traveling library that sent her a selection of "classics" from New York. A kind of *Reader's*

Digest before its time, it consisted of pieces that were condensed or simply summarized versions of great books: *The Iliad, The Odyssey, The Human Comedy*—all in a single booklet. Fanny read in a desultory fashion.

During the year 1873, however, it was not literature that changed her life, nor the afternoon concerts at the theaters in San Francisco, but a walk she took every Sunday with the children and hundreds of others.

At the corner of Mission and 14th Streets, extending over many acres, were the Woodwards Gardens. In this wonderful amusement park you could find a botanical garden, a zoo, an aquarium, mechanical swans on an artificial lake, and Chinese giants disguised as dragons, the Disneyland of the nineteenth century. And the centerpiece: culture! "A unique spectacle" boasts the advertising brochure. "In a well-lit pavilion hung with red velvet, with deep carpets and comfortable pillows for the visitor's convenience, under good light and with a clear view, all the masterpieces of history have been assembled here solely for the pleasure of San Franciscans. From now on, crossing oceans to bury yourself in the old museums of France and Italy is pointless: For a few cents, the Woodwards Gardens offers you that journey." This was the first art gallery, the first exhibition of paintings in the Far West.

And they were all painted by an artist who would give new meaning to the aspirations of the Oakland household. His name was Virgil Williams.

Curiously, I picked up Virgil Williams' trail earlier in the miners' camp at Austin, during the period when Fanny was there. The local paper registers his passage on the Wells Fargo stagecoaches during the same month. The coincidence stops there, however, because they did not meet in Nevada. Williams, originally from New England, had previously studied in Rome, where he had married the daughter of an American painter established at the Villa Medicis. This was an unhappy marriage that ended about ten years later in divorce, when the artist took up residence in Boston. One morning Williams had been visited in his studio by a Mr. Robert Woodwards, a speculator who had gotten rich from the silver mines of Virginia City and had come east looking for good investments. Woodwards' visit concluded with the purchase of Williams' entire studio, walls, canvases, preliminary drawings, palettes and all. And the painter signed a contract agreeing to come and create in Woodwards' San Francisco amusement park a gallery in which all the masterpieces of the world would be displayed. For months Williams was paid to travel around to the museums of Europe, copying frantically. Ten years later he would have liked to burn every canvas and never hear another word about this project, which had consumed his soul and his art.

Having become *the* preeminent painter of San Francisco, Virgil Williams had thrown himself into creating the first art association of the American West. He had made contact with all the museums of Europe, and by way of encouragement and solidarity, the city of Paris had shipped the plaster casts of several statues from the Louvre to San Francisco. Flattered, the chamber of commerce had opened the cases with great ceremony, only to make the horrified discovery that limbs and heads were missing! The transport company was brought to court. Incredible as it may seem, the suit was won: The transport company had to pay damages and interest on the missing arms of the Venus de Milo.

Virgil Williams then understood the urgency and the necessity of opening an academy of fine arts in San Francisco. This school, which he directed until his death, would become the famous School of Design.

And when Belle Osbourne, sixteen and very gifted at caricature, showed the desire to take lessons there, Fanny, who had heard of the director, enrolled her immediately—and herself as well.

This is the beginning of the mysterious influences, echoes, and coincidences that marked the lives of mother and daughter. Whether accomplices or rivals, they would trail after each other for the next half century through all their adventures across the seas.

For the moment, Fanny Osbourne had just celebrated her thirty-fourth birthday. She was beginning to live.

San Francisco School of Design—1874–1875

This was my idea of Heaven! Belle writes. *To do what I liked better than anything in the world, and at the same time have it dignified by such stodgy words as "study" and "work."* . . . *I was taken out of high school and sent three days a week to the School*

*of Design in San Francisco. . . . Going back and forth on the train
and ferry I began to notice the attention my mother attracted and
realized how very pretty she was. At the art school she won the
medal in the first competition. This did not seem to have much
effect on her at the time. But after her death I found, squeezed in
her jewelry box, a little leather disk at the bottom of a black box,
the medal she had taken with her everywhere, even to the end.*

The drawing school was above the fabulous California Market at
the corner of Market and Pine streets. Food seemed to be a
constant presence in Fanny's destiny, and between the fragrant
melons, the bulging avocados, the piles of crabs and lobsters, stood
the little door that opened onto a stairway. A few steps up and you
were led from the animated street into a huge, glass-enclosed room.
The light fell powerfully on ten or so impressive castings mounted
on pedestals. The Victory of Samothrace, the Discus Thrower, and
the Venus de Milo stood between the easels.

Twenty or so white-smocked students of all ages and both sexes
stood in a group around their teacher. Powerful, handsome, with a
blond goatee and pensive black eyes, very deep-set, Virgil Williams
had the distinction, the reserve, the generosity of an ideal teacher.
Above all, he had a passion for beauty and knew how to communicate
it. His prudish Protestant education had not stunted his enthusiasm:
Virgil Williams liked nothing so much as discovering a work worthy
of admiration which he would praise to all and sundry. He nurtured
the first generation of California landscape painters, who labored
to render the desert light, Death Valley at sunset, the rosy dawn
breaking on the craggy peaks of Yosemite's high country. Virgil
Williams's teaching left an indelible mark on his students.

"For the exam at the end of the year, I am asking you to draw the
right hand of the Venus de Milo as you imagine it. Get your charcoal!"

Belle, along with the other young people, hurled herself
unthinkingly at her drawing paper. Fanny stood alone at the foot
of the statue, her eyes shining, her mouth half-open, plunged into
an intense physical happiness.

"Do you like her?" murmured Virgil Williams, amused.

"Yes," she answered, without looking at him, as if afraid of being
distracted from her pleasure. "The light, the movement, the
material. It's as if I had never seen them before. And you?"

He smiled at her naiveté. Mrs. Osbourne was among his oldest and most gifted students. Her utter lack of culture delighted him. She literally knew nothing. Swept by great gusts of powerful emotion, her intoxication with beauty left a lasting imprint. A teacher's ideal student: a virgin sensibility coupled with maturity.

She had no idea, no image, no point of reference, and so Fanny's excitement was all the more naked and profound. Williams had merely to glance at her drawings. In every exercise there was the same purity of line, the same audacious use of color. Something awkward and powerful made her copy immediately recognizable. The joy before an aesthetic ideal, which this woman managed to express without understanding—he sometimes wondered if this wasn't the very definition of art.

"Get to work, Mrs. Osbourne. Get to work!"

The sun was at its zenith. It was beginning to be quite hot. With her mouth set, her curls sticking to her head, her back bent, Fanny dragged her easel to the Venus. Side by side with her daughter and the other young people, she set to work.

As usual, she was the last to finish. Night was falling on the statues. The fog flowed down from the hills, stretching like an awning in the sky, already covering the roofs down to the sea, where the ferryboat would not wait. Fanny shivered, throwing her shawl over her shoulders and crossing the deserted studio. Her boots raised a blue dust that enveloped her and seemed to pursue her. At the door, she held her rolled-up drawing out to a figure who tucked it into a large bag.

"And what if I were not here to close up after you?"

A hat trimmed with long feathers, a tangle of brocades and silks, ten jade necklaces, a chain at the waist where a crowd of trinkets clinked together, a penknife, a pencil box, a coin purse, the five keys to the school: Dora Norton Williams had also been Virgil's favorite student before he married her three years earlier in Boston. A mediocre portraitist but very gifted at still lives, Dora Norton took herself seriously, wanted to be a painter, and claimed her freedom as an artist and her right to speak her mind. *She was a thin little Yankee woman, very authoritarian,* Belle would say of Dora, who had made several disagreeable comments on her talent. *She was always determined to tell the truth, and her studied frankness could turn into the most dreadful vulgarity.*

"Your eyes are bloodshot, Mrs. Osbourne," commented Dora,

giving the key a final turn. "Your cheeks are on fire, and your hands are red."

"I got excited," Fanny conceded, by way of excuse. "As if something important were at stake. I've made you wait, and for what? For a poor drawing of the Venus de Milo's hand. Was it worth it?"

"What do you expect?" Dora remarked. "An aesthetic pleasure is not a salary to be cashed in. Once tasted, it must evaporate slowly like perfume."

The woman nearing forty who was speaking this way in her dry voice must have known how to win Fanny's respect by her moral courage, her whimsy, and her decade of experience in the art world, for she would be Fanny's lifelong friend and only female confidante besides her daughter.

At seventy and eighty, all the same, Fanny and Dora would manage to quarrel and break with each other.

Comparing the dates, I am astonished to discover that Fanny's adventure at the San Francisco School of Design lasted only one year. Yet it transformed her profoundly.

The woman who did not speak, who moved very little and in shadow, the passionate lover of Austin, the Oakland homemaker, became a blue-stocking, half aesthete, half bohemian.

Certainly Mrs. Osbourne was learning to draw, and she had talent. But it was the "artist's life" that particularly attracted Fanny at this period. At the Williams's home, under Dora's aegis, she visited with other painters, the musician Oscar Weil, and the poet Charles Warren Stoddard, who had just returned from the Pacific and wrote stories à la Pierre Loti. Tahiti, Hawaii, the Marquesas, he was the first to introduce the South Seas into Fanny's imagination. She was carried away listening to his tales, sharing conversations, devouring the books they exchanged. During this short period of a year, she allied herself with all the people who were going to matter in her life until her entry into the literary circles of London, all those who would make her a woman who was permanently different from the rejected wife of a court stenographer. Sam, however, was part of the circle that included her new friends. He was long acquainted with Virgil Williams, and with another man whom Fanny would make her accomplice and mentor, the lawyer Timothy Rearden.

*
**

"Is that how you see me, Mr. Rearden? Sweet, romantic, a bit naive?"

The man whose studio Fanny had invaded above the big Mercantile Library was fluent in ancient Greek, could translate medieval German ballads, tried his hand at Latin poetry, and indeed embodied all that San Francisco considered most learned—and most chauvinistic. Having come west at the age of eighteen from Cleveland, Ohio, Timothy Rearden hoped, like everyone else, to get rich in California. Fascinated by adventure without liking it, he had found a job as accountant at the Mint and prudently pursued his legal studies. He left behind him a widowed mother and an unmarried sister whom he thought he would care for, once he'd made his fortune.

He was destined not to make a fortune and to abandon them both in Ohio, never returning home. But he was plagued by feelings of guilt, and wrote to them every Sunday for twenty years. The two women kept all his letters, which can be found today, along with a few photographs, in the Bancroft Library at the University of California in Berkeley.

The photographs show a large mustache draped over a firm mouth, a short nose with flaring nostrils, and something intense in his gaze, almost hard. Rearden seems very much alive. The soft knot of his tie, the shimmering silk, the jacket of cut velvet, make him seem quite modern. His sensitivity is perceptible in the slightly frowning expression of the eyebrows, and his tenderness in the childish dimple in his chin. Unlike his contemporaries, who pose and express nothing before the camera's objective eye, Rearden is obviously made uncomfortable by the instrument, even irritated.

"You think I'm vain, don't you, Mr. Rearden?"

Fanny negligently threw her burning cigarette butt at the hearth, covering one of the square tiles that framed the fireplace with ashes. Rearden was very proud of these antique tiles.

"Stop smoking, Mrs. Osbourne. You are affecting a manner your husband should forbid."

"When it comes to manners, Mr. Rearden, my husband appreciates only the most vulgar. You should know!"

During his legal studies, Rearden had met John Lloyd, who had introduced him to his former partner, Sam Osbourne. When Fanny was away in Indiana the three men had gotten into the habit of meeting every Sunday to chat. As different from each other as possible—Osbourne the charmer, Lloyd the apprentice banker, Rearden the intellectual—they had in common the need to exchange ideas in a world uniquely geared to action.

With a few journalists from the *Overland Monthly,* the three companions founded what would become one of the most exclusive clubs in the West: the Bohemian Club.

It had all begun very modestly with a collection for the rent of a comfortable place to get together and talk about music, painting, and literature. Rearden had found a site above the California Market that was too burdensome for the little group, which sublet a part of it to one of its members, Virgil Williams. He had made it his drawing school. The upper floor was quickly becoming the cultural center of the city. The School of Design on one side, the Bohemian Club on the other; the group, under the aegis of Williams and Rearden, had chosen the owl as a mascot. The bird of Athena, goddess of wisdom and symbol of the night, suited these young men, journalists, lawyers, navigators, and artists, who had all come from elsewhere. Tempted by adventure, seduced by the West Coast's eternal spring, a number of European painters would bring to San Francisco, through the Bohemian Club, their experience of the true bohemian life of the Latin Quarter and the Parisian ateliers.

"Have you heard of Paris, Mr. Rearden? No, of course not. You're only interested in your books, your solitude, your bachelor frustrations. Go on, get up on your high horse, take on your grand airs, and look down on your equals."

This time he was tempted to throw her out the door. He contented himself with throwing the new cigarette she was about to light into the fireplace.

"You're annoying me!" he barked.

She shrugged her shoulders at him.

"Poor friend!"

Settled on the arm of an old leather armchair, her legs crossed, she swung her boot lightly, staring at its toe.

"Come on, admit that I frighten you. Do come closer, Mr. Rearden. Don't be afraid I'll make you late. You are meeting your cronies from the Bohemian Club this evening, aren't you? I know it, Mr. Osbourne has used your meeting as a pretext not to come back to Oakland this weekend. Tell me, then, what's happening on the other side of Mr. Williams's studio—I'm dying of curiosity."

As she swung her leg back and forth, Rearden again came close to throwing her out. Since she'd been studying at the drawing school, Mrs. Osbourne was no longer the same. She was coy with everyone, and with him she was a plain flirt. Sam had made a big mistake letting his wife frequent ateliers and consort with artists. Freedom to learn? What nonsense! Fanny's metamorphosis tended to confirm Rearden's theories. In July 1868 in the *Overland Monthly,* he had written an essay on the question: "Favoring Female Conventionalism," in which he had demonstrated the inanity of women's emancipation.

"Your paradoxes make me laugh, Mr. Rearden. Can you tell me how I am different from your mother and your sister? From what I've heard, your mother supported you. She worked to pay for your studies, didn't she? And you don't take responsibility for your sister, that I know of. Isn't she a schoolteacher, who earns a living back home? I will earn a living one day, too—and unlike Mr. Osbourne, who throws away his pay on mistresses, I will sell my pictures to support my children!"

Timothy Rearden, the man who was usually so quick to judge women, was at a loss as to how to label this little lady. At first he had seen her as the perfect housewife, the type men marry. Tonight she seemed to be more the type they seduced. The new Mrs. Osbourne attracted him, disturbed him, drove him crazy as the former Fanny had never done. That small, graceful body, that birdlike chatter, her ruffles, her perfume. He resisted. In the first place, she was Sam's wife, and Rearden was loyal to his friends. In the second place, would his advances be welcome? In his uncertainty, Rearden preferred to abstain.

"Isn't it true, Mr. Rearden, that you think I'm hysterical?"

He shot her a scornful look: "Oh no, my poor girl! Lord, the females of San Francisco all want to pass for hysterics! It's a fashion, I suppose, a fancy . . . Good Lord, if women would only understand how charming they are when they don't complicate things. Be quiet, be agreeable, be content with what you have, and your life will be beautiful."

"Content? But there must be someone to love and understand you."

"My dear, it's absurd to expect people in love to understand each other. Understanding is not needed for love, just as love is not needed for mutual understanding. I, for instance . . ."

He came closer, placed his arms on the two armrests, and leaned over. A handsome fellow, sensual lips, flaring nostrils. She avoided him, jumping to her feet.

"You! You are an egoist who doesn't love or understand anyone!"

She crushed her fresh cigarette on a new tile, something she knew would exasperate Rearden, and went on: "Anyone, except perhaps the beautiful Mona Wills, who just ran off to Europe with a German violinist. Ah, Vienna, London, Paris!" she teased. "Paris, Mr. Rearden!"

He reddened. Touché. The only woman Rearden had ever been in love with had indeed just run off with a foreigner. She smiled: "All right, Othello, what are you giving me to read this week?"

Rearden's lips curled into a nasty smile. "For Madame Osbourne, *Madame Bovary* will do, the story of a hag who poisons the life of her family and her own in the process. It comes to us from the Paris you seem so enamored of."

She shrugged her shoulders, held out her hand, took the volume and left without thanking him. Their relationship would never be more cordial.

Timid to the point of discomfort, they would hide their mutual sympathy behind constant attacks that led to actual scuffles, though neither could remember why. *You ask me what I have done to Rearden,* she writes in 1880 to her friend Dora Williams. *Ask him. He might know. As for me, I don't have the slightest idea.* They would cross swords like two adolescents; they would play at war out of modesty, prudishness, alternately skirmishing and calling a truce.

One never knows what may or may not offend Rearden . . . she speculates again. *I wonder if I was too much trouble for him. I suppose so . . . That he may be a little mad, I do not deny; but then the society and friendship of mad people are so infinitely preferable to other's.* Rearden was not always so tolerant. In a letter to his mother on the subject of divorced women, he writes: *I feel toward them as I do toward toads, somehow as if they were sticky.*

Yet in spite of all his noisy condescension toward this "little lady," Rearden would later manage Fanny's Oakland property, refuse fees she couldn't pay him, secretly buy a painting of hers for a sum greater than its value, and frequently help her out of financial difficulties. And against his better principles, Rearden was the one who would file for her divorce.

As for Fanny, she proclaims in her correspondence to Dora: *I can only say I am very fond of that sham cynic . . . You,* she adds, *and he are the only two people with whom I feel familiar enough to pour out nonsense.*

But on this evening in December 1874, descending Timothy Rearden's stairs, Fanny was overcome by a sudden sadness: *That old sarcastic Rearden only cares for mean women. If I were a little nicer, he would show me the door immediately. My nasty remarks—that's what he likes in me. Well, he's gonna get it!*

*

For the moment, what was especially galling to her was the status quo with Sam. *When I was alone with my father,* Belle recounts, *he was always gay and companionable, but when my mother joined us there was often tension, an atmosphere of suppressed feelings that chilled me.*

One day we were in the sitting room of our cottage in East Oakland. My mother was sewing; I was curled up on the floor, leaning against my father's knee as he read aloud from Vanity Fair *... He had reached the place in the story where Captain Osborne goes to war, and his wife Amelia discovers he has betrayed her with Becky Sharp. I was listening with interest when my mother interrupted in an icy voice: "I wonder that you dare read your own story, Captain Osbourne!" My father jumped up, red in the face: "God Almighty, woman! Can't you ever forget?" And then I was sent out of the room.*

This rancor cost Fanny dearly. This time it was one of her famous "brain fevers" that verged on psychosis. She heard Sam's jaunty boot on the steps, she heard his whistle calling the children, she breathed in the honeyed perfume of his tobacco and her stomach, her heart, everything inside her clenched. "There he is ... He's here." She felt no hatred but a tension, a repulsion so vivid it made her nauseous. Every weekend, Sam's arrival sent her into bouts of fever. She shivered, then caught herself, vacillating between a cold, controlled politeness and attacks of aggression. The East Oakland cottage was a combat zone on the weekends. Friends began to stay away. Even John Lloyd gave up his Sunday meal. The Osbournes spent these final days of the week alone, no visitors or outings. What was the point of a social life together when Sam was taking his mistress around to all their friends? They no longer communicated except through the children.

"Belle, isn't it time to eat?" Sam would ask, famished.

"Hervey, it's cold. Tell your father to put your jacket on!"

She could no longer manage to address him directly, and he made no effort to speak to her. She was afraid, he was distrustful. Neither of them attempted a reconciliation. They were too cautious to risk a word, a gesture. This cautiousness was their only point of agreement. Sam wandered from one room to the other, hoping that Fanny would not notice him. She made every room her own, hoping that Sam wouldn't stay.

The first flowers were trembling in the garden. The dogs were playing under the fruit trees. The warmth of April had never seemed so mild, the shade of the shrubbery so sensual. But they remained unmoved. Even Sam the charmer. His mouth had a mean twist when he gave Fanny money for the week. Despite his apparent good humor, he took pleasure in refusing to allot her a fixed sum. He waited for her to ask, and before giving her a penny demanded to see her account book and the money in her purse. Only then did Sam give in. He was not stingy, he simply spent everything he earned on his cronies. His San Francisco women cost him dearly, so he was constantly short of cash and revived his old dream of getting rich in the mines. He speculated, staked his wages on new concessions in Nevada, and believed, depending on the moment, that he was either a millionaire or bankrupt. Fanny was thrown into rages at the thought that after all his disasters, Sam was still susceptible to gold fever and preferred the comfort of his mistress to his children's. This recurrent rage of hers infuriated Sam. "A very intelligent boy" Timothy Rearden would say of him, "but utterly lacking any sense of family."

This particular Sunday evening, with the younger children sleeping and Belle reading in bed, they found themselves alone. Ordinarily, they would hurry to their separate quarters. The cold, gray night was dark and damp. The fog shrouded the garden, which was filled with the muffled sound of a stream running under the earth, the first rustlings of spring. They stood there, on either side of the porch, leaning on the railing. The smoke from his pipe mingled with the smoke from her cigarettes. Far off, as if imprisoned in a cloud, the lights of San Francisco glimmered on the sea. They might have been happy.

The serenity of this moment suspended them both in the same

feeling of expectation. The trickle of water in the garden and the sea beyond filled them for a moment with the desire to reach out to one another, to join together. A gesture would have perhaps been enough to change their fate. But this desire quickly vanished, and there they were, left with only a vague bitterness. Now each tried to forget the other's presence, to steal a little solitary, secret joy from this night. Murmuring "good night," Sam was the first to leave the porch. The next day at dawn he took the ferry. Two hours later, Fanny made her escape.

To occupy the boys during her absences in San Francisco, she had engaged a governess whom Timothy Rearden had found for her. Still another service Rearden rendered. Originally from Ohio like him, Miss Kate Moss, with her hair piled in a stiff chignon, accepted the very irregular pay that depended on the good will of Mr. Osbourne, whom she adored. Passionate, authoritarian, and highly literate, she lacked charm and ruled her world with an iron hand. She had even succeeded in bringing a semblance of order to Belle's life, forcibly inculcating the rudiments of grammar and French, and compelling her to study piano three times a week. Miss Kate announced loud and clear that this girl was too much a part of her mother's existence. The same activities, the same schedule, the same visitors. And Belle was only sixteen years old! Fanny, who was not the sort to brook contradiction, listened to Miss Kate's criticisms. And the two women shared the same tenderness for the child with the long blond curls who was crowned "Prince of Clouds" on the morning of his fourth birthday.

"Look, Mama," cried Hervey, "the lady coming there . . . she is beautiful! She looks like a fairy."

Sitting on the porch steps, Fanny was drawing her son's profile. She raised her head. A young woman was coming up the path. Wearing a flat little hat teetering on an enormous hairpiece, a fitted dress quite inappropriate for the afternoon, long boots of red leather, and striped stockings, she approached, smiling. Fanny rose.

"What right do you have to come here?"

The woman hesitated, stammered: "There is no reason why I can't come here."

"There is an excellent one. Get out!"

The other woman flushed, and drew back.

"You should be a little more polite. I'm coming for your sake—

it's a courtesy call I'm paying. After all, we do have things in common, and it's in your interest that we get along. Why not come to visit us from time to time in San Francisco, with the children? Sam would like that. It would make everyone more comfy. And then for the children . . ."

She touched Hervey's cheek as he looked at her, utterly won over. Fanny snatched up her son.

"Get out!"

"Listen to you!"

"Miss Kate!" Fanny shouted at the top of her lungs. The heavy young woman appeared from behind the mosquito net. "Take Hervey away!"

The governess left with the child and closed the door. At that moment, Fanny curled her tongue between her teeth as she'd seen the miners do, and spat the biggest wad of phlegm she could produce into her visitor's face. She had aimed at her face but it fell wetly on the lace at her bosom. The other woman was dumbstruck: "Oh!"

She looked at her chest but did not attempt to clean herself off. She held her breasts as far as possible from the spittle, turned on her heel, and departed, her train wagging furiously behind her. Fanny's gaze followed her as she went. Then, shaken by a spasm, Fanny hung onto the railing and began to laugh and laugh, a child's wild laughter. She didn't think she was capable of doing something so disgusting! How did she dare? She could not believe it. How did she dare? She had never seen this woman before, how could she be so sure this was Sam's mistress? Intuition! Hearing the click of the gate, spying the little red hat and boots, she had been certain: This was the woman Sam preferred to her. Her laughter subsided. This woman was not even pretty. Fanny mentally reviewed the thick waist, the large hands, the dyed hair. And Sam preferred this woman to her. She had imagined her like the widow Kelly, blond, proud, and formidable. Instead she was just fluff, filth. And Sam preferred this woman to her. She found great pleasure in her rival's plainness, and even greater disappointment. He was spending three-quarters of his time with this hag. Sam was truly mediocre. At first she took comfort in this thought.

Then she looked around her. The little house, the garden she loved so much. Even more mediocre than she had imagined. Suddenly the idea of Sam's insignificance overwhelmed her. And she was going to spend her life here as "Mrs. Osbourne, the wife of the court clerk, a woman with vague literary and artistic aspirations." Squeezed into the role of blue-stocking, frustrated by her husband's infidelities, yet unlike the heroine of the French book Timothy Rearden had lent her, she did not take a lover. A lover? Rearden, that was it! Why not? For a moment she imagined Rearden embracing her, his beautiful hand on her breast, his mustache against her mouth. He would treat her like a whore the moment he had possessed her. In the eyes of everyone here she would never be anyone but Mrs. O, more or less virtuous, more or less inconstant. At the drawing school, she would become at best a competent craftsman. She might decorate porcelain plates or illustrate ladies' magazines.

She looked again at the expanse of her garden. The tiger lilies were out, the roses were blazing. What more could she do here? She thought about her house. She had changed the curtains ten times, she had recarpeted her room, redecorated the parlor. What more could she accomplish?

Her gaze wandered toward San Francisco Bay. The fog was rolling in like white gauze, crawling up the sides of Mount Tamalpais, revealing a series of little valleys where ribbons of clouds cascaded toward the sea.

And over the Bay itself a hard light still filtered through the mist, illuminating a ship without sails. With its two standing masts, its prow, its skeletal rigging striping the ocean, it seemed elongated, drawn toward a spot on the horizon, a tiny black point, the tugboat that was perhaps pulling it toward the sea. Yet the ship seemed stationary, nailed against the rose-colored sky. The whole bay had taken on the tints of a color print. Like some holy spirit, a seagull swooping down and veering in front of the boat seemed to point the way. At that moment, Fanny made a decision.

*

"I'm leaving, Mr. Rearden!"

"Ah, yes? Bon voyage."

"Stop it, Mr. Rearden, I'm serious. I'm leaving."

She had climbed up to his floor, four steps at a time, and burst in without knocking. He was working in front of the fire, his pipe in his mouth.

"The Old World!" she gasped, decisively.

"That's not too far away."

"Rearden, I have to talk to you, it's serious, I need to ask you for advice."

"Between me and women like you, two oceans aren't enough . . ."

"Rearden, please!"

"Go to the devil!"

She did an aboutface, slammed the door, and stormed onto Cable Car 10. Hanging on the outside, her skirts dragging along the wooden streets, she jumped off at the Williams's.

*

"Dora, I'm leaving."

"Yes? What a good idea! And where are you going?"

"To the Old World!"

"What an original idea," Dora said ironically, as Fanny caught her in her kitchen.

"Do you think Mr. Williams would agree to give me some addresses? Recommendations to his acquaintances? Names?"

"Of course he will!"

Leaving the stove, Dora took her friend to the parlor, made her sit down, and served her tea.

"How I envy you, my dear. Rome is the only place to study! Rome or Paris. You are doing the right thing. As gifted as you are, you will have no trouble getting recognition. If only I could. But with my husband's responsibilities . . . We will help you! We will give you recommendations, we will find you a good teacher! You will exhibit at the Salon! You will make much faster progress there, much faster, far from material cares, from your house, your garden that keeps you so busy, without all those children."

"My children? I'm taking them with me!"

"Good Lord, what for?"

*

"Of course, all three! You don't imagine, John, that I am going to leave my children?"

"But with all due respect, Mrs. Osbourne, what will you do in Europe?"

"I will paint."

"What will you live on?"

"I will work. It won't be the first time!"

John Lloyd was well placed to know what part of her life Fanny was alluding to.

"But in those days you were not responsible for three children, and you were living in your own country. How will you communicate?"

She shrugged her shoulders.

"I will manage!"

"And Sam? The children? What about Sam?"

"Sam," she interrupted, "Sam has his life, and I have mine. The children? Tell me! He doesn't see them more than once a month! And busy as he is, a little more, a little less, it doesn't make much difference."

"Does he know about this project?"

"I have not managed to find him." Playfully, Fanny smiled for the first time in a long while. "Perhaps I might pay a visit to his lady friend, make her—what did she call it?—a courtesy call?"

*

"Never!" Sam shouted.

"If not," she retorted, "I'll file for divorce!"

"You're crazy, I'll have you locked up! First you spit in people's faces, then you want to tear your children away from their house, from their family, from their father. The Old World—you'll see it in a mad house!"

"Or in a coffin!" she growled. Then, changing her tone: "Sam, listen to me. We cannot go on this way." Her voice was soft and lilting again, like a stream running under ice. "I'm tired . . ."

Falling onto the sofa, she gently pulled Sam down beside her. The photograph of Jacob Vandegrift, in John Lloyd's gold frame, was enthroned above them. Their whole past, a whole life was in this sitting room. Eighteen years of conjugal memories. On the door of the wood-burning stove was a label with the worlds HOME AND COMFORT. The cat was rolling on the carpet. The designs of the carpets echoed the wallpaper, which harmonized with the upholstery on the armchairs. On the rocking chairs, even the most rustic ones, were cushions that Belle and Fanny had embroidered. In the windows stood Belle's ceramics and Fanny's drawings. Amusing drawings of the pitiful camp at Austin, with its mounds of bristling stakes, its tents flanked by barrels in the guise of chimneys.

Caricatures of Sam and John Lloyd dressed as prospectors, hats over their eyes, worn-down boots, and shovels over their shoulders: *We are not suited for manual labor.* Staggered on the piano, with its fringed shawl, were photographs of Belle in her first fancy dress, of Hervey at two months. And under a glass globe, a piece of the only silver-streaked stone Sam had ever found.

"I'm suffocating," she said. "I need to be alone, I need time. I would like to go back to the farm."

"Go. Spend a few months with your parents in Indiana. I'm very fond of the farm, too. Perhaps I might even join you."

"No."

Vexed, he jumped to his feet.

"We are married, you know!"

She let her hand fall back on the armrest.

"Barely—Sam, let me leave."

He walked off a few paces, his back turned to her.

"And the children?"

She was quiet. He did an aboutface, repeating: "And the children?"

"For Belle, for her training, Europe would be an invaluable experience . . ."

"If you go, Fanny, you go alone."

She lowered her eyes, murmuring: "I cannot live without them."

"Then stay here."

He was leaving the room.

"Sam," she cried, "they are my children, I cannot abandon them!" She added more softly: "And I cannot stay!"

"And what about me, Fanny? They're my children, too!"

"For all that you see them!" she spat out bitterly.

"Do you think it's pleasant coming here for the weekend? This house is hell!"

"Ah," she exclaimed, triumphantly, "you see, then, that things have to change, that I have to go away."

He kept quiet. She pushed her advantage: "Sam, give us a year. It's true that I am difficult. It's true that I'm unpleasant, a real shrew—I don't like myself this way any more than you do," she said, sadly. "You love this woman. You have your life, a job. But I have only my children. Let me leave, let me become somebody! When I am proud of myself, things will go better between us."

*
**

In the month of March, 1875, Fanny transplanted her flowers to the greenhouse. The neighbors would water the plants. She covered her photo laboratory, packed her trunks and closed the cottage. Sam would live in San Francisco and send a money order each month for one year, though he didn't specify the sum. He would do it for the children. How on earth did she manage to convince him?

The man who hated scenes and fled from explanations and histrionics didn't get a moment's peace once Fanny took it into her head to leave. In Oakland she pestered and begged, in San Francisco it was even worse: "Let her get out of here with her kids, that hysteric!" his mistress screamed, enchanted at the idea of getting rid of Mrs. Osbourne. At the Bohemian Club, the tone was different, but Fanny's project pursued him everywhere. Rearden and John Lloyd, who despite their reserve loved nothing more than gossip, never stopped talking about it. Only Virgil Williams kept quiet, and his silence was even more eloquent. Hurt that one of his students would want to study elsewhere, he was content to say that they were all free to choose their teachers, and in any case Europe could not be a bad experience. He graciously emphasized how unforgettable it was.

On the landing, posted at the door to the School of Design, Dora organized a support committee: "Mrs. Osbourne could not possibly stay chained all her life to that Sam, a failure who doesn't give her a dime."

She approved of scandal and adventure. She trumpeted her support so loud and clear that the school, the club, and her salon were abuzz with Mrs. Osbourne's projected departure.

Assailed by doubts, Fanny had been losing sleep and, absorbed in her preparations, stayed away. But one evening, at the end of one of her last classes, Timothy Rearden came to collect her.

"I have to talk to you," he growled, leading her between the stalls of oysters and scallops.

"I thought it was not proper to talk to me. Write me, Rearden, I'm in a hurry."

He caught her by the elbow.

"I am walking you to the Market Street tram."

From street to street, their faces striped by the shadows of tele-graph wires or bathed in golden sunlight, they walked up and down, crossing intersections, suddenly plunging into pockets of blue sky or leaning against the grade of a steep hill. Whipped by the cold ocean wind, they wrapped themselves up in their scarves, or unbut-toned their coats in the summer heat.

"It is not proper for a woman to go abroad alone."

"Proper—is this the only word you know? You'll die of respectability."

"And you will, too, my dear. Everyone here condemns you."

"Would you be sorry to see me go, Rearden? That would be news to me—Mr. Timothy Rearden misses 'that little woman'?"

"Keep quiet and show a little sense for once. You are not really going to leave Sam, are you?"

"Why not?"

"Because, Mrs. Osbourne, a lady of your age, as charming as she may be, does not leave her husband."

"Mind your own business!"

"And you—look at you, the clock is ticking. Your youth is behind you and soon, my dear, you will be gray!" Rearden noted with some pleasure that despite her years, Mrs. Osbourne still knew how to blush. "Calm down, my girl. You're turning as dark as an Indian."

She felt like tearing his eyes out or pulling his mustache away from that lurking smile. Rearden was expecting her to explode. She contained herself. Without relenting, as if she were trying to shake him off, in a slightly breathless voice she adopted a half-playful, half-reasonable tone:

"Do you hate women so much, my poor friend, that you always try to humiliate them? What have they done to you? And me, what am I doing that is so reprehensible? I am not separating from my husband, as you would like to believe, I'm not leaving Sam. I am not spending my children's inheritance, I'm not selling anything, the house is still here, and yet God knows I need the money! I am not even taking the trouble to rent the place. This is a study trip. What's so wrong with that?"

The horses pulling the tramcar connecting Market Street to the Embarcadero had just turned the corner. On this Friday evening, the car was crammed full. Fanny passed the stop and followed on foot among the crowd of men hastening toward the ocean. Rearden caught her.

"Indeed, about these studies . . ."

They passed groups of Chinese with shaved crowns and long braids down their backs. They mingled in the crowd of Malaysian coolies, Mexican *vaqueros*, orthodox Jews—all the nationalities, colors, and races that Rearden despised.

"I don't want to listen to you anymore, Rearden. I hate your narrow-mindedness and your vulgarity."

"One more word—"

"Enough!"

"My girl, you're going to listen to me. All your talent, your artistic pretensions, are just a lot of nonsense and a waste of time! You will never become a great painter."

This time he had gotten to her. With the wind knocked out of her, she had to stop. He had just attacked what was most precious to her. But Rearden did not pause at her imploring look.

"Finally," he went on, "let me remind you how rough it is for a mature woman who chooses to turn her back on society. You hope to live in harmony with yourself—that's it, isn't it? Follow your instinct wherever it takes you? What nonsense! You better know that a woman who leaves the straight and narrow is lost forever. If you go away, if you leave Sam, you are done for. There—I've said all I had to say. Now you do as you wish," he concluded. With no transition, with the same grumbling manner, he took a small packet out of his overcoat pocket and held it out to her. "I found something rather nice on your friend Rubens. For this sort of thing, it's well written. Read it carefully, this little book might interest you."

He brought her to the ferry landing, then turned and retraced his steps.

She fluttered, like a wounded sparrow, from the freight area to the warehouses, coming back to the wharf and standing still at the water's edge. She would have liked to embark instantly, just disappear, and begin again from scratch. She stood for a long time looking at the glimmer of the little waves dying at her feet.

*

Early the next day, Fanny heard the click of the gate. Sam, his face haggard, his eyes red, smelling of whiskey, let himself sink onto the porch step in front of her. He growled between his teeth: "I am coming back to live with you."

"Oh, Sam," she sighed.

"I've left that woman. I'm coming back to live with you!"

She looked at his bent neck, his slumped shoulders, his hands hanging down: a beaten dog. Fanny instinctively respected weakness. Her father used to tell how as a young girl at the races in Indianapolis, she had openly spurned the favorite and staked all her money on the nag that needed most encouragement. Seeing Sam so defeated, she was gripped by a rush of feeling. Affection? Compassion? Fear?

"I am coming back to live with you," he repeated.

His voice was hard and hateful. He was surly, ready to bite. She thought for a moment.

"It won't work," she said.

"And why not? It worked fine for ten years!"

She shrugged her shoulders and went into the house. He stayed seated, the dampness of the wood soaking his trousers, and then turned toward the door: "Fanny!" he shouted. "You're not taking my children thousands of miles away . . . Not for six months, not for a year! Europe is a continent, a world, a whole life! You are tearing them away from their home, despite them, despite me. And all for what?"

For what? Fanny stood still, her face torn with feeling. For what?

"To give them a chance to be educated, so Belle can become a real artist."

She was deceiving him, and she knew it. She remained standing in the hall, paralyzed with fear. What should she do? Stay? Take up her life again with Sam?

A month from now he would go strolling off again with some creature on his arm, an old mistress or a new one, and he would come here on Sundays, quibble over the household expenses, and leave again to spend his money elsewhere. And all their life she would be confined to this role of housewife, dissatisfied with everything and especially with herself. Fanny's gaze fell on her reflection in the hall mirror. Between the black eyebrows, two quite visible creases were giving her face a tense expression. At the corners of her lips, two others accented the naturally pouting curve of her mouth. The clock was ticking, Rearden was right.

Thin, almost too thin, her bust bound in a man's jacket that clung to her waist and fitted tightly over her hips, the thighs hampered by her bustled skirt that closed in front and behind along its entire length in a stream of beveled jade buttons, tens of black, shiny drops—she conjured up some amphibious animal. She imagined herself in a few years. It seemed to her that she would not have a drop of moisture left in her skin, or blood in her heart. A dry stick. What should she do? If she did not go away now, it would be too late.

"You take full responsibility for it, Fanny. You are stealing Sammy's and Hervey's childhood from me. You are stealing Belle's youth. You are stealing my children!"

*
**

On April 28, 1875, Fanny was ready. She closed up the cottage, she sent her trunks to the station. Miss Kate and the children were told that they would be leaving for Indiana. From there, they would go to New York, where Miss Kate would stay with one of her aunts. Fanny, with Belle (sixteen), Samuel Lloyd (seven), and Hervey (four), would depart for Belgium. A year of study at the celebrated Academy of Painting in Antwerp.

Why Antwerp rather than Paris or Rome, as Dora suggested? Because Rearden had given her a book on Rubens, or because a Belgian port city seemed more reassuring to Sam than a great capital? Because from New York to Paris, Antwerp was a stopping point along the way? Perhaps, in her impatience, she had simply chosen the first ship she could find.

One thing I'm sure of is that Fanny did not know how to find Belgium on the map, or whether it was a kingdom, an empire, or a republic. As for the language they spoke there—a total mystery. Anyway, she didn't know a word of Flemish or French. Besides, she forgot that Sam would not send her money, or only the minimum, that she had no safety net, no friends or relations in Europe. And she was entirely unaware of the fact that the Academy of Painting in Antwerp was closed to women. She was leaving for nothing.

*

In this second half of the nineteenth century, Europe saw many an American adventuress arriving on her shores. None, however, came at the age of thirty-five, encumbered with a family, and penniless.

Fanny was about to take art and the Old World by storm.

Part Two

The Stormy Petrel 1875–1880

IV

Against the Odds

*Living is like the bubbles in
champagne, simply living!*

—Fanny Osbourne

Seaward—July 1875

Standing on the second-class deck, very straight and upright near
the bulwark, a woman in a striped cotton dress held her three
children close. They made a pretty picture. The sons, both very
blond, were fighting over a pair of binoculars and talking about the
sea. The older, in knickerbockers and a fitted jacket, neat curls and
a bow tie, seemed perhaps too reasonable, too passive for a boy
his age. The little one was full of life. Dressed in a sailor suit, his
dark, intense eyes half hidden beneath thick lashes, he let the wind
take his breath away. Then he stuck out his tongue and tasted the
salt without letting go either of the binoculars he held in one hand
or of his sister, who held him by the other. The beauty of the
young girl in a Scotch plaid dress, a square shawl thrown over her
shoulder, was offset by the boys' light charm. Very brown and
earthy, she laughed and swayed for the exclusive benefit of the
passengers playing at shuffleboard behind her. At every shot she
knew that a man's gaze was lingering on her waist, on her shining
hair that fell in two long curls. She was innocent but very knowing.
    The mother, more somber and austere, her neck and ears

123

unadorned and only a simple gold cross at her collar, watched over her family. Her burning eyes followed the wake of the ship as it broke and disappeared from sight. Her veil of cream-colored dotted Swiss lay flat against her straight nose, against her curved forehead and narrow temples, filtering that cameolike profile, that splendid, smooth, amber skin so cleanly framed against the ocean. She seemed quite still, but everything in her was humming. Her little boot was bouncing to the vibrations of the engines, the red ends of her belt were tangled with her hat ribbons, the gray raw silk of her striped dress flattened against her bustle, opened out into a fan under the pouf, and cascaded in short folds to the deck.

"Mama, are we there yet?" the youngest boy, Hervey, asked impatiently.

"Where are we going to live?" Samuel Lloyd worried.

"And what about Papa?" Belle inquired.

"Papa will come!" Fanny enfolded her children in that intense gaze whose confidence and faith were so reassuring. "We," she murmured, "we are going to have adventures that no one in San Francisco has ever had before. Not even the prospectors!"

Fanny's prophetic style, her husky, veiled tone so full of contained excitement, that bubbling spring running hidden to the sea set her children dreaming. They moved closer to her and stood quite still.

Antwerp—August–October 1875

It was, after all, just as I said it would be, she writes to Dora. *We dropped right out without time even to let our friends know.* San Francisco-Antwerp, via Indianapolis. Twenty-five years before the first airplane flights, half a century before Lindbergh, Fanny seemed to travel around the world with the greatest of ease. To appreciate such a trip, I must remember that she first embarked on the Western Pacific Railroad to Vallejo; from there, she took the California Pacific to Sacramento, then the Central Pacific to Ogden, the Union Pacific as far as Omaha, and another change to Indianapolis; a local train brought her to Clayton or Danville, and a buggy to the Vandegrift farm.

At the end of these twelve days of uninterrupted travel, lashed into her corset, sitting on seats with no back support or headrest and no place to lie down at night, with two young children and more than a hundred stops, plus a missed connection that forced her to wait twenty-four hours in the Omaha station, she spent just a week with her family. Then she was off again on a journey so daunting it frightens me, and this was something she did repeatedly, eagerly, until late in life.

After many moving adventures by field and by flood we are at length domiciled at the heart of the old city of Antwerp. I say flood advisedly, for we were blockaded by the floods in Indiana for a longer time than I liked. Track and bridges were washed away. At last I grew too impatient to wait longer, and hired a driver warranted to obey orders, an old country omnibus, and two stout horses. With my children and trunks I drove right through the flooded country. We plunged over embankments into foaming torrents, at the risk of being swept away and drowned, half a dozen times. Only one bridge was left standing, and men were waiting to warn people off it as being unsafe: we went over it, and afterwards it fell. I do not think I should dare do such a thing again, for I risked not only my own life, but that of the children. After all, though it was a fortunate thing that I had been so desperate, for my tickets were limited, and the time having run out, they were useless from Indianapolis to New York. . . . I arrived at New York, too, at a fortunate time, as the vessel going out was almost empty, and I only had to pay one hundred and seventy dollars for my whole party, all the way to Antwerp, and had two of the best cabins on the ship. I will never again believe anything that is said about the Englishman's want of chivalry. The fact of our being American ladies traveling alone caused us to be treated with the greatest consideration and respect. So fearful were the officers that something might happen to us that some one of them stayed by us and took care of us until they saw us safely on board the channel steamer which carried us to Antwerp. . . . We arrived at Antwerp at eleven in the evening. The custom house officers came on board but no entreaties of the captain would induce them to look at our things that night. It was very dark and raining, and there were only half enough beds on board the boat for the passengers. I watched for a chance to get near the best-natured-looking of the officials, tried to look as helpless as possible, it was very easy to do, I can assure you, I had only to look as I felt, and said "We are American ladies alone; you see how unpleasant it will be to remain here all night; I trust to your courtesy!" My trunks were down in an instant, the lids lifted, and closed again, and two men were carrying them out amid the curses, loud and deep, of the Englishmen who were compelled to wait until morning. The captain, as soon as he saw our trunks were being opened, rushed out and engaged a carriage for us, and in a few minutes we found ourselves at the hotel San Antoine. We were taken to our room, it was so crowded they could give us but one, where we took off our things and sat down to rest. At that moment, as we were all sitting silent, the midnight chimes rang out from Nôtre Dame spire, which was very near us. I then realized that I was in Antwerp. I held my breath to listen, with tears in my eyes, and my heart in my mouth. I think I felt as Mr. Williams did when he first caught sight of Rome. It was a moment in my life that I shall be loath to forget. I was sentimental enough to imagine it a welcome to the Old World, and to accept it as a good omen.

Entirely taken up by her enthusiasm, Fanny was not deterred by the catastrophic discovery that her journey had been useless.

But good Lord, cried the director of the Academy when I presented myself to him the next day, good Lord, why, why were you not a boy? I could learn more in one year here at the Academy than in five years at home. The director, however, is going to interest himself in my studies so I hope my time will not be altogether thrown away. He advises some six months hard work at anatomy here, then a year at Paris and another at Rome. I shall do just what he tells me as closely as possible.

How would she pay for this? Fanny never raised the question. While many gifted young girls took private classes, while the exhibition at the Salon was not closed to them, and some even achieved success—I am thinking of the American Mary Cassatt, of Berthe Morisot, of Eva Gonzales, of Marie Bashkirtseff—they were all sustained at first by their own money or that of family or friends.

Friends? Oh, I have some too! she exclaims rather innocently. The owners of the hotel du Bien Être, the Gerhardts. The most delightful people. They have petted us to death, nearly.

Fanny had no social prejudice. She always refused to belong to any class and resisted the notion of milieu. Even in London she would make no concessions to British snobbery, she would not bow to their codes. Ultimately, Fanny was the antithesis of an intellectual, the opposite of an "adventuress." People interested her only for emotional reasons. She loved, she hated, and from her feelings, and from those alone, came every one of her ideas and actions. The freedom to feel was her whole ethics, and the moral inheritance she wanted to leave her children.

The old Flemish mother, a stately dame, puts her arms around us and talks caressingly in her own language, we answer in our own, and all laugh merrily. I told them at first that their charges were more than I cared to pay, so they set to work to find a place for me. They have found one after much trouble, just the second door to themselves. They thought it much better for me to live alone than to divide a house with someone. "You know," said the old lady, "the rest might object if the children cried, or were noisy. I have had eleven and I understand that." This of course was translated, the husband speaks some English. I suppose I could tell you much about Antwerp that you do not already know. The things which struck me most were the crookedness of the streets and the dirt ... You start out in one direction and the street turns and twists and you imagine that in the main you are traveling in the opposite direction from which you started, and the last floors of the houses almost touch above our heads. Nothing is like it is at home! Here muzzled dogs pull wagons and milk churns, at every intersection there are statues of saints and madonnas lit by candles, but the most extraordinary thing of all is the way people dress. What a mascarade! The men wear enormous trousers and short jackets, the women huge headdresses and long coats. We are located three hundred feet from the middle of this giant, costumed population, who take us for dwarfs or children. Belle has come back from taking a third or fourth look at Rubens' Descent from the Cross. Little Sam is infatuated with Rubens. He comes home and tries to copy the pictures with pen and ink and cries because they are not like Rubens'.

Belle says if you wish to know anything about the house to tell you that it is a four-story brownstone front, just around the corner from the palace; all of which is true. The stove is brown from age and dirt, it is four stories high, but only one room deep; in fact there are only five rooms, the tiniest little rooms imaginable, and a tiny hall . . . The rooms are so small that we shall have to stay one in a room, and Miss Kate, I think, will sit on the outside doorstep. You may wonder what I did with Miss Kate . . .

Miss Kate? Didn't Fanny leave the governess with her relatives in New York? This brings up Fanny's odd relations with the people in her service. She was either "loathed or slavishly adored; indifference was impossible," as Stevenson would describe it. Some of her employees would follow her to the ends of the earth, and Miss Kate began the series of extreme devotion with a certain sense of melodrama.

As they were about to depart from New York to Liverpool the previous August 2 on *The City of Brooklyn*, the governess had found it difficult to separate from Fanny and the children.

"Take me with you!" she had begged.

"Look, Miss Kate, you know that with what my husband will send me in Europe, I would not be able to pay you."

"But I will work for nothing!"

"My poor Miss Kate, I could not even feed you!"

"I will not eat!"

Fanny had glanced skeptically at Miss Kate's large bulk and even larger mouth.

"Take care of yourself, dear Miss Kate. Do it out of friendship for us. I will let you know when we are going to return, and you will come to join us again in East Oakland. Good-bye!"

Without much success she had tried to embrace the governess, who had wandered off sniffling. Sadly, Fanny had watched her disappear.

During the crossing, Fanny and Belle had been chatting with a court of young men on the second-class deck: two of them were so fascinated that they would pursue the women for several years. The first, a rich Southerner, a plantation owner from Kentucky, was set on marrying the daughter; the other, a New York surgeon, was bent on seducing the mother. So they were flirting when suddenly up rushed an imposing lady who threw herself at their feet.

"I love you! Keep me! Forgive me, forgive me. I have been hiding in the hold for ten days. I bought a third-class ticket. I am staying with you. You cannot get rid of me now!"

Surprised and very moved, Fanny raised Miss Kate to her feet. The two women embraced.

The were about to share long, sleepless vigils, a nightmare from which neither of them would fully recover.

Paris—October 1875–April 1876

Paris was full of confusion, a rubbish-strewn shambles, a charnel house. Four years after the massacres of the Commune—which claimed almost twenty-two thousand victims, more dead in a single week than in six years of the French Revolution—Fanny alighted at the Gare du Nord.

Our last days in Antwerp were hurried, tragic ones, Belle recalls. *By the time we were settled in our new house, my little brother Hervey was taken ill with a fever. The doctor, a Frenchman recommended by Papa Gerhardt, confessed that he did not know what the matter was and advised my mother to take the little boy to Paris, where there was a doctor famous for his success in children's ailments. We were ready to leave before the week was out. How my mother managed it is a mystery. She didn't know a word of French. All the same we were soon settled in a sunny little apartment on the rue de Naples, the new doctor was attending Hervey whose health improved at once . . .*

Bombarded by the Prussians, burned down by the Communards, pulverized by Haussmann's building projects, the poetry of Paris as Fanny discovered it was the poetry of a city in ruins.

Crumbling walls, cinders, soot, the Tuileries burned, the Hôtel de Ville, the prefecture, the Archives, the d'Orsay Palace, stones, pits, holes, not a tree left standing. The famous streets—Avenue Royale, rue de Rivoli, rue de Lille—gutted. A total of 200 condemned buildings.

On the Avenue de l'Opera, the houses were collapsing as the former owners auctioned off their belongings. They were laying a straight line from the Theatre-Français to the Opera. The roof of the new temple of music and dance, all gold on a black background, marked the horizon. On the heights of Montmartre, masked by a gigantic palisade, stood the white stones of Sacre-Coeur. This was a golden era for anyone interested in painting. Millet and Corot, the precursors of the Barbizon School, had just died. But the word

"Impressionism" had been pronounced for the first time the previous spring. Monet was painting his series on the Gare Saint-Lazare. Renoir was living on rue Saint-George, Degas on rue de Douai, Henry James was coming to visit Turgenev, and a few doors away, in a garret in the European quarter, a certain Mrs. Samuel Osbourne found lodging for herself and her children. She arrived at the most exciting moment, when the history of art was about to tumble into the twentieth century. Fanny was unaware of this.

She was engaged on another front, in a battle that would consume her body and soul until the final defeat. "Art, life, for us it was all the same thing," writes her countryman, the painter Will Low, who was studying in Paris at the same period. Fanny was indeed fighting for life with all her incredible energy, battling life, art, death, throwing herself into the breach.

From this first hand-to-hand combat, from her terrible failure, Fanny would retain all the traits that so aggravated her detractors: the obsession with "saving" those she loved; the mania for diagnosis, the fear of bad omens; a zeal for thwarting fate. Even her children reproached her for this obstinacy in trying to prevent illness, in making dire predictions, and despairing when no one took her seriously.

For the moment, her letters to Dora Williams and Timothy Rearden revealed nothing. Not only didn't she complain, she embroidered. Dora admired her, Rearden blamed her: she was bluffing. How could she admit to them how she was really spending her time in Paris? Fanny's silences were always more eloquent than her words. Anyone reading between the lines can sense her anguish.

October 1875—Fanny to Dora

Dear Mrs. Williams,

I dreamt of you and your husband last night, and though the dream was not a pleasant one, (I thought I had quarrelled with you), still it served the purpose of reminding me that I owed you a letter. So long a period does not elapse between my letters to you, as between yours to me, and my duties are more manifold than yours.

We are, as I suppose you know, now in Paris. It may interest you, as I believe you have some thought of ultimately coming here, to know something of our way of living. Of course our apartments are on a flat; we have the whole floor, and are as private as though in our own house. For fifteen dollars, and two dollars a month to the concierge. We have two large bedrooms, a pretty little salon, a small entrance hall, and a very large elegant dining room, to say nothing of a kitchen with a little charcoal range, a porcelain stove of great elegance in the dining room, and immense mirrors in every room. Our furniture is of the most primitive character, mostly made by myself. We have a hydrant in the kitchen (no charge for water) which comes, not from the Seine, as in most houses, but from an artesian well, and is consequently pure, and also cold as ice, and gas if we choose to pay for it.

I am charmed with the French style of painting, but then I know but little, and may not be a judge. I have not as yet seen all the best pictures, but so far have seen nothing that I liked so well as some of Rubens. Belle and I, after asking the advice of several artists have begun studying at a Monsieur Julian's academy. His atelier was founded about fifteen years ago on rue Fontaine, with branches all over Paris. One of them, miraculously, is reserved for women. Absolutely everyone comes, and it promises to be exciting.

October–November 1875—Fanny to Rearden

Dear Mr. Rearden,

Everything is going well.

Since we arrived in Paris everyone's health is better. With Hervey's illness, I have not yet been able to go to the Julian Academy. But he is doing better. All the same, I think they give enormous doses of quinine here. Hervey takes seven grains for a dose. When it is mixed with water it almost fills a table spoon. The poor little thing has suffered so much that he takes the bitter dose eagerly, hoping it will alleviate his pain. Although he is still very thin and pale, I am not so worried.

November 1875—Fanny to Dora

You ask me for news of my bohemian life. I am full of it! Belle, who goes every day to the atelier, says that next Monday Mr. Julian gives a fancy dress party for the ladies' class, with the provision that no gentleman except personal friends of the ladies shall be admitted, and that no invitations are to be extended to the gentlemen's class, and no young lady is to go without a chaperon. Of course Belle's heart will be broken if she does not go, so I shall have to go with her, but not in costume, I assure you. It is going to be an excessively bohemian affair ... At the head of the grand staircase a nude model will stand, posed as a statue, with a lamp in his hand. The passages are to be lighted by Chinese lanterns, and pages in buttons are to be stationed at intervals to prevent people from wandering off and becoming lost. The supper, which will be served in M. Julian's private room, will consist simply of brioche, cakes, wine, and fruit, but the meagerness of the fare will be made up by the fashionable hour at which it is served, two o'clock. I think it is going to be awfully funny.

Of course I wouldn't notice any of Mr. Rearden's nonsense, I know him too well, though he is certainly what you said, still I admire him for more than for some qualities of his mind as you say; for many kind and generous actions, for his tenderness for children, for his refined tastes, and for a certain sort of childishness of manner, which seems so at variance with his character. To me he is a strange and curious creature.

I was not particularly surprised at the news of your cousin's marriage. You are quite right about thinking anything of the kind impossible for Belle. She had an opportunity of the same kind on the boat, except that it was much more advantageous. A planter from Kentucky asked me for her hand, but his offer was instantly rejected with scorn by me, as well as herself. I will tell you about it someday, but don't speak of it to anyone at all, please. It never was thought for a moment, though many mothers would have jumped at the chance of getting several hundred thousand dollars into the family. Don't speak of it to my husband even.

My little Hervey is still quite ill, it almost seems as though he never would get better. The doctor says that I must not look for much improvement under three months yet.

As ever,

Fanny M. O.

November 1875—Fanny to Rearden

Dear Mr. Rearden,

Everyone has gone to bed but Miss Kate and myself. Little Hervey is still quite ill. I sent for one of the great Paris doctors who said all sorts of things ailed the child and that he was threatened with scrofulous consumption. The treatment is very tedious and unpleasant to the child. We have to paint his side every night for a month with some drug so powerful that everyone in the room is almost blinded by it.

Of course I am very tired and hardly fit for study. Still until the last three days I have gone every day to the art school. It is called the best for women in Paris, and is crowded to suffocation with ladies from every quarter of the globe, Swedes, Russians, and four or five other Americans.

The entrance is from the Passage des Panoramas and is a narrow winding stairway, perfectly dark and excessively dirty. The atelier is on the third floor and consists of two rooms, one large and one small and both very dirty and uncomfortably crowded. One side of the room is occupied by a platform for the model. The ladies all crowd around with their easels. You have to come at dawn to get a good place, otherwise you see literally nothing. If you are too close, you see nothing either. With Hervey's illness, it is difficult for me to come on time.

When a stranger comes on any business, Mr. Julian, the director, puts on airs of the greatest dignity, but as soon as the door closes he rushes in, climbs upon a stool, the only place where there is any room for him, and he and the school talk the person who has just left over from top to toe. It is a very French habit that would suit you well.

We have the model who sits for the head in the morning and for the nude figure in the afternoon. One week we have a male model and the next week a female. The men are vaguely covered, the women in the nude. It's fine with me to draw them nude, but I must say that when the woman perched on the platform laughs and jokes with Mr. Julian, or puts on her underwear in front of us, still speaking to him, she stops being a model and becomes a woman, and I don't like this very much. Today someone found out that the female model could sing, so this afternoon they called up Mr. Julian from the speaking tube and had her sing songs and waltz for them.

Wouldn't that be shocking in San Francisco? A couple of Yankee old maids who are studying have almost lost their senses. We have pleasant times all through the week until Saturday comes; nine o'clock in the morning brings Mr. Fleury, the corrector, who is one of the great painters of France. He is excessively significant and very disagreeable. His business is not to praise, only to point out faults, which he does with the greatest unction, seeming delighted when he has found anything very bad indeed. He is received in dead silence, and leaves a depression of spirits behind him. I was away a good deal last week, so . . . I turned my easel to the wall and he did not notice it. Mrs. M., however, had, and just as he was about to go, maliciously called his attention to it, and showed him with great eagerness, to whom the drawing belonged. To my great surprise, and hers, too, he praised it more than anything that had been done, saying it was so innocent, natural and truthful, and that I was to keep on in exactly that style without regarding what was said to others.

Don't let us talk of John at all. I would rather not. It doesn't seem fair when he and you are not so friendly as formerly, to even speak of him in a joking way. I am very well aware that any amount of sentiment is quite wasted when lavished upon me, still it is a comfortable feeling that I have one friend in the world. That I know I have in John, and he is the only one.

To answer your question, I believe in women's rights in a general sense, but not for myself. Nature meant me for one of those creatures so despised by the "strong-minded" whom they call derisively the "clinging vine." I do not want to be the stately oak and stand alone, it makes me lonesome to think of the oak with no shelter nor support except what it provides for itself.

It is bitterly cold here. There has been a heavy fall of snow and we have been compelled to keep two fires in one room and then cannot keep warm. Cold weather is one of the things that I "do despise."

By the time you receive this it will be Christmas. I wish you a very Merry Christmas except that I would like to have you feel just a little pang of regret that I am so far away, at least that Miss Kate is.

You tell me that you only mean the kind and pleasant things that you say. Immediately upon reading which, I looked through your letter to find them, but with no success. Did you forget to put that sheet of your letter into the envelope? Write to me anyhow, whatever you say. Nobody else writes and your letters are at least something.

Fanny M. O.

Since writing the above which I forgot to send, I have received your registered letter. Thank you as much for remembering me as for the present. I had my money, all I had, in my lap, and was counting up with a pencil and paper to see if I could afford to buy anything for Belle and the children. My husband said in his last that he would not be able to send me anything at all, more than my usual allowance, which just does meet expenses. I had sadly concluded that I should have to let Christmas pass by. I am sure you will not mind that I took the most of the money for them instead of for myself. It gives me much more pleasure to use it that way, and I know that is what you meant.

January 1876—Fanny to Rearden

Dear Mr. Rearden,

I am glad you found my letter amusing. It is more than I can say of yours. My days are so stupid and my evenings so tiresome, though I am glad of letters of any kind. I could read an almanac or a hymnbook.

If I am spiteful and need to have my claws cut, it is at least a feminine weakness, and not an astonishing one under the circumstances. How do you sharpen yours? On your friend's back?

I have not attended the art school for some time on account of Hervey's illness. For two weeks I nor Miss Kate have not gone to bed until some time in the morning, and then we only take naps. Hervey is better tonight, so, though it is only seven o'clock Miss Kate is going to bed now—only think how good I am, sitting up to write to you.

I am amused at your idea of rue de Naples. It may have been a street of elegant structures before the war, but was heavily shelled by the Prussians, and torn to pieces by the communists [1871 Commurards], so that though the structures are of recent date, there are very few of them. On each side of our house are ruins. The street is rather narrow, and quite short, only a few blocks in length and very quiet. I like it for the latter reason, and then it is on the highest ground in the city. We are within a couple of blocks of the Parc de Monceau; it is a pretty place, quiet and shady, and will be a fine place for the boys in the summer.

Do you know anything about my doctor? He has been in Paris for twenty-five years, but came from your town where his father was a doctor before him. His name is Johnstone, and he is quite celebrated as a physician. What do you think? I want to trust him, but I am not sure. I am no longer sure of anything. Is Hervey being well cared for? Write soon and tell me what you think of him. It is urgent.

February—Fanny to Dora

You ask me who we are seeing? No one. We don't know a soul here. The evenings are long for Sammy and Belle, who sit up at their little brother's bedside. Please say nothing about this to Rearden, it would make him only too happy. Since you really want to know the truth, we are very poor. My children are always cold and I cannot manage to keep them fed properly. Belle, who is never defeated, can get away with it. Even on an empty stomach she continues to go to the Julian Academy. On the way, she chats with the merchants, who think she is a little housemaid, and give her food. My daughter is so good-natured, fate will not crush her. But seeing Sammy so miserably glued to the bakery windows, I know that my little boy is always hungry. I enrolled him at the local school, but because of his blond hair and foreign accent they treat him like a Prussian. He does not complain, but he is easily discouraged, he is so sensitive, so full of imagination. And now he is thin and pale, and has a frequent cough.

All the money my husband sends goes for Hervey's medicine and for doctors. I tried to find work, but who will look after my sick child? Miss Kate cannot do more. She has lost in excess of twenty pounds. I try to tempt my littlest with grapes and expensive cakes but now he cannot swallow anything. His eyes are bright and feverish and he trembles all the time. I have done all I can.

Mr. Osbourne no doubt does what he can, but we don't have anything. He does not understand.

February 1876—Fanny to Rearden

Come, don't quarrel with me. I feel lonely and dreary enough without that. Your sarcasm, I suppose you meant it for that, about my bright letter, though, didn't hurt my feelings at all for I know that they are just as stupid as possible; but I have been quite ill . . . I have been so anxious and distressed about my sweet pretty baby.

I believe that Sam does miss us very much indeed. I had no idea that he would. I thought it would be a sort of weight off his mind to have us gone once more. His letter quite touched my heart and I wish you could cheer him up a bit. Somehow I didn't seem to succeed and yet I have tried very hard. I don't like to be selfish, and it makes me feel so if I thought he is unhappy at our absence. I didn't know I should miss him as I do. It was very pitiful to hear my little Hervey in his delirium calling and calling for his father; it made me feel as if I had no right to have him so far away. I will add only one more bit, and that is this: please don't write cross letters to me. If you do I shall cry.

March 1876—Fanny to Rearden

It is six weeks now since I have gone to bed before morning. Hervey has been and still is very ill indeed—don't say a word of it to his father. He is out of immediate danger now I think.

With the fatigue and anxiety I have grown so thin that if my looks depend only upon eyes and plumpness, as you say, then I have only eyes left; indeed I am hardly anything but eyes. The ladies at the art school asked me to pose for them as "Sorrow." If Mr. Julian pays me I will do it, I am so in need of money. It would certainly be the first time my troubles did me any good.

You tell me not to let the doctors fool me about Hervey. I don't need doctors for that. And my doctor is so kind and good that I almost love him; I believe I should, did he not remind me so much of you.

As to the model of the Pantheon, that will have to wait until I am able to go over to the other side of the city to see about it. I generally go to bed about three in the morning, sleep snatches of ten minutes until daylight, get up feeling like a person in a dream or walking in their sleep, give Hervey a medicated bath, change and arrange his poultices and get his medicine ready for the day, eat my breakfast, take a Guarana powder to settle my senses a little, read what letters may have come, find it noon and my painting teacher come, paint till dark, eat my dinner, and sit up another night. Now do you wonder that I write wandering letters?

I have given over going to the atelier for a month past, to my heartfelt sorrow. Such another opportunity I shall never have while I live again. Belle, however, goes every day and is making wonderful progress. I am very proud of my girl, so good and so handsome and so talented. It does not seem to me that there are three such children in the world as mine. I suppose every mother thinks that, but do you not think that my Belle is superior to most girls? And she is not equal to my boys. Doesn't it seem that these children ought to be happiness enough for one woman's life? If I lose one of them I shall die—I forgot that I am writing to you who cannot understand me.

Next week I am going to take Hervey every morning outside the city to drink fresh blood.

As I write, his symptoms have changed for the worse. I hope it will pass off. He is coughing with a hard rasping cough. In my haste to go to him I have blotted my letter all over.

Cable from Paris, March 1, 1876, Fanny to Sam

Impossible to move Hervey. Come at any price. Come quickly.

Cable from Montreal, March 14, 1876, Sam to Fanny

I will be in Paris two weeks from Tuesday.

Cable from Liverpool, March 29, 1876, Sam to Fanny

Telegraph about Hervey.

Cable from London, March 29, 1876, Sam to Fanny

I leave tonight via New Haven and Dieppe. Reach Paris noon tomorrow.

Same Day, Fanny to Sam

Still living.

April 1876, Timothy Rearden to Fanny

Dear Mrs. Osbourne,
   This is what happens when a woman, a mother, goes gallivanting around like a young girl! If you had stayed sensibly at home as I advised, none of this would have happened. What an idea, to drag your children around on such an adventure. And now, you've been in Paris for five months, without money, with a sick little boy whom you cannot care for. And you are studying, you say, less than in San Francisco? A fine thing. Hervey must have caught a cold, if not some contagious illness in Belgium or on the boat. Let this be a lesson to you!
   Now that the deed is done, you might as well stay in Europe. Learn a little anatomy in France and work on your colors, that will not be amiss.
   You thought you were being strong to leave your country when you were merely being irresponsible. Between us, my dear, whatever happens you've got it coming. You have confused courage with lack of conscience, and this blindness has cost you dear. Stop your nonsense, then, and save your children.

Paris, April 5, 1876, Sam to Timothy Rearden

   My dear Tim,
   I saw a letter in your handwriting brought into the room by the concierge, the other day, and Mrs. Osbourne read it at the bedside of a sick little boy. Something it contained, I am afraid, gave her some offense. She did not show it to me, but intimated that it

contained something that grated harshly on her feelings, wrought up as they were with watching for fifteen weeks at the little boy's side. But whatever it was, of course I know was nothing that was intentionally said—only it happened to come mal apropos. Our poor little boy died this morning at five o'clock, and his mother is almost paralyzed with grief. I will remain with her until her condition will allow me to leave her and then will speed right home. I may not be many days behind this letter, but I knew you were anxious to hear from us all, and I write to you among the first to whom I turn for sympathy in our bereavement. Write to Mrs. Osbourne for she never stood in such need of kind words and friendly messages as now.

Several Weeks Later, Fanny to Rearden

Dear Mr. Rearden,

. . . In one letter you told me to cut my baby's curls and try to make him more of a boy like Sammy. I cut off the yellow curls, and that is all I have left of my pretty boy. You thought him not as manly as Sammy because of his pretty face and the yellow curls. There was never a boy so brave. His death was hideous and a continual torture, and his appearance was so dreadful that strangers could not look upon him, and Sam was afraid of him. Though I tried to prepare his father, he gave a cry of horror and covering his face with his hands fell upon his knees. And my poor brave boy, knowing what it was, for he grew very precocious in dying, tried to comfort his father, patting his bent head with his little hand, and smiling such a smile that I pray no human being may ever have the terror and misery of beholding.

The doctors say that it was a most interesting and extraordinary case, that of my boy, so feeble in body, and yet a month in dying, kept alive by sheer force of will. I never left him day or night, taking only three out of the twenty-four for sleep on his pillow, except on his birthday, when I went to the toy shop and bought him some playthings. Such a pitiful, heartbreaking birthday that was.

I did not dare leave him because every few hours he bled in a new place. I shall never forget the smell of blood. He would say, "Blood, mama, get the things; wait till I am ready." Then he would clasp one hand in the other, close his eyes, and say "now," would clench his teeth and wait, and not a moan or cry or tremble would be perceptible, though the pain made him deathly sick afterwards. Everyone ran from the room when he said blood; his father stayed once until he saw the probe, and then he too turned pale and ran away. None could see what my boy could bear. Through all his sufferings he never lost his mind. I only wish he had been unconscious. When in the most violent convulsions, his bones snapping in and out of joint like the crack of a whip, and covered with blood, he lay back in my arms, looking into my eyes and listening to my words through it all. I couldn't bear that he should suffer terror of mind as well as anguish of body, so I tried to speak encouraging, comforting words into his ear; he could hardly hear, the rush of blood having torn one drum entirely away and perforating the other, but no one can conceive what agony it was to me, and so it went on day after day, such terrible days! His bones had cut through the skin and lay bare, and yet there was no word of complaint through it all. The only thing he asked for was that he might see the sky and grass once more, and we both watched every morning eagerly for the bright warm day when it was promised that his father would carry him out to ride.

One awful day I smelled blood and could not find it. I looked all day, my boy growing weaker all the time but I could not find it. At night I burned all the front off my hair looking at his throat with a candle but I could find nothing; he was bleeding internally. He asked that his father should sing a song that he had heard long ago. Something, he said, about goodbye to the old home and the young folks playing round the little cabin door, once he woke and said, "Lie down beside me." After that he never spoke again.

His father tried to comfort me by saying he died so peacefully, but I heard him cry, a dreadful moaning cry, just before he died, my brave boy who had never cried before through it all. I knew then that he was dying and that the cry was involuntary. He never would have cried like that if he had known that I heard it. There is no comfort for me; there can be none but to give me back my child.

The weather changed and the first bright day my boy went out to ride as I had promised him, but he rode alone and never came back.

Christmas you sent me some money to get a present for myself. I spent it mostly for the children. Hervey had seen a pretty dress that he wanted so I got it for him, telling him Mr. Rearden gave it to him. He kept it very carefully to wear when he went home that you might see it. He wears it now, and you will never see him in his pretty dress. He wished me to thank you for it, and for the animals you gave him and to say goodbye to you for him. He bade everybody goodbye. It is too cruel that my child should die. They try to comfort me by telling me that he is better where he lies, that he would have been deaf and dumb and probably deformed, had he lived. That only makes me feel that he must be tired lying so long on his back, and that I must dig him up and turn him over. Then they talk to me of heaven; what sort of a heaven would it be for my baby alone, without his mother. It cannot be, I cannot believe that he is dead, though the knowledge of it is always with me sleeping or waking. As I followed him to his grave walking behind the little white coffin, would you believe I tried to call Hervey's attention to the pretty pitiful sight?

Fanny M. O.

The morning of April 8, 1876, the morning of the burial, an icy, bitter blast raked people's faces and twisted the trees. The spring they thought had finally come after months of severe weather was once more just a memory. Snow was falling everywhere. It burned the new buds, ravaged the leaves, broke the twigs. It glistened in the sky, on the sand, between the crosses with a greenish light. Five figures were threading their way through the cemetery of Saint-Germain. They wandered among the least expensive graves and burial vaults in Paris, less expensive than Montmartre, less expensive than Père-Lachaise. But the Osbournes were so poor that even here they could offer their child only a temporary resting place. In ten years, little Hervey's bones were to be thrown into a common grave.

The terror of this eventuality would pursue Fanny daily—the common grave. Every day for ten years, she would worry about finding the money to avoid the common grave.

In November 1884, and again in April 1886, Robert Louis Stevenson, then her husband, would send numerous letters to his lawyer and friend, Charles Baxter: *Please look up the papers you have about Hervey Osbourne's grave, find the address of the* marbrier, *take up your best French quill, and see that the concession is assured for some while longer. This is* immediate . . . *For God's sake, see about the boy's grave in Paris at once; I feel sure the concession runs near an end.*

With the death of her child, Fanny's robust constitution was broken. She would never regain her formidable pioneer's good health, or her mental equilibrium. She had hallucinations, memory lapses and dizziness. She did not manage to reach out to Sam again. They lived alone in their deep sadness. And when Sam gently suggested that she come home with him, Fanny did not respond. She felt that this time he had no enthusiasm for resuming their life together, especially since he'd settled his latest mistress in the Oakland cottage. Fanny knew this from their neighbors.

Hand in hand, Sam and Belle walked sadly through the spring-time streets of Paris. Fanny remained prostrate at home. In 1911, three years before her own death, she would write: *My Hervey would have been a man of forty had he lived, and yet I am grieving and longing for my little child as though he had just gone.*

All her life she would express her maternal anguish, year after year. *Day or night I carry with me the memory of my child.*

And as if the horror of this mourning were not enough, she had to face another loss: the man who meant more to her than anyone in the world, her father.

Jacob Vandegrift had lost his mind. *I should not be at all surprised if the next letter brought me news of his death,* she wrote to Rearden in the spring. *A short time ago his favorite sister, one whom I greatly resembled, starved herself to death while insane. But I always forget when writing to you that you are only interested in things that are amusing.*

The Vandegrift family seemed to have suffered from a certain mental fragility. Several of them committed suicide. A cousin of Fanny's hanged himself. And she, with her "brain fever," would endure more than one attack in which memory loss would be the least of it.

This time, madness took hold of her in earnest. She was a phantom, frightening even to Sam, who knew what she was thinking. He read it in her eyes: "If you hadn't spent everything on your mistress, if you had sent us something to live on, even the least bit, I would have managed to save Hervey!"

"If only you hadn't gone away," he countered mentally. "It was this journey, Fanny, that killed our son."

"I have accused myself plenty! If only you knew . . . But you did not want to know! Why didn't you help me? Why did you leave me so alone?"

"You should have stayed home!"

They buried themselves in silent accusations, two blocks of suffering and hate. Until the day when the doctor who had cared for Hervey, observing Sammy's drawn face, commented: "Madame, you must take this child to the country right away! It's urgent—he will contract tuberculosis."

Terrified at the idea of losing her second son, Fanny reacted. An American acquaintance recommended "Grez-sur-Loing," a peaceful little village near Barbizon. This was the headquarters of a group of English-speaking artists. Unfortunately, this inn was closed to families. Wives, at least respectable wives, were entirely unwelcome. The painters chased out all middle-class families and their brats. But the hotel was not very expensive, the food was healthy, and the countryside was restful. One Sunday, Fanny and Sam took the train from Paris to Bourron-Marlotte, then the coach to Grez. This day spent in private conversation did not bring them any closer. But on the return trip, Fanny moved out of her lodgings in rue de Naples. She put the little she owned into the storeroom and accompanied Sam to the train leaving for le Havre, where he would embark on April 14, 1876 on the *Péreire*.

The same day, a coach deposited his family at the edge of the Fontainebleau forest, in the courtyard of a village inn. Destiny beckoned.

Grez-sur-Loing—first summer—May to September 1876

HOTEL CHEVILLON. GARDENS AND SHRUBBERY. FISHING BOATS. PLEASURE BOATS. The sign, displaying a pig cavorting at a table so tempting that Saint Anthony covers his face, grated furiously at the end of its chains at every squall.

At dawn, the storm subsided. It had rained for three days and three nights. In the paved courtyard of the inn, the roofs of the old building were crumbling beneath the weight of soaked and spongy tiles. Slippery grasses grew between the flagstones of the landing. The new-leafed vine tumbled softly over the additions and storeroom, and the branches of the weeping willow swept the ground. The garden wall, which made a terraced descent to the river, spread a pale gray light. On the steep bank, the hulls of overturned canoes were dripping and greasy, as though back from a long crossing.

The last drops of rain could be heard trickling from the rosebushes and wrinkling the black surface of the water. From the square grid of the kitchen garden rose a fragrant, cooling air. The thin crescent moon, a white line like a nail paring, shone palely above the poplars. The reflection of a tower could be seen distorted by the current. Clusters of clouds vanished beneath the arches of the bridge. On the opposite bank floated a thick bluish mist, the sun rising through the trees of the pine forest.

*

"Mrs. Osbourne," Miss Kate called as she came down that morning. "I must speak to you!"

The wooden stairs creaked under her weight. Her boots clacked on the cold tiles of the large dining room. Fanny, dark and straight in the shadows, held her hands toward the hearth where a fire of kindling flickered. An oil lamp was burning in front of the window and shed a soft golden light on the panes. Outside, the early morning looked gray. On the long refectory table, Ernestine, the niece of the house, was setting out bowls for breakfast.

"What is it, Miss Kate?"

"It's just that this place is too uncomfortable to stay any longer. It's primitive here!"

"Primitive?" Fanny repeated, catching a footstool with the end of her boot. "Miss Kate, where is your sense of adventure?"

She sat down. The governess came over to her.

"I haven't slept a wink. There are not even shutters at the windows!"

"It's still dark anyway."

"Exactly! And for sleep, which the doctor said Samuel Lloyd needed, this hotel is a disaster!"

"Sammy never wakes up before noon, he is exhausted by evening, he is eating enough for four," Fanny answered, annoyed. "You agree with me, Miss Kate, that the food is wonderful. You, who so love a good meal, you ought to appreciate . . ."

Miss Kate did not react. Swallowing, she held her hands toward the fire and sententiously asked: "Why didn't you go home with Mr. Osbourne? As I was writing to Timothy, who also told me in his letter—"

"Would you please mind your own business."

"Rearden is my friend, and this is my business. Could you explain what we are doing in this hovel?"

"You may pack your bags, if you like, I won't stop you."

"But you are stopping your poor children! And you are shutting them up between four walls covered with monstrous black graffiti. Belle is sleeping under a naked woman, and there are even naked men!"

"Miss Kate, the attraction of vice is getting to you."

"Those ghastly charcoal drawings!"

"Student sketches and caricatures of French politicians."

"It's shocking! How can the innkeepers allow these vandals to perpetrate such horrors?" She beat her hand nervously against her skirt. "And it sticks to everything. There, on my sleeve, is it charcoal or oil paint?"

"Miss Kate," sighed Fanny, "what is it that's bothering you this morning?"

"There is only one bathroom for the whole floor!"

"Which is used only by Samuel Lloyd, Belle, you, and me."

"For the moment! But Madame Chevillon told me yesterday that before the end of this week her hotel will be full of a dozen of their regulars, trailing the whole Latin Quarter behind them. A bearded, long-haired horde—and dirty, too! Can you imagine all these men carousing all night in our hallway?"

"The little painter we found when we came didn't seem very disorderly to me."

"That's because he is American, because he is alone, and because he washes. But wait till the English arrive!"

"Well?"

"A group of drunkards who force their dogs and their women to drink. Last summer, under this very table, they killed two bull terriers with absinthe!"

They sat together at the end of the long plank table, where fifteen empty chairs were lined up. Ernestine served them fragrant coffee. Then, holding a loaf of whole wheat bread against her white apron, she cut it into slices which she distributed generously. Miss Kate seemed to calm down. Her gaze drifted toward the window where the oil lamp had just expired.

"These gray roofs, these gray walls, and the endless clouds depress me."

"It's strange," Fanny murmured, "but I like this landscape."

"There are no high mountains here set against the vast, crystal-clear blue of our Sierras! It's so beautiful at home," Miss Kate went on, "It's grand! Here, everything is sad and shabby."

"I think I like the stone bridge with its arches," Fanny replied, almost in a whisper, "the ruined tower, the old church and this terraced garden sloping down to the water—the calm and solitude. I love to hear the lapping of the current and the voices of the laundresses beneath the church. The sheets they wash there must be so fresh and soft."

"Frankly, Mrs. Osbourne, I did not come to France to listen to peasant women wash their linen among fish and water lilies!"

"And why did you come?" Fanny asked impatiently.

"To be of service to you!" exclaimed Miss Kate. "And it seems to me I have done more than my share!"

"Who says you have not?"

"You might show me some gratitude!"

"Miss Kate, you are so ill-tempered."

"Perhaps, Mrs. Osbourne, but how would you have managed without me when poor Hervey was bleeding . . ."

The governess stopped, lowered her eyes, and sighed deeply. Ernestine was coming and going around the table without understanding a word of the women's conversation. Fanny went pale and silent.

"I believe you're trying to tell me something, Miss Kate," she said at last.

"You don't need me anymore. Sammy runs through the countryside and fishes for trout from the bridge. Belle explores the ruins of the castle and dreams. As for you, whether it is rainy or windy, at dawn you take your colors and your parasol and you go to paint. I'm bored."

"I understand," said Fanny.

"I have an aunt in Paris. She is rich. She has offered me a position as her companion."

"And you have accepted?"

"I wanted to see how it would be here, first."

"Have you seen?"

Miss Kate nodded her head. Fanny rose. She went to the window and leaned her forehead against the glass. Outside, the light seemed caught in the spiderwebs, and the drops of water trembled on the silver grape vines. The last bond with Hervey was unraveling. Miss Kate, her witness, her companion, had shared such love for the child. Like two allies unable to bear the horror of their defeat, they tore away from each other. Despite her emotion, Fanny felt neither the wish nor the strength to detain the governess. She had only regret—for her son.

Since their arrival in Grez, it seemed to her that she was floating in a vague somnolence somewhere between absence and calm. Her blood was beginning to flow again, a tide that ran ineluctably, like the river at the bottom of the garden. The cold of the pane pulled Fanny out of her torpor.

"When do you want to leave?"

"Right away."

"We must wake the children."

"It should be a beautiful day," commented Miss Kate, by way of conclusion.

A few hours later, a long white handkerchief was waving from the carriage window en route to the train. Miss Kate managed an honorable exit. She had shed a few tears and promised to write. Mother Chevillon and her niece, in bonnets and wooden shoes, Fanny and Belle in mourning, Sammy, his fishing rod and his basket in hand, watched the plump arm wave between the elms and disappear.

"She brought us bad luck," the little boy commented laconically.

"Sam," cried Belle, "you mustn't say that!"

"But it's true!"

During these last three days in Grez, the governess had tried to impede the boy's new-found freedom. Sammy was feeling happy for the first time. Since Hervey's death, his mother seemed solicitous and tender in a way that he intended to enjoy fully. Miss Kate, with her dreadful predictions of the bearded hordes who would chase him from paradise, her incessant harping about the discomfort of the inn, had spoiled his pleasure. Poor Miss Kate. Yet she wasn't the only one to complain about Grez. Thirteen years before, the Goncourt brothers had noted in their *Journal* the hardness of the beds at the Chevillons'. This did not stop them from spending three summers there, and from starting their novel *Manette Salomon* there on the refectory table. How could an American woman from Ohio understand that this hotel, which she considered a hovel, had welcomed as its guests the finest flower of the bohemian world and the Latin Quarter?

The place had been "discovered" by two Italian painters walking in the Fontainebleau Forest. Members of the French Academy, officers of the Legion of Honor, they had their introductions to the court of Napoleon III but chose instead to settle at Jules Chevillon's in 1863. The younger of the two, Joseph Palizzi, even built himself a studio on the grounds of the inn. It was still there when Fanny arrived.

After that, other Italians, several Spaniards, and soon the entire colony of foreigners who studied during the winter in the Parisian ateliers migrated to Grez. Two and a half hours by train from the capital, but more pleasant and less popular than Barbizon, where the presence of Diaz, Millet, and Corot, the masters, had drawn hundreds of disciples, Grez had the advantage of its situation on the banks of the Loing. The river was ideal for the landscape painters. The play of water and light offered an inexhaustible subject for study and inspiration. For the athletic and the idle, there were the joys of sailing and rowing. From every corner of the world, these men of all inclinations and ages were in agreement on one point: The inn never had rooms for snobs, tourists, and middle-class families. For forty years, until the First World War, the Chevillon family would untiringly and cheerfully nurture and cultivate generations of artists. Writers, painters, and musicians recognized today in their own countries, from the Palizzi brothers to the Goncourts, from August Strindberg to Robert Louis Stevenson, from Theodore Robinson to Carl Lindstrom, all these now famous men had passed through the Hotel Chevillon. Today in Paris and New York the galleries are exhibiting what is justifiably called the School of Grez.

*

Under the pale May sun, the wall of the wheat fields rustled and quivered. Blue thistles and white dandelions were gently blooming in the hard earth. The poplars stood unmoving along the riverbank. The Loing wound between small islands, heavy as a track of pale straw. Fish darted beneath the waterlilies. At a distance, by one of the arches of the bridge, the reddish figure of a cow could be seen drinking at the river. The solemn peace of the country at midday. In the shelter of a large, cream-colored parasol, Fanny was trying to capture the softness of this spring. She had placed her easel on the bank, ground and mixed her colors. She heard Sammy's voice on the bridge, where he was fishing with Mimi and Kiki Chevillon, his new friends. Beside her, beneath the same umbrella, Belle's intent profile was leaning over a drawing she was going to send her father. Fanny was reborn.

"But who gave these females our Grez address?"

"I did," conceded a tall, handsome American affecting New England manners and answering to the Gallic name of Pasdessus.

This admission provoked a revolt on the platform of the Bourron station. They were five or six young men just off the train, who now hesitated over where to spend their holiday. Aside from their gesticulations, the noisy use of the English language, and the habit of calling each other by their last names, they had in common the oddity of their dress. They looked as if they were in costume, though just what they were supposed to be was hard to say. Their "unique" getups, however, made them immediately identifiable. From Barbizon to Cernay-la-Ville, from Montigny to Grez, the colonies of artists knew that the blue beret and the walking stick could only belong to the Irish painter O'Meara. The man with the soft thatch of hair, in leather knickerbockers and unlikely striped red stockings, was clearly the landscape painter Stevenson, the Scotsman who looked like a gypsy. The one with the black velvet jacket and the rucksack was his cousin, his alter ego, the one they called "the other Stevenson." By a family aberration, they were both named Robert. The older cousin, present here, Robert Alan Mowbray Stevenson, called Bob, was studying painting in Paris. The "other," Robert Louis Stevenson, called Louis, his junior by three years, was interested in literature and visited France only intermittently. For the moment, he was moping at his parents' home in Edinburgh. As for the frail Robinson, the asthmatic painter with the head of a gargoyle, he wore a yellow scarf tucked across his chest to protect him from the dampness of the forest.

"It was you, Pasdessus?" shouted O'Meara, brandishing his stick.

"They were working in the passage of the Panoramas, in the studio above me, at Julian's," he explained.

"'They?' How many of them are there?"

"Two."

"How old?"

"Mother and daughter."

"Bravo: an old hag and a marriageable young lady. Very good, Pasdessus!" jeered Bob Stevenson.

"And a kid brother, too!"

"Still, if the girl were alone . . ."

"But chaperoned by her old mother, nothing doing!"

"They've had some bad luck," explained Pasdessus. "They were looking for a quiet place, it was early in the season, I had no idea they would settle in!"

"Barbizon," Robinson gently interjected, "The last time I went to Barbizon it was crawling with English women. I left the place."

"If these women should stay here for good," threatened O'Meara, "we'd better move on."

Boxes of paints on their backs, easels under their arms, the group had crossed the road and settled themselves at the station café. Seated side by side, the American, the Scotsman, and the Irishman formed a rather attractive trio, three types of youthful male beauty: O'Meara, redheaded, thin, and strong; Stevenson, restless, dark, and supple, his eyes intense and mouth sensual beneath its mustache; Pasdessus, taller, slower, and perhaps more blasé, with his blond head like the sculpture of an athlete. Together they emptied several bottles of new wine which the barkeeper hastened to bring, knowing their taste. Stevenson clucked his tongue:

"We've had to be tactful and patient to create this colony . . ."

". . . we've had to work to win over the locals."

". . . to inspire the innkeeper's trust."

". . . to teach him to give us unlimited credit."

There was silence while each of them thought.

"With their demands and their money, Pasdessus's females are going to drive up the prices."

"Lower credit."

"Good-bye, freedom!"

"The philistines are everywhere. The forest is covered with the greasy litter they leave behind after their Sunday picnics."

"These ladies don't seem so bad," timidly ventured a young man whose bald head, round figure, and conservative clothing made him quite as noticeable as the others.

"Bloomer," interjected O'Meara, "are you going over to the enemy?"

"He's in love!" bantered Stevenson.

"I thought you only stroked your canvases."

The little man blushed and kept quiet. This was the guest to whom Miss Kate had alluded, the only other occupant of the inn

since the Osbournes' arrival at the beginning of May. Fanny had
not exchanged a word with him the entire month. Had they chatted
in the evenings, sitting at either end of the long table deep in this
little French village, they would have discovered a common past. Originally from California, Bloomer knew Virgil Williams. Today the works
of these two artists are hung together at the Oakland Museum.

"So, Pasdessus, since you are responsible for this disaster, it's
going to be your job," ordered Stevenson, as prince of this bohemia.
"I will await your news at Madame Antony's place in Moret. Her
inn is not as good as the Hotel Chevillon, but at least we can work
in peace there. To throw these females out I place any means at
your disposal. Shoot them if necessary."

He tossed some coins on the table, paying the bill as usual with
the last of a comfortable legacy he would soon exhaust. Then with
a quick step, he headed for the forest.

"I'll come with you," clamored O'Meara, brandishing his stick.

They both disappeared around the bend.

Pasdessus and Robinson climbed with Bloomer into the carriage
that had driven them from Grez. None of them could imagine with
what anguish those ladies awaited their arrival at the inn.

*

In the last week of May, they caught no glimpse of either mother
or daughter. Despite the racket that continued till dawn, the ladies
rose early and disappeared into the countryside before the painters
had opened their eyes. Only the peasants, groups of them filing
toward the fields, crossed their path between the high walls of corn
and the green furrows. The two dark figures, their walking sticks
in hand, carried their work materials done up like bundles of kindling on their shoulders: folding chairs, parasol, easels, canvases,
boxes of colors. A picnic basket was slung on their hips, a plaid
throw or shawl tied at the waist. They painted all day in some
mysterious spot in the forest and reappeared only at dusk. Their
slow steps slid over the wet grass, their voices murmuring softly in
the evening coolness as they walked side by side. Passing by, they
nodded almost imperceptibly to the peasants they'd met that morning, following behind the girls driving their herds down to the river.
Sometimes the "beautiful American," as they called her in the vil-

lage, stroked the haunches of the animals while her daughter collected flowers along the riverbank. They did not linger.

How did they slip back into the inn unperceived? Were they abetted by the Chevillons? Why didn't they come down to the table at the sound of Ernestine's dinner bell? How did they manage to eat?

This mysterious feminine presence excited the curiosity of these young men. Pasdessus, to obtain his pardon, was now insisting that the petticoats rustling upstairs belonged to attractive women.

"The little blond boy we see on the bridge with the Chevillon children would augur well for their appearance. Are they really pretty?"

"Oh, but the child does not look at all like them!" commented the wise and enigmatic Bloomer, who enjoyed an advantage over his friends: he had actually seen them.

The artists were constantly aware of these women, yet they were not a hindrance. The inn was now full of young painters, and life flowed on as it did each year. Until May, until the opening of the Salon, the deliberation of the jury and awarding of medals, the painters came to Grez only on weekends. But with the closing of the Beaux-Arts and the private ateliers, they flocked by the hundreds to their summer places just outside Paris. To hell with artificial light and professional models! For three months, the Latin Quarter worked "on motives," sketches, studies, and drawings that would be refined in the ateliers the following winter. By mid-June, all the villages around the Fontainebleau Forest were bristling with easels.

"But where is the husband?" one of the newcomers wondered.

"Someplace in California."

"Does the mother run around?"

"Ah, as to that, who knows?" Pasdessus intervened, enhancing the mystery.

Bloomer shook his head: "She's neither prudish nor flippant."

"Proper, then?"

"Different. In other times, this woman would have been a Medicis, a Bonaparte, a conspirator or rebel, someone who demands protection and obedience. She sets me dreaming. If she would agree, I would paint her as a queen, a captive queen. She is entirely out of the ordinary!"

"And the daughter?"

"Exquisite!" Pasdessus enthused. "Huge black eyes in a sweet little face. And such a mouth—so fresh and juicy!"

"You like the girl, Pasdessus?"

This question was asked by the latest arrival, another Scots land-scape painter, a friend of the two Stevenson cousins, who was studying color with Carolus Duran at his studio on Boulevard Montparnasse. Mr. William Simpson was called Simpson Senior to distinguish him from his brother Walter. Simpson Senior's mascot was the monkey he always carried on his shoulder. The poor bull terrier dead drunk under the table last year, alluded to by Miss Kate, had belonged to him. This summer he'd replaced him to some advantage with an alcoholic marmoset.

"Although I much prefer the company of monkeys, perhaps we should ask these ladies to dinner? A proper invitation, made quite respectfully. Pasdessus would woo the daughter, Bloomer the mother. We could amuse ourselves flattering them, coaxing them, and then, just when they've let down their guard, we boot them out!"

This proposal, made between absinthe and vermouth at one of the little round tables in the garden, was widely approved. They stationed themselves at all the paths leading to the inn, on the riverbanks, in the kitchen, a lookout system charged with inter-cepting the fugitives. Fanny and Belle, returning from one of their outings, were caught in the net. It was Robinson, the asthmatic Robinson with his yellow muffler, who brought them in.

"Ladies, my friends and I would be very honored if you would agree to share our supper this evening."

"That is very kind of you, sir, but my daughter and I simply want some peace and quiet."

"And we appreciate our solitude," Belle insisted with her clear, pretty voice.

He had to let them go. They passed by and disappeared.

Robinson's shyness and his polite approach nonetheless facilitated the long-dreaded occasion on which the two parties came together.

"Farewell freedom!" The first evening the two Osbourne ladies took their seats at the end of the table, their silence and reserve cast such a pall over the meal that the painters met to consult after supper.

"Intolerable! We must immediately call Stevenson back from Moret. He will get them out of here. Let O'Meara come, too!"

"It's urgent: the 'other Stevenson' is arriving from Edinburgh at the beginning of July."

"He will have very little time, as usual."

"Those bores will chase him away."

"He already prefers Barbizon to Grez."

"Anyway, Barbizon is spoiled," muttered Robinson, who continued to bemoan the invasion of English ladies studying in the field of his master Millet.

"If either of the Stevensons deserts the Chevillons', we will lose them both and Grez will be spoiled, too!"

So they dispatched a village boy on a donkey to Moret with their call for help.

*

The following day, supper did not seem quite so bad. The intruders were quiet, but their silence was no longer hostile. Neither prudish nor arrogant, they were listening, interested. And what conversation there was around the table at the Chevillons—a regular fireworks, a tower of Babel! Fifteen young people speaking in various languages discussed art, gesticulating wildly. French, Swedes, Scots, Americans, with their different accents, all talking about art, art, art. In search of their aesthetic ideal, they came from all over the world to study in Paris, making sacrifices they would never admit to. Sons of respectable families, bourgeois, petty bourgeois, they exchanged ideas with the conviction that the history of painting depended on their beliefs and their work. Their attitudes were a mixture of self-confidence and respect for the masters, enthusiasm and doubt. The panelled walls in the dining room hung with drawings, sketches, and portraits bore witness to their talent or lack of it. Candles burned on the table, the flames flickering through the night. The young men burned with an ardor that was mirrored in Fanny's eyes, and echoed in Belle's heart. The painters felt it.

By the third evening, they were talking openly in front of the women, and for them, about the Salon, the jury, the medals, their careers. They helped themselves to wine, stroked the cats, smoked, and doodled.

"Robinson, where did you work today?"

"At the intersection of the Fin-du-Monde. But I couldn't do anything. I didn't have any white. And you?"

"I didn't work either. I was looking for subjects."

"And you, ladies?" asked Pasdessus.

"In the forest."

"It's best to wait a little for the forest. The woods are not as beautiful as they will be soon, in summer."

"For me, the forest in this season has the piquancy of bitter beer," murmured Fanny.

"Well said!" exclaimed Pasdessus. "And the young lady, what does she do?"

The young girl's dark eyes glittered. "Oh, I just follow my mother!"

During the day, they were silent again, they became invisible. Nothing changed their habits. They continued to rise early, to picnic alone in the country, and to take their evening meal at the end of the table.

Belle answered, Fanny listened. A sphinx. She did not engage in conversation. Far from irritating these young men, her silence intrigued them. They were twenty, twenty-five years old. Like the miners of Austin, this feminine attention stimulated them. In her presence, the banter was noisier, and sometimes more clever. They were all dying to perform for the "beautiful American," to make her smile. And especially to win her daughter.

Belle in all her seventeen-year-old splendor was as seductive, perhaps more seductive than Fanny. She would always seem more accessible. Belle had inherited Sam's optimism, humor, and disregard for tomorrow. As a woman, she would be charming and gay with her friends, and as a wife, easy to live with, qualifiers that hardly apply to her mother! She had neither Fanny's intelligence nor her depth, but she did have her bravura, her whimsy, and her kind of beauty.

They looked alike. Belle was buxom and romantic where Fanny was dramatic, but they had the same intense eyes in a little gypsy face, the same grace, the same sensuality. Just as the Southern planter fell for Belle on the boat from Antwerp, her dinner companions at the Chevillon table were completely won over.

The last half of June came and went. Madame Chevillon had taken it upon herself to inform the painters of the Osbourne family's misfortune. Mourning made the two figures crossing the bridge at Grez, bent beneath their easels, even more touching. The young men tried to soften their loss with kindness. Corn grew golden in the sun. Water lilies glistened under the arches. Belle accepted their attention, Fanny tolerated it. Neither of them was attached.

But everything was about to change when the dark Stevenson arrived to rescue his companions. He appeared at the Chevillons' inn on the first morning of July.

*

"Mama, I've seen him!" Belle shouted charging into the room.

"We know that," Samuel Lloyd interrupted, "We saw you from the window, you were talking with him."

"So?" Fanny asked.

"He approached me in the courtyard."

The threat of the "two Stevensons" weighed more heavily than ever. During the last weeks, the painters had described these young bourgeois from Edinburgh as the most bohemian and gifted of the little band. With his monkey and his bottle of absinthe, Simpson Senior led them to expect the worst from the eccentricities of these Scotsmen. Magicians, that's what they were. And fierce chauvinists.

"So?" Fanny repeated.

"So . . . he is handsome!"

"Silly," Sammy said.

"He took off his hat to speak to me, then he bowed and introduced himself. He's called Bob."

Sammy shrugged his shoulders.

"He looked like he was pulling your leg."

"Not at all! He was smiling in a very friendly way."

"Oh yeah? That's what you say. He was just showing his teeth, like the wolf in 'Little Red Riding Hood,' ready to jump on you and eat you up, old girl."

"Shut up!" ordered Belle, pushing him away. "This kid is impossible since he's been playing with Kiki Chevillon!"

Their three shadows danced on the whitewashed walls, mingling with the caricatures of Thiers, Gambetta, and several other local celebrities. Fanny, leaning over one of the beds, was organizing their things for the day. With authority she pushed a straw boater onto her son's head and donned her own hat.

"Let's go!"

Clear and cheerful, her voice rang out in the summer morning. Belle raised her head. The shadow of a smile floated on her mother's lips, expression that mingled defiance and humor. It surprised the adolescent.

"So what?" Fanny countered in response to her daughter's questioning look. "We are not going to let ourselves be chased away by this crazy Scotsman!"

Belle gave a little laugh. It was the first time since Hervey's death that she heard Fanny express a desire and a need—to stay in Grez. That day, they walked down the hall clicking their heels on the bare floor.

I have already met him, Fanny would write to Rearden, *I suppose you would say in the most artful manner. I was helping Sammy fish and I caught the gentleman as he was rowing by in a little boat, by the back of his collar in such a way that he had to land and asked me to disengage him. I did not manage to do it. Belle has drawn a picture of it for her father amongst some others.*

A hundred and thirty years later, these drawings still exist. The caption reads: MAMA MAKES THE ACQUAINTANCE OF THE ENGLISHMAN. There is a whole series: ADVENTURES IN GREZ.

Upright in the front of the same canoe, the gentleman paddles along, whistling. Behind him, seated single file, two feminine figures allow themselves to be carried along. One is facing forward, her face hidden beneath a huge hat. The other, bare-headed, is half turned. The caption beneath reads: WE GO OFF IN A BOAT.

This outing would take them into deep waters. But to everyone's surprise it is the boatman, enchanted by these two sirens, who would get caught in the rapids.

*
**

Bob Stevenson: painter, musician, philosopher, art critic. He held a degree from Cambridge University. His friends considered him a genius, "a genius in the most basic sense of the word," they would say.

There was in him a something mystical, the poet Henley writes, *which I, who was as close to him as his shirt, never quite fathomed. . . . I think, as I sit here grieving for both, that we shall get ten Lewises, or an hundred even, or ever we get a Bob. Nothing like him has ever passed through my hands.*

Bob Stevenson had the nonchalant distinction of a gentleman, the free ways of a bohemian. Strikingly handsome, suntanned, with glowing black eyes and a sensual mustache, he was said to have adventures, love affairs, and a mysterious penchant for excess. Belle imagined he was a Polish prince traveling incognito, Sammy thought he was a terrible Mexican *vaquero*. His Grez friends told how he divided his patrimony into ten equal portions, how he spent one portion every year, and at the end of the tenth year intended to commit suicide. *I never saw him lay out a few coppers for tobacco without a quivery feeling that he had shortened his life,* Samuel Lloyd would write. Bob Stevenson was the man whose presence electrified the atmosphere at Grez.

At his cradle the Good Fairy said: "I give him all the gifts, and he may do anything," Henley goes on, though his passionate feelings of friendship would soon be offended at the influence of certain American ladies. *But her wicked sister smiled, and answered: "He shall have so much brains that he shall be merely futile." The Bad Fairy was wrong, in part; for he created art-criticism in England, and his creation will not cheerfully be let die. But as an artist he was inarticulate; so that so far the Wicked Fairy was justified.*

A being touched by grace—Fanny was not mistaken about that. *Stevenson* [Bob] *the boating man, is also called Adonis, and Apollo because of his wonderful grace and perfect figure,* she writes to Rearden, not without a disturbing return to coquetry. *He is exactly like one of Ouida's heroes with the hand of steel in the glove of velvet, and with all that . . . He is the best painter here, a charming musician, speaks all languages, does any sort of feats of strength and has no ambition. Strangely enough he reminds both Belle and me of you.*

Is this a compliment to Timothy Rearden or to Bob Stevenson?

What Fanny did not know was that under the arbors, in the courtyard of the inn, chatting with the Osbourne ladies and listening to their laughter, the gentleman had fallen in love with Belle and her charms. Bob Stevenson was one of those men who give themselves unstintingly. He was also at that point in his life when a man chooses to plunge in.

Nothing to be alarmed about, he wrote to his cousin, the "other Stevenson," who was waiting somewhere else in France for news of the expulsion. *Nothing to be alarmed about. You can come.*

But before this happened, the game became more complicated still by the arrival of a last contender: with a blue beret over his

eye and his shillelagh in his hand, the hot-blooded Irishman
O'Meara—Frank to his friends—made his appearance.

*
**

"Lincoln would never have won the war without us, and the
audacity, the nerve, the strategic genius of the Irish. Believe me,
Miss Osbourne, a few Irishmen more or less and the victory would
have gone to the other side."

Sitting by the fire, his serious, warm voice sang of love and death.
With his helmet of wild red curls, his glittering eyes full of life, at
twenty O'Meara had the rectitude, the flame and purity of a very
young man. He was a fervent Catholic with a tendency to arro-
gance, and played the aristocrat though he was originally from the
Dublin middle classes, the youngest son of a large family of modest
means. Of all the Grez regulars, O'Meara was the one who loved the
village most passionately. He returned there in the winter to work for
long months in solitude. And his loyalty to the inn would not flag: He
returned for eleven consecutive years. "I revive in contact with this
nature," he confessed to Madame Chevillon, who had a special soft
spot for this boy. O'Meara came to Grez for the gray-toned landscapes
that inspired him: the watery skies, the bluish softness of the mist,
the violet-tinted air, the light line of reeds and willows.

On fine days, he put down his brushes. An enemy of the Impres-
sionist School, he eschewed hard lines, detested pronounced shadows,
and simply refused to work in the sun. From July to September
he became just a good summer companion.

Anticipating the foggy, rainy mornings so dreaded by his friends,
he organized naval battles on the Loing River, excursions to the
forest, and singing contests around the fire.

"Do you like Bizet's *Carmen,* mademoiselle?

"Oh, apart from *La Fille de Madame Angot* I don't know anything about French music. I don't know anything about music at
all, in France or anywhere else."

"You play the piano, don't you?"

"Yeah, I plunk on it!"

Belle's naturalness, her absence of any intellectual pretension coupled with a real artistic sense seduced the Irishman's virgin heart.

O'Meara added to his program of summer pleasures the education of this American girl who admitted so candidly to knowing nothing. Holy bread for a purist like him! Even before Bob Stevenson had finished softening the ladies up, O'Meara took the young girl under his wing, constituted himself her guide and mentor, and made it his mission to reform her education, religious as well as aesthetic.

"We say *yes*, not *yeah*—you do have a dreadful accent, Miss Osbourne! You make mistakes in English usage with every sentence. Our language is rich: Use it correctly!"

Titillated by his protective tone, moved by his male authority, Belle corrected the pronunciation he thought so vulgar. She accepted his reproaches even more graciously as the handsome O'Meara seemed to have tied his shillelagh to her apron strings: He carried her umbrella, set up her easel, mixed her colors. From the cellar where the girl helped her new friend Ernestine make butter, to the kitchens where, under the tutelage of Madame Chevillion, she was initiated into the art of beating eggs for an omelette and grinding coffee beans just right, Frank O'Meara never left her side. In his crafty way he eluded Fanny's surveillance and managed to get the girl alone.

Despite the disorder, the bottles and cigarette butts left lying around, the boots, the clogs, the paintbrushes, the drying canvases, the ambiance of the inn was more like a club than a hovel. The little colony respected an implicit morality and the rules of life. Work, congeniality, resourcefulness, striving toward an aesthetic ideal. No revolutionary ideas, nothing anarchic. Only Bob Stevenson's high wit, the eclecticism of his knowledge, his formidable intelligence that exploded in the most trivial of his statements, brought a touch of madness to the dining table.

"You're smiling?" he said triumphantly one evening looking at Fanny. "Wait till Louis gets here! He really has a sense of humor. I am only a poor cad but Louis is a true and good man."

Mrs. Osbourne would not agree.

*
**

"Don't you find there's good old French romance in the air?" Pasdessus whispered to Belle on this night of July 6, 1876.

Every evening at the end of the meal, between the cherry tart and the plum brandy, the hieratic sculptor carried on his seduction. As they ate, he preened in his seat, and while the talk became more personal, he would pay her several compliments. This evening, over dessert, his courtship was interrupted by an opening chord O'Meara was playing on the piano. An old crate, that piano, and tinny to boot! He'd had several glasses of wine too many, and was feeling no pain. The piano had been a collective purchase—each had given as he could—bought the previous year from a local dealer in secondhand instruments who was charged with tuning it from time to time. When the painters brought their models and mistresses down from Paris for an evening of waltzing on the banks of the Loing, the old crate provided a rhythmic accompaniment.

O'Meara's song soared to the roof, a romance praising a girl revolutionary, a brunette with glowing eyes. He articulated every word, and with his body half turned on the bench, his eyes riveted on Belle's face, he sang only for her. Blushing, enthralled, she tried to meet his gaze.

Bob Stevenson and Fanny were observing the scene. Both felt they were witnessing an event which, in their anxiety, in their impotence, they called "the birth of love." They had been thinking that the first flirtation did not mean much, that there had to be a beginning to everything, that this emotion, too, would pass. Bob Stevenson noted forlornly that a surprising beauty emanated from O'Meara's body as it strained toward the young girl. The piano fell silent.

There was a moment, before the applause, when no one moved. At just this instant they heard the cry of an animal, perhaps a cat, a cry of distress and desire, an infinite plaint that tore the silence and seemed to echo through the night to the other side of the river.

"That's love, all right, if I'm not mistaken!" clamored Pasdessus.

"How can you speak of love, you don't know anything about it," O'Meara retorted, firmly taking his place next to Belle.

"What do you know?"

"One can only wait until a blind man is touched by the romance of a sunset," Bob joked with a mocking smile.

"And who says I'm not crazy about Mademoiselle?" joked the sculptor, attempting to take Belle's hand and kiss it.

"Let her go, Pasdessus!" Stevenson intervened again. "Many lovable people miss each other in the world or meet at the wrong time. That's your situation."

Ernestine served the coffee in the tall blue faience cups. The oil lamps smoked on the table, the cigarettes, the pipes and the steam from the coffee wrapped them all in a bluish haze. Outside, the swallows skimmed the riverbanks. The sun was setting, violet, between the clouds. A slight breeze pushed the mists from the river against the windowpanes.

"I beg your pardon! Since falling in love is the illogical adventure par excellence, the one thing we are tempted to call supernatural, there is nothing to stop Mademoiselle from loving me!"

Belle, embarrassed, sought her mother's help. But Fanny's eyes were fixed elsewhere, toward the knocking on the Dutch door that was half opened onto the street. The lanterns hung above the entrance lit up a man's face.

His gaunt face thin as a knife blade was framed by straight, ash blond hair. His drooping mustache fell like fine thread onto his mischievous smile. He had a delicate, straight nose and his high, prominent cheekbones emphasized the unusual separation of his eyebrows. His large, almond-shaped eyes sparkled eagerly in the light, and the warmth of their expression was striking as they observed Fanny Osbourne.

Years later, Robert Louis Stevenson claimed to have been lovestruck in the street. He would say he was smitten with Fanny as he spied her through the half-open door, this young woman so dignified in her deep mourning, so noble and natural amidst the gesticulating artists. He would describe the indulgence, the mystery of her half-smile, the candlelight dancing in her golden eyes. Belle would add that she herself was surprised by her mother's expression, intense and fascinated. It was this expression of Fanny's that would reveal to the girl the man who was destined to change their lives.

But their life was not going to change for some time yet.

"Louis Stevenson!"

"Look who's here!"

"Where the devil have you been?"

"We've been waiting all month for you!"

Leaning on the door, he leaped nimbly into the room.

He was twenty-five years old, stood roughly five feet ten inches tall and weighed 118 pounds. He would preserve this gaunt and youthful look all his life.

His boots were all worn down and he had a rucksack slung over his bent shoulders. He wore an old velvet jacket with no buttons or lapel, and an open, collarless shirt. Robert Louis Stevenson's slovenly appearance had already earned him several arrests by overzealous policemen and a few nights in jail for loitering. Anyone who knew how to look, however, would have noted that he had all the self-assurance of a bohemian from a respectable family. With his law degree and acceptance to the Edinburgh bar the year before, his father had given him an advance against his inheritance, a decent amount which he lent, spent, and shared unstintingly. Money did not matter to Stevenson, or comfort. But freedom, yes. His rucksack contained a volume of poems by Charles d'Orléans, an excellent bottle of cabernet sauvignon, tobacco, a pen and paper. No comb or razor, or change of linen. He got a shave from the local barbers en route, had his things washed by local washerwomen, and threw out his worn shirt—habits more expensive than the luxury of a suitcase! But Robert Louis Stevenson had no possessions, neither on him nor elsewhere. Traveling so light, however, did not stop him from living well. His charm and sparkling talk earned him membership in one of the most exclusive clubs in London, the Savile Club, where he occasionally stayed. His literary mentor was Sidney Colvin, a curator at the British Museum and one of the eminent members of the British intelligentsia. Stevenson's first articles appeared in *Cornhill* magazine, edited by Leslie Stephen, son-in-law of Thackaray and future father of Virginia Woolf. Louis would show up unannounced and stay with one of these friends for a few days or a few weeks, then disappear again. *You must not be vexed at my absences,* he wrote to his mother. *You must understand that I shall be a nomad, more or less, until my days be done. You don't know how I used to long for it in the old days; how I used to go and look at trains leaving, and wish to go with them.*

An only child, fragile and overprotected by his family, he remained very attached to his parents with whom he had clashed since adolescence. In their elegant house in Edinburgh's upper-class New Town, there were endless scenes of unexpected violence between a fanatically religious father and this boy who doubted and questioned. *And now, you know, I have a little more that is solid under my feet, you must take my nomadic habits as part of me,* he pleaded to his mother. *Just wait till I have hit my stride, and you will see that I shall pass more of my life with you than elsewhere; only take me as I am, and give me time.*

London, Paris, Menton, Montigny, Barbizon, Grez: Robert Louis Stevenson was a great walker and traveled everywhere on foot, alone or with friends. Friendship had a vital place in his heart.

He was received at Grez with much joking, hugging, and back-slapping, rather like a long lost child, something between a mascot and a hero. Bob hugged him, led him to the table, offered him his place next to Mrs. Osbourne, and solemnly introduced him: "My cousin, Mr. Stevenson, a young man who writes."

Robert Louis Stevenson bent forward, waving away the characterization and corrected: "Who wants to write, or at least hopes to write one day . . ."

"Don't listen to him, Mrs. Osbourne," Bob interrupted. "This young man is a genius. He is the most talented of us all, and what's more, he knows it. He is as self-sufficient and smug as any bourgeois. I am sure he imagines that one day they'll even publish his letters. *The Letters of R.L.S.* Oh yes, you'll be famous, my boy! 'What?' You'll ask. 'Louis, famous? So simple, so cheerful, so natural, such a nice chap. Just like us, only kinder?' Don't you believe it! He looks puny, but he's strong, he's as hard as the granite of the lighthouses his ancestors built! Look at him with his eyes so full of life, his curly mustache, he already sees the titles of his books on the backs of the sandwich-board men in London."

"Bob, you are a monster—but I love you!" exclaimed Louis, hugging him with a burst of laughter. "I always thought, and I still think, that in having you as a master and procurer I have been favored by the gods. My dreadful cousin, madame," he continued, turning toward Fanny, nearly upsetting her glass, "surely surprises you by his playing, his painting, his writing. But when he transmigrates (it is the only word) from one point of view to another with a swiftness and completeness that leaves a merely logical mind panting in the rear, and in an incredibly brief space of time helps you to view a question upon every side, what a delight! Yes, madame, his insane lucidity will amaze you, his singular humorous eloquence, and a power of method that brings the whole of life into the focus of the subject at hand. As for me, I owe him everything! He came to pull me out of bed when I was languishing with a cough in Edinburgh, dragged me to free air, showed me that real life is found out of doors, that the true God was not made of this mediocre bourgeois fabric, that one needed to cleanse one's soul and mind of ready-made habits, principles, and formulas. He taught me to go on alone, free. And sometimes to plunge into the infinite."

Robert Louis Stevenson was talkative, gesticulating, getting up, sitting down again.

"And your father?" Bob cut in.

"He hasn't changed. He still thinks that a man who does not believe in Christ and the Church must be a rascal, a madman, or an idiot. He laments what he calls my straying and attributes it to youth. But if youth is not quite right in its opinion, there is a strong probability that age is not much more so. A man hardly finds he has been wrong at every preceding stage of his career, only to deduce the astonishing conclusion that he is at last entirely right!"

That evening, the Osbourne ladies had some difficulty following the conversation. Fanny was not attuned to the charm of this voice, this verve, this exuberant talk, which everyone agreed was unparalleled. Like the police, she found something "strange" about Robert Louis Stevenson. And when he began laughing, his mouth wide open, in such a sudden, shrill volley, she would firmly label him "hysterical." Only the cousins' mutual admiration and their freely expressed tenderness would find favor in her eyes. But of the two Stevensons Bob was the one she would prefer until autumn.

"Mama, he is amazing!"

"Who?"

"Louis!" exclaims Samuel Lloyd.

"Don't say 'Louis' but 'Lewis,'" Belle corrected him sharply with an excellent British accent redolent of Irish and Scots. "Lou-ou-iss," she repeated sententiously.

"Poor girl!" Sammy retorted, turning around. "He's just as funny as Bob, Mama! Even funnier! We were with Mimi and Kiki on the bridge when Louis came looking for us. And you know what he did? He took us for a boat ride. It was wonderful! He attacked all the canoes single file, we lay down in the bottoms, closed our eyes, and let the current carry us. And guess, guess where we woke up? At the underground entrance to the castle of La Reine Blanche! This evening we're going to explore it with lanterns. Can I go? Please—Louis will come to ask your permission. Say yes, Mama!"

Appealing to attractive women through the intermediary of their children was an old practice of Robert Louis Stevenson's. He had done it with two Russian women on holiday at Menton, whose little girls were enchanted by him. This passion for children, his knowledge of their world and their dreams, would bring him luck: It was for Sammy, to amuse and distract the boy, that Stevenson would some day write the work that would bring him fame and fortune, *Treasure Island*.

R. L. S. always paid children the compliment of being serious, no matter what mocking light might dance in his brilliant brown eyes, Samuel Lloyd would write, *and I instantly elected him to a high place in my esteem.*

*

Sammy had not been the only one. Before him, another boy had been dazzled by this playmate and extolled his qualities to his mother, the very beautiful and very intellectual Mrs. Sitwell, Robert Louis Stevenson's first love.

Stevenson had been writing to this woman every day for three years. She was his confidante, muse, and madonna. Married with children, separated from her obscure husband, much older than her young admirer, she was now thirty-six, or eleven years older than her. Like Fanny. Mrs. Osbourne and Mrs. Sitwell had evidently married at the same age—seventeen—when Louis was still playing with toy soldiers. Both women had sailed to the ends of the earth while he, a little boy leaning over his maps in his room in Edinburgh, had dreamed of traveling far away.

Mrs. Sitwell had also known the harsh life of colonial places: Sydney, Calcutta, Bombay. With a Mona Lisa smile and a steady gaze, she seemed rather distant; her admirers found she had the exotic charm of an Indian princess. She had tiny hands and feet, dark hair and eyes, an aquiline nose, amber skin—like Fanny. Unhappy in her marriage, she supported her children teaching literature and giving herself over to the pleasures of the mind. She would also lose one of her children, a son, under dreadful circumstances.

But the extraordinary series of coincidences that linked the destinies of these women did not stop here. Mrs. Sitwell's first name, inscribed in the civil registry, was Frances, the name Fanny Vandegrift was given at her christening. And Frances Sitwell's nickname, used only by those closest to her, was, of course, Fanny.

Fanny Sitwell, Fanny Osbourne, the Englishwoman, the American woman: two faces of the same dream?

For the moment, Louis had neither the time nor the leisure to court Fanny O. He was staying only three days in Grez before setting off on other adventures. He left her with his best publicity agent, however, Bob, who would lavishly sing his praises.

*
**

Bob spent the summer at the inn. In the peaceful village on the banks of the Loing he would create an odd *tableau vivant,* a mixture of Manet and Watteau, *Le Dejeuner sur l'herbe,* and *Les Fêtes galantes.*

Ballads sung to the guitar, boating excursions, languorous siestas in the hammocks. Fanny's little foot swung idly, brushing the grass, skimming the water, amber and highly arched, naked. Beneath the gaze of her fifteen admirers, she gradually shed her melancholy. She was alive again. At thirty-six, she found the self she was before marriage. More daring than the boys of Clayton and Danville, she once slid down the snow-laden slopes of the Vandegrift farm. Now, in her purple espadrilles, her black bathing costume with the short, revealing skirt, her red shawl tied around her hips, she was magnificent. No one put as much energy into their canoe games, into rocking her opponent's skiff and spilling him into the rapids, and she didn't even know how to swim. *I can manage a canoe perfectly, just as I would ride a horse, and am sunburned and blackened and bruised until you would hardly know me,* she bragged to Rearden.

She painted, they watched, she swam, they saved her from drowning. In the evenings they exhibited their day's work in the courtyard of the inn. Beneath the arbors they observed, criticized, discussed art and literature, history and morality. They settled their accounts on the river in these mock naval battles. Reigning over a coterie of young men, Fanny was living out a dream. She meted out justice under her tree. She presided at supper in the evening, and her throne was reserved next to the fireplace.

A modest regional wine, coffee imbibed with half-closed eyes in the big cups, apricots burnished by the sun—the garden of the inn was transformed into a voyage to Cythera, where amorous intrigues entangled them. Fanny was attracted to Bob, Bob to Belle, Belle to O'Meara. No one declared himself, and emotions rose and fell, darting and humming like the thousand dragonflies on the Loing.

*
**

Fanny raised her head toward the full moon, then, as if exhausted by violent sensation, rested it on the back of the armchair. The night was too cloying, too dark. She was suffocating this evening. The garden, drowned in shadow, had suddenly disappeared. The river glistened and meandered into darkness, a huge necklace of jade knotted with the silken foothills of tiny islands. Fanny's dark face had that gravity of warrior peoples. The brown braids still damp from bathing hugged the curve of her shoulders, her breasts. She widened her eyes a little, as if a distant and luminous vision excited her interest. She sighed. The image of Hervey haunted her memory, her heart, her hands, more living, more palpable than ever in these summer nights. She felt his weight on her. She could still feel her child's soft curls between her fingers, his little body in her arms, breathe his scent. Even more than the idea of death Hervey's physical absence tormented her with desire. She needed to carry him, to caress him, to hug him.

Only when every muscle of her back and stomach was stiff and aching from physical effort, only then was Fanny released from this emptiness. Her neck rolled back on the chair. She knew Bob was nearby. Why wasn't he here?

*
**

Pale and smooth, the last new-mown hay lay before them. Fanny and Bob were taking the path to the fields. The earth was burning under the sun of midday. The spiky blue thistles, the blood-red poppies were gray with dust. They veered off on a path along the sudden walls of the cornfield. In the cloudless sky, a swallow was following them. Its sharp chirping made them lift their heads.

"It's coming with us," Fanny remarked with satisfaction.

Bob glanced at the bird. A promise of happiness. Fanny felt good. First the long walk in the sun, then something shining in Bob's eyes, something affectionate as he spoke to her of the future, a kind of solicitude she had been missing for a long time. They had left during the siesta hour, and their departure was noted with interest by the little group. They had walked on in silence, then Bob began speaking, gossiping and commenting about the artists the Osbourne ladies should or shouldn't see in Paris this winter.

"Pasdessus is not the man for you. He seems likely enough, but don't trust him. He is not a gentleman."

"And who is a gentleman?"

"Louis Stevenson, my cousin, whom you seemed to set so little store by."

She shrugged her shoulders.

"And you?" she asked. "Are you a gentleman?"

He laughed.

"Especially not me. I'm the black sheep of the family. On his deathbed, one of our young cousins called my uncle, Louis's father, to warn him that I would bring misfortune to his house. Mine was not very prosperous. My father spent thirteen years of his life holed up at home with neurasthenia."

Fanny remained silent. She knew the rumors about the two Stevensons. It was said that they inherited an enormous fortune which they would not be able to enjoy. It was said that men in their family died young and mad, victims of generations of intermarriage.

"My father is also going to die mad," she confessed. "Who knows if I will not follow in his footsteps?"

"Suicide seems to me the best solution."

They forced a laugh.

"One of my friends, who rather resembles you, writes me this morning that I am already a toothless old hag who would do better to rejoin the ranks."

"Don't do anything like that, Mrs. Osbourne. Continue to exist just as you are! It's that fellow who has forgotten how to live."

He took her elbow and led her under the young pine trees.

"Believe me, when my cousin returns, pay attention to him. He could teach you many things."

"What sorts of things?"

"Reading, for example."

"Thank you very much, I already know my alphabet."

"Don't be silly! You've come to Europe to learn, haven't you? Because you are pursuing an ideal of beauty? You believe in your art, don't you? Louis has only the highest respect for his! He is, I think, a man of letters to the very tips of his fingers. And as much as he loves literature, no one has thought about it with more passion and honesty."

"And what about you?" she repeated.

Bob shrugged his shoulders. His eyes glittered with contempt.

"I can't be compared to him. I—I drift like a feather, whimsical—and lazy. Some artists need optimal conditions for work, a temperate climate, good health, an income of a thousand pounds a year, the calm of a monastery, and universal approbation. They sharpen their pencils endlessly before getting down to work. Others work in the hull

of a boat, under bridges, spitting their lungs out, a mob of creditors at
their heels. I belong to the first category, Louis to the second. He
spent all his childhood scribbling, shut up or shoved around from one
health spa to another, it never mattered: Intellectually, he's a steve-
dore! I think he has always done what he wanted!"

"And you?" she insisted.

Bob thought a moment. His clogs clattered on the stones.

"I, too, have always done what I wanted. But what do I want?
Every adventure, every idea, I set off in all directions. I have genius, if you will, but genius without talent is nothing."

"I would say it's the other way around, that talent without genius
means nothing."

"You're wrong. Louis is someone who has talent, enormous talent! And one can lean on him. You should see him again in Paris!"

"How about Frank O'Meara?" she asked suddenly. "Should we
see O'Meara again?"

Bob leaned over and looked her in the eye. She recognized that
strange, almost hostile male look. It was Rearden's expression when
she had wounded him. She blanched.

"You would have to ask your daughter that question, Madame."

"Belle is young," she answered lightly. "How could she know?"

"Yes, she is young."

Fanny read such suffering, such tension on Bob's face that her
heart contracted. And immediately a vague, familiar sadness invaded
her. It was that old feeling of losing someone dear that she'd had since
the birth of her daughter, since Sam's departure for the Civil War.

"Let's leave the woods," she said, "I find this atmosphere stifling."

They went down to the riverbank. She suddenly felt better
amidst the gorse, amidst the insects buzzing and beating their
wings. She knew what Bob was going through. Weren't this young
man's feelings predictable? He was twenty-eight years old, she was
thirty-six. Yet she felt something like the pain of betrayal, the pain
she'd felt as a young woman when Sam no longer looked at her, when
he was in love with someone else. This time, there was no jealousy,
just an enormous sympathy for her companion's emotional turmoil.
And an immediate and total acceptance of her defeat as a woman.

She plunged her two hands into the reeds to feel closer to the
water and the earth, to that hot, humming, prolific nature. They
did not utter Belle's name.

"With Pasdessus," Bob merely said, "love is merely a complication of feeling, with Simpson Senior a flirtation, with O'Meara an obsession. But with me," he said, "it is a sickness, and since you know that I am considered mad, you also know that for such people lovesickness is always serious."

They exchanged a look, and for the first time Fanny saw tears in a man's eyes. She leaned on Bob's arm, and with his elbow he squeezed her little hand against him.

"Let's go back," he said. "The others are going to think I've murdered you."

They laughed a little, then, clinging to one another, returned to the inn.

*
**

That night, as usual, Fanny sat alone in the fresh evening air of the garden. The wind wafted the warm scent of newly cut corn. Behind her, the door jamb clicked. She heard laughter, shouting, conversation in the dining room. A hurried, familiar step slipped over the grass. Bob. Her cheeks grew hot. Her fingers resting on the arms of her chair dug deep into the wicker. The steps stopped, made a half turn, and again she heard the click, the noise of laughter, conversations, and the door closed. Bob had not felt the need to join her. She was old. Rearden had won. *A toothless old hag.*

"Are you sad, Mrs. Osbourne?" asked a voice beside her.

It was the voice of the cousin, the "other Stevenson," who had come to Grez that afternoon. He had just completed an incredible canoe trip from Antwerp to Pontoise, and from there along the banks of the Loing. His appearance with Walter, Simpson Senior's brother, had created quite a stir at the inn. Everyone had seen them at the bottom of the garden, unkempt beneath their hats. They were returning from fifteen days of shipwrecks, storms, solitude, and visions along the canals of France and Belgium. This was the raw material for Robert Louis Stevenson's first book, *An Inland Voyage.*

"Should I be cheerful?"

She did not look at him. Louis Stevenson sat down, cross-legged, at her feet.

"Are you thinking about your husband?"

"About him. About my children. About myself."

"And . . . ?"

He rolled a cigarette, which he held out to her, half turning. Instinctively she took it. Their faces joined above the flame. Stevenson's brown gaze fixed on her, enveloped her in warmth.

"And," she took a puff, hesitating, "I was thinking that I have not made a success of my life."

"Nonsense!"

With a leap he jumped to his feet. Smoking, gesticulating, one hand stroking his mustache, the other sweeping the air, he began to turn around the armchair.

"I saw you in July, you were leaving the inn at dawn. You work."

"Not enough."

"I have seen what you're doing, your canvas *Le Pont de Grez* drying against the wall . . ."

She tried to follow with her eyes his elongated silhouette as he leaped right and left in a kind of Saint Vitus dance. She gave up, it was making her dizzy.

"Yes, *Le Pont de Grez*, painted how many thousands of times?"

"I have seen the studies of all the students of the Latin Quarter exhibited on the walls of the Salon at the Academy. And I thought none of them had the candor of yours!"

"You mean naiveté?"

He burst out laughing. He kept on talking, walking back and forth from one tree to the other, behind or in front of her.

"The life of the novice in any art is punctuated by small successes amidst a litany of failures. You must bear it all. It's a long-distance course. First step, the painter or writer plays with his material. He is like a child who keeps turning a kaleidoscope. Step two, the game is played by the rules. He uses the bits of colored glass in the service of formal representation. This step seems long and painful. Those who keep going can be counted on the fingers of one hand. Step three, he breathes life into his representations, gives meaning to facts . . ."

"You have seen what I've done. Do you think that my talent justifies spending another winter in Paris?"

For a moment, Robert Louis Stevenson stopped. A smile danced in his eyes.

"Beware of those who let themselves be lured too soon by toadies!" he mocked, drawing on the glowing butt of his cigarette.

She insisted: "Bob claims that you know how to recognize what is good from what isn't, he speaks of your critical sense. I need to know! Because if I don't have that kind of talent in me, my presence in Europe is unacceptable. My . . . my . . ." she hesitated, "my pretensions are too costly to others!"

Louis turned his lively gaze toward the face of this woman tortured by doubt, fear, and the fierce determination to persevere.

"Only you will one day be able to answer that question," he pronounced gravely, continuing to pace up and down. "But I can tell you that when people admonish me, saying, 'You're wasting your time scratching out little scraps of literature. Why do you write only articles? Why don't you publish a great book?' I mistrust them! If my guardian angel did let me fall, if I did succumb too quickly to the desire for greatness without developing the tools of my art, I would put my writing in jeopardy forever. We artists always tend either to be in a hurry or to put off the dangerous day of creation, to postpone the leap into the unknown. That said, there is no Mozart in painting or in literature. Take your time. Work, study, copy the masters. Learn technique. For the moment you belong to that category of artists who find Grez an ideal refuge. In the slang of the colony, we call them 'snoozers.' Snoozing is part of an artistic education. But it is only one step in the great adventure."

"My purpose, during my years in France, is to succeed in representing life!"

"A wager lost in advance! Life is many-faceted, infinite, illogical. A work of art is clear, rational, reductive . . ."

She smiled.

"If you believe in the supremacy of life over art, why on earth do you want to write?"

He answered without stopping to turn around: "It's a quest."

"Then the pleasure you find in this quest is enough in itself?"

"Certainly." He repeated: "The pleasure of things is enough in itself. And you?" he asked, suddenly standing still before her.

She raised her face.

"What do you mean, me?"

"You—you ask questions, you listen, but you don't say much about yourself. It takes two to have a conversation."

"I haven't anything to say."

"Nothing to say? I have never known a woman like you. You are so . . . so different. So American!"

Vexed, she crushed her cigarette in the grass. "And what does that mean?"

"You embody all the drama, all the dreams of a new world. Look, while we are hammering out an 'aesthetic' in the most civilized garden on the planet, I imagine you carrying your six-shooter in your pocket. You aren't from here! You belong to the world of gold miners, of professional gamblers, trappers. With your ten fingers you can do anything—kill or create. When you walk, you move like a raging flood. You smell like campfires and sage brush, you will be loved by those who dream of the Sierras, of canyons and forests . . ."

She sighed, but kept still. She stared before her at the dark mass of trees. He noticed her gaze lost in the woods.

"That forest is a great fountain of youth!" he exclaimed. "François I, Ronsard, and many other disappointed men withdrew to this place. Of all the hidden places of Europe, it is perhaps the best spot to catch your breath. You are right to work there every day. In this wood, the artist can learn to feel the poetry of life, of the earth. When you have become a master of your art, this memory will protect you from a sad reproduction of life."

"Sadness is something you do not seem to know about," she said with an edge of hostility.

"Here I am living a moment of peace, a moment of freedom. I am content. This ideal might not be very elevated, but it is accessible and simple. When I'm done, I'll buckle on my rucksack and take to the road again."

"What a moralist! You talk like a religious lady from Indiana!"

He burst into childish laughter. "Come hear me tomorrow, I am mounting the pulpit. I have arranged it with the village priest, I am preaching a sermon. If my father could hear me, he would have a heart attack! You will come? It will be quite absurd."

September. The trees were yellowing. One by one, the painters were returning to their ateliers. Bob's words had borne fruit. As a first sign of maturity, perhaps, Fanny renounced her romantic attraction to him. She followed his advice and became interested in the "other Stevenson," whose gaiety amused her.

The gaiety of Stevenson was his cardinal quality in those early days, his friend, the poet Edmund Gosse, would write. *A childish mirth leaped and danced in him; he seemed to skip upon the hills of life. He was simply bubbling with quips and jests; his inherent earnestness or passion about abstract things was incessantly relieved by jocosity; and when he had built one of his intellectual castles in the sand, a wave of humor was sure to sweep and destroy it. I cannot, for the life of me, recall any of his jokes; and written down in cold blood, they might not be funny if I did. They were not wit so much as humanity, the many-sided outlook upon life. I am anxious that his laughter-loving mood should not be forgotten. He was often in the old days, excessively and delightfully silly—silly with the silliness of an inspired schoolboy.*

Intrigued, Fanny let him carry her easel, her paint box, her umbrella. O'Meara followed the daughter, Louis the mother. He joined her when she went to paint in the forest. He read under the big parasol, he wrote at her feet. At supper, they sat side by side. In the evenings, when Stevenson had finished his article and Fanny her sketch, they sat together under the willow trees along the river and talked. She found in Robert Louis Stevenson the same kind of artistic and literary mentor she did in Rearden, minus the aggression.

Through stage after stage of growing pleasure and embarrassment, they can read the expression of their own trouble in the other's eyes. There is no declaration so called, Louis wrote in October, in an essay entitled "On Falling in Love." A promising title. The die is cast. As for Fanny, she confides in Rearden with that strange mixture of modesty, hostility, and artfulness that characterizes their friendship: *You are quite right. I shall miss my bohemian friends when I get home ... mostly the two mad Stevensons who with all their suffering are men out of spirits, but so filled with the joyfulness of mere living that their presence is exhilarating. I never heard one of them say a cynical thing. With all the wild stories I have heard of them fresh in my mind, I still consider them the truest gentlemen and nothing can make anything less.*

Was this panegyric meant to make Rearden jealous? Or did it illustrate Fanny's initial fascination?

Whatever the case, the little group at Grez no longer knew which of the Stevenson cousins the beautiful American preferred. Gossip was rife. The cousins, Frank O'Meara, and the Osbourne family extended their stay at the inn late into the autumn.

On their return to Paris, Fanny and her children would no longer feel the awful solitude of penniless foreigners.

My health is beginning to improve, and the doctor says that my memory will soon be as good as it ever was; it was only from what he calls a nervous crisis, that it was so impaired, caused by loss of sleep and anxiety. I am to give up attempting to keep house, so we will move once more, this time to No. 5 rue Douay, she writes to Rearden. *You say that a nervous crisis comes from advancing age; that is what ails Stevenson, so they say, and he is some years younger than I am. I do wish he wouldn't burst into tears in such an unexpected way; it is so embarrassing. One does not know what to do, whether to offer him a pocket handkerchief, or look out of the window. As my handkerchief generally has charcoal upon it, I choose the latter alternative. He will be in Paris in January on business connected with some dramas of his that have been trans-lated into French, so I suppose Belle and I will go to the theatre sometimes with him. I like him very much, he is the wittiest man I ever met, but when he begins to laugh, if he is not stopped in time, he goes into hysterics, and has to have his fingers bent back to bring him to himself again; and when his feelings are touched he throws himself headlong on the floor and bursts into tears; and you never know when either thing is going to happen. I like him very much but there are times when it is a little embarrassing to be in his company; and sometimes, I imagine, not altogether safe. Once we were going over to the other side in a cab when he began laughing, and couldn't stop, and asked me to bend his fingers back. I didn't like to do it, so he laughed harder and harder, and told me that I had better for if I didn't he would bend my fingers back and break every bone in them, which he proceeded to do, and I only saved them by suddenly biting his hand till it bled, when he immediately came to his senses and begged pardon, but I couldn't use my hands for more than a day afterwards.*

A curious way to get acquainted. As usual Fanny exaggerates, she dramatizes the scene. A good way to express her anxiety, her fear of a man who dares to feel his deepest emotions and express them in laughter and tears, with no false modesty.

The ideal story, Robert Louis Stevenson writes, *is that of two people who go into love step for step, like a pair of children ventur-ing into a dark room.*

V

A Passionate Kindness

*The essence of love is kindness; and
indeed it may be best defined
as passionate kindness;
kindness, so to speak, run mad
and become importunate and violent.*

—Robert Louis Stevenson

Paris—second winter, October 1876–April 1877

"Belle, come here!"

If the girl who was lifting the latch so carefully had hoped to get in without being heard, it was wasted effort; the boards of the parquet floor had creaked. So she shut the door behind her, noisily dropped her portfolio under the coat rack, undid the twenty buttons of her frock coat, and untied her hat which she placed on the chest. Then, stepping up to the mirror, she examined her face. Her lips were swollen, her mouth too red, her eyes too bright.

"Belle, I am waiting!" came her mother's impatient voice from the living room.

"I'm coming!"

Still looking at her reflection, she smoothed the curls of her short bangs, redid the first knot of her sheath, leaned over to inspect the others, a total of seven big blue velvet knots descending in a straight line from her chest to her boots. The blouse, the blue-striped skirt

178

with no flounces or pleats, hugged her figure, emphasizing her bust and her hips, molding her bottom, and fanned out at the knee in a darker draping of cotton.

"Belle!"

She sashayed down the little hall where the wallpaper was peeling off in strips. Moth-eaten hangings, a neogothic buffet, a fireplace in false Italian marble—modest as it was, this apartment bore little resemblance to the garret of the previous year. Sam regularly sent his stipend, a small sum that nonetheless arrived punctually. The Osbournes had gone from near destitution to the ease of organized poverty. The apartment's entrance hall, situated under the maid's rooms on the last floor of the main staircase, opened onto two rooms occupied by two American ladies, a certain Margaret Wright and her daughter from Illinois, distant relations of the sculptor Pasdessus, the man who had given Fanny the address of the Hotel Chevillon. The Wright ladies, who also had a son Sammy's age, were equally inspired by artistic ambition, which had brought them to Paris, but they did not encroach directly on Belle and Fanny's territory. They preferred the beaches of Normandy to the Fontainebleau Forest, the School of Honfleur to Barbizon, and disdained any country holiday on the banks of the Loing, which they thought provincial. Sharing the kitchen and sitting room went quite smoothly. Paired by age, the mothers, daughters, and sons shared the same interests. The narrow hallway bustled with rustling dresses, laughter, and the doorbell's incessant ring. Visitors took turns in the sitting room, where the Anglo-Saxon bohemia of the Left Bank came to mingle with the middle-class American ladies of New Athens.

Belle stopped on the threshold of the sitting room. Fanny sat facing her with her back to the hearth.

"Do you know what time it is?" she asked coldly.

"Ten o'clock, I think," the girl said lightly.

"I thought we had agreed that your Irishman would bring you home before dark."

"Don't call him 'your Irishman,' please, Mama! His name is O'Meara!"

"Don't change the subject," ordered Fanny without raising her voice. "We had an agreement. You aren't respecting it. I am going to be forced to take you home with me from the atelier."

"Mama!"

Belle thought to win her mother over and started to run to her. But her doeskin armor, the system of cords and bones that held her straight, narrow skirt hampered her step. The time was past when women hid their hips under the cage of a crinoline, thought Fanny, long, long past the time of her youth. Belle tried tenderly to push her mother into the armchair, crouch at her feet, and put her head in her lap. Fanny resisted.

"Stop your wheedling! My goodness, you would flirt with anybody!"

Both dressed in blue, both dark, slim, the same size, the same energy, mother and daughter fought for a moment. Fanny dropped into the armchair.

"Belle, I am not joking! Stand still! Listen to me . . ."

"Listen to me, too, Mama . . . With O'Meara, we're not doing anything bad. Do you want me to tell you why I'm late: We forgot the time at the Louvre, in front of the Velasquezes."

"Forgot, really? At the Louvre? At ten o'clock at night?"

Fanny pushed her daughter away. Settling at the foot of the armchair, Belle raised her little face, a mixture of naughtiness and innocence.

"After the Louvre, we walked to the Luxembourg Gardens."

"Belle, cut out these lies, will you? The Luxembourg Gardens close at six o'clock!"

"Then, we went as far as Montparnasse . . . O'Meara wanted to show me Carolus Duran's studio, where he works with Bob. We met Sargent there, one of their friends, an American from Boston. We went back to their rooms."

"Belle," cried Fanny. "You went to O'Meara's rooms?"

"Mama, look, there were three of us! They live together above the atelier. Just as we do at the Julian, they have to register Monday mornings at dawn to have a good place for the week. The French students who live in the neighborhood beat them to it every time. O'Meara, Bob, and Sargent have solved the problem by living right in the building. This way they register on Sunday evenings. The others may come at four in the morning, but O'Meara and his friends will have the best places! We should do the same. Find an apartment in the Passage des Panoramas rather than wasting an hour in the morning, an hour in the evening, and crossing Paris in the dark!"

"Don't talk nonsense, from here to the Passage des Panoramas takes us barely twenty minutes! In any case, crossing Paris in the dark doesn't seem to bother you much, my girl!"

"You neither, Mama. It seems to me you came back very late with Louis Tuesday evening."

"Belle, that's enough!"

"And you have not told me where you went together," Belle added, teasing.

Fanny hesitated. What authority could she have with her daughter, and why was she forcing herself to use it?

"I'm afraid for you, Belle. You're so . . . so young."

"But you're young, too, Mama! What are you afraid of?"

"That you are getting too involved, Belle."

"Mama, he loves me!"

"These years in France will come to an end. They cannot last. One day we'll have to go, Belle."

"When?" the girl asked anxiously.

"One day . . . soon."

"But when?"

"When your father stops sending us money. When he asks us to come back. This period shouldn't count, it's a parenthesis. Our life is in San Francisco. One day we will have to leave all our friends here. We will never see them again. Do you understand?"

Belle shook her head.

"No! O'Meara loves me, and in Ireland, that's for life."

"Has he proposed to you?"

"Mama!"

"What 'Mama?' Has he asked you to be his wife, yes or no?"

"But he cannot!"

"Why not?"

"He hasn't any money, you know that!"

"Poverty never prevented a young man from starting a family."

"And his career? First he must succeed! And there are his parents . . ."

Fanny took her daughter's head between her hands.

"You have answered my question, Belle. With O'Meara, as with everyone here, it is temporary. Never lose sight of this reality, dear. It is temporary." She made a pained gesture: "All this! Paris . . ."

"And Louis?"

"Bob and Louis, too."

Belle disengaged herself: "I don't want to hear anymore, Mama! You always predict the worst."

"That is not the worst, Belle."

The girl paled and stepped back again.

"Are you going to stop me from seeing O'Meara?"

"No, that wouldn't do any good. You would just do it secretly. I don't want you to lie to me, I don't want you to cheat, I want you to confide in me. You can see O'Meara. All I ask is that you respect the terms of our agreement. You will not come in after ten o'clock, you will not go to his rooms, you will not do anything irreparable."

To every condition, the girl nodded in passionate consent.

Fanny insisted: "Do you understand? Nothing irreparable, without talking to me first ... O'Meara is young, and you, Belle, you are so impulsive, so passionate."

"Oh Mama, don't be so naive! I may be a flirt, but I'm not about to give myself to him, if that's what you are trying to say!"

Fanny, almost embarrassed, kept quiet. Belle went on: "Listen, I'm going to tell you everything. I like him more than the others, it's true. I've let him kiss me, that's all. The only thing that matters for me is to become a great artist! How can I explain it to you? Aesthetically, he and I understand each other. After working so hard all day at the atelier, it's so wonderful to see him standing at the door! I know that with him I am going to keep learning. When we walk side by side through the streets of Paris, when he shows me all those art galleries I didn't even know existed, when he explains to me about the old masters he admires, you cannot imagine my happiness. I have never known such a feeling. At the Louvre, he teaches me about Velasquez and Dürer. At the Cluny Museum he tells me about the horrible French Revolution. He describes scene by scene, all the murders. He talks to me about his religion, he opens the doors of Nôtre-Dame for me, he plunges my hand into the icy water of the baptismal font, he lights a candle to Saint Anthony, and together we make a secret wish, the same one I'm sure! Do you understand?"

Fanny caressed her daughter's cheek.

"I understand. If you only knew how I understand. Now go to bed. We have to get up at five o'clock tomorrow."

"And we'll be the first to register at the studio, and we'll have the best places to work, and this month, Mama, we'll win the medal and send it to Papa!"

"Yes, we will send it to your father!"

*

As mother and daughter, they had an astonishing relationship for their time. The Osbourne ladies seem to have skipped over the

Victorians and their successors and really belong to the end of the twentieth century. What mother of the 1870's, even in America, would have spoken to her child with such frankness? What daughter would have answered so openly? They were to be passionate friends and deadly rivals.

The day would soon come when, like many young women today, Belle would feel nothing but rebellion and anger at her mother. "You are stifling me!" she would soon cry. "Let me live. I am not you!" Torments, outbursts, and criticisms, regrets and reconciliations followed each other by turns until Belle became a mother as well, and recognized Fanny's contradictions in herself.

Now, in November 1876, together they pursued the goal they had both set for themselves: to paint.

*
**

"This is the first time I've posed for women, and even if I have to die of hunger, I swear it will be the last!"

The door slammed shut. His crown of thorns on his head, his long hair flying, Balducci, the most celebrated Christ of Paris, bolted down the Passage des Panoramas.

Indeed, the ladies of the Julian Academy had a charming way of torturing their models. The rule of the studios was quite strict: A pose should not be held for more than a quarter of an hour at a time, with a five-minute break every hour for male models, every half-hour for females. These ladies took no notice. They ordered the model to assume the most arduous position, head turned, torso arched, arms extended. They were more callous, competitive, and indefatigable than anyone in the art world. The hall was full to bursting with women, and on the walls an anatomical hand, a torso, and Dante's death mask danced strange sarabandes. The atmosphere of the atelier was so charged with electricity that any inconsiderate gesture, any intemperate look at a neighbor's sketch, was enough to overturn the easels like a ninepin hit by a bowling ball. A spectacular tension existed for one simple reason: necessity.

The teachers of the "men's" section benevolently dispensed their knowledge in exchange for their student's handiwork on large paintings and official commissions, and the male students assumed only the cost of the models and the rent of the halls; the ladies, on the other hand, paid for everything. They paid by subscription for the models and the large studio, and they paid the masters. So having saved their pennies over the years, they wanted their money's worth. As for the wealthy women artists, with the exception of the Russian aristocrat Marie Bashkirtseff, they preferred private lessons to the promiscuity of the ateliers.

Poor and lonely, these women arrived at the Julian Academy from all over the world with the dream of studying art in Paris. They were Spanish, Swedish, Swiss, English, American, with blond curls, gray chignons, curl-papers, eyeglasses, all shapes and ages. Each of them had sacrificed a family, a country, or a husband to their passion for beauty; each had renounced security to pursue the ideal. The ladies' studio of the Julian Academy was a hotbed of petty rivalries, as well as a proving ground for proud heroics.

They worked fifteen hours a day. They shared lodgings by twos and fours, formed alliances, cliques, and coteries. They did not shrink from any trickery to please the corrector, or get his attention, or eclipse their more talented companions. With the firm notion that "an artistic nature always expresses something of its inner beauty in its physical aspect," each woman cultivated a particular type of beauty and a "look" in harmony with her work. The dark Spaniard, taken by Raphael's virgins, tinted her hair to look like a blond Venetian. The Swiss woman, in love with El Greco, starved herself. The English woman wore unattractive spectacles and shapeless old boots to prove she was interested only in her work. As for the oldest of the Swedish women, she arrived at the studio with her face wrapped in a piece of linen, which she knotted at the top of her head like an Easter egg. She said she was suffering from terrible toothaches but would work anyway! They worked until noon, took only an hour for lunch, carried on with their work until five o'clock, and were even zealous enough to take courses in the evenings. During their rest time they arranged themselves in groups in the waiting room; some washed their brushes in the large sink, others peeled oranges. Perched on tables, sitting on the floor, they munched their picnic lunches and commented on the ranking that took place at the end of the week—and which was always unfair! Or they compared prices at the market in rue des Martyrs with those in rue de Buci.

"Who wants to know where I found this delicious Gruyère?" an Englishwoman might ask, her hair in curl-papers and her mouth full.

"Where?" the others would wonder.

"On the Left Bank, at the *crèmerie* where Carolus Duran's students go."

"How much was it?"

"Six sous!"

"And you pay twelve for your bus ticket? What a bargain!"

This was followed by the usual discussion on the cost of living in Paris and the thousands of ways to dress cheaply. Each woman boasted of her frugality, a surprising rivalry in which artistic delight vied with pragmatism. Only one woman found favor in their eyes. This was Sophie, the maid, who fed the fire in the stove, swept up the shavings from the pencils, straightened the cushions on the platform, and changed the draperies between posing sessions. She had made a specialty of spying on Tony Robert Fleury, the "corrector," when he commented on the progress of this or that student to Monsieur Julian. She hurried to repeat his comments to the interested parties. The ladies' spirits for the next week depended on Sophie's tattle.

This morning in December, just before the midday break, the forest of easels swayed in the breeze of the usual excitement. The students had recognized Robert Fleury's heavy step behind the door. The model who was playing a bacchante arched her torso lasciviously, while each woman concentrated on her work. The corrector entered heavily, passed from easel to easel, commented on this line, criticized that proportion, drew a big charcoal mark across a figure, retouched several drawings, tore, erased, distributed a few "not bads," and departed with a "good day, ladies!" that left everyone in a daze.

"Let's buy him flowers," purred the blond-tinted Spaniard, one of the few elect who had been awarded a "not bad."

"You still believe that bribes will work?" retorted Fanny, who had unhappily incurred the master's censure.

"It is unquestionably the case," he had said to her loud and clear, "that you are not as gifted for drawing as for painting. The pictorial side, color—that is all coming along fine. But you're not making any progress in construction or form. And that is the foundation of everything! You have put the cart before the horse, and now you are just treading water. Don't waste your time that way. Yes, you're floundering, that's obvious! And you are so adept, it's aggravating."

Fanny's heart beat wildly with shame.

"I am not happy about it either, but I don't know how to improve."

"I have wanted to speak to you for some time. You must try to get beyond this impasse any way you can."

"Tell me what I must draw. A skeleton, a perspective? I will copy anything you tell me to."

"Very well. Come to see me on Saturday at my place. We'll see what we can do."

*
**

"That's where it stands," she confessed pitifully to Louis Stevenson when he came to collect her for supper at rue de Douai. "I went to Robert Fleury's this morning. He lives quite nearby, at 69, that part was easy. They told me to leave my drawings. Monsieur Tony Robert Fleury is on vacation until January 8."

Every evening, O'Meara, Bob, and Louis would leave the Left Bank, cross the Seine, and climb the four floors to the Osbourne lodgings. They would go out all together, or in pairs, and Bob would join up with one of the couples.

*

One Stevenson cousin was taken with the daughter, the other with the mother—and for the same reasons. Fanny and Belle were neither courtesans nor innocents, but a different type of woman, a new breed that excited and intrigued them.

Young ladies from respectable families had never attracted either Bob or Louis. Both preferred loose women. Edinburgh gossip had it that Louis was once so taken with a prostitute, he announced their engagement to his father. This was merely unfounded prattle, a silly rumor. But clearly at twenty-six, Louis loved either ladies of the night or intellectuals, who fell under the spell of his charming wit. They might counsel him, protect him, educate him, push him, but they did not become his mistresses. They remained the wives of his friends, the companions of his teachers, older women. Even Mrs. Fanny Sitwell, with whom he corresponded daily, continued to keep him at a certain distance. Although separated from her husband, she respected the conventions. She would only give herself to Stevenson's mentor, the man who would be her lifelong companion,

Sidney Colvin, when they finally married after her first husband's death. This was to happen in 1903, when they were aged fifty-eight and sixty-four respectively. They had waited a quarter of a century.

To Stevenson, the son of a prosperous and established Edinburgh family, Fanny Osbourne belonged to no class in particular, and certainly not to Victorian society. Neither bourgeois nor prostitute, neither aristocrat nor blue-stocking, she existed in a kind of "no man's land," a mysterious and distant world that excited his imagination. In his eyes, Fanny meant adventure.

As for her, the rejected wife of an Oakland clerk, this young man's nervousness, his enthusiasm, his taste for words and ideas, his determination to become a writer seemed to embody the artistic sensibility that so obsessed her.

They talked about everything together. That was all they did: talk and walk. She listened to him with that passionate attention men found so seductive. Louis told her about his childhood as a frail only child, the extraordinary goodness of his parents but also their disapproval of his desire to write. He confided to her their religious conflict, which took on such wretched proportions for his father. In evoking the suffering he had inflicted on a loved one, Louis dissolved in tears. These were the famous hysterical attacks Fanny described to Rearden. But what Fanny hid from her friend in San Francisco was that listening to Stevenson, she wept with him. Fanny knew all about the necessity of hurting those she cherished, and the unbearable remorse that followed. But inured to the coarseness of adventurers, she had never met a man who dared to weep in front of her. Far from seeing this as a sign of weakness, she read it as proof of courage, the courage of his feelings, which was characteristic of Robert Louis Stevenson. If Fanny minimized the extent of her interest in writing to Rearden, she would express it all winter at the Julian Academy, painting the banks of the Loing, the bridge at Grez, the garden of the Hotel Chevillon. She did not sense the danger. She imagined she was virtuous, wise, strong enough to resist Robert Louis Stevenson's formidable lust for life, for creation. She allowed herself to be caught. She bloomed in his wake. Louis, like Bob, was a being touched by grace. Whoever met him fell under the spell of his talk and his kindness. And Fanny did answer his letters when he was away in Scotland. There had been no need for grand declarations; with absence, their feelings had crystallized. Some days after

Christmas, on January 2, 1877, Louis had hurried toward rue de Douai. Until the end of the art school's vacation period, Mrs. Osbourne had agreed to stroll with him around Paris. Arms linked, they browsed in the book stalls along the quays, they had supper at the *crèmerie* in Montparnasse, they explored New Athens, the general quarter of the Impressionists.

"Usually, I rest pretty content with the prospect of being misunderstood," he explained as they left the art store at the corner of rue des Martyrs where she bought her tubes of paint and canvases.

They strolled by the church of Nôtre-Dame-de-Lorette and came out on rue du Faubourg-Montmartre, heading toward the great boulevards. In the narrow warren of streets, the omnibuses could barely pass one another. The horses pawed the ground, while the high wheel of a large bicycle tried to thread its way among the carriages and dust carts.

"Truth between human beings is so rare," he continued, "so fleeting. Most people manage to be only partially honest, and generally we are content with our failures. But I cannot bear to have you mistake my meaning and my emotions; my pride revolts at the idea that you love me by mistake—for this or that quality but not for myself!"

She laughed.

"But who says I love you?"

Like Bob that summer, Louis squeezed the little hand resting on his arm, keeping it there, pressed in the heat of his elbow, in the velvet of his jacket. This rush of affection had no resemblance to his cousin's gentleness. Fanny did not dare withdraw her hand. She blushed. "Is this love?" she thought.

She felt jubilant. Was this it, at last, the thing she had coveted for so long, that had returned to her, she thought, with Hervey's birth, and had been lost forever with his death?

She felt serene in the certainty of her power. She was loved, loved by a wonderfully intelligent young man. Much more intelligent than Sam, even more intelligent than Rearden! She looked admiringly at the emaciated face above her.

With his gold-embroidered skullcap over his eye, his red sailor's scarf around his neck, his flannel shirt open on a chest rosy with the cold, his threadbare velvet jacket and ulster, Robert Louis Stevenson's awkward bearing attracted everyone's attention. The peddlers who plied their wares at all seasons up and down the muddy streets grumbled at his passage. The housemaids and shopgirls giggled as they stared at him. Fanny, usually so careful of her appearance, never felt a moment's embarrassment at her companion's originality.

"I like you very much," she admits. "And I don't love you. Do we agree?"

He laughed.

"Not at all!"

"I could be your mother," she purred, playing the coquette.

"My mother wanted me to be an engineer, not you, you would not like me as an engineer, would you? An engineer like my mother's husband. My parents love each other as much as they ever did: children of lovers are orphans. Mind you, I understand her admiration for my father: He is sometimes very witty, and when he does not feel obliged to be strict, he is very tender. And how clever! The lighthouses he has built, the optical instruments he has invented, save thousands of sailors each year. Thanks to my father, people's lives are a little better. His existence will have been useful. As for me, I am good only for causing him worry."

"To each his own. Your essays are superb. I've never read anything as well written as your article on the forest at Fontainebleau!"

He smiled.

"You flatter me. And yet," he continued, turning serious again, "when I listen to you, my personal vanity exists no longer. I even believe that I would take a perilous pleasure in telling you all my weak points, just to hear you accept and condone them one by one."

"For example?"

"I'm no Hercules. My poor health forces me to spend one day out of two in bed."

"But that's not a fault! You bear it all without complaint. At Grez, I heard you cough whole nights, it was heartbreaking! Yet the next day you were the most cheerful and enthusiastic of the bunch. I would call that courage!"

"What joy to hear you defend me!" he exalted with the greedy face of a child satisfying a sweet tooth. "More . . . I am lazy."

"You—lazy? You always have a pencil and paper in your hand! You write all the time. You work more than any of us!"

"I am temperamental."

"You're . . ." Fanny thought a moment. "No, temperamental, that's probably right. You are violent. But it's always to defend a good cause!"

Continuing their walk, they looked at each other with

amazement, admiring what life force they both shared. "Bob is right," he thought. "This woman has grit!" "Bob is right," she thought. "Morally, this boy is a rock!" If such a man loved her, she would enjoy that love. What risk was she running? She was eleven years older than he. She felt old enough to keep him in check. Yes, she was old, and she was wise. Hadn't she resisted John Lloyd's love when she thought she was widowed? Hadn't she resisted Rearden paying court to her when she felt humiliated and betrayed? What risk was she running with Louis? He was such a young man, almost an adolescent. It was an impossible love, but that love would last. It would last at least until the inevitable separation. She would take care that nothing ugly, nothing base, nothing malicious should mar their affection. Between them there would be a tenderness of her own devising, like the tiger lilies, "Fanny's lilies," which she had planted at the Chevillon's, in the garden of the inn, and which would perhaps bloom in springtime. Belle and O'Meara would love each other, too, with the same purity. Why should she persist in spoiling their pleasure? What fear or cowardice was she obeying? What dread? If Belle should become involved, so what? This was the essence of life: the attachment to others worthy of being loved. O'Meara was worthy. Convention be damned! They would dare to love, and then, when the time came, they would leave, carrying with them the magic of those past moments. They would forget nothing, and go on.

After this examination of conscience, Fanny resolutely went on her way along the muddy Parisian sidewalks.

For the whole Osbourne family, the winter was turning into a daydream.

*
**

Monsieur L. STEVENSON
5, rue de Douai
Paris (9e)

If Louis was faithful to his Left Bank impulses to wander and moved from hotel to hotel, his intimacy with Mrs. Osbourne grew such that he had his mail sent to her address. Was Fanny his home port, his anchor? The idea that he might compromise her reputation never occurred to either of them.

Coming home that evening, she put the pile of envelopes addressed to Louis on the hall table. She left the rest of the mail there as well, which consisted of one envelope. She had recognized the writing only too well.

She relit the fire in the sitting room, scattered her drawings around the floor, and with her legs folded under her big skirts, her fingers yellow from rolling cigarettes, contemplated her work. Weak, very weak. She could not get past the stage of lady painter. Again, the paintings, the watercolors—that still life, this blue vase, this little yellow book—were rather good. But the drawings had no structure or proportion. Kneeling, the end of a cigarette in her mouth, she brought the drawings closer to the flames to see them better and understand. The fire warmed her cheeks, ambered her curved forehead, burnished her bangs, where a few white hairs glistened among the black curls.

Belle joined her before the fire.

"It's for you," she insisted, holding out the envelope. "It's from Papa." Without enthusiasm Fanny unsealed the light envelope:

Thanks for your letter and your good news. Here, too, everything is going well! The house is in good shape, and if the garden is not as pretty as it was, it is being maintained. The San Francisco Stock Exchange has continued to decline and I will not be able to cable you this month's money. I hope that you will understand. I will try to come in the spring. If I sell a few feet of my claim on the Comstock Lode, we will have a good time. Tell Belle that I will take her to the theater. Tell Sammy that I am training a big pony for him from Kansas. He will find it in the stable when he returns. I will write to them both while waiting to hug them. We'll all come home together in June; it's a good time to travel. Mrs. Williams speaks of you often, as do John Lloyd and Rearden.

Faithfully yours,
Sam

"What does he say?" asked Belle.

"That he will write to you."

"But what else?"

"That he is not sending any money this month. That he is going to come."

"He's coming! Really?" The girl's face lit up with joy. "When?"

Fanny shrugged her shoulders. Sam—she hadn't thought about him since his last payment, he had been relegated to a dusty corner of her mind. This letter, which reminded her of his existence, surprised her. A disagreeable intrusion! Sam would not send money? As usual, just like last year. Was he going to let them die of hunger again? And what about the rent? How would she pay the rent? And the third trimester at the atelier? And Sam was planning on coming to rue de Douai. Fanny looked around the room, so lively and warm with its red marble fireplace, the deep love seats, the ramshackle pedestal table. She savored its charm for the first time. Sammy was stretched out in front of the hearth playing with toy soldiers. Belle rushed into the front hall: O'Meara was coming! This was Fanny's family, her world, her friends. A wave of affection swept over her when her daughter's boyfriend, the handsome, redheaded Irishman, leaned over to greet her. And Sam was going to come and tear them away. She watched Belle slipping on her frock coat, tying her hat strings, impatient to go out with her beau.

A wave of nostalgia helped to fix this moment in Fanny's memory. The fear of losing everything sharpened her pleasure. The doors clicked shut. A step in the hallway made the worn floorboards creak.

"Have you read it?"

Winded, red-faced, crying out in that Scots accent with its rolling, ever present "r," Robert Louis Stevenson had just appeared in the doorway.

"Have you read it?" he cried. "A review of my article!"

"But which one?" asked Belle, who prided herself in knowing her friends' work.

" *'On Falling in Love'* in the February *Cornhill*! Listen: "This sensitive and perceptive essay is perhaps the most brilliant analysis ever written on this subject. We strongly suggest that readers keep an eye on the promising talent of a certain Stevenson.' "

Fanny's eyes flashed. She knew all too well the source of Louis's inspiration. With her eyes fixed on the flames, a sphinxlike smile on her lips, she radiated pride. And if that night she spared him her praise, she kept calling him, with a gay, ironic tenderness, *"a certain Stevenson."*

February 1877

Don't laugh when I tell you that I have been helping to get up an English conservative newspaper called London. *The first two numbers have come out and it seems to be successful. I did not write for the paper. I wouldn't because I couldn't, but I helped choose the staff of writers for it, and examined manuscripts and accepted and rejected things. . . .*

And then, the other mad Stevenson has been here, the gentleman whom I am allowed to know, and he has been very ill and I have read and answered all his letters for him.

Secretary, nurse, collaborator, critic: In this letter addressed to Rearden, Fanny describes point by point the existence she is going to lead for the next twenty years.

Half the day too, I paint, she concludes. Only half? In the eyes of her American friends, such dilettantism could not justify such a prolonged stay in Paris. Half-time at the Julian Academy? Thinking of hardworking ladies at the studio, it is surprising how casually Fanny Osbourne allowed herself to be outstripped by the less gifted. *I don't expect to become a great painter, I never did. I haven't the talent. I only paint and study because it pleases me to know just what there is in me* . . . she writes again. With the modesty of defeat? Where are her fine certainties about her vocation? The day will soon come when Fanny will roundly deny ever having studied painting. *An artist, me? What an idea!*

This pathetic renunciation was as yet unconscious. During this period Fanny does not seem to have experienced any sense of failure. She threw herself with enthusiasm into a new mission: to shore up Louis's talent. She had a flash of intuition, overwhelming and intoxicating, that at her side superior work was being created, work that would surpass them all. The merit of this intuition is clearly hers. Robert Louis Stevenson at twenty-seven was nobody. His writings, though recognized by the critics, were mere augurings of the future.

Articles, essays, poems, projects, Fanny read, intuitively understood—and began to efface herself. But she did not withdraw. Beneath her humility was hidden the same demand, the eternal need, the only requirement of her nature: to create.

How could the obscure wife of a court stenographer ever have dreamed of helping to found a magazine that would be read by all the English intellectuals? Even more amazing, Henley, the editor-in-chief, would sing her praises after the publication of the second issue, William Ernest Henley whom Robert Louis Stevenson thought one of the greatest poets of his time. Louis had told Fanny of their old friendship. Theirs had been a painful and romantic meeting. Henley suffered from a bone disease. At eighteen, he'd had one foot amputated. Several of his poems had been noticed by Stevenson's sponsor, Leslie Stephen, editor of the *Cornhill*. On a trip to Edinburgh, Stephen had introduced his two protégés to one another: He had brought Stevenson to Henley, who was languishing in a Scottish hospital. The two young men had been struck by one another. Stevenson had returned every day to visit this giant who wrote his verses despite the greatest suffering. Momentarily out of pain, Henley threw himself body and soul into the literary life. Louis, upon his return to Grez, had told him of his feelings for the American woman. He had described her to him. Henley fell under the spell by proxy and published a series of poems to the glory of great ladies of his time. The first poem is entitled "The Californian." Without ever having seen her, he sings of the exoticism of her beauty, the symmetry of her slim, firm figure, the dangerous lights in her reddish brown eyes with *a feline gleam that sets you thinking*. He expresses both attraction and repulsion for the unknown woman who seduced his friend. This was the first and last time Henley would praise the merits of Fanny Osbourne.

> *A passion flatters her, but she*
> *Is icy hard unless she shares.*
> *Unprejudiced, quite indifferent, free,*
> *She pardons everything—and dares.*
> *Et voila! There's her photograph,*
> *I wonder, will she recognize it?*
> *I think she'll greet it with a laugh*
> *And—very coldly—analyze it.*

A faithful visual portrait, filtered through the prism of Louis's love. As to the rest, Henley was mistaken. Fanny may have been daring, but she did not pardon. She would remember everything, criticisms and insults. And Henley would as well. Between these two titans of rancor there would soon be war.

In April of 1877, however, the homage paid to her by such a man was seductive. Through Louis, Fanny had just entered a world of which none of her American friends, even the most brilliant, could have any idea. Those she so admired, Virgil Williams, Timothy Rearden, were wallowing in mediocrity.

*
**

"The summer light, the 'true sun' as the Impressionists say, is given ridiculous importance at the Durand-Ruel gallery!" shouted O'Meara.

"A thousand pardons," Bob retorted, stoking the fire. "But what a surprise, what a gift to our miserable, boring times, what a miracle, this eruption of new ideas! Manet, Renoir—finally, an original creation!"

"Come on! In Renoir there's no more mystery—one of the major attractions of painting! All the fantasies of imagination have given way to a passion for the real: This is the death of art!"

Evening was falling in the little sitting room in rue de Douai. In the soft light of the lamps, Fanny sat enthroned, wrapped in her silence. Belle reigned alone over this little coterie. The whole group was gathering for a last time before going off in different directions. They counted on meeting up again in Grez in May.

Louis was leaving the next day for England. He had traveled incessantly all winter between Edinburgh, London, and Paris. Now, he was going home for an indefinite period of time. How would he find Fanny upon his return? Who could say if he would find her at all; Sam was arriving in a few weeks and meant to take her back with him.

The idea of the "husband" plagued them both. But the different nature of their fears was expressed by mutual exasperation. Yet God knows they had given each other enough tokens of trust. Hadn't Fanny allowed Louis to pay for her trimester of study at the atelier? And hadn't Louis paid her rent for March? Sharing his funds with her and taking responsibility for certain expenses since he had the means seemed natural to them both. Until these last days when, without apparent reason, they had closed up like two oysters and gotten on each other's nerves.

On the eve of Louis's departure and Sam's arrival, the past

reasserted itself. She breathed deeply Hervey's sweet scent, she felt her baby's curls against her cheek, her child's caress on her forehead, the plump, awkward little hands feeling her mouth. She missed her little boy as if he had just died. Belle's laughter brought her back to reality and tormented her. Belle was so forgetful. Fanny resented the girl's happiness, the love she so clearly felt. How could she forget that the first anniversary of her brother's death was only seven days away. In nine years, the common grave.

Stevenson took no more part in the conversation than Fanny. He was distressed by the husband's imminent arrival. Sam Osbourne: even the name put him in a rage. The woman he loved belonged to Sam Osbourne. He was jealous, but what right did he have? What was he to her? Nothing, neither friend nor lover. They had exchanged not even a caress. Belle may have embraced O'Meara in dark corners, but Louis had never touched Fanny.

Strangely, neither of them had felt the need for a carnal union. Until the announcement of Sam's arrival. The existence of this man abruptly conjured up images and dreams. The odious idea that Fanny had lived before their meeting, the idea that she had drawn breath before their eyes met, that she had loved before that July night at the Hotel Chevillon, haunted and tormented him.

As for Fanny, what was she feeling? Watching her enthroned above the gathering, sober and inscrutable, without a glance in his direction, without a word for their friends, Louis asked himself the question for the first time. What was she feeling? Tenderness mixed with irony? A quasi-maternal indulgence? *A passionate kindness?* Hervey's death must have left a void in her life; did Louis merely serve to fill the void?

Stevenson's optimism led him naturally to believe that his feelings were reciprocated. But what sort of attraction could a mother, a foreigner, a thirty-six-year-old wife feel for such a young man? Physical desire? The facts tended to prove that their intimacy did not depend on unfettered passion. Then, did she love him? No, how could she? Where would she find place for such a feeling? She was thinking of her dead child, of her husband, of her return home.

Louis tried to catch her eye. It was useless.

Eyes fixed, lips slack, feet together, she was a sphinx. He could not approach her. Had the intimacy of the last months been merely an illusion? She and her husband had shared a long past, fifteen years, the birth of three children, a mourning they had borne together. In the balance, Robert Louis Stevenson did not count for much: questionable health, dwindling reources, a literary career still in the future. Sam the adventurer against Louis the bohemian. With no experience of life or knowledge of women, Stevenson cut a pale figure.

And did he love her? Suddenly he doubted it. Fanny's muteness, her coldness, sent him back to himself and made him want to run away. He had bought his ticket to London. She had not tried to dissuade him. Both of them knew that Sam's presence in Paris was going to change the rules and double the stakes. This summer, either Mrs. Osbourne would go back to California—exit the American romance—or Louis would find Fanny again at Grez, and they would belong to each other.

". . . In the use of color, the Impressionists have made a real discovery," Bob shouted, gesturing wildly. "Before them, only Velasquez had recognized that light shifted the tones. What do you think, Louis?"

"I don't care," he answered dryly. "I am not a painter! I am only trying to write."

He turned toward Fanny, she did not react, she had not been listening. She was imagining Sam, Sam at O'Meara's age, as she had found him in Austin at the end of her journey across the Isthmus of Panama. Sam dressed as a miner with his cowboy boots, his old hat over his eyes, his pickaxe at his hip and his six-shooter. Indeed, with a pile of papers in his fist, his shares in the silver of the Comstock Lode. What on earth would this cowboy do in Paris? How could this Oakland clerk understand the discussions of this little group?

Worn out in advance, Fanny was confusing the shame she would soon feel introducing her philistine of a husband to the artists of Grez with the dreadful anger that kept her awake nights: She continued to hold Sam responsible for Hervey's death. Out of lack of concern and stinginess, he had allowed their child to suffer. While Hervey twisted in pain, Sam was drinking in the bars of San Francisco, running to whores and the theater, spending happy days in their cottage with one or another of his conquests. Perhaps he even put his mistresses in the children's rooms, in Hervey's room.

If this man was counting on taking her back to the house where their son was born, on shutting her up behind the white picket fence in Oakland, he had another think coming!

Let him come, she was ready for him. She would not return, not this year or next. "Never," she swore to herself.

R. L. Stevenson and Mrs. Osbourne parted without a word. They did not try to explain. Was this a pact or a misunderstanding? Louis left on April 2. Fanny stayed on in rue de Douai.

If they had taken the trouble to understand, they would have read the same fury in each other's eyes and the same impatience. An impatience to settle things one way or the other.

Sam arrived in May.

*
**

There was an explosion of steam, a vibration of girders, the glass roof clouded over. In the blue jet of smoke and gas, the locomotive surged into the station.

Black and monumental, it bore down on the two women and the child waiting on the tracks. As if prepared to stop the machine themselves, they pushed through the lines. One of the women blew her nose, the other sneezed. All three had a cold, and the smoke made it worse.

"You have such a red nose, Papa won't recognize you," Sammy whispered in his sister's ear.

"That's not funny!"

Belle hopped around with impatience. Fanny coughed, her eyes red under the gauze of her veil, a handkerchief to her lips, her right hand clasping the handle of her umbrella. The rails screeched, the brakes ground. There was a shaking. The monster chugged in, then veered off, entering the station on another platform!

"We are going to miss your father!"

Obsessed by the image of Sam burdened and bewildered, she saw him lost, distracted, unable to find his way in the cavernous station. She began to run. She ran through the Saint-Lazare station, that temple of modernity, that antechamber of all dreams and all departures, which in this month of May 1877 was the subject of eight of Monet's paintings.

Sam had jumped onto the platform. She saw him from a distance, his powerful blond head above the crowd. She recognized him at once. She had forgotten how elegant and civilized he was, more distinguished than all the artists she'd kept company with during the winter. He walked over to her, fending off the crowd. The journey had not exhausted him, his face was fresh, beaming with a big smile. He reached her, caught her, hugged her, enveloped her. She let herself go, let herself slip, unresisting. A vast feeling of well-being came over her; she closed her eyes. Reassured, she breathed in the honeyed scent of his tobacco. She nestled in the sweetness of his neck, the softness of the skin just where his beard began. She no longer wondered why she loved him. The rediscovery was immediate and total. The bond could not be broken. She accepted it.

*
**

Belle would remember their week in Paris as a time of unprecedented happiness. All four of them basking in the same serenity, the Osbournes lived for themselves on rue de Douai. The family was reconstituted. By some miracle, the Wright ladies had gone off to Normandy, leaving them quite free to love each other. With its large windows open onto the roofs of Paris, the apartment echoed with Yankee songs, which Fanny accompanied on the guitar, and the Irish ballads Belle taught her father. There were romantic suppers on the sitting-room rug, picnics at the table on the balcony, and they went out all together to explore Montmartre and the New Athens quarter. At Place Saint-Georges, in the murmuring jet of water, Fanny marveled as she listened to the man she had thought such an ignoramus asking a thousand questions. Who owns this house? Who is Monsieur Thiers? Why did they burn down his mansion? How did he managed to rebuild it at the expense of the Republic?

Sam wanted to see everything in Paris, to know everything, understand everything. One tour of the Louvre wasn't enough, he explored every room for three days until closing time. He returned several times to Nôtre-Dame without tiring of it. He visited the third exhibition of the Impressionists, whose simplicity of subject and natural execution delighted him. To everyone's surprise, he was interested in modern painting and even intended to buy a canvas representing a garden. He cabled to San Francisco for funds that never arrived. Sam had such charm! He told his beloved son about the terrifying adventures of desperados who were put on trial in San Francisco. He paid court to his lovely daughter, assuring her of the unswerving loyalty of her former suitors. He told his wife the story of the latest artistic events in which he took part.

"I just organized an exhibition of Muybridge's photographic panorama in the rooms of the Bohemian Club. It's enormous, Fan, just imagine: sixteen panels placed end to end representing the city, the Bay, and Mount Tamalpais. Sumptuous! You should take up photography again!"

This miraculous harmony lasted an entire week.

On the last evening in May, Belle came to sit tenderly on her father's lap.

"Papa, I would like you to meet one of our friends, Mama's and mine."

"Someone you care for, my dear?" Sam's blue eyes twinkled teasingly. "An Irishman, perhaps?"

Belle blushed.

"You already know everything?"

"Me? I don't know anything! So you want to introduce me to an Irishman? A lousy bunch!"

"Papa, stop teasing . . . He is waiting in the hall."

"Ask him in, silly girl!"

It was with some concern that Fanny watched her husband shake hands with one of the most ferocious defenders of Grez. The meeting was a collision of two worlds, the two parts of herself. Which would triumph, San Francisco or Paris? Would she go home? Would she stay?

"Sir," the Irishman said, "we are a little band of artists who love nature and stay every spring at an inn along a river. We are having a party at the end of the week. Would you like to join us?"

Sam did not sense the danger. If he had seen his wife's expression, perhaps he would have declined. Grez was the one place in the world where Fanny felt reborn. Her fiefdom, her lair— instinctively she rebelled at the notion of Sam at Grez. She wanted to keep the inn, the garden, and the river her own secrets. The memory of these places was dear to her. She would even agree never to go back to Grez again, yes, she would agree never to see the banks of the Loing again, and La Reine Blanche's tower. But for Sam to know Grez seemed a desecration.

"I was there only once and found it a charming place," he replied casually.

"But my husband prefers to visit the capital."

"Not at all . . . I'll come with pleasure!"

"Come on, Sam, there is nothing to do in Grez. You haven't traveled all this way, across a continent, just to sit in a little village!"

"Why not? You like it so much, you spend your life there."

"But I go there to work."

He laughed.

"I know, my wife is an artist, an intellectual, a thinker." Sam looked at her intently. "You, Fanny, a thinker?" he joked. "What on earth have you found in Grez, what treasure in the earth, in the water?"

"Certainly not gold!" she cut in.

Hovering between humor and hatred, between laughter and tears, for a moment they took each other's measure.

"Are you afraid I'm not refined enough to appreciate it?" he asked with sudden bitterness.

"I didn't mean that. Only life in Grez is not to your taste."

"Who knows? I would be happy to see this place again that you are protecting with such passion. It must be very charming indeed for you to prefer it to our cottage in Oakland, very comfortable for you to spend my money on it!"

The polite smile masked the same old resentment, resentment for the times when Sam took revenge on his wife by demanding to see the accounts before giving her a penny for the children.

*
**

"What is the husband doing now?" growled Simpson Senior, watching him on the river.

Sam had jumped into the boat that Louis had used the year before. An excellent rower, he was heading toward the bridge. Behind him his son and the little Chevillon boys were kneeling on the benches, leaning toward the reflection of the arches where the fish darted.

"That was O'Meara's bright idea," Bob retorted. "He thought it clever to bring his future father-in-law."

In the courtyard that swept down to the Loing, in the shade of a tall pine tree, the two Scotsmen gloomily sipped their absinthe.

Simpson's marmoset lost its balance at every gulp, tottered, and clung with all fours to its master's white jacket.

"I told you so!" Simpson moralized. "Why on earth did you welcome those hags last year? This is the beginning of the end—they were sure to attract tourists!"

"He is not atrocious, the husband," Bob replied with a smile that was both fierce and scornful.

"Even sweet and good-natured!" Simpson chipped in.

"His hearty, primitive laughter warms your heart . . ."

"And what does she think of him?"

Simpson gestured with his chin toward the opposite bank. Under their large parasols, two blue-clad figures could be seen among the willows and rushes. Fanny and Belle watched the boat pass under the bridge.

"Mama!" cried Sammy, waving. "We are going to ride the rapids! Papa is going to take us fishing at the falls. We'll bring you lunch."

"She?" Bob thought a while without taking his eyes off the group. "Who knows? What such a woman could find in a fellow like that is a mystery to me!"

Simpson could not figure out if Bob was referring to Sam or O'Meara, to the mother or the daughter.

The two women went off along the tow path. They were assailed by a thousand scents of grass, trees, and earth. The murmur of the water bugs rose around them, the furtive movements of a rat plunging into the river. The grass rustled at their feet. A snake disappeared under a rock. Behind them the stone bridge receded, and on the opposite bank were the U-shaped buildings of the Hotel Chevillon, the painters sitting under the trees in the courtyard, the fiery bank of tiger lilies sloping on trellises down to the river. In the depths of the green water, the rosy walls formed impenetrable islands.

"I had forgotten how much Papa likes children," Belle commented without taking her eyes off the boat that disappeared around a bend in the river.

With his back and large shoulders playing under the blond brim of his hat, Sam more than ever embodied youth and strength.

"He loves them as much as Louis does," the girl went on. "Mama, don't you think they are very much alike?"

"Who?"

"Papa and Louis."

Fanny, taken by surprise, threw Belle an agitated look.

"Not at all!"

"Oh yes, I tell you, they're the same kind of man."

"They have nothing in common. Nothing!"

"Papa is very handsome, Louis is rather plain. But apart from that . . ."

"Apart from that, your father is forty years old. And Mr. Stevenson's consumption . . ."

"He is consumptive?" cried Belle.

Fanny gestured impatiently.

"I'm just guessing. He coughs a lot. I suppose he spits blood. It looks like it. Whatever it is, his poor health overshadows his life, and I doubt he'll reach your father's age."

"I'm not saying that Papa and Louis resemble each other physically! But their gaiety, their optimism . . . I don't know. The way they have, both of them, of taking life with good humor. In their company, I feel like everything is possible. With Louis, with Papa, nothing sad can happen. They keep you from harm!"

"You feel safe with your father?"

The doubt, the vehemence of Fanny's tone, told the young woman that the harmony of their first days together had already turned to discord.

They left the river and headed toward the woods. Taking small steps, they crossed the plain, their boots kicking the pebbles along the path, climbed a steep slope, and descended in a rut. In the distance, the copse surged up from the earth. The rows of wheat, a tender green, converged toward the white horizon and veered off at a right angle, hugging the contours of the hillocks. The two women began to disappear in the solemn silence of the fields, lost in the depths of a vast nature.

"In Paris, though, you seemed . . ." Belle began.

"In Paris, everything was different, your father was different."

Belle did not press her. Fanny was quiet. She was thinking of the first happiness of their arrival in Grez five days ago—it seemed a century.

*
**

When the coach from Bourron had swept down the main street, when the walls of the old hotel, the alignment of its windows and its porch had come into view at the turn of the road, when she recognized the familiar figures of Madame Chevillon and Ernestine in their aprons and white caps, Fanny had felt a rush of joy. At that moment, she had been happy to be back at Grez in the company of her husband.

A mistake. This time, the miracle did not happen. From the first evening, Sam monopolized the conversation and drank more than he should. His gaiety may have found favor in Ernestine's eyes, but to the Chevillons he seemed unworthy of his wife. In the kitchen he was labeled "ordinary," in the dining room "coarse." Fanny could feel it.

Under the crossfire of such scrutiny Sam thought he had to play the adventurer, the goldhunter. He hooted at his own jokes, described ghastly murders, regaled them with stories of holdups he hadn't witnessed. He bluffed and got on everybody's nerves. The year before the painters had accepted the presence of two pretty women whose silence and discretion had won them over, but they detested this swaggering, boastful tourist. Bob and Simpson Senior were the first to express their dismay; they simply couldn't bear the way the Osbourne family—and especially Sam's presence—lent a certain bourgeois atmosphere to the garden at Grez. This American who kept congratulating himself on the good value and low prices at the Chevillons' would certainly publicize the inn to his cronies in Oakland. Soon all of California would come to Grez! "This was the beginning of the end!" Simpson exaggerated the danger and Bob acted in bad faith. But they did everything possible to label Sam Osbourne "undesirable."

Was Sam bored in Grez? Probably. Walking through the forest, searching for a subject, finding the right spot, planting the parasol, setting up the easel, opening the folding chairs, and sitting there the entire day with nothing but visual pleasure, without even the dream of making a fortune—what monotony! Still, if only the solitary walker through this wood might encounter bandits, that would be something. There was no adventure in Grez.

"But look around!" Fanny exclaimed. "Have you ever seen such a beautiful forest? Here, the forest is like the sea, it changes its aspect every hour of the day."

"Just like at home!"

She shrugged her shoulders.

"At home, the belfries do not date from the twelfth century and the towers are not haunted by La Reine Blanche."

"Maybe so. But our churches and our houses are better built than these ruins!"

In three days along the banks of the Loing, the gulf between them had become unbridgeable; and then, as if on purpose, Sam had multiplied his sins.

Not content to hit the bottle, he managed to insinuate himself into the local cottages. Without knowing a word of French, he did a little skirt chasing and heart breaking, seriously violating the Grez code of honor. The artists sketched the shepherdesses, painted the wood workers, even drew the farmers in their yards and painted the lace makers in their rooms, but they would never seduce the daughters or wives of the local peasants. This was the golden rule which accounted for the good relations between the colonies of painters and the natives. Sam broke the rule.

Another gaffe: He had a blue, lavender-scented letter delivered by express messenger from Bourron, a letter posted in San Francisco that had arrived from Paris. He hid it in his wallet, read it secretly, but no one was fooled. And when Sam thought he had found the convivial atmosphere so dear to his heart at O'Meara's little party and boasted of his amorous prowess, expatiating on the details of his recent conquests, he signed his marching orders. And gave the final blow to his marriage.

"Do you think Grez is a saloon?"

Heartbroken, Fanny had watched Sam wrap himself in that vulgarity, which she now characterized as "chronic." She felt no anger, no jealousy, only an insurmountable irritation.

The Parisian honeymoon had been an illusion, a last burst of passion. But love subsided again, empty as air, leaving a heap of ashes. She recognized this and resigned herself. For the first time, Sam's behavior did not concern her. She defended herself against his shame by affecting indifference. But the last drunken spree, the latest boasting, had triggered her explosion.

"Are you really stupid enough to humiliate me in front of my friends? How can you expect to take me back to Oakland, to your girlfriends and your booze?"

Sam listened to her, passive. She was raising her voice. The afternoon was hot. In the shade of the reeds and birch trees, with only the buzzing of the insects and the unexpected leap of a carp, her vehemence broke the country silence. She tramped back and forth along the bank, her foot sometimes slipping in the slime, her dress catching on the roots. Leaning against a tree trunk, his face turned up to the sky, Sam was chewing on a piece of grass. She went on, her head lowered, pacing continually, seeing nothing: "That's your idea, is it? To park me in Oakland while you play the man-about-town in San Francisco?"

"How long am I supposed to finance your escapades?" he cut in coldly. "Your escapades and Belle's."

She stopped and faced him.

"And what does that mean?"

"That you are a bad influence on my daughter!"

He had struck a chord. She weakened.

"I thought you were getting along very well with O'Meara."

"That's not the point; I'm finished paying for this. I'm taking Belle and Sammy with me. You're free to follow us."

"Free? You must be kidding! You claim to want me back, but you are cheating everyone, you're tricking me. It's just a show! If you really wanted to take me back, you wouldn't have gotten so drunk, and you wouldn't have had those letters from your mistress sent here! How could I want to return to that?"

Suddenly desperate, she clung to him.

"How can I return to that? You've taken away any desire I might have had!"

He brushed her off and retreated to their room.

The letter he received the following day, in addition to a second blue envelope, provided him with the pretext he was looking for. It was signed Harry Muir, his new associate, who was pressing him to return to San Francisco. The Stock Exchange was plummeting again. Neither Harry, Lloyd, nor Rearden could take responsibility for selling his shares in his place. Their message was clear: Osbourne had to jump on the first boat home. A prolonged absence would involve an irreparable loss of his investments, guaranteed bankruptcy.

To her father's great distress, Belle declined the offer to embark with him. She was so persuasive that he promised to send a stipend each month until the end of her studies at the Julian Academy. In exchange, he made his wife and daughter promise to return to Oakland the following summer, no matter what. They promised. A year from today, in June 1878, the Osbournes would be reunited in California.

Watching him climb into the coach for Bourron, Belle dissolved in tears. She felt torn between her passion for her father and her desire to be an artist. Neither Sam nor Fanny had mentioned her attachment to the Irishman.

*
**

On June 9, 1877, Sam Osbourne arrived in London, where he embarked for San Francisco via Montreal. On June 19, Louis Stevenson arrived in London and departed for Grez via Paris.

Pasdessus, the younger Simpson, Robinson, and Bloomer arrived with him. The troop was complete. The long tables of guests under the arbors, the naval battles on the Loing, the exhibitions of paintings in the yard of the inn could be joyously resumed in the July sun.

But that summer, the great number of their admirers would not protect Belle or Fanny from love.

Grez-sur-Loing—second summer—June to September 1877

"So, Madame Osbourne, your husband has left for good?" asked the rough voice of Madame Chevillon.

Sitting in the blue shade of the pine tree in the yard, her knees spread wide beneath her gray skirt, her neck down, the innkeeper was furiously polishing the handles of a large leather jug. At every shake, the ends of the *marmotte*, the traditional scarf she had wrapped around her head, flopped like two little rabbit's ears. The indigo of the scarf deepened the brown of this peasant woman's face, which expressed both cunning and goodness. With her left hand brandishing the jug, which shone in the sun, and her right hand supporting her back, Mother Chevillon got up with a sigh:

"Men—they're best when they're gone! I know something about that. You do, too, don't you?" The two women exchanged an understanding look. "Good riddance, I say!"

Fanny, her Mona Lisa smile playing around her lips, watched the stocky figure disappear beneath the porch.

She felt unburdened, liberated, relieved. Since Sam's departure, she had bustled around like an adolescent delighted to rediscover the odors, the secrets, the magic of a vacation house. Step by step she was reclaiming her village, which hadn't given her a moment's pleasure during her husband's stay. In Sam's presence, she had felt obliged to be a one-woman chamber of commerce. "Grez—its bell, its tower, its river." As if she were seeking to justify her interminable absence from Oakland by the beauty of the place.

Now at the end of June, she found it all again, its gray cobblestones, its grid of narrow paths, its low gates in the walls, those stone walls topped with red tiles that descended in parallel lines toward the river. Fanny untiringly repeated the trajectory that led from the inn. First, she walked along the main street of Grez, turned toward the bridge, there to the left, under the sign of Saint Anthony and the pig. Then, inhaling the perfume of the honeysuckle clinging to the porch and entering the courtyard, she descended the stairs that led into the garden and walked along the short passage under four chestnut trees to the Loing. Here, the bathing costumes were drying on the hulls of overturned boats, the oars leaning against the first arch of the bridge. The river meandered mysteriously through an archipelago of islands, lapping against the steep roofs of the wash houses and docks, and disappeared, swallowed up in a tunnel of greenery. She crossed back through the garden toward the inn and climbed the little stairway leading to the yard, contemplating for a moment the old building covered with vines, the roofs flecked with moss, the balconies of the two new wings of the inn. She entered through the main French doors, and observed the dining room to the right with its refectory table, to the left, the bar with its floor of stamped earth and the vast mantel over the fireplace holding jugs, bottles, vases in all shapes and colors. She breathed in the scent of burnt wood, smoke, and wine that lingered among the round tables and rattan chairs. Then she continued into the dampness of the hall, took the cold stone stairs leading up to the first floor, through the corridor, leaving on the left the rooms on the street side and stopping on the right at number 12. She rested her palm on the icy porcelain of the button, opened the door without a key, crossed the white room and stood at the open casement window. From the flowering garden, with its blue shade under the chestnut trees and its golden pools, rose the damp scent of roses and the river. Between the poplars on the opposite bank, clusters of white parasols gleamed dry and hard in the sun of this first morning of summer.

"Do you think she's taken the plunge?" inquired the hieratic sculptor Pasdessus, who had a particular interest in Mrs. Osbourne's virtue.

Standing with his head bare, his arms dangling in the river, he let himself be rocked by the little waves. His handsome blond beard fluttered at every breath.

"It would surprise me," murmured Robinson, stretched out on the bank.

In the heat of the day his gargoyle's head emerged from a yellow scarf. Who would have predicted that the asthmatic Robinson would become the most celebrated painter of the group, soon to be a companion of Monet's at Giverny. He remains one of the American Impressionists most in demand on the art market today.

"When will she succumb, do you think?" insisted Pasdessus.

It was before lunch, the time for taking a dip, when the painters gathered on the banks of the Loing to comment on the morning's work and plan the evening's festivities.

Our favorite amusement has consisted in going off in two's and three's to talk about the rest, Fanny writes to Rearden. *Talk about women being gossips, I never saw any like men!*

She could not have had any doubts that her chastity was the focal point of all this chatter. Since his arrival, Louis had monopolized her. The little group now knew which of the two Stevensons "the beautiful American" preferred. He read and wrote at her feet. At the table she saved him the chair beside her throne. In the evenings they went off alone together.

"I think you're all wrong: They've been having an affair for ages!" announced Pasdessus, caressing the waterlilies. "What do you think he was doing with her at rue de Douai all winter?"

Simpson Senior, casually turned over on the hull of a boat, blew a few puffs from his pipe into the cloudless blue sky.

"It will all happen when Louis returns."

"He's leaving?" cried the others.

Simpson watched the untiring starlings circle above them.

"Don't worry, we have time before he goes. He's leaving for a few days in August, for the wedding of our friend Charles Baxter. He's his oldest friend, they did all sorts of outrageous things at the university, they must have gotten drunk and slept with their first whore together. Charles Baxter's marriage is the end of an era, and it's a blow to Louis. The passage to adulthood. Even Henley, of the *London* magazine, was married this winter. All his friends are settling down, and Louis is always thinking about love. Yes, I wager it will happen on his return from the wedding, after he sees Baxter happy with his wife. It's well known that love is as contagious as an epidemic. Jealousy, too—just look at yourselves, gentlemen!"

"I'll take that bet," said Pasdessus. "A bottle of champagne that Louis is already a fortunate man!"

"Two bottles that he will be when he returns."

"Three that he will never become Mrs. Osbourne's lover!" threw in the chivalrous Robinson, who hadn't the money to buy himself a beer.

A delicious heat filtered through the trellis. The dappled light shifted through the broken shade of vine leaves, the clustered shadows of tiny grapes ran quivering under the table. Large bumblebees buzzed in the glasses holding the last drops of red wine. In the heavy, perfumed air, the lilacs that wreathed the inn with an ocean of mauve mingled with the odor of freshly brewed coffee, bread hot from the oven, and blond tobacco. In bathing costumes and shirtsleeves, bare feet or espadrilles, the artists lingered that summer for hours, gossiping under the arbor. Belle, sitting between Pasdessus and O'Meara, laughingly let her head roll back on the armchair. Fanny, at the end of the table, presided in a huge seat. The chair on her right was empty. She brought her knees up under her chin, leaning her brown head on her wide purple skirt. She crouched this way, staring with her luminous black eyes, wide open, her beautiful, watchful cat's eyes.

"Where are our Scotsmen?" inquired the latest arrival, an older man who swayed through the grass towards the table.

With his white mustache, his large panama hat, his three-piece suit, and the Legion of Honor rosette in his button-hole, his nonchalant distinction evoked some English officer on leave in the colonies. He was the Italian Joseph Palizzi, the painter who had "discovered" Grez nearly fifteen years earlier. Palizzi occupied a wing of the inn, which he had converted into his studio. He received new recruits there, to whom he opened his wine cellar and his portfolios. Half a century of painting—a visit to Palizzi took nights and days. Fanny, who knew how to listen, had completely seduced the aging painter.

"Louis isn't here?" he said, surprised, kissing the hand she held out to him.

"He is leaving at the end of the month for Edinburgh. At the moment, he is in Moret."

"What on earth is he doing in Moret when you are at Grez, my dear?"

Belle, leaning toward Palizzi, shouted into his deaf ear: "Louis is buying a barge!"

"What the deuce—a barge? What for?"

"To live in!" answered the young girl.

"It's a good idea," Fanny approved. "Don't you think so, Monsieur Palizzi?"

"I thought he hadn't any money!"

"Those are middle-class considerations," cried O'Meara.

"O'Meara is right," chimed in Belle, who had learned her lessons well.

"Why attach yourself to one place," the Irishman went on, "staying in the same place like some common banker? What do you think, Pasdessus, you always have ideas on every subject."

"Me?"

Above Belle's little brown head the two young men took each other's measure. They both stuck close to the young girl and monopolized her as if she had granted them each special favors. But O'Meara considered her his, and Pasdessus disagreed. At every meal, with stubborn amiability, the sculptor relentlessly addressed himself to Belle, as if he wanted to prevent anyone else from getting a word in. O'Meara, mad with jealousy, defended himself only with sudden sallies, a series of gratuitous attacks. Pasdessus answered him politely with a shower of innuendos.

"Indeed," he said, "if the land is too populated, the canals are free."

"My friends, it's done! The papers are signed, the deal is concluded."

Running, smoking, gesticulating, Louis had stormed in from nowhere—he never arrived from a particular direction, never seemed to enter either from the inn or the river or the garden, which always made his appearances rather surprising.

"It's done!" he repeated, exulting. "The old girl is lounging about a few miles from here. She is awaiting our wishes, the minx!"

He came and stood before Fanny, who blinked her eyes and raised her head a little. She did not say a word. Pasdessus and O'Meara watched them closely. Louis, sitting astride the empty chair, was already tracing the lines of a fork on the tablecloth.

"This winter, we begin in the South. We go slowly through the canals of the Midi across the whole French countryside. We will be in Paris in May for the opening of the Salon. We'll berth it at the Concorde!"

Fanny loved it, this whirlwind of impossible dreams that haunted Louis Stevenson's imagination. Unlike others, he actually realized his craziest projects. Despite his poor health, despite the money problems that had begun to plague him, he was traveling around the country like some Don Quixote, she thought. "Don Quixote crossed with the Good Samaritan," she concluded shrewdly. Louis would marshal an army for the happiness of others. Yes, she loved it, that generosity that brought a troop of itinerant singers to Grez whom all the inns of the region had banished; and she loved him for offering these vagabonds his royalties on the short story they had inspired him to write. Had he been truly rich, Fanny would not have been touched. But wasn't he secretly spending the last pennies of his inheritance to buy a new wardrobe for the painter Bloomer, who had been chased out of the Louvre because of his wretched clothes?

With his skinny arms and narrow shoulders, this boy was Fanny's idea of courage and vitality.

"There will be wine, books," he went on enthusiastically, "a hedonistic community where artists from all over will live freely!"

"And we will grow old on the deck," Robinson said, wrapping his muffler snugly against his chest, "old men with flourishing beards watering their geraniums."

"Wait a minute, wait a minute," shouted Pasdessus. "What about the ladies? Where will we put the ladies?"

"I suggest setting up a bridal suite," Louis replied. "Those who choose to pair off like bourgeois will have the right to live one month under a ceiling of naked angels. Bob will paint them for us, Pasdessus will sculpt Venus's breasts, and O'Meara heavenly roses . . ."

"There will also be a canary," murmured Simpson Senior, whose drunken monkey had just passed out under the table. "A canary in a golden cage above the bed."

"And what is she called, your barge?" Belle asked excitedly.

"The Eleven Thousand Virgins of Cologne."

"The Eleven Thousand Vergers?"

"Virgins, Monsieur Palizzi, virgins."

"Ah, very good."

*
**

Canoe battles, painting competitions, charades, composing verses to
set rhymes, the games went on. But nature's palette deepened from yellow to ocher, from red to violet; her textures thickened. Bob roamed
alone through the countryside, or went from one couple to the other. Or
he disappeared to Moret to survey, he claimed, the work on *The Eleven
Thousand Virgins,* which was being carried out at great expense.

The Stevenson cousins' dream barge would never be pulled by
a horse tramping along the towpath. The carpenter in Moret would
have it impounded in September. The young men would run out
of money and even have to give him the *Arethuse* and the *Cigarette,*
the canoes Louis and Simpson had used to travel the canals from
Antwerp to Pontoise. For the moment, however, nothing could
dampen their good humor.

With his contagious laughter, his energy, his poetry, Louis led
the dance. Joy exploded at Grez. A joy less innocent than last
summer's, something heavy and intoxicating that buzzed around
them and seemed perilously close to happiness.

*
**

"I will return in mid-August, in ten days. Will you wait for me?"

After lunch, which stretched until mid-afternoon, Louis and
Fanny were in the habit of going for a stroll. The others, beginning
their siesta in the hammocks or on the grass, watched them go.
Belle, flanked by O'Meara and Pasdessus, left as well. Their joint
attentions protected the girl, or at least that was Fanny's hope.

Down in the orchards peasants were picking the first apricots,
whose fragrance drifted on the wind. Fat white clouds trooped
across the blue sky and were reflected in the water. The church
bells rang, announcing vespers. A mist rose nearby, enveloping all
the countryside in a veil of warmth. In the center of the main road
leading to Nemours, Louis and Fanny walked side by side.

From behind, their figures under their large hats offered a contrast verging on caricature: she very short and dark, he very lanky
and blond. Feature by feature they were opposites—a little purple
patch, an endless white line. The back of her neck, where the curls
were gathered, rested on rather round, broad shoulders that seemed
almost masculine next to the fragility of her companion. Standing at

her full height, she scarcely reached Louis's shoulder blades, which jutted out, pointing like two wings under the thin fabric of his shirt. She seemed to glide, still and concentrated, without swaying her hips or swinging her arms, while he meandered ahead, right and left, his birdlike head on a neck and body that moved forward jerkily. And yet they were perfectly in step, walking effortlessly to the same rhythm, welded together by their very dissimilarity.

They were heading toward the forest. On either side of them the reapers were plunged to their chests in the wheat, which rasped like raw silk.

The couple crossed the fields, took the path through the heather, and entered the woods. Louis undid his foulard and whistled. An expression of childlike sensuality lit up his face. He caught the branch of a pine tree and breathed deeply.

"This scent, what a pleasure . . . There is nothing more alive than a tree!"

Fanny smiled. They followed the narrow forest path.

"An absence is a dead break in a relation. Yet I will not write to you," he said. "Letters are in vain for the purposes of intimacy, they are useless to people who understand each other."

Embarrassed, she interrupted: "Look at the bell flowers, how they are growing on the moss! Oh, strawberries!"

He held out his foulard. Fanny fervently gathered the fruit. She placed them carefully in the scarf. They took up their walk again, both deep in their own thoughts.

"In the end, it's still the best way!" she exclaimed abruptly. I will squeeze a little lemon juice over them, add a few mint leaves, I will ask Mother Chevillon for some cream, and we will eat them at—"

"Is that what you were thinking of all this time?" he cried. "Strawberries!"

"Does that surprise you? I love to think about food. Don't you?"

"Yes," he granted. "But I was hoping all the same that you were thinking of something else."

She laughed.

"What a Jesuit you are, Louis! I see you salivate at every meal. You love to eat and drink!"

"And to love."

She frowned. "I thought that those who know how to love don't need to talk about it."

They were quiet for a moment, then Louis asked her seriously: "Why did you bring your husband to Grez?"

She shrugged her shoulders. "I had no choice."

"That wasn't very tactful!"

"Are you angry about it?"

"Yes."

They were quiet again.

"I suppose," he went on with a sigh, "that jealousy is part of love."

"It is a low feeling!"

"Why 'low'? It is part of it, that's all. Even if, in the present case, it is not really a matter of jealousy."

"Of what, then? Why do you reproach me? On whose behalf are you questioning my honesty? My husband's or yours?"

"I'm not questioning anything! I don't suspect you. Just the idea that you could live without me is painful. I would have wanted us to discover the world together."

"What a cliché!"

"You know too much, Fanny, and yet you are missing the main thing!"

"And what is the main thing?"

"Kindness. To love kindly."

"Yes, that would be very nice," she said simply. "But kindness in love does not exist."

"Why deny it?" he said, his words spilling out. "Why do you want to torture us?"

"If I am torturing you, I must leave," she cut in, quickening her step.

He held her tightly by the arm. "Stop this affectation now!"

She pulled away. "You want to talk of love. Fine, let's talk about it: What I want is a love that takes nothing away from anyone! And I am not thinking about my husband, contrary to what you might believe. His stay in Grez, for which you reproach me, has ended our relation. It's over."

"Does he know it?"

"Probably."

They spoke in half whispers, a pressing murmur.

"Will you have the strength to leave him?"

"The strength?" she sneered. "The strength! You are 'strong.' You can turn around and leave any time you want. Someday you will marry a girl of your own age and class who will please your father. And I am strong, too, in my way. Strong the way people are in the Sierras when they have a long road behind them and only dreams ahead."

She remained in suspense, uncertain of her dreams.

"The ideal thing," she went on, "is to wait a long time for happiness, let that happiness come, let it be intense, let it be swift, and then, when it's over, let it go. Then I will go back to my husband and spend the rest of my days in silence and obscurity."

"But what you're saying is monstrous!"

"*C'est la vie*," she said, "and it's better than nothing."

"Your way of putting your husband into the equation, of toying with the idea of separation between you and me, shocks and repulses me!"

Again they were quiet.

"You are right," she murmured. "Do you forgive me?"

He smiled his young man's smile. "Madame and sweetheart, so far as I have gone in life I have never yet been able to discover what forgiveness means. So I will just tell you again that you are not very tactful."

"But you do understand me a little?"

"God knows; I should think it highly unlikely."

Frustrated, furious, she quickened her step. "Then what's the point of all this discussion?"

She strode boldly into the woods. Suddenly, like a mare that takes the bit between its teeth, she began to run. She wove between the tree trunks, her face raised to the sun. He followed her and caught her. She felt her companion's breathing becoming irregular. He began to cough, he had to stop. A terrible fit racked his chest, and his eyes filled with tears. He grew white to the lips. Frightened, she made him sit down. He collapsed onto the moss. "My God, it's my fault!" she gasped. She kneeled beside him, took his head on her knees, wiped his forehead and leaned over him, murmuring soothing words as she would to a child. As she had to Hervey. Louis remained stretched out, his eyes closed. Fine drops of perspiration veiled his forehead. Under the drooping mustache, his mouth was pinched together. His nostrils were closed. "What if he were to die?" She was afraid. She continued to stroke him gently. This emaciated face reminded her of the face of her little son as he battled his illness.

Little by little, Louis began to breathe normally again. At last, he inhaled deeply and Fanny heard him murmur: "Breathing, what a miracle!" He smiled like a dreamer waking up, and then he opened his eyes and looked at her. A fresh, cheerful look full of youthful good spirits.

"Are you all right?" he laughed. "Are you feeling better?"

"Me?" she gasped.

"You are positively green! Did you think I was going to expire?"

"I saw how much you were suffering."

He grew serious. "When I was lying here and you put my head on your lap, I was conscious of everything. When you leaned over me, I felt you push my hair off my forehead and felt your hands trembling."

"I was afraid for you."

"I felt that, too. Your compassion encircled me . . ."

"Hush now, rest."

He wrapped her in a tender and satisfied smile, jumped to his feet, and, taking her hand, helped her up. He held her. Disturbed, she wanted to pull away.

"Look at me," he said.

She looked at him anxiously. Louis thought he could read a prayer in her eyes. He did not take her in his arms. Not yet.

"Could you love me some day?" he asked her. "Could you?"

Fanny lowered her head. She felt the young man's heart beating against her chest, small, startled pulsations that entered her flesh. This wild beating moved her so strongly that she looked back up at him. A look suffused with tenderness. Her face had become serene once more, washed of all distrust and soothed.

"Yes, I could," she murmured.

"Then everything will be all right."

They both heaved a deep sigh of contentment, and without adding anything more, took the path back.

*
**

"Bob?"

"Hello, Louis. How are you?"

"What are you doing here?"

"It's siesta time. Have a seat!"

With his arms folded behind his neck, Bob made a slight attempt to move over a little. His body, bare and tanned under his blue peasant blouse, disappeared entirely in the grass. Only his face with his eyes closed and his two big wooden clogs stuck out. Louis sat down cross-legged. Surprising, thought Bob, how Louis's mere presence brings a whiff of bohemia to the neighborhood.

"So," Bob asked, "are you fitting out *The Eleven Thousand Virgins of Cologne*?"

"Why aren't you either at Moret or Grez? Bob, the barge was your idea! Without you it doesn't exist."

"I'm having a siesta," he repeated soberly, "and I am studying. I would like to study the raw, almost phosphorescent light here. And the plump peasant women. Forever painting the Loing is wearing out my brush."

"Where are you staying? Why don't you come to the Chevillons'?"

"It isn't comfortable to be the predictable Bob: he's always at Montparnasse, at Montmartre, he's always at Moret or Grez."

"What's eating you?"

Louis looked at his cousin with concern.

"I'm staying at the Laurent pension, it's better that way."

"For whom?"

Without opening his eyes, Bob gestured with his chin.

"For them—the O'Mearas, the Pasdessuses, all their flirtations! I can't bear it anymore! I'll end up giving one of them a beating and drowning the other. Belle isn't even concerned about my feelings!"

"She's eighteen years old, Bob. Remember how absorbed you are by the strength of your own emotions at eighteen. If you don't speak to her about it, how do you expect her to know?"

"You know as well as I do that she is in love with O'Meara. But you can do something for me." Bob blinked his black eyes looking thoughtfully at the sky. "You have some influence with Belle's mother, I believe."

"In a manner of speaking."

"Belle is as attractive as Fanny, isn't she? When she leans back a little ... And that chest, that line to her neck—that's difficult to forget! That golden down on the back of her neck, the matte skin that seems to flow with honey, not blood ... and those arms!"

"I know," sighed Louis Stevenson. "When we become obsessed with such a woman, something has to happen. When such a woman haunts our imagination—that womanly flesh with a manly heart— she plays a double role, she is strange, a kind of hermaphrodite."

"When such a woman haunts our imagination," Bob took up, "well then, you have to possess her."

"Better, marry her."

Bob turned an incredulous face toward Louis.

"Marry her?" he cried. "You're joking!"

"Probably."

"Are you thinking of marriage yourself?"

"In theory."

"You are moving fast. Might I remind you that she is no longer young, your fiancée? She is married, the mother of a family, American—all the virtues."

"Can I count on your support?"

"Certainly. At best, I will be very flattered to have you as a father-in-law. But everything depends on the lady. Is she informed?"

"No. But in the woods the other day, I read kindness in her eyes and we closed the match."

"You're crazy, Louis."

"I know," he admitted. "But this woman is the country that God or the devil meant me for. I believe that, I have been sure of it for nearly a year.

"But to think of marriage!"

Louis smiled and sighed: "On this field, no man is of any use until he has dared everything."

*
**

The water seemed leaden. The boat, as it left the riverbank behind, flowed in a magical torpor. Louis's agitation, his abrupt gestures, that cascading laughter, had suddenly fallen quiet, like the wind. He was rowing slowly, with precision. His oars cut silently through the water. With his hat tilted over his eye, he tenderly watched the little brown body steering across from him. Fanny's chest was prominent under a light dress. Her thin, muscular arms rolled, her mouth fluttered, red and full. She had the sun in her eyes, in her flesh, in her blood. The boat glided without wrinkling the water. They floated between two skies, outside of time and space. Little by little the steep riverbanks closed in, the branches of the weeping willows plunging into the field of flowering waterlilies caressed their faces, their shoulders and backs. They traveled down a canal. Slowly they glided beneath a vault of greenery. In the depths was the reflection of an incandescent cloth that moved away as they came near. Fanny, her eyes staring, did not take her gaze off it. She slowly dropped the tiller. She got up, leaned sleepily on Louis's shoulder, and lay down prone beside him. Suspended on the river, her arms extended, she wiped the drops of water from the prow and the long aquatic plants that rolled themselves around her fists.

Standing in the middle of the boat, Louis maneuvered to land. By sight he measured the water level and the fall of the bow rocking white on the blossoming green and pink. The slight impulse that pushed them forward subsided, and the boat touched ground on a bed of gravel. It stabilized on the bank of the narrow canal. Louis went to moor it to the root of a willow and returned to sit above the motionless form. Fanny's reflected face, her curls, her hand, were floating on the water as the insects swam nervously for the mere pleasure of disturbing her image. The dragonflies swooped here and there. With her chin on her fist, she curled up but remained still. She felt her heart beating against the boat, beating so loudly that Louis would surely hear. He looked at her neck with its brown tendrils of hair. He put out his hand, resting his long fingers lightly on her neck. She shuddered.

"Fanny," he murmured, "we cannot go on like this."

"No, we cannot go on like this."

Then, turning her slowly around, Louis took her in his arms.

*
**

The croaking frogs already announced the coming of evening when he released her. She was resting her head on his chest, curled up, peaceful.

"There's an animal," she whispered. "Listen, there . . ."

A tuft of grass moved, the head of a marten appeared among the reeds and plunged in. The waters were rose, hyacinth, and gold. The blue foliage was reflected again on the smooth surface of the canal. A cover of dampness rose from the river where a pale, very pale, crescent moon shone. Happy, aching, they slowly made their way home.

*
**

That night Louis traveled to Edinburgh to be present at his friend's marriage. Fanny, standing on the threshold of her room, listened to the regular breathing of her son Sammy, who was sleeping half naked on the folding bed beside hers. She waited for Belle, watching in anguish the beams of warmth that filled the room with a trembling white light. The air was laden with a heady scent of woods and fields. A rustling suddenly shook the pear tree at the window, and the hard fruit fell on the grass. She heard the thunder, but very far away, a deep rolling sound. What would happen now? She had made her decision and had no regrets. She felt rich and tired, the way she did after the harvesting in Indiana. Oh, she was not in a hurry. This evening, she wanted to rest, to savor the present, her youth and beauty like a rose blossoming in the heat.

At the bottom of the garden, on the bank where she had recently fought with Sam, she suddenly perceived the tall figure of O'Meara brandishing his stick, pacing up and down. She understood that he was addressing passionate words to her daughter, and the scene taking place below disturbed her. Belle, hidden by the hedge, stood still, throbbing in the summer heat.

*
**

In Louis's absence, a harsh wind blew through Grez. The sky was charged with electricity, the air heavy with storm warnings. On the evening of August 5, 1877, a thunderbolt struck the Hotel Chevillon: O'Meara slapped Pasdessus in the face. The sculptor sent him sprawling straight into the jugs at the fireplace. Belle, throwing herself across her bed, was sobbing. The witnesses, Simpson Senior and Bloomer, sold the piano in the dining room to buy weapons. The place and hour of the duel were set: pistols, at dawn on August 10, in a clearing in the Fontainebleau forest. Fanny and Bob united in their efforts to heap scorn and ridicule on the affair, and succeeded at the last minute in stopping the massacre. But a new turn of events complicated matters further: the Southerner they had met on the ship from Antwerp, the rich Kentucky planter in love with Belle, showed up in Grez. As a prudent mother, Fanny had apparently kept in touch with this departed suitor. Having forbidden him to speak of marriage before Belle turned eighteen, she had later sent the young man their address. So he was coming in person to ask for her hand.

Under the watchful eye of Bob, O'Meara, and Pasdessus, who surveyed the new couple as they stood side by side, Belle and her intended talked at the foot of the tower. The Southerner offered her his hand and his fortune: "You can continue to paint," he conceded. "I am not absolutely opposed to it."

With a firmness that was not usual with her toward her suitors,

Belle politely sent him packing, to O'Meara's great relief. To the great regret of Mrs. Osbourne, who knew that such an opportunity would not present itself again.

*
**

Henceforth all the guests at Grez were driven by a single idea, and each gave himself to it with fervor and consistency. O'Meara, Pasdessus, and Bob loved Belle and hated each other. Belle loved O'Meara, but when Pasdessus looked at her so avidly—when ordinarily he was so inexpressive—his greed fascinated and excited her. Bob made her laugh, and when he joked with her, when he lashed O'Meara and Pasdessus with his contempt, he made her cry. Fanny herself no longer knew where to turn, what attitude to adopt toward her daughter, or toward O'Meara and Pasdessus? Torn between her responsibilities as a mother and her complicity as a woman, between reason and dreams, she fled. But she fled forward.

During the torrid nights when no one at the inn could sleep, she thought she heard Louis's warm breath, she felt Louis's desire like a burning hand on her. She walked down to the river. Standing still, she let the evening breeze caress her feverish flesh. The Loing sent little black waves rushing against her feet, against her ankles, as if it, too, desired her.

Mama is ever so much better and is getting prettier every day, Belle writes to Rearden. And for good reason! The rediscovery of pleasure seemed to agree with Fanny. At least that was Louis's opinion when he rejoined her on August 16, 1877.

The miracle of his presence restored the gaiety to Grez. He concerned himself with each of them. He reassured Belle, mothered Bob, warded off Pasdessus, exhorted O'Meara to work.

With Fanny the rapport was instantaneous. They no longer got caught up in those stinging remarks, fits of sulkiness, and bickering that had been usual in their friendship, occasional bloody disputes that would be revived in their middle age. At the end of such a long courtship, their physical accord was immediate and total. They were united, they understood each other perfectly. And there was no need for grand declarations. If they chatted endlessly, they talked of everything but love. Not a gesture, not a word that betrayed their affection, No flirtation or excessive delicacy. But Louis and Fanny's liaison was no longer a secret to anyone. They all talked and gossiped about it. And the gallant Robinson had lost his bet! In such circumstances, how could Fanny stop Belle's flirtation?

Now Mrs. Osbourne was a loose woman. In becoming Louis Stevenson's mistress, she joined the cohort of Parisian girls who shared the artists' lives. Yes, now there was no difference between her and the models who frequented the bohemia of the studios by the hundreds. Deeply conservative, the painters loved these women for a season, they loved them but they did not respect them. Fanny had been able to reign over Grez, presiding over meals and games, because she belonged to no one. And because she worked. By throwing her hat into the ring, Mrs. Osbourne lost everything. She lost Grez, she lost Paris and San Francisco. The worst prophecies of her mentor Rearden had come true. Didn't he predict that she would be corrupted by the dissolute life of the ateliers, that far from her husband, far from her world she would fall like a common tart?

The unbelievable thing is that Fanny seems to have left the last bit of firm ground with the greatest spontaneity. And with no regrets.

This year, when the black, heavy plums fell one by one under her window, when the vine leaves turned russet on the walls of the inn and the rain-dampened winds shook the four chestnut trees in the garden, Fanny did not linger on the banks of the Loing. She packed up for Paris. To her son Sammy's great regret, whom she consoled for the departure by telling him: "But you know, Luly is not staying in Grez." Luly, the nickname young Osbourne had given his good friend Louis. "Luly is coming too!"

Paris—1877–1878—third winter

I am not so young as I once was; there is a relish of time in me. I find myself heavy and a little sad-hearted in comparison with the past, Louis writes to the happy husband, Baxter. *And above all laughter, that old uncontrollable hyperbolical laughter that took you by the midriff and kept you crowing till the tears came . . . is all extinct . . . But . . . though nothing can bring back that hour of splendor in the grass and glory in the flower, I pretend to be a pretty sound and merry liver after all . . . We are a little too old for green sickness and Wertherism*°, he goes on. *If we haven't cleared our spirits of that unripe rubbish by this time, I wonder how we expect to die.*

Had Simpson Senior been right when he claimed that Baxter's marriage put an end to Louis's adolescence, that it marked the onset of maturity for the whole little band of friends? Whatever the case, Stevenson's song of triumph seemed as far as possible from any ode to joy, the ecstatic aria of satisfied lovers.

They were lovers living from day to day, for Louis and Fanny's future in this puritanical period did not seem very auspicious. Thirty-seven years old, with a marriageable daughter, a little boy to raise, and a husband in the wings, Mrs. Osbourne did not exactly embody the idea of the maiden one fell for with impunity. Nor was she the good-hearted whore, or even the sort of woman who initiated men into sensual love. Nothing, however, cast a shadow on their passion. They were living what they already called a "romance of destiny." In Paris, as in Grez, they understood each other and surrendered themselves unreservedly to the pleasures of the flesh. This wouldn't last long. By the month of October, Louis again found himself in bed, not with love but an infectious conjunctivitis. Fanny no longer even bothered to preserve appearances. She sheltered him in the new apartment she occupied with the Wright ladies at 5 rue Ravignan; Louis Stevenson lived openly in her room and shared her bed.

She looked after him, although she was not feeling much better herself. During the last mock battle in Moret, during the last shipwreck, her foot and Bob's were crushed between two canoes. Bob ended a heavy season with a broken big toe and escaped to his sister's in Scotland. Fanny, with a sprained ankle and torn calf muscle, limped on crutches. Day after day, Louis lay with his eyes shut. The halt and the blind—a fine beginning for romance. But they were undaunted.

In November, the situation became critical. Louis's eyelids were swollen and oozing, Fanny's ankle was not healing. She was panic-stricken. What doctor could she call on for advice? Her helplessness again reminded her of Hervey's illness. What if Louis were to lose his sight permanently? What madness it was to take this boy in,

---

° *The Sorrows of Young Werther* (1774), by Goethe, in which the lovelorn hero commits suicide, was one of the "best sellers" of German Romanticism and had a profound effect on its generation.

when her own health was so fragile! Her telegrams to Bob went unanswered. What should she do?

Once again braving all conventions, Fanny entrusted Belle and Sammy to the Wright ladies and took her young lover to London. She took him to Sidney Colvin, Louis's intellectual and moral mentor. Mr. Colvin was a professor at Cambridge University, soon to be a curator of the British Museum, and a founding member of the Savile Club: not the sort of man to deal with the mistresses of his protégés! She defied all this.

Two months after their first embrace, Fanny Osbourne got a taste of the life she would lead for the next twenty years: a quest for health across the world to save Robert Louis Stevenson's life.

I don't suppose any of this will interest you, she writes with her customary aggressiveness to Timothy Rearden, *but I have read books until I am tired, and it's so dull lying in bed day after day for so long. Only think, I have spent all but a few days out of three months in bed. It is very dreary, though . . . the doctor says that I may go about in another month if I am careful. A month looks a long time and it is dull.*

I had a poor boy go blind in my house and fall so ill that he was said to be beyond hope. I telegraphed his friends in London, and took him to them. His friends wouldn't let me go back immediately as I had meant to do, so I had my foot operated upon there by some great doctor, and then fell very ill myself and had to stay there in bed for three weeks.

I was with very curious people in London, the leaders of the Purists. I was so out of place in their house that a corner was arranged, or disarranged, for me. They wrapped me in yellow shawls and spread a tiger skin over my sofa, and another by me. Everything else was of dull pale blue or green, so that I had quite the feeling of being a sort of Pocahontas in my corner. This seems most incongruous to have the solemn Mr. Colvin, a professor at Cambridge, and the stately, beautiful Mrs. Sitwell sit by me and talk in the most correct English about the progress of literature and the arts. I was rather afraid of them, but they didn't seem to mind and occasionally came down to my level and petted me as one would stroke a kitten. They called me Fanny directly, but didn't ask me to say Frances and Sidney to them. I wanted to because it was so unsuitable and would have been so funny, but I didn't dare.

I must tell you how nice the people in London were. I was told beforehand that they must never know that I had ever dreamed of smoking a cigarette, and that one puff of tobacco smoke would be a desecration and pollute their house forever. One afternoon a Mr. Henley, who had written a poem about me last winter without knowing me or ever having seen me, and Mr. Leslie Stephen, Thackeray's son-in-law, were brought to see me. I was very much interested in their talk and forgot where I was, and suddenly finding a cigarette in my pocket began smoking it quite calmly. Not the slightest notice was taken of it, but when they were gone, instead of killing me as I expected, Mr. Colvin went out and bought some Turkish tobacco and papers and made me teach him and Mrs. Sitwell to roll cigarettes. Now I call that real politeness.

This was her first contact with the people who "discovered" most of the great English writers of their time, the men who would publish Kipling, Conrad, Hardy, Wells, Yeats, Shaw. And Robert Louis Stevenson. The band of intellectuals who would influence and censure his work even after his death, Fanny's future rivals, whom she would soon qualify as *fiends disguised as friends*. In ten years, she would stir up trouble between Henley and Stevenson, provoking the literary quarrel of the century's end. For the moment she returned to the Julian Academy.

What impression did she make in London on her young lover's patrons? With what chaste eye did the cerebral Fanny Sitwell observe the immodest Fanny Osbourne, her rival and replacement in Louis Stevenson's affections?

I imagine that Colvin was rather surprised by this woman, and felt a pinch of condescension, a dash of sympathy, in short a cocktail of contradictory feelings mingling amusement and indifference. Nothing absorbing, nothing intense. Almost a relief.

Compared to Louis's taste for fishing in more troubled waters, this temporary companion seemed a lesser evil. Mrs. Osbourne had her feet on the ground. She took care of the boy's health, she seemed endowed, despite her extravagance, with a solid practical sense. What more could one ask for in a mistress? This liaison with an older woman could only calm Louis and give him a sense of himself. At least this is what Mrs. Sitwell explained, whose wisdom and wit had enormous credit with the Stevenson parents. She magnanimously pleaded her protégé's new cause. For the father, distressed by Robert Louis Stevenson's endless sojourns in France, was threatening to cut him off and break all relations with him if he did not return to Edinburgh immediately.

Neither Sidney Colvin nor Mrs. Sitwell imagined for a moment that this Fanny was going to leave her mark on their lives, that they would have to reckon with her, with her literary tastes, her influence, and her fanaticism in the forty years to come.

*
**

"My father is coming tomorrow to rue Ravignan!"

"What?" she shouted.

"You know that I have written him about you . . ."

"But I never imagined he would come to visit us!"

"I'm the one who asked him to make this trip. I want him to know you, I want him to meet Belle and Sammy!"

"This is suicide!"

"No, it's nerve."

"Your father cannot possibly accept me: I am married, older, an American. It's an impossible love story. What's the point of this meeting, would you please tell me?"

"To try and be honest with those we love. To look things in the face. I will not make you live with me in secret nor will I play tricks with my family. I wish to be right with the world as far as I can. It's an impossible love story, you say. Very well: We are living an impossible love story. That's clear."

"Very clear! After this scene with your father—"

"I shall know where I stand, and either be well off and free to help you provide for your children or quite a beggar. But we will be together, in the same boat, Fanny!"

Fanny was still cautious and refused to play the supplicant. She would not meet her lover's father but waited at home while Louis, sitting in a café, explained what he modestly called "the new complications of his existence." This conversation rather reassured the senior Stevenson. The scandal was nowhere near Edinburgh, and the lady had a husband somewhere else. There was no need to demand an immediate breakup. Louis's passion for a matron ten years his senior would pass. Besides, sooner or later the American woman would return to her California. Patience!

The old gentleman, touched by his son's sincerity, agreed to welcome him without any reproach and even gave him a new advance against his inheritance. They agreed that Louis would spend Christmas in Edinburgh. He could not hope for more. He had won, they had all gained some time. But the question was, how much?

Until spring Louis and Fanny forgot their financial worries, their health problems, their anguish, their separations. Without rent to pay and children to feed they would even have forgotten Sam's existence and the promise to return to America in June.

Belle's romance was in full flower. The girl became secretly engaged to O'Meara. The idea of "marriage" was in the air. *The man who should hold back from marriage is in a same case with him who runs away from battle,* writes Louis. A curious comparison for a lover about to commit himself. As far as he was concerned, forethought and realism were involved in even the most utopian state of mind. He asks his legal counselor Baxter: *Can a man, a British subject of age, marry an American (of age, if necessary) in Scotland? If so, with what delay and under what conditions? Would this be easier managed in England by special license?*

At the beginning of March they had to return to reality. Sam Osbourne did not send his meager stipend. April, May, still nothing. Their financial situation was nearly catastrophic. By a miracle, Louis found a job that justified his presence in Paris. He served as private secretary to one of his old teachers, an engineer and member of the jury for the World Fair taking place at the Trocadero Palace, built especially for the occasion. And as good things never arrive singly, the London publication of his first book, *An Inland Voyage* (the story of his adventure with Simpson on the canals of Antwerp), brought him twenty pounds sterling and some good reviews. He judged it with that severity he applied only to himself: *not badly written, thin, mildly cheery and a bit puffed up.* If he underestimated his work, his earnings that year allowed him to pay Fanny's most pressing debts. She did not ask Sam to send his long overdue money order. In June, there was neither a check nor a message. Sam was cutting off their livelihood and burning his bridges. He played dead.

On July 1, the dreaded telegram arrived: *"Come home."*

Fanny, ignoring the ultimatum, moved to Grez. The Osbourne family took up his summer quarters in the hammocks under the blue shade of the willows. But Belle and Sammy alone would be able to enjoy the beauty of the garden.

*
**

The winter had changed Fanny. It had made her more self-confident, and much more humble.

Her contact with Robert Louis Stevenson, whom she had seen writing, correcting, and rereading *An Inland Voyage*, his work and life one and the same, made her aware that it made no appreciable difference to her whether she mixed her colors or left them in their tubes. Certainly she had talent, energy, and tenacity; but not power and passion. She painted like an amateur. How could she justify her presence in Paris, how could she continue at the Julian, knowing that at best she would paint sweet, ladylike watercolors? It was unbearable to discover her own mediocrity.

And it was painful to discover that her situation among the painters of Grez had changed. The artists treated her as an equal only, it seems paradoxically, because she seemed "virtuous" to them. Fanny now found herself in the category of the familiar women who shared their daily lives in Paris, women for whom Grez was off limits. The Chevillon Inn would soon be closed, all right, and then what? she thought. San Francisco was out, too. Fine. But what about Indianapolis and Edinburgh? Louis, with his youthful spirit, kept repeating that there was such a thing as divorce, that he would marry her, that he was prepared to introduce his wife to England. Fanny was aware, however, that the scandal of divorce would cut them off from both their worlds. As for living together outside of marriage, this would permanently ruin her reputation as a woman, her authority as a mother, and bring shame to her and her children. Besides, maybe Louis would take up with a nice Scots girl of his own age and class, as she predicted he would. And even if he continued to love Fanny Osbourne after she had sacrificed everything for him, how would he support Belle and little Sammy?

Grez—June–July 1878—third summer

As the evening cooled, the pungent scents of summer rose from the banks and fields. The perfume of the roses on the trellis did not make her drunk, only slightly nauseated. Facing the river, Fanny shivered in her big rattan armchair. The shade of the flowers and plants dappled her feet like a lattice, like a net. She raised her head and watched the thin white crescent in the colorless, vitreous sky.

Fanny heard the click of glasses behind her. In the shifting moonlight she recognized Ernestine's lace cap and Mother Chevillon's blue headscarf as they moved around the dining table. They were setting the table for four only. It was mid-summer and the inn was empty. The piano, sold last August, left a gloomy gray hole amid the sketches and drawings. Scalded by the complications of last summer, Pasdessus, Bob, the two Simpsons, Bloomer, and Robinson had preferred to set up their easels eighteen kilometers away, at Mother Anthony's in Moret. They temporarily ceded the ground to the Irishman O'Meara, who had conquered Belle. The young people, entirely absorbed in their love, did not even notice the desertion.

"What is Belle doing?" Fanny wondered, as she did much of the day. In the evening twilight she could make out only the row of poplars that, like a barrier of lances, stood between her and the opposite bank. Below, the cry of a cat, a bird, a duck perhaps, made her jump. It was the same urgent call, the infinite plaint that had torn the night that evening in July when Robert Louis Stevenson's face had appeared in the door frame. It was a cry of distress, a song of love and hate. The letter she had to write to Sam should resemble that cry. She would find the words to express as much impatience, as much desperation and spite as the clamor of that animal down there on the riverbank.

*

This tenth morning in Grez, Fanny settled herself under the arbor. Once more she was trying to write to Sam. From her shady retreat, her gaze plunged into the sun-burnished world, alighting on her carpet of tiger lilies. She saw nothing, imagined nothing. She could no more conjure up her garden in Oakland than the apartment on rue Ravignan. Should she go or stay?

Taking up her pen, she drew a vertical line down the white paper. At the top of each column, two names: Sam and Louis, advantages, disadvantages. Again, she tried to think rationally, and nothing, absolutely nothing, came to mind. Not a single idea. Only Louis's arrival, which she was expecting that very day, could pull her out of this ghastly torpor, an abyss of doubts which, in her anguish, she could no longer even name.

Louis. She leaned her head against the back of her chair. What did she love in Louis? The fire in his dark, wide-set eyes, the delicacy of his face, that sweet and irresistible something in his smile? His long, nervous hands or that eternal cigarette, the ash half consumed, squeezed between his index and middle finger? His quick step, the birdlike grace of that elastic, frail body inhabited by a will of iron? His physical courage, the fact that he had not complained for a moment when he thought he had lost his sight, and never spoke of his health or his suffering, of his probable tuberculosis? Or his moral courage, his way of confronting situations and their consequences?

She admired the way he had defended their liaison to his father when no one had asked him for explanations, when most people in his place would have kept quiet. Louis was always ready to pay for his mistakes, but wouldn't allow ambiguity in human relations. What did she love in Louis? She opened her tobacco pouch, rolled a cigarette between her agile fingers, and, leaning back again, let herself be distracted by the fugitive pleasure of the first few puffs. What did she love in Louis? His humanity. Stevenson was a hundred times more alive than anyone she had ever known! With him there was nothing conventional, nothing ready-made, nothing artificial. She loved his rejection of everything commonplace, his rejection of codes and conventions. She loved his mistrust of all prudent or restrictive rules except those his conscience could accept. Louis's conscience was utterly personal, and always under scrutiny. Fanny loved that, too, that constant need to live in harmony with himself. In others, she thought, this habit of introspection, of self-examination, of self-questioning, would lead to narcissism. In him it led only to a marvelous generosity. And if he played a role, if he worked with childlike passion to make life a story, a drama, a tale, the character he played was himself. Louis was shifting and various, a poet for whom the world was filled with enchantment and romance. He was an artist in revolt against moral cowardice, unfulfilled beliefs, empty conventions, and he had a fierce hatred of respectability, a horror of comfort. He worked at creating for himself a morality as distant as possible from the coldness of Mosaic law, as close to the teachings of Christ, a morality that would respond to his demands for charity and joy. Louis: generous, heroic, tender, a sensitive man devoid of sentimentality. "Action, Fanny, action!" An adventurer who wanted to experience everything, not simply the most agreeable things but everything that was part of the human condition. She thought again of the relations he maintained with his highly conventional family. Basically, Louis liked nothing so much as finding himself in the thick of battle, amidst moral dilemmas, in difficult social positions, for the sole pleasure of grappling with himself, putting himself on the line, assuring himself that he was behaving according to his personal code of honor, duty, and kindness. This need to struggle with himself found a thousand echoes in Fanny. But in that frail body and delicate constitution, Louis's pugnacity overwhelmed her.

Moved by the harsh contrast between this man's physical weakness and his inner strength, Fanny gave a sigh and lowered her head.

After all, what was so tragic about her situation? She would be neither the first woman to separate from her husband nor the only mother to live with her lover. And the scandal, as the elder Stevenson had very rightly seen, the scandal was being played out far from their family circles and hurt no one. As for Sam, what on earth did Sam have to complain about. Wasn't he living openly with his mistress, in full view of everyone in San Francisco? Fanny even began to say to herself that after all, the poor woman—her husband's concubine—was treated rather badly. She blushed with retrospective shame, remembering that she herself had spit in her face. Yes, she was badly treated. And especially by Sam! How would Louis have behaved in his place? Fanny put aside the question; the two cases were not comparable.

Louis Stevenson and Fanny Osbourne were living "a romance of destiny." The meeting between two beings so different and so close could happen only once in a thousand years. This was a love worth living. How would she provide for her children? How would she finance Sammy's education? Well, she would work! It wouldn't be the first time she'd had to take care of herself. But work at what? Her talent did not allow her to hope for a major career. But she could paint porcelain plates, that was very popular. Though from what she could judge of the girls working in cottage industries whom the artists occasionally used as models, these young women seemed to find it rather difficult to make ends meet. And what about her talents as a seamstress, why hadn't she thought of that? In Virginia City and San Francisco, her skill with the needle had brought her a little nest egg and a fine reputation. In Paris, the seamstresses strained their eyes and ruined their health for a pittance. Never mind, Fanny Osbourne would always manage! She smiled, thinking that with Louis and his imagination, his energy, his sense of humor, she was not likely to wallow in sadness and boredom. No, she wouldn't. But Belle and Sammy? Without Sam's stipend, poverty awaited them, the poverty that had killed Hervey. Was she going to flirt with death a second time? How could she make a deliberate choice to plunge her two remaining children back into such horror? Oh, the danger was not so great, the Stevenson parents were not lacking in feeling or fortune. And as for him, the reviews of his first essays, the praise that greeted his first book, the respect he commanded from men like Henley and Colvin confirmed her certainty: Louis had genius!

What did she love in Stevenson? Fanny had dared to ask herself this question. Indeed, she loved the creator.

She had felt a flush of emotion reading Louis's first texts, and enthusiasm at the purity of his style, the finesse of his analyses. She had the inner conviction that she was witnessing the birth of a great writer.

As for her, the gods or the devil had refused her the power to create a work of art. On this point Fanny knew the answer to the very first question posed two summers ago in the little wood at Grez. She belonged to that category of artists who would never get to the next stage, to those Stevenson called the "Snoozers." A snoozer—so be it. But deep in her half-sleep, Fanny Osbourne had a real artistic sense and a yearning toward the ideal. She was brilliant at seeing the beauty of a future painting in an awkward study or line drawing. Intuitive and visionary, she was infallibly gifted, as Stevenson himself said, at divining the character of people, their human value, their artistic potential. Infallibly gifted at guiding another's talent toward its potential.

With the wisdom of her advice, with the solidity of her support, she would lead him to the pinnacle of success. She already saw him in the pantheon of immortals. How could she hesitate even a moment between her little garden in Oakland, and the greatest adventure of a lifetime!

She took up her pen. *Dear Sam* . . . She crushed out her cigarette with a nervous gesture and, grabbing her tobacco pouch, rolled another. At that moment she spied Belle in the grass on the riverbank. O'Meara was holding her and kissing her full on the mouth. They did not even take the trouble to conceal themselves. It struck her that her daughter had fallen, too, that she now belonged, like herself, to the class of hussies and loose women. And she was struck by the certainty that O'Meara would not marry Belle, that he might make her pregnant. It was her own example, her fault; she was leading her daughter into disaster. Wasn't the tragic case of Hervey enough? She thought she could hear Rearden's accusing voice.

For a moment she'd had the sense that the lawyer's grasp was dragging her down, that Stevenson's influence was raising her up. Rearden represented fear, Louis hope—hope? She gave a mocking laugh. The hope of compromising her daughter? Again, the memory of Hervey, her remorse at having led him on such an adventure, swept over her.

What a blind egotist she was. Because she was bored with her decent American husband, because she had crossed the ocean to play the artist, because she had taken a lover to pass the time, because she was enmeshed in what she took for a passion, was she ready to let Belle throw away her future? Fanny Vandegrift's life was behind her. She had ruined it. Fine. Was that a reason to sacrifice her children? This ridiculous comedy had to come to an end. She had to dismantle the bomb, to stop the machine while there was still time.

Taking a new sheet of paper, she wrote: *As agreed, we will be home in August.*

Fanny sealed the letter and, with the envelope in her hand, went up to her room four steps at a time.

*
**

With no explanation to either Belle or Sammy, the next day she took her children and left Grez. She went back to Paris, packed her things, gave up the apartment, canceled her registration at the studio. And she broke her daughter's heart. For years to come, Belle would not forgive her for that haste and brutality.

*

"You are engaged, all right. Is he marrying you, yes or no? This is the moment to choose."

"Mama, not right away, it's impossible!"

"Then we are leaving. Your father is waiting for us. It's time to go."

"Why must I break with O'Meara? Because your affair with Louis isn't going anywhere?"

"I am not asking you to break up, just to settle down and get married."

"You're the one to say this to me? You dare?"

Wracked with suffering and uncertainty, Fanny stiffened.

"The adventure in Paris is over, you have learned everything you can at the Julian. It is time to prove yourself at home. We shall see what Virgil Williams thinks of your progress."

Then, softening, she tried to approach Belle and murmured: "I only want your happiness, Belle. If O'Meara makes you his wife, I will give my consent. Even if it means that you are living far away from me, even if it means you are staying in France."

"That's a lie! You cannot bear it that I'm happy! Because your life is behind you, you want to destroy mine. Because I'm young, because I'm pretty, because O'Meara loves me, you're choking with jealousy! You're always accusing Papa of hypocrisy, but you're the one, Mama, you're the one who's deceitful!"

"Get out of here or I'll slap you! It's high time for a little discipline. I've brought you up very badly, my girl, and now I'm paying for it!"

*
**

Belle was obliged to put it to her lover: marriage or separation. Before this dramatic choice, the Irishman recoiled. He loved Belle, he loved her to distraction. But he preferred work, silence, the gray skies of Grez to the ruckus of the Osbourne ladies. Despairing, betrayed by everyone she loved, Belle made her farewells. On the platform of the Gare du Nord she sacrificed O'Meara, her first love, to maternal tyranny. The train and boat that separated the young people took her to London. They would never see each other again.

No Man's Land—London—July–August 1878

I am living the final days of my passion. They are steep, Stevenson writes to Baxter. *Afterwards, everything will be gone.*

They spent these final days in a modest family pension in Chelsea, the last stop en route to the boat leaving from Liverpool for New York.

Of this English stay, Fanny would preserve only the memory of those big, wide-set eyes suspended above hers, of that laughter, that childish smile. In her disarray, it seemed to her that Hervey was dying for the second time.

"I cannot separate you from me, even in thought. Are you going to speak to your family?" he asked.

"Yes, I will talk to my husband."

"Your husband, Fanny, is me! You are Mrs. Robert Louis Stevenson."

"Yes," she replied, in a tone of infinite sadness, "in a way . . ."

"If I let you leave, it is so you can ask for a divorce!"

"Let's stop talking about that, please."

Overwhelmed by the suffering he saw on her little face, by her evasive look that was usually so honest, terrified by her avoidance, Louis insisted: "Swear to me that you are leaving only to clarify the situation. You are leaving to return a free woman."

"Oh, yes, certainly . . . of course."

"Fanny, there can be no question of pride, of weakness, of a power struggle between us. Listen!" he begged, trying to attract her wandering attention. "Listen: Absence makes no difference, or distance."

"Of course," she repeated softly.

He observed her and concluded: "I am coming with you! I will not leave you alone with that man! You will explain how things are, and I will bring you back."

She smiled, an expression full of sadness, of grace and knowledge. "What will you use for money?"

"Give me until September. I will have enough for our passage. It's decided, I will accompany you!"

"No, certainly not! Your presence would compromise everything. It would only exasperate Sam. No. I must put my affairs in order alone. I will stop in Indiana, I will speak to my family, to my mother, to my sisters. If only I could see my father! If only I could explain to him . . ."

Tears came to her eyes. She lowered her head. In August 1876, four months to the day after Hervey's death, her father Jacob Vandegrift had died. Overwhelmed by suffering as she was then, she had felt only a vague sorrow. Now she was going to revisit the farm, the big, red brick house, the dogs, the horses—without him. She imagined him standing in the turn of the road as she'd left him, a forceful, lively man in full maturity. The anchor, the harbor where she took refuge. The Vandegrift house without him—how was it possible? In losing Louis, in losing the love of her life, Fanny suddenly realized how much she missed her father. Jacob would have known what to do!

"Go back ... But what else can I do?" she cried to him, her face on fire, her chest heaving. "What else can I do?" She began to walk. She paced back and forth, and in her agitation borrowed Louis's gestures, his sudden pauses and starts. "How can you imagine that I'm not thinking of divorce? That's all I think of, that's all I think of," she repeated. "Not a day goes by, or a night, or a moment when I don't dwell on this obsession, and I have to banish the thought for fear of going mad. I'm afraid, I'm afraid of losing my mind, like my father."

Louis saw the depth of anguish in her eyes. Empty of himself, full of her, he lost his sentences, his words. He had no more eloquence, nothing but that furious tension and mute, lurking violence characteristic of Fanny.

"But let's think it out!" she went on mechanically. "Let's think it out. How can I ask for a divorce? Sam will not agree to it. He is too afraid of the judgment of his family, even if he never sees them. He will be afraid of displeasing his pals, his club, Rearden. Divorce, no, he will not agree to it. I would have to have something against him. But I'm the one at fault! I'm the one who deserted the family home, I'm the one who took his children away from him. And I'm the one," she tossed out with a kind of desperate rage, "I'm the one who is cheating on him!"

"Fanny, calm down! No one can force you to stay married against your will!"

"You believe that, do you?" she mocked. "Truly?"

Immunized by the anguish of this break, they held one another without moving. They could not even make love anymore. Louis began again: "Swear that if you need to, you will call me! That is my only condition: You will call me and I will come!"

"I will call you. But these are the final days, Louis. The future is not important now. Let's take the little we have. That's all there is."

In their room in Chelsea, they lost themselves in work. Louis was writing numerous articles for Henley's *London* magazine. He read everything to Fanny first. She listened, she made corrections and suggestions. Every word, every phrase was passed through the crucible of her judgment.

The intensity, the success of this last experience comforted them both with the absolute certainty of a unique intimacy. "*A perfect relation*," Louis writes to Baxter. An intellectual communion that sublimated—if need be—sentiment and physical desire.

Meanwhile, the hour of parting was drawing near, Fanny's son would write in his Intimate Portrait of R.L.S. *I had not the slightest perception of the quandary my mother and R.L.S. were in*, Sammy goes on in the chapter entitled "Stevenson at Twenty-eight," *nor what agonies of mind their approaching separation was bringing; and doubtless I prattled endlessly about "going home," and enjoyed all our preparations, while to them that imminent August spelled the knell of everything that made life worth living.*

But when the time came I had my own tragedy of parting, and the picture lives with me as clearly as though it were yesterday. We were standing in front of our compartment, and the moment to say good-bye had come. It was terribly short and sudden and final, and before I could realize it, R.L.S. was walking down the long length of the platform, a diminishing figure in a brown ulster. My eyes followed him hoping that he would look back. But he never turned, and finally disappeared in the crowd. Words cannot express the sense of bereavement, of desolation that suddenly struck at my heart. I knew I would never see him again.

The jolting train lurched toward the ocean carrying a woman's body. The stiff neck rolled on the headrest. The face, eyes closed, was impassive. The downturned mouth, the pinched nose, the hollow cheeks: Fanny had ceased to exist.

At her side, forehead against the glass, a girl was sobbing with rage and pain. She would be twenty years old next month. Her mother sat silently, rocked by the motion of the train. Matronly and shrewish, aging and unloved, she would die with a man she despised. This journey to France was a hideous failure. Yet she had found what she had come to find—a destiny worthy of her. Life had won out, and she renounced it.

Without talent, without a career, without Hervey, without her father, Mrs. Sam Osbourne was sailing into the void. She was returning to her point of departure, this time without hope.

VI

A Romance of Destiny

Hope is so strong that it has conquered fear.

—Robert Louis Stevenson

San Francisco—Winter 1878–1879

"How is Mrs. Osbourne this evening?" Virgil Williams asked kindly as he took his place in his wife's sitting room. "What does the doctor say?"

Dora raised an eyebrow but, unusual for her, refrained from comment. Her hair sleekly parted in the middle, chains and trinkets jingling, she was filling the tea cups.

"It was predictable!" Rearden muttered, stirring his tea.

They were all gathered here, all of Fanny's longtime friends, allies, and beaux, for the customary ceremony of tea and scones at the Williams's. Only Sam was missing; he was detained at the courts by the trial of a Mrs. Chadwick, who was accused of pumping six bullets into her husband with her pocket derringer.

"Poor Sam!" Rearden sighed, puffing on the pipe clenched in his teeth.

"Poor Fanny!" Dora retorted. The lawyer's unfailing chauvinism always roused her combative spirit. She was deeply distressed by Mrs. Osbourne's persistent prostration and mental disarray. Fanny was on the verge of madness. Rearden knew this. He relit his pipe.

"That's what happens when women want to go off on their own.

The machine breaks down. And the victims are their husbands, as usual!"

"Rearden, your nasty irony isn't funny!"

"Indeed," he went on, "the story is even sad. The wife of a fine fellow abandons him,"—Rearden dwelt on "abandons"—"she disappears for three years. She cuts him off from his children. And when she comes back, one of those little ones is missing. The lady sulks and wanders around the house like a ghost."

"This 'fine fellow,' as you call him, doesn't seem to have suffered much during that long absence. He consoled himself rather quickly, it seems to me. Didn't he move a young lady into his wife's house, a cheap actress of the lowest sort, whom all you gentlemen seem to find very attractive?"

Virgil Williams, John Lloyd, and Timothy Rearden, all embarrassed by this attack, looked away.

"Now this young lady," Dora resumed, "didn't she turn your friend's house upside down? The whole house—the master bedroom, the wife's workshop, her dark room, her parlor. And why did she spare only Hervey's room?"

"Out of loyalty to his memory," suggested John Lloyd.

With his short blond curls now turning gray, his ruddy complexion tanned by the San Francisco air, his deliberate gestures, his double-breasted suit, the former Austin miner finally looked like the banker he had dreamed of becoming. The beautiful Mrs. Osbourne's return may have given him a few sleepless nights, her nearness may had disrupted his plans and stirred his memories, but he congratulated himself on escaping with his fate intact. This woman was a source of complications.

"How easy it is for you to justify Sam!" Dora stormed. "Out of loyalty to his memory, you say? Out of revenge! Sam could have cleared Hervey's room out before Fanny's arrival! I can see him opening the door, showing his poor wife the stuffed bears sitting in a row, the orderly array of toys, the little blue sailor suit hanging in the same place in the cupboard. 'Take a good look, my dear. And breathe in that lingering baby scent. He's all that's missing!' Even I, who have no children, even I," she repeated," who don't particularly care for them, have never been able to set foot in that room. How much worse it is for her! What cruelty! It's not surprising she hasn't said a word since that day. She cannot speak, she cannot eat . . ."

"She doesn't recognize anyone," John Lloyd added sadly.

"We're lucky that Sam, out of loyalty to his memory, didn't kill her on the spot."

Feelings of friendship pushed the faithful Dora to embroider on the facts—friendship, and a taste for melodrama. Fanny had not been struck speechless upon seeing her son's room, she hadn't collapsed on the very day of her return to Sam's house. An onlooker would have thought that their reunion on the platform of the Sacramento station took place, if not joyfully, at least peacefully and kindly. That onlooker would have been mistaken.

Sam's mother, on a visit to Indiana, had foreseen what would happen. She confessed she was shocked by Fanny's lack of enthusiasm at the idea of rejoining her husband, pained by her indifference, and quite troubled by her physical transformation. Indeed, Fanny had not stinted in that direction. In a gesture of foolish audacity for the 1870's, she had cut her hair very short. Was the sacrifice of her hair a sign of widowhood, of mourning for her lost love, or for her father? Or—as with many women—did she signify her inner revolt by a radical change in appearance?

In the photo, taken soon after this period, Fanny's scandalous hairdo suits her marvelously. A face like a Greek statue, the head of a Pre-Raphaelite page: the straight nose, the full lips, the jutting chin, and that helmet of black curls on her forehead and temples. With that modern look it is hard to imagine her lashed into a corset, difficult to picture her crushed under layers of skirts, stifled by a profusion of frogs and loops. Yet it was the submissive mother, the dutiful wife who walked through the white gate in Oakland on Sam's arm.

She was silent about her adulterous passion for a young Scottish author. She had not mentioned it to her mother or her sisters, not even to Jo, her old accomplice. Jo, George Marshall's widow, was now remarried to a Danville banker; the word "divorce" would have shocked her. Perhaps Dora would understand. After all, hadn't she involved herself with a divorced man when she married Virgil Williams? Yet it would do no good to tell her. The past was dead, and Fanny with it. Only Belle knew her secret. To avoid any intimacy with her daughter and to deflect Belle's hostility, Fanny had brought with her to California her youngest sister, twenty-two-year-old Nellie. Aunt Nellie and her niece Belle were thick as thieves.

Mrs. Osbourne had settled in again. There were the neighbors, the visits, the garden. It was all as if Fanny had never left.

Sam slept in San Francisco. He came home weekends, bringing along Rearden, Lloyd, and the Williamses, who lunched in Oakland every Sunday. Once again Fanny presided over a long table. But compared to Louis's intelligence and Bob's flights of fancy, the chatter of Sam Osbourne's friends seemed heavy-handed and tedious. So what? Looking neither ahead nor behind, Fanny simply went on. She did not write to Louis, or Bob, or anyone. For the first six months at least, silence.

And step by step, little by little, she sank into a depression. She had hearing and visual problems, memory loss, exhaustion—attacks of psychotic symptoms. Her future detractors would say that she suffered from recurrent mental illness, something like schizophrenia. This attack was but one in a long series, some more serious than others.

Whatever the case, her effort to leave Robert Louis Stevenson, her renunciation, led to what in all modesty she called "brain fever." This time, it was a black fever, a string of obsessions that consumed her body and soul.

"It's all over," she repeated to herself during her interminable sleepless nights. "It's all over." She saw Grez, the river, the boat where they had made love for the first time. She felt her lover's kisses on her shoulder. She lay down, she got up, she walked down the hall. She stood in front of Hervey's room. She waited. No, she would not go in. "It's impossible." She returned to her bed. Hervey, Louis . . . "What is impossible? Can it really be over? No, Louis is going to come! But why would he come?" She would write to him! She got up again, walked to her desk, opened the ink bottle. "I am doing what he asked me to do . . . *If you need me, you will call me and I will come* . . . and what if he didn't come? *If you need me* . . . But let me see, did I do my hair today?" She put down her pen and tottered to the mirror. She did not hear the clock in the sitting room strike midnight. "He mustn't find me without my hair done. He mustn't find me with my eyes red . . ." She came up to the mirror, then withdrew. That puffy face, those hollow eyes, those haggard cheeks, who was it? She pushed her curls back off her forehead. "But it's me! I must make myself up quickly, before he comes." She ran her hand through her hair, then stopped: "Am I going mad?"

Terrified, she caught herself and went back to her big, empty bed.

*

What on earth happened in Paris?" Dora would wonder again and again.

"None of us reckoned on how shaken she was by Hervey's death."

"Hervey would be seven years old today," calculated John Lloyd, who had been so attached to Fanny's children.

At this moment the door opened. Sam and Belle came in. Father and daughter were always together now, a handsome couple. He was charm incarnate. Time seems to have spared him. Photographs from the period show the same face with a trim blond beard, the sensual mouth under the mustache, the eyes sparkling with the same kindness, the same mischief. At moments, however, strange currents crossed his blue gaze, fleeting expressions suggesting that perhaps life was not as simple for this man as it seemed. Witness his drunken sprees, secretly indulged in the lower depths of San Francisco. Everyone there knew that Osbourne didn't go home each evening to his mistress but frequented even more sordid places. He could go for months without women and alcohol, but his sober periods alternated with attacks of debauchery in which he haunted the brothels of Chinatown. He never talked about these mysterious descents into hell. He plunged in, then pulled himself out. The pleasure of his charm and his open gaiety, shadowed by the sense that dark battles were being fought in his soul, made Sam all the dearer to his friends. Belle spared him neither her tenderness nor her admiration. And she tossed in a little ostentation to torment her mother.

"Mama is exaggerating," Belle responded to their friends' questions. "She is making herself sick. She doesn't make any effort!"

"They've prescribed sedatives," Sam went on, "but our poor Oakland quack doesn't have a clue!"

"There is nothing to understand," grumbled Rearden.

"Miss Belle, let's see what you have to show us in your portfolio today," suggested Virgil Williams with a smile, unwilling to pursue this painful conversation.

The girl untied the ribbon and brought out several drawings. Everyone at the San Francisco School of Design agreed that she had made real progress in France, a spectacular development. The study trip was an obvious success.

"Very interesting, anatomical drawings," Mr. Williams commented. "If only we could find teachers for our school of the caliber of your Monsieur Robert Fleury."

"Well, then," Dora bitterly concluded, "all's well that ends well!"

Without registering her sarcasm, Sam looked adoringly at his very charming daughter. How on earth would he have gotten her back if Fanny had chosen to stay in Paris? What leverage would he have had? He could have cut off his children's stipend, but at what cost? Mrs. Osbourne's present nervous state suggested that in any case she would have collapsed, pulling Belle and Sammy down with her. Osbourne gave a long sigh of relief.

More than 6,000 miles away, by a marble fireplace between family portraits and silver candelabra, a Scottish engineer and his wife heaved exactly the same sigh. The Stevensons' patience had borne fruit. Reason had triumphed. Distance forever separated their only son from this older American woman. Now he simply needed distraction and occupation.

Robert Louis Stevenson was engaged in this pursuit himself. Fifteen days after taking Fanny Osbourne to the boat-train, he had returned to France, intending to visit the Cevennes on foot. But this time neither Simpson, nor Bob, nor any of his usual traveling companions followed him in his wanderings. He traveled alone across one of the poorest, wildest, most beautiful regions of his adopted country. With only a blanket and sleeping bag, he slept out under the stars. For food: sausage, chocolate, and water. And he was alone for two weeks. *And yet even while I was exulting in my solitude*, he wrote in his second book, *Travels with a Donkey in the Cevennes. I wished a companion to lie near me in the starlight, silent and not moving, but ever within touch. For there is a fellowship more quiet even than solitude, and which, rightly understood, is solitude made perfect. And to live out of doors with the woman a man loves is of all lives the most complete and free.*

For now, he had to be satisfied with conversations and arguments with Modestine, his she-ass. Seen from a certain angle, she reminded him of a certain lady of his acquaintance. This hard journey would inspire him to write a story full of charm and tenderness. ... *lots of [Travels with a Donkey]*, he confided humorously to Bob, *is mere protestations to F.*

Time did not mute Louis's suffering. He missed everything about

Fanny, her incredible vitality, her jumble of contradictions, her silences, her faith in him, her enthusiasm for literary work. Every week of absence seemed to him more unbearable. However, *to F. I never write letters*, he admits to Colvin. *All that people want by letters has been done between us. We are acquainted; why go on with more introductions? I cannot change so much, but she would still have the clue and recognize every thought.*

What a transformation, this silence! It was not like R.L.S. in love to put down his pen. Witness the dozens of bottles of ink spilled to confide the slightest movements of his soul to Mrs. Sitwell, a correspondence that would fill several volumes.

Louis seldom spoke, and had trouble working. He thought only of joining her. What decision had she made so far away? Was she still thinking of divorce, or had she changed her mind after seeing the father of her children? Would she stay with Sam Osbourne? These uncertainties demoralized him. Would he ever see her again? If so, what could he offer her? How could she agree to share such a precarious existence? *Louis had been to pieces,* Colvin writes to Henley, *and was together, or nearly together again, when he went away yesterday week.*

All his friends in London and Edinburgh were waiting impatiently for him to get past this obstacle. In February 1879, despair won out. *I want—I want—a holiday; I want to be happy; I want the moon or the sun or something, I want the object of my affections badly anyway; and a big forest; and fine summer wind and a camp under the stars,* he writes to his friend, the poet Edmund Gosse. *I envy you your wife,* he goes on, *your home, your child—I was going to say your cat. There would be cats in my home too if I could but get it. I may seem to you the 'impersonation of life,' but my life is the impersonation of waiting.*

*
**

"Wait? Wait for what? What are you waiting for, Fanny?"
She gave Sam a look full of hatred.
"The end."
Embarrassed, he tried to laugh.
"You may be waiting a long time!"

She did not brighten. Sitting at the foot of her bed, that big bed with sculpted columns where Hervey was born, where Sam had loved other women, Osbourne was preparing his final ploy. God, how his wife irritated him. She had been so full of life, but now her face was painful to look at, thin and sallow. Her ridiculous short hair plastered down on her forehead made it seem even lower and more obtuse since her return, Yes, she exasperated him. Not only was she pretentious and a blue-stocking, but she was mad. She was destroying herself for the sole pleasure of tormenting everyone.

"Stop your histrionics. There's nothing wrong with you. The doctor says there's nothing! All your complaints, your dizziness, your memory loss, your deliriums, are imaginary."

"And my fever of 104 degrees the other week?" she murmured. "I didn't make it up! My sister Nellie took my temperature every evening: she told you. I had 104 degrees, I was delirious."

"You have no fever today, you are not delirious, and you are getting out of here."

"And going where?"

Sam made a vague gesture. "There are plenty of places to go. California is huge!"

Fanny crawled back under her covers. "Leave me alone. Get out! Get out!" she repeated with a gesture of horror. "Or else . . ."

A strange light came into her eyes, which she lowered. She opened them again and gave him a black look. They took each other's measure as though to engage in another battle of wills. But Sam seemed utterly fearless. She understood that for the last twenty years he had feared her, feared her demands, her complications, her contradictions. In the old days he would have done anything to avoid this scene, but tonight he was ready to do battle.

She recognized that she no longer touched him on any level, not even in some obscure way connected to the past. This sudden realization threw her into an abyss of terror.

"Or else," she repeated in a voice punctuated by the beating of her heart, "give me my freedom!"

Sam shook his head and sighed. "When you wanted to leave, I let you leave . . . I let you take my children! Your decision caused me such torments—your decision, not mine. You have no idea how I suffered in your absence! The possibility that I could suffer never crossed your mind. It's always like that with you. You don't give a damn about the feelings of others. But you won't fool me a second time. 'Let me go,' you kept repeating. 'Let me become somebody. When I am proud of myself, everything will go better between us.' And I went along with it," he remarked, bitterly. "Are you proud of yourself today? Do you really believe that things are better between us? I listened to you, Fanny, to your misfortune and mine. And look what's happened. Now I will decide. If I've done you any wrong, you have certainly taken your revenge. We're even. Now this is what I have to say: We still have twenty or so years to spend together, so let's live them comfortably."

She jeered: "Comfort, Sam? What does that mean to you, cheating on each other? Mutual cuckoldry?"

"Paris has made you vulgar."

"Not more vulgar than you. I have done nothing that you don't do daily. In France—"

"I don't want to know what you did there!"

"What? Your charming daughter hasn't told you?"

"Shut up! And leave Belle out of this! You have lost all common sense."

"Ah, you see, I'm crazy, but you were just saying there was nothing wrong with me! You claimed that my illness was imaginary!"

"Look, get this straight: If you leave, I won't stop you, but at the age of forty, you will have to survive as best you can. You will live on your charms, I don't doubt. But you won't get a penny from me. And I keep Belle and Sammy. In your state you're incapable of raising your son and marrying off your daughter. They stay with me!"

Tense, concentrating, she was trying to follow his explanation. Her mind, confused by months of emotional exhaustion, could no longer reason. A single question burned on her lips, a request she dared not formulate. "Does this mean," she asked, "does this mean that . . ." She raised herself on her pillows. "Does this mean that you would grant me a . . . divorce?"

"Don't even think about it."

She had expected this answer, and dreaded it. "Why?" she asked timidly. She had already stopped listening.

"Belle and Sammy have had enough shocks, enough insecurity. I will not subject them to the scandal of a divorce. In any case, my children will not be children of divorced parents."

Seeing the kind of apathy that met his response, Sam pushed his advantage.

"This chapter is closed," he said with a new firmness. "So I propose that we attempt a reconciliation. I agree that it's not easy here. Let's go away together for a week, without Belle and Sammy, without your sister Nellie. Let's take a vacation. We could visit the coast south of San Francisco. Turn to the wind, to the sea, to life in the great outdoors. That's what you need, Fanny. Go horseback riding, sleeping out under the stars—you'll find peace again. And I will, too," he added to himself.

Louis had got quite a sane letter from an intelligible address in Spanish California, Colvin writes to Henley on February 6, 1879, *where, after wild storms, intercepted flights, and the Lord knows what more, she was for the present quiet among old friends of her own . . . What next, who shall tell?*

Monterey—Southern California
February–October 1879

"This is the most beautiful of the old California towns. But please, don't tell anyone! If rich people discovered it, they would pave the streets, they would destroy the old houses, they would build hotels and shops. In five years, this paradise would be ruined! We could say good-bye to the charm of Monterey."

This prophecy was uttered at the train's arrival by an old student of Virgil William's, Joseph Dwight Strong, twenty-six years old— "Joe Strong" to his friends. At this final stop of the narrow-gauge railway he had just run into an old crush from his youth in San Francisco. Her name was Belle Osbourne. She had alighted covered with dust and accompanied by her young aunt and little brother.

There was really no station, no platform, no depot. At the foot of the only train car, two carriages were waiting. Horseman passed by at a trot on Mexican saddles, wearing big sombreros, shouting orders in Spanish. And in the distance, a huge crescent of white sand flanked by dark cypress tress extended beyond the sleepy village.

Less than 150 miles from San Francisco, Monterey was a complete change, an expedition to a foreign country. It was really a plunge into the American past. A hundred years old, the former capital of California, Spanish, Mexican, only recently American,

Monterey was redolent with history. It was the first city to be attacked by pirates, the site of the first newspaper west of the Mississippi, the first court of justice, the first constitution, the first hotel, the first wharf, and the first pool room.

My father and mother disappeared together a week, Belle recounts. *And we were very surprised to receive in Oakland a telegram asking us to join them in Monterey. My father was waiting for us at the train. While the porter piled up our luggage, he told us that he had rented an entire wing of a huge house, the Casa Bonifacio, where our mother was settled; that their vacation together had gone well; that she was feeling better; that she was the one who had asked to stay, and wanted us to come . . . One of the horsemen who was passing by at a gallop jumped down and came to greet us. He resembled a young German with his very short hair and big blond mustache, He was Joe Strong, the most famous young artist in California, the king of Monterey, whose charm opened doors here to old Spanish society . . .*

Belle and Joe had met six years earlier, in 1873, on the ferry that crossed the bay from Oakland to San Francisco. Belle, then fourteen years old, was on her way, without a chaperon but accompanied by a classmate, to a matinee at the Baldwin Theater. Very proud of their first long dresses, their first corsets, their first bustles, the adolescents resisted the desire to buy some candy and strolled instead on the deck to the sounds of a band. *We were talking of the pleasant day ahead,* Belle remembers, *when we noticed that a couple of young men were looking at us with interest. Demurely, out of the corner of my eye I discovered that the taller one was making a sketch of me . . . Just before the boat arrived at the San Francisco side, a schoolboy friend appeared, and we sent him over to ask the artist if we could see the sketch. It was a daring thing to do and we both felt that we were outraging the conventions, but our curiosity was too strong for us. The young artist signed the sketch and it was brought over to us with his compliments. . . . This was signed "Jos. D. Strong, Jr." We bowed discreetly and smiled our thanks; the two young men took off their hats, and we thought the incident was over. We went to Papa's office and were given our theater tickets and money for our lunch of fried oysters and coffee at the California Market. Before half past two we were in our seats at the Baldwin Theater. The play was a musical comedy called Ixion. As Nellie and I were looking about pleasantly at the rapidly filling theater, a voice behind us said, "Good day." Looking over our shoulders, who should we see but the two young men! Without exactly knowing how it was done I found Joe Strong sitting beside me and his friend by my friend.* [This would be the same Reginald Birch who so brilliantly illustrated *Little Lord Fauntleroy.*] *They must have used a good deal of ingenuity to get those two theater tickets, for our seats were reserved ones in the dress circle and the house was crowded.*

I was wearing lemon-colored kid gloves fastened with gold buttons like cuff links with little gold chains, Belle goes on. *The young man beside me artfully admired them and finally succeeded in removing one so that he could hold my hand under the program.*

In 1873, at the age of fourteen, Belle was making an early start! And the story doesn't end here. Joe Strong had sent Reginald Birch's father, an Oakland notable, to pay a visit to the young lady's parents. The old gentleman was the bearer of a message. He asked Mrs. Osbourne if young Belle could come to pose at his son's studio, which he shared with Joe Strong. To buttress his request, he recalled that Strong had just finished doing a portrait of the mayor of Oakland. The picture had been so successful that the city had taken up a collection to send the artist to study in Munich. Escorted this time by Miss Kate, Belle had visited the young men at their studio until their departure for Germany. So ended the first episode.

Years later, returning from Europe a little before the Osbourne ladies, Joe had answered the urgent summons of another of his friends, the poet Charles Warren Stoddard, a pillar, like himself and Sam Osbourne, of the Bohemian Club. Stoddard, who would one day introduce Robert Louis Stevenson to the poetry of the Pacific Islands, was seeking a calm, dreamy, exotic place to write his elegies. *Leave San Francisco right away and come down here,* he wrote to Joe Strong. *This place is ideal for painting what's around you. There is everything! Fishing boats aground on the shore, whaling ships, enormous rolling waves that rush into the breakers, and above it all the ruins of a Spanish castle, and the Carmel mission, you cannot imagine how picturesque it is.* Joe hurried down, bringing with him several exuberant regulars of the

Bohemian Club. They rented apartments in the Mexican haciendas from the locals. And so they established the first artists' colony in the country west of the Rockies. A second Grez. A less chauvinistic and more exotic Grez, which Mrs. Osbourne, her daughter, and her sister would enliven with their passions.

Once again, Fanny was at the forefront of a trend, the first woman painter in a long line of artists to savor the charm of Carmel and Monterey, the first to move to these now legendary places. Afterwards, several generations would choose to make their homes on the peninsula: A whole band of artists would soon come, whose hero was the mythic figure of a certain Robert Louis Stevenson. And their ringleader would be Jack London.

There were no business affairs to conduct, no gold mines to exploit, nothing but this beach enclosed by rugged rocks where the rolling waves broke. Stranded on the sand were the black hulls of old whaling ships and the stray carcasses of the huge dismembered mammals. At one end of the bay lay the straggling village crushed by the sun. It could have been Seville or Cordoba. Behind thick white walls with red tiled roofs burst vibrant plants, vines, huge tropical flowers, a vivid natural world riotous with colors and cries. The broad, unpaved main street was trampled only by occasional galloping *vaqueros*. Down below, across the horizon, lay the blue Pacific. On the beachfront stood a jumble of tall houses festooned with wrought iron balconies, wooden stairs, striated lattice-work screens and shutters. At the intersection of the streets that disappeared between the adobe walls and wound under the arcades and over bridges, old Spanish cannons stood black against the blue sky; now people used them as hitching posts. The clank of spurs echoed up and down the uneven steps of the wooden sidewalks. Through heavy, half-opened doors one caught a glimpse of cool patios, courtyards paved in mosaic tile, variegated pots where clusters of geraniums bloomed, and Moorish fountains spewing jets of water.

We passed a porch and there, amidst the fruit trees, under the trellis of roses, I recognized my mother, who was making furniture with an ax and hammer. Her cheeks were red from the effort, a smile was on her lips, and for the first time in months she seemed alive.

Did the salt smell of the sea, the perfume of sap and cypress trees, the flowers draped over the walls, the Monterey spring bring peace and renewal to Fanny's overheated mind?

Could the miracle of the first summer at Grez, whose memory continued to haunt her, happen all over again?

For Belle, the magical experience did happen again. O'Meara was forgotten, his vows of love and his betrayal. As in Grez, Belle's gaiety and beauty won her the allegiance of the whole little community. She made friends at the grocer's. She gossiped and flitted about the street, she danced and flirted at the beach. And then, as in Grez, she got involved, predictably succumbing to the charms of the group's leader, Joe Strong.

As for Nellie, with her long tresses and schoolgirl manner, Nellie the intellectual, so devoted to her older sister, she, too, soon deserted Fanny's company to chose a *novio* in town. She took a friend of Joe's, the owner of a local saloon, the handsome Adulfo Sanchez, last scion of an aristocratic Mexican family.

In Monterey, social background didn't count, Belle and Nellie recall. *You danced until dawn, and enthusiastically, with the old butcher, the young baker, or the attractive barman.*

Serenades by moonlight, fandangos under the cypress trees, picnics by the sea, pounding hearts and wild laughter—Fanny no longer shared any of this with the young people. She and her daughter had no common secrets, pleasures, or projects. Belle kept her resolutely at a distance. Mrs. Osbourne henceforth belonged to the older generation, and Belle made her feel it—all the more as the girl openly took Sam's part in the quarrels that once again marred the peace of the great white-washed rooms. *It shocks me now to remember how little I noticed that my father's visits grew fewer and fewer. At first, he joined us over the weekends, going back to San Francisco on Sunday nights; then, several weeks would pass, and often when he did come, Nellie and I would be sent away while he and my mother held agitated conferences. My mother was relieved by his absence. In the garden of the Casa Bonifacio, she set to work again. She was painting miniatures, small, very lifelike portraits. She prevailed on me to sit for her, but the results were always so uncomplimentary, or, perhaps, so true to life that I wept on seeing them.*

Scotland—Near Edinburgh

Swanston Cottage—The Stevensons' Country House—June 1879

"It is shameful and indecent that my own son should behave like the lowest of philistines, that he should pursue the adulterous woman and ask her to leave her husband, to betray her children!"

Outside the rain was falling steadily, clouding the glass of the two bow windows that looked out on the vast lawn. A wet summer. The water gathered in pools in front of the old country house and ran into the foundations, eroding the crumbling stone walls at the bottom of the garden. Black-faced sheep browsed in the grass, so newly green it seemed yellow in the sun. But this year in Scotland there was little sun. The heavy clouds pressed against the flues of the four square chimneys that flanked the slate roof. The fire was permanently lit in the drawing room, the dining room, and bedrooms; Thomas Stevenson was suffering from rheumatism, his wife Margaret was coughing, and their son was going stir crazy. From his mother he had inherited his weak constitution and his incurable optimism, from his father the violence of his convictions and his concern for honesty.

"You are contradicting yourself, Father!" Louis allowed himself. He got up and paced from one end of the table to the other, where his parents were seated. "I have so often heard you defending the rights of women! You talk about their right to freedom, their right to happiness." He leaned toward his father. "I thought you were so generous and progressive, some of your ideas even seem revolutionary . . . Didn't you say that a mistreated wife should be able to divorce without her husband's consent, that divorce should be a woman's privilege . . . And now you claim—"

"That you do not have the right to disturb the peace of a household, to meddle in a home that isn't your own. If you continue to pursue such a disloyal deed, you make my whole life a failure!"

There was nothing limited about Thomas Stevenson, nothing mean or narrow-minded. The biographers who have tried to turn Louis's father into a petty bourgeois tyrant have been misguided.

This stern face framed by its mutton-chop whiskers harbored a youthful, twinkling eye under the bristling brows, and an expression both curious and tender. Thomas Stevenson was indeed conservative, and a fierce Calvinist. Like his son, whom he loved and with whom he continually fought, he tried to live in harmony with himself, with his code of honor, with his faith. His religious belief was a mixture of sober principles and fanaticism. A theologian, physicist, and engineer, he was a man in constant motion, a man who sought, groped, doubted, and sometimes made mistakes. His character was an odd blend of dry humor, whimsy, even eccentricity, as well as intransigence and rigor.

"I beg of you," he pleaded, "not to inflict on me the most terrible suffering of my existence. Don't force me to disown you!"

"Lou," his mother intervened, an elegant, pious, and cheerful lady who adored her husband.

Margaret Balfour Stevenson belonged to the old Scottish upper middle class. Without being really pretty, she had a delicate manner and elegant features that lent her a quiet charm. With her narrow face, her hawklike nose, her gray, glowing eyes, she was spirited and still preserved a youthful grace. Some thought her saintly. Only her coughing fits, Thomas's attacks of spleen, and the violent altercations with Louis managed to crease her smooth, curved forehead.

"Lou," she repeated tenderly, catching her son's hand, "sit down."

She forced him to take his place beside her. And to prevent him from moving, she left her slender hand on the young man's arm. She wore a large medallion on her wrist representing "Lou at four years," an enamel portrait held by a bracelet of Lou's blond baby curls.

"Dear, try to understand your father. He is suffering to see you suffer—"

"What does it matter?" cut in Thomas bitterly. "He does not care! I am used to his insults and indifference . . . But what egotism my son displays toward this woman he claims to love!"

Turning his heavy figure at the end of the room toward Louis's frail body, Thomas rose in a great show of strength. Theatrical, accusatory, he walked toward his son.

"How dare you ask her to sacrifice her family without offering her anything in return?"

"I beg your pardon, but I mean to marry her!"

"A fine thing! You must have a profession, my son, to play the paterfamilias. You must have an income and a certain sense of responsibility—which you seem to lack entirely! You are twenty-nine years old, Louis, and you are still living on the allowance I give you."

At this remark, Louis, escaping from his mother, jumped to his feet. Both of them trembling with rage, father and son took each other's measure. The one, massive, red-faced, his square jaw shaking, the other with a face like a knife blade, purple with humiliation, his huge eyes bloodshot.

"You can bequeath your whole fortune to your charities," he began to shout. "I don't want a penny! I'm the first to say that a child who doesn't share his parents' beliefs has no right to their bank account. I've always understood your generosity as an advance! I keep a precise accounting and, believe me, I will make it a point of honor to reimburse you to the last pound!"

Thomas had just touched a sensitive chord. Unlike most young people of his class and generation, Robert Louis Stevenson spent his father's money only with a bad conscience. At a time when sons of good families lived off their incomes, he considered the many advantages of his birth to be a loan from society, a loan that he hoped someday to repay.

"Only morality can be a legacy," he went on indignantly, "so I ask nothing from you!"

"Lou, oh Lou, that isn't what your father meant . . ."

"I would be very curious to know the total earnings from your author's rights," insisted Thomas.

When he thought he was in the right, he never let up. Nor did Louis.

"How much has your *Travels with a Donkey in the Cevennes* brought you?" Thomas went on, pitilessly ironic. "Thirty pounds? If you really loved this woman, you would leave her alone. Or else, my boy, you would hang out your shingle, open a law office, and earn your living! As for that poor mother at the other end of the world—"

"Who we don't doubt for a moment, my dear, is utterly charming . . . Only think, Lou, that in ten years she will be my age!"

Louis threw his mother a grateful look. He knew that, while sticking by her husband, she was trying to divert the argument from the dangerous course it had taken. He seized the opportunity.

"But you are ravishing, Mother."

"Don't be silly, you know what I mean," she continued lightly. "I understand that you don't find certain young ladies very entertaining. But the sister of your friend Walter Simpson, for example. She is very original, and she still belongs to an excellent Edinburgh family."

"Eve Simpson is very lively, Mother, I easily grant you that, she is literate, intelligent, more intelligent than Fanny perhaps. But—"

"But what?" interrupted Thomas, who had seemed to calm down at the other end of the room. "But it would be too simple to take up with a woman who lives down the street! I warn you, my boy, if you set off in pursuit of this American woman, I'm finished with you!"

His voice trembled a little. His mouth seemed to weaken. "Don't force me to disown you, my son."

Seeing this passionate old face so anguished, Louis no longer doubted his father's sincerity. "He is afraid," he thought. "He is so afraid for me that if he dared, he would weep. That is certainly the worst of it: He is afraid. And I'm torturing him!"

Thomas shook his head, collected himself, and murmured: "I am begging you, Louis."

The two men exchanged a pleading look.

Monterey—Casa Bonifacio—July 1879

Fanny was alone. She had sought support from her mother and confessed to her sisters that she wanted a divorce, provoking a general outcry of indignation. The Vandegrift family had never held Sam responsible for his wife's departure to Europe, but now they blamed him for allowing her to leave. Separation— that was the cause of all their misfortune! And as for divorce, inconceivable!

Her sisters did not deny that Sam Osbourne was a bit shallow, sometimes irresponsible, perhaps unfaithful. But what couple didn't have such problems? They were part of married life, and indeed of life itself. Why on earth did Fanny suddenly feel the need to complicate a situation that was not even worth mentioning? Divorce? How could she? Their poor father would have turned over in his grave. His daughters had to respect his memory and his name.

The Vandegrifts, the Osbournes, and the Stevensons presented a united front. Three worlds, three clans that reacted in precisely the same way: with clenched teeth and furrowed brows. Indignant letters rained down from Indiana.

And Fanny's relations with Belle became even more difficult.

"I don't want you to continue seeing this Joe Strong. He's not worth it. You're wasting your talent and your youth with him!"

"And what if I like him?"

"You'll quickly forget him, my girl. Like your Irishman, that poor O'Meara you said was the love of your life. The way you carried on! I know just what you need. I'm thinking of a marriage much more to your advantage than hanging about with that bunch of would-be artists!"

Why this sudden scorn for bohemian life, this crude concern with respectability? Did Fanny want to prevent her daughter from making the mistake she had made by loving Robert Louis Stevenson? Was she trying to spare Belle her own torments, her doubts, her bouts of anguish? This, at least, is what she told herself to justify her harshness, her stance as a mother concerned only with her child's future material well-being. Deep down Fanny continued to mock such things, but she feared that Belle was too quickly becoming involved in a new romance. She knew the girl's horror of suffering, her frantic taste for pleasure, and her passion for love. As a mature woman, she recognized the flamboyant Joe Strong's talent, and his weakness. Her fear made her predict disaster, and she multiplied her blunders. Of course Sam took his daughter's side. He supported Belle's right to happiness.

"Happiness," Fanny jeered, "happiness, what does your father know about that?"

"Much more than you do! If it's that planter from Kentucky you want me to marry, I'm not interested. He bores me, he's stupid!"

"Not as stupid as Joe Strong! He plays at follow-the-leader, he thinks he's a great painter. But I give him five years, five years before he burns out. Perhaps he was gifted at eighteen, but now he is undisciplined, he shows no character or determination. He's a failure, you will see, a nobody!"

Belle defied her and let her talk. At the beginning of July, the dutiful Nellie made her contribution by announcing her intention to marry Adulfo Sanchez. As for Belle, she became secretly engaged to Joe Strong.

*
**

On the ground floor of the Casa Bonifacio, in the big room with the vaulted ceilings and whitewashed walls that served as her bedroom, Fanny paced up and down. Her bare feet on the cold flagstones, she circled repeatedly from the big canopy bed to the marble washstand, from the porcelain pitcher that held fresh water to the painted wooden trunk filled with her dresses. Every time she passed the casement window level with the garden, Fanny, with an old childish gesture, flung back the tresses she no longer had. She distinctly heard the voices of Nellie and Belle gossiping above her. Fanny would have liked so much to go to sleep. But when she stretched out on the bed, someone or something threatening seemed to approach her. She had to stay alert. A draft suddenly moved the curtain. She heard steps in the garden. They were coming. She opened her night table, took out her derringer, loaded it, and moved to the window. The first notes of a guitar rose into the evening air: a love song in Spanish, a raucous, violent cry. Four young men's voices lifted toward the first floor. Adulfo Sanchez's rich baritone was dominant. On the floor above, little steps ran to the window. They struck a match, put the candle on the balcony, and courted in the moonlight. The fools! Fanny was shaken with disgust. For this display of emotion Belle and Nellie would sell their souls, ruin their lives. Shoddy goods! Why protect them? Against whom? What should she do? Spoil the moment? Interrupt the serenade? Chase the young men away? Their silhouettes threw long shadows against the walls barred by the geometric line of the guitars. She put her pistol back in the drawer and closed it.

She stood there at the foot of the bed, her arms hanging down against her nightgown, an old woman's chaste nightgown. She felt a hundred years old. Why did she stay here? No one here needed her. Oh yes, she stayed to raise her son and marry off her daughter. Why couldn't she recover the warmth and tenderness that had once given her life meaning? Her husband did not love her. Her daughter despised her. She had no more reason for living. Only little Sammy still showed her some affection, but he preferred riding horses and playing with boys his own age. She was tired. If only these bellowings would stop! She threw herself on her bed, pushed her head into the pillows. She wanted to think about Louis. Let him come, let him come! She tried to visualize him, but they had been apart for a year and his image was fading. What could she hope for? To see him, to hold him, to burden him with all her responsibilities? If he came, what would happen? Another scandal! Belle would accuse her again. His arrival would not bring her peace. She couldn't escape, not even in her dreams! She would have liked to think of something absolutely peaceful, something that would involve no choice, that would bring no reproach, like the orange carpet of tiger lilies in the garden of the old Vandegrift house, a red and silken sea that rose up before her, shutting off the view.

She must have dozed, for when she woke she heard no guitar, no men's voices, no girls' murmuring. Silence. But someone was standing above her, motionless at the foot of her bed. Louis! She recognized that thin figure, those hunched shoulders. Louis! His great dark eyes were staring at her, and his mouth opened with a dry cough that seemed to rattle his teeth. A death's head! An alien, menacing Louis, a skeleton that threatened to take her.

"What's happening?" she asked.

"Nothing. I've come to find you. I'm taking you back."

The voice was Sam's voice, that drawling Southern voice that swallowed its words. Sam had caught her and held her.

"You said that everything would be fine!" she murmured.

"But Fanny, everything is fine!"

Ready to argue as she always did with him, to insult and accuse him, she stood up. But the room was empty. It was another of her dreadful nightmares. Tomorrow, tomorrow she would end it . . . she would write to Louis.

At dawn that morning of July 30, 1879, Fanny Osbourne was at the telegraph office in Monterey. She sent off a message of ten words to Swanston Cottage.

What did the telegram say? No one knows. Robert Louis Stevenson destroyed it. Did she speak of madness and death? Did she confide her desire to end it all? Or was she trying to break off their relationship? I tend to think that she begged Stevenson to save her from herself.

Whatever the case, her appeal must have been urgent enough for Louis to answer the same day: *Hold tight. I will be with you in one month.*

Swanston, Edinburgh, London, Glasgow, New York, San Francisco—Louis's quest—August 1879

He left Swanston Cottage, passed through Edinburgh, and hurried to
London, where he counted on borrowing money from his friends for the
crossing. But all of them, Colvin, Henley, and Mrs. Sitwell, disapproved
of this journey. This was the first conflict in the long rivalry between
Fanny Osbourne and Robert Louis Stevenson's intimates, and they
fought to detain him. By leaving England, Louis would destroy his literary career. He would cut himself off from his contacts in the publishing
world. Above all, he would quarrel with his parents. And what on earth
would he do in Monterey, on the husband's home ground?

To prevent him from going, his friends refused to give him
money and support. Even so, Stevenson obtained a small advance
against future essays. He bought a second class ticket and committed one of the only cruelties of his life by allowing his parents to
believe that he would see them on vacation the following day.

That day, August 7, 1879, he embarked among the emigrants on
the *Devonia* for New York. In his pocket he carried a little book
of black Morocco leather, the work of theology his father had written. And he brought these religious reflections from Glasgow to
New York, from Monterey to San Francisco. Nine months later, he
would make a gift of the book to the only man who seemed worthy
of it: the pastor who would marry him to Fanny Osbourne. Meanwhile, Robert Louis Stevenson would grow up. This journey to
America would forever change his style and his vision.

*So you see he has gone to the Far West, ill, and with every
condition to make him worse,* Colvin writes to Henley. *If it wasn't
for the frailness, I wouldn't mind, but if that spirit will go playing
fast and loose with its body, the body will someday decline the
association—and we shall be left without our friend.—Of course if
he does live, he will come out somehow or another having turned
it all to good—and it's no use doing anything but hope. But I can't
help fearing as much as hoping.*

Despite his compassion, Colvin would always refuse to imagine
his protégé's odyssey. He would even refuse to hear about it when
Stevenson tried to tell him.

I seem to have died last night, Louis confides to him the morning of his voyage. *I can say honestly I have at this moment neither [sic] a hope, or fear, or an inclination; except a mild one for a bottle of wine, which I must resist. I have just made my will and am reading Aimard's novels!* Que le monde est bête! *God bless you all and keep you, is the prayer of the husk which once contained R.L.S.*

Only to Bob did Louis dare to speak of Fanny. When the ship set sail, he wrote: *F. seems to be very ill. At least I must try and get her to do one of two things. I hope to be back in a month or two; but . . . it is a wild world.*

In train after train hurtling west, R.L.S. crossed a whole continent in search of the woman he loved. He saw the Great Plains, the mountains and deserts of America, he knew cold and hunger. He wrote the story of his adventures in two volumes that cannot be paraphrased, two small masterpieces: *The Amateur Emigrant* and *Crossing the Plains.* His friends refused to acknowledge these works. His father purchased the copyright of his book to prevent it from coming out—judging it unworthy of his son's talent. Robert Louis Stevenson's world could not accept the fact that this scion of a respectable family had chosen to touch bottom—out of love, and utterly alone.

He traveled in such conditions that Fanny would find not the romantic bohemian of Grez but the skeleton of her nightmares.

In order to join her in Monterey, Stevenson would lose nearly fifteen pounds in twenty-three days and contract an illness the doctors would soon call consumption.

He would leave his address only with Charles Baxter: *c/o Jos. D. Strong, Monterey, Calif., to be given to no one, not even the Queen.*

The irony was that so as not to provoke Sam's jealousy, Joe Strong acted as a cover for his future mother-in-law's love affairs.

Monterey—August 1879

In the heart of the peaceful, sun-washed village, passions ignite. While a lover from the other side of the world embarks in pursuit of the mother, an undesirable neighbor steals the daughter. What amazing love affairs those Osbourne ladies had! On August 9, 1879, two days after Robert Louis Stevenson sailed on the *Devonia,* Joe Strong made his move.

My mother threw a bombshell into our camp, writes Belle in her autobiography, *by telling Joe that she was arranging a very good marriage for me. I had reason to believe the man she had in mind was the tall Kentuckian, for later I sat next to a Southerner at a dinner party who reproached me for jilting his friend. Joe was very much upset by this news and hurried to San Francisco for a talk with my father. On his way back he stopped at Salinas and got a marriage license.*

Taking me for a walk on the beach he told me he had my father's consent. Then he begged me to marry him at once without telling anybody. We could go to the cottage in East Oakland, get any clothes I needed and then we'd find rooms in San Francisco, where there was much work waiting for him. And I could do illustrating for a weekly paper. It all sounded delightful.

We climbed over the rocks hand in hand till we came to the "Pacific Grove Retreat." Here Joe led me to a cottage where a minister and his wife were waiting, and almost before I realized what was happening, we were married.

I wore an old gray dress and shabby scuffed shoes that I kept for walking on the bench. We laughed hilariously over my wedding outfit, for I hadn't even a hand bag.

The incredible thing is that Belle prudently returned that very evening to sleep under the maternal roof. For almost a month Fanny would be unaware that her daughter, her accomplice, her companion, was now a married woman.

They were both torn between impatience and anguish, each keeping her secrets, waiting for something to happen. Fanny was hoping for the arrival of her young lover, which she mentioned to no one. Belle was counting the days until her twenty-first birthday, so that she could escape with her lawful husband. The atmosphere at the Casa Bonifacio during the month of August 1879 was charged with tension.

And the sentimental imbroglio was to become further complicated by the apparently simple relations between Aunt Nellie and the handsome Adulfo: their engagement had unleashed another family drama. Nellie had sent the family in Indiana a photo of her Mexican fiancé. Horrors! The youngest Vandegrift girl was going to marry a black man! The sisters held the scandalous Fanny responsible for this new disaster.

After all, hadn't Fanny brought her sister Cora to California ten years earlier, in 1868? And hadn't she married Cora off to Osbourne's partner, Sam Orr, who had disappeared with him in the Sierras? Orr was a man who couldn't seem to shake the gold fever that periodically gripped him, but now it was the Orrs who most bitterly stormed against Nellie's union with the owner of a Mexican saloon. In the meantime, Joe Strong had secretly delivered a telegram from Stevenson. He was on his way. To hide his visit any longer would seem suspect. What should Fanny do? What should she say, and to whom? To prepare Sam's friends, she chose Rearden, whose intelligence and shrewdness she knew all too well.

I hear, she writes, *that my literary friend from Scotland has accepted an engagement to come to America and lecture; which I think great nonsense and have written to tell him so. I have also advised him not to mind the pretty talk of the reviews, but to stick to his own legitimate walk in literature. He has a line that belongs to him alone and would be an idiot to leave it for money and flattery. Later on if he works and lives he will get both fame and money, I am sure.*

An act of faith and a tissue of lies, sincerity, and deceit—a curious mixture. Belle was not fooled. At the end of the month, her father's rival was to make his appearance in Monterey.

Monterey—Friday, August 30, 1879—5:30 P.M.

I remember his walking into the room, and the outcry of delight that greeted him, Fanny's son would write forty years later, *the incoherence, the laughter, the tears; the heart-welling joy of reunion.*

On this late afternoon, the patches of light and shadow fractured the large room on the ground floor. The last rays of the sun fell starkly on the dark furniture, the elaborately carved sofas of the Casa Bonifacio, playing in the scrolls of the balustrade, burnishing the upholstery of the armchairs, pricking the velvet of the footstools

and prie-dieux. Elsewhere vases floated in the half-light, along with
the golden pendulum of the grandfather clock—a puzzle of a thousand broken pieces. Drifting in from the garden and suffusing the
room was a bittersweet odor of perfume and salt, the sea air laden
with a mellow, honeyed fragrance. The roses of the Casa Bonifacio
belonged to the legend of Monterey. In the village, they called this
house "the adobe of the Sherman roses." People told how a young
man, later the Union's General Sherman, one of the heroes of the
Civil War, had loved the Bonifacio's daughter. When they parted,
he swore to return and marry her, and as a token of his fidelity
planted a rose bush at her door. Forty years later, the roses clung
to all the walls of the house, while Nichina Bonifacio shriveled
under her mantilla, dividing her time between her old mother, her
passion for her beautiful garden, and her anger at her tenants' son. It
was open war between the child and the elderly señorita. Sammy was
amusing himself learning to lasso the cow and the calf in the corral
on the pony his father had just given him. "Poor old maid," Fanny
sighed as she bent over her sewing machine. "Her flowers may have
flourished, but love dies in this house."

Sitting at the east window, her back to the sun, Fanny pedaled
energetically, keeping the lace of the skirt she was making aligned
under the needle.

With her long garnet skirt, her plum-colored blouse buttoned to
the chin, her starched sleeves, her white collar and gold cross, she
looked so dutiful this evening, serious and calm. "Since I know
Louis has arrived in New York, it's strange, I'm less eager to see
him. I'm not very sure I really want him to come . . ."

But for her helmet of black curls and the crispness of her profile,
she would have embodied the image of feminine sweetness—but
for her fingers yellowed with nicotine, the cigarette that burned
endlessly in the jumble of bobbins, pins, and snippets. "As my
symptoms disappear when the doctor arrives, his visit doesn't seem
quite necessary."

"Sammy, are you working?" she asked the child stretched out at
her feet on the tile floor. "Recite your declensions for me . . . You
know, I think Luly's coming."

She had already made this seemingly innocuous remark the evening before, she had said it in a strange tone of voice, with excitement in her eyes: "I have news for you. Luly's coming."

"When?" Sammy asked again, thrilled.

"Soon."

"Will he stay long?"

"I don't know . . . Now let me hear those declensions."

Sitting cross-legged, Sammy intoned his Latin, which he was trying to learn from the big dictionaries Timothy Rearden had sent him.

The hum of the sewing machine kept them from hearing either the housekeeper's steps, the light knock at the door, or the click of the lock, until the señorita suddenly announced behind them: "A visitor for you."

Fanny did not need to turn around to knock over her chair or run to him. Louis stood against the light. She noticed his worn blue suit, the cheap sheen of the coat he'd flung over his shoulders, the collapsing bag at his feet. In the shadow of that odd, melon-shaped hat, she could not see his face, but throwing herself into his arms she thought she had forgotten how lanky and frail he was. They stood entwined, weeping together, laughing, murmuring incoherent words.

Until that moment, Sammy writes, *I had never thought of him as being in ill health. On the contrary, in vigor and vitality he had always seemed among the foremost of those young men at Grez . . . Now he looked ill, even to my childish gaze; the brilliancy of his eyes emphasized the thinness and pallor of his face. His clothes, no longer picturesque but merely shabby, hung loosely on his shrunken body.*

What Sammy does not say here is that Robert Louis Stevenson's ears, neck, and hands were swollen with an itchy red rash, which he scratched continually.

"Sammy, dear," she babbled, "go quickly and find the wine and tacos I ordered at the grocer's . . . Find Belle and Nellie. Tell them Luly is here!"

They stood face-to-face, paralyzed with emotion. In the absence of a third person, a strange discomfort prevented them from embracing.

"Are you disappointed?" he asked with a strained smile.

She hesitated. This momentary pause before answering tore the traveler's heart. She understood how her silence affected him, and in a great burst of feeling, pressed herself against him.

"Don't be silly. But I did not expect to see you so soon, not this evening. It's the weekend," she tossed out. "Sam comes down here tomorrow."

"Good. We won't waste any time."

He closed his arms around her, and this time, kissed her. He thought she felt no pleasure in this caress. He was wrong. But for God knows what reason, Fanny told herself that she absolutely had to make an effort of will. She tried to recover herself. He restrained her. She disengaged.

"Your caresses hurt me," she murmured, "because I love you so much."

"Then I am going to hurt you and squeeze you until your bones are imprinted in my flesh!"

She laughed, embarrassed. "You would have trouble doing that. I've gotten heavier, haven't I? Since I received your telegram, I've gained ten pounds! And you, let me look at you . . ."

She drew back, tilted her little head, narrowed her eyes and scrutinized him, the way she scrutinized objects before painting them. Her heart was wrenched. "You're so thin," she said, putting on a cheerful voice. "But I'll fatten you up!"

She had resumed her maternal housewife's voice as she prepared the glasses and dishes. She made him sit down at the table. "I bet you've eaten nothing all day." She placed a bowl of guacamole in front of him. "Have you ever tasted avocado?"

"I had forgotten what an actress you are! You drag me onto your ground so I won't talk to you about us—"

"It's a Mexican recipe . . ."

"Ah, Fanny," he laughed, "love will never make you lose your footing. You will always keep the tip of your heel on firm ground. The same mare hitched to the same wagon!"

"And you, the same bird who burns his wings in the same sun. Tell me about your trip. Talk to me about your work. Have you something new to show me before the others arrive?"

"I am drowning in ink and have not stopped scribbling! From New York I sent Colvin the longest novella I've ever written, *The Story of a Lie.*"

"You are going to read it to me . . ."

"Not now."

He looked at her inquiringly: "You're so afraid I'll touch you that you'd make up anything to keep me busy."

She did not answer.

He had removed his arm from Fanny's shoulder and she had withdrawn. Sitting beside each other on the same bench, he wounded by her prudence which he mistook for indifference, she distressed by his exhaustion, they conversed like two old acquaintances. They pretended to take up the conversation where they had left off last August. Having once waited so impatiently, they were now overcome by the same sadness and fear.

"I had always imagined the race of emigrants to be like the Vikings going off to conquer the New World," Stevenson went on in a livelier way. "The people whose wretchedness and filth I shared on the *Devonia* did not quite fit this picture ... Alcoholism is not pleasant, Fanny, and poverty does not exactly encourage self-transcendence ..."

She nodded her head: "I know." And to prevent him from changing the subject, she insisted: "And so?"

"So ... compared to the first-class passengers, the runaways, the failures, the desperate emigrants in steerage are still much more human and dignified ... I always thought one man was as good as another, and I have never been politically involved. Yet, for God-sake, when the elegant young ladies and their escorts from the upper deck came to take a look at us as if we were monkeys, I was appalled at the insults these people managed to convey by their very presence! They pretended to hide their contempt beneath a condescending smile, but I would willingly have given them a good thrashing ... Well, I suppose I learned a lot from this voyage. And your country, Fanny, is splendid beyond my wildest dreams. I don't regret having come," he insisted, as if to reassure himself. "It was now or never. I've cut the cord. Now I've got to rely on myself, I must stand alone. The road behind me I see clearly. As for the future ..."

She smiled hesitantly.

"Come what may," he repeated, "I have no regrets."

The anguish of this last statement seemed to touch Fanny, who let herself lean against him. "Nobody here is saying that you shouldn't have come ... Nobody!"

This time she was the one to put her lips on the young man's parched mouth. He held her little body, which no longer resisted. Love had finally caught up with them, but not for long. The door opened wide.

"There are too many months, too many minutes to catch up on," Belle said unpleasantly. "Hello, Louis. I did not even know that you were in America!"

Nellie and Sammy were swallowed up in her wake.

Fanny recovered her wits and her maternal severity to growl: "Where were you?"

"With my aunt," Belle answered in the same tone.

Blond and round, affecting not to remark her sister's disarray and Belle's aggressiveness, Nellie took the hand Stevenson held out to her.

"Fanny has told me so much about your talents ... It seems that you are the Walter Scott of our generation. I so love Walter Scott."

"And I, Miss Vandegrift, I've not been here more than an hour and I've heard nothing but praise for your charms. It seems that along with Walter Scott you are very partial to someone singing under your windows at night ..."

Nellie blushed and Belle could not help laughing. "I know," Belle teased, "I know where you got this information!"

"You stopped at Sanchez's saloon?" cried Fanny.

"I would have thought, Mama, that you were close enough to him to notice," Belle remarked ironically. "Louis, you smell of whiskey from thirty feet away!"

"My dear, I was so afraid of showing up in the state I was in that the first thing I did after twelve days on the train was to buoy myself up!"

"Precisely," Fanny cut in. "It is time to think of supper."

"There are six of us," Belle informed her. "I invited Joe. At this point, I think you will not object."

Mother and daughter exchanged a hostile look. Fanny chose to keep quiet. Sammy, delighted at finding his old friend once more, begged: "Tell us about your adventures! What are you going to do now? Will you stay long?"

He had come of course as The Amateur Emigrant, *but he wasn't there because he wished to study the manners and customs of the New World; he was there because he loved Fanny Osbourne,* Belle comments. *All of his talk was to her; Nellie, Sammy, and I hardly existed.*

Did Belle succumb to Louis's charm that evening? Two years earlier, Miss Osbourne had written to Rearden: *The other Stevenson is not handsome, no that he is not, but as soon as he opens his mouth, as soon as he speaks, I would rather listen to him talk than read the most interesting book I ever saw.*

*
**

The night of August 31, 1879, was a sleepless one at the Casa Bonifacio. On the first floor, in the big bed she shared with her aunt, Belle nursed her anger. So, her hypocrite of a mother had prevented her from loving Joe Strong while she was waiting for her own lover to arrive. This was the last week Belle would spend under this roof! She would soon flee with Joe. They would take their things to the Oakland cottage and seek protection with her father in San Francisco. She wouldn't even tell Nellie. Nellie insisted on regarding this ailing Scotsman as Fanny's protégé—"a literary friendship." How naive of her! When the scandal of Fanny's love affair would finally break, the Sanchez family would take a stand against Nellie's marriage to Adulfo.

That evening Fanny did not hear the murmurs of the two girls. Stretched out fully dressed on the patchwork quilt, she was thinking. And what she discovered in herself terrified her: "He is here . . . he is here! This ought to be happiness. And I feel nothing, I am dried up! I am hard and mean—Belle is right. I have the luck to know a man who loves me enough to cross the world, and yet I feel no more joy than this? A man I admire, a man I respect, the most generous, courageous person. His family has disinherited him because of me. And this is how I welcome him? He has traveled day and night, he hasn't taken the time to sleep once in a bed, he arrives ill, full of hope, and this is how I welcome him!"

She could not move. Her hands and feet were icy. "And he has no doubts! Wasn't this what I was wishing for? Someone who knows what he wants. He has come to encourage my separation from Sam. Wasn't that what I asked him to do? He's the only person in the world who cares about my life, the only one, and I treat him like this, the man who supports and protects me."

This time, she shifted around. Folding her knees, she sat in the middle of the bed. "Protects me? How could he protect me? He's poor and ill. Perhaps he's dying! Ah," she shivered, "it doesn't cost him much to offer me his hand and his future! A scab-covered hand and a nonexistent future . . . A talented boy, certainly. Yes, he has genius, I'm sure of it! But will we have time to prove it?

And what if he dies? What will become of Belle and Sammy? Suppose I divorce Sam and Louis dies . . . Rearden will have the last laugh! If Louis dies, what will I do?" She raised her face toward the canopy above her bed and, with her eyes wide open, lost herself in contemplation of the pompons and drapery. "After all, Sam is not such a bad father. He pays the rent on this house. The cottage in Oakland belongs to him. Louis is so poor now he's dying of hunger—how will he feed Sammy? Am I going to watch my son lose twenty pounds in a month? And that cough! That rash covering his hands, will it soon cover my child's hands too? My God, what should I do?"

She twisted around and slipped under the linen sheets, which she pulled up to her chin. "I owe Sam nothing, I'm sure of that. He has no claim to my loyalty. And when I think of his behavior during Hervey's illness . . ."

She pictured Sam, so blond and handsome, arriving tomorrow by train. But tonight even her anger seemed exhausted. Anger, love, all the feelings that had overwhelmed her in recent years.

At the age of forty was she finally self-contained, impervious to passions? That was the question: Should she play it safe and stay married to Sam, or gamble on glory by tying herself to Louis? "It's all the same," she sighed. "Sam is irresponsible, Louis is ill; one could disappear, the other might die . . ." Her indifference to the possibility of these disasters struck her. She called on her conscience one last time. "I am a monster. That poor boy has risked his life, his future, his past. I have lost everything, even any moral sense. If Louis hadn't defied his parents for my sake, he wouldn't be in such a state today. I'm the only person he has left in the world!"

She felt nothing, not even compassion, the sympathy that usually mobilized her energy, her old tenderness for victims.

Exasperated with herself, in a last outburst she lost her temper: "But I did not expect him so soon—he's landed on my doorstep without any warning! If only he had given me a little time, so I might at least have prepared Belle."

Two streets away, in the little room that Joe Strong rented for him at Señora Reese's house, Robert Louis Stevenson found no rest. The distrust on his landlady's face when she took the seven dollars payable in advance from his scab-covered hand brought home to him the effect he was having on women. Seven dollars, that left him without a cent. Impossible to stay here more than a week. He was thinking neither of Fanny's coldness, nor of Scotland, nor of the future. Nor was he thinking of his friends' predictions: "When you arrive in Monterey, Louis, what will you do?" But he was thinking of money. If only Henley would manage to sell the piece they had written together. If Colvin could only round up thirty dollars for *The Story of a Lie*. If only Baxter would scrape together the fifty dollars his publisher owed him. In Louis's mind he was still rolling across the Great Plains, his ears filled with the churning of the axle and the plaintive whistle of the locomotive.

*
**

I had looked forward eagerly to [my father's] visit, Sammy recounts, *and it was disconcerting to find him so preoccupied and with so little time to devote to me. He seemed forever to be talking with my mother in a seclusion I was not allowed to disturb. Once as I was studying my lessons in an adjoining room and felt that strangely disturbing quality in their subdued voices—reproaches on her side and a most affecting explanation on his of his financial straits at the time of my little brother's death—I suddenly overheard my mother say with an intensity that went through me like a knife: "Oh Sam, forgive me!"*

"Don't come near me! I beg of you, go away!"

Surprised, terrified, Robert Louis Stevenson stopped under the trellis that led to the Casa Bonifacio. What he was dreading had just happened: She was dismissing him. It took his breath away. With his hand on his stomach, he bent over in pain. His tight trousers accentuated his dreadful thinness. A skeleton that barely cast a shadow. His face was marked by anguish, the tension of the past weekend, the husband's presence in Monterey, the uncertainty over how he should behave—should he introduce himself to Sam or wait discreetly for the conclusion of negotiations? The oval of his face had lengthened, his mustache seemed finer and sparser.

"I beg of you, go away," she repeated.

Hysterical, with her blouse unbuttoned, she waved him off toward the bottom of the garden. This was the end of the adventure. He had her answer: She was rejecting him.

"You must leave right away! Nellie is ill, it's diphtheria! I've sent Sammy and Belle to live in the hotel. Their father has returned to San Francisco, he is paying for their room. The children mustn't live here while I am nursing her. Diphtheria is horribly contagious! It can be fatal. And in the state you're in, you'll catch it. The membranes have pushed into her throat. I must burn them every half-hour, day and night. If she were to die far from home, I would be responsible, I brought her here. When my sister is better, I'll send for you. I beg of you, don't come in. The diphtheria would kill you."

"But what about you?" he asked coming toward her.

"Me?" she jeered. "Me—I'm indestructible!"

Fifteen years later, on the eve of his own death, Robert Louis Stevenson described his wife to one of his friends: *Hellish energy relieved by fortnights of entire hibernation . . . Doctors everybody, will doctor you, cannot be doctored herself.*

*

Because he did not have enough money to stay in Monterey and understood that his physical presence was working to his disadvantage, and because he thought that visiting the country could only fuel his travel writing, Robert Louis Stevenson left town. *I am still thirty pound to the good,* he writes to Baxter on September 9. *You had better send me fifty of that hundred in circular letters or something to San Francisco. My news is nil. I know nothing, I go out camping, that is all I know. Today I leave, and shall likely be three weeks in camp. I shall send you a letter from there with more guts than this, and now say good-bye to you, having had the itch and a broken heart.*

He buried himself in adventure in the back country. Joe Strong, concerned with pleasing his new mother-in-law who was still unaware of their bond, provided Stevenson with a cart and two horses. The young men pushed on together to the last outpost of civilization, the last ranch before the untamed mountains. They were only three years apart and had many things in common. Each of them was inextricably enmeshed in emotional complications with mother and daughter; each reigned over a circle of his own and took his art seriously. Why not collaborate—a series of articles on the United States, signed "R.L.S." and illustrated by "J.D.S."? They would take up this idea again ten years later as they traveled together toward the archipelago of Samoa. But for the time being Stevenson was already riding ahead to explore the canyons of Carmel Valley on horseback.

The bourgeois Scot, the bohemian of Grez, was transforming himself into a lone cowboy. At their first encounter Fanny had embodied adventure, life in the fresh air and open spaces, and now she seemed to be keeping one of her promises: In her wake, Robert Louis Stevenson entered into the legend of the West. His friends, receiving his letters, would not understand the importance of the change. They could see no difference between Louis's solitary walks through the Cevennes and his wanderings through the California mountains. But the difference was his flirtation with death.

His head was spinning. He had a ringing in his ears, and his legs no longer held him in the saddle. The pebbles danced before his eyes. The reins slipped out of his hands and he collapsed. *For three days and three nights I stayed there, lying under a tree, in a kind of stupor,* he writes a month later to the poet Gosse. *My mind roamed the countryside, . . . By a miracle, a bear hunter came upon me . . . He found me very sick and took me to his ranch.*

Here is another curious start in my life, he tells Colvin. *I am living at an angora goat ranch in the Coast Line Mountains, 18 miles from Monterey. I was camping out, but got so sick that the two rancheros took me in and tended me. One is an old bear hunter, 72 years old, and a captain from the Mexican war; the other a pilgrim and one who was out with the bear flag and under Fremont when California was taken by the states.*

Trappers, pioneers, gold seekers: a far cry from the damp streetlamps of Edinburgh, those beacons in the night that beckoned the sick child behind the closed window to travel through the world.

East Oakland—mid-September 1879

The cottage door banged. Belle, who was emptying the contents of her dressing table into a traveling bag, jumped to attention. For a moment she was tempted to flee. Fanny was already standing at the threshold of the room. Her face was distorted with rage, her lips gray with dust, her mouth curved downward, her staring eyes lit with anger and madness. In pursuit of the fugitives, she must have made timely connections between Monterey and Oakland. Nor had Belle expected her to cross the last feet that separated them so quickly. With one hand Fanny grabbed her bag, and with the other administered the first slap in the face Belle had ever received. She lost her balance and stumbled against the little pedestal table, which rocked back and forth. Joe Strong, his arms full of his wife's dresses, rushed out of the dressing room.

"I won't allow it!" he yelled at his mother-in-law.

Her brief glance told him quite clearly what she thought of him—a nonentity. Joe Strong was not, however, unattractive in his traveling coat. Photographs from the period show him sprouting a big, waxed mustache, a trim beard, short coiffed hair. He is a bit dandified, perhaps, with something ostentatiously powerful in his pose. "A weakling," Fanny would say, "a slug, a leech."

Relaxed, sociable, Joe's friends found him endowed with real kindness and a true sense of camaraderie. "With the sole desire to amuse himself," his mother-in-law would be more precise. "I foresee only dramas and disasters with this kind of man. His is a false kindness. He will suck Belle dry and leave only skin and bones." She was forgetting the fact that Joe Strong had talent, more talent than all the Osbournes put together. Not only that, he knew how to sell himself. Few artists have enjoyed the favor he did with the new ruling class of San Francisco. They fought over his portraits, commissions rained down. Avid to please, Joe molded his art to the demand and rendered all the services asked of him. In his middle age, this marvelous compliance would become obsequiousness.

From small compromises to greater acts of cowardice, his penchant for facility, his passion for the sun and the bottle, would lead him on a slow descent into hell. He would collapse, body and soul. "Out of laziness, all this ruin out of laziness!" his mother-in-law would conclude.

"You, how dare you?" she asked, addressing only her daughter.

Belle looked at her warily, rubbing her cheek, and cried: "I am doing what I want . . . I'm twenty-one!"

"You were still a minor when this fool carried you off."

"I had my father's consent."

"Your father?" Fanny repeated. She had blanched and reeled under the blow.

"He knows everything, from the beginning," Belle announced triumphantly.

"He knew all along?"

"Everything! Joe asked him for my hand, and Papa gave him his blessing."

"Traitor!" Fanny exploded, though Belle did not know if the insult was addressed to her.

So during all their conversations of the past weekend, while Fanny had admitted her own love affair to him and begged his forgiveness, Sam had betrayed her again! He knew that their daughter was married and he had told her nothing. He had given his consent to this marriage without taking the trouble to discuss it with her.

"As usual, your father didn't think twice about it. He would do anything to look good, even sacrifice your future."

"He found us an apartment next to his office," Belle insisted, conscious of the effect of her words.

Her mother would never forgive her for seeking refuge against her with Sam, for confiding in him what she was hiding from her.

". . . Two big, high-ceilinged rooms with a kitchenette and a little bathroom," Joe Strong insisted, wanting to show that he would take care of Belle.

"If you should pay us a visit, we live at 7 New Montgomery Street . . . Come to see us when you like," added the girl, without knowing whether, by this phrase, she was hoping to make peace or tossing out a last gesture of defiance.

"Of all the worthless idiots, you take the cake!" Fanny grimaced. "You cannot imagine, my girl, what a weight you've taken off my back!"

Papa met us there after the painful interview with my mother. My dear father! When I remember him, it is always with his arms open wide to love and comfort me. He helped us arrange the rooms, invited us to dinner at Frank's, and when we parted, filled my hand bag with twenty-dollar gold pieces. Bless him!

*
**

"Once and for all you have to accept not being the center of the world. The idea that your poor husband could know secrets that you don't, that's what is driving you crazy!"

"You're mistaken, Rearden. I have never felt calmer. This marriage changes everything for me. The necessity of preserving the family's respectability was tormenting me. Settling Belle's future was my obsession. Her behavior frees me. And then, there's one less mouth to feed—not a negligible consideration."

They were walking on the endless beach of white sand, their feet stumbling over whale bones. Night was falling. She went on: "And stop saying 'your poor husband' when you mention Sam!"

"What do you want me to say, my dear?"

She shrugged her shoulders: "Sam wasn't much of a husband. We haven't even managed to talk to each other about our children."

"Belle's mystifications merely wound your female pride."

"And my feelings as a mother," she added, reflecting.

"If you like," he conceded. "But let's drop this nonsense. You did not ask me to take four trains and waste two days going back and forth to talk to me about your maternal woes. Just between us, you have raised your daughter so badly, she runs off with the first man to come along. When it comes down to it, she is just following your example."

"You do not know how right you are," she retorted sarcastically. "If I begged you to come—"

"It's because you want something from me . . . You only remember me when you need me. How can I be of use to you, my dear, what service can I render?"

"If you think that, go to hell!"

She left him and walked quickly back toward town. Rearden continued along the seashore. Half turning, she observed his figure, which time had thickened. Had she loved him? Stockier than before, with a graying mustache, Rearden was losing his hair. Yet he was no different. Would he ever change? As a young man he was charming, but age was turning him into an old curmudgeon. With his cut-velvet jacket whipped by the wind, his silk cravat blown against his face, he was rather touching. She retraced her steps, slipped her little hand under his arm, and begged: "Rearden, let's stop quarreling once and for all, what do you say?"

He pretended not to have heard her. With utter indifference he did not hold out his elbow and let her hand fall.

"Do you remember," she took up lightly, "do you remember that walk we took together? It was just before my departure for Europe . . ."

"Yes, so?"

"You made fun of my artistic pretensions. You warned me that I would never become a great painter . . . you were right!"

"Happy to hear you say so."

"But the young man I spoke to you about, you know, my Scottish friend, I would like you to read his books . . . I would like you to meet him. He never stops working! He has almost finished the story of his travels; I would like you to tell me what you think of it. It's good, it's very good, I think. No doubt you would have some suggestions about magazines where he might place his articles. During my sister's diphtheria, he camped out in the mountains. He has returned to Monterey. He nearly died. If he had died, Rearden, I would have lost—"

"What does it matter to me what you'd have lost! Who do you take me for, your father confessor?"

She said very quickly: "You must help me win custody of my son!"

"Good God, Mrs. Osbourne, what are you talking about?"

"I'm not asking anything from Sam, I'd leave him my dowry and the thousand dollars he owes my family . . . But I want my son, and the right to raise him in Europe."

Rearden had reddened. He was embarrassed and now hoped only to be rid of her. He quickened his step. "What do all your intrigues have to do with me?"

"I thought you were a lawyer, Rearden. I've given your name and handed in my request at the courthouse. I beg of you, take my case. I know what you're going to say," she went on, spilling out a torrent of words to prevent him from answering. "All your arguments I made to myself two days ago. Today, I don't know where I'm going. I don't even know whether the man I want to be with will live long enough to marry me. I am certain of only one thing: This man is worth the risk. Please, just agree to meet him and you will judge for yourself." She burst out in her tinkling laughter. "Then, Judge Rearden, if you like, you will marry us!"

He pushed her away. "I'm disgusted by your simperings, your

stupidity outrages me, and your vulgarity embarrasses me. I don't know how to respond to this utter nonsense, whether to laugh or cry! The ridicule will kill you."

"And you—you'll die of fear, Rearden." This time, Fanny stood her ground. "You may laugh," she cried in his face, "laugh to your heart's content. But you're a dead man and I am alive!"

Abruptly turning her back to the ocean, she left him standing there and climbed the dune to the pine forest. Against all expectation, he followed her.

"And I have found what your prudence will never give you!" she screamed into the wind that raised the sand and bent the cypress trees above her on the promontory. "Take your train home, go back to your books."

Behind her, Rearden lost his balance on the slope. Without waiting for him, she set off on the path that skirted the woods. At this height, the rumbling of the ocean became a roar. It rose ever more deafening, more disturbing. In the distance, the beam from the lighthouse swung across the huge drifts of fog advancing toward the coast. Between the trees, the foam of the great waves broke against the black rocks enclosing Monterey Bay.

"Take all the risks you want," Rearden thundered in conclusion. "But once and for all, do not mix me up in your affairs!"

She sighed and, suddenly softening, murmured: "Do you really believe I don't know the risks, as you call them? The difference in age, the lack of money, illness. Even if I become Mrs. Louis Stevenson one day, pleasure is over for me."

Rearden jeered. "I suppose you find that very grand, the sacrifice!"

She reflected a moment before replying quietly: "And the fear that paralyzes you, Rearden, I know what it's like. The fear of losing the only man in the world who cared for me . . . the fear of losing the most generous being on earth . . . I am in love, of course, but more than my love for him is my admiration, which grows each day. He gives good for evil, the air he breathes is so right, so pure, never polluted by malice. Even yours couldn't shake him! He would find a thousand excuses for you this evening. I have no choice, Rearden. I am afraid, but I have no choice. I accept the inevitable. My decision is made."

"Go ahead, commit suicide! Only have you thought what others will say?"

"What others? The goats in Monterey? The cows in San Francisco? Oh, I see—suppose the grasshoppers in Indiana should find out!"

She gave him a look he didn't quite know how to interpret. In the darkness, Rearden thought he saw her laughing.

*
**

In coming here I did the right thing, Louis congratulates himself in a letter he begs Baxter to keep private and confidential. *I have not only got Fanny patched up again and in health, but the effect of my arrival has straightened up everything.*

Fanny would no longer vacillate. She took up the challenge and did not back down. This nineteenth-century woman was willing to sacrifice everything at the age of forty for a dying man. Her only terror, a wracking anguish, was the thought of losing her maternal rights. That anguish would torment her to the end. Yet she charged ahead.

Hope had conquered fear.

*

I knew nothing of what all this meant until shortly afterward as I was taking a walk with Stevenson, Samuel Lloyd would recount forty years later. *He was silent and absorbed: I might not have been there at all for any attention he paid me. Ordinarily a walk with him was a great treat and a richly imaginative affair, for at a moment's notice I might find myself a pirate, or a redskin, or a young naval officer with secret despatches for a famous spy, or some other similar and tingling masquerade. But this walk had been thoroughly dull; we had remained ourselves, and not a breath of romance had touched us; and Luly's pace had been so fast, besides, that my little legs were tired.*

All at once he spoke, and here again was this strange, new intonation, so colorless and yet so troubling, that had recently affected the speech of all my elders. "I want to tell you something," he said. "You may not like it, but I hope you will. I am going to marry your mother."

I could not have uttered a word to save my life. I was stricken dumb. The question of whether I were pleased or not did not enter my mind at all. I walked on in a kind of stupefaction, with an uncontrollable impulse to cry—yet I did not cry—and was possessed of an agonizing feeling that I ought to speak, but I did not know how, nor what.

But all I know is that at last my hand crept into Luly's, and in that mutual pressure a rapturous sense of tenderness and contentment came flooding over me. It was thus we returned, still silent, still hand in hand, still giving each other little squeezes, and passed under the roses into the house.

*

As now arranged, there is to be a private divorce in January, Stevenson exults, *and yours truly will be a married man as soon thereafter as the law and decency permit. The only question is whether I shall be alive for the ceremony.*

The law, decency? Rearden let himself be caught. On a second trip to Monterey he met "Mrs. Osbourne's literary friend." They did not speak about money or love or the future. Just what did they say to each other? By the end of the conversation, the lawyer was astonished that a man of such intelligence, such culture, could be interested in this little woman from Indiana. In any case, if these people wanted to hang themselves from the same tree, that was their business. His business, henceforth, was to put the rope around their necks.

"That's the end of the bohemian life! Short hair, cigarettes, painting—all that nonsense is over! You are going to listen to me: You will reenter respectable society."

By the end of that night at the Casa Bonifacio, with Nellie out of danger and Belle married, Fanny had faced the thought that Louis might have died in the mountains, and she had suddenly became conscious of the power of their attachment. But if she imagined she was out of the woods because she no longer doubted her feelings, she was mistaken.

The subsequent days promised to plunge her into despair. For Mrs. Osbourne, the war of attrition had only just begun.

Rearden insisted she suspend her meetings with Robert Louis

Stevenson. He insisted that the lovers must not see each other until the end of the divorce proceedings, and God only knew how many months these would drag on. Louis would stay in Monterey, and she would go back to Sam's house.

"Don't ask me to do that!" she implored. "Now not, now that Louis ... that we are together again! If I leave him now, he is going to die!"

"Show a little common sense and a modicum of decency! You must go to Oakland, and you must go alone, to face your husband. He is distraught, he is indecisive ... Do not exasperate and humiliate him! If you flaunt your liaison, you lose your freedom and your son ... You have a bad reputation, my dear. Your indiscretions would justify taking Sammy from your custody. Consider what you've done, tearing your children away from their father to drag them off to Paris! And I know many people who would support such a decision. Belle doesn't make things easy for you. If you stay here in Monterey, if you go on with your 'literary friendship,' some of Sam's pals—the least refined, I grant you—some of them will be delighted to drag you through the gutter before you can make a fool of him. Do I make myself clear?"

*
**

I am now all alone in Monterey, Louis writes to Colvin.

Pride made R.L.S. sweeten the truth. Rolled up in a blanket on the floor, he was dying of hunger and spitting blood.

Once again, he would owe his life to the intervention of a stranger, Jules Simoneau, who ran a modest Monterey restaurant; seeing that Stevenson failed to appear two days in a row for his only meal, the man went and forced his door open. He found Louis delirious, took him home, tended him and saved his life.

A hundred and fifty miles away, cloistered behind the white picket fence of her cottage, Fanny felt powerless and tormented, yearning to battle with the death that threatened to take her love from her. From now on, wherever she was, in Edinburgh, Davos, Hyères, or Samoa, her gratitude to Simoneau prompted her to look out for his interests. As an old lady, she would give him a pension, pay for his burial, and build him a mausoleum.

His writing was suffering, Louis wrote to Henley. For the time being he was hanging on as best he could. It was a hard fight, and he felt it was probably pretty worthless. But if Henley disliked his *Travels with a Donkey* so much, why hadn't he told Louis when it came out instead of hitting him with it just when his health was failing, along with his finances and his hopes?

These were the pathetic questionings of a man abandoned by his peers.

In other times and places, Fanny would remember their cruelty. She would also remember the generosity of the poorest and simplest people, the Portuguese sailor, the two Italian fishermen, the Mexican cowboy who went out of their way to save this Scottish writer who meant nothing to them. Robert Louis Stevenson's magnetism attracted not only London intellectuals, those "fiends disguised as friends," as his wife would say. They had used Stevenson, she would claim, for their own ends and their own glory.

Stevenson's biographers do indeed debate the roles played by the journalist William Ernest Henley, Professor Colvin, the poet Edmund Gosse, and many others. The "pro-Fanny" biographers accuse them of self-interest and financial indiscretion. The others, the "anti-Fanny" forces, accuse her of jealousy and coarseness toward these men devoted to furthering her husband's career.

Despite his outcries, his criticism and gossiping, Henley continually struggled to place Louis's writings. He sold Stevenson's manuscripts advantageously. Had he been willing to accept a percentage of the rights—as Louis repeatedly proposed—their relations would likely have been less problematic. But how could Henley officially be his friend's "agent"? Less formal arrangements seemed more natural: Robert Louis Stevenson dug into his own pocket and Henley helped himself.

This is a strange constant in Stevenson's relationships: Whoever draws close to him attempts to take over the man and the work. The kind of love he elicits seems inevitably transformed into some inordinate passion. The simplicity of his character is legendary—a legend orchestrated by Fanny, who wanted to see him as completely pure. And certainly he was pure, but complex as well.

Pitying his physical infirmities, admiring his firmness of soul, his

prodigious generosity and no less prodigious narcissism, the slightest acquaintance would become intimately attached to him. His life
and his reputation have been affected by this. A century after his
death he continues to belong to the readers he has touched. His
admirers regard R.L.S. as a private preserve, and their emotional
reaction has resulted in his work's double fate: both famous and
half-forgotten.

London—The Savile Club—winter 1879

"We must cut him off! He mustn't receive another penny, no
one here must publish a single line of his. He must finally be made
to understand how his writings from America affect us!" Henley
thundered, letting himself sink from his full height into an armchair
that groaned beneath his weight.

With his impressive stature and stentorian voice, he shouted
through the wainscotted dining room of the Savile Club. Beyond
the vast windows, between the billowing curtains, stood the shadowy alignment of columns on Savile Row, the grillwork and display
windows that glistened like metal plates in the London night. This
protected ambiance, the clinking of carafes and glasses, this exclusively male cacophony had been created by a group of intellectuals
as a meeting place for brilliant talkers and men of letters, without
regard for wealth or social status. The dues for the Savile Club
remained as low as possible to encourage the membership of young
men from every social background; but the club was becoming
bourgeois. The traditional dining table, at which members were
accustomed to take their meals for a fixed price and at specified
hours, was already a thing of the past. It was still the heart of the
dining room, but the gentlemen could also choose to dine in dress
coats after the theater, in groups of two or six. The bouquets of
roses, the silver, the ballet of waiters spoke clearly of abundance.

Knowing each of the eccentricities and all the demands of the
members, the butler arranged Mr. Henley's crutches under the
pedestal table and set a flask of whiskey at his right. During supper,
the journalist used to drink it neat, every glass making him louder,
more lyrical, and more voluble. By dessert, his ideas crackled in an
explosion of words, a conflagration of wit, almost genius. Henley
was fascinating, as susceptible as an old woman, and formidable.

With his red beard trimmed like Rodin's and his amputated leg, which he affected not to mind, he haunted the theaters, the publishing houses, and bars, borrowing from his brother, the Shakespearean actor Teddy Henley, a real sense of the theatrical and a flair for effect. Unfortunately, the plays he persisted in writing were not up to the standard of either his poetry or his reviews.

". . . The first part of *The Amateur Emigrant* I received yesterday is utterly worthless, badly written and devoid of interest . . . Who cares about his stories of the United States? To hell with the American fawn!"

Professor Sydney Colvin and the poet Edmund Gosse sighed in agreement. All three men were of modest origins but belonged to social classes that usually do not mix. But they had in common a passion for literature and an equally passionate sympathy for Robert Louis Stevenson. Each one boasted of discovering the young Scotsman and playing a role in his career.

Colvin had met him first. He had known him five years earlier through their go-between, Mrs. Sitwell, who was close to one of Louis's female cousins. Colvin had introduced him to his circle of friends, even here at the Savile Club, where he was one of the founding members. Stevenson in turn had introduced him to Henley, to whom he had been introduced by the editor of the *Cornhill* magazine. Louis turned out to be the most "clubable" of men, and attached himself, around this same table, to Edmund Gosse, who haunted the club on a regular basis and could always be found in the smoking room or the library.

Unlike the friendships of Louis's childhood, these three men were English, they were over thirty, and published something every year. Sydney Colvin wrote papers and gave lectures. Henley held court in the publishing houses. Edmund Gosse, an intimate of the Pre-Raphaelites, wrote volumes of poetry but made his living as a translator for the ministry of commerce.

"I don't know how to answer him," sighed Colvin. "He has stopped progressing, he is in decline . . ."

Precise, polished, precious, Professor Colvin provided an almost comical contrast to the journalist Henley. He was as finicky as Henley could be slovenly. Colvin had intelligence without genius, but he was endowed with a tact, a finesse that his noisier colleague lacked. Furthermore, he knew how to be cruel, and his understatement cut more deeply than Henley's hyperbole.

"What I have read," he murmured, clasping his hands, "does not seem to me what he has done best. But he is very ill . . . his physical weakness is affecting his writing. That worries me. He is very low."

"The last time I saw him," Gosse intervened, "on the eve of his departure, I bet sixpence with myself that we should never see his face again."

Less intimate with Stevenson than the other two, Gosse could allow himself to be more indulgent.

"Lewis must return! . . . Lewis must understand that nothing good will come of staying with those savages! . . ." cried Henley, stubbornly insisting on calling the absent Stevenson by the name he was christened with.

Stevenson's parents had Frenchified his name long ago, and no one wrote anything but Louis; this use of "Lewis," however, was proof of their intimacy. Long after Robert Louis Stevenson's death, Henley would stubbornly ignore any other spelling. "Lewis . . . the Lewis I knew . . ." he would repeat nostalgically.

"Louis is much too ill to hear the sad truth about his writing," Colvin whispered.

"On the contrary!" Henley cut in, "Don't delay because he is ill. He absolutely must be made to see that England and a quiet life are what he wants and must have if he means to make—I won't say a reputation—but money in literature. Come back he must, the sooner the better. Married or unmarried—*je m'en fiche*. I don't believe that our letters will have any effect at all in preventing his marriage. He has gone too far to retract. He has acted and gushed and excited himself, playing the knight in shining armor. All we can hope is to make him get through his book quickly and come back quickly. Between us, if he is as ill as he claims, that woman is a damn slut for abandoning him in that hole!"

"Do you think that she's after his family's money, Colvin?" inquired Edmund Gosse, who had himself made an advantageous marriage.

With his thick ash-blond hair, which he wore combed back and parted in the middle, his little round, gold-framed glasses and his dandified elegance, Gosse's single passionate affair had been with a popular sculptor. Without being openly homosexual, his masculine friendships, and his literary affinity with Henry James would soon raise a good deal of gossip.

"The vulgarity of the Americans is in vogue these days," he resumed. "A fashion that won't last long . . . The girls of Boston or Philadelphia have their fortunes and their youth, at least! This woman must be a dreadful adventuress . . ."

"I long hoped that she would be charitable enough," Henley cut in, "generous enough to renounce Lewis. She would have shown herself worthy of him had she let him go his own way. But this woman does not have that kind of generosity, let's not speak of her anymore . . . but I think he should know that Monterey will never produce anything worth a damn!"

Monterey—East Oakland—December 18, 1879–March 18, 1880

Father desperately ill. Come home at once, Margaret Stevenson wired on Christmas Eve.

Fanny seriously ill too. I won't desert my wife, Robert Louis Stevenson wired back. His wife? In the moral sense only.

For Osbourne has us by the hair, he writes to Baxter. *He is trying to find out how much I am worth. On some days, he demands money, on others he claims respect.*

They continued to struggle, and Robert Louis Stevenson grew weaker. He was down with malaria, probably contracted crossing the Great Plains. In addition to the "fevers," he was suffering from a pleurisy that was tearing his lungs, an eczema that made him itch horribly, and toothaches that would have driven the most Spartan man mad. Plus malnutrition, solitude, and anguish. He had become a skeleton held together with a little flesh and blood.

As for Fanny, with Sam's hesitations, Belle's furious ranting against her parents' divorce, Louis's absence and her fear of hearing he was dead each day, she once again plunged into depression. She suffered from memory loss, delirium, dizziness, and now endless stupors, which her sister Nellie could hardly pull her out of.

"This is emotional blackmail!" Rearden fumed, "melodrama! A hysterical fuss! You want your lover to come to San Francisco? You're setting yourself up for the torments of Tantalus! I warn you, Stevenson will not set foot in East Oakland. Even if he were at death's door, I forbid you to come near him until you are legally divorced. If someone sees you together, the agreement we have just wrung from Sam will be annulled. Your husband is behaving graciously. He accepts my attempt to arrange a divorce by mutual consent, on the sole condition that you respect the proprieties ... that's the least you can do. Even if you are free by the spring, there can be no question of remarrying before a year is up! Do I have your word?"

"And Sammy?"

"Your husband will see to his needs ... He is a generous man, whose open-handedness we all admire. You must live up to his standard!"

*

Bad conscience. Added to their troubles was an acute feeling of guilt that would rob them of their pride in loving each other, of their happiness together. The roles had been reversed. Sam played the generous lord and gallant knight, Louis was cast as the villain and the unworthy son. In Edinburgh, his father lay dying, perhaps, a father whose only beloved son had just refused him even the solace of reconciliation. "It would take me so long to get home," Stevenson reasoned, "that my father would be either dead or cured by the time I arrive ... If I return, what will happen to Fanny?"

A painful choice.

I pass henceforth as the greatest egotist on earth.

If Fanny rarely examined her conscience, Louis, who did so constantly, was in torment: *It is so difficult to behave well; and in that matter, I get more dissatisfied with myself.*

And how could Louis calmly accept the fact that his enemy was gentleman enough to support the woman and child he was so graciously allowing to leave? This moral crisis was, if possible, worsening his physical collapse. Stevenson was tormented by the anguishing thought that Osbourne was perhaps his superior. Meanwhile, he discovered the amazing number of similarities that bound him to his rival. Was Sam Louis's alter ego?

Two years earlier, Belle had made an innocent remark to her mother: "I had forgotten how much Papa loves children," she had said, watching him rowing at Grez. "He loves them as much as Louis . . . Don't you think they resemble each other?" All her life Fanny would refuse to acknowledge that her two husbands had anything in common. She denied the evidence.

Both men were gifted raconteurs and played the tin whistle; they had a way with children, a talent for telling them fireside tales; they loved the same woman, cultivated the same sense of humor, and even professed the same respect for the same quality, kindness. They both knew how to charm. Fanny was well placed to know of their amorous conquests, and especially the love of their friends. Masculine friendship held as central a place in Sam's life and in his wanderings as literary friendships did in Louis's. Their choices, their rebellions, their philosophies were similar. As young men they both rebelled against the strict religiosity of a father. They both studied law, they both chose adventure. And they both fought against intolerance.

Chinatown was burned last night . . . writes Sam, *the white people stood by and looked on and made not the least exertion in the world to help the poor devils get out their goods.*

And is it Sam or Louis who goes on: *Of all the stupid ill-feelings the sentiment of my fellow Caucasians toward our companions in the Chinese car was the most stupid, and the worst.*

Is it Sam or Louis who would write to young Sammy: *Whatever the bent of your feeling may be now, remember, that it is the part of wisdom to hear both sides: that it is only the half baked who are extremist.* Is it Louis or Sam who would advise the boastful child: *It is well for you to cherish a pride in the scenery of your own country, but let us be just and concede that there are things abroad that are just as good, and often better.*

How could Louis despise someone so close, how could he wound Sam without hurting himself? This theme of the double, of role reversal, of false appearances will haunt all of Robert Louis Stevenson's work. There is not a novel in which the hero's kindness doesn't resemble the egotism of the monster, in which the villain does not become strangely sympathetic to the reader. Shifting contrasts, the play of light and shadow, the soul of his characters moves in waters that are never as pure or as murky as the narrator would have us believe.

San Francisco—end of December 1879—end of March 1880

Was the divorce final in mid-January? A few weeks earlier? A month later? This remains a mystery. The San Francisco earthquake and fire of 1906 destroyed the city and burned all the civic records. No one knows the exact date of the divorce of Samuel Osbourne and Frances Matilda Vandegrift. Neither of them would inform their families. A hidden divorce. Just as Belle continued to live at home like a good girl for nearly a month after she was legally married, so Fanny as a divorcée would remain "Sam's wife" for the Vandegrifts and her neighbors until her distant remarriage.

This was the end of an epoch. The next one began under terrible auspices.

Stevenson's effort to meet his own needs, his determination to stand alone without paternal aid was to end in failure during the winter of 1880. He could not earn a living. Dailies, bi-weeklies, monthlies, annuals, he combed all the publishing houses in the futile search for a job. Here and there he managed to place a poem or an article, but this hardly paid his rent. If the world refused to employ his intellectual capacities, what would become of him? *Louis is a man without hands,* Fanny would say with a smile. If he hammered a nail, he crushed his finger; if he tried to gather wood for a fire, he found only damp twigs or dragged in enormous logs that wouldn't burn. He was incapable of doing addition or subtraction. He forgot to record his checks, he misplaced everything.

Stevenson was a seductive soul, but in practical life he was a disaster. In East Oakland, Fanny was painting continuously. She even tried to write. Six months earlier she had managed to place one of her illustrated stories in a children's magazine—she boasted in a letter to Rearden of making 350 dollars on her own. Was this bluff or exaggeration? The miracle would not be repeated, her works would not bring her another penny. This being the case, how could they stay in California? They would have to seek their fortunes elsewhere. But where? Should they return to Edinburgh defeated? What would become of Sammy, of his education, if London and San Francisco continued to reject Louis's work? Where would they live? Once more, Rearden's dire predictions threatened to come true.

It was with a feeling of compromised pride that Fanny finally introduced her lover—that young prodigy who would henceforth be referred to as "the fiancé"—to her dear and formidable confidante Dora Williams. Compared to Sam, he was no great shakes: *In his shabby velvet coat, the unbecoming crocheted tie his mother had made him, he surely looked singular,* Dora Williams, who was recuperating from an illness at the time, would recall. *But there was a certain air about him that made you know unmistakably that he was a gentleman. He came again the next day for something he had left behind and, finding me better, he remained awhile and we entered into conversation, and I may add, a lifelong friendship. . . . There was an instant charm of manner which seemed to come from earnestness and went straight to the heart. My remembrance of the conversation is that we rashly plunged into matters of national agreement and disagreement as between our respective countries; things coming to the surface generally whenever one of the Queen's subjects (be he English or Scotch especially) talks with an American. His point of view struck me as being at once new, broad, and finely humane, the point of view of a man capable of doing justice without either assumption or flattery.*

While we were earnestly talking and Stevenson had for the moment paused in his walk and was leaning his slight figure on the mantelpiece, my husband came in, and glanced at him very curiously. I hastened to introduce them to each other. He afterward told me he thought some tramp had got into the room and I could not get him out, so peculiar and foreign was the appearance of my visitor. Stevenson often laughed at the joke about his appearance.

From that hour, however, they became fast friends . . . He often came to cheer my invalidism and to talk over the ever new theme of The Marriage, *as with a lover's fond egotism he called the approaching event.*

Loiterers on Kearny Street in busy downtown in San Francisco simply observed, a few days before Christmas 1879, a cadaverous man who looked as though he had just come out of the hospital.

Nearby, at 608 Bush Street, a plaque nailed up in 1972 notes Robert Louis Stevenson's passage. Here, we read, Stevenson wrote "essays, poems, an autobiography, fiction." All in three months! It was this impressive list of works, torments, and privations, that would result in the infirmity ever afterward responsible for his many changes of address. *He was skeleton thin, and you could see his teeth in the hollows of his cheeks. His long, graceful hands seemed transparent. All the buttons on his coat were missing,* his landlady, Mrs. Carson, said in response to numerous journalists who came to interview her at the beginning of the century. *I was quite leery of him and did not want to take him as a lodger. He must have read something of this in my face, for he smiled and looked at me with such distress and so kindly that I could not refuse to show him the lodging. It was a large room with two windows, nothing luxurious. It was the table that seemed to please him, and the fireplace.* It had been raining incessantly in San Francisco since November. A searing wind blew off the sea. The newspapers spread the alarm for respiratory patients. The stranger went away without engaging the room but came back toward evening and said he would take it. With only a valise and a knapsack, he moved in for the winter. *And afterward,* Mrs. Carson said, *when I came to know him, I loved him like my own child.*

. . . I must say that he was very discreet . . . He never received visitors. He spent Christmas alone, and I don't think he spoke to anyone at all during the holidays . . . At the end of January a lady came to see him two or three times a week. They would go out to stroll around town. He used to take her to the less respectable neighborhoods, to Chinatown, to all the picturesque places where he loved to see the throngs of people hurrying by . . . Sometimes he would take another woman, her sister I think, and they would dine in some cheap restaurant. They usually saw each other in the evenings . . . Our family, the other tenants in our fourteen-room house, and the Bush Street neighbors all came to know his strict schedule, which varied little from day to day.

When I'd go up to his room in the morning to build the fire, he was always in bed writing—seems as though he was always writing, and I'd want to be talking to him, for when anything came into my head I wanted to tell it to him; he could always understand. So I'd be fussing around the room, talking to him, when I'd think maybe I'd be disturbing him. But he'd say, "No, go on, Mrs. Carson, I can write and talk to you at the same time."

On days when he wasn't feeling well it might be as late as nine-

thirty when he came downstairs and opened the front door on his way to a ten-cent breakfast. He would come back and go to work at his authoring until around two o'clock, when he would go out to walk God knows where, unless he tried to find some wood in the courtyard for his fire, and then he would work again until evening. He would go out to dine around six o'clock, but the truth is, he saved his pennies by skipping meals. He was living on forty-five cents a day, forty-five cents to feed himself—you couldn't even buy two bottles of milk for that price! The poor boy, I saw him so weakened by hunger that sometimes he couldn't even get out of his bed. Wrapped up in his muffler, propped up on his pillows, he kept on writing. When I would ask him what he was working on, he would answer, "Oh, things." It seems that many great men have known times of poverty like this. Many writers have worked in attic rooms, fasting and freezing. But I think all the same that few were as close to literally dying of hunger. In February he weighed a hundred pounds ... Still, when my four-year-old son Robbie, who adored him, caught pneumonia, it was Mr. Stevenson, my lodger on the second floor, who fought to save him, leaving aside his writing for more than a week to care for my little boy day and night ... Thanks to his efforts, Robbie survived. But he collapsed! This time, the doctor said he was lost. This was in the month of March. The woman whom I had seen many times crossed the Bay each day in the storm. She would arrive soaked to the bone and spend the day at his bedside, leaving him only quite late. She took her ferry back across the heaving sea, but at dawn I found her there again. Against the advice of the doctor who did not want the sick man moved, she took him back with her one day on the ferry and installed him in a hotel in East Oakland. From what I learned later, she had been prevented from caring for him in her house, which still belonged to her ex-husband. But how could they pay for a hotel? She didn't have a penny. Shortly after the divorce, it seems that the father of her children had lost the job he'd had with the court in San Francisco.

Dora Williams took up the thread ten years later to a journalist from the *Indianapolis Journal. Osbourne was a noted storyteller and had always a pleasant way about him that made him generally liked; but finally people found out that he was far from pleasant at home. He had 5,000 dollars a year as I say, but he spent it on anybody's family but his own ... Osbourne said that he would support the boy*

[Sammy], *and Mr. Stevenson sent him papers to make Osbourne settle an allowance upon him. But Osbourne did nothing about it in the end, so Stevenson assumed the guardianship of the boy.*

If Louis could barely manage to survive alone on forty-five cents a day, how could he assume responsibility for a house, the education of a child, and medical care? Fanny's worries knew no bounds.

"Marry him immediately," counseled Dora. "Marry him on his stretcher. Let him die as your husband!"

Joyous prospects, which two doctors—one from Oakland, the other from San Francisco—seriously envisaged.

The terrible Christmas of 1879, spent in fasting and solitude, had marked the first stage—the divorce. With Easter a new period began that would end at the top of a mountain overlooking the waters of the South Seas. In April 1880, at Tubb's Hotel in East Oakland, Robert Louis Stevenson suffered a hemorrhage. This was the first. After pleurisy and malaria, here it was, the illness everyone had feared. In twenty years, none of the numerous practitioners called to his bedside had pronounced the cause of his "weak lungs" with any certainty. This time they were specific. Doctor Bamford diagnosed galloping consumption. Fanny thought all was lost. Louis wrote to Colvin that even if the doctor were to give him a year to live, even if he hesitated to give him a month, he had to keep fighting and to see what could be accomplished in a week.

During this week battling his illness, during the weeks of April and all the months to come, Louis and Fanny would win a reprieve of fourteen years.

*

Come what may—Rearden, neighbors, family, and convention— she braved them all. Fanny moved Louis to Sam's house. By this gesture she alienated the sympathy of her last accomplice, Nellie, whose marriage to Adulfo Sanchez she compromised. Nonetheless, she set up her lover's bed in the parlor, and carried her own mattress downstairs to be with him.

And she alone tended him. He spit blood, he vomited, he suffered from diarrhea. Cold sweats soaked his sheets. Cramps locked his jaws. He was wracked by coughing fits. He lost the strength to see or speak. She moistened his lips, bathed his temples, she no longer knew whether she was waking or sleeping . . . Hervey! She would not lose her child a second time. She carried him, changed him, soothed him. Back and forth she went, from kitchen to bed. She would repeat these gestures, begun that spring, day and night for the rest of their life together.

East Oakland—April–May 1880

Leaving the pantry, her arms laden with a heavy tray, she already saw him in her mind, Louis's face as the young man she had known, that face which had changed so much during these last weeks. Was this death approaching? Was it the final triumph of life that gave him that strange expression of calm and maturity? Or was this man, now concerned with the fate of racial minorities and the unemployed, this man who in his delirium enumerated the symptoms of hunger one by one, was he no longer the gentleman from Edinburgh? What did he have in common with the bohemian of former times, whose taste and humor ran toward slumming in the lower depths? Or was this a revelation of inner worlds she didn't quite understand?

Barefoot in her long white nightgown, she entered the veranda and walked past the closed windows of the house. Above her, Nellie was sleeping behind the tangle of climbing roses that clung to the shutters of Belle's old apartment. Sammy, home from boarding school for the Easter vacation, was in the room he had formerly shared with Hervey, the big nursery on the first floor. She had settled Louis in the huge room on the ground floor, the only one that opened directly onto the garden. Every morning she entertained the dream of taking him out there . . . Yes, she would settle him there beginning tomorrow, weather permitting. After the exceptional harshness of this winter, a rainy spring had begun. Last Sunday, Easter Sunday, she had still seen patches of snow on Mount Tamalpais. The clock in the hall had just struck midnight. Beneath her feet, the wood was damp. The petals of the roses clinging to the balustrades spilled over in the form of an urn, dripping rosewater on the steps. The sea breeze swept between the railings and made the porch swing creak. Along the horizon the rays from the lighthouse pitched on the sea, and above them, in

the distance, in clusters of golden drops, the gaslights were extin-
guished on the hills of San Francisco. Unreal—that was the impression she'd had in these last days. Since Louis's move to the cottage,
she was living someone else's life. No, Louis did not seem to have
aged. This change in him during his illness was not because of his
thinness, or his extreme weakness, or the necessity of remaining
absolutely immobile when for him, speaking had always meant
walking back and forth or running. But what did it mean, this
transformation in his gaze? Could she enjoy it? Should she worry
all over again? She remembered the weak sound of his voice, she
heard the words he had pronounced the evening before, the words
she had spoken to him. She imagined other words, words she would
use when he got well, and the meals, the sumptuous meals she
would prepare for him! This past winter, when he was living in
San Francisco, when he was suffering from hunger on a bench in
Portsmouth Square, hadn't he told her of the feasts he'd enjoyed in
his dreams? She would make those feasts come true! This evening,
tomorrow, she would know how to whet his appetite—if only it
would return!

Still laden with her tray, she pushed the screen door open with
her foot. He was sitting in his camp bed facing the French doors,
leaning against the pillows, his head thrown back and his eyes
closed. He was dozing. She stopped a moment on the threshold
and looked at him. His thin mustache had grown so long that a
shadow shaped like a horseshoe framed his pinched lips. His fingers, white and nearly transparent, dreadfully long and thin, held
the sheets to his chest. His slightly retracted ring finger gave the
whole hand the narrow, tapering form of a shell. She noticed a
swift, nearly imperceptible shudder cross one of his cheeks. He
was not sleeping, he was fighting some pain . . . Where did it hurt?
She quickly approached the bed. Above Louis hung the photograph
of Jacob Vandegrift in the gold frame John Lloyd had given her.
He opened his eyes and followed her with his gaze. What was he
thinking? She rested the tray on the bedside table, and he slowly
turned his head toward her. Did this new slowness mean that he
was taking the whole parlor into his field of vision, all the objects?
Was he looking at the portrait of Sam between the two windows?
The caricatures of Sam dressed like a miner? The stone that represented Sam's first silver find? The drawings of the camp at Austin,
the watercolor of Virginia City? Was this the gaze of a convalescent,

lingering on things and assessing another man's twenty-five years of married life? She approached him softly and wiped her hand across her forehead. If only the anguish, the pity, the compassion, the suffering of others were not so exhausting. She tried to smile as she caught his gaze. He was going to speak. The voice, that warm voice, was still the same.

"I was listening to the rustle of your skirt, your steps outside . . . your cold little feet coming toward me, those sounds so full of promise." He sighed, took her hand, and placed it against his unshaven cheek. "Please forgive me," he said, his eyes burning. Full of new anxiety, he was staring at her. She wanted to escape.

"Good Lord, for what?" she asked lightly. She had already turned toward the little table. "A midnight supper! A good chicken broth like they used to make at the *cremerie* on rue Ravignan."

"The terrible thing," he went on, clinging to her hand, "is that you are going to tie yourself forever to a man who is incapable of taking care of himself!"

"I put asparagus tips in it . . . not those thick white ones . . . the little green ones."

". . . to a man who will never be able to take care of you!"

She took the tray with both hands and put it with the steaming plate on his knees. "That's my lot, I'm used to it. No one has ever taken care of me. You know, when I was little, it bothered me. I didn't want to be like the oak tree standing all alone. I wanted something to lean on, some support—"

"And I," he cut in bitterly, "I'm hopeless, I belong to a race of parasites! Yes, I always end up standing on my own two legs, but until now the feet belonged to my father. And now these feet are yours!"

She shrugged her shoulders. "Nonsense! Do you want me to tell you why you love me? Because I'm not as strong as I seem. If I really were an oak or some magnificent tree, I'm not sure you would have followed me here. What you like most about me is my weak, morbid side, and you're the only one who sees it. And you," she went on, "beneath your fragile appearance, you're a rock! You know that, too. She held a spoonful of soup out to him and he took it. "The asparagus have the strength and flavor of the earth!"

"All right," he agreed, bringing a little tip sensually to his mouth.

Teasing her, he closed his eyes and murmured, "All right, I feel it, yes I feel it, the strength of the earth!"

"Go on, pull my leg!"

"And I took my betrothed for an artist, for a woman of letters, for an intellectual . . . Deep down, Madam and sweetheart, you are nothing but a peasant!"

"Very true . . . and when I plant a seed, I plant my heart with it . . . And I even feel closer to God when I see my little green tender leaves sprouting . . ."

He listened to her avidly. Fanny's pleasures, Fanny's secrets, Fanny's needs—what did he really know about her? His gaze rested on the tiny fist plumping his pillow, a dark little patch the color of honey against the whiteness of the linen, that adept hand with such short, tapered fingers. One of those boyish fingers would soon wear his wedding ring.

"It's true, it's true," she went on in a livelier way, "just put me in a pea patch and I'm filled with happiness seeing my own little peas. And when my roses bloom on the veranda, I feel almost as joyful as when you read me one of your poems."

"I cannot swallow . . . Forgive me, I cannot."

She seemed so disappointed that he cried: "Don't worry, I don't want to die, and for one simple reason: I haven't done anything to warrant an honorable exit. I will live, Fanny, and I'm no longer afraid for my work. My ideas are changing. I have been telling you that for a long time. I'm just in search of my new vein . . . I'll find it. I know I shall do better work than ever before, despite what they all say—Colvin, Henley . . ."

"There are just jealous of your talent, they know they could never create."

"Create." They were both caught up in the same delirium, the same vision, the same faith. "But mind you, it won't be like my other work. My sympathies and interests have changed. I don't even know if I'm the same man since I've lived with you, or if my friends and family would still recognize me. And perhaps I don't really know them anymore. . . . Yet I do love my father—he's the person I love most in the world along with you. But when I rode those trains across the country to find you, I was uprooted from my past . . . I'll write no more travel stories, nothing picturesque or beautiful. Only the moral and the tragic interest me now, only people and human drama."

*
**

They were no longer separated by San Francisco Bay. Their mattresses lay side by side, and they spent every night spinning out projects. Yet they did not speak about their passion, or about happiness or the future. She wrote down what he dictated, he corrected it, and she proofread.

From now on Robert Louis Stevenson would not compose a single line, a paragraph, a page, or a book that he had not submitted to Fanny's scrutiny.

At certain hours of the day they both felt the same fatigue, and said to each other: "How sweet life is when you are not suffering, when you are working." Life gave him pleasure when Fanny opened the shutters onto the veranda, when she came in from the garden, her hair and skin permeated with the warm odors of springtime. A bee sometimes strayed into the room, and its buzzing spoke to him of Fanny's skirts and the sun-soaked roses. At these moments he dozed, and his dreams took him back to Grez. Fanny's face caught the reflection of the river, a bright light dancing in small golden patches on her neck, on her mouth, in her eyes. In his dreams he became that patch of light and settled in the corner of her lips. Fanny, untiring and tender, never spoke words of love, but when she helped him up, he leaned on her with all his weight, on that little brown body he wanted to embrace. Would he ever recover the strength to be a man? How could he ask for forgiveness for this physical weakness?

Yet there was none of the depressing atmosphere of sickness, Nellie reports, *he refused to be the regulation sick man. Every day he worked for a few hours at least, while I acted as amanuensis in order to save him the physical labour of writing. In this way the first rough draft of* Prince Otto *was written . . . While engaged in dictating, he had a habit of walking up and down the room, his pace growing faster and faster as his enthusiasm rose. We feared that this was not very good for him, so we quietly devised a scheme to prevent it, without his knowledge, by hemming him in with tables and chairs, so that each time he sprang up to walk he sank back discouraged at the sight of the obstructions. When I recall the sleep-*

less care with which Mrs. Stevenson watched over him at that critical point in his life, it seems to me that it is not too much to say that the world owes it to her that he lived to produce his best works.

*
**

"Read," he fidgeted. "I am asking you to read! Go on, I tell you, whatever my mother writes, I want to hear it!"

When Robert Louis Stevenson spoke in this tone of voice, when he gave an order, it was better to comply. Fearing an explosion, she sighed and reopened the envelope.

We cannot understand why you have never attended to our request for information as to your plans, she deciphered in a neutral tone, lowering her voice almost to a murmur. *I must repeat again what we have said over and over before: that we can tell nothing because we know nothing. We do not even know the names of any of your friends in San Francisco. So for any favour give us a story to tell . . . You have behaved like a fool ever since you left us, running risks which you were not fit for and you have surprised and disappointed me much for I had thought you had learned to take care of yourself.*

"I cannot reach them," Louis cut in with an impatient gesture. "They do not understand . . . They will never understand what I am trying to do with my life . . . Go on," he ordered.

Drink champagne as a tonic.

A this line, they both burst out laughing. "They just don't get the point!" Louis scoffed.

"But we must tell them the truth!" she urged. "They think you have put yourself in this state deliberately, that you are living in artificial poverty."

"I have been trying to tell them what I felt for twenty years! They don't listen to me, they don't see me as I am. It doesn't do any good to shout and carry on, they don't know me . . . Can people love each other so much and understand each other so little?" he sighed. "They don't give me a chance!"

Indeed, there were terrible misunderstandings between them. Henry James was probably the only one to denounce this lack of awareness on the part of the family: *My visit was a bit tarnished by the rather heavy presence of the parents,* he would write to Sydney Colvin eight years later. *They stay with him too long ... I do not understand how they fail to notice how much they tire him!*

Lack of awareness, yes, but they were also misunderstood. They had twice sent him money orders that were returned. The day after their son's departure, Thomas and Margaret had written to New York "general delivery," since Louis had left them no forwarding address. As he had never gone to collect his mail, he knew nothing of their concern.

Fanny sensed the moral tortures he endured, the feeling of guilt that gnawed at him, as well as his certainty that he had behaved well, his anger, his rebellion at not being acknowledged. These conflicts, aggravated by his financial woes, threatened and slowed his recovery. This was a danger that she could not tolerate. Along with the role of sick nurse, Fanny had now taken on the function of protective go-between. From now on, she would meddle in everything to save his life or simplify it, playing a benevolent role on the chessboard of his fate, throwing herself between the man she loved and the harshness of the world. To Mrs. R.L.S., this ministry—or this fault—would be worth many vexations; it would also cost her her reputation. But Fanny sacrificed her own story to Stevenson's comfort and memory, with no regrets.

And since tact did not restrain her, since the words "delicacy" and "discretion" did not belong to her vocabulary—Fanny's famous nerve so criticized by Rearden—she would commit an act that might lead to disaster, to a bloody quarrel with Louis, to an irreparable break with Edinburgh.

She wrote secretly to the Stevenson parents. The difficulty of composing such a letter did not dampen her spirits. Someone else would have taken hours or days finding just the right tone. Fanny did not even pose this as a problem. Would she address herself to Thomas Stevenson as a potential daughter-in-law? As a woman in love? As a mother? As a nurse? Should she beg the paternal pardon? Should she plead her own case—in humility or anger?

This missive has not survived. I am left only with conjectures, and am tempted to think that she spoke plainly, as a doctor to the head of the family. And I trust her to have concocted a heartrending description of the sufferings and ailments of the man who was their common concern.

An atmosphere of mystery floated over the Oakland cottage. At the home of Jacob's daughters, the desk drawers concealed more than one dangerous letter. Fanny was not the only one sending secret messages. At night, in the darkness of her room, Nellie frantically scratched away. Behind her sister's back she sent letter after letter to the Vandegrifts in Indiana. Through Sam Orr—Sam Osbourne's great friend—Fanny's sisters and mother came to hear the scandalous news of the divorce. *You spoke of my keeping things secret from you. It is true that I've done so—it has been for two reasons—one: that things might be prevented and you never be worried by them—the second because I could never bring myself to the point of writing to you of things so painful. Yet now I see it must be done, since I find myself utterly unable to do anything. In the first place about the divorce. As to the cause which led to it I cannot tell you anything—But the divorce is not the most of the trouble—the worst is that Fan is about to be married to Louis Stevenson, of whom you have often heard her speak. This was kept secret from me as long as possible, but as soon as I found out I did everything in my power, as you may well think, to prevent it. But there is no use—I have given up in despair. I cannot express to you the worry that I have suffered on account of all this—enough to affect my health very seriously. But Adulfo thinks that will be all right when we are married and I shall be away from this—All this is quite as heavy a trouble to him as to me, if not worse, for to his people such things are worse then death. Certainly his confidence in me must be great not to have been shaken. But I must tell you in the midst of all these troubles Mr. Orr ordered me never to come inside his house unless I would give up Adulfo. I will not give up the man who is devoted to me heart and soul, and who stands by me like a man through everything—But I must say one thing and that is that it is hard for me to say anything against Fan, for in all my anger toward her she has always heaped every kindness upon me. And I must say I am sure that she is a good woman—no better ever lived—but she is weak and has had an unhappy life. I hope you will think of that.*

Now about Louis Stevenson—He belongs to a good family, is perfectly honest, and has great talent. He is quite able to support her, and will also take upon himself the support and education of Sammy. I am bound to say that if circumstances were different I could not say a word about him. Now I know it will be hard for you to believe when you get the news, that there is not yet time to stop it. But I assure you that I could not do anything with her that you could not—besides, in the present state of affairs, scandal will be far worse if she is not married than if she is—one reason that I did not write you before was that I was sure that Mr. Stevenson was dying and that thus the matter would be settled—but he seems to be regaining his health. I know how this blow will fall upon you, but I have done all I could to avert it, and now I am helpless.

Two days after this letter, dated April 19, 1880, a telegram from Edinburgh addressed to Mr. Robert Louis Stevenson arrived at the garden gate in Oakland.

*

That morning, the first fine one they'd had, Fanny had brought the furniture out on the lawn. She had spent a sleepless night. Mute and sullen, she had let Louis finish his breakfast with Nellie while she spread the throws in the patches of sunlight, brought down the rocking chair, the table, the writing desk, and the basket of medications. Between the veranda and the grass, she came and went with a quick, energetic step. But her waist had grown thicker during the winter, her breasts fuller. It had been an abrupt transition from the slim young woman of Grez to this maturity. At the beginning of the spring, too absorbed by Louis's illness, she had forgotten her birthday. On March 10, Fanny had turned forty. Her cameo profile had become sharper over time. The first gray strands curling on her forehead deepened the color of her face, making her seem even browner than before. She was forty. So what? Her impassive gaze was as direct as ever, boring with the same penetration, the same vigilance. It was an unbending gaze. Her bad mood this morning made it almost mean. Really, Nellie and Louis's latest fad was exasperating, pretending to speak only Spanish! And their indifference when she had suggested they finish the meal without her, their laughter as they drained their glasses, speaking in a gib-

berish they claimed was "an introduction to Adulfo's culture"—
how ridiculous!

Standing under a huge purple parasol she was trying to open,
Fanny suddenly spied at the end of the walk the person she'd been
waiting for. She ran quickly through the bushes and reappeared in
the distance, near the gate.

"It arrived yesterday evening," said the postman. "Addressed to
the gentleman staying with you."

"I'll take it to him myself. Thank you. Good-bye."

She folded the paper in the pocket of her apron and made her
way slowly back toward the cottage. Along the path, a warm breeze
whispered through the beds of red tulips. She stopped to potter in
the garden, her head down, inscrutable. This is what had disturbed
her during the night. She was waiting for it, she knew this answer
would arrive today. Why on earth hadn't his parents written to her?
The contents of this telegram could kill him! She would open it
. . . she would check it . . . And if his father's reaction was not
suitable, let him go to the devil. This insult would be drowned in
the Atlantic, she would see to that!

Fanny spied Louis rocking in the armchair she had prepared for
him. Little did he care where she was, what she was doing or
thinking. Sitting in the sun with Nellie, he was carrying on, rolling
his "r's" in a speech about Lope de Vega's *Punishment without
Vengeance*. Nellie, at his feet, was rolling with laughter, flat on her
stomach on the throw that Fanny had arranged for Louis's legs.
His feet especially must be dry, he mustn't catch cold! A speech
above love, no doubt. How pretty Nellie looked this morning. Her
shapely dress showed off her waist and fit snugly over her hips.
Her long blond braids glistened in the sun. Every time he rocked,
he seemed to plunge down on her, no doubt noticing all the pleats,
knots, tassels, all the poufs and flounces. And Nellie, looking for
words in the dictionary, refolding her legs, showing her stockings,
waving her little boots in the air . . . Louis and Nellie were the
same generation. Nellie was born in . . . Fanny calculated. She was
barely five years younger than he, and intellectual as well! The
intellectual of the family. Nellie's library contained more novels
than all the parlor shelves. Why hadn't Louis fallen in love with
Nellie? With Nellie or Belle? His few friends in San Francisco
belonged to the same circle, Joe Strong's circle. Since his convalescence, he had been seeking the company of young people his own

age. How could he stand that idiot Strong? If Fanny thought he'd changed during his illness, she'd been wrong! With the return of health, he was recovering his gaiety. Raising her head again, she glimpsed the two of them, Louis and Nellie, laughing together. She felt then like a middle-aged woman warming herself in the sun by taking a turn around the garden. She would let them enjoy themselves. She would not go to them, since they hardly needed her. Even Chuchu, the setter spaniel, had not followed her to the bottom of the garden. She saw him there, curled up on the throw. If Chuchu preferred their company, let them take care of him! Nurse, cook, warder . . . Fanny fed the dogs and nursed the sick. But as for laughter and pleasure, when life was happier, who would bother with her? Irritated, she followed the fence around the house, drew water from the well, and went to the kitchen garden. During Louis's illness she had sadly neglected her rows of little cabbages. She strolled peacefully along the paths, watering her beds of vegetables. But she was looking elsewhere. She was looking at the couple there on the grass. What were they saying? Was Stevenson murmuring in Nellie's ear: "The finest things lead nowhere, the finest ideas have no future, and the finest adventures are those we do not undertake?"

If he was uttering these words, would Nellie think he was courting her? Would she blush? Would she answer sententiously that he spoke the way he wrote? Or would she keep silent, thinking that he was chatting away not to find but to seek? That he explored words the way he explored life, for the pleasure of seeing, for the pleasure of revealing. Would Nellie understand that the pleasure of this quest was enough, an end in itself? And how would she respond if Stevenson, in his warm voice, told her: "There is a dark little pond, lilacs, and a stone bench at the bottom of the garden . . . that's where we ought to be sitting . . ."

While the fine silver droplets gathered on her plants, Fanny imagined them, Nellie and Louis, ambling down the paths, settling under the shelter of the tall trees. From there they could glimpse the veranda and the little blue figure of Mother Fanny watering her cabbages.

"I think we ought to join her," Nellie would whisper.

"You're right," Louis would answer. "But let's stay just a moment longer in this quiet."

"She'll come looking for us."

The shadow of the leaves would tremble on the lawn at their feet. The sun would set in a torrent of reddish light. The last rays would settle full on Nellie's face, tingeing her blue eyes with a green that reflected all the little pulsations in the air. Fanny had such a wretchedly clear vision of things. Abandoned to her fears and her demons, she would one day know how to transform anguish into hallucination. Now, with a beating heart, she imagined to herself a Louis sliding along the bench toward the young girl.

"We might leave the garden."

"But what will Fanny say?"

"That dampness is fatal for consumptives ... that I will come down with a fever and die of it this evening!"

"It's risky ..."

"It's risky,' he would admit, "but to get scolded together would strengthen our friendship!"

Fanny put down the watering can, got up, wiped her hand across her forehead in a gesture that had become habitual since Louis's illness. And what if he were to die like Hervey? She could taste and smell the salty odor of blood. She wanted to vomit. A few feet from her, on the lawn flooded with sun, Louis was alive! And she had just been feeling the same shameful feeling she'd harbored for twenty years with Sam—jealousy! How could she confuse the two men? What madness, what shame in subjecting herself to such torments! Poor Louis ... poor Nellie. Still jabbering in Spanish, they were continuing to read their piece, leafing through grammars and dictionaries, arguing, shrieking with laughter.

They did not see her coming, but when she was there, they both uttered the same cry: "You have a letter for me?"

She was expecting anything but that question. Taken up short, she began by lying: "No letter ..." She blushed, agitated, and mumbled: "A telegram."

"From Baxter ... He is sending me money."

"I don't think so."

"And for me?" Nellie interrupted.

"Nothing."

The two women watched Louis tear open the paper. The umbrella cast a purple glow on their faces. Standing still under the canopy, they evoked the image of two priestesses in the service of a divinity.

I remember the day this word came from his father, Nellie wrote.

"Listen," he began shouting. "Listen, Fanny," he repeated with a nasal accent exaggerated by emotion. Standing up, he was trembling all over. *Be sure you want for nothing that you require, as long as we have a penny. We shall do our best. We shall receive your wife. You can count on two hundred and fifty pounds annually!"*

Fanny's relief was boundless. Louis's happiness was complete. This time everyone accepted their union, and they would accept everyone's support and pardon. Thomas Stevenson had just saved his son, Fanny Osbourne was triumphant. They had won.

Wednesday, May 19, 1880

Lying on her back in the four-poster bed in her old room, her arms behind her head, her large eyes open, she was watching the dawn break on her last morning as a single woman. A bright day streamed through the mauve and mustard floral designs of the curtains, lifting the darkness from the trunks and boxes. She had finished her preparations late the night before, alone. Louis had crossed the bay on Tuesday, yesterday. He would end his bachelor life at his old rooming house on Bush Street and tie up the last details in San Francisco: find a pastor of his father's denomination, buy two modestly priced wedding rings, perhaps silver rings at a Chinese jeweler; purchase a marriage license; send fifteen dollars to the fund for widows of the Scottish bar.

It was not my bliss that I was interested in when I was married; it was a sort of marriage in extremis; and if I am where I am, it is thanks to the care of that lady, who married me when I was a mere complication of cough and bones, much fitter for an emblem of mortality than a bridegroom. Yes, fifteen dollars to the widow's fund that would leave Fanny with a small pension after the burial. But who knows? she thought, stretching, full of uncharacteristic optimism. Who knows, maybe Louis will live forever? His father's letter had done more for his recovery than all the treatments and specialists.

In evoking his parents' generosity, Fanny's heart swelled with gratitude and fear. Those Scottish puritans seemed to accept her, the aging American divorcée. But they were accepting her from a distance. And now Louis wanted to go home. Relieved and thankful, he wanted to return and live with them! That was his project for the autumn, that they should all live together, with Sammy, with his father and mother, in the old Edinburgh house. What would happen? She preferred not to think about it.

Louis's inner peace now depended on his father's approval, and Fanny knew it. She knew, moreover, that she could not allow herself another failed marriage. Success would depend on the impression she would make . . . How would they welcome her, with her midwestern accent, her cap of gray curls, her gypsy complexion, so dark that in Monterey they took her for a half-breed, her six-shooter in her garter and her young scamp of a son at her heels?

She brushed away these thoughts and rose. What on earth was she forgetting? Sammy . . . Sammy and the dog Chuchu would join them in the hills near San Francisco when she'd found a place to spend their honeymoon in the open air. The sun, before the grayness of Scotland, a dry breeze before the English rains—this would complete Louis's convalescence. What was she forgetting? Big white dustcovers protected the furniture . . . As on the eve of her departure for Antwerp, she had repotted her plants and put them in the greenhouse. Sam had promised to put the cottage in her name. Hadn't he bought the property with her dowry? But you couldn't count on Sam Osbourne's promises. It was said that he was keeping company with a dark little lady who looked very much like his first wife. Sam and women! Fanny didn't want to think about that anymore either. Belle would come to take the knick-knacks during the week. She had already taken her piano and her favorite childhood souvenirs. Nellie would live with the Strongs until her own marriage in September. One of the two cats would leave with Nellie for Monterey, the other would stay here. Her pony Clavel was sold . . . Clavel was perhaps her only regret. Since she was anxious about the life that awaited her in the old town of Edinburgh, she had this need for exercise, this nostalgia for violent movement, for a last ride. She could go to sleep only by imagining herself rocked back and forth on a galloping horse. In dreams she saw herself riding straight across the rich land of a huge plateau. Seated squarely in her saddle, her reins long, she entered a stand of trees. She was plunging ahead, passing under the branches that brushed her back, crouched down, her chest against the saddlehorn, ready to jump ditches. Between the tree trunks, the dark plain, the clearings, the green openings in the hedges, everything was sweeping past. Everything was falling thick and fast, blowing in gusts, perfumes, roses, the past . . .

Two o'clock in the afternoon. At the Embarcadero, waiting for the ferry, the minutes ticked by slowly. A forest was burning in the back country. Even the sea air was heavy with smoke. The passengers were looking at the sky and anxiously questioning each other on the likelihood of a shower in these last May days. This is it, she said to herself, this is it, she repeated to convince herself, this is the day, the hour of my marriage to Louis. She felt the way she did before a competition at the Julian Academy: too weak to choose a pencil, too heavy to raise her arm, too vacant to visualize her drawing. She could not think anymore, she knew nothing. She stood in the waiting room, her mind a haze, and kept her eyes fixed on the painting she had looked at daily during the past winter when she was taking the boat to nurse Louis on Bush Street, and every day of all the previous winters when she had crossed the bay to study at the School of Design. It was a two-masted schooner with unfurled sails swelled by the wind, fresh and lively, against a sky flecked with gray clouds. The bronze-green waves, unbroken, rose like a powerful breath. They jostled each other near the boat and lapped at the prow. It was this scene, Fanny remembered, that had fueled her desire to leave Sam, her need to live alone, her obsession with leaving for Antwerp. At the bottom of the painting was a plate engraved with the name *The Casco*.

On the deck of the ferry, the wind caught in her skirts and slowed her step. She made out behind her the gathering squalls that pushed against the bulwarks. She stiffened and arched her back, and stepped firmly forward. She felt the lace of her underskirts caress her knees. She resisted, it was delicious! On the ferry's funnel, a fat white seagull cried sharply. It was laughing by fits and starts between the trails of smoke from the engines, the ribbons of mist rising from the sea, the haze from the burning pine forest. Fanny watched, her face smooth and free, her curls plastered against her plumed hat, and the bird looked back at her. For a moment they surveyed each other with the same round, black eye, buxom little ladies boldly braving the upper air. The seagull, suddenly dropping onto the water, bobbed before her.

It was then that she perceived, quite close, the red and cluttered mass of San Francisco, the quays bursting with carriages, the horses, the bales and bundles, the swarm of men waiting in the mud. Among the Chinese, the Kanakas, the sailors, the cowboys, she recognized, bucking the crowd, the slim figure of Robert Louis Stevenson. She had always thought he was tall, but it was his thinness that accounted for the illusion. He stood hardly more than five feet ten inches. Bareheaded, his straight hair parted in the middle and falling to his shoulders, he wore his traveling suit of blue serge. One hand at his mustache, the eternal cigarette between two fingers, the other hand in his pocket, he strode toward the embarcadero. He had an ungainly walk that looked like his arms, his legs, his head were all functioning separately, at cross-purposes. She let go of the railing, came down the stairs, and stepped onto the gangplank.

"I have everything!" he cried, seeing her.

They did not greet each other, no kiss or embrace, no sign of affection. He took her familiarly by the elbow and led her with his quick step along the jetty.

"I've found him, the Reverend Dr. William Anderson Scott, pastor of St. John's Presbyterian Church on Post Street. Not only has he published eleven books and built a cathedral, he's escaped lynching three times! There's a reverend after my own heart . . . He is waiting for us."

"Now?" she cried.

She stopped still, planting her little boots on the wooden planks. He had to help her. She could not go back and she could not go on. He looked at her in surprise.

"Didn't we agree to marry today?" he asked.

"Yes, but . . ."

He smiled: "Ah, that . . . Are you afraid? If I were expecting . . ."

"We have no witnesses," she announced quickly.

"True. I hadn't thought of that."

"In America, you need two witnesses . . . Otherwise, it is impossible. You need at least two witnesses."

"There are bound to be a few bums on the street where the Reverend Scott lives . . ." he teased.

Still, she would not move. Beneath her, the surf had just broken against the piles of the jetty.

He took her once more by the elbow and tried to make her walk. "What on earth were you thinking about standing all alone on the boat?"

"Nothing."

"What scared you? What disturbed you?"

"I was watching the seagulls."

"The Williamses will be our witnesses. The trolley stops right at their door. We will pick them up on the way. Come on," he ordered.

Seated side by side on the Geary Street trolley, they did not say a word. It was warm. The horses climbed up toward the leaden sky. Riveted to the bench, her face blank, her forehead beaded with drops of sweat, Fanny seemed ready for the slaughterhouse, not a love match. It was finally Dora's babbling that pulled her from her torpor.

"You are marrying right now? What a charming idea! My dears, I am so happy for you! You have waited so long for this moment. And when I think of what it cost you in blood, tears, and sacrifice!"

The thin little lady grabbed her hat and her umbrella.

"I hardly imagined I would be maid of honor . . . at my age! At ours, my dear Fanny!" She burst into her metallic laughter that mingled with the tinkling of her bracelets. "What a shame Mr. Williams is not in town today! As best man I propose Rearden: He will do very nicely!"

"He isn't speaking to me since the divorce. He is applying for the post of judge—I guess I'm not proper enough for him," Fanny grumbled.

"Damned Rearden," clucked Dora, "he's always so disagreeable! But I know he has a very valuable wedding gift for you."

"He sent it to me: a funeral urn."

"So you can carry Louis's ashes with you?"

"Do you think it's funny?"

"Unless he meant the vase for your lovely remains . . . In any case, you can be sure it's authentic!"

The three of them climbed up the street, small gossiping figures waving their arms and making their way toward that event which had cost them, as Dora tactfully remarked, "so much blood and tears." On board the *Devonia* a year earlier, Stevenson had written so lucidly: *The woman I love is somewhat of my handiwork; and the great lover, like the great painter, is he who can so embellish his subject as to make her more than human, whilst yet by cunning art he has so based his apotheosis on the nature of the case that the woman can go on being a true woman, and give her character*

*free play, and show little littleness or cherish spite, or be greedy of
common pleasures, and he continue to worship without a thought
of incongruity.*

This sort of analysis, and the almost total absence of great female
characters in the work of Robert Louis Stevenson, has led some of
his biographers to claim that he was not happily married. Certain
scholars even claim that he never loved Fanny Osbourne, that he
simply followed her to the United States out of a sense of duty, in
order to make this unhappy mistress a respectable woman.

Not a single admirer of Stevenson who knew of my research on
the controversial character of his wife failed to ask me whether I
honestly thought he was happy in his marriage. I answered that
after all, he said it himself, and repeated it: *My marriage is the
best decision I ever made, the most intelligent act of my life!*

"Do you know that she was not just eleven years older than he,
but sixteen!"

"We have Fanny Vandegrift's birth certificate. The San Francisco
civic records may have burned, but the Indianapolis archives are
intact."

"But do you know that she was black?"

More than a century after the wedding, the wife's exoticism still
gives rise to fantasy.

*

"My friends, we are gathered here today to join together in the
presence of Jesus Christ our Lord and of this noble assembly . . ."

The assembly was reduced to the strict minimum.

New rumors: People said that in the presence of Belle, Joe,
Sammy, and Nellie, Sam Osbourne led his ex-wife to the altar and,
with his own hand, before the Reverend Scott, gave her to Robert
Louis Stevenson. A thousand other stories of this marriage still
make the rounds, gossip circulated by the wagging tongue of Fanny's future daughter-in-law. There were only five people present:
the pastor Scott and his wife, who served as the second witness,
Dora Williams, Louis, and Fanny.

"Do you, Fanny Vandegrift Osbourne, agree to take this man,
Louis, as your lawful wedded husband, in sickness and in health,

for richer or poorer, renouncing all other men until death do you part?"

She murmured: "Yes."

"Do you, Robert Louis Balfour Stevenson . . ."

The long green drapes were pulled. No shaft of light played on the clusters of lamps and the wood paneling that covered the pastor's austere parlor. Deep in the shadows, on a round table, a tray had been set, a tea service in blue faience. At the far end of the room a single ray of sunlight fell on the people grouped together around the fireplace. It came through the pseudo-Gothic west windows, through little squares of red tinted glass.

"In the name of the Father, I declare you man and wife . . . Now, Mr. Stevenson, you may kiss the bride!"

Standing side by side, they made no gesture to embrace. No doubt they found it superfluous to express their passion in public: They had proved it to each other. The tenderness of the long look they exchanged, the triumph, their intoxicated smiles, sealed the pact.

It had taken three years to arrive at this moment, and it was over in ten minutes. Neither of them would remember it, but henceforth, the record of marriages performed by the Reverend Scott would read:

Married by me at my residence 19 May, 1880,
Robert Louise [sic] Stevenson, born Edinboro', Scotland,
white, single, 30 years old, resides in Oakland, Cal.
Fannie [sic] Osbourne, born Indianapolis, Indiana, 40 years,
widowed, white, resides in Oakland.
Certificate to be sent to Mrs. Virgil Williams,
719 Geary Street, City.

Fanny, a "widow"? Why would she bravely admit her age but lie about her past? What could have prompted her to describe herself as Sam's widow?

Last-minute cowardice at Rearden's sarcastic remarks? Weakness in the face of the inevitable contempt of Scottish society? A belated wish to reenter the ranks? "Widow"—what could be more respectable!

I am tempted to think that in her usual way, Fanny simply eliminated what disturbed her, killed what she didn't like. In burying her ex-husband, she was offering herself a new beginning, a clean slate.

For the first time and last time in their common history, the Civil War veteran, gold seeker of Virginia City, clerk at the San Francisco Courthouse, Sam Osbourne, was going to help further her enterprise.

Six years later, in October 1886, at the entrance to a comfortable villa in Bournemouth, England, a large envelope would arrive. It was a letter from Dora, along with several newspaper clippings. The headlines and small print all posed the same question: WHAT HAS BECOME OF SAM OSBOURNE ESQ.?

The clippings would record that after remarrying a woman who resembled his first wife almost feature by feature, Sam Osbourne did not show up at his home one day after the usual court session in San Francisco. On that autumn night, his wife and supper would wait for him in vain.

Had he once again changed his life? Had he secretly embarked on a sailing ship? Had he been "shanghaied"—forcibly abducted to serve as a sailor in some sea caper? Was he murdered in a brothel and thrown into the ocean?

Or had the instability, the anguish, the obscure currents that had troubled him all his life, dogged his soul? Did Fanny Vandegrift's husband commit suicide?

Several days after his disappearance, a bag of clothing that might have belonged to him was found on the seashore. No one, however, could identify these remnants with certainty. This time, the lone cowboy did not reappear. His children never knew what had happened to their much loved father.

So ended this long story of love and hate bound together before God one icy Christmas evening. The winter roses had decked the little house in Indianapolis, and the bride had been only seventeen years old.

If we stop to think of it, both of Fanny's husbands met romantic ends. Each in his own way escaped oblivion, each evaded the grave. And they both became legendary; the elusive Sam forever preserved his mystery.

During the next twenty years, rumors about him continued to circulate. Belle would tell that during the First World War, witnesses claimed to have met Sam Osbourne in South Africa. Others would write about him, claiming to have seen Sam Osbourne at the races in New Orleans. What should we think? For the little girl who saw her father come back unscathed from an Indian massacre, the hope of finding him again would never die.

*

His demise, or escape, left his second wife, Rebecca Paul—"Paulie" to her friends—in despair, and in financial straits. Fanny had written about her after her wedding in 1881: *I am not deeply complimented by the choice of a successor to my former position . . . Belle may have an ornamental father, but you can hardly say that she has an ornamental stepmother. Well, I don't envy her. . . . How curious both he and I should have chosen invalids. However I flatter myself that my invalid is of a different sort.*

Fanny was hard on Paulie, who was a bit deaf. Without knowing her, she called her ugly. This is yet another example of her prejudice. She claimed to be unaware of their resemblance, the similarity of their complexion, stature, and looks. But all of their contemporaries were quite specific: the two Mrs. Osbournes, Fanny and Paulie, were alike—except in character! The second was thought to be sweet and rather insipid. Yet the two women would eventually meet, and the one most touched by this meeting was not the one you would expect.

If Paulie's impoverishment reassured Fanny that she had made the right choice, it also awakened her compassion. *It could have been me,* she confided to Dora. Fanny then made over a pension to Paulie, though nothing obliged her to do so. Playing the *grande dame*, in a formidable rush of generosity she granted Sam's widow a comfortable living. Taking revenge on fate, Mrs. R. L. S. saved Mrs. Osbourne.

She even indulged in the luxury of rewriting history. Unrelenting when it came to Sam's memory, accusing him of never supporting his son, she erased her ex-husband from the civic records. Henceforth, little Sammy would be called "Lloyd," Lloyd Osbourne, the name the reader now finds bound to that of Robert Louis Stevenson on the works that stepfather and stepson signed together.

Fanny was too complacent; eventually she would lose this battle. Just before the Second World War, when Lloyd Osbourne, at the age of sixty-eight, had a last son, he would baptize him Samuel Osbourne.

*
**

For the moment, the past was suspended in a no man's land where the first loves of Miss Vandegrift no longer existed, despite the fact that less than a year after her own marriage, she would become a grandmother: Belle would give birth to a little Osbourne-Strong. Yet Fanny would give up everything—her own story, her secrets, her dreams, her well-being, her health. She was so busy coming between her husband and death that she would forget her own needs and demands, even her joy in attracting him. Fanny, formerly so aware of her appearance with the painters of Grez, so frivolous and "flirtatious" with Rearden, would deprive herself, with Louis, of all the little pleasures of her life as a woman.

Did Stevenson grasp the magnitude of this sacrifice? Was he ever conscious of the fact that in working together for the emergence of that great writer they both dreamed of, they would mutilate one soul that should have survived? What do we think of his tendency to reckon without her when he had less need of her services; of his inclination to carry on alone when he had recovered his health? Was it independence, narcissism, hardness of heart? He would ask himself the same question. *My dearest fellow*, he wrote to her in May 1888, preparing to set off on the great adventure in the South Seas, *This will not reach you till some time after our wedding day, which as usual has taken me aback ... Not that I think so much of that day; if I had some other dates I could think more of them; ... the day when I looked through the window* [at Grez], *or the day when I came to see you in Paris after the first absence, for example. But the marriage day we know, and it was a mighty good day for me; for you I wish I was sure.*

He wouldn't be too concerned, and could count on Fanny's instinct, her formidable instinct for self-preservation. Indeed, if this wife gave all she had, she never lost sight of the goal: to create, to triumph over her own death. With her eye on that prize, she aimed for immortality.

Part Three

The Lioness
1880–1914

VII

Mrs. Robert Louis Stevenson

Honour, anger, valour, fire;
A love that life could never tire,
Death quench or evil stir,
The mighty master
Gave to her.

—Robert Louis Stevenson

London—The Savile Club—August 18, 1880

"So?" inquired the poet Edmund Gosse, taking his seat in one of the spacious leather armchairs recently acquired for the smoking room.

"So, if I had known that the old parents would come down from Edinburgh to greet them at the boat," sighed Sidney Colvin, putting down his paper, "I would not have traveled all the way from London to Liverpool!"

He took a moment to savor a small sip of sherry.

Gosse sat self-importantly in the big chair. He lifted the cup of coffee he had brought in from the dining room, and in the shadowy light his blue gaze fixed on the bindings of several dictionaries that gleamed above the frail Professor Colvin.

"I returned this morning," the professor went on softly. "Exhausting!"

"How were they?"

"The parents? I'm bound to say the old folks put a most brave and most kind face on it indeed."

"The poor people," sighed Gosse, whose eyes twinkled with amusement behind his little glasses. "If one thinks of Thomas Stevenson ..." He let his sentence trail off, smiling at the image in his mind. "The austere, bourgeois, the puritanical engineer, the famous builder of lighthouses, who is going to escort the aging American mistress of his atheist son to all the drawing rooms of Edinburgh."

Colvin stroked his short, pointed brown beard. "Louis certainly did play an outrageous trick on them. And bringing them that little twelve-year-old grandson, who guzzles his food and sops up his gravy ... The child wolfed down everything he could swallow as the waiters looked on aghast. What a spectacle!"

"Poor people," repeated Gosse, delighted.

"The little boy is not a bad chap. But the daughter-in-law—I understand that in their eyes, she may seem hardly presentable ..."

"I appreciate your understatement, Colvin, but let's call a spade a spade: This woman is the devil himself as far as they're concerned!"

The green lampshade made their faces even paler. In suits and white cravats, the two of them embodied a race of intellectuals whose aestheticism posed no threat to the values of Victorian society.

"I daresay it made things more pleasant, my being there," Colvin murmured. "I convinced them to wait at the hotel while I took the tugboat out to the ship."

"And then?"

"And then I found Louis better than I'd thought. He finally went to the dentist, and his new teeth seem somewhat to have improved the shape of his mouth. Nonetheless, he seemed very weak."

"As ill as she said?"

"Weak and easily flustered. And so small you could put your thumb and finger around his thigh."

"Is he happy?"

"Marriage seems to suit him. America has not changed him too much. When I had him alone talking in the smoking room it was almost exactly like old times."

Colvin paused, musing: "And it is clear enough that he likes his new condition so far and is at peace in it."

Rolling the stem of his glass between his fingers, he sighed: "But whether you or I will ever get reconciled to the little determined brown face and white teeth and grizzling (for that's what it's up to) hair, which we are to see beside him in future—that's another matter."

A smile floated on Gosse's lips: "Ah, but we are broad-minded, you and I . . . You, my dear fellow, you positively exude goodness. You are flexible and tolerant . . . But Henley—in his last letter he calls this *the whim of a sick child who played 'husband and wife' with a schoolgirl of forty . . .*"

"A schoolgirl, if you like . . . But—just between us—of the two Mrs. Stevensons present yesterday at the family meal, it was the elder who seemed fresh and youthful!"

This spoken by the friend whom Fanny would think of at the time as her closest ally.

Liverpool—Northwestern Hotel August 18, 1880

"So?" Fanny asked, timidly sitting on the bed. "Did I behave properly?"

"Properly?" Louis cried.

"But I even refrained from smoking until coffee was served," she murmured miserably.

"Properly?" he thundered. "You made me look ridiculous! Here I go to all this trouble to prepare my family, I write to my father, I write to my mother to warn them . . . I introduce my wife to them as an exotic adventuress, a cigarette in her mouth and a pistol in her belt—and what do they find? A nice little middle-class lady who discusses chiffons and agrees with everything they say!"

"But I was sincere!" she roused herself, delighted.

"That's the worst of it!"

"So . . . Do you think they liked me?"

His mocking gaze was both tender and teasing. She was wearing a dress of black grosgrain silk, stripped of her usual ornaments. Only a band of beaded jet trim enclosed the high collar and wristbands of the bodice. A thin black ribbon held her curls. From the front, it looked as though she were wearing her hair in a low chignon.

"Madame Louis, you will never stop surprising me! You seemed so perfectly at home between my serious friend Colvin and my very dour father . . . So totally at ease! I had to ask myself what I was doing there myself, in my old suit, with my cigarettes and my long hair, amongst all those solid citizens, and the most dignified of all—my bourgeois wife!"

Her cheeks flushed with pleasure, her little hands on her knees, she gurgled like a convent girl discovering the world: "Very well, you are finally going to learn to comb your hair! Your mother was telling me that she had never managed to get you to change for dinner . . . Your mother," she enthused, "I adore her. She is so like you! She has your way of looking on the good side of things! Yes, I adore her! But your father . . . well, we shall see," she mumbled. "We shall see. I haven't made up my mind about him."

"On this point, I should be grateful if both you and my father would be a little forbearing. All you can think of is judging! Judging . . ."

This time Robert Louis Stevenson shot Fanny a look that was anything but indulgent: "The two of you—when you like someone, you adore them. When you don't like someone, you destroy everything until you've managed to eliminate them. Even if you have to immolate yourselves in the process . . . you're both wicked partisans!"

*

"So?" asked Margaret Stevenson, walking ahead of her husband into their apartment. "What did you think of her?"

Thomas Stevenson unbuttoned his evening jacket and walked heavily into the dressing room between their bedrooms. She followed him.

"Well," she repeated. "What did you think of her?"

"Better," he grumbled, lifting the pitcher to wash his hands. "Better than I expected."

"More distinguished, isn't she?" Margaret went on, without taking her eyes off the mirror in which her husband's congested face was reflected. "You know, I wouldn't be at all ashamed to take her to church! With her hair done properly and decently dressed, she will do quite nicely in our pew."

He set down the pitcher with a bang and turned toward her: "Don't get carried away, I beg you, Maggy. Don't get carried away!"

"Of course we must select hats, gloves, some jewelry for her. If you will allow it, I would like to make her a gift of the brooch your mother gave me at our marriage . . . She looks after Lou so well! She is so tenderly devoted to him. Did you see how she makes sure he doesn't finish the bottle of champagne? How kindly she remarked to him that it was late, how firmly she made him say goodnight. I am sure that without her—"

"Without her, without that ridiculous escapade—"

"What's done is done," Margaret cut in lightly but a little sharply. "I do not want to know about the past. They are intelligent enough not to speak of it. Now it's up to us to make the best of a bad bargain."

"Without her," Thomas stubbornly continued, "our son would not be in this alarming state of health. He will have to consult your brother, Doctor Balfour, when we return to Edinburgh. I thought he was terribly thin and weak."

"It's Fanny who saved him . . ."

" 'Fanny?' You already call her Fanny?"

Margaret burst into the tinkling laughter she knew was so seductive. "I found her rather charming . . . rather entertaining! And her little boy, what a darling! Don't you think he resembles Lou at the same age? The chambermaid immediately asked me if he was his son. Isn't it extraordinary? We never managed to get Lou to grow up, and there he is, the head of a family!"

"Head? He would love to think so. The father of a schoolboy at thirty. Still another game!"

"But we all think the boy resembles Lou much more than his mother . . . You might give him the old nursery . . . It will be so nice to have young people in the house again!"

"We shall see," the old gentleman mumbled. "We shall see! That woman, I have not yet made up my mind about her."

*

I am sure, Belle, that you would like his parents awfully, wrote the twelve-year-old adolescent they would still call Sammy for a few more years. *She and her husband are awfully nice people.*

Mama got several presents. I cannot write what they are now. I will let Mama write that.

Mama is just now speaking with Mrs. Stevenson on the subject of clothes. . . . I forgot to say that at the Northwestern Hotel, they burnt no gas or lamps, only miserable candles that give a feeble glaze. Also there is no running water, not even plumbing. . . .
This is what Mama bought today:
a dinner dress
a walking dress
a walking cape
a white cloak
a cornet with yellow feathers
ruffling
lace collar and cuffs
three pairs of gloves
one white lace tie
one black lace tie
fake red cherries
I think that is all, Belle, I certainly think that's enough.

Give my love to all,
a brat to be made over,
Sam Osbourne

First impressions? Amazingly favorable on both sides! They had all so dreaded this moment that reality eased the pressure. Each expecting the worst, they were all equally relieved. But how long would the pleasure of this reassurance last? Long rainy Edinburgh days lay ahead with all of them living under the same roof. Along with the seasonal organization of charity events, the five o'clock teas, church *en famille* on Sundays, prayers at the supper table.

And ahead lay social acceptance in one of the most puritanical cities of the British Empire.

Edinburgh—17 Heriot Row—August 21, 1880

A narrow facade of large gray stone fronted the three-story house. The high, sash-windows with small, square panes of glass framed in white flanked a wooden black lacquered door with its gleaming brass fittings—knocker, doorknob, mounting for the post box. A small porch was enclosed by a polished grillwork that extended down to the flickering gaslight of one streetlamp and over to the next, climbed up five steps, and festooned the porch next door as well. Tall, identical houses with vertical lines from their eaves and their doors stood side by side along the mist-shrouded street facing the chestnuts trees in the park. There, children with hoops and sticks followed their imposing nurses. These were the legendary nannies hired by the well-to-do families, who passed from one generation to the other and spent their entire living pushing the same black baby carriages toward the new neighborhoods of Edinburgh, the "new town." This was a whole city built at the end of the eighteenth century in reaction to the medieval disorder, the labyrinth of little streets on the walls, the wretched poverty of old Edinburgh's ancient hills. A whole city inherited from the century of the Enlightenment, a city without shadow, a rational city with broad, parallel avenues, vast perspectives, swept by an icy wind from the sea that frosted the cobblestones, the twisting trees in the squares, and the tall statues at the street corners.

"You are not going to behave as you did at the hotel!"

"Yes, Mama."

"Look at me: I'm not joking! You will not guzzle your food! This is a family dinner in our honor ... Do you understand?"

"I understand: They are introducing us and it makes you nervous."

"You will take modest portions and you will eat everything."

"Even their awful jam with leg of lamb?" Sammy protested.

"Everything," Fanny replied.

Changing her tone, she whirled around and asked gaily: "How do you think I look, my boy?"

The child appraised her knowingly. Later, Samuel Lloyd would love women, he would love their elegance. The collar of his mother's gray outfit was closed with a large white organdy knot. The sleeves revealed the roundness of her arms beneath the openings in the lace. At her wrist, the same cascade of organdy fell on her bare hand.

"Do you think my hands look red?" she asked, holding them out to the child. "Can you see I have worked with my hands?"

"If only Belle could be here to admire you!" he whistled. Sammy looked around and heaved a big sigh. "Everything is so chic here!

Did you see the drawing room? The enormous curtains ... your shoes sink into the carpet. And that portrait of Mrs. Stevenson— she is so pretty! And Luly's room, have you seen the toy soldiers? He was sure lucky to grow up in this house. He must have felt so secure!"

Fanny caught her son and held him against her. Surprised by this gesture of tenderness, the boy relaxed in her arms: "You smell good," he murmured. "I love being secure ... you smell like Mrs. Stevenson."

On the ground floor, in the huge dining room, an extension had been added to the mahogany table. Between the two tall windows that looked out on Heriot Row, the sideboard seemed to be collapsing beneath the weight of crystal and carafes. The two doors at the end of the room kept banging. One opened onto the servants' quarters, the other onto the office of Thomas Stevenson. With its bookshelves and its ebony desk, it was the only brutally austere room in the house. Over the rest, the large drawing room on the first floor, the bedroom with its silks, its chintzes, and its little varnished desk, Margaret Stevenson's gaiety had prevailed.

This evening, the impending visit from his nephew and niece was doing nothing to improve Thomas's already dark mood. Bob Stevenson was coming to Heriot Row for the first time in six years. Bob, the atheist corrupter, the adored cousin ... Everyone here remembered the dreadful scene in which Thomas Stevenson had accused him of perverting his son, and closed his door to him forever. This scandal dated from the time when Thomas had discovered among Louis's papers the secret charter of the society the two boys had founded: the "L. J. R.," Liberty, Justice, and Reverence. The first article, written in Bob's hand, began with the words: *Disregard everything our parents have taught us.*

In honoring the newlyweds, Margaret was making a sacrifice and Bob was coming to supper. He was coming from London with his sister, the splendid and unhappy Katherine, who against the family's wishes had married a free thinker, an Englishman of the worst sort, who drank and beat her. Katherine was now trying to live separated from her husband, and through the intermediary of Louis's friend, William Ernest Henley, was publishing a few short stories and articles that allowed her to survive with her two children. The new

generation of Stevensons was hardly fulfilling their elders' promise.
Louis had also invited his old university friend, Charles Baxter and
his wife; and Walter Simpson, his traveling companion along the
canals of Antwerp, with his sister Eve, the girl they all thought
Louis should have married. They were the children of the inventor
of chloroform, the famous Dr. Simpson who lived across the park.

They were all from respectable Edinburgh families, of course.
Thomas was also waiting for Miss Alison Cunningham, "Cummy,"
Louis's former governess, whom Robert Louis Stevenson would call
his second mother and his first wife. Cummy—that name evoked so
many memories for Thomas Stevenson. How long had Cummy been
with them? Fifteen years? Louis's whole childhood and youth . . .
Thomas felt old this evening, old and disoriented. Sitting at his
desk, his hands resting on the blotting pad of his writing table, he
raised his eyes and sighed. His gaze stopped for a moment on the
ceiling frieze, on the little sculpted medallions that crowned the
shelves of his library. Margaret might well spend her days with her
daughter-in-law, instructing her on fashion, presenting her to the
organizers of her charity events, but she knew no more about Fanny
Vandegrift today than when she'd first arrived. Thomas had heard
the servants whispering about a Scotsman who left for Africa and
returned "married to a negress." He had heard them commenting
that "for a foreigner Mrs. Louis did not speak English too badly."
A negress? A foreigner? An adventuress? Who was he dealing with?
She hadn't made a false step since she'd come on stage. Had this
woman studied her role so well that she could behave with such
aplomb? Far from growing impatient with the customs of the
house, she had eased into their life and become part of the scenery.
It seemed to Thomas that she'd always been there. Was this the
suppleness of a snake, the imitative behavior of a chameleon? Had
her ascent to the upper bourgeoisie been so long and carefully
planned that today she could thoroughly enjoy it? Had she married
Louis just to belong to the Stevenson clan? He could no more
imagine her among the half-naked Comanches, among the gold
miners of Nevada and the bearded painters of Barbizon, than he
could imagine Louis married to another woman. Margaret was right
on this point. The adroitness with which the Vandegrift woman
maneuvered their son was spectacular. Thomas knew that Louis was
impossible to discipline—and difficult to care for. The astonishing
thing was that the presence of this new pawn in the family chess

game eased their relationships with each other. But he was suspicious. They would see her in society this evening—how would she behave in public? Would she manage to charm the governess as she had the mother? Fanny Vandegrift seemed groomed for the profession of cajoler. Her most recent coup had been to recognize the precise species of kangaroo vine that Maggy was struggling to grow on the first floor, at the drawing-room windows. This kind of erudition would not cut any ice with Alison Cunningham—she would know how to judge Fanny Vandegrift. In spite of her extreme kindness, Cummy was a little jealous of any influence over Louis, especially any influence that wasn't Scottish. Indeed, in the past she'd looked askance at Louis's English friends! With great satisfaction, Thomas remembered the violence of the governess as she showed those apostates and free thinkers the door.

He was shaken from his daydreams by a doorbell ringing, by the noisy laughter of his niece and nephew, Katherine and Bob Stevenson. He heard Louis leap down the steps four at a time to welcome them under the big lantern in the entrance hall.

*

"O that ye would altogether hold your peace! and it should be your wisdom," read Thomas Stevenson in his thundering voice. Standing at his place, the big family Bible in his hands, he was reciting the verses from the Book of Job that he had chosen for this evening. *"Hear now my reasoning, and harken to the pleadings of my lips."* His guests were attentive. Feeling the gaze of the head of the house upon them, they all bowed their heads and collected their thoughts. In this paneled dining room lit by silver candelabras, each of them experienced a vague discomfort. *"Will ye speak wickedly for God? and talk deceitfully for him?"* Thomas inquired, and he hardly needed the prompting of the page to declaim the poetry he knew by heart.

In the silence they could hear the breathing of Mr. Baxter's pregnant wife, who was fatigued by the long-standing grace. And they could hear the clinking of the dishes, which the new maid was piling behind Thomas Stevenson on the buffet between the two windows. Margaret, helpless at the other end of the table, watched this ancillary ballet, whose inefficiency was equaled only by its indiscretion. The noises of the glass, the clinking of the plates seemed to grow louder as Thomas raised his voice. She knew that this racket was disturbing him. She already recognized the signs of mounting anger in certain inflections of her husband's voice. *"As one man mocketh another, do ye so mock Him?"* Thomas shouted.

Who would lightning strike this evening? Even Cummy, who dreaded no one but God, asked herself this question. The prospect of supper at the table with her old employers made her anxious. She was sixty years old, tall and straight as a ramrod, with a fine face and clear eyes, an authoritarian mind that was both intelligent and dignified.

Louis exchanged a look with his mother; he had recognized the same menace in his father's voice, which continued: *"Shall not his excellency make you afraid? and his dread fall upon you?"*

This evening, if the conversation touched on religion, Louis would grovel before his father. Once upon a time he had considered it his duty as an honest man always to tell the truth, his duty as a son not to compromise his convictions, not to deceive his father about his faith. But he had just gotten what he wanted from life, his choice of a career and their acceptance of his wife. Henceforth he would bow to family piety, smiling with tenderness and indulgence. Who would be the victim of this storm? Bob the bohemian? In six years, he had changed none of his habits. Gifted with numerous talents, he had accomplished nothing. Katherine, who was rocking from one foot to the other, Katherine so fine, so distinguished, whose ethereal blondness was a magnificent counterpoint to her brother's gypsy looks? Louis watched his cousins with the same tenderness, both of them so caustic and brilliant. Fanny? Fanny would know how to deflect the blow. Raising his head, Louis observed his wife. Her hands joined in a pose that was not a gesture of prayer, she stood at her full height to the right of the master of the house. A head shorter than the other women, she held Thomas's gaze and seemed to listen to him with greater attention. If Louis's optimism had not been much surprised by the understanding—the miraculous complicity—between Fanny and Margaret, Fanny's adaptation to her new life staggered him. Only a month ago this pioneer woman had chosen a ghost town for their honeymoon and settled their sleeping bags in what remained of an old gold mine; in the old mine shafts she had stored the goat's milk she'd obtained with her own hands, and then invited him to sun bathe entirely naked in the hills not far from San Francisco.

How could he have foreseen that this woman would flourish in his parents' house, amidst the eighteenth-century furnishings, the lace shawls, and grace before meals?

"All my inward friends abhorred me: and they whom I loved are turned against me. My bone cleaveth to my skin and to my flesh, and I am escaped with the skin of my teeth." Thomas shouted, while behind him a dish clattered. He closed the book with a furious bang. "I want you," he growled, "to read the following verses at my burial. These are my last wishes."

The young servant girl who had broken the dish was now serving soup to the guests and offered him a plate.

"This soup is cold!" he exclaimed, violently setting down his soup spoon. "Haven't you understood anything my wife has tried so hard to teach you for the past fifteen days? You must recover the soup tureen after each serving! This isn't a mystery! But you do not listen, you just do what's in your own head, a peasant girl's empty head!"

The girl lowered her head and blushed under her bonnet. She was shaken with sobs while the pitiless master went on: "Go back where you came from! You will be more at home on a farm than in this house . . ."

"It is I, sir, who will not stay a moment longer in a house where the servants are mistreated!" Fanny Vandegrift spoke in an icy voice. Standing up, flushed with rage, she shot a scornful look at her father-in-law: "It is monstrous to humiliate a girl who is trying to learn her job! You ought to be ashamed!"

If Fanny could have seen the expression on her husband's face she would perhaps have thought twice. Louis, Margaret, and Cummy were horrified and speechless. The whole table kept their eyes riveted on the old gentleman and his daughter-in-law. The maid began to cry. Fanny continued: "You find it highly moral, perhaps, to insult someone who cannot answer you back?"

"Sit down, my dear . . . sit down."

Known for the violence of his anger, Thomas Stevenson had not flinched: "Sit down, my dear," he repeated.

Calmly, Fanny obeyed and resumed her place. Thomas patted her on the hand. Stupefied, no one seemed to understand what had just happened. Even Louis remained silent. Only Fanny and Thomas had begun to eat. This was the moment the lawyer Charles Baxter chose to make a toast to the newlyweds. Several years older than Louis, massive, ruddy, with a bushy mustache, he was the only one of Louis's friends with a lucrative profession. Mr. Baxter's respectability, however, did not curb his penchant for the bottle. In his prime, he had been a ladies' man and thumbed his nose at the bourgeoisie. He still had the gift of gab and was a wit besides. Raising his glass, he turned to Fanny: "You have become, dear Mrs. Stevenson, a citizen of one of the most exclusive circles in Great Britain," he began, "a self-confident society, whose most active members, those who work for its edification, are gathered here this evening . . ."

"Are you speaking for yourself, Charles?" Thomas commented ironically, apparently having recovered his cheer.

"For myself, sir, for your illustrious family, for Louis, and above all for madam. I should like to say to her that if the solidity of our gray streets, the prosperity of our sober esplanades has given her the impression that Edinburgh is a closed city, isolated from the world . . ."

Baxter smiled, leaving his sentence suspended in mid-air. He stood up solemnly and, holding out his arm, addressed Fanny rather ironically: ". . . I should like to tell her that if we seem narrow to her on the outside, we also know how to be tolerant. We are easy, madam, Louis would even say we are kind, and you know that coming from him this word is no small compliment. Once we are sure that our customs are accepted and our values recognized, we have the flexibility of a family toward all its members, as eccentric as they may be! You belong henceforth to a kind of club, a regiment that would hold you to very high standards at first, but that will accept all strayings, all lapses, once the first obstacles are surmounted."

Baxter paused, and, dropping his teasing tone, turned his blue gaze full of affection on Louis: "You must know, above all, madam, that a man born into this circle never leaves it! He can live away from it, he can distance himself through time and space: He will always return to Scotland in his dreams and in his heart."

Charles Baxter raised his glass high and thundered in the glow of the dining room: "Welcome to Edinburgh, Mrs. Robert Louis Stevenson!"

This cry was repeated by all the company. Even old Miss Alison Cunningham said it with particular warmth. As for Mr. Thomas Stevenson, he emptied the bottle with uncharacteristic good spirit.

The miracle had happened. How on earth had Fanny done it? This remains a mystery. By the end of this dinner, she had charmed the man whom she already called, with tender irony, "Master Tommy." Their understanding would be total and definitive. Without a shred of hypocrisy, she would acquiesce in her father-in-law's judgments, and he would swear only by the wisdom of his son's wife.

They had in common a complex nature that swung between extremes, between love and brutality, tenderness and fervor, despair and laughter. They shared the same vision of the world, the same pessimism, and the same good sense. They understood each other in all things, to such a degree that the old gentleman would soon make Louis promise not to publish anything without his wife's approval.

Six years later, when Thomas Stevenson decided to help his children settle by buying them a house, he did not put the property in his son's name but in Fanny's. In his will, he would leave his wife Margaret an income, and instruct her to bequeath the Stevenson family assets to Mrs. Robert Louis Stevenson if she should survive Louis, an inheritance passing to his daughter-in-law's children, Belle and Lloyd Osbourne, after their mother's death.

In the role of sensible matron devoted to their son, Fanny knew how to win over Louis's parents. But that very devotion was to provoke disapprobation from other sources.

London—October 1880

Her personality was almost as vivid as [Stevenson's]. She was small, dark-complexioned, eager, devoted; of squarish build—supple and elastic; her hands and feet were small and beautifully modeled, though busy; her head had a crop of close-waving, thick black hair. she had a build and character that somehow suggested Napoleon, with a firm setting of jaw and beautifully precise and delicate modeling of the nose and lips; her eyes were full of sex and mystery as they changed from fire or fun to gloom or tenderness . . . She had deep and rich capacities alike for tragedy and humor, Colvin reminisced in *Memories and Notes. All her moods, thoughts, and instincts were vividly genuine and her own, and in her daily talk,*

*like her letters, there was a play of character and feeling and choice
and colour of words.*

Of all Louis's friends, Colvin was the one with whom Fanny got
on best. Let us say with whom she argued least. Between Mrs.
Robert Louis Stevenson and the others, all the others—Walter
Simpson, Charles Baxter, even Bob Stevenson, and certainly William Ernest Henley—the cycle of estrangement and reconciliation
would go on for twenty years. Whether momentary quarrels or
lifelong grudges, their relations would never be simple.

She was one of the strangest people who have lived in our time,
wrote Edmund Gosse. . . . *a sort of savage nature in some ways,
but very lovable—extraordinarily passionate and unlike everyone
else in her violent feelings and unrestrained way of expressing
them—full of gaiety, and with a genius for expressing things picturesquely, but not literary. I think R. L. S. must have caught some
of his ways of feeling from her . . .*

Gosse is said to be the only one of Louis's old friends to have
cheerfully accepted his marriage. Wrong! *He and I had a quarrel
once and he bears malice,* Fanny wrote the very week of their
meeting, *so I don't like him; but I believe he is, or thinks he is,
honestly fond of Louis. He is a poet, and like most of his walk in
literature, very good at business, smooth, silken, like a purring cat,
very witty, rather maliciously so, but vain beyond belief. That is
why he cannot forgive me. I was the unintentional cause of his
acting in a way he was bitterly ashamed of afterwards.*

Fanny, partial? No doubt, but she was shrewd as well. This first
judgment will find many echoes among Gosse's friends, who would
forgive his vanity, preferring to emphasize his sense of humor and
charm. Long after Louis's death, she would finally admit that he
was the only one who had been kind to her, he and Mrs. Sitwell.

Yet relations between the two women would not always be peaceful. The day would come when Fanny could not tolerate the prudishness of her counterpart.

It does indeed seem that no one escaped her resentment, with
the single exception of Henry James. He alone found grace in her
eyes. She continued to feel admiration and affection for him,
though in the end he resisted her and refused to be the executor
of Stevenson's literary estate. She would forgive him for this, too,
perhaps because James was the only one of the group never to
have known Louis without Fanny, the only one who didn't feel

nostalgic for the Louis of former times, for the Stevenson before America and his marriage.

At the end of this first Scottish summer, a cold, rainy summer, Louis's uncle, Dr. George Balfour, once again became alarmed at the state of his nephew's lungs and sent him immediately to the sanatorium at Davos. On the way to Switzerland, Louis stopped in London, met his old friends, and introduced them to his wife. Six months after their marriage, Fanny's official entry into English literary circles seemed more like an ending.

The night we arrived, before I had my hat off which covered a frightful headache, Bob, Henley, and Mr. Colvin were in the rooms. They stayed until twelve and after . . .

"Basically, realism is merely a question of method," Henley stormed, his red beard smelling of whisky, his crutches leaving their imprint in the carpet from the window to the bed, where Fanny was sitting.

"Art, whether it is realistic or idealistic," purred Colvin, his hands joined in the armchair, "appeals to the same feeling, and aims at the same goal."

"Artistic vision," Bob remarked, sprawling on the cushions, "might be a sort of partial blindness!"

"Precisely!" shouted Louis, his face lost in a haze of smoke, a glass of wine in one hand, a cigarette in the other. He hadn't stopped pacing the room, gesturing and spewing paradoxes, his eyes burning with excitement. "Look at Balzac, he leaves nothing in shadow. He says everything, drowning in detail and missing his mark. There is only one art in the world, the art of omission! If I knew how, if only I could omit—I want nothing else. A man who has mastered the art of omission could create *The Iliad* from a trivial newspaper article."

For no one in the world will I stop in London another hour after the time set. It is a most unhealthful place at this season, and Louis knows far too many people to get a moment's rest . . . Company comes in at all hours from early morning till late at night, so that

*I almost never have a moment alone . . . It is not good for my mind,
nor my body either, to sit smiling at Louis's friends until I feel like
a hypocritical Cheshire cat, talking stiff nothings with one and another in order to let Louis have a chance with the one he cares the
most for, and all the time furtively watching the clock and thirsting
for their blood because they stay so late . . .*

How could Fanny take so little pleasure in the intellectual elite
of her day? How could the artist who had formerly complained
about the cultural desert of Oakland take so little interest in the
aesthetic reflections of London? How could the adventuress who
rolled her own cigarettes and chain-smoked rail so against late
hours, culinary excess, and heated discussions? Had marriage and
respectability changed her into a bourgeois housewife?

Fanny may not have changed, but Louis had become an invalid—
a circumstance he preferred to forget. How could she relish the
brilliant exchanges between Stevenson and Henley when she knew
that excitement, smoke, and whiskey would provoke a relapse? She
knew that at any moment Louis might bring his handkerchief to
his mouth and she would spot the crimson drop that signaled a
hemorrhage; that he would spend discouraging weeks after such an
attack confined to his bed. Henley would have no knowledge of
the suffering, the horror of those weeks. But Fanny would.

Those she suspected of egotism or carelessness toward her husband had better look out. Having failed to save Hervey, she attacked in advance anything that threatened Louis's health or peace
of mind. The silences were over, the mystery vanished. The impassive sphinx of Austin Camp expressed herself quite clearly in
London.

Surely some of Fanny's innate wisdom deserted her here, along
with the reticence that had won the hearts of the miners of Nevada,
the painters of Grez, and the puritans of Edinburgh. The woman
who had known how to adapt herself to such different settings
would alienate the English intelligentsia in one week. They began
to murmur that her influence on Stevenson threatened to adulterate
his future works, that he would never become the great writer he
promised to be, that the grasp of this little American woman from
the Midwest would break his spirit and reduce his work to medioc-

rity. *If we do not soon get away from London, I shall become an embittered woman*, she concluded.

When in mid-October 1880, Fanny Stevenson escorted Louis to Switzerland, the chips were down and the roles set. They would not change for seven years.

From this moment on, Mrs. Robert Louis Stevenson was regarded as a dominating wife who meddled in what she knew nothing about. A watchdog: faithful, no doubt, but tedious.

Imagining the Fanny of the English period, I cannot help feeling a certain anger at the injustice that is still done to this woman. Nailed to the place her husband assigns her, bound by the requirements of his illness, mummified in the eyes of the world—she has so little freedom.

Certainly, she chose this life out of love, some will say out of ambition; she put herself first, and consequently took all the blows. But Louis was the star; it was Louis who suffered and Louis who created. Fanny was content to keep watch—to exercise surveillance, the meanest will insist. Henceforth, a few adjectives will be enough to describe her, two or three attitudes sum her up. This woman who for forty years had never stopped growing, seeking, progressing, is suddenly arrested, fixed. Her head and heart stop expanding. Morally, nothing happens to her. She will spend seven long, joyless years that pass uneventfully as far as she is concerned. And when she tries to step outside her assigned role, heaven help her! When Fanny is impelled to collaborate with her husband, to sign her name along with his, she will discover that the word "Vandegrift" on the title page is invisible to the critics. *I thought in the beginning that I shouldn't mind being Louis's scapegoat, but it is rather hard to be treated like a comma—and a superfluous one at that.*

Davos—Saint Marcel—Hyères—1880–1884

Seeking a climate that would benefit Louis's health, Fanny accompanied him on a frenzied, anxious search that kept them wandering around Europe for some years. They went from Switzerland to France, from the Alps to the Mediterranean, with several detours via Scotland, London, and Paris, detours that destroyed in a few days the improvements won during long months of solitude and rest. Every new stay raised her wild hopes for a cure. Every relapse dragged her down into an abyss of anguish. This was a grim existence, tense and wearing.

It is depressing to live with dying people . . . But may Davos forgive me! It has done so much for Louis that I am ashamed to say anything against it.

There was a sanatorium, two hotels, several chalets and chains of snowcapped mountains looming on every side. No volume, no color, always the same walks, always the same straight river, and the snow.

Graves dotted the mountainside in this village where all the inhabitants, including the shopkeepers, were consumptives. Hatreds, jealousies, and love affairs were carried on with great intensity, as though the living had to throw themselves into extreme passions to prove to themselves that they were still alive. Among the patients at the hotel, invalids of every country and nationality, gossip was rife about this odd couple. She was so tiny, so robust, as stocky as he was fragile and lanky. She was as dark as he was pale, as secret, as tragic as he was voluble and sociable. The Stevensons: People whispered about their difference in age, the husband's long hair, the wife's short hair, the stepson's upbringing.

The impromptu arrival of Louis's first love, Mrs. Sitwell, would have come as a pleasant diversion from the heavy tedium of Davos if she were not accompanying her dying son. Side by side, the two Fannies nursed the adolescent. This was a wretched way of reconnecting with the past, of taking up the broken threads of a former life . . . a sad echo of Hervey's death. Mrs. Sitwell would lose her child in April.

Fanny would return to Davos two winters in a row. The altitude was not good for her heart, she suffered from dizziness and palpitations. Never mind. Since the mountains seemed to strengthen Louis, she neglected her own health. What mattered was that he should become the great writer they dreamed of: *Take thou the writing: thine it is*, he would write, dedicating his last book to her.

Strangely, Fanny would not recognize the talent of the first novel that would make him famous. Because he began it on vacation with his parents, because he wrote it to distract Samuel Lloyd from the Scottish rain and to dream with his father over the stories they used to tell each other in the old days, because he published it in serialized form in a children's magazine, Fanny disdained the masterpiece that would bring glory to the man whose genius she believed in. She would not be the only one to disdain *Treasure Island*. It would take two years before the serialized novel was published as a separate volume and became a best-seller, two years of making ends meet, of not knowing how to pay for treatments, doctors, hotels, or how to subsidize her son's education. It was Louis's father who paid the family's bills. It was Thomas who continued to sign checks and send money orders. This was a humiliating situation for an author who was turning thirty-five and never stopped working. From his bed Stevenson produced *Prince Otto, The New Thousand and One Nights, A Child's Garden of Verses*. He wrote essays that Leslie Stephen published in his journal, literary criticism, lead articles that Henley tried to place. These were small *succès d'estime* that allowed him, when the doctor in Davos finally agreed to let him leave, to rent a house in the suburbs of Marseilles. The doctor's orders were precise: "Live at least twelve miles from the Mediterranean, near a pine forest." They left the snowbound inferno for the sun.

*

Heat: She loved the sun more than anything. Fanny was exultant: After all those years in hotels, she was finally going to live in her own home. She ran to antique shops, hemmed curtains, fashioned tablecloths from old dresses, and built some furniture with boards. As she had done for Sam in Virginia City, in fifteen days she organized a comfortable house for Louis. They moved in October. By December they were once again living in a hotel. The humidity, the mosquitos, and an epidemic of diphtheria had brought Louis a new series of hemorrhages. The two years spent in Davos ended in the most serious attack he'd ever had.

Fanny had to close the house alone, while Louis left to convalesce in Nice. He neglected to wire her that he'd arrived safely. She went mad with anxiety. What if he had died on the way? She abruptly abandoned her moving chores and set off. From town to town, from station to station, she followed his footsteps as far as

Toulon. At Toulon she reflected that perhaps a letter was waiting for her in Marseille. She took the train back. In Marseille, no message. She returned to Nice and finally found Louis comfortably settled at the hotel.

This woman, who was the very incarnation of practical sense and efficiency, was now considered by the London crowd to be quite mad. Colvin, the reasonable professor whom she had frantically wired for help, called Mrs. Robert Louis Stevenson "insane." She laughed at this, but she bore him a grudge. She held it against him, not that he'd criticized her, but that he hadn't dropped everything to fly to Louis's aid.

Indefatigable, she discovered in Hyères a resort recommended for respiratory patients, a tiny chalet built for the Paris Universal Exposition and brought piece by piece to the bottom of a Provençal garden. This doll house seduced them both so much that they rented it for nine years, with the Stevenson parents' backing. Fanny moved in. She began to plant clumps of trees. And it was at Hyères, four years after their marriage, that success caught up with them. Prime Minister Gladstone, they said, stayed up all night to finish *Treasure Island*. The serialized novel, finally published as a separate volume, sold by the thousands.

Intoxicated by his success, Louis invited his old pals Henley and Baxter to celebrate the event. He would pay all their expenses and show them a good time. She was incensed at the idea that the men she called "bloodsuckers" should come to exhaust Louis with their bouts of drinking and gossiping, and that afterwards Stevenson would pay their bills. She hardly had any sense of money, and no one would ever accuse her of stinginess; but as the woman who paid the bills, she knew the value of a penny and took no pleasure in sharing it with men she didn't like and who largely returned the favor. When they arrived at Hyères, Fanny sulked. As a result, Louis proposed to his friends that the men go off together to amuse themselves in Nice. He caught a cold there which degenerated into lung congestion, complicated by a kidney infection. Distressed, Henley and Baxter beat a hasty retreat to England. They withdrew, anticipating Fanny. She spent the next fifteen anguished days nursing him in Nice, alone as usual in a foreign town.

Her telegrams preparing England for the death of Robert Louis Stevenson irritated the salons and clubs with her taste for melodrama. Bob finally crossed the Channel, helped Fanny take Louis back to Hyères, and then departed. Their understanding at Grez was not part of this life. When Louis began to convalesce, there was suddenly a new catastrophe, an epidemic of cholera sweeping the south of France. All around Stevenson, people were dropping like flies. His fragility suggested that he would not escape the contagion. Fanny canceled the lease and convinced him to flee: *I was only happy once; that was at Hyères; it came to an end for a variety of reasons, decline of health, change of place, increase of money, age.*

For Mrs. Robert Louis Stevenson, happiness meant Louis, and saving his life. Fanny's story during these years of frenzied movement, these years so well documented by the biographers of Robert Louis Stevenson, is reduced to this unity of purpose.

But what can we say about Fanny Vandegrift? That the tension and anguish occasioned by the seriousness of Stevenson's relapses at Hyères, and the series of hemorrhages that would soon keep him bedridden in Bournemouth, finally eroded her nervous system? That her husband's illness undermined her already tenuous sense of social convention? It is easy to understand her detractors' irritation, to smile at the exaggeration of some of her requests. When she discovered, for example, that some visitors had cold symptoms, she was not content to forbid entrance until they were completely well; she then demanded that they pass inspection. This was the height of absurdity: Each one had to hold his handkerchief to the window for Fanny to inspect. She had the eye of Cerberus, and only immaculate handkerchiefs could enter! She rightly maintained that a cold is a contagious infection which, if Louis caught it, could lead to a hemorrhage. Fairly soon this theory of contagion would be scientifically established, but Fanny's precautions are still cited as merely one of her crotchets.

Her determination to defend irrational intuitions, her impulsive decisions, her courage and her energy in times of crisis raised Fanny Vandegrift to the rank of heroine. But this lofty role of wife and nurse left no room for her own development. Intellectually and emotionally, Mrs. R. L. S. stood still.

And because Fanny did not change during her time in England, telling her story for the period between 1880 and 1888 means passing quickly over these years which were so rich for the history of literature, years she herself would remember only as shadowed by impending death. And yet she made great efforts to fit the mold; and she succeeded.

Great Britain—1884–1887

They moved to Bournemouth, where Samuel Lloyd, more English than the natives, had been at boarding school for some years. Thomas Stevenson then decided to offer his daughter-in-law the house, that safe haven she had dreamed of. *I suppose it is my Dutch blood that makes me so fond of a real home, something that is our own, and in which there can be no change except that which we choose to make ourselves.* In just these terms Sam Osbourne's wife had formerly described to her sisters the little cottage in Oakland. *A house of my own.* For her, this house would finally mean security; for Stevenson, boredom. Fanny would bloom in this peaceful bourgeois life. And Louis would feel trapped.

Yet during their three years of sedentary life at Bournemouth, Stevenson would become "R. L. S.," those three famous initials whose renown would reach Indianapolis, Oakland, even Hawaii, where Belle was leading the good life. Along with Joe Strong, who had become official painter to the court of King Kalakaua, Belle would finally celebrate her mother's remarriage.

Mrs. Stevenson played the Anglo-Saxon nurse. She lost any trace of an American accent, and her drawing room at Bournemouth entered into literary legend as "the Blue Room." She presided at conversations between Robert Louis Stevenson and Henry James, and figures—a rare detail for a portrait—in the background of the famous painting "Stevenson," signed by John Singer Sargent. This work, commissioned by rich Bostonians who wanted to hang the image of their favorite author over their fireplace, bore witness to the vogue of R. L. S. in the United States. If Fanny became anglicized, Louis drew closer to America.

Comfortable in her new role as mistress of the house, Mrs. R. L. S. was cowed by no one, not even by William Ernest Henley and his visits to Bournemouth. Even as she kept an eye on the level of the whiskey supply, she would go so far as to encourage the two men to collaborate. This was a mistake. The plays Stevenson and Henley wrote together were total failures. Their association would exhaust Louis's strength and embitter Henley, who would not forgive Fanny for her suggestions; Fanny would hold a grudge against Henley for never taking her advice to heart, and each would blame the other for the poor quality of the work.

Because she was American and he was scornful of America, because she was a woman and he thought the "weaker sex" had nothing to contribute to intellectual discussion, because he thought her heavy-handed and illiterate, and because he was exclusive and jealous, Henley was pained by Fanny's influence over Louis. He tried to ignore her, and kept her at a distance. If he could have, he would have muzzled her and locked her up. He was doubly wrong.

Actually, Louis's most conspicuous success owed much to Fanny's critical sense. When he read her the first draft of *The Strange Case of Dr. Jekyll and Mr. Hyde*, she was the only one not to applaud.

"You're missing the point," she commented.

Furious, he demanded an explanation.

"You make Dr. Jekyll a hypocrite, the bad man pretending to be good. But he should be like all of us, both bad and good."

Louis threw the sheets of paper at Fanny's face, gathered them up and slammed the door. He burned his work and began again. For three days and nights he rewrote his story, following his wife's advice point by point: "Get beyond anecdote"; "Sublimate the supernatural"; "Aim at allegory."

The week of its publication, the Archbishop of Canterbury based his sermon on the parable of Dr. Jekyll and Mr. Hyde. The *London Times* published a six-page review. The expression "Jekyll and Hyde" passed into the English language. This was to be Fanny's triumph: Robert Louis Stevenson could and should have confidence in her! Following his father's wishes, he would subsequently submit all his writings to his wife's judgment. She stood as proof of his purpose. They were symbiotically joined.

This communion, however, did not prevent conflict. The Stevensons argued violently. Louis was still the reckless patient, devoured by the need to live and act. A frustrated, difficult invalid, he kept dreaming of travel and adventure. Fanny's despotism as a worried, intrusive, demanding nurse irritated him. Louis's irresponsibility exasperated her. He was impatient, she explosive. He insulted her, she slung it back. A neighbor would say later that hearing their quarrels, she did not know whether to cry "murder" and call the police or to retreat on tiptoe. Their mutual savagery reached such heights that it would take them several days to settle down after these battles. Fanny generally concluded by calling Louis a "flimsy canary bird." He would answer that "there was no use in turning life into King Lear."

Yet Louis was the one who almost dragged his family into tragedy. Reading the newspapers, he was so moved by the martyrdom of Ireland that he decided to go there and offer himself to the holocaust, so that the murder of a well-known author, along with his wife and stepson, might attract the world's attention to the violation of human rights and misfortunes of this province. Let this massacre of a celebrated family stop the barbaric acts perpetrated by civilization and discredit the murderers!

Fanny was not charmed by the idea of collective immolation. Louis was impervious to her opinion, however, and went to pack his bags. To die for a great cause, that was certainly more heroic than to die of sickness and boredom—off to the sacrifice! "This is utterly absurd," she sighed. "It's absurd, but if you're going, I'll go too."

*

Once more she left her fabulous garden and her house. Once more she prepared to set off. But it would not be for the "Irish massacre." A few days before their departure, a telegram from Margaret reached them. Thomas Stevenson was dying.

Struck down by a new series of hemorrhages, Louis would not be present at his father's funeral.

Edinburgh—May 13, 1887

Drawn by a team of six horses, the hearse arrived at the cemetery. Draped in a black flag stitched with silver palm leaves and covered with white flowers according to the wishes of the deceased, the coffin was shouldered by six men of the family, six of Louis's cousins, who carried the remains along the paths. Bob Stevenson led the mourners and, as pallbearer, replaced the absent son. Shaking with fever, consigned by his uncle, Dr. Balfour, to his old nursery room, Robert Louis Stevenson had watched the cortege as it made its way down the street. Edinburgh was giving the engineer and scholar a semiofficial funeral, the most imposing ceremony ever organized by the city for a private citizens.

Silently, hidden behind their veils, the women gathered around the burial vault. First came the widow, supported by Katherine and Fanny; then Cummy and numerous notables' wives; the nuns of the Mary Magdalene Mission of Edinburgh, which Thomas Stevenson had helped to establish; the ladies associated with the charities Thomas continued to support; a huge crowd of the faithful of the Presbyterian Church of Scotland, of which he had been one of the most active members; and finally his friends, his associates, and his butler, the devoted John, who held Thomas's beloved skye terriers on a leash. In his homily, the minister did not forget to mention the deceased's fondness for animals, his passion for dogs, whom he used to say "possessed a soul." In addition, the reverend emphasized that if engineer Thomas Stevenson's name had not reached London, it was because he had always refused to patent his inventions in the area of optics, alleging that his appointment by the government obliged him to put his talents in the service of the state without seeking celebrity.

At the graveside, Bob read the verses from the Book of Job that Thomas had taken care to recopy, those verses he had begun to read during Fanny's first dinner in Edinburgh and had labeled "my last wishes."

Fanny Stevenson replaced the shawl that was slipping off Margaret's thin shoulders. Not a tear fell behind the old lady's veil, but she was leaning with all her frail weight on her daughter-in-law's arm. Solid and straight, Mrs. R. L. S. stood there, unmoving, long after the grave had been filled. Bob, bareheaded, his face nearly covered by his scarf, was already on his way. He was ill himself. Katherine took him by the elbow, helping him to avoid the puddles in the hollows of the paths.

In the now empty cemetery, three figures, pillars of the Stevenson clan, remained in meditation: Margaret, Cummy, and Fanny. Beside these three women, standing a little to the left, was one man—Lloyd Osbourne. It was Thomas Stevenson's generosity that had made possible his gentleman's education. At nineteen, he had the self-assurance, the dry humor, and the cool manner of the well-bred young Englishman. In addition, he had that very British hint of eccentricity which the perfection of his bearing did not betray.

With what pride—and what gratitude on this day of mourning—

Fanny Vandegrift observed her son. The work of Master Tommy. It was miraculous that Lloyd had been lucky enough to assimilate the values of this milieu, to bloom in this financial security. Jacob's daughter had never known such an opportunity. Until her meeting with Louis. She had never belonged to any milieu, she thought, she had never been part of any society. Since her first return to Indiana twenty years ago, she had felt uprooted. She had been a stranger in Paris, in Grez, even in Oakland and San Francisco. Now, seven years after her arrival at Heriot Row, she finally knew the satisfaction of belonging to that upper middle class whose praises Baxter had sung. She wanted proof of it in her son's gentility. Who would have imagined that this tall boy with the pale complexion was the son of a prospector, an adventurer who had just gone off to sea without leaving an address. The news of Sam's disappearance had just arrived in Bournemouth the month before. What shame, what scandal, what mediocrity were hidden by his father's flight? From now on, Lloyd would fear only one thing: that Sam Osbourne should land in England to tell the tale. Lloyd stood with his monocle in his eye, his long, ungloved hand in a pocket, his umbrella over his arm, a pure product of the Scottish gentry and the best guarantee of his mother's social standing—or so she thought.

I returned soon after [the funeral], *but my mother and R. L. S. remained several weeks. In the course of time two letters arrived, the first from my mother—such a heartbroken letter—saying that the doctors had ordered R. L. S. to leave England at once for Colorado as the only means of prolonging his life. England was ended for him; he was never to set foot in it again. She wrote of her "little nest" and the unendurable wrench it would be to leave it. "Life had been too happy in Skerryvore—the envying gods had struck it down." It was all in this strain of anguish at abandoning her home for a future that loomed before her black indeed.*

Expecting to find R. L. S.'s in a similar note of tragedy, I opened it—when it arrived a day or two later—with a sinking heart. But it was cheerful, almost jubilant; the prospect of Colorado or New Mexico seemed to fill him with joy. Were we not to live in the wilds with rifles on our walls and bearskins on our mud floors! Sombreros, ha, ha! Mustangs, silver spurs, spaciousness, picturesque freedom; "Scottie" of the something or other ranch! There was not a word about cozy nests, nor envying gods, nor eternal farewells to happiness. None whatever. "Vive la vie sauvage!" He was plainly glad to be off, and the sooner the better . . . One might have thought that this was the ideal moment to go to Ireland; why Colorado and an uncertain search for health when in three weeks the whole matter could be so easily and definitely settled by bullets in our backs? But the mad idea had dropped from his mind, never to be mentioned again . . . I have often wondered since whether the Irish venture had not its origin in an unsuspected desire to leave "Skerryvore" at any price. Hopelessly embedded there, locked in and double-locked, had he not seized on this as the one possible means of escape?

Yes, they had to leave. But how could they leave Bournemouth, Edinburgh, Scotland, England, leaving Margaret Stevenson alone in her sorrow? And Fanny, once more sacrificing her own desire to stay, would find a way to satisfy her husband's wishes.

You have only Louis left now, and I could not take him away from you, even for his good . . . Come with us, dear, and let us try to be to you what we can, even though that may be little . . . Dr. Scott says that [Louis's illness could be] cured by a total change, and strongly advises the American plan. But we will not leave you. After all there is something left you to do. There is the dear old man's boy; yours too, but his as well. You and I have a mission in life, a sacred one. Let us join hands, for our work is one.

Her detractors have accused Fanny of fighting with everyone closest to her husband, of trying to clear a space around him that only she could fill. But she would live with the old lady for seven years, and God knows Louis was close to his mother. For a wife devoured by jealousy, the presence of such a rival would have been a fine occasion for angry scenes. Yet Fanny never tried to supplant the woman she very tenderly called "Aunt Maggy."

In the close quarters of a sailing ship, on cannibal islands, the two Stevenson ladies would stand at the side of the man they both loved, in perfect harmony.

On August 28, 1887, nearly seven years to the day after their return from America, Fanny and Louis set off in the opposite direction, bound for the United States. Traveling with them were Aunt Maggy, Lloyd, and Valentine Roch, a servant hired in Hyères. The illustrious author traveling with his entourage: The times of crossing in steerage were over! This was the height of Louis's popularity: The two captains of the tugboats that hauled the steamer into New York harbor were called "Jekyll and Hyde" by their crews because of their contrasting characters. This was fame.

New York and the Adirondacks, U.S.A.—August 1887–May 1888

On the docks of New York, important American publishers tracked him down and waited on his whim. Journalists took his hotel suite by storm. On Broadway, the theatrical adaptation of *The Strange Case of Dr. Jekyll and Mr. Hyde* played to sold-out houses. Yes, this was fame American style, the fame that William Ernest Henley and friends scorned or, Fanny would say, "envied."

Mrs. R. L. S. may have been intoxicated by this triumph over her obscure beginnings, but she would always detest interviews, publicity, and public life. She made great efforts to find a restful place that suited Louis's health, a retreat far from the hubbub of New York. The excitement, the success, had just provoked a new relapse, which precluded the long trip to the sanatorium in Colorado. Where should they go?

Belle's former suitor Ernest Pasdessus, the American sculptor who eleven years earlier in Paris had recommended Grez-sur-Loing, now suggested they try Saranac, a mountain village in the Adirondacks where a famous specialist on tuberculosis had a clinic for "lungers."

The little group settled into a log cabin in October 1887. For Fanny it was the pioneer life all over again. She chopped wood, shoveled snow, shot game. The hems of her skirts were edged with constellations of ice. At night the thermometer plunged to fifteen below. She sat at her husband's bedside until dawn. As always, Louis's cold degenerated into hemorrhages. Bedridden, he continued to write *The Master of Ballantrae*.

And there in the Adirondacks mountains, thousands of miles

from London, the old rivalry between Mrs. Robert Louis Stevenson and Louis's friends led to that famous "Stevenson-Henley" quarrel which would end relations between the protagonists.

The bomb had been wired a month earlier at Bournemouth when Fanny, seeking a closer bond with Louis's literary companions, linked herself quite intimately with the muse of the little group, Bob's sister Katherine. As gifted and charming as all the Stevensons, Katherine shared Fanny's literary ambitions. She wrote. But Katherine—unlike Fanny—was personally supported by Henley, who made an effort to place her stories in magazines. In Henley's eyes, Katherine belonged to an elite from which he generally excluded women, hence his near fanatical admiration.

One evening by the fire in the Blue Room, they had all listened to Katherine read one of her stories. "They" was Stevenson, Henley, and Fanny. When Katherine had put down her sheets of paper, Mrs. R. L. S. had, in her usual way, made criticisms and suggestions. Katherine had been annoyed by her advice, but Fanny insisted. They raised their voices. The two women finally agreed that if Katherine did not manage to sell her story as she had written it, Fanny would be free to rework it. The business rested there, for the moment. °

Some months later, pressed by Fanny, Katherine confessed that her story had not been accepted anywhere. She then gave Fanny permission—rather grudgingly—to change it as she liked.

Newly arrived in New York, Mrs. Robert Louis Stevenson hastily published her version in the *Scribner's* of May 1888. This story, entitled "The Nixie," was signed Fanny Vandegrift Stevenson. Shipped to London, this issue would fall into Henley's hands. Mustering his most acidic tones, he sent a "private and confidential" note to Saranac.

In the letter, which he addressed only to Louis, Henley said little about the matter. He spoke of his melancholy, the failure of their plays, the latest bit of club gossip. Then, in the course of two paragraphs, he slipped in six lines that would decide Fanny's future:

I read 'The Nixie' with considerable amazement. It's Katherine's; surely it's Katherine's? The situation, the environment, the principal figure—voyons! There are even reminiscences of phrase and imagery, parallel incident—que sais-je? It is all better focused, no doubt; but I think it has lost as much (at least) as it has gained; and why there wasn't a double signature is what I've not been able to understand.

In short, Henley accused Fanny of plagiarism; worse, of theft. In literary circles this is a serious charge. It can damage a reputation for life. All the more so as Henley circulated "The Nixie" and expressed his amazement to all and sundry.

A frenzied exchange of letters between Louis, Henley, Katherine, the faithful devotee Baxter, and finally Fanny crisscrossed the Atlantic. Stevenson demanded a complete retraction and apologies from Henley. He demanded that Katherine explain and establish the truth of the matter. The letters crossed each other, were lost, provoking contretemps and misunderstandings. The tone got increasingly heated and the debate more poisonous.

Henley was astonished by the violence of Louis's reaction, by his stubborn defense of the indefensible, and would not take back a single word. He even publicized the quarrel. This estrangement of the famous literary journalist and the successful author had its literary echoes. The incident resulted in Louis's relapse. For Henley, its outcome was a hatred of Fanny, a resentment so fierce, so painful, that nothing, not even the death of the protagonists would appease it.

This horror of "la Vandegrift" would end by spoiling all his feelings for "Lewis," *the man who was my most faithful friend, the being who, excepting my wife Anna, was most dear to me.*

In 1901, seven years after Robert Louis Stevenson's death, it was William Ernest Henley who would write the article that for several generations consigned the author of *Dr. Jekyll and Mr. Hyde* to the rank of a children's author, *a seraph in chocolate, this barley-sugar of a real man.*

*

More than a century after this fight to the death between two friends, between two brothers—the theme of *The Master of Ballantrae*, which Stevenson wrote the month of his quarrel with Henley—how are we to judge the situation? What parts did Fanny and Katherine play, the two women they each claimed to defend and protect, and used to wound each other?

Did Fanny really steal an idea, a story, rights, a reputation that did not belong to her? Did she receive a fee that the author of the work desperately needed to make ends meet?

As Katherine's text has not survived, it is impossible to compare the two versions of "The Nixie" and therefore difficult to make any judgment. But it is quite a surprise to discover the weakness of the published work. The irony is that such a trivial piece of writing could provoke such a tempest. "A matter of principle," the combined voices of Henley, Louis, Katherine, and Fanny whisper in my ear, "a matter of principle!" In his letters to Baxter, Louis takes great care to review the facts. And this so-called restating of the facts provoked Henley's outcries. From these facts, as Stevenson recounts them, issues a portrait of his wife with all Fanny's weaknesses and her impatience that conforms to what I know of Jacob Vandegrift's daughter.

I can imagine her motivated by a thirst for recognition, a desperate need to prove that in artistic matters she could not be wrong; an obsession with establishing Henley's negligence, when he so scorned her; an eagerness to demonstrate the journalist's inability to publish Katherine's story, when rewritten in her own style, signed in her own name, it was published by one of America's most important magazines. Let us add, if we like, a good dose of pretension and blindness: Fanny chose to ignore the fact that in the same issue Louis had signed an article which was the pride of the magazine: that probably *Scribner's* accepted her "Nixie" just because her name was "Mrs. R. L. S." Tactless, unable to let go of an idea—that was Fanny Vandegrift.

But Fanny genuinely had no idea that she might be pillaging someone else's work. *Katherine claimed that she was no longer interested in the text*, she insists, *that I could modify it as I liked, that my suggestions had seriously changed its meaning, that the story I told her did not resemble her novella. I did not for a second imagine that she might want to sign it!*

And let us be clear on one point: "The Nixie" was not their first collaboration. Fanny seems to have had a longstanding habit of editing Katherine's stories, giving her the benefit of their association. I found evidence of this collaboration in a letter from Davos dated 1881, seven years before the incident:

Dear Katherine often writes, Fanny tells her mother-in-law. *She sent me a paper which she hoped I could place for her in America. It was too much to ask Louis to do, so I rewrote the whole of it and sent it to my magazine. I do hope she will get something for it, though it will not be much. I am not sure, now that I come to think of it, that Katherine would wish me to speak of it, so I had better say this in confidence.*

The affair would never have reached such proportions if Louis had not been trying in this final quarrel to settle an old score with Henley. *I fear I have come to an end with Henley; the Lord knows if I have not tried to be a friend to him, the Lord knows even that I have not altogether failed. There is not one of that crew that I have not helped in every kind of strait, with money, with service, and that I was not willing to have risked my life for; and yet the years come, and every year there is a fresh outburst against me and mine . . .* Louis writes to Baxter. *And I have forgiven and forgiven and forgotten and forgotten . . . I knew long ago, how Henley tried to make trouble for me, and I not only held my peace when I had the evidence; I willingly forgave also . . .*

But, I do not see how it is possible for me to return to England, Fanny rambles on to the same correspondent, *after the disgrace that has been put upon me by Louis's friends. Had Henley only been satisfied with making the charge to me, I should have been bound to say nothing to Louis on account of the ill effect of such a thing upon his health. As it is, they have nearly, perhaps quite, murdered him. It is very hard for me to keep on living! I may not be able to, but must try for my dear Louis's sake. If I cannot, then I leave my curse upon the murderers and slanderers. I had done them nothing but kindness, ever, nor surely had Louis.*

Since this horrible untrue charge has been made against me, I have received not one letter from all those I considered my friends in England . . . I think it is almost better that we were both out of such a world. . . . I have always had courage before, but I feel beaten now. They say that one is supported by the consciousness of innocence. That is not true. . . . It's the injustice—the injustice that eats my soul. . . . If it so happens that I must go back to perfidious Albion, I shall learn to be false. For Louis's sake I shall pretend to be their friend still— while he lives; but that in my heart I can ever forgive those who have borne false witness against me—! . . . While they eat their bread from my hand—and oh, they will do that—I shall smile and wish it were poison that might wither their bodies as they have my heart.

This time, Fanny had confided Louis to the care of the servant Valentine, consigned him to his mother's vigilance and Lloyd's affection, and left them all in Saranac. This was the first separation in eight years.

She had gone alone to Indiana, where she wanted to see her mother again. Then, in March 1888, she continued on to San Francisco. She hoped to meet her sisters, Cora Orr and Nellie Sanchez, overcome as she was with an urgent need to renew ties with her own world before the return to Bournemouth, a need she thought she would never feel.

*
**

In the luxurious Pullman car carrying her toward her past, Mrs. R. L. S. could not sleep. She stared at the corner of the compartment, at the crystal of the liquor cabinet dancing with purple port, and blue curaçau. Big bouquets of tiger lilies, which she had confessed to journalists were her favorite flower, stood in vases. A small attention from the admirers of Robert Louis Stevenson. How things had changed in eight years! Louis was famous, Sam dead or defeated. How would she find San Francisco? And Rearden? And John Lloyd? The first had become a judge on the State Supreme Court, the second a founder of the Bank of California; they had both just married very young women. And Dora? Her confidante, her only friend . . . Impatiently she imagined all they would have to tell each other. Poor Dora—she was now a widow. In December 1886, the news of Virgil Williams' death had reached Bournemouth. He had been Fanny's teacher, the man who had introduced her to art. She only now understood how her life would be changed by this loss.

The train pulled into the station at Omaha, jolting her out of her reveries. Here, too, what transformations! To cross the United States now took only ten days. She could, if she liked, stay in this same car and have her meals served to her compartment, she had only to ring the bell . . . Fanny rolled her little head back against the headrest and closed her eyes. How far removed she felt from her first days at the School of Design! She could still see Belle painting at her side, her pretty daughter. How she missed her daughter! Why had Belle kept this terrible silence for the past eight years? In her letters, dear Dora would say that it was surely Joe who prevented Belle from writing. But Fanny knew her daughter too well not to know that she still held a grudge against her for her scandalous marriage to Louis. Or perhaps Belle imagined that Fanny, who was at home in the best Scottish drawing rooms, should have sent her money, a lot of money. Yes, surely that was it: Belle thought she was very rich and very stingy. The young woman no doubt reproached her mother for not coming to her aid when her little boy was born. How could Fanny make her understand that the money belonged to Thomas Stevenson, and that until these last few years . . . The shaking of the train as it started off jolted Fanny back into her seat. Again, she closed her eyes. These last few years . . . But she could not sleep. She hadn't a single happy memory from these last years at Bournemouth. She straightened up against the cushions. How on earth could that be? Wasn't she miserable at the thought of leaving her pretty house? Didn't she have a single regret for these eight years? Hadn't Louis made her happy? Imagining his thin figure, the gestures of his long slender hands, his brown eyes, his laughter, and especially his voice, his warm, teasing voice, she felt a contentment much more exciting than her impatience to arrive in San Francisco. She had never loved Louis more passionately than she did today. Living with him was living as close as possible to Christ's teaching . . . Fanny smiled at this thought. The least one could say is that she had never shared her father-in-law's religious convictions. She had acquiesced in everything, save the fanaticism of his faith. But Louis's goodness, his generosity, his way of returning good for bad—how she admired it! If only she had known how to acquire a little of the tolerance he practiced. She let her forehead roll against the window . . . What a shame that Louis had not succeeded in teaching her kindness. From the beginning of this trip, the memory, the remorse at her violence, had deprived her of sleep. Remorse, yes, but Henley—hadn't she been right? Certainly for the past eight years Mrs. R. L. S. should have taken training in indulgence. But to forgive Henley? That idea revolted her! In the end, it was Louis who might have shown some lucidity—and a little more reason with age. Fanny suddenly remembered a scene in which she had tried to warn him. Louis, as usual, hadn't wanted to listen.

"I truly believe that Henley takes your money with one hand," she had told him, "while he is preparing to knock you down with the other. Only he doesn't quite have the courage. He is waiting until you're gone, until you cannot defend yourself . . ."

"Shush!" he had ordered her. "I only want to imagine Henley with his open hand held out!" He had laughed: "And stop thinking ill of people."

"I don't think ill. I am only trying to protect you!"

It was Louis's levity, his carelessness that always gave her the impression that "she saw only the bad side of people and things."

And yet, how Fanny missed his gaiety since their separation! She should never have undertaken this trip. In her husband's absence, every day on the train seemed endless. She tried to imagine him at Saranac, to visualize what he was doing, the state of his health. She had even consulted her deck of cards: The king of hearts told her that he was doing well, "but not as well as he should have." And what anguish she had felt in New York, waking up alone in her big bed! When his illness gave them both some respite, their physical understanding was still complete. At Hyères, Fanny had even thought she was pregnant. A false alarm. Pregnant at forty-four? That would have been a fine thing . . . She smiled at the thought. But would he one day regret not having a child of his own? He claimed that he was much too afraid of passing on his bad health to his progeny, that he wouldn't do such a thing to his worst enemy, that his intimacy with his stepson had satisfied all his desires for paternity. And it was true that Louis and Lloyd had a close and untroubled relationship. The disappearance of Sam Osbourne had left Stevenson responsible, morally and financially, for the young man. Fanny rejoiced in that. And Lloyd seemed on many fronts much more reasonable than Louis. Now they were even thinking of collaborating. That the two great loves of her life should find each other on literary ground charmed her. Lloyd, the antithesis of his sister, was a model son. But . . . did Louis love her? At this wrenching question, Fanny straightened her back. She sat upright in her seat, taking care not to lean either on the armrest or against the window. She had just forgotten her forty-eighth birthday. The image of her reflection on the glass did not show too much damage. Had she aged much? Louis, who always teased her, assured her that she was no different from the respectable matron he had introduced to his parents eight years earlier. He repeated to whoever would listen that his marriage was a matriarchy, that his wife ruled over all things, that she led the dance with the violence of her emotions. Nonsense! Those who let themselves be fooled by this speech were highly naive. Nothing and no one had ever forced Louis to do anything he didn't want to do. Their conjugal life rested on this pact, which stipulated his absolute power, his good will toward her, and her occasional right to veto. Although they had tried to use their tenderness to escape the power struggle, they had loved each other without illusion for eight long years. After their romantic beginnings, time had transformed the two children who had entered love as they would enter into a dark room into a couple of fraternal warriors—accomplices or rivals—two halves of the same androgynous being. And besides, Fanny's ambiguous, "hermaphrodite" aspect attracted Louis—a woman's body with a man's stout heart, grace, and strength. At this idea—the idea of her own strength—Fanny was overcome by a strange feeling of guilt, though she could not see why. This feeling always overtook her when Stevenson reproached her for her violence and her partiality. How had she let him down this time? How had she betrayed him? Hadn't her vigilance helped him to fulfill his promise as a writer? But Louis was also an invalid at constant risk. During the past eight years, Fanny's battles against his illness had resolved nothing. Despite the stability of their life at Bournemouth, the rest, the prudence, Louis's health was as precarious as ever. Bournemouth. As Fanny was traveling back to her past, to her world, all she remembered of Bournemouth was the curtain of rain that obscured the horizon on all sides, a trellis of drops that hemmed her in like the knots of an inivisible net. The death of Master Tommy, whom she had so loved, had finally put an end to her desire, her need to be accepted in Great Britain. The image of the villa Mr. Stevenson had offered her, the house she at first regretted, her furniture, her rugs, her blue drawing room, her garden—that image, especially, weighed heavily on her. Henley's monstrous accusations, and the others' failure to come to her defense, made the idea of returning unbearable.

The midday sun shone hot on the glass. As she leaned her temple against the window, her cameo profile, her straight nose, her drooping mouth, seemed framed against the ocher landscape of the Nevada desert. Suddenly a flame ignited in her gold-and-blackberry eyes. She no longer saw the Scottish mists, or the eternal snow of Davos. Instead, a blue vastness rose before her like a powerful breath. A dream—she had a dream in her head for the first time in eight years!

San Francisco—May–August 1888

"Belle! You came from Honolulu? You crossed the Pacific to see me? You made that long voyage?"

Fanny's happiness took their breath away, both of them. Getting off the train in Sacramento, she had seen her daughter waiting for her at the end of the platform. Belle, with her seven-year-old son, Austin Strong, Fanny's grandson. If Mrs. R. L. S. could have, she would have dissolved in tears. But Fanny had not cried since Hervey's death.

*

Small and dark in their blue dresses, mother and daughter leaned against the railing of the jetty in San Francisco. The wind whipped their curls, which danced around their strongly sensual faces. The two women squinted and continued to stare at the ocean, opening their lips slightly in a smile. But they were not smiling. The light undulating on the Pacific, the rocking of the waves, the incessant rhythm of the ocean, made them deliciously dizzy. On the embarcadero where fifteen years earlier Rearden had lectured Fanny, where Louis had come to meet her on the morning of their wedding, the two women were waiting for the Oakland ferry. They hoped to go meet the tenants living in their cottage, and make sure that everything was in order.

"And your work?" Fanny asked, without taking her eyes off the ocean. "How is the drawing coming? And Joe? Tell me, how is he getting on?"

"But Mama, I should be asking you all these questions . . ."

"Me? That's of no interest! But Louis . . ."

"I know: Louis is famous. His Majesty, my friend King Kalakaua of Hawaii swears by *Treasure Island* . . . But you, tell me a little about yourself. I see that you haven't lost your taste for feathers and frills."

"Here I do as I like. If you'd seen me at Bournemouth, it was quite another story."

The two women gave the same conspiratorial giggle.

"You must have known all the celebrities in England," Belle insisted.

"It's you, my girl, who are consorting with kings! As for me, apart from Louis and his parents, I loved only my dog."

"Mama!" Belle scoffed.

"I swear to you, he was a very brave animal. The only honest soul I met in Great Britain. He died last year."

"But in your letters to Dora, you spoke of all the writers you visited, Henry James, Thomas Hardy, Professor Colvin."

Fanny made a tired gesture. "Oh, in my letters to Dora . . . You know, I had to amuse her. She is so sad, so lonely without Mr. Williams. I couldn't just go on about Louis for five pages? And you . . . You, my girl? Tell me about you. You have grown up."

Fanny's dark gaze rested on her child. Belle was now a woman of thirty. "How are things with Joe?"

Belle straightened up. "Fine," she said coldly. "Just fine."

The two women hesitated a moment.

"Austin seems to me the most courageous little boy I've ever seen," Fanny went on, in a laudable desire for reconciliation. "I just heard him hold his own against a big strapping fellow. Are you thinking of having other children?"

Belle's expression cut her short. Had she said something wrong? Should she apologize?

"All I wanted to suggest," she began awkwardly, "is that when your brothers were born . . ."

"Be quiet, Mama! For once in your life, be quiet!"

My God, was their reunion dissolving into a new quarrel? Finding Belle again had been such a joy, the idea that she had made such a trip, taken such trouble . . . And now Fanny was going to lose her again.

"Mama, there is something I did not tell you . . . Something I could not write you about . . . Something . . ."

The young woman's voice broke. The ferry had just pulled up. They had to stand aside to let the passengers disembark. Behind them the Oakland-bound passengers were lining up, pressing them against the barrier.

"What is it?" Fanny finally murmured.

Belle remained silent a moment. The crowd preparing to embark jostled them and pushed by.

"In Hawaii, I had another child . . ."

Fanny's face, her lips, her eyes suddenly drained of color. All her blood had rushed to her heart.

"A boy," Belle went on.

The mother groped for her daughter's hand, while Belle took a deep breath:

"I baptized him . . ."

"Hervey," murmured Fanny.

Belle nodded.

"He had blue eyes . . . and long blond curls . . ."

"And you buried him . . ."

Belle fell against her mother, who held her and rocked her for a long time. The two women clung to each other, picturing the sons they had lost. It was Fanny who was finally able to speak.

"And what if we were to come visit you in Hawaii?" she whispered in her daughter's ear. "If we were to come and spend some time with you?" she repeated, as if the idea had just come to her.

To both of them these questions seemed to be the natural conclusion to their common bereavement.

"That would be nice," Belle said with simplicity.

Still holding hands, they turned toward the bay. They stood there dreamily, leaning on the railing. They were waiting for the next boat.

"Do you remember," Fanny asked. "Do you remember that painting in the waiting room of the embarcadero in Oakland? A yacht under full sail . . ."

"The *Casco*."

"That's it, the *Casco*! Doesn't it belong to someone in Oakland?"

"Doctor Merritt . . . He was a friend of Papa's from the Bohemian Club."

"I seem to remember that this doctor supported his yacht by renting it out to private parties for luxury crossings . . . Am I mistaken? The *Casco* has sailed in the South Pacific . . ."

"But Mama, what about Louis? Shouldn't consumptives live in the mountains? The humidity and warmth of the Pacific . . . Hawaii's tropical . . . for his health . . ."

"The cold, the snow, the mountains have done him no good. The doctors are wrong! It's the English rains that are killing him! I say that Louis needs the ocean, that he needs the sun and a boat

... If I could only find a schooner, we would come to join you. And we would sail as far from London as possible!"

*
**

A few days after this conversation, Mrs. Robert Louis Stevenson went down to the telegraph office of the Occidental Hotel and sent a message addressed to her husband in New York state: *Can secure splendid seagoing schooner* Casco *for seven hundred and fifty a month with most comfortable accommodation for six aft and six forward. Can be ready for sea in ten days. Reply immediately.*

The verdict would come that same evening, a crackling on the line that crossed the continent from East to West: *Blessed girl, take the yacht and expect us in ten days.*

*

The Old World closed behind Robert Louis Stevenson, Fanny Vandegrift's universe snatched him up and never let him go. Louis would never see Europe again, or Henley, or Baxter, or Colvin, or Bob, or Katherine. On the vast ocean, Fanny would soon have her love all to herself, or almost.

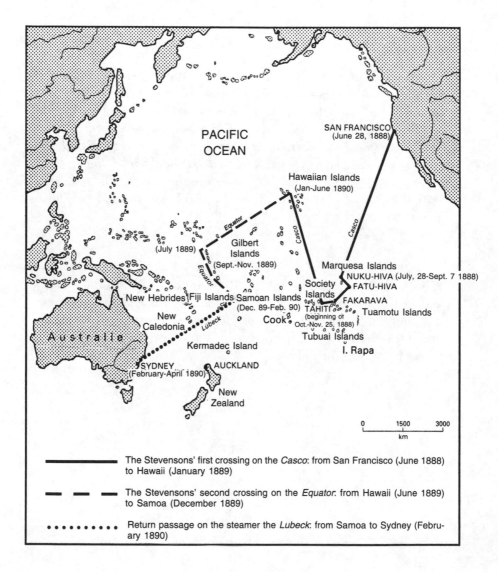

PACIFIC
OCEAN

SAN FRANCISCO
(June 28, 1888)

Hawaiian Islands
(Jan-June 1890)

Equator

(July 1889)

Gilbert
Islands
(Sept.-Nov. 1889)

Equator

Marquesa Islands
NUKU-HIVA (July, 28-Sept. 7 1888)

Society
Islands

FATU-HIVA

New Hebrides Fiji Islands Samoan Islands

FAKARAVA

New
Caledonia

(Dec. 89-Feb. 90)

TAHITI
(beginning ot
Oct.-Nov. 25, 1888)

Tuamotu Islands

Lubeck

Cook

Australia

Kermadec Island

Tubuai Islands
I. Rapa

SYDNEY
(February-April 1890)

AUCKLAND

New
Zealand

0   1500   3000
km

─────────── The Stevensons' first crossing on the *Casco*: from San Francisco (June 1888)
to Hawaii (January 1889)

─ ─ ─ ─ ─ The Stevensons' second crossing on the *Equator*: from Hawaii (June 1889)
to Samoa (December 1889)

• • • • • • • • • • Return passage on the steamer the *Lubeck*: from Samoa to Sydney (February 1890)

VIII

The Sirens' Song

This climate; these voyagings;
these landfalls at dawn; new islands
peaking from the morningbank;
new forested harbors;
new passing alarms of squalls and surf;
new interests of gentle natives,
—the whole tale of my life
is better to me than any poem.

—Robert Louis Stevenson

San Francisco—The Marquesas
The Tuamotu Archipelago—Tahiti—Hawaii
June 28, 1888–January 25, 1889
Aboard the *Casco*

A flat sea lay under a blue vault of the sky, belted with long fiery
bands of clouds tapering off in rose-colored trails, narrowing, cut
with white, the pure white of a tube of gouache applied impasto.
On the edge of the mist-shrouded horizon slipped a dark shadow:
A two-master under sail skirted the soft wisps of changeable rose.
The yacht might set its course toward those luminous bands, but
they kept receding. They were a mirage, one of the many mirages
of the Pacific, distant ribbons of gauze against the sunset.
The wind blew in the rigging. The halyard slapped against the

361

mast, the timbers groaned. The *Casco* sailed freely on the emerald waters. This was their tenth day at sea.

Once past the Golden Gate in San Francisco, the ocean had swelled, surging against the portholes and onto the deck, heaving itself against the closed doors of the cabin. From her bunk Fanny had watched the trunks, the packets of books, the cartons of clothing, slide across the floor. Even the photographic equipment, the typewriter, the banjo, the guitar, and the playing cards had tumbled down at every swell. A fine beginning for a cruise of seven months.

"Seven months!" Captain Otis had exclaimed, exasperated, seven months wandering around the Pacific with this crew—two Swedes, a Russian, a Finn, a Chinese cook who, for God knows what reason, wanted to pass for Japanese—a band of incompetents who had, none of them, sailed for more than a month. And why all this fuss? So that this human zoo, this troop of invalids and women, could stroll among the Pacific islanders.

Relations between the captain and his passengers had begun inauspiciously.

How the devil had that Mrs. R. L. Stevenson, the craziest of the lot, managed to persuade Dr. Merritt to entrust them with the *Casco*? The doctor didn't need her money, he was supposed to be a millionaire! "You may think your husband loves you," he had answered Fanny during their first conversation; "but see here, I love my schooner even more." The truth was that Fanny had anticipated things somewhat by telegraphing to New York that she had engaged the yacht. "My ship is not a toy! It takes prizes in the regattas. It's swift and light . . . and what comfort! Have you been inside? Have you felt the velvet seats, admired the mahogany table, the Venetian mirrors, the brass doorknobs, and my Persian rug? To charter such a jewel would cost your dear, madam, very dear!"

"That isn't a problem . . . the price, I mean," she had answered, disdainfully. "McClure Publishing Company has made my husband a lucrative offer for his stories of the voyage. He will write up his adventures in the South Seas each month, and the New York newspapers will finance our cruise. Furthermore, Mr. Stevenson has just come into a small inheritance." She had insisted on the word "small," emphasizing this with a wave of her hand. "So . . ."

"So, has Mr. Stevenson ever sailed anywhere besides the canals of France and Belgium? Do you know if he's used to sea-going, or has any sense of the responsibilities involved? There must be strict discipline aboard a ship. I understand that your husband's had rather a taste for the bohemian life, and fragile health besides!"

"Come and meet him, Doctor. Then we will talk."

The meeting between Merritt and Stevenson was held in the flower-filled room occupied by the celebrated author at the Occidental Hotel in San Francisco. Exhausted from his latest crossing of the United States, weakened by the winter at Saranac, Louis had received him in bed—a rather feeble way of reassuring the owner of the yacht. What charm had the patient worked on Dr. Merritt, what fund of seduction and tenacity had his old siren of a wife deployed to win the doctor over? "Very well, my dear, are you happy?" he had concluded, signing a contract for June through January. "On one condition, however: I'll lease you my yacht only if you take my skipper. Captain Albert Otis is part of the deal."

*

"*Please* don't talk to the man at the wheel today, Mrs. Stevenson. *Today* I want him to steer," the captain cautioned drily.

Thirty years old, robust, his very blond hair cropped short, vain, brutal, and shrewd, with a gift for observation and impeccable logic, the captain hated his female boss and took a dim view of the others. With good luck, he doubted the crossing would last as long as they anticipated. One look at the chattering skeleton who paid the bill was enough to know that he wouldn't last the voyage. The captain had seen to the necessary Bible, plank, and flag for a burial at sea. He was particularly exasperated by the invalid's mother, a Scottish lady nearly sixty, who insisted on saying grace before meals, bored him with her admiration for her son and his books, and took absurd risks on deck. Her myriad hat boxes containing dozens of widow's caps in the style of Queen Victoria, all starch and white organdy streamers, cluttered up too many shelves.

When her daughter-in-law asked, "What would you do, Captain, if my mother-in-law were to fall overboard?" Otis merely replied, "Put it in the log, madam."

Yet "Aunt Maggy," as they called her, did surprisingly well in the heavy weather that plagued the *Casco* for days. Well forward in the bows, holding tight to the rail, she had laughed delightedly as the prow plunged on through the heavy swell. And then there was the servant—imagine, a servant on a boat! they would have to unload her at the first port. She was a Swiss girl who would surely sleep with the whole crew, the captain wagered. "Ten to one she'll be big trouble . . . A fine pretext for a mutiny!" Add to this Madam's son from her first marriage—a great stringbean of twenty, so nearsighted he wore magnifying lenses for glasses. This snob with the British accent thought it was fashionable to have his ear pierced at the port in San Francisco: Now he wore a gold ring in his right lobe. And finally, the linchpin of this menagerie, Mrs. R. L. S., ten years older than her husband, who had laid in provisions for seven months for eleven people. Nearly ten thousand meals, daily rations of chicory and tobacco, hundreds of gifts for the natives, even a wardrobe she had designed for her mother-in-law, her servant, and herself, before they could finally face the tropical dog days.

Since the thermometer was climbing to 90 degrees, this lady was walking around without her stockings or corset, barefoot, her body drowning in one of those huge nightgowns, the *holoku*, which the missionaries had imposed on the natives. The servant Valentine and Aunt Maggy would still cling for some days to their stockings and usual attire before donning this flowered, cotton sack dress, an ample gown with a large flounce at the hem, the sleeves tight at the wrists, a high collar, with the only flourish a square piece at the breast.

With a cigarette in her mouth, her short hair under her straw hat, Mrs. R. L. S. was working in the galley, considerably improving the usual fare of the crew. The men doted on her delicacies and her dreadful chatter. Fortunately, some days she could not get out of bed. Seasickness, from which she suffered horribly, kept her nailed to her bunk.

"And on a seven-month cruise," Captain Otis jeered, watching her tottering toward the railing, her handkerchief at her lips. "Didn't you know you'd be seasick?"

"No, I knew it . . . I hate the water . . . I'm afraid of the waves, I despise the ocean. But my husband needs it so badly!" she said, hiccuping. "This adventure is an old dream of his . . . he has talked about it since I've known him. And then, look at him: He is revived!"

The captain's blue eyes followed her motioning arm: On the deck, bareheaded and bare chested, Stevenson was sunning himself while making some notes, responding flexibly to the rolling of the vessel, and nothing, not even the water suddenly washing over the railing, could disturb him.

"Look at him, Captain," she repeated.

The enchantment that transfigured the features of this little woman cut short Otis's grumbling. Before the spectacle of this half-naked, suntanned man in full possession of his capacities, she seemed to have completely forgotten her illness and recovered buried feelings, the strong, direct, and unambiguous attraction of her youth.

"For a sick man like him," the skipper groused, returning to his charts, "an ocean voyage is a dangerous gamble!"

"But that's just what makes my husband's life worth living. All his life he has wandered in search of health—in Europe, in the United States—and he always ended up wracked with fever, coughing his lung outs. Do you know what it is, Captain, to be confined to a room, forever imprisoned between two sheets? Now, look at him! His skin has changed color and even texture—I've never seen him so free with his body. It almost looks like his cells are reconstituting. As we approach the tropics, his vertebrae, his bones, his blood, his marrow, everything in him seems to soften, everything is flowing . . ."

*

Day after day the sun caught fire. Night after night the moon blazed. And the miracle happened: a month without setting foot on land and not a single relapse. No more hemorrhage, no more cough, no more cold! All those winters in the mountains had just been a dead end. Fanny was triumphant. Louis boasted that he was as black as a prune, that only his aristocratic behind retained the vile whiteness of the North. *I hate the sea and I am afraid of it*, Fanny conceded, *but I love the tropical weather . . . and to see my two boys so happy*. Lloyd, Louis, and Aunt Maggy were jubilant. And they were not the only ones. For all of them, even the captain, this crossing was a revelation.

Belle would recount that she could not believe her eyes or ears when she saw Otis disembark on the quay in Honolulu. She had rather anxiously observed the sailor's brutality in San Francisco, his aggressiveness toward her mother and her younger brother. Six months later, in January 1889, Belle heard this same man use expressions so literary that only his passengers understood him, rolling his "r's" like a Scotsman and swearing only by the beauty of old Edinburgh. She even saw him desert the gambling dens of Hawaii for the endless parties of whist with the only partner who had ever succeeded in beating him, Aunt Maggy. The young captain admitted it. He'd lost all his bets. With the possible exception of the escapades of the servant girl, whom Mrs. R. L. S. had caught in the arms of the second mate. It was well known that women on a boat are nothing but trouble. But Otis henceforth acknowledged that the natives of Indiana, the "Hoosiers," had "a lot of cheek and, damn it all, real nerve!"

*
**

They all needed nerve to bear up during the storms and battle a gray sea roiling in the wind and foaming in impotent fury. Nerve to land on unknown shores, live side by side with the natives, spend months at a time without any contact with Whites; to weave sleeping mats and straw hats, fish for their food, understand and respect the local customs; and to enjoy all this unfamiliarity and discomfort. And it took nerve to tear themselves away from the magic of this life on the beach and set out again on a storm-tossed sea. *What sadness to go away and leave our new friends so far behind*, Aunt Maggy regretted. *I wonder if in my sleep I will walk in the shade of the coconut trees, if I will hear the breakers rolling over the coral reef.*

*

But the most intense moment of this first long voyage, the moment that forever altered their senses and their consciousness, would not be the surprise of Tahiti's black beaches, or the splendor of the Hawaiian dawn when the twisted tops of the coconut trees stood black against the orange wash of sky, when the sun surged up between the palms to ignite the bands of fog drifting toward the breakers. Nor would it be the sunsets at sea, the bright red improbable stripes, the full, heavy clouds weighing on the Pacific like blood-drenched silk. No. The vision that would transfix them was a pale phantasmagoria of mist and rocks, Nuku Hiva, their first port of call. *The first experience can never be repeated. The first love, the first sunrise, the first South Sea island are memories apart and touched a virginity of sense,* Stevenson wrote.

Fanny glimpsed her first island at four o'clock in the morning on July 28, 1888: Nuka Hiva, one of the Marquesas. The Stevensons could only recall what Melville wrote about it. Held by the French and populated until 1855 with the most ferocious cannibals in all of Polynesia, Nuka Hiva was their first entry into a culture none of them knew much about; but when scores of canoes surrounded the *Casco,* they did indeed remember that less than three years earlier the men there were still devouring their brothers.

A hoard of natives clambered aboard and spread out on the deck. They loudly hawked their goods, gesturing boldly, and jostled the passengers, insulting them when they understood that the white men did not want to buy their coconuts, their bananas, their mats and baskets.

Aunt Maggy did not bat an eye as the barebreasted women brutally tugged on the ribbons of her bonnet, fingered her skirts, and pulled off her mittens. *It was impossible to believe that these people are not totally dressed with their magnificent tattoos,* her daughter-in-law calmly noted.

Perhaps Fanny remembered her experience with the Piutes of Austin and the Shoshones of Virginia City. Was it out of loyalty to her past, her sympathy and respect for those Native Americans, that she decided to offer—not to sell—the chief and his women the purple velvet curtains and the furnishings they coveted? When the Marquesans understood the meaning of Louis and Fanny's gesticulations, their aggressiveness was transformed into laughter and squeals of joy.

The *Casco* would remain several weeks at anchor in the bay; it would leave laden with gifts. *I could never have dreamed that such places exist, and such races!* Louis exclaimed.

From now on, the legends of the islands haunted their imaginations. Fanny admired the beauty of the natives, the kindness of their welcome; Louis's curiosity was captivated by the fate of Polynesia. What role did the white man play in the evolution of these races that had prospered over the centuries and yet had gradually begun to disappear in the past fifty years? What about the missionaries who trampled on these ancient civilizations, burned their idols and sacred objects, forbade nudity, prohibited traditional costumes and dances, in order to imbue these people with notions of sin and evil? What about the crowd of traders who trafficked in copra, coconut meat from which the West extracted oil, and who sold weapons and alcohol to the natives, who thought only of profit as they battered down the wall between two worlds?

Fifty years before such ideas were fashionable, Mrs. Robert Louis Stevenson railed against the heresies of colonialism. Louis was fired with questions. As for Aunt Maggy, she did not miss the church service but was nonetheless fascinated by the local inhabitants and their customs.

I wish you could see her, Fanny notes affectionately, *this lady in her fluted bonnet, who walks on the beach in the moonlight with a gentleman clad only in a handkerchief.*

It is a strange life, echoed the old Scotswoman, *irresponsible and wild. I wonder if we shall ever return to civilization.*

And they always came back to the magic of that first landing. They had sailed into a little bay backed against the green-clad mountains, a beach snug between two outcroppings of rocks, and palm trees lying horizontally with their branches stroking the sea. That morning in July the yacht turned upon her heel, and the anchor plunged. *It was a small sound, a great event,* Robert Louis Stevenson would write. *My soul went down with these moorings whence no windlass may extract nor any diver fish it up; and I, and some part of my ship's company, were from that hour the bondslaves of the isles.*

*

Nothing, not even Belle's descriptions, had prepared them for the world that awaited them 2,500 miles north of Tahiti's idyllic beaches, in Honolulu.

Geographically, Hawaii belongs to Polynesia. In reality, the seven principal islands of the archipelago are Hawaiian only in the beauty of their landscapes. Under the influence of Protestant missionaries and the money of big American landowners, the native population was being increasingly replaced by Asian workers and losing its place in the local economy. The Whites possessed the land, the Chinese worked it, and the Polynesians sadly watched as their paradise slipped away.

But this assessment did not reckon on the ambition of their sovereign and the megalomania of the dynasty that had taken power seven years before. The king of Hawaii was counting on Western wealth, on an army, on a fleet, on a court, in order to justify his power and extend it. He would see in the illustrious Robert Louis Stevenson the bard, the herald of his cause.

Honolulu—January 25–June 25 1889

The chamberlain struck the polished parquet with a great blow of his halberd. "His Majesty, King Kalakaua the First of Hawaii!"

The crowd of courtiers jostled each other to let him pass. There were naval officers in the uniforms of many countries, Chinese mandarins in silk robes, Japanese dignitaries, all races and dress. In the blue drawing room reserved for private audiences, a host of Polynesian valets had closed the shutters made of rare woods and pulled the purple velvet curtains across the seven French doors. In broad daylight the sovereign used only electric light, which burned from brass chandeliers fitted with countless light bulbs. On a background of indigo damask, portraits of King Louis-Philippe and Queen Victoria sat enthroned between the two likenesses of their "illustrious cousins": David Kalakaua stood in a gold frame not far from Kapi'Olani, his wife, a strong woman in a very low-cut dress by the Parisian couturier Worth, her chest hung with the rather impressive Royal Order of Oceania. This decoration had been designed by a certain Mrs. Joe Strong.

"When he gets to us," Belle whispered in her mother's ear, pushing her to the first row of ladies, "you go down!"

"But I don't know how to curtsy!"

"Never mind, just lean with your bust, bend your knees, and raise the hem of your *holoku*. Go on!"

Uncertain what to do, Fanny bent all the way down to the floral carpet.

"Sire, allow me to introduce to you," Belle's voice twittered above her, "Mrs. Robert Louis Stevenson."

"Please, Madam . . ."

A large, dark hand had taken hers and was raising her up. "It is we who are touched to see you among us. The books of your illustrious husband enchant our nights. As for your daughter, she delights our court. Her courage henceforth belongs to the history of the realm."

This florid language, so full of hidden meanings that Fanny could not understand, was spoken in English by a perfect man of the world. Two hundred and fifty pounds, almost six feet tall, in his fifties, dressed all in white from head to foot, wearing an immaculate three-piece suit whose elegance was not eclipsed by the profusion of jewels—a ruby-headed stick pin, assorted cufflinks, numerous rings—the huge king of Hawaii was an imposing sight.

He had built this palace less than five years before, a cube of cut stone flanked by pseudo-Venetian columns of stucco and marble, and set in a park full of fruits and flowers that delighted the soul of Fanny Vandegrift. Fanny would never have imagined that such a place might exist in the Pacific. There were coffered ceilings, friezes of Greek dancing girls, little round mirrors that reflected the sun or shimmered at night when the lamps were lit, a fairyland.

In the hall, under the portraits of the ten last kings of Hawaii, large niches sheltered a collection of cloisonné vases and statues of nudes. Two caryatids flanked the central stairway, an enormous stairway of precious woods and sculpted banisters.

This marvel was the result of long travels undertaken by the king during his reign. He had been the first sovereign to visit the United States in 1874 and was familiar with San Francisco and New York. Seven years later, in 1881, he had set off on a tour of the world. David Kalakaua had stayed in most of the European capitals: Vienna, London, Paris. His private car had gone as far as Moscow and Peking, his yacht to Bombay. From this experience, which no other local monarch had known, he had returned to the Pacific with a dream. That dream was to give Hawaii back to the Hawaiians, to revive the legends and traditions of his country, to free Polynesia from the economic yoke of Western civilization.

To this end, he had organized his own coronation and modernized his capital. In January 1889, Honolulu could flatter itself with being the most modern city in the world. Telephone lines crisscrossed the sky; dispensing with gas and candles, the streetlamps were lit by electricity. Many streets had been paved.

And at the celebrations for his coronation, the king had committed another act of rebellion: He had reestablished the custom of the traditional dance, the "hula," forbidden for decades by the missionaries. Every evening, to the sound of ukuleles, the royal dancers writhed half-naked on the palace lawn.

A few hours later, the curtain of the new opera house had gone up before the royal box, a huge canvas operated by a hydraulic system where, against a background of blue skies and Alpine peaks, the rose colored steps of a marble stairway disappeared into the waters of Lake Como. An extraordinary mixture of genres!

Arriving in this unique city, Belle and Joe had been seduced by the sovereign's liveliness, his megalomania, and his intelligence. David Kalakaua was both childish and cultivated, powerful and perhaps doomed. A fairy tale prince. The pomp and intrigues of his court appealed to the Strongs' passion for pleasure; the balls and constant plotting satisfied their taste for risk and adventure.

For six years now, Joe had been the regime's official painter. Belle designed afternoon dresses for the queen and painted the multicolored fish the royal fishermen brought her in the early morning, before the palace kitchens claimed them. To the sound of Viennese operettas, amidst the popping of champagne bottles, the couple let themselves be compromised.

"What did His Majesty mean about your courage?" Fanny asked in the street car that was taking them to the beach at Waikiki.

Through the open window, the wind ruffled the ostrich plumes of their hats. Their fists closed around on the handles of their umbrellas, arms folded, weighed down by the trains of their *holokus,* a tumble of pastel muslin in the Hawaiian style, they looked like two pretty dolls. They were caught in a traffic jam. Big machines for laying asphalt frightened the horses, a chaos of wagons and buggies filled the downtown. Between the palm trees rose apartment buildings with cut stone facades, very similar to those on Fifth Avenue in New York.

A single glance at Honolulu had been enough for Robert Louis Stevenson to declare that the city was much too civilized for his taste. So he had settled at the seashore, far from the cars and telephones.

"What is this courage that makes you worthy of belonging to the history of his country?" Fanny repeated.

"I did him a great service," Belle whispered with a sibylline smile.

"What sort of service?"

The young woman lowered her voice. "I cannot tell you about it here . . ."

"Why not?"

"People might hear us . . ."

Fanny glanced around her. There was no one. She half turned. The tram was nearly empty. Only two people of mixed race were taking seats behind them. "But—"

"This is not the place!" Belle cut in.

An explosion of fanfare drew their attention to the music pavilion in the park.

"Herr Berger, the king's Austrian kapellmeister, who rehearses the Royal Hawaiian Band every day at this hour," Belle commented.

The brass covered her voice. She took advantage of this to murmur: "This is a breeding ground for conspiracies. You will very soon see that for yourself. Two clans are vying for power: the king's party, the nationalist party that wants to unite the Polynesian islands, and the missionaries' party, which is trying to overthrow the monarchy and replace it with an American administration."

"And who are you for?"

"Guess!"

"Why him?"

"Because the Whites hate him," Belle heatedly explained. "They accuse him of being an operetta monarch who empties the coffers of the state. They treat him like a drunk . . ."

"Does he drink?"

"Can he ever! He can down six bottles of champagne in an afternoon without the alcohol affecting him at all . . . The missionaries are after his hide."

"Surely you're exaggerating."

"No! The word 'missionary' has lost any religious meaning here. To be a 'missionary' means to belong to a political party. Like the Republicans and Democrats in San Francisco. The leaders are the sons and grandsons of ministers who came to convert the Hawaiians at the beginning of the century. They made a fortune in sugarcane and own all the banana plantations today; they are rich American businessmen."

"Wasn't your husband's father a missionary to Hawaii before living near us in Oakland?"

"Joe's sister was born here. The Strongs still have relatives in Honolulu, but we don't visit them anymore! Those 'missionaries' have only one purpose: to take the archipelago away from the natives and annex to the United States. For ten years now, they've been trying to overthrow the king. They are plotting coups d'etat in the name of civilization!"

"Of civilization?" Fanny remarked indignantly. "But Kalakaua is the height of civilization!"

"Exactly! And they don't like that, the hypocrites! The king dreams of expanding the archipelago, he is trying to create a confederation of all the islands the Whites have not yet appropriated. Joe will tell you: He accompanied one of Kalakaua's delegations to Samoa. As an artist for the government, he took photographs there, he made sketches. Our friend Henry Poor, whose house you are living in on Waikiki, went on this expedition as well. He saw King Laupepa of Samoa. An agreement between the two kings was signed, and what a slap in the face it was for the Western powers that rule the island with such contempt for the Samoans! If Kalakaua succeeds, the Whites will lose their foothold."

The blazing look the two women exchanged reassured Belle, and her pretty face was flushed with joy. She had finally found her mother again. What diabolical wiles she'd had to use to wrest Fanny away from Louis, to have her to herself for a little while! This introduction to the king, this interminable tram ride through the traffic—these were merely maneuvers to find Fanny once more.

In Stevenson's presence, the rest of the world could be collapsing and Mrs. R. L. S. wouldn't give a damn. At least that was her daughter's impression. Even Austin, her grandson who had charmed her so in San Francisco, had become invisible. It was Louis; Belle's old rancor for her father's rival, that hostility she wasn't able to conceal, was poisoning family relations all over again. And Fanny was not even aware of it.

What a disappointment the arrival of the *Casco* had been for Belle. After all these months of waiting and worry, the young woman could not get over it. At Christmas, the port authorities of Hawaii had given up the yacht for lost; friends of the Strongs no longer dared mention it, since shipwreck seemed the only explanation. Sighting the yacht, Belle had run joyfully to the port, jumped into a boat, and gone out to meet them. In her haste she could have drowned. And not a look from Fanny! Not an embrace, not a word to let her know how eager her mother had been to see her again. Louis, Louis, Louis, there was nothing but Louis!

Rich, famous, in good health, Stevenson's recent transformations made his joy in life and his aplomb more exasperating than ever to his stepdaughter. From now on, he assumed the right to exercise his authority over his wife's family. But it was not from him that Belle expected help. Her salvation was her mother. This had been a big mistake. Fanny would never save anyone but Louis, the young woman thought bitterly. "My reunion with Mama was just an illusion. Just when I need her, all she can think of is his happiness . . . Just when my life is foundering, she discovers the joys of marriage . . . and those joys surely come first."

The seven months of this endless cruise had clearly tightened the bonds between the couple. If Belle thought last May that she'd detected a slight distance between Mrs. Stevenson and her dear husband, she had been wrong. In reaching the shores of these new worlds, Louis and Fanny had rediscovered each other. Their reactions to the beauty of people and things was identical; their emotions, their curiosity toward the natives; their sympathy, their common enthusiasm, the whole adventure had comforted them with the absolute certainty of an almost spiritual symbiosis—a romance of destiny. On board the *Casco*, thought Belle, they must have taken up their liaison where they'd left off at the Chevillons', when they made love in the canoe at Grez. How long ago it all seemed! Love? For Belle love now meant an affair with a bank employee and a brief passion for a naval officer who had shipped out again. Love meant only adultery. And the maternal tenderness she felt for her little boy.

She had to confess failure. Fanny had won all her bets. Her predictions had come to pass. And if her mother had not yet said "I told you so!" as the daughter dreaded, it seemed implicit in the severity of Fanny's gaze, in the anxiety in her voice when she asked about Belle's life, and in their silence.

Joe was a skirt chaser. Joe was a drinker. Joe smoked opium. He worked less and less and devoted most of his energy to concealing unpaid bills, hiding his debts from his wife. Under the ostentation and ease of their existence, the Strongs were tottering on the brink of ruin.

Like her husband, Belle preferred to forget the disintegration of her life, throwing herself headlong into pleasure and action. The idea of initiating her mother into politics, of guiding her, of winning her to her cause intoxicated the young woman and excited Fanny.

"Louis must make the acquaintance of your king! For his articles on the South Seas . . . He would surely have a thousand questions to ask . . ."

"And Kalakaua himself is a man of letters. He has composed the words to the national anthem and just published a collection of legends. It's the first book in English that tells the old stories of his country."

With the same agility, mother and daughter jumped on the tram that left them off 1,500 feet from the beach. Their little boots sank to the same depth in the sand, the same fire lit up their eyes.

"Louis might be able to help him," Fanny continued. "His pen would attract the world's attention to what America is doing in Hawaii."

"Tomorrow, if you like, I will organize a meeting between Kalakaua, your husband, and my brother!"

*

On Monday, January 27, 1889, Louis and Lloyd went to Iolani Palace for a private meeting with the king. Forty-eight hours later, His Gracious Majesty returned the courtesy and settled himself on the seats of the *Casco* for a little cup of tea. When it came to tea, the half a dozen bottles mentioned by Belle proved to underestimate the monarch's capacity. Stevenson and his entourage would remember the gaiety of this afternoon long afterwards. Captain Otis surpassed himself on the accordion, Lloyd sang Scottish ballads, Belle swayed in dance, and Louis recited the most recent of his poems to the glory of Polynesia.

As for Fanny, she listened. Fascinated, she gazed at this giant who was bubbling over with projects and dreams. Did she guess that Kalakaua had already lost the battle? That the Whites had virtually annexed his country? Did she sense that in January of

1889 the days were already numbered for this monarch and his
throne? Or as a middle-class woman from the Midwest, was she
simply impressed by power? Whatever the case, she took sides.
Accompanying Kalakaua to the gangway, Mrs. Robert Louis
Stevenson announced loud and clear that she would support his
cause. In her usual way, Fanny took the side of the weak.

The following Sunday, February 3, she invited His Majesty to
come celebrate with them in the largest of the four bungalows the
Stevensons occupied on Waikiki Beach. The move of the whole
tribe had proved to be too expensive for them to keep the *Casco*
anchored at the quay; Louis had sent the yacht back to its owner.
He released their servant Valentine, who would marry and settle
down somewhere near San Francisco.

The group of bamboo cabins provided space for each of them
to work at his own projects. Lloyd developed his photographs in a
windowless hut, his darkroom. Fanny planted her easel in the little
house that served as her general headquarters. Louis wrote some
distance away, in a hut covered with straw mats and surrounded
by two layers of barbed wire to keep out the curious, he claimed.
The little group met on the veranda of the big house for meals
orchestrated by Fanny and her cook, Ah Fu.

This is a strange story, too, the story of Ah Fu, the young Chinese
cook they had met in the Marquesas. Hired by Mrs. Robert Louis
Stevenson, he was passionately attached to his mistress, who
dreaded only his intrusions in their conversations and his swearing,
which made all the traders in the Pacific go pale. Ah Fu would
follow the Stevensons in all their wanderings until the day he would
ask leave to return to China for a last visit to his old mother, a last
visit before returning to spend the rest of his days with Louis and
Fanny. Permission was granted. Fanny sewed his wages into the
lining of his clothes, she hemmed his jacket and trousers with gold
pieces. And they never heard from him again. Despite her efforts,
she could find no trace of Ah Fu. The cook used to say that he
had learned everything from her.

Raw fish or grilled pig, Fanny's culinary talents lost nothing by
her visits to the islands. Curious about everything, respectful of
local traditions, she learned native recipes. If we keep in mind that
most American women living in Honolulu had never tasted boiled
taro root paste, the Hawaiian delicacy, and turned up their noses
at the very idea of plunging their fingers into the shared poi bowl,

Fanny's open mind—like Belle's—is all the more surprising. The village chiefs would agree that no woman, white or Polynesian, knew how to grill kiwi over ashes, cook taro under stone, and prepare fafaru like the woman they called "Pani." Pani was also the name the Indians of Austin had given her.

In six months no one knew better than Pani the rules of etiquette and how to treat kings. But the high point of the party she gave for Kalakaua was the quasi-feudal moment when the Stevensons made a gift to the sovereign of the most beautiful pearl in their collection, accompanied by several verses by the poet to the glory of the monarch:

The right, my liege, is ancient as the lyre
For bards to give to kings what kings admire.

The photographs taken that day bear witness to the profusion of dishes, the floral arrangements, the decorated platters. The gestures of the company, Fanny's hands in the bowls, Aunt Maggy's posture as she sits cross-legged to the right of the king, all suggest that the Stevenson clan had chosen its camp.

Fanny's enthusiasm, Belle's influence, Louis's sympathy for Kalakaua's expansionist ambitions, the literary affinities between the two men would lead to Robert Louis Stevenson's first political involvement in the South Pacific. The generosity of the gesture would be equaled only by its absurdity.

Though he knew practically nothing about the history of Samoa, that small archipelago thousands of miles southwest of Hawaii, Louis was going to send his first letter to the editor-in-chief of the *Times* of London. This was an incendiary article in which Louis demands the world's acceptance of a federation of Hawaii and Samoa, as well as its admiration and respect for David Kalakaua, who was up against the great Western powers. Stevenson was still unaware that Kalakaua's expedition, in which Joe Strong had participated, had ended in the most formidable drinking bout the capital of Apia had ever known, and that the Hawaiians had abandoned themselves to excess and foolishness.

But the word "Samoa" was thrown down, and Stevenson's quest began. In an irony of fate, he opened fire with a defense of the archipelago, several islands among the thousands that dot the Pacific, which he would soon choose as his land of exile.

Robert Louis Stevenson to Charles Baxter

Honolulu, February 8, 1889
My dear Charles,
 . . . The cruise has been a great success, both as to matter, fun, and health; and yet, Lord, man! we're pleased to be ashore! . . . Altogether, this foolhardy venture is achieved, and if I have but nine months of life and any kind of health, I shall have both eaten my cake and got it back again with usury. But man, there have been days when I felt guilty, and thought I was in no position for the head of a house. . . .
 . . . My wife is in no great shakes: she is the one who has suffered most. My mother has had a Huge Old Time. Lloyd is first chop. I am so well that I do not know myself—sea bathing, if you please, and what is far more dangerous, entertaining and being entertained by His Majesty here, who is a very fine, intelligent fellow, but O, Charles! what a crop for the drink! He carries it, too, like a mountain with a sparrow on its shoulders. We calculated five bottles of champagne in three hours and a half (afternoon) and the sovereign quite presentable, although perceptibly more dignified at the end.
 . . . I have no word from [Henley], and shall not try to write in the midst of my scurry. He little understands the harm he did me. . . . As for Katherine . . . I do not wish to see her.
 All these clouds, and the extraordinary health I enjoy, and variety of interests I find among these islands, would tempt me to remain here— only for Lloyd, who is not well placed in such countries for permanency, and a little to Colvin, to whom I feel I owe a sort of filial duty.

Robert Louis Stevenson to Henry James

Honolulu, March 1889
My dear James,
 Yes—I own up—I am untrue to friendship and (what is less, but still considerable) to civilization. I am not coming home for another year. There it is, cold and bald . . . But look here, and judge me tenderly. I have had more fun and pleasure of my life these past months than ever before, and more health than any time in ten long years. . . . and though the sea is a deathful place, I like to be there, and like squalls (when they are over); and to draw near to a new island, I cannot say how much I like. In short, I take another

*year of this sort of life, and mean to try to work down among the
poisoned arrows, and mean (if it may be) to come back again when
the thing is through, and converse with Henry James as heretofore.*

Fanny Stevenson to Fanny Sitwell

*Honolulu, toward the end of March 1889
My dear friend,*
    *... We think of trying yet one more voyage. We are a little
uncertain as to how we shall go ... but the "unregenerate" islands
we must see. I suppose we shall be off sometime in June. ... It
seems a pity to return to England until [Louis's] health is firmly
reestablished, and also a pity not to see all that we can see quite
easily starting from this place: and which will be our only opportunity in life. Of course there is the usual risk from hostile natives,
and the horrible sea, but a positive risk is so much more wholesome
than a negative one, and it is all such joy to Louis and Lloyd.*
    *... As for myself, I have had more cares than I was really fit
for. To keep house on a yacht is no easy thing. When Louis and I
broke loose from the ship and lived alone amongst the natives, I
got on very well. It was when I was deathly seasick, and the question was put to me by the cook, "What shall we have for the cabin
dinner, what for tomorrow's breakfast, what for lunch" and what
about the sailors' food? Please come and look at the biscuits, for
the weevils have got into them, and show me how to make yeast
that will rise of itself, and smell the pork which seems pretty high,
and give me directions about making a pudding with molasses—
and what is to be done about the bugs?—etc., etc. In the midst of
heavy dangerous weather, when I was lying on the floor clutching
a basin, down comes the mate with a cracked head, and I must
needs cut off the hair matted with blood, wash and dress the wound,
and administer restoratives. I do not like being "the lady of the
yacht," but shore! O, then I felt I was repaid for all.*

Robert Louis Stevenson to Sidney Colvin

*Honolulu, April 2, 1889
My dear Colvin,*
    *... I am outright ashamed of my news, which is that we are not
coming home for another year. I cannot but hope it may continue*

the vast improvement of my health: I think it good for Fanny and Lloyd; and we have all a taste for this wandering and dangerous life. My mother I send home, to my relief, as this part of our cruise will be (if we can carry it out) rather difficult in places. Here is the idea: About the middle of June (unless the Boston Board objects) we sail from Honolulu in the missionary ship (barkentine auxiliary steamer) Morning Star: she takes us through the Gilberts and Marshalls, and drops us (this is my great idea) on Ponape, one of the volcanic islands of the Carolines. Here we stay marooned among a doubtful population, with a Spanish vice-governor and five native kings, and a sprinkling of missionaries all at loggerheads, on the chance of fetching a passage to Sydney in a trader, a labor ship or (maybe, but this appears too bright) a ship of war. . . . You can see for yourself how much variety and adventure this promises, and that it is not devoid of danger at the best; but if we can pull it off in safety, gives me a fine book of travel, and Lloyd a fine lecture and diorama, which should vastly better our finances.

. . . I cannot say why I like the sea; no man is more cynically and constantly alive to its perils; I regard it as the highest form of gambling; and yet I love the sea as much as I hate gambling. . . .

Robert Louis Stevenson to Charles Baxter

Honolulu, April 12, 1889
My dear Charles,
    . . . I take my backgoing son-in-law [Joseph Strong] along with me. This family has been a sore trouble to me, but Joe is a good photographer, and the idea is to get up a diorama and let Lloyd lecture, and try to start a little money, honestly got, for this Skimpolian household. Joe is a loveable fellow, but I tell you, and you know, I would rather have to deal with D___ than one of these truculent fools who do not know the meaning of money. It is heartbreaking; but there—the burthen is on the back, and the diorama is an honest and hopeful pitch to lighten it. What think ye?

Robert Louis Stevenson to Charles Baxter

Honolulu, May 8, 1889
My Dear Charles,
    . . . I must now turn to a point of business. This new cruise of

ours is somewhat venturesome, and I think it needful to warn you not to be in a hurry to suppose us dead. In these ill-charted seas, it is quite on the cards we might be cast on some unvisited or very rarely visited island; that there we might lie for a long time, even years, unheard of, and yet turn up smiling at the hinder end. So do not let me be "rowpit" [sold at auction] *till you get some certainty we have gone to Davy Jones in a squall or graced the feast of some barbarian in the character of long pig. . . . .*

Robert Louis Stevenson to his friend Will Low, an American painter living in New York

Honolulu, May 9, 1889
. . . O Low, I love the Polynesian: This civilization of ours is a dingy, ungentlemanly business; it drops out too much of man, and too much of that the very beauty of the poor beast; who has his beauties in spite of Zola and Co. . . . But if you could live, the only white folk, in a Polynesian village; and drink that warm, light vin du pays *of human affection and enjoy that simple dignity of all about you . . .*

Waikiki—Louis's Bungalow
The night of May 10, 1889

"Poor Aunt Maggy . . ."
The air was still. There was a full moon. Through the open casement, the sea glistened, black and smooth as a two-way mirror. No lamp was burning in the hut. From the shadows emerged the pallor of the long shell necklaces that decorated the window frames, the stacks of manuscript, the pages of books piled on the two tables, raw silks, a trouser leg, a shirt sleeve hanging softly on the back of a chair. From the ceiling, two white mosquito nets fell like a canopy to enclose two little camp beds pushed together against the partition. The pillows were placed against the wall, facing the ocean.

Stretched out with their ashtrays on their blankets, Louis and Fanny smoked in silence. They loved this moment, peaceful and mysterious, this chatting in the dark. At dawn, Ah Fu would wake them, at six o'clock, work would begin. Fanny would immediately go out, leaving Louis alone with his page and his cup of tea. He stopped writing only at dusk. Louis may have been a bohemian at heart, a restless soul, but he willingly yoked himself to an iron discipline.

When it came down to it, Louis never loosened the vise. The problem, Fanny thought, was that he asked as much of others as he did of himself. As for Belle and Joe, she reckoned a little severely, how could they answer to such demands? The life the couple led seemed mediocre and doomed to failure . . . But could one do one's best for someone in spite of them? How could they help Belle if the young woman did not want to help herself?

All these reflections buzzed in her head, mingling with the humming of the mosquitos, with the chords of the guitar Lloyd was strumming far down the beach, with the lapping of the waves at the shore.

"Your mother's courage as she climbed the gangplank this morning," she went on, "her dignity on the desk of the *Umatilla* moved me. I was watching her, so straight and dignified in the crowd. She seemed to disappear under all the leis Belle had put around her neck. Her little face lost in the flowers. That was all you could see, just her face—and not a tear!"

She stood up, pushed aside the white netting to light the antimosquito powder whose smoke mingled with the smoke of her cigarette.

"Poor Aunt Maggy," she repeated. "To make that long voyage all alone—without you!" Fanny closed her lips around her cigarette, stopping to add: "Without you, her son, whom she may never see again . . ."

With his arms beneath his head, his back against the pillows, Louis, upset by his mother's departure, dragged loudly on his cigarette. His short, well-barbered hair he owed to his stepdaughter's scissors. Belle, always preoccupied by physical appearance, took pleasure in lecturing her stepfather on the laxness of his grooming. During the weekends the young woman spent at Waikiki, she would constantly joke about the potential beauty of Fanny's husband. Aunt Maggy had approved.

"My mother," he murmured tenderly. "Who could have imagined that my mother, coddled by her husband for thirty years, spoiled by life, utterly content in the company of proper ladies, who could have imagined she would find such pleasure in the discomfort of a ship, the dangers of the ocean?"

"And the company of natives!"

They both fell silent a moment: Each of them was thinking of the old lady's unexpected whimsy.

"She distinguished herself this afternoon by one of her replies, which sums her up entirely," Fanny smiled. "On the deck of the ship, the king was speaking to her about his orchestra, which was playing *"Aloha Oe"*—you know how very proud he is of his brasses and his drum rolls. 'Madam, how do you like the music of the Royal Hawaiian Band?' Kalakaua asked her. 'Oh, do not worry, it's no bother . . . I don't mind it at all.' That answer is so much her, her wonderful charm! Her kindness. And her extraordinary lack of awareness!"

"All the same, I think she will do better waiting at Heriot Row for our return. I would rather know she is safe, near her sister. When it comes to it, she couldn't go on here . . . And then I wanted to spare her."

Louis turned his tanned face toward the twin bed where his wife was resting. "Fanny," he went on, "there is one more thing I must do before leaving Hawaii. I was waiting for my mother's departure . . . I am going away too."

She stood up, livid and dramatic, sensing danger. "Where?"

"I will not be gone long: I want to visit Molokai.

"The leper island? But that's a hellhole! They say that the living no longer take the trouble to bury the dead."

As if this litany of horrors could dissuade Louis, Fanny went on breathlessly, describing a catalogue of lurid images.

". . . they throw them in the lakes, where they rot, and the ground of the cemeteries is so hard and stony, they bury cadavers, hundreds of them, sticking out of the earth. They say that dogs and pigs come to dig up the corpses, that the stench reeks all the way out to the boats plying the coast!"

This visit to Molokai was just like the "Irish plan"—stuff and nonsense! Quick, describe everything to him so there won't be any question of going: "People say that leprosy doesn't just affect the body," she continued, "that it destroys all the mental and moral faculties of the unfortunate victim. There seems to be total anarchy on Molokai. The lepers brew their own alcohol, and carry on violent, drunken orgies day and night!"

Louis gestured impatiently: "Why should they live differently? These people have no hope of a cure. Every leper knows he'll only be worse tomorrow. Is it so surprising, that they live only for today? For pleasure? For the small pleasures they can grasp from the moment?"

"But what would you do there? The crossing to Molokai is a voyage of no return. The wives say good-bye to their husbands as if they are attending a funeral! The Honolulu papers are full of accounts of the hearings on inheritances: A leper on Molokai is considered legally and civilly dead. What would you do there, Louis, among those disfigured men and women, those children who survive in a moral distress I dare not imagine—"

"Exactly. The least one can do is to go and see."

"But this is morbid foolishness!"

"Last month at the cathedral, at Father Damien's funeral, I couldn't stop thinking about it: I had been living in Hawaii for three months and I hadn't even met the man who had given his life, a few miles from here, caring for the sick, easing the last days of those most unfortunate people, to make the horror a little bearable. I will not leave Honolulu before honoring his memory by going to Molokai, where he lived, where he died. I will not sail on the *Equator* before seeing his work, before witnessing it."

"Louis, Damien's work is just a few houses built on the promontory of the island! A church, a Catholic village ... What are you going to do on Molokai? It's almost shocking to think that a healthy man should want to risk that descent into hell."

"That, Fanny, is your way of looking at it. Always negative! I consider it my duty to undertake this voyage."

"But what about the leprosy? Louis, leprosy is a contagious disease, and Father Damien died of it, something you seem to forget! Careless as you are, you'll be sure to catch it ... I'm coming with you!"

"No. I'm going alone. You stay here and prepare for our next trip. We'll leave after I return, and you have plenty to do here! You are the only one who can find the photographic equipment we need; a duck hammock for each person; a patent organ like the commandant's at Taiohae; cheap cigars as gifts; revolvers; permanganate of potash; lineament for the head and sulphur; a fine tooth comb. And see to your daughter! If we take Joe, we cannot leave Belle in Hawaii ... Honolulu, with its intrigues and pleasures, is a vile place for a frivolous young woman. I've decided that we'll pay all of the Strongs' debts in Honolulu. We shall take them under our wing until Joe is in a state to support the needs of his family. They must both change their habits."

"But Belle adores them, those habits, those intrigues and pleasures . . . She's happy in Honolulu. Where do you want her to go?"

Louis gave Fanny a look that shut her up. The era was past when, bedridden and ill, he let her take the initiative when it came to medicine and life as well. Health had finally come with a vengeance, along with age and money, and the liberal bohemian was changing. Certainly he had never admitted that they challenged his authority. But he was now burdened with new responsibilities. And Fanny rejoiced. She loved it that Belle, Joe, and Austin considered him the head of the family. She loved it that all their lives, Aunt Maggy's included, revolved around the man she considered a genius. She loved it, too, that he surrounded himself with her tribe, her children—their children.

On Waikiki, Louis had established several rules of conduct that made their life together easier. Neither Belle, nor Joe, nor Lloyd thought to flaunt them. These rules were simple, fair, and practical. But anyone who violated them should beware. Behavior that Louis judged inappropriate threw him into a rage. Rule #1: Everything of a confidential nature, heard at his table or in his house, was sacred and must not be repeated on any account. Rule #2: Tardiness at mealtimes would not be tolerated. Nor would there be argumentative conversations, irritating or provocative remarks. Louis believed in general, agreeable conversation, with no disputes. Otherwise, silence. Rule #3: Small talk was not allowed. "How is your mother, I saw you yesterday at the concert, you were ravishing this evening"—all such empty remarks were forbidden. Rule #4: Books had to be treated with respect; every book borrowed ought to be returned in a week; a book destroyed or lost had to be replaced. And anyone who liked a work had to remember the name of the author.

More than ever he detested anyone making a fuss over him and his health. It made him nervous when Belle coddled him, running to put a pillow under his head; he was exasperated when Joe rushed to carry his luggage. But Louis seemed unaware of his wife's vigilance. He did not realize that at the first sign of fatigue, Fanny encouraged guests to leave; and that they would hurry away despite his insistence that they stay. Nor did he realize that she protected him from the indiscretion of his admirers, from tedium as much as from drafts.

Mrs. R. L. S. could signal to Lloyd with a look to close the window. With a gesture she would send him to fetch a shawl. And she kept the door closed to undesirable visitors. Stevenson accepted all this. And the strength he enjoyed this evening he owed to his wife, that strength which managed to persuade her.

"Talk to your daughter . . . Since she refuses to be separated from Austin by sailing on the *Equator*, I want her to leave with him for Australia. Convince her!"

"If your father could only hear you!" Fanny remarked humorously. "Remember how you resented his attempt to run your life. And all your friends who called me authoritarian!" She laughed: "Ah well, I've found my master! As for Belle, you will convince her yourself. She won't accept anything from me."

"Very well. I will speak to her when I return from Molokai."

"The minister of health will never allow you to go!" she said triumphantly.

"I have already got permission: I am leaving on the twenty-first."

Furious, exasperated, she jumped out of bed. He watched her pace around the table, the chairs, again and again, like a lioness in a cage, in a highly agitated state.

"It's ridiculous," she was saying. "It's ridiculous! You've just spent ten years in bed, ten years flirting with death . . . and just when you're finally enjoying good health, you're going to throw yourself into the lion's den. It's ridiculous! Swear to me, at least, that you won't touch anything, swear to me that you will wear gloves."

"Gloves—Fanny, I will put on gloves to brave your . . ." Louis smiled, an expression full of humor and tenderness: ". . . our daughter."

Belle Strong would preserve a rather painful memory of that interview:

One afternoon, only a week or two before they left, I was called to Louis's cottage where he and my mother were waiting for me. Then, as head of the family, Louis told me the plans that he had made for me, my mother agreeing to everything he said.

I was to leave Honolulu by the next steamer. Tickets had been bought and a cabin engaged for Austin and me on the Mariposa *to Sydney, Australia. When there, we were to put up at a boarding house already chosen, and draw on Towne and Company, bankers, for a certain sum every month.*

"And what do I do then?" I asked.

"Wait till called for," said Louis.

When they first spoke of taking another cruise, there must have been some mention of my going with them, for I remember declaring that I would not leave Austin in a boarding school under any circumstances. That idea was soon dropped and I had looked forward to staying on in Honolulu for the rest of my life.

It was a stormy interview. I think these memoirs show that I was rather a meek person, doing pretty much as I was told. I remember making a joke of it and saying I always obeyed the nearest man. But this time I rebelled. I loved Honolulu. I had many friends there, and I could earn my own living as I had proved in the past. They did not believe that at all, and thought I'd be safer in Sydney living on a weekly allowance; then, when their voyage was ended, we would meet there and make further plans.

*

A few weeks before this altercation, on that evening in May 1889, Louis had made his plans without Fanny. This was the first time.

Robert Louis Stevenson to Fanny

Molokai, May 22, 1889

Dear Fanny,

. . . To tell you the truth, I was so cowed with fear and disgust that I dared not go back on the adventure in the interests of my own self-respect. Presently we came up with the leper promontory: lowland, quite bare and bleak and harsh, a little town of wooden houses, two churches, a landing stair, all unsightly, sour, northerly, lying athwart the sunrise, with the great wall of the pali cutting the world out on the south. Our lepers were sent on the first boat, about a dozen, one poor child very horrid, one white man, leaving a large grown family behind him in Honolulu, and then into the second stepped the sisters and myself. I do not know how it would have been with me had the sisters not been there. My horror of the horrible is about my weakest point; but the moral loveliness at my elbow blotted all else out; and when I found that one of them

*was crying, poor soul, quietly under her veil, I cried a little myself;
then I felt as right as a trivet, only a little crushed to be there so
uselessly. I thought it was a sin and a shame she should feel unhappy; I turned round to her, and said something like this: "Ladies,
God Himself is here to give you welcome. I'm sure it is good for
me to be beside you; I hope it will be blessed to me; I thank you
for myself and the good you do me." It seemed to cheer her up;
but indeed I had scarce said it when we were at the landing stairs,
and there was a great crowd, hundreds of (God save us!) panto-
mime masks in poor human flesh, waiting to receive the sisters and
the new patients.*

*Every hand was offered: I had gloves, but I had made up my
mind on the boat's voyage not to give my hand; that seemed less
offensive than the gloves. So the sisters and I went up among that
crew, and presently I got aside (for I felt I had no business there)
and set off on foot across the promontory, carrying my wrap and
the camera. All horror was quite gone from me: to see these dread
creatures smile and look happy was beautiful. . . . One woman was
pretty, and spoke good English, and was infinitely engaging, and
(in the old phrase) towardly; she thought I was the new white
patient; and when she found I was only a visitor, a curious change
came in her face and voice—the only sad thing, morally sad, I
mean—that I met that morning.*

*

The creation of the leper colony that Robert Louis Stevenson
had come to visit dated back twenty years or so, when the minister
of health, concerned with confining the epidemic, had bought land
on the least populous, most arid island of the archipelago. The first
convoy of patients had been dropped there in January 1866, without
provisions, medication, doctors, means of support, help, or infra-
structure of any sort. They had counted on occupying the newly
vacated house of the peasants and cultivating the attached lands
until death overtook them.

Four years later, the promontory of Kalaupapa consisted of two
hundred and seventy-nine outcasts.

The police tracked down lepers throughout the realm. The doctors of Honolulu who made a diagnosis of leprosy incurred reprisals
from families who had to see one of their own sent to this living

hell. Some patients arrived handcuffed for defending themselves
against the sheriff and his men.

In 1873, five years before the minister of health decided to send
the first doctor to Molokai, a Belgian priest took it upon himself
to stop there. He was born Joseph de Veuster. They called him
Father Damien. His arrival was no different from that of the ordinary leper. He found no help, not even a roof for shelter. A carpenter by training, he rolled up his sleeves and set to work. He worked
hard, shared all he possessed with the needy, comforted the dying,
encouraged the living. And for fourteen years he harassed the ministry of health with his constant demands for subsidy. Some then
accused him of diverting private donations earmarked for particular
purposes into his pet projects, which favored "his" lepers, those of
the Catholic confession.

Whatever the case, for hundreds of these unfortunates Father
Damien was the only ray of hope in a dark world. Neglecting his
own health, he took constant risks. "My life is in God's hands," he
replied to the doctor he had finally obtained for his island. Ten
years after his arrival, Father Damien was infected with leprosy.
He spent the four last months of his life tormented by the fear
that he hadn't earned the right to heaven.

Robert Louis Stevenson to Sidney Colvin

Honolulu, June 1889
My dear Colvin,
    . . . I can only say that the sight of so much courage, cheerfulness,
and devotion strung me too high to mind the infinite pity and
horror of the sights.
    . . . I have seen sights that cannot be told, and heard stories that
cannot be repeated: yet I never admired my poor race so much,
nor (strange as it may seem) loved life more than in the settlement.
A horror of moral beauty broods over the place: that's like bad
Victor Hugo, but it is the only way I can express the sense that
lived with me all these days. And this even though it was in great
part Catholic, and my sympathies flew never with so much difficulty
as toward Catholic virtues. . . . Of old Damien, whose weaknesses
and worse perhaps I heard fully, I think only the more. It was a
European peasant: dirty, bigoted, untruthful, unwise, tricky, but
superb with generosity, residual candor and fundamental good hu-

mour: Convince him he had done wrong (it might take hours of insult) and he would undo what he had done and like his corrector better. A man, with all the grime and paltriness of mankind, but a saint and hero all the more for that....

Did Fanny understand the importance of such a trip? Did she recognize the moral shock, the spiritual transformation Louis had undergone without her?

Robert Louis Stevenson's encounter with the suffering of others, the discovery of compassion and hope bolstered the writer in his faith in humanity, and gave him an even greater passion for life. The essayist, the novelist, the literary critic, would become politically engaged. It was difficult for those who had stayed ashore, difficult for Fanny to follow him along this path fueled by emotions she had not shared. But Fanny Vandegrift was not a woman to be left behind. She would share, support, and sometimes even outdistance her husband's dream.

Six months after Louis's visit to Molokai, when the Stevensons dropped anchor in Samoa before joining Belle in Sydney, Fanny read in the local paper that the project to erect a monument in Honolulu to the memory of Father Damien had just been abandoned. The interruption of work was due to the publication in an Australian religious paper of a letter signed by the Rev. Dr. C.M. Hyde, a powerful man in Hawaiian affairs, that revealed Damien's moral lapses.

As soon as she landed in Australia, Fanny ran to the libraries. She located the edition of the *Sydney Presbyterian*, found the Reverend Hyde's letter, and read it aloud to Louis. Indignant at what he had just heard, embittered by the stupidity and vileness of this attack on the memory of a dead man, Stevenson shut himself up in his room.

In *An Open Letter to the Rev. Dr. Hyde of Honolulu*, the words that burst from his pen continue to shock some of his admirers today. Some of his biographers condemn the violence and cruelty he deploys to destroy the Rev. Dr. Hyde. He himself repented of it. And while he may have smiled at the coincidence of the name "Hyde," his remorse at having destroyed a man, even one bereft of charity, would haunt him for many years. He would renounce his author's royalties to his pamphlet: *This letter to Dr. Hyde is yours or any man's,* he wrote to his publisher. *I will never touch a penny in remuneration; I do not stick at murder, I draw the line at cannibalism.*

A good thrashing—perhaps! But we still find in Stevenson's voice a generosity, a breadth, a scope worthy of the greatest pamphleteers, a caustic tone that can match the best of Voltaire. And above all the evocative power of the visionary.

One afternoon in Sydney, Belle recalls, *we were summoned to the Oxford Hotel, the whole family assembling. Giving instructions that no one was to be admitted under any circumstances, Louis announced with unusual gravity that he had written something he wanted us to hear. When we had taken our seats round the center table he stood before us with a manuscript in his hand. I had never seen him so serious or so deeply stirred. He explained that the article he had written would probably involve him in a suit for libel, which, if lost, might mean poverty for us all. He felt he had no right to print it without consulting us, but hoped we would take the risk, for he wanted to publish it at his own expense and send a copy to prominent people all over the world. Whether he should do this or not rested with us. He would abide by our decision.*

Then, in his deep voice vibrating with emotion, with heightened color and blazing eyes he read aloud the Father Damien Letter.

Never in all my life have I ever heard anything so dramatic, so magnificent. There was deep feeling in every sentence—scorn, indignation, biting irony, infinite pity—and invective that fairly scorched and sizzled. The tears were in his eyes when he finished. Throwing the manuscript on the table he turned to his wife.

The look that Louis and Fanny exchanged would remain engraved forever upon the memories of the others present. She had risen. They had stood for a moment face to face. They were both feverish with emotion. Then, holding out her hands to him in a gesture of enthusiasm, she cried: "Publish!"

"Fanny, you understand that if I publish this, it may mean poverty again?"

"Publish!"

"Poverty and scandal? If there is a trial, we will be dragged through the mud ... The Protestant missionaries will fall upon us, which means that we won't be able to stay in the Pacific. If we return to Scotland, we'll have the whole Presbyterian Church on our backs."

"Publish! You must send it everywhere . . . to Queen Victoria, to President Harrison. Belle and I are going to make envelopes right away. Ah, you must also send it to Sadi-Carnot, to the Archbishop of Canterbury. And then to the Vatican, to the Pope!"

*

A century after Robert Louis Stevenson's outcry, several monuments are standing to the memory of the priest of Molokai.

It was recently ruled in Rome, during a trial of beatification, that Father Damien deserves to be ranked among the blessed. Beatification is the first step toward canonization. *Well, the man who tried to do what Damien did is my father . . . and the father of all who love goodness; and he was your father too [the Rev. Dr. Hyde], if God had given you the grace to see it.*

Hawaii—The Gilbert Islands—The Samoan Islands
June–December 1889, on board the *Equator*

"Do you know why I love the Pacific?" shouted Louis as loud as he could.

His question was answered by a shot. Joe Strong, napping in a hammock, pushed off the hat that was covering his face. Above him, seated on the roof of the cabin, her legs dangling barefoot in the sun, the little blue-clad figure of his mother-in-law was emptying her revolvers into the shark that had stupidly decided to follow in their wake. Fanny kept her arms held out, the sleeves of her *holoku* flapping in the wind with the snap of a flag. Her strange shadow danced on the ocean.

"Because the Pacific is a strange place. The nineteenth century exists there only in spots!" cried Louis.

Joe twisted around to watch him against the light.

"Because the South Seas are a no man's land of the ages, a stirabout of epochs and races, barbarisms and civilizations, virtues and crimes!"

Joe replaced his hat and went back to sleep, wondering if Louis

was talking about the South Seas or about Fanny Stevenson. All
ages and races, all crimes and virtues—that was Mrs. R. L. S.

"Touché!" she cried triumphantly, jumping to her feet. "He's
done to a turn! Go on, boys, lift him up."

On the aft deck, the two sailors awaiting the results of the hunt
lowered the net, which they arduously lifted by way of a pulley.

"Shark steaks—delicious. We'll eat them this evening," she commented complacently. "Leave it there. I'll gut it right away."

The sailors obeyed. They would not have thought to resist. This
woman embodied a maternal figure clearly tinged with a little sorcery. They all feared her powers as much as they respected her
endurance. Didn't she know how to relieve fevers? To cure
wounds? To prepare meals? Even Captain Reid, a twenty-five-year-
old Scotsman—a hard case who would end in prison for having
sold a stolen boat—even Reid complied.

The splendors of the *Casco* were over. The *Equator* was a little
trading schooner that collected the copra gathered from around
Polynesia and Melanesia by the traders. It belonged to a San Francisco company, and did not take passengers. This was another of
Fanny's coups. She had furnished the vessel and even managed to
install two additional bunks for Joe and Ah Fu. She agreed, despite
her seasickness, to sleep on the floor, rolled in a cover, squeezed
between her son and the fat boatswain's mate, a rather unprepos-
sessing Norwegian. She had left her husband the only cabin, ceding
to him all the luxuries and comforts so that he might write in peace.

It was a strange paradox that this passion for Louis's work, this
symbiosis in artistic expression, the creative communion that had
fascinated them both from the first days of their liaison, the eternal
struggle for elaboration of the work, was now becoming, in July
1890, a violent source of discord aboard the *Equator*.

"If you persist," she went on angrily when they jumped down
on the deck together to lean over the enormous beast, "I warn
you . . ."

They had continued this discussion at all hours of the day and
night, at random, confronting each other as violently as they had
in Bournemouth, when the young neighbor woman had hesitated
between calling the police or retreating on tiptoe.

"It would be a shame for you to do such a scientific and imper-
sonal thing, a doctoral thesis on the Pacific! What a waste! Why,
with my own feeble hand I could write a book that the whole world

would jump at. And you, when I think that you have put nothing in your diary but statistics! Your readers will be bored to death at your comparisons of the Protestant and Catholic missions. They couldn't care less about the etymology of the world pronounced "io" in Tahitian! Who gives a damn that it comes from "oi" in Hawaiian? You are not a linguist, you don't know anything about these things. Leave the erudition to the ethnologists, and do what you know best. You're a writer. There is no one living who understands the people of Polynesia as you do and can tell their stories as you can! People are dying to hear about Ori A Ori, your friendship with him, how you became blood brothers with the cannibal chief of the Marquesas, the strange stories they told, and the extraordinary adventures we've had. To think that you would spoil such a subject!"

"On the contrary, this will be my greatest book . . . my masterpiece. This work will be unique, it will be worthy of my idea of literature, embracing all genres, mixing the demands of science with anecdote, savagery with civilization, the beautiful with the monstrous. I will teach the mysteries of Polynesia to the whole world!"

" 'Teach!' " She tapped her foot impatiently on the deck, and the crouching sailors who were taking the fish from the net raised their heads to look at the couple. "Who asked you to teach, Louis? Your readers want you to entertain them."

"Entertaining is not enough for me, Fanny! I must go further."

"And what does that mean—to go further? To bore? To pontificate? You are betraying your public, and you are betraying the Polynesians by making science more important than the human dramas we are here to witness!"

"You want me to remain the Stevenson the public knows—young, light, caustic . . . People develop, Fanny! It is a writer's duty to grow."

"Not you, not me—we do not change! You know what I am going to do? I'm going to write about your project to Colvin, you respect his judgment. He will agree with me, you'll see!"

"Once and for all, Fanny, mind your own business! You will not write to Colvin . . ."

"Oh yes I will! I'm going to tell your mentor what you're doing. A scientific book! You will see his reaction. 'The duty to grow'—

who are you kidding? No one writes out of duty! Or rather, yes: You have the duty to respect your reader by making him dream!"

"What do you know about a writer's duty? You should know, my dear, that your advice in artistic matters is to be followed only with the greatest circumspection! The truth is, you understand nothing . . ."

Stevenson stopped short. This was a mine field. "Art" was now a taboo word between them, the only subject they could not discuss.

"Nonetheless," Fanny growled, her teeth clenched. "Nonetheless, you have been successful only when you've followed my advice."

"Let's not confuse things: I don't owe my success to your artistic sense but to your commercial instincts," he replied coldly. "You have the narrow mind of the greater public that thinks a book must be interesting."

She blanched. "It is the greater public's narrow mind that finances your cruises, my boy!"

"Who is saying otherwise? I believe, along with you, that my first duty is to feed my family!"

"I never said," she shouted, wounded to the quick, "I never said such a thing!"

"I agree with you," he went on, pitilessly, "that producing masterpieces must take second place in a writer's life. But stop interfering!"

Then, in one of the explosions of fury Lloyd had come to dread, Stevenson thundered: "For the last time, Fanny, my work belongs to me!"

Joe Strong, keeping score with delight in this argument, which for once didn't have to do with his laziness, was hard put to say which of the two combatants had won this round.

But the great scientific work Robert Louis Stevenson dreamed of and carried within him for many years was never written.

Would Fanny and Louis sense that in this confrontation—whose dramatic outcome did not depend on either financial difficulties, the husband's alcoholism, or the wife's infidelities, as it did with the Strongs—they could kill their reason for being together?

"I have a sensational idea!" Louis announced that evening, after making peace and taking particular delight in the shark steak. "This is a plan that will allow us to combine business and pleasure, a project that will give us a base in the Pacific. Lloyd and I are going to write an adventure novel that will make us a fortune. With all that money we will buy a schooner and support ourselves trading in copra! What do you say to that, Madam and sweetheart?"

"Bravo!" Fanny exclaimed.

She continued to hate the ocean, but if this was the price of Louis's health, fine, she had no regrets at being the wife of a trader. She was graciously prepared to be nauseated for the rest of her days.

"The company will be called Jekyll and Hyde. And in memory of the Stevenson firm that built all those lighthouses in Great Britain, we'll call the schooner the *Northern Lights*."

"That's one way of continuing their work," Fanny remarked, not without irony.

As it happened, Louis would renounce this dream himself.

After a stop in Buritari, in the Gilbert Islands, where the Stevenson party almost got themselves killed by a population drunk on the white man's alcohol and armed with traders' rifles, they recognized the vileness and corruption of the traders' world. They felt no regrets at moving on to other adventures.

A hundred or so miles from Buritari, the *Equator* put in at Apemama, capital of King Tembinok'. Bellicose, cruel, deceitful, Tembinok' reigned over a miniature empire of atolls. His name filled the war songs of the archipelago. The Whites called him the "legendary despot," or the "Napoleon of the Gilberts."

King Kalakaua was underdeveloped by comparison to the warrior Tembinok'. He weighed three hundred pounds and stood about six feet tall. *A beaked profile like Dante's in the mask, a mane of long black hair, the eye brilliant, imperious, and inquiring. . . . His voice matched it well, being shrill, powerful, and uncanny, with a note like a sea-bird's. Where there are no fashions, he dresses . . . "to his own heart." Now he wears a woman's frock, now a naval uniform, now . . . trousers and a singular jacket with shirt tails, and cut and fit wonderful for island workmanship, the material always handsome, sometimes green velvet, sometimes cardinal red silk. This masquerade becomes him admirably . . . , Tembinok' is never ridiculous.*

The sun shone on the brass plates engraved with the name SINGER. Plunging into the slack waters of the lagoon were one, two, ten sewing machines, which sunk straight to the bottom of the ocean. When Tembinok' 's oarsmen threw his sewing machines into the water as anchors for their canoes, the flotilla was impressive. The only inconvenience was that the Napoleon of the Gilberts did not allow any stranger to reside on his islands. His father had executed all the Whites who had tried to establish trading posts there. Today only one trader remained, a coward who lived in terror of the king's caprice. "I have the power," he would say to Robert Louis Stevenson. Precisely: Tembinok' had the power. That and his politics made him a man after Louis's own heart, taking from civilization what seemed agreeable and rejecting the rest. The agreeable things were weapons, tobacco, and fabrics—the king's special favorites were moire and silk velvet. In short, all the merchandise the trading vessels could sell him.

In his bamboo palace, hundreds of grandfather clocks and music boxes, bits of bicycles, umbrellas, nails, and ovens stood rotting and rusting. It did not matter that Tembinok' had no use for them. When he saw an object he liked, he wanted it. His idea was to prevent others from acquiring the goods he might covet. As a consequence, he was highly interested in the boats sailing into the lagoons. And the men of the *Equator* polished the brasses and washed the deck to welcome and impress him. For Fanny had hoped that the king would make an exception to his rule and allow them to spend fifteen days there while the schooner pursued its business through the Gilbert Islands.

She was not aware that Tembinok' 's lagoons had no fish, that the coconut palms sheltered no birds, that edible roots were rare, and that they would all get sick living on coconut and kegs of salt beef. However, Tembinok' appreciated a fine welcome, and God knows Fanny's cooking must have seemed delectable!

While soldiers armed to the teeth to defend the king's wives drank kava with "Pani," Louis and Tembinok' got acquainted discussing poetry on the beach. They were mutually charmed. From the few missionaries he had encountered, Tembinok' had learned how to put his own language down on paper. His wordy, florid English, picked up here and there, allowed him to compose what the two men called lyric poetry: "Lovers, the beach, the coconut trees ... Not always true. Beautiful all the same." He was even working on a chronicle of his reign, in which he recounted, among other things, the visit of an emissary from King Kalakaua, who had made him sign a federation treaty. But as far as Tembinok' was concerned, if he dreamed of a league of the Pacific islands, it was to use it to extend his territory at the expense of Hawaii and others like it.

Their stay amidst the Apemama mosquitos was surely too long to be idyllic, three months camping on the beach, afraid they might never see the *Equator* again; but the two parties would not say good-bye without shedding a few tears. At the king's request, Fanny made a sketch for his national flag, a black shark on a striped background. She would have this flag embroidered in Sydney and bring it back to him in a few months. The Stevensons decidedly did not belong to the "civilized world." In Tembinok' 's eyes, the white race was usually divided into three categories: minor thieves, major thieves, and thieves who robbed him on a grand scale. Standing on the shore, he composed a poem to the glory of the first Westerners who had never tried to cheat him. Their reunion promised to be an emotional one. Now, only too happy to leave this pitiless land, Fanny set off for Samoa, an archipelago the old explorers had called "Navigators Islands."

Upolu—The Samoan Islands
December 1889

Halfway between the horizon and the shore the *Equator* skirted a fringe of foam that surged, subsided, and surged again, a scarcely perceptible line that flowed and flamed like a tongue of white sparks on the gray sea. The coral reef. In this spot the roar of the Pacific was dulled, and an implosion took place in which the human ear could not distinguish the ebb and flow of the great waves breaking against the coral wall before being sucked back out to sea. And Fanny knew that there, on the distant island, fishermen were pulling in their nets, wading thigh deep in the lagoon, followed by women and children who also heard this incessant rumbling, this eternal sound of the deep more powerful than any force on earth.

In the last hours of daylight, the *Equator* was seeking a break in the coral reef that allowed entry into the harbor of Apia. Upolu was the largest and most populous island of the archipelago, consisting of over 400 square miles and 35,000 natives at the last missionary census. Apia, the village capital, nestled at the foot of a mountain chain, drowsed there at the edge of the lagoon. Only the cathedral stood out, massive and white, almost phosphorescent, against the dark, leafy green of the slopes.

The crests of the mountains disappeared into a heavy, leaden sky that looked like rain. The heat was so close that Fanny felt the humidity on her neck, the moisture frizzing the curls on her forehead.

She experienced the same emotion with every landing. She stared feverishly at the narrow strand of beach, where the trunks of palm trees, crushed by the weight of the clouds, leaned over the ocean and stretched toward the horizon with their forlorn fronds licking the waves, dead in the lagoon.

This was a gray basin flatter than a pond and rimmed by a sandy beach so pale it seemed transparent, smooth as a steel blade. In Samoa it was the sand that mirrored the water, the water that was reflected in the sand; only the jutting black lava rocks, dark masses, disturbed the palm groves climbing toward the slopes, reminding sailors that they were approaching land.

On December 7, 1889, just before sunset, the wives of missionaries, traders, planters, the little colonial society sauntered down to witness the arrival of a trading boat. All the Whites of Apia squinted their eyes. Even the three rival consuls, watching from their villas beneath their respective national flags—German, British, and American—exchanged circumspect looks as the passengers disembarked at the port.

In a cotton pajama top open to the navel, a yachting cap, long hair, barefoot, the first of the band jumped ashore brandishing a tin whistle. His companion, a guitar slung over the back of her flowered holoku, her face tanned under an enormous native hat, a purple scarf around her neck, a striped shawl over her shoulders, leaped behind him and trotted at his side. Then came two young people, one in a faded striped vest, an earring in one ear, his eyes hidden behind dark glasses, and a violin in one hand; the other, with a huge mustache, his torso belted with a flowered pareo, a cockatoo on his shoulder and an accordion across his chest. A Chinese man, the top of his head entirely shaved, his long queue swinging like a metronome, brought up the rear.

This prepossessing party had just filed out of the boat of Henry J. Moors, the most influential trader in Apia, an American whom the consuls suspected of arming the native factions. What were the relations between Moors and these itinerant musicians?

I took them for a troop of wandering players, confessed a local pastor. *I thought they were down-at-heels entertainers who were coming to sing here with the hope of earning a few dollars in the bars of Apia for their crossing to Sydney.*

The Rev. Mr. Clarke was not mistaken. They were indeed players, but of a particular sort. He could not have imagined that the guitarist and the tin whistle player would eventually defy the hegemony of local white society; that as rebels against stupidity and rapacity, they would espouse the Samoans' cause; and that in token of their gratitude, generations after civil war and outside exploitation had torn Samoa apart, Samoan postage stamps would bear the picture of Robert Louis Stevenson, whom they affectionately called "Tusitala," the Teller of Tales.

Apia—Samoa—December 1889–February 1890

Letter from Fanny to Margaret Stevenson

Christmas 1889
Dear Aunt Maggy,

This place is far more splendid than we would have imagined in our wildest dreams. I have never seen anything so strange . . . you may think that all the Pacific Islands are rather alike, and that Joe's descriptions and his enthusiasm for Kalakaua's expedition have perhaps influenced our judgment, that we could only be impressed or disappointed in our landing here. This is not true, as Upolu is even more magical.

Compared to the Marquesas or Tahiti, the charm of Samoa does not immediately strike you, there is nothing spectacular about it. Apia, the capital, even struck us as quite uninteresting, with a single street meandering along the bay, a row of huts that at best shelter small general stores, at worst brothels and bars. The view of the strait is spoiled by the skeletons of six warships. Imagine the black hulls rolling in the tropical storms, and they cannot even be destroyed by explosives for fear of blowing up the village along with them! The pitiful history of these boats illustrates the stupidity of the three powers that govern the island.

Briefly, for twenty years four royal native families have been vying with each other for power. In the 1870's the Germans, the English, and the Americans took advantage of the situation to force the Samoans to sell them their land in exchange for weapons. And the Germans were most successful. A company from Hamburg owns the largest palm groves in all the South Seas, and they have a thriving copra trade. In order to prevent them from exercising too much power over this part of the Pacific, an American, Colonel Steinberger, concluded an agreement with King Laupepa, one of the pretenders to the throne, that allowed him to reign for four years, after which he would pass the throne to the three other kings in turn. So each dynasty would reign every twelve years—under the thumb of the American colonel appointed prime minister. The idea evidently did not please the Germans or the English, who made common cause to overthrow him, along with his constitution, leaving Samoa in the hands of partisan factions that continued to be armed by one or another of the three white powers. Heroically, Laupepa gave himself up, thus avoiding civil war. The Germans deported him, and you must know that for a native Samoan, living far from his island is a fate worse than death.

Then, you see, the Germans being mysterious for no apparent reason, spared no expense: They dragged Laupepa around the world for two years without ever telling him what they'd decided to do with him or his destination. The deposed king was taken as far as the high seas near Bremen, where he barely caught a glimpse of the lights before sailing back in the other direction to New Caledonia. Meanwhile, Mataafa, the German's former candidate, Laupepa's ex-rival, had organized a resistance to the white occupation in support of the exiled king. The three powers then formed a coalition to send in the war ships I mentioned. Can you imagine such a flotilla sailing into the tiny port of Apia? Hundreds of men and more than forty cannons. Germany, Great Britain, and the United States, three big dogs sniffing after the same bone—a little bit of gristle.

But nature joined the fray! As if the heavens wanted to take revenge on human stupidity, they concocted one of the most violent cyclones in history. The unbelievable thing is that the captains of the three fleets had seen it coming, for on the day of March 16, 1889, the barometer had suddenly dropped. But neither the Americans nor the Germans nor the English wanted to be the first to withdraw. Yet they could tell at a glance that this bay forms a *basin where the waves become violent as they are dashed against the sea wall of the coral reef. At the last moment, one of the English boats chose to brave the cyclone and flee. Thrown against each other, the six battleships with their crews sank on the spot. After this carnage, in which more than one hundred and ninety sailors perished without the natives firing a single shot, the three powers reconnoitered in Berlin to sign a treaty. What a farce! This agreement, which was not ratified by any native representative, very generously stipulated that Samoa would remain independent and governed by a king whom the three powers would choose for the people. This king, hand-picked and kept in power by the Whites, would govern the country with the agreement and support of the three consuls, each representing one of the powers. You can just imagine the muddle. They restored Laupepa whom they had exiled, and banished Mataafa, who had supported Laupepa. They removed the throne from the two other families, who continued to claim their rights, while the three consuls fought amongst themselves. The only parties whose dignity saved the situation were, as usual, the natives.*

I understand Joe's sympathy and fascination with the Samoans. The men are built like statues, with broad torsos that move muscle by muscle and very slowly. They all wear lava lavas, *a big piece of red or blue fabric with white flowers, as we had seen in Tahiti. But they knot it on the side, and Louis claims that they wear the* lava lava *the way the Scots wear the kilt. It seems that these people have cultivated the art of gesture and plastic movement as if they had no artistic expressions but their own beauty. They have a way of moving in slow motion, one part at a time. The upper body straight, head held high, their eyes looking into the distance . . . Forms seem to hold a central place here, and the aesthetic sense of their society seems to run much deeper than in ours. Every moment of their life strives toward an ideal of beauty. The village boys, for example, choose one or several girlfriends who advise them on their hair styling, who know just which curls and waves suit their particular hairdo, and put a kind of passion into decorating them with flowers or leaves. The men and women groom each other while chatting on the steps of the fales. The most elegant men tint their hair with a concoction of quicklime and lemon. This operation takes several days, and they saunter around with their heads all white, like marquis of the eighteenth century who have stuck huge red flowers in their wigs* . . .

Their houses and gardens are jealously tended. I believe that weeding is their only activity. They keep their lawns cut close and sprinkled with flowers. Otherwise, they hardly move. They can sit still for hours watching the ocean. What are they thinking about? . . . *They haven't an ounce of aggression, just forebearing kindness. But there is something deeply and utterly foreign about them. They are nonetheless Christians, and very practicing. Missionaries of all confessions agree that getting them to accept Christianity was rather easy. The Samoans had long expected our God, who was thought to be more powerful and generous then theirs, judging by the wealth of the Whites. Sundays please them particularly, the churches and temples are full to bursting, and the services are interminable. The faithful like nothing better than the endless hymns which they chant in their most beautiful finery* . . . *Yet these people seem more different from us than all the other native peoples, even those of the cannibal islands. There is something absent about them that fascinates and intrigues me. I am not sure I'll ever be able to understand them* . . . *I am also struck by their language and their vocal inflections. It's a kind of whispering. They murmur, and I sometimes have trouble hearing them. Even the children do not scream. They laugh, they run, but noiselessly. In this sense, the atmosphere of Samoa is extremely different from Tahiti. At the port, when families from Savai'i and Manono, Upolu's neighboring islands, meet, they don't call out to each other. Clearly they still feel tension or emotion, but here again acts and words seem withheld and muted. An embrace, a murmur, and whole villages of them disappear in a damp cloud in the direction of the "bush" that borders on the town. Mr. Moors, the American trader who is putting us up, told me that demonstrativeness is considered ill-bred. The Whites haven't any idea how important etiquette is here. It will take months, perhaps years, before I know the rules.*

Months? Years? Their stay in Samoa was expected to last only until February. Louis and Fanny had sent the *Equator* on its way and counted on returning on the *Lübeck*, the steamer that plied the route between San Francisco, the islands, and Sydney. Belle and Austin were waiting for them. The Stevensons thought of making financial arrangements for the Strongs in Australia before their own return to England.

*

A white man, deeply tanned, was walking on the level ground at the edge of the coral reef. Armed with a harpoon, he kept his eyes on the gaps between the fingers of coral. The black crest of the sea wall stood out of the water, festooned with clusters of plants drying in the sun, an array of aquatic fauna that gave off a nauseating odor of slime and algae. In the distance, enclosing the beach, rocks of black lava rose ever higher and more menacing, all the way up to the coconut trees. Directly below, the basin flattened out, hollowed beneath the sun like an empty cup. A native woman was advancing slowly along the shore. She was carrying a large basket against her hip. She sat down. Upon closer inspection one could see that she, too, was white. No Samoan would have mistaken her for one of their own. She had walked too energetically down the beach just now, and she had crouched too quickly on the sand. Even her stillness, her silence, was different from the Samoan reverie.

Yet she was suffused with an unaccustomed sense of peace. She put her arms around her legs and rested her chin on her knees without taking her eyes off the thin figure stalking around the coral. She could not get used to this marvelous development: At the age of thirty-nine, for the first time in his life, Louis was fishing, Louis was swimming, Louis was riding horses—he had even danced on Christmas Eve. Next May, he would return to London. What madness! She was convinced that what Robert Louis Stevenson needed was the sun, the sea, a tropical climate; the warmth of the ocean, not the high altitude of the mountains; and never to go more than ten degrees north or south of the equator. He was now thinking of settling in Madera, of spending the winter there, and returning every summer to England. To take such a risk simply to see Colvin again, who was bored by their travel stories, and Henley, whom Louis had finally forgiven, that whole bunch who basically, she thought, didn't give a damn about him! "While here . . . here," she was thinking. "Why not stay here?"

She perceived some distance behind her, between the palms that fringed the shore, the slow activity of a Samoan village. There were five or six houses without walls or partitions, with an oval roof of pandanus leaves supported by twenty posts. Raised on a bed of black stones, the *fale* consisted of a single huge, elliptically shaped room, open on all sides. Between the posts painted bright blue, red, or vivid yellow, shades were rolled down for the night, protecting those inside from wind and rain. From the central post of the *fale* hung the calabash of water and cups carved from coconuts. On the fine gravel strewn over the floor stood the furniture, wooden boxes where the women stowed the *lava lavas*, the cloths that could be hung to partition the house into several alcoves, and the sleeping mats of woven straw. What more could anyone want? thought Fanny. Nature provided for their needs. The women manufactured clothing from tree bark, which they wove and dyed. They had only to bend down to gather bread fruit, coconuts, and taro roots. The sea was swarming with fish, and catching them seemed to be the most delightful sport; Louis, who had never been able to do anything with his hands, loved it. The biggest problem, she thought, the only question was the effect of permanent residence in the South Seas on Louis's work. Would he find it difficult to write here? Would his production suffer? Would he manage to get published? Would he be cutting himself off from the papers and the reviewers? Would he lose his readers? Here in these remote islands, would he miss the intellectual contact with his peers? Even granting that Louis would need very little in the way of income to survive in Samoa, would he manage to earn a living?

As she had done before in Grez when she had tried to choose between Sam and Louis, weighing the advantages and disadvantages of one against the other, she traced a line in the sand with her index finger. On each side she listed the pros and cons.

"Samoa has an advantage," she went on, "a great advantage over the other Pacific islands. The ship going between Australia and San Francisco stops here once a month. The mail takes only thirty days to reach Europe. Upolu is only a week's travel from New Zealand, and from there the telegraph line to London takes less than a minute. But what about Louis's work? Granting that he could correspond with his publishers, correct his proofs, publish without hindrance, would Louis's work suffer from his isolation? No, she concluded. The yield of the past two years had never been better, and it was so richly inspired. And his capacity for work—no, there was no reason to think that their settlement in the South Seas would prevent him from producing. Besides, here he could be a writer and a planter as well!

She heard behind her the constant humming of the bush, disturbing, various . . . Give her this virgin land, this jungle, this forest, these waterfalls and birds, give her these huge trees, these flowers, this soil and its mud, and Fanny Vandegrift would turn it into gold. She would knead the humus until she transformed it into huge fields of vanilla, tobacco, and cocoa. She was already imagining a large clearing where her plantings stood in rows, she could feel the black seeds between her fingers and smell the fresh odor of the damp earth.

Evening was coming on. The tide was rising. The palm trees on the strand seemed illuminated by the moon, as if the ocean had been merely scenery lit by stage lights. Blinded, she saw the shadows of long canoes lining the shore. The silhouettes of the oarsmen disappeared swiftly behind the coconut trees, reappeared between them, and went on in silence. The water flowed back into the basin. Louis was walking slowly back against the dying light, brandishing his enormous net laden with fish. To her right Fanny sensed the inhabitants of the village advancing over the close-cropped grass that muffled the echo of bare feet. The odor of smoke, the murmur of women rose from the little lean-tos that served as kitchens. A herd of small black pigs was trotting at the edge of the sand; a half-starved white dog wandered by; chickens pecked here and there. Three voices intoned a hymn. The *"Ave Maria"* rose in the evening air. In the last rays of the sun, the oil lamps were lit in the houses. Then the darkness reached even to the residence of the chief, and the slow chant of prayer rose along the shore.

This was the secret hour when the silence of the water was most profound. And Louis took his place beside her on the beach.

Sydney—February 5, 1890

My dear Aunt Maggy, Belle would write a month later.

One morning as I was in bed and lazily wondering whether I had better get up with a wrench or take one more little cat-nap, I heard a wild flying upstairs and the little housemaid burst in with "Mrs. Strong! Mr. Strong!!" and in walked Joe. Though he looked very well indeed, I was sorry to hear that he had been so ill in

Samoa that they sent him on here ahead of the rest for treatment. Indeed he was so bad—weakness of the heart—that the doctor in Samoa told Mama he did not think he would live to reach Sydney. . . .

After Joe left Samoa Mama grew anxious about him, especially after what the doctor said, so she sent Lloyd up by the next streamer to look after him. Lloyd looks well and is fairly brimming over with enthusiasm about the South Seas and the voyage of the Equator . . .

Have you read by the cable that Louis has bought a "home" in Samoa and is going to build a grand place there? They arrive here (Mama and Louis) the day after tomorrow. I will not send this till I see them so that I can tell you how they look and what they said, and what I said, and what they said when I said that! . . .

Lloyd is adding a note to this—

Love, B.

The place in Samoa is two miles behind Apia; is called "Vailima," "The Five Rivers" after the five streams that cross it. Its highest elevation is 1500 feet, lowest 600 feet, area near 400 acres, with fine big trees . . .

L.O.

There is beautiful soil; it is not broken—and picturesque—very few mosquitoes.

L.O.

P.S. Lloyd tells me that they are going to grow vanilla, cocoa, and oranges, which should bring in a lot of money. Lloyd is thinking of setting up a saw mill on one of the river banks. It seems that Mama is talking about creating a distillery and making perfume. She thinks she has found the ylang-ylang tree. In New York, one drop of ylang-ylang extract sells for seven dollars. Louis is dreaming of creating a club in Apia, where there would be books, paper, a billiard table, and tea.

Belle

One detail Lloyd and Belle omitted from their postscripts was that there was nothing on this land but a tangle of bushes, trees, roots, and vines. Vailima was the jungle.

Before seeing those tree trunks for myself, touching those ferns, those stalks, that ivy, and being pricked bloody by their thorns and swollen with their poison, I had never gauged the extent of the Stevensons' task.

The muscles of five men, the open arms of two giants, would not reach around the frailest of the banyan trees. And if by some miracle the axes or explosives managed to demolish them, the steaming earth would simply feed on their remains to produce new branches full of vigorous sap. In Vailima clinging plants, riotous, twining, and sinuous, wove a net between earth and sky in which nature strangled anyone who tried to subdue it.

Despite their descriptions and numerous photographs, I had not fully recognized the madness of their enterprise.

Nor does Lloyd say that no road linked this property to the capital; that during the rainy season, the few paths leading down to Apia were transformed into torrents of mud; that the rains fell from October to May, and the winds took the roofs off the houses; that the 400 Whites, civil servants and traders, thrown together by fate on this remote island, preferred to foment intrigues and mix cocktails rather than cultivate land in the interior; that the 35,000 Samoans scorned manual labor, and that at the beginning of this year, 1890, they were forming factions and arming themselves for a new civil war. Finally, he had forgotten to write that if barrels of gunpowder and cases of champagne crowded the commercial warehouses, it was impossible to find a box of nails, a shovel, a spade, or a trowel anywhere in town. The colonist who hoped to settle there had to import everything by slow ships from far away New Zealand or Australia, or even from San Francisco.

Sydney—February–April 1890

The lift landed gently in the opulent lobby of Sydney's most elegant hotel, and the grillwork opened under the noses of the waiting guests to let a man through.

"What do you take me for?" he shouted, heading toward the reception desk. "I ask for a suite on the first floor, I'm taken to the fourth . . ."

The manager scornfully watched the approach of this unlikely figure. His straw hat was unraveling, his suit seemed to have spent the last six months bundled up in a trunk to judge by the smell of camphor and mothballs.

"I ask for three big, airy rooms and they give me a closet! And you haven't brought up my bags!"

The traveler pointed to his luggage and the bystanders turned to look. Tortoise shell, coconuts, a wealth of shells in calabashes were bound together by a network of string. There were drums in fishing nets, a machete, straw mats, weapons, masks, chests, packing cases—the result of two years' worth of shopping in the South Seas—a pile guaranteed to make even the least snobbish of the elevator operators worry about the character of these guests. This hodgepodge, which only the man himself thought worthy of a gentleman's gear, was being minded by his wife. More conscious than he of the oddity of their baggage, she wore a vague, sphinxlike smile, both ironic and embarrassed. In this temple of civilization, on the polished parquet floor beneath those tapestries of silk and velvet, *I suddenly realized*, Belle relates, *that the two* [of them] *were as odd looking as* [their] *belongings*.

The manager let them know they were unwelcome, and advised them to go to a less fashionable hotel. The hotel management would have cause to repent such high-handed behavior. The day after his arrival, the name of Robert Louis Stevenson was in all the papers. If he had thought he was famous in New York and San Francisco, his success in Sydney surpassed all his hopes. His books—his entire corpus—were displayed in the windows of all the bookstores. Through photographs, articles, editorials, and interviews, the Australian public would get to know his physical appearance, his habits, and his projects: He was to spend several days here before setting off again to summer in Europe. Summer only . . .

*
**

"But my mother was planning to return to Samoa after their trip to England!" Belle whispered, while behind the partition they could hear the sounds of a dreadful coughing fit. "Mr. Stevenson has business to deal with at home. He has to see his publisher in London, rent his house in Bournemouth . . . His own mother still lives in Edinburgh, and . . ."

"The patient's present state will brook no delay, Mrs. Strong! He must leave by the first boat for Samoa, since that is . . ."

"But the docks are closed down, Doctor. Not a single ship is sailing. There's a strike . . . My stepfather must stay here at least until the end of the strike!"

"Then . . ." Dr. Ross made a despairing gesture.

Closing the door to the sickroom behind her, Fanny raised her face toward the doctor. She seemed paler, rather gray beneath her sunburn. Her lips, left untouched by the weather, suddenly seemed to sag. She had just turned fifty. The circles under her eyes, the creases in her neck, the calluses and spots on her little hands all spoke clearly of a wearing life. Belle had not seen her weep since Hervey's death, and now her gaze suddenly seemed to drift off. Then the words she had been repeating in her mind for fifteen years burst out like a cry: "Is my husband going to die?"

"If you do not take him away from Sydney as soon as possible, I cannot answer for the consequences."

Louis had no sooner set foot on the cold, damp quay in this Australian winter than the inevitable had happened. He had caught a cold that had degenerated into a hemhorrage. He was shaking with fever in a room at the Union Club, and spitting blood. Outside, the rain drummed on the flagstones.

"Take your husband to the tropics, settle him on some island, and stay there! As for any visits to England, which your daughter mentioned to me, there can be no question of such a thing, madam. Not now, not ever! Do you understand me? Your place in Samoa will not be simply a second home . . . you are condemned to exile. It is quite clear that you mustn't leave the Pacific again."

The figure of a woman could be seen wandering around Sydney's deserted quays. With her hands in the pockets of her soaking raincoat, without hat or gloves, she was going from one pier to another, searching between the piled up crates, rifling through the sheds, scaling the gangplanks, prowling the deserted decks of all the ships. No one. The few sailors strolling on the docks sent her to find their captains at the Blue Parrot or the Edentata, the taverns where they all spent their pay waiting for a settlement of the conflicts between the gun runners and the supercargoes.

The cold rain flayed her face. She had lost the habit of it, this fear. She thought she had entirely forgotten it, but now the nightmare reasserted itself, more intense than ever. "Dear God, let me die before he does." The last time was in Tahiti in October 1888. The climate of Papeete had been no better for Louis than the rains of Sydney. How ironic that compared to a summer in Scotland, the temperature of these two cities seemed mild.

She did not feel the burning salt drying her lips, nor did she smell the odor of the oily copra, dried coconut meat, lining the docks. She did not hear the gulls calling or the rigging whipping against the masts. Fanny was haunted by a single image, Louis falling back on his bed after a coughing fit, haggard and exhausted, as he had done in Oakland, Edinburgh, Davos, Marseille, Hyères, and Bournemouth. Despite the gusts of wind that took her breath away, she saw only that thin face in which even those large eyes, so full of vigor and life, no longer seemed responsive. The eyelids closed, so pale and fine they appeared molded to the dead globes. Dead? "If he were to die . . . If he were to leave me . . ." She could no longer bear this idea, which had obsessed her for fifteen years. The rediscovery of suffering sent her spinning. "All right, let him die! Three days will do it . . . Let him stay three more days in Sydney and let him die! Let's be done with it! And then I'll throw myself into the sea." This was not the first time she had imagined the turgid green wave pulling her down, or pictured her naked body, stiff and dripping, laid out on the quay. She visualized the hundreds of masts above her, dancing like the skeletons of fragmented fish. They would bury her near Louis. Their shoulders would touch, their hips and legs would be soldered together in a single block of stone. Yes, let him stay here and be done with it!

Only the prospect of her own death could soothe her now. For two years they had wandered the Pacific only to come to this: to end it all in a hotel room in the heart of the first civilized city they had found. Two years and this was the result! Yet at moments she felt hopeful. In Tahiti, too, they had given Louis up for lost. In Tahiti, too, the doctor had ordered them to go to sea. But there, too, it had been impossible to set sail. The *Casco* had then needed crucial repairs. So they hadn't been able to set sail there either, she repeated to herself, as tears of helpless rage rolled down her face—tears or rain. In Tahiti she had decided to take him to the other side of the island, to Tautira, that little village known for its beauty and the purity of its air. They said it didn't rain there, that it was warm . . . But where could she take Louis here, in Australia?

In Tahiti, as here, they had needed to go far away, to the other side of the island, to escape the dampness. It was forty miles between Papeete and Tautira, forty miles of forests with twenty-one streams to cross. The sole means of transport had been a wagon and two horses that belonged to a Chinese man. In living memory the happy owner of such a rarity had never wanted to sell or rent it, or hire himself out along with his team. One morning at sunrise she had gone on foot from Papeete. At midday she had returned, by wagon. Fanny no longer remembered how she had convinced the man. He spoke no English, she spoke no French, but she had gotten the cart. In retrospect, her success seemed easy. At least she had found someone to talk to! Here there was no one. This port full of ships was a ghost port.

How she found out about the Janet Nichol *I have no idea,* Belle recalled. *It was a trading schooner, manned by Solomon Island black boys and bound for the Line Islands. Having no white sailors aboard it was unaffected by the strike and preparing for an early departure.*

I was present when one of the owners, Mr. Henderson, called on my mother . . . She was busily packing for she had learned the Janet *was leaving next day. Her caller, very serious and firm, sat in a big chair, telling her, while my mother continued packing, that he couldn't possibly take any passengers.*

He went into details about the discomfort of such a trip for a sick man. Also there were no accommodations for ladies. When he stopped for breath, my mother, still packing, remarked that there would be three of them—her husband, her son, and herself.

Again Mr. Henderson declared he could not, would not, take any passengers. I left the room on an errand for my mother, stopping to tell Lloyd, who was waiting anxiously, that there was no hope at all. When I got back I was astonished to hear Mr. Henderson giving instructions how to reach the Janet *(owing to the strike she was anchored out in the harbor) and warning my mother to be sure her party was on time.*

It was cold and drizzling when we set out next morning, a sorry company in a big rowboat. Louis was laid out on a board, rolled like a mummy in a blanket; his wife sat beside him, silent and watchful of his comfort. Lloyd, Joe, and I crouched miserably in our seats, too dejected for conversation.

The Janet Nichol *was painted black and perfectly answered the old cliché, "long, low, and rakish." As we neared her I noticed how she rolled, and was not surprised to hear, later, that she was known throughout the Islands as the "Jumping Jenny." . . . She had high bulwarks and there was some trouble getting Louis over the side and into his cabin. . . .*

We were heavy-hearted as we left the Janet Nichol; *Louis looked so ill we thought we might never see him again. It seemed terrible for him to be going away in that sloppy ship with drunken men and inky-black savages, and I didn't like the thought of my mother being the only woman on board with not even Ah Fu to look after her.*

Fortunately letters arrived very soon from Auckland where the schooner stopped for supplies, and later from Samoa. To our surprise we learned the travelers were having a glorious time. Louis had recovered as soon as they struck warm weather . . . They were planning on staying on the Janet Nichol *five months, stopping in all the islands, paying a visit to their friend Tembinok', gathering material for the next book.*

*

The month of August would see them all reunited in Sydney—where Louis fell ill all over again! This time, the game was up. The nomad who used to boast of having spent at least one night in no fewer than two hundred and thirty-one cities in Europe, the vagabond who had begged his mother to accept his wandering ways, had cause to remember that as a twenty-five-year-old dreamer he had written to Fanny Sitwell, his first love:

A civil servant from New Zealand came to dinner at Heriot Row this evening and told me that I had no business to stay in Europe; that I should find all I cared for and all that was good for me in the Navigator Islands . . . beautiful places, green forever; perfect shapes of men and women, with red flowers in their hair; and nothing to do but study oratory and etiquette, sit in the sun, and pick up the fruits as they fall. Navigator's Island is the place; absolute balm for the weary . . .

So the wanderer was finally ready to put down his bags and drop anchor forever. And he would be only half joking when he called his house and lands a return to the feudal legacy of his ancestors.

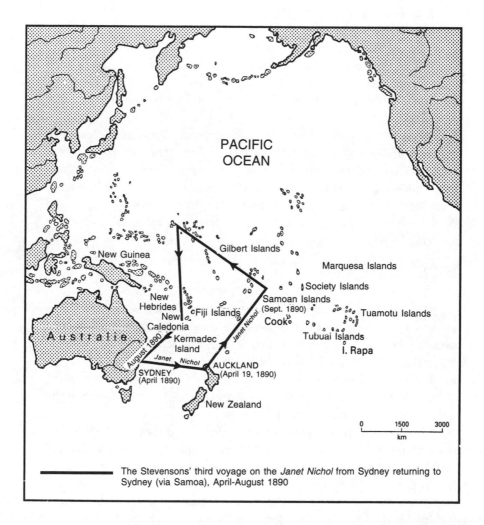

PACIFIC
OCEAN

New Guinea

Gilbert Islands

Marquesa Islands

Society Islands

New
Hebrides
New
Caledonia
Fiji Islands
Samoan Islands
(Sept. 1890)
Cook
Tuamotu Islands

Australie

Kermadec
Island
Tubuai Islands
I. Rapa

Janet Nichol

August 1890

Janet   Nichol
AUCKLAND
(April 19, 1890)
SYDNEY
(April 1890)

New Zealand

0   1500   3000
km

The Stevensons' third voyage on the *Janet Nichol* from Sydney returning to
Sydney (via Samoa), April-August 1890

Vailima would be the domain of the "Stevenson clan," Louis's "empire."

The Stevensons took time only to put in provisions of plants and seeds, tools and poultry. Then they returned alone to their land, the two of them, to undertake a task that couldn't have been accomplished by twenty men.

Fanny sent Lloyd to England to sell the Bournemouth house and garden where she had once thought to settle. He would bring back with him to the Pacific the furnishings of the blue drawing room, and all the odds and ends of that bourgeois villa. He would bring Aunt Maggy with him as well, who would spend a happy old age and, she hoped, a peaceful if expatriot end near her only child. As for Belle and Joe, who continued to live in Sydney on the income provided by their stepfather, if they had hoped to escape the family life Fanny was concocting for them on her island, they were very much mistaken!

The Stevensons were counting on them for the month of May, when the house would be built, when Fanny and Louis would have worked for six months trimming, mowing, and digging. "And my life in the future," thought Robert Louis Stevenson, "promises to consist of many rainy days, a lot of weeding, some correspondence, and devilish little food!" Unless, once again, Fanny could save the situation. She rolled up her sleeves, jammed on her hat, and buckled down to work. "While my chickens are not fenced in," she said to Louis, "I'll be reduced to hunting down the omelette in the wild." So she began by building a chicken coop. She would then build a pigsty, a trough, and a stable, drive in sixty stakes around almost two thousand feet of enclosure, clear five acres herself, and hoe a kitchen garden where she would one day grow lettuce, tomatoes, artichokes, cabbage, zuccini, peas, onions, radishes, and even asparagus. For the moment, they suffered from scarcity. *Our dinner—the lowest we have ever been—consisted of an avocado pear between Fanny and me ..."*

They had no way of getting down to Apia, nor the time to lay in provisions. Fanny tried to put together a team of ten Samoan workers, who knew no more about gardening than they did about carpentry, *Fanny was to have rested ... Lafaele began making a duck house; she let him be; the duck house fell down, and she had to set her hand to it. He was then to make a drinking place for the pigs; she let be again, and he made a stair by which the pigs will probably escape this evening, and she was near weeping . . . Then she had to cook the dinner; then, of course, like a fool and a woman, must wait dinner for me and make a flurry of herself . . .*

The scene of their exploits was described to their mutual friend, Henry James, by the painter John LaFarge and the man of letters Henry Adams, rich Americans who were sailing through the Pacific for pleasure and health, as Louis had done earlier on the *Casco*:

The Stevensons' Vailima: a clearing dotted with burned stumps . . . a two-storey Irish shanty . . . squalor like a railroad navvy's board hut . . . a man so thin and emaciated that he looked like a bundle of sticks in a bag, with . . . dirty striped pajamas, the baggy legs tucked into coarse woolen stockings, one of which was bright brown in color, the other a purplish dark tone . . . a woman . . . [in] the usual missionary nightgown, which was no cleaner than her husband's shirt and drawers, but she omitted the stockings . . . Her complexion and eyes were dark and strong, like a half-breed Mexican . . . Though I could not forget the dirt and squalor, I found Stevenson extremely entertaining . . .

Both La Farge and I came round to a sort of liking for Mrs. Stevenson, who is more human than her husband. Stevenson is airu *[sic]—uncanny. His fragility passes description but his endurance passes his fragility . . . Their travels have broken his wife up; she is a victim to rheumatism which is becoming paralysis, and, I suspect, dyspepsia; she says that their voyages have caused it; but Stevenson gloats over discomforts and thinks that every traveller should sail for months in small cutters rancid with cocoa-nut oil and mouldy with constant rain . . . instead of buying so much land, they might have purchased soap.*

IX

Stevenson's Folly: Villa Vailima

Fanny V. de G. Stevenson
The Weird Woman
Native Name: Tamaitai
. . . If you don't get on with her, it's a pity about
your visit. She runs the show . . . a violent friend,
a brimstone enemy. . . . Is always either loathed or
slavishly adored; indifference impossible.
The natives think her uncanny and that devils
serve her. Dreams dreams, and sees visions.

—Robert Louis Stevenson
(from a letter to James M. Barrie)

Samoa—Vailima I—September 1890–May 1891

"You know all about it, Mrs. Stevenson—attacking the virgin forest, subduing a rebellious nature, taming it," conceded the trader Henry J. Moors. "But—"

"But what?" Fanny cut in dryly.

Late this afternoon toward sundown, the mysterious, mountainous bush country on Mount Vaea to the left of the cottage resounded with shrill cries, like the voices of merry children. The

417

calls of the birds seemed strangely human in the tops of the tall trees that Fanny had spared in the heart of the clearing.

"But . . ."

Moors smiled somewhat condescendingly. She had not expected his visit and had received him barefoot as usual, dressed in her habitual blue *holoku* soiled with sweat and mud. Regretfully setting down her weeding tool, she had led him by the outside ladder to the second floor, to the room that served as the parlor. The ground floor was entirely occupied by the families of her Samoan staff, and by her equipment. "How can a white woman live in such a mess?" the trader wondered. Through the door at the other end of the room he caught a glimpse of her bedroom. "Some boudoir!" he thought. Indeed, the room did present an extraordinary picture. Among the dresses on a big coatrack dangled bridles, halters, and saddle girths. On a box that must have been her dressing table, amidst her tooth brush, her comb, and toilet articles, lay a scattering of tools: a hammer, pruning sheers, pliers, and chisels. On the wall which she had adorned with yellowish tapa, between the harness and necklaces of sharks teeth, hung a bucket, a sculpted lance, and an oil lamp. Her camp bed seemed to have strayed between two cases of ammunition.

"When Lafaele loses the same thing twice," she felt obliged to explain, "I ask him to bring it up to my room. It's the only way we can find it again." She got up to close the door. "Before you arrived, I surprised him in the process of lighting the fire with alcohol, something I've told him a thousand times not to do. 'Bring the alcohol to my room!' I told him as always. But . . ." Fanny pointed to the alcohol drum Moors was sitting on. "I can put up with everything in my room but explosives." She smiled, amused. "Let's hope my guests' ardor won't light it."

Moors did not seem to get the joke.

Powerful, hairy, and fourteen years younger than his hostess, this American owned one of the most important trading posts in Samoa. Besides a grocery-hardware store in town, he also owned the Tivoli Hotel, a palm grove, and several coasting vessels. He was an independent copra trader whose nuptial arrangements with a native woman had incurred the censure of local white society. He continued to be received, however—provided he came without his wife. Fanny greatly preferred the parties at Moors's house to the tea dances at the consuls'. His marriage and his business linked him closely with Samoan interests. Shrewd, ambitious, with a real knowledge of the peoples of Polynesia, Moors liked nothing better than playing a role, and he was power hungry. He had been quick to take under his wing the most illustrious father-in-law of his old pal, Joe Strong. It was Moors who had found Vailima for Robert Louis Stevenson and negotiated the transaction. And Moors had taken it upon himself to clear the first twelve acres of land and build this first "cottage"—the wretched hovel described by the friends of Henry James—which would shelter the Stevensons while they were building their home.

"But," he went on, resting his hat on the table covered with a rose-colored shawl belonging to the mistress of the house, "it takes time to grow coffee, Mrs. Stevenson . . . It doesn't happen, as you seem to think, in one, or two, or even three years . . . You need a minimum of five years before the trees bear fruit. And during those five years your plants will be uprooted by hurricanes, and choked by weeds, roots, and ferns. And you'd better watch out or the toxic *tui-tui* plant will poison all your crops."

"I know that one," she said grimly, holding her red and swollen hands.

Moors just glanced at them and went on: "The *tui-tui* is going to destroy your coffee plants just when you think they're about to flower. Here we plant around six hundred feet per acre. What Samoans are going to do such donkey's work? They don't even cultivate their own land, the word 'work' means nothing to them. If you're counting on luring them with good pay, you have to understand that their wages are just pocket money as far as they're concerned. They don't need it to live on, but they'll 'borrow' freely from you with many fine promises. The notion of 'theft' isn't as clear here as it is with us. Of course you might do like the Germans and hire what we call 'black boys' . . . Surely you've noticed them along the paths to Apia—miserable, cringing creatures with downcast eyes? You can't mistake them for Samoans! They're small, thin, and black as the devil, imported from the Solomon Islands on those ships people here call black birders. I dealt in this trade myself for the plantations in Hawaii, and I wish you lots of luck! They're stupid and understand nothing but the stick! Get your whip ready and lock them up. The Samoans despise their ugliness and fear their customs. For good reason: The black boys on the German plantations are cannibals, they'd as soon make a meal of each other.

Oh yes! If you choose this system, you're cutting yourself off from the native population of the island. In fact, I discovered something about Vailima that I didn't know. Your woods and that mountain, Mount Vaea, are a hideout for all the black boys who run away from the plantations. Surely you've heard strange noises in the night? I'm afraid the *aitus* are not the only ones to disturb your sleep."

"Why," she asked coldly, "have you come to tell me all this, Moors? What do you want me to do? Pack my bags?"

"Precisely, Mrs. Stevenson. Your husband is in Sydney again. You are alone here. The rainy season is beginning. It isn't prudent. I've come to offer you my hospitality."

"That's very kind of you . . . But who would carry on the work if I go to town? You know why my husband has just left for Australia? To meet his mother. He's bringing her back by the next boat. Everything must be ready for her arrival. I have less than a month left."

Through the window of the cottage Fanny cast a discouraged look at the site. An enormous, menacing black cloud had enveloped the frame of Villa Vailima, a large cube of wood with two verandas running the length of both floors, upstairs and down. The wind shook the posts, raised the disjointed planks of the porch, and rattled the sheet iron roof. There were a total of nine rooms, a wash house, and several bathrooms. More than six hundred square feet of floor space. They had planned a hall paneled in California redwood, with a magnificent polished parquet floor large enough for a hundred dancers and a piano.

It had taken at least twenty cost estimates and hundreds of drawings before they could agree on the final plan. "I want it to be on a grand scale," Louis had explained to them. "What I love here is the space. Even if there's nothing else in the house, I will have my drawing room thirty feet long! . . . I want to see the ocean from my bed, and the top of this mountain . . ."

The left wing of the residence was almost leaning against the slope of Mount Vaea. Dense and mysterious, the woods climbed like an abrupt wall, so near the windows that furrows of mud could be seen between the trees.

This time, Moors had followed her gaze. "Right," he continued. "That's what I'd like to talk to you about. You have delusions of grandeur! No one has ever built such a house on these islands.

Have you thought of what this property is going to cost you? Louis already owes me seven thousand dollars . . ."

"He will reimburse you, Mr. Moors. I can count on you to recover every cent."

Moors' face remained impassive. "How many thousands of books will he have to sell to reimburse me, madam?"

"Five years from now, as you were saying yourself, five years from now my coffee trees will have grown. I'm also planning to cultivate cocoa. Vailima will be self-sufficient and it will free my husband from having to support us. We will not live on his royalties, Mr. Moors, but on the earnings of my plantation!"

The trader scoffed: "Ah, I can see that dreamer in the family isn't your husband, madam, it's you!"

"Me? I would be just as happy with a *fale*. But not Louis . . . Louis dreams of a palace. You know as well as I, Moors, how much he loves to entertain. He wants Vailima's sumptuous hospitality to be known as far off as Fiji and Tonga—and even in London."

"But this fireplace you insist on building, that's *your* idea, isn't it? There isn't a single fireplace in all of Polynesia! You'll have to import every brick from San Francisco, at ten cents a piece. And to bring them here from Apia, along with the sand and cement—how will you do it? You can't get through on horseback, huge fallen trees block your path every few feet and it's as muddy as a bog. Do you know how much the fireplace alone will set you back? More than a thousand dollars! If that isn't self-indulgent, I don't know what is. A perfectly useless whim!"

"Useless, Moors?" Fanny exploded. "You're forgetting that Mr. Stevenson is a sick man . . . The weeding he's bragged about these past few months is the first physical labor he's ever been able to do. When he told you how crazy he was for outdoor work, how much he loved coming home at the end of the day covered with mud, drenched with sweat and rain, it was the exhilaration of a man who had lived until the age of forty like a weevil in a biscuit. If he goes on writing furiously and loves life so much, it's because he knows that in a split second it might all be over. And now, look at the weather, Mr. Moors. Just look!"

The dark cloud had finally exploded. Torrents of water were streaming down the windows. The cottage swayed and creaked, shaken by every gust. A downpour beat a tattoo on the iron roof with persistent, maddening regularity.

"This is only the beginning of the rainy season, you were saying . . . Do you smell this room? Everything is already damp, even the walls. At night, my shoes get soggy. And you have the nerve to say that a fireplace wouldn't be useful? You don't seem to understand, Moors, that a cold can kill Louis. Without a fire, how would I dry his things? How would I dry his damp sheets? If he catches a cold," she insisted, "he's finished. As for the cost of this whim, don't worry about it."

Moors, exasperated, rose and took his hat. "I thought you had your feet on the ground," he grumbled. "I mistook you for the practical one in the family. I see you share his folly." He descended the ladder in the downpour, muttering between his teeth: "His folly without his charm and his talent . . . That woman is nothing but a peasant."

"Peasant." Standing in the rain, Fanny gave the trader a murderous look as he untied his horse. Had Louis confided in that swindler Moors? "Peasant," that word the trader had not meant Mrs. Stevenson to hear, had wounded her to the quick. She was a peasant: This was the great theory Louis had announced to her before his departure for Sydney. He had claimed he'd made an ultimate discovery about his wife, that she had *"the soul of a peasant."* A peasant, not because she loved to work the land, but because she was intoxicated by ownership. If Fanny had been the artist she thought she was for twenty years, owning a little land wouldn't have thrilled her so or made her so furious at this analysis. He had assured her, moreover, of his enormous respect for peasant folk, his great admiration for that mysterious universe, which was even more interesting than the world of the artist. Besides, in his view, no one had the right to call himself an artist if he couldn't provide for his family's needs.

Louis's paradoxes had cast Fanny into a turmoil of worry and doubt. Did he think her mind was so absorbed in the material world, so unsophisticated and obtuse, that she didn't understand what contempt he had for her? Of course he had contempt for her, just as Henley did. And he dared to patch together the remnants of his earlier doctrine of art for art's sake with his new philosophy of the artist whose sole justification was to provide for daily needs! His theories were good for nothing but legitimizing his own reversals and contradictions. The single constant was his own craving for importance. As for his good conscience, he preserved it on his wife's back, and at her expense. Obviously, witticisms didn't cost him much! He was delighted by the discovery of his new physical powers; and she would help him enjoy them. Wasn't that what he expected? If he thought he no longer needed her, she would prove him wrong! Without her, without the peasant woman, Louis's castles in Spain would collapse like a house of cards. Without her the artist would cease to exist! Yes, the peasant woman would prove it to him.

Had Robert Louis Stevenson ever been aware that by constantly drawing Fanny's attention to the features of her personality that did not accord with the image she had of herself, he was inviting anguish? That his constant reminders of her own limitations left her empty, and uncertain of her own identity? That it was her failures at the School of Design and the Julian Academy that had led her to sublimate her creative aspirations in this passionate love? Others would not be fooled.

After Fanny's death her children would be determined to purge her journal of any allusions to wounded pride, any signs of tension between their mother and stepfather. They would freely delete any sentences that might have betrayed Fanny's despair. Did Belle and Lloyd recognize in these shards of doubt and anguish the first indications of the tragedy that was about to befall them?

*
**

She was stretched out in the dark under her mosquito net, listening to the storm, her eyes riveted on the roof. It was going to collapse on her bed. Any minute the sheet iron could let in a flood of water. That continual noise of gravel exploding against the window was driving her crazy. The barometer had suddenly dropped during the evening—this was the forerunner of a hurricane, she knew it. But why worry? Lafaele, the native Hercules who helped her in her rustic labors, was sleeping on the ground floor with his wife . . . unless the woman had made her way to Apia during the first showers; she was engaged in prostitution and would often leave him alone, curled on up his mat, shaken with sobs. Poor Lafaele was wearing Fanny out. Just yesterday she had sent him to town to find the new delivery of the seeds she had ordered from Sydney containing all the trees for the orchard, the exotic flowers she was going to distill as perfume, even the buffalo grass she was impatient to plant in the paddock. She was counting on that grass to feed her livestock. "Very precious things, Lafaele. Pay attention, Lafaele. Take very good care of the little labels. Without the little labels, I can't do anything with the seeds . . ." Lafaele had been more than delicate. Upon his return to Vailima, he had proudly held out his treasure, a little packet carefully wrapped in a banana leaf. Opening it up, Fanny had discovered all her labels in a jumble. What could she say? How could she scold him? This giant and the tiny "Tamaitai,"—"madam"—in Samoan, had become attached to each other. Since Louis's departure, he had been calling her "Mama." This dependence did not reassure her. At the moment she wondered if he wasn't more afraid than she was.

In the uproar, a squall shook the cottage. Fanny felt as if it had pitched to the ground. The trees outside were crushed with the cracking sounds of teeth being pulled. She could see nothing, but she felt the new disorder of the room. She searched for the matches, finding the box on a chest. She squinted and lifted her arm to the barometer above the bed. The mercury was amazingly low, lower than the sailors had reported during the cyclone that had destroyed six warships in the waters of Apia and drowned all the crews. "This is going to be terrifying," she announced to herself. The rain pouring down on the roof seemed like the vestige of an enormous wave that had broken on the coral reef and was rising again in a turbulent rush toward Vailima. The match went out, plunging her again into darkness. She still had time to see that the coatrack with all the bridles, halters, and dresses, had been overturned by the last blast of wind. Her hairbrush and her toilet articles were lying on the ground amongst the tools. She measured the violence of the gusts that had shaken the cottage. And the worst was yet to come. Better be prepared. She shouted: "Lafaele!" She put on her shoes and grabbed the mosquito net. The Samoan appeared in the doorway. The curls of his black hair, which he dyed red, were plastered down on his forehead, his naked torso was dripping, his *lava lava* was sticking to his thighs.

"Lafaele, carry this mattress, these candles, the table and the mosquito net to the stable!"

"Me not go to the stable! Ghost there, spirit ... Not go there, not go there!"

She put her bundle in his arms and pushed him outside.

Choked by the wind and rain, they crossed the clearing. They had to step over several fallen coconut trees and floundered in the mud before managing to open the door. Lafaele rushed to set things down and leave again.

The water was streaming in. Curled up, her feet in a puddle, Fanny watched fearfully through the gaps in the planks, staring at the frame of the large house that might be swept away at any moment. She was imagining Aunt Maggy's arrival, her joyous exclamations when the saw the room her daughter-in-law was preparing for her. It was to be a peaceful green room facing the garden, with a private entrance and a small antechamber hung with the British flag, the Union Jack that had flown over the *Casco*. Would Aunt Maggy like Vailima? Everything had to be ready ... First impressions were so important!

The gusts came in quick succession and shook the stables, the crazed roosters crowed as though it were morning, the pigs squealed, knocking against the sides of their stalls, the horses whinnied hysterically and pawed the ground. The shadow of Villa Vailima had vanished in a sheet of rain, and yet not for a moment did Fanny regret having chosen such a place of exile.

The two months of Louis's absence along with the frightening letter from Aunt Maggy announcing the news of his relapse in Sydney—the ever renewed threat of death—had swept away other griefs and vexations. Only nostalgia remained. She had understood, she believed, that he had never sought to humiliate her, that he simply thought in paradoxes, that their arguments of the weeks previous to his departure had been simply due to exhaustion. The consequences of Fanny Stevenson's well-known susceptibility.

With some perspective, she recognized that they had never been closer, more united, than during this winter. God knows their life had been hard. Together they had struggled to bring order out of chaos, they had fought against nature and men, against sky and earth, against the inertia of their native boys, against their own ignorance and the social and ethical rules of the country they had chosen to live and die in. Go back to Europe? Return to America? They had both done their mourning. Louis had painfully resigned himself to never seeing his friends again. He knew that he would never again walk through the drawing room at Heriot Row, through his father's study and his old nursery; that he would never make that grand entrance into the Savile Club he had fantasized about these past two years. How he had dreamed of that dramatic, joyful entrance—the return of a glorious, suntanned Stevenson, powerful, bubbling over with stories to make his friends' hair stand on end. That was not to be. They were exiled for life, both of them, and Fanny wouldn't have thought of leaving Louis stranded on his island in Samoa while she enjoyed a visit to Dora or Rearden, to her mother and sisters.

No, nothing had equalled the magic of these last months together. Bent toward the earth—their earth—they had dug side by side beneath a white sun, laughing as the sweat dripped along their noses and mingled in a single drop on the same little spear of grass . . . And what excitement exploring the boundaries of their domain together! Leaning on each other in the bush, helping each other through the mud, walking single file as they cleared a path, struggling with the dripping lianas tufted with orchids overhead, hacking through the underbrush, feeling it give way with that morbid cracking sound they knew so well. She would see the great canes topple with a swipe of the machete, while the short grass stubbornly thrust beneath her skirt, scraping her ankles and calves all the way to her knees. This was the price they had to pay for the great happiness of suddenly discovering an unsuspected banana grove, the glistening, fruit-laden trees which they would uproot and replant. "I think we have something deep and strong," she reflected as she shook with fear and cold. "My house, my land, will be kind and gentle to me. They will never betray me."

On this last thought, Fanny Stevenson, chilled and alone, dozed off with the dream of her great house lit up at the foot of Mount Vaea.

Vailima II—May 1891–July 1892

It was their twelfth wedding anniversary today, May 19, 1891. Fanny could hardly believe it, or that they had been living in the bush for more than two years now. Everything in Vailima seemed so settled, so polished and civilized.

The big house was painted a dull blue, its shutters, posts, and railings picked out in Venetian red, with wide verandas upstairs and down; in front, a beautiful, sweeping green lawn sloped gently down to the long stone wall separating the garden from the paddock and stable. On the grass, as though at random, stood the tall, stately trees that had escaped both axe and hurricane. Behind this area, double hedges of hibiscus dotted with purple flowers as big as hands enclosed the garden. The yellow and green rows of lemon trees bore so much fruit that some of it was used to polish the parquet floor of the large salon; the big, round oranges, hard as balls, were rubbed together beneath the waterfall to make an unguent that left the hair soft, perfumed, and silky. Endless flower-beds rimmed the bottom of the terrace with carpets of jasmine, tube roses, and gardenias that exuded a suffocating perfume.

In a Scottish kilt, his torso shining with coconut oil, a tall Samoan boy prepared the armchairs for the cocktail hour on the veranda. To the left the stream flowed down to the foot of the mountain in a series of falls that plummeted into a basin of fresh water. The laughter of the young servants taking a swim mingled with the water's babbling song. In the distance, the bells of the cathedral rang out for vespers. The sound of a ship's whistle rose from the waters of Apia: a man-of-war must have been maneuvering in its dangerous waters. In a straight line above the treetops, as far as the eye could see, stretched the ocean. You could even spot the line of foam, the place where the gray of the high seas met the turquoise of the lagoon. In the surrounding countryside, the hills surged to the horizon, vast vistas open to the wind. Everywhere, you could hear the powerful whisper of the bush. Not another roof in sight, not a field or crops, except those belonging to the immense property. Villa Vailima seemed to stand alone on the island in dignity, solidity, and permanence: the seat of Louis's newly created clan.

He would soon preside, beneath the portraits of his mentor Sidney Colvin and his father Thomas, at a long ebony table laden with silver and crystal, all the things Lloyd had brought last year from the villa at Bournemouth. The splendid Faamua, whom they jokingly called the Butler or, depending on their whim, the Minx, a Samoan woman dressed in scarcely more than a handkerchief, would pour the French wines into goblets at each place. And they would sample the homemade raisin bread, the little peas and pineapples from the garden. Aunt Maggy, swathed in a black silk skirt for dinner, would bless the meal. Young Austin would regale them with an account of his swim in the pool. Lloyd would report the latest waspish gossip from Apia and the rumors of war. Joe would carp about the ugliness of the consuls' wives. And the daughter of the house, Belle, thirty-four years old, who now acted as secretary to the master, would enthusiastically praise his work. Flattered, Louis would promise to read "their" work at dessert. Only Fanny's place would remain empty. She arrived late to every meal. Her manners shocked Aunt Maggy, drove Belle to despair, and exasperated Louis. They had to say grace without her and serve the soup.

"Austin, do you know where your grandmother is?" the head of the family would finally ask impatiently.

"At the coffee plantation," the child would answer. "Or maybe in her kitchen garden . . . Or else she's securing the footbridge across the river . . . or maybe grooming her horse . . . unless she's looking after the disgusting black boy who arrived this afternoon . . ."

"I saw her crossing the lawn, she was carrying a breadfruit tree three times her size," Belle would comment. "That good-for-nothing Lafaele was toddling after her hardly burdened with a spade."

"Austin, go and find her!"

That was the moment she would choose to make her appearance. She would stand still for a few moments, a tiny blue-clad figure in the doorway with the enormous sliding door that opened onto the veranda. If the tall yellow silk drapes were pulled, she would stand hidden behind them, unless her breath agitating the silver stitching of the fabric gave her away. Barefoot and dirty, her hair in her eyes, she would come in, holding out her hands, murmuring in a reproachful voice: "I was working!"

"This isn't the best time for gardening," Aunt Maggy would grumble.

"I'm bleeding," she would protest.

"Didn't you hear the conch?" Louis would ask. "It was blown three times. Where were you?"

"In the cocoa plantations . . . there are twelve thousand plants by now!"

"The cocoa could wait . . . sit down."

But she would not sit down. She walked slowly around the table showing everyone the palms of her hands.

"I'm bleeding."

"But why didn't you put on gloves?" Louis would inquire looking at the raw flesh of her fingers, nicked at every joint.

"Because Belle lost them."

"That's not true!" the younger woman would cry. "They're hanging on their nail in the wash house."

Fanny would stop for a moment, then ferociously lash out at her daughter: "Do you dare to say I'm lying?"

"I didn't say that, but . . ."

"The gloves were not in the wash house . . ."

She would slip around her own chair.

"Otherwise, do you think I'd be crazy enough to pull the *tui-tui* with my bare hands? Perhaps my son-in-law hid them so I would hurt myself?" she would insinuate, coming dangerously close to Joe, who looked down into his plate. "Or perhaps he sold them? This wouldn't be the first time he's sold things behind our back. Things that belong to us," she would say in a threatening tone, leaning over his shoulder. "You are living on our generosity, Joe. Do you think that's the way to treat us? Do you think we don't know the gossip you spread around Apia about Belle and this house? When I think that you're plotting with the consuls to deport us!"

Joe would not react, but Belle would dissolve in tears.

"Fanny, sit down," Louis would cut in coldly, "and eat!"

She would turn toward him, outraged: "Are you taking her side again? Her husband does nothing all day long, he claims to be going to the dentist, but that's just a pretext to stroll around Apia . . . He does nothing, nothing! Except steal the key to the wine cellar to get drunk at night and add water to all the Bordeaux he opens! How can you claim you don't know? They suck us dry while I'm exhausting myself to maintain this plantation! Look at my hands! Look! This is what your property, your land, your house have done to them . . . the hands of a peasant!"

*

These brief, unpredictable explosions left Fanny terrified and remorseful. What had she done? What was happening to her? She did not understand. Less than an hour after one of her tirades had plunged her whole family into anguish, throwing Louis into one of his rages from which it would take him two days to recover, she would fall all over herself to beg their pardon. She would wander through the house, humbly knocking on every door, asking forgiveness of her mother-in-law, her daughter, her husband . . . She was confused and felt such hatred for herself.

The following week, her kindness, her many attentions, her total sacrifice of herself, of her health and well-being, would win everyone over. Order returned to Vailima. Everyone would attribute her temperamental outbursts to fatigue. Doctor Funk, the German doctor attached to the plantations, did indeed call Mr. Stevenson's attention to his wife's physical exhaustion.

"I know," he would answer, "she does too much . . . she doesn't know when to stop. But . . ."

"It's easy to tell me to sit down," Fanny would retort, "Only things don't get done by themselves. Someone has to take care of them!"

Now it was Louis's turn to learn how irritating he could be with his helpless concern, constantly saying "Take a rest," "Put on your shawl," "Go get your shoes . . ." to someone who cannot hear.

"Who will look after the sowing if I don't do it? Who? Joe, maybe? Or you?"

Every exchange turned into a discussion and ended in a quarrel. These disputes became more frequent, ever more violent and irrational.

*
**

It had all begun a year earlier, five months to the day after the arrival of Belle, Joe, and Austin; Aunt Maggy and her Australian maid; and Lloyd with the furniture, the rugs, the silver, the porcelain tea services, the Rodin sculpture, the bas-relief of Louis by St. Gaudens—all the things from Louis's past. Hundreds of packing cases that Fanny had to clear at the port and bring up to Vailima with the help of her boys. The leather-covered Chippendale chairs, the sideboard with all those copper knobs, the two Indian Buddhas brought from Delhi by a brother of Aunt Maggy's, every souvenir, every knickknack, had found its place quite naturally in this house that Fanny had spent the last six months carefully planning and preparing. No one had really appreciated the extent of her effort. The bookshelves in Louis's study awaited his books. And the piano, the last piece to come to Vailima, had only to slide under the huge cover of woven coconut leaves she had designed to protect the instrument from the dampness.

In her personal bathroom, Aunt Maggy had only to turn the faucets to take a shower: A system of pipelines brought the water from a mountain stream by a whole network of cisterns and tubes designed and built by her daughter-in-law. An ice machine rumbled at the bottom of the garden, operated by a generator, so that Austin might have a sherbet for dessert. And armed with a level, a spade, and ropes, the presiding priestess had just finished designing a tennis court for the young people's pleasure.

The Strongs thought they had come to paradise. How could they have resisted the exhilaration of belonging to Vailima, a land whose beauty they judged unequalled, the intoxication of participating in the glory of the family that now passed for the most powerful on the island?

Prestige and beauty, the keystones of the indigenous social system, had impressed the Samoans sufficiently for them to take an interest in Vailima.

Moors had not exaggerated the difficulty of getting help from the native peoples. And Fanny had very quickly understood that the plantation depended on the competence of her staff. Without servants, Vailima could not function.

At the advice of the Apia residents, she had first tried to employ Whites. This was a failure. Some drank, some ran away, others left if they were offered better pay. Against all warnings she had then hired Lafaele and his promiscuous wife. Three months later, Mrs. Lafaele lay at the bottom of the bay, pushed off a cliff by one of her customers. The day of her burial, the widower had taken a new wife. This time she was a ravishing Samoan woman from the neighboring village. Fanny had employed her to do washing and

housekeeping. Faamua had brought her girlfriends, who were fascinated by the mystery and luxury of the house.

The Samoans had seen the trees fall, had watched the bricks,
the wood, the quicklime, transported through the mud; they had seen
the silver, the porcelain, the fabrics, the cases of wine and books,
without really understanding the source of all these riches. Their
owner did not traffic in copra, he did not own a shop in town, or a
hotel or bar. He sold neither guns nor alcohol. He did not com-
mand warships or have any political power. He had not financed
this dwelling, larger and more luxuriously furnished than the resi-
dences of the three consuls, with tax money. How had he done it?
Did he have some mysterious power? Chance would provide them
with an answer. Shortly after the completion of Vailima, they had
read in the missionary journal published by the Rev. Mr. Clarke a
translation of Louis's story *The Bottle Imp*—the first fiction ever
translated into the Samoan language. It tells the story of the Hawaiian owner of a genie trapped in a magic bottle who carries out all
his master's wishes. Unused to making distinctions between fiction
and reality, the readers had naturally deduced that this bottle belonged to the teller of the tale, Tusitala. They clung to this explanation. The genie had obeyed him. Tusitala was truly a great chief,
whose power had manifested itself in all sorts of wealth and sorcery,
too; in the eyes of the natives, both husband and wife participated
in the supernatural. The woman they called Tamaitai, "Madam,"
looked after her family, healing them with her power. She could
even banish spirits! Nothing escaped her—mistakes, neglect, de-
lays—she saw everything, she had eyes in the back of her head.

It was natural for Fanny to encourage this way of thinking. She
had always had faith in her intuitions and believed in her instinct.
She "felt" it when a horse got loose at the bottom of the garden,
when Lafaele was sleeping far from her in the shade of the banana
trees, when a letter or a visitor was about to arrive. She fancied
herself something of a "medium."

She may have owed her talents as a healer to her apprenticeship
with the Indians of Austin, to the time-honored recipes of her
Indiana grandmother, and to ten years of reading the British medical journal, the *Lancet*. She had kept abreast of the latest discover-
ies and the newest drugs, which she imported from San Francisco.
Otherwise, she resorted to bluff and stagecraft: "You know," she

would say to Lafaele, "that no spirit would dare to attack a man who belongs to me?" "I know!" he would agree. "But one year ago Tamaitai was not aware of my existence, and the spirit took advantage of it to slip into my foot. He is going to eat my leg." "Close your eyes," she would order, placing her hands on him and murmuring incantations.

If the natives feared ridicule, Fanny knew them too well to make light of their superstitions: She measured herself against their traditional lore and enjoyed playing at witchcraft.

To learn from them as much as they learn from us: This aphorism which had guided Louis's curiosity during his two years of travel had dictated the entire organization of Vailima.

He had observed that a Samoan village was composed of twenty or so *fales*; that each one was headed by a *matai*, whose title was either chief or orator. In the assemblies of the chiefs, each *matai* occupied the place his ancestors had held before him. He represented the members of his household, for which he was responsible. This household extended from the family—parents, wives, children—to the group of fifteen to twenty persons linked to the *matai* by blood, marriage, and the very common practice of adoption. As an economic entity, the members of the household depended on the *matai*, whom they obeyed blindly. They worked for him, and under his direction. In return, the *matai* provided for the material welfare of each one. He owed them justice, welcome, and protection.

This system could not help but find an echo in the man who had written to his mother in 1886: *I have perhaps inherited my quasi-feudal ways with the servants from you. The unhappy fate of the bourgeois master who chose to ostracize his domestics—his "family" in the old Scottish sense of the term—to avoid any intimacy with them, shelter them far away, deprive them of all the joys of the house, awaits us at every turn. This segregation between masters and servants creates impossible human relations, and throws everyone into confusion.*

Robert Louis Stevenson had detested the Bournemouth property owners' lack of generosity toward anything or anybody that did not concern them directly, and he had hated their domestic arrangements too much to reproduce them in Samoa. In the purest Scottish tradition, in the Samoan fashion, Tusitala's employees would not be his valets but members of one clan who would share the joys and sorrows of their chief. The Samoans' conventionality, their taste for systems—though they seemed the most free, relaxed people in the world—their passion for an ordered and regulated existence, their need to distill beauty from chaos, all these elements combined to ensure that Robert Louis Stevenson got the very best from them, and they from him.

Louis would demand of his flock the obedience they owed to the *matai*, and the immediate execution of his orders. Each person's work was assigned to him, lists of instructions distributed, proclamations tacked to the large bulletin board in the great hall. If there was a theft or a serious act of negligence, the guilty party would be tried before a court of justice. In the presence of the whole "family," Robert Louis Stevenson would hear the story of the delinquency told by the accused himself. The master would review the case, and rule on it. He would explain the rationale and consequences of the punishment, which was never applied the same day. Sentenced to pay a fine, the convicted man would pay it to the collection plate at his church, whether Catholic or Protestant.

With the power of the lord, Tusitala had shouldered his responsibilities.

Even when his work absorbed him, when he was writing in a frenzy, when the mail boat was threatening to sail without his manuscripts and letters, he participated in the life of his clan members. At any hour of the day or night, on all possible subjects— domestic quarrels, neighborly relations, payment of taxes—they could come to consult him. He was always ready to listen, to support, to help anyone who needed his services. He received the relatives of those under his protection, he built their *fales* on his land, he gave them lavish native ceremonies and splendid meals. *I must tell you of our feast*, he wrote rather proudly to Sidney Colvin. *It was long promised to the boys, and came off yesterday in one of their new houses.... We sat down thirty strong. You should have seen our procession, going (about two o'clock), all in our best clothes, to the hall of feasting! All in our Sunday's best. The new house had been hurriedly finished; the rafters decorated with flowers; the floor spread, native style, with green leaves; we had given a big porker, twenty-five pounds of fresh beef, a tin of biscuits, cocoanuts, etc. Our places were all arranged with much care: the native ladies of the house facing our party; the sides filled up by*

the men . . . After the feast was over, we had kava, and the calling
of the kava was a very elaborate affair.

The originality of Louis's perspective on the Pacific Islands had
led him to make a study of native societies, and not only of their
differences but especially of their similarities to Western civilization. Stevenson had understood that these Samoan "barbarians"
were prouder of their lineage, more punctilious in matters of tradition than a Spanish hidalgo. The glory of the *matai* reflected on all
the members of the house, as the glory of a Highland chieftain had
done in former times. Nostalgia for his country had made the history of Scotland dear to his heart, and his imagination was fired by
the idea that Vailima might become the embodiment of the works
of his father and his ancestors.

Tusitala had therefore selected several visible details that would
signal his belonging to a clan whose aristocracy flattered them all.
As a sign of recognition, Fanny had cut the *lava lavas* of those
under his protection in the shape of a kilt: green squares barred
with yellow on a red background, the royal tartan of the Stuarts.

Belle, who was enchanted by the external aspect of people and
things, quickly became interested in the imposing presence of the
"Vailima folk." She had in common with them an easy disposition
and a concern for the aesthetic. The day after her arrival she had
quite naturally taken in hand the supervision of the staff, and assumed the management of the household, the kitchen, the table
service. In short, she played the role of head housekeeper. This
was a heavy task, with fourteen people to feed each day, seven of
the servants with large families, parents and cousins of all sorts, to
whom Vailima owed hospitality.

Aunt Maggy had chosen to shepherd the spiritual life of this
little flock. She led prayers they all said together every morning in
the great hall. She had no difficulty imposing this ritual. The Samoans, religious by nature, liked nothing better than to come together
to sing hymns.

Lloyd acted as steward of the place. His meticulousness, his taste
for order, his hunger for authority were satisfied by organizing the
work and keeping the books.

Joe, such a mixture of vice and weakness, had taken over the
teams of agricultural workers. His friend Moors, a harsh judge of

his talents as overseer, used to say that Joe had too much artistic sense not to snore in the sun under the cocoa trees.

In the beginning, however, he had made real efforts. The family had watched him disappear into the bush, wearing a safari helmet, booted, belted, a spade in his hand and a parrot on his shoulder. Halfway between an African explorer and an officer in the Indian army, with his curly mustache and wobbly legs, the sight of Joe bringing up the rear had been wrenching for Belle. What had happened to the young *vaquero* who had galloped in the dust of Monterey? What connection was there between this pathetic nonentity eaten up by opium, alcohol, and hatred, and the gifted, charming painter of San Francisco? His flute was heard setting a rhythm for the boys' work, and his voice counting the seeds they planted. But his ineptitude was equalled only by his hypocrisy. Full of apparent goodwill, he had pretended to be interested in the efficiency of his teams, the cost of their food, and their pay. Joe was trying to demonstrate his gratitude. He knew only too well that for close to two years he had been living off Robert Louis Stevenson's generosity. And Strong could not accept such magnanimity from someone he had long regarded as his alter ego. Only three years younger than Louis, Joe had judged his own talent infinitely superior to this writer of best-sellers. And his health infinitely more precarious! His heart murmur had nearly killed him last year. And Louis had sent him in this heat and humidity to supervise a bunch of incompetents? Joe suspected that Louis wanted him to die. This had been Fanny's single-minded idea since their time in Monterey—to free Belle from her marriage. Yes, that was it: Fanny had been trying to get rid of him all along.

"Besides, it's a custom in this family," Joe grumbled, lying beside his wife in the first bed the Stevensons had shared in Vailima.

They were living in the cottage Moors had built three years earlier. Austin was sleeping in the old sitting room.

"They get rid of anyone who's outlived their usefulness."

"What are you talking about?" Belle asked impatiently, suspecting him of drinking again.

"Look at your mother. As long as Louis needed her for his work, as long as he needed her judgment and critical ear, he acknowledged her sense of story telling, her taste and intuition in artistic matters. Now that he feels sure of himself, of his genius, he keeps her down in the mud."

Belle shrugged her shoulders.

"She has too much to do! Without her, Vailima would not exist."

"Right. Louis may have gotten his hands dirty at first, but he quickly retreated to his tower. Deep down, beneath his kindly airs, he's just as crazy as she is! If I were your mother, I wouldn't trust a man who flatters himself by inventing only sympathetic murderers, cutthroats more likable than their victims! That's him, all right— he's written the most bloodthirsty stories in all of literature, hasn't he? He's never better than when he's imagining scenes of violence, grisly deaths . . . Horrible things are going on here, I'm sure of it. Look how he pens your mother up with her chickens and pigs, how he squeezes her into her role as peasant."

"Shut up, you're delirious! Mama likes nothing better, the earth, the 'mud' as you call it . . ."

"Come on! She's afraid of the past, she's afraid of the future. All she's got is the present, and she clings to it: This place is her triumph! You've seen her expression—remember the fever in her eyes the day we arrived? Her pride at showing us all her efforts, her success?"

"I've seen," Belle concluded, keeping her mosquito net firmly closed. She had seen one of those poisonous hairy centipedes, as long as her hand, on the door frame, and her fear of it kept her awake.

"And I've seen that their marriage is a great success!" she went on. "Each completes the other and still has his own life . . . I admire them and I envy them."

Joe sneered: "The only problem is that to prove how happy they are they need witnesses . . . When they're all alone they're bored to death with each other, that's why we're all here, to distract them from themselves, to act as clowns and foils."

"Poor Joe! You, a foil?" hooted Belle. "As for being a clown . . . "

Joe thought it preferable to keep quiet. "I never wanted to come here," he thought furiously, turning to the wall. "It was Belle, she forced me!"

And Strong could not forgive Stevenson for that. What had happened between his wife and Louis during their stepfather's last stay in Sydney? "Nothing!" the young woman had assured him.

"What did he say to you?" her husband had asked. "What did he do to make you suddenly give in to all his wishes? I thought you couldn't stand his need to run our life, I thought his noisy exuberance exasperated you. In Hawaii you resented him for using his success, his power, and his filthy money to cut you off from your mother . . ."

"His filthy money, Joe, is what supports your son! Where would we be without him? Do you think I don't know that you sold paintings in Honolulu and never said a word about it? That you were lying and taking his money while you spent your own earnings behind his back? You just drank it all and smoked it all away! Without Louis's filthy money, as you call it, your son would never have been able to go to school."

"And you think Austin is going to learn something here?"

"Louis will give him history lessons, Aunt Maggy will do literature . . . Anyway, where do you want us to go? We're lucky to have parents generous enough to take us in, and I'm certainly glad to have a place here . . . If only we wanted it, we could be happy in Vailima, too."

"Happy? Have you seen the state your mother is in?"

"Of course. It's up to us to relieve the pressure. I could fill in for her while she goes on holiday and gets some rest."

In August 1891, two months after the Strongs had settled in, the family had convinced Fanny that she needed a change of air for the sake of her health. Too weak, too exhausted to resist, she had let them put her on the first boat to set sail. She was to spend fifteen peaceful days alone on Fiji.

It was then that I really got acquainted with my brother, Belle explains, *and learned, in spite of his superior air, his fine manners and his English accent, that he was a true grandson of Cynthia Osbourne. Rolling up his sleeves, he joined me in the kitchen. Like our blessed grandmother, what Lloyd did he did well; we soon had the place as neat as a new pin.*

When Fanny returned from Fiji, bringing with her an Indian cook acquired at great expense, she had found her ovens manned by the new boy Belle had hired. He was called Talolo, and would become one of the pillars of domestic life at Vailima. Bringing the members of his family with him, Talolo was to obey only the young mistress who had trained him. He worshipped Belle and called her "Teuila," "the lady who enhances everything she touches," "the Adorner."

Another thing Fanny had found changed upon her return was the way Louis used his time.

One day when Stevenson had seemed troubled by the pile of letters that needed finishing before the monthly mail boat was set to lift anchor, Belle—"Teuila"—had asked: "Would it help if you dictate your letters to me, or if I answer the unimportant mail or recopy your notes?"

"Good idea. Let's try it!"

Their collaboration had turned out to be such a success that Belle settled in Louis's study. There Fanny would find her daughter bent over her husband's work.

Belle had just reached the same age as her mother when Louis had met her at the Hotel Chevillon: thirty-four. And Belle looked just like the Fanny of those days.

Writing her autobiography thirty years later, Belle would tell the story of this alliance, the moment when she and her stepfather had renewed their mutual understanding from the days in Grez.

It wasn't until Louis came alone to Sydney on a business trip that we had the talk that was to influence my whole future life. He always referred to it as "the time we got acquainted."

He stayed, as usual, at the Union Club. One day he asked me to go shopping with him for supplies to be sent to Vailima. My mother had made out a list and I remember how we puzzled over "Some aluminum paint and a reasonable quantity of confectioners' sugar."

. . . We sat down on a bench . . . Before us were lawns and winding paths; green branches met over our heads. It was a peaceful spot and for some reason I was emboldened to speak to Louis as I had never done before. Quite suddenly I burst out with all I had wanted to say for months.

I begged him to let us stay in Sydney. I was very grateful for all he had done for us, I said, but I hated being a burden on him. Besides, it wasn't necessary; we could take care of ourselves. The Bulletin *had offered me a steady job to write a theatrical column. Friends assured me I could easily get pupils in drawing and painting, and if that wasn't enough I could always form a dancing class.*

"Building the new house in Samoa and starting a plantation must be a heavy expense to you," I said. "Why should we add to it? You work so hard; you're not well . . ." Here I began to cry.

Then he gave me his side. It is the only time I ever knew him to be despondent in any way. He described the despair he felt when told he could never go back to London, to his home in Bournemouth; he would never see his native city Edinburgh again. Sentenced to exile for the rest of his life, what he wanted now was to make that exile bearable.

"You and Lloyd are all the family I have," he said. "I want a home and a family, my family, round me."

He told me, too, that Lloyd's great ambition had been to go to Oxford but he had given it up to stay with Louis and our mother in Samoa.

We talked till late, going back over old scores, clearing up old misunderstandings. Though I admired Louis and respected him, there had always been a hidden antagonism between us. Perhaps because I had adored my father, I was unconsciously critical of him. Even if he was the head of our family, I saw no reason why he should plan my life.

But now all was changed. He talked with such kindness, such understanding, that every bit of resentment I had held toward him melted away, and I felt myself to be truly his loving daughter.

Strange echoes of another life. Joe now seemed like Louis's younger self, an irresponsible self who didn't know how to grow up; Louis treated him with the indulgence his own father had previously shown toward him. Young Austin had reached Lloyd's age when they had lived in Monterey; and Belle was going through the same hellish, hateful quarrels Fanny had experienced with Sam. Like her mother, she had found refuge and comfort with Robert Louis Stevenson.

*
**

The sun was still shining in those last days of December 1891, but the rainy season was at hand and the wind blew incessantly. On the beaches, everything seemed to be in constant motion, the leaves of the coconut trees crackled at every gust. In the villages, the lengths of red-flowered fabric were blowing like flags on the clotheslines, and the fishing nets tangled together. In Vailima, the *lava lavas* of the women crossing the lawn opened suddenly on their breasts, the men's kilts clung to their thighs, and the clouds scudded in swiftly from the sea. They trailed a dark vapor in their wake that settled for a moment on the red sheet iron of the roof. In the distance, the ocean changed from blue to gray-green. They heard the implosion of the waves on the coral reef, a dull, continuous noise that broke the silence of Vailima. The scents of water, lemon balm, and wood smoke filled the air.

Fanny had set down her spade to sew on the veranda. This was usually Belle's job, but for some time now Tamaitai claimed to enjoy this peaceful occupation. She was making jackets for the servants to complement their best uniforms to be worn on holidays. She had sent for a striped material that went nicely with the tartan of the loincloths.

Sitting in the shade, she created the illusion of calm and made everyone think that things were in order at Vailima.

But Fanny could not endure this work for long. Basting, gathering, hemming did not sufficiently occupy her mind. She was disturbed by certain thoughts. It was nothing personal, she was not worried about Lafaele's blunders or Joe's swindling. What troubled her was that the Whites were once again preparing to betray the trust of the Samoans. The Berlin treaty stipulated that the natives could elect their own king. The line of the great chief Mataafa, his titles and tradition, made him chief of chiefs, the natural heir to the throne. But Germany, England, and the United States had secretly agreed that Mataafa would not be eligible. This was the doing of the Germans, who had never forgiven him for challenging them when they had deported Laupepa. They had persuaded the two other white powers to go along with their decision to pass over him. Of course the Samoans were completely unaware of this new arrangement.

Four years earlier, when King Laupepa, broken by exile, had received the kingship from the Whites, he had reached an understanding with Mataafa, who consented to make no demands and stay in the background until the next elections. Mataafa had kept his word. During this period he had lived in Mali, his fiefdom, in a kind of retirement. "Now Laupepa's legitimate reign is coming to an end, and the Whites won't respect the agreement to let the people choose their own king!" she grumbled to herself. "Yet the old warrior Mataafa is not only the most powerful of the *matais*, he is a gentleman. He has done so much for Samoa! He supported the king during his exile. He defeated the three powers. He refused all honors, resisted temptations that might have shackled his loyalty. And now we Whites are breaking our promises and forcing him to take up arms against his brothers! It was all a trap . . . what injustice!"

Was it her usual compassion for the underdog that was making her so sad, or did Fanny see some similarity between Mataafa's unhappy fate and her own? Her fingers fidgeted on the fabric. She finally put down the sewing and returned to her cocoa plants. All last week even Lloyd and Louis had rolled up their sleeves. They had filled the hundreds of little baskets she had placed under the veranda with earth, making sure no stone or insect slipped in. But she had to plant the cocoa seeds herself. Scalded by earlier experience, she would not leave this task to anyone else.

Fanny vividly remembered the day she had entrusted a whole bag of vanilla seeds to Lafaele, with precise planting instructions. The next morning, she had discovered all the seeds planted upside down. Lafaele, mortified, had offered to replant them, but just then she had spied the *Lübeck* in the coastal waters. The mail! It was delivered only once a month. Quickly she had sent him into town to bring back the enormous waterproof bag full of letters, which he carried directly up to Louis's room. Crosscurrents had delayed the boat. Waiting for Lafaele to return, Fanny and Belle had spent the day replanting each seed. At dawn the following day, they had gone to inspect their work. They had been amazed to discover that while they slept, Lafaele had replanted all the seeds the other way round, "to give Tamaitai a big surprise." He had certainly done that. She had set the seedlings upright again, but they had been so damaged by all this handling that they died.

This time, she would watch over her cocoa plants. The planting took one week. At the end of her labors, Fanny killed the pig and gave a great feast that was the talk of the villages. And every day during the planting period she had served hot chocolate to her helpers, a sweet and creamy delicacy, so that everyone here might know its nutritional qualities, its exquisite taste, and understand the value of their efforts.

Apia—April 1892

"No one ever saw a Samoan run except at Vailima!" Moors conceded with a chuckle. Behind the bar of his hotel, the American

trader was offering a whiskey to his personal enemy, the British
consul Sir Berry Cusack-Smith. The cathedral clock had just struck
twelve noon. He gestured to his guest to sit down at one of the
little tables.

This was a custom in Apia. Two Whites might spend weeks without talking to each other, their wives would cross paths without
greeting, until, perhaps at a dance given by the municipality, the
enemies would find themselves face to face in a quadrille. They
would enjoy dancing together and agree to meet for a drink. Each
would try to pump the other for information before they had another falling out.

With his straight hair parted on the side, sporting a large, waxed
mustache, Cusack-Smith's birdlike head bent close to the beefy
face of Henry Moors. The contrast between the consul's stiff-
collared officer's jacket with the gold buttons and the trader's short-
sleeved madras shirt, open on his chest, offered an amusing sight.
The two men toasted each other. They were alone. Through the
window looking out on Beach Road they could see the parade of
red umbrellas and clusters of colorful *lava lavas*. In groups of threes
and fours the natives were protecting themselves from the sudden,
brief cloudbursts that came at the end of the rainy season.

"My wife complains that she cannot get anything out of them,"
sighed the functionary. "It's much worse than in India . . . She says
the natives are uncurably slow, stupid, and lazy. How does Mrs.
Stevenson manage?"

"She's gradually replaced her Protestant boys with Catholics."

Cusack-Smith raised his eyebrows: "The Catholics, Moors, belong to Chief Mataafa. And Mataafa is a rebel!"

"And that's why you're after him . . . because Mataafa and his
Catholics have escaped the influence of your missionaries?"

Of the three consuls, the Britisher flattered himself on being the
most liberal. His small face expressed only a slight annoyance.

"I am afraid you did not read this morning's proclamation on
the sanctions against the partisans of Mataafa . . . Don't talk too
much, Moors, or I shall have to arrest you."

Laupepa, Mataafa—what difference did it make? Cusack-Smith
certainly didn't give a damn. Neither of them mattered. No, the
important thing was that England should preserve its right to intervene in the country's affairs, its influence equal to that of its two
partners. Germany, the most powerful since it owned the greatest

number of plantations, was dead set against Mataafa. Fine. England and America would throw it that bone. Why disturb the already precarious balance of power? Why fight amongst themselves over a couple of "Negro kings"?

The balance of power had seemed threatened, however, by the cries of indignation raised by the most celebrated resident of Upolu and a British citizen besides. Robert Louis Stevenson demanded that the three nations respect the Berlin Treaty, which stipulated Samoa's independence and the right to choose its chief of state. He advised a reconciliation between Laupepa and Mataafa, which would allow the two chiefs to rule together. He thought, rightly, that this would avert a war. But the consuls wanted no part of such a coalition. That was their only point of agreement: to keep the people divided, to continue governing without the Samoans.

Robert Louis Stevenson's letters to the London *Times* angrily exposed the negligence and dishonesty of the white civil servants. His aim was to have them recalled, and his protests attracted a good deal of antipathy from the local white community. The nationals of the three Western countries were hoping he would pack his bags. Which of the two camps would prevail? Stevensons's position not only aggravated the political powers. Every time a new letter appeared Colvin complained that he'd had enough of hearing Louis defend "his beloved Blacks—or Chocolates," whose fate was of interest to no one.

Fanny and Moors were alone in supporting her husband. She knew, however, what it might cost them to oppose the politics of Great Britain and the United States, their home countries: the loss of Vailima. The decree that outlawed the partisans of Mataafa explicitly threatened the Stevensons with deportation. As for Moors, the consuls hoped to catch him delivering arms to Mataafa's troops.

"You've questioned me on what goes on at Vailima," the trader went on in a neutral tone. "It's Stevenson you ought to interrogate! He's the one who runs the plantation. Just between us, what a sinkhole! It's swallowed up all his royalties. He works damn hard, he gets up at five in the morning to write. He told me the other day that in one year he'd finished *The Wrecker*, edited *The History of Samoa*, written *The Beach of Falesa*, practically finished *Catriona*, and begun research for a biography of his grandfather. He must have published a grand total of nearly two thousand pages, not counting his letters and articles. He has no choice: Vailima and

the support of almost twenty people would suck a Rockefeller dry
in five years. Do you know they've managed to reclaim only fifteen
acres out of 325? And I personally cleared twelve of them!" he
declared ironically. "Poor Stevenson, it's a hell of a burden . . . Not
to speak of his son-in-law's philandering with Faamua, the wife of
his boy, and his stepson's affair with Dr. Funk's adopted daughter . . ."

"You're joking!" exclaimed the consul, shocked and delighted.
"Lloyd with—"

"Hell, he's twenty-four years old, and the girl is pretty . . ."

"But she's a native!"

Moors, who was married to a native, gave Cusack-Smith a menacing look: "So?"

"I am surprised, that's all . . . Lloyd Osbourne always seemed
so proper!"

"He's a cold fish, you might say. But he's hot-blooded all right,
he loves the girls, that's plain! He must get it from his father. I've
heard that Madam's first husband was a hell of a chaser."

"And the old dowager, how does she take all this?"

"By squabbling with her daughter-in-law."

"Heavens!" Cusack-Smith exclaimed, charmed by Moors's
coarseness. "I thought they got along . . ."

"They do get along. But they're two females . . . Shut up in the
same pen, they argue . . . about the Catholics. Like you and me,
old Mrs. Stevenson is a Protestant. So every morning she reads
from the Protestant service. But as you know, there is a longstanding rivalry between our missionaries and the Catholic fathers . . .
And sure enough, the flock of papists at Vailima refuses to read
the Protestant prayers! Old Mrs. Stevenson complained about it to
Fanny, but Fanny retorted that at Vailima freedom of religion will
be respected. She won't force anyone to pray. I think this answer
threw the old lady into a fury."

"What a family!" Cusack-Smith sighed, getting up.

"And that's just the beginning!" Moors jeeringly remarked. "I
wish Louis lots of luck trying to keep order among all those spong-
ers . . . He will have a harder time than you or me avoiding war
with Mataafa," he concluded with a wink as he accompanied the
consul to the door. He held him a moment by the elbow. "Tell
me, Cusack, speaking of family, I heard that the wife of Lord
Jersey, your governor-general, the head, if I'm not mistaken, of all

the British colonies in these troubled waters . . . that his better half is going to pay us a visit? Does that mean Queen Victoria has taken an interest in our island?"

Cusack-Smith disengaged himself from the powerful arm that had slipped under his. "Lady Jersey's yacht will be anchored in our bay, but her visit is not in any way official! She will be received by Bazett Haggard, our land commissioner. She is not coming down to my office—it's purely a private visit for recreational purposes."

"But there will surely be some balls in her honor?" the trader insisted. "Lady Jersey is reputed to be a great socialite, a fearless sportswoman . . . Some polo matches, perhaps?"

"Not before August, Moors, not before August . . ."

"Let's hope, old boy, that between now and then you'll manage to keep order . . ."

"Let's hope that between now and then Mataafa and his village will be wiped off the map!"

The consul remounted his horse. And Moors watched this thin figure, dressed in colonial whites, move off between the yellow croton bushes, the administrative buildings, and the warehouses. After the cloudburst, the sun was beating down on the puddles. Mount Vaea, which plummeted into the bay, exuded a humid, stifling warmth. Apia was a city in name only. There were no quays at the port, simply a wooden jetty and a pontoon landing. There were no paved streets, only muddy paths. The cathedral alone, all white with its colorful windows, high walls, and buttresses, gave the capital the illusion of existing. Moors saw the consul take up a trot toward the Malinu'u peninsula where the king lived. What was he going to do at Laupepa's? His Majesty lived in a *fale* hardly worthy of a chief. Just opposite, in the same village, the minister of justice was building his new and luxurious residence. "Another one of their stupidities," thought Moors. "These white idiots don't understand that by humiliating Laupepa, by keeping him in this deprived state, they are diminishing his prestige and making him unpopular . . ."

Moors let the screen door of the Tivoli Hotel fall shut behind him and went down to the street himself to untie his horse. The building was at the corner of the road that led to Vailima. There stood the cottages of several white men married to Samoan women. With their little fences and verandas, these were the only real houses in Apia, the residential quarter. At some distance, under the mango trees of the gardens, were clusters of *fales* where the white men had to receive the enormous families of their native wives. A duty of hospitality that they could not avoid. The expense of providing for these relatives, who settled in to stay, drained their resources as civil servants and restricted them to a life spent in these enclosures.

*
**

"If Lloyd marries that girl, he doesn't know what he's getting into," Joe jeered.

"Mind your own business," his wife objected.

Strong knocked over the small black pigs that the washerwomen had attached to the feet of their ironing boards. The three young girls wore red *lava lavas* on their hips, their chests covered by bandanas knotted at the neck. They were perspiring, and their little breasts were pointing provocatively under the scarves. Joe had nothing to do there, in the wash house. Belle, who was supervising her crew, suspected him of coming to flirt with Faamua, the "Minx," as Louis called her. Lafaele's second wife was also very generous with her charms.

"You're right," Joe agreed. "When a man has decided to do something stupid . . ."

"Lloyd has not decided anything."

"I'm not so sure. But of course your mother will decide for him . . . She is going to send him off for a few weeks to San Francisco, and everything will be settled until next time. Your brother is quite right to enjoy himself with the girls here. As for marrying them . . . he's not so dumb! I've seen the sort of fellows who take that risk. It never works!"

"What never works," Belle retorted, giving him ground, "is drinking, cheating on your wife, and wasting your life!"

She went out. Joe approached the "Minx" and took her in his arms, while the other two girls broke into giggles.

*
**

Joe was still cause for concern. Not content to cheat on Belle with the servants under their own roof and to spread outrageous rumors about his wife and mother-in-law in town, he openly flaunted his affair with a native woman. This attachment, formed on his first visit to Samoa with King Kalakaua's embassy, had taken on the proportions of a scandal when Joe installed his mistress in a little bungalow at the Stevensons' expense.

This final vulgarity signaled his doom. Louis filed for a divorce on Belle's behalf, which was granted by the court of Apia. He also asked to be made sole guardian of the Strongs' child, Austin. Like Fanny's son "Sammy" before him, Belle's son would grow up with Robert Louis Stevenson as his only masculine and paternal figure.

Austin and Belle, Fanny writes to her sister Nellie, *have moved from the cottage to the big house. Belle has a room on the first floor, near Louis' study. She is officially his secretary and even earns forty dollars a month. She is going to take his dictation. We are waiting for the visit of a nephew of Aunt Maggy's, a Balfour cousin whom Louis has never seen. He will live with Lloyd in the cottage the Strongs have vacated.*

Not a word about Fanny's suffering. Some time ago, it must have seemed like ages, Louis wouldn't have written a single line without submitting it to her; not a paragraph went to the publisher without her approval. Nowadays, she along with everyone else enjoyed Louis reading from his work in progress after lunch. But her criticism carried less weight than Lloyd's. It was Lloyd who took notes, Lloyd who answered the author's questions, Lloyd whose judgment the writer most anxiously sought.

Lloyd had already collaborated with Robert Louis Stevenson on *The Wrecker.* Colvin may not have appreciated this adventure story, but it was very popular with readers. The authors weren't as pleased with their second collaboration, *The Ebb Tide,* and left it in a drawer. There it would remain until the arrival of Graham Balfour, the cousin Fanny mentions in her letter.

He was a twenty-three-year-old Scotsman, a young man of distinction and a whimsical turn of mind. He had a degree from Oxford, a fund of intellectual curiosity, a literary soul, and he was enthusiastic about this last story. Louis and Lloyd found Graham an ideal companion, and his visit, which was to last a month, stretched out to a year. The trio understood each other implicitly, and the "young people" promised to find plenty to entertain them at Vailima.

That winter the inhabitants of Apia would hear more about the ailments of Fanny Stevenson than about the health of her illustrious husband.

Vailima III—August 1892–July 1893

Lloyd, looking at his mother's small figure, gently closed the door. She was suffering dreadfully from lower back pain. Dr. Funk had diagnosed kidney problems, which were not eased by morphine.

Lying on the couch in her room, she had received her son with the hesitant smile that had moved him since childhood. For him, and for him alone, she had preserved the patience, the silence, and the enveloping sweetness that he sought in native women. Lloyd liked small women with very dark skin and intense black eyes. Women like his mother.

Fanny had not showered her son with tenderness or caresses, coaxing words or whispered endearments. Yet Lloyd had never doubted her love. She had loved him, protected him, and watched over him. As long as Fanny lived, nothing could hurt Lloyd Osbourne. He felt it, and always had.

Lloyd had shared everything with her—joy as well as sorrow. Together they had lost Hervey and discovered Grez. Together they had loved Louis, Aunt Maggy, and England. This, at least, was Lloyd's impression until the falling out with Henley. Young Lloyd had dearly loved Henley, that poet bursting with life. He considered him his literary mentor. Fanny's fight with Henley had been awful for Lloyd, and then there was Henley's terrible silence, his refusal to answer the young man's letters. Lloyd had not expressed the pain of this rejection, but his mother knew it. She knew everything. In his way he felt about her something akin to the veneration displayed by the natives, a curious mixture of love and fear. He distrusted her powers, he kept her at a distance, but he could not live far from her. Like Lafaele, who knew how to invent any pretext to come to her room, and who, once there, was petrified with fear, Lloyd never entered his mother's room without a feeling of apprehension. Fanny's mystery remained intact. The tigerskin on the sofa and the footprint traced on the ceiling gave him the same turn it did the servants. Like Lafaele, who would smile politely when Fanny explained to him that this footprint was only a track made on the varnish by some worker, that it had been made *before* the plank was nailed to the ceiling, Lloyd accepted his mother's words yet could not dislodge his sense of the uncanny. Tamaitai could summon spirits. Her room was a place where the *aitus* roamed free.

Yet the place had nothing disturbing about it. It no longer resembled the storeroom of former times. Fanny's quarters occupied the right wing of the house, and the large bay windows, set at an angle, opened onto the sea and one of the tennis courts. This double exposure made the room so light that the green walls seemed blue in the sun. The long topaz curtains around the bed, the ocher window seats, the Turkish rug with a floral design in yellow, so thick one's bare feet sank into it up to the ankle, were all comfortably inviting.

Lloyd took the hand she held out to him and sat on the bench beside her. This gesture was uncharacteristic of them. It was hard to believe that this blond young man nearly six feet tall, his upright posture accentuated by his nearsightedness, was really Fanny's son. When Fanny stood up, she scarcely reached his chest. At fifty-two, she was still as graceful, as quick as he seemed stiff and slow, as emotional and violent as he seemed cold. The whole Vandegrift inheritance ran in Lloyd's veins; the north wind blew in his caustic tone and dry sense of humor.

"Look," she said, pointing to the landscape.

Between the treetops he glimpsed the vast ocean gleaming in the sun.

"You'll never see it just this way again . . . This hour is fleeting, but let's prolong the pleasure for a moment . . ."

She was aware of Lloyd's surprise, his near anxiety, and smiled: "Do you think I'm acting a little strangely? Forgive me . . . Funk prescribed a drug. I feel much better, but perhaps it puts me in a peculiar state . . . You see," she went on, taking her son's hand, "I'm so sorry that Aunt Maggy is unhappy here . . . She is unhappy, isn't she? She would like to convince us to give up the plantation and move to the colonies, New Zealand perhaps. All the same, I think she would be happier at Vailima if she were busy with something. But I don't manage to find anything to interest her. It's so difficult for me to imagine that she might prefer a social life, a world where ladies call on each other and leave engraved visiting cards, where there's a real church, real social gatherings, Sunday rest . . . that anyone might prefer such things to the paradaisical life we lead here. One feels so close to God at Vailima!"

Again, Lloyd gave his mother a worried look. Was it really the new medication that was putting her in this ecstatic state so unfamiliar to him?

"Tell me," she went on with her voice of former times, a low, uninflected voice that he hadn't heard since they had moved to Samoa, that cool flowing voice, strange and insidious. "Tell me, how is Belle? You know how she is, always ready to follow some man, as long as he's handsome and talented enough. I must say that compared to the horrible Joe, Graham Balfour is a delight. He has quite naturally become part of the family. But she's forgetting that he is twenty-three years old. And she . . ."

Lloyd refrained from remarking that Louis hadn't been much older when his mother had fallen in love with him. There were eleven years between Graham Balfour and Belle, as there were between Louis and Fanny.

"Your sister is so flighty, do talk to her . . . she'll listen to you. She won't accept anything from me. If Graham could fall in love with her, fine! I'd be the first to congratulate them. But this young man is not for her . . . I don't want to see her suffer, do you understand? And I don't want people in London to say that we all throw ourselves on Louis's family . . . Lady Jersey would be only too happy to gossip about my daughter making a spectacle of herself!"

"Lady Jersey?" Lloyd exclaimed. "Surely not! She has taken a liking to Belle, the two of them are as thick as thieves. The countess is politeness itself, Mama, and she is a great admirer of Louis. She knows his work by heart—even *A Footnote to History*! Tomorrow we shall take her to meet Mataafa."

If Lloyd had seen his mother's expression, he would surely have held his tongue.

Without saying a word, she got up, crossed the room, and went down the hall.

"You claim to be working for peace, Louis," she exploded, bursting into his study, "but if you do this, you're going to set off a war!"

"If I do what?" he asked impatiently.

He would not tolerate any interruption when he was dictating. Belle, with the manuscript on her lap, shrunk down on her little stool.

"If you take Lady Jersey to Mataafa's camp! This woman, who you claim is so brilliant, so courageous, so literary . . . This woman is the wife of the governor-general of New South Wales. She represents the Queen . . . 'your' queen, who considers Mataafa a rebel, a fanatic, a sworn enemy . . ."

Louis contained himself, put his papers down, and taking Fanny by the elbow, led her to the couch he used as a bed. Belle took advantage of this move to slip off.

"Precisely," he said, trying to seem calm. "Lady Jersey will testify to Mataafa's goodwill, she will judge his wisdom, she will see for herself that he has always restrained his troops, that he is not seeking war, that without him, without his efforts, Upolu would be devastated today!"

"The meeting of an official personage like Lady Jersey with Mataafa is going to put the British consul in an impossible position in relation to the other two powers. Are you trying to exasperate the Germans? How are you going to prove to them that England is not betraying its commitments to them, that Great Britain is not supporting Mataafa behind their backs?"

Resisting his pressure, Fanny refused to sit down. While he settled himself against the pillows, she stood above him and kept talking: "You are going to force Lord Jersey and Cusack-Smith to attack Mataafa to prove their good faith! The Germans have been waiting for that, the backing of the English, to crush him . . ."

"No one needs to know that the lady who accompanies me is the wife of the governor; it's not the first time I've paid a visit to Mataafa in his village . . . I'll introduce her as my cousin, Miss Amelia Balfour . . ."

"You mean you're going to lie to Mataafa as well? You're not only behaving badly but stupidly. You think you'll fool him? There are no secrets on this island, rumors proliferate like trails of gunpowder. Mataafa will not be tricked. And the consuls will know about this meeting the moment it happens!"

Louis had jumped to his feet. They glared at each other. "Fanny, you are so pesimistic! You are always imagining the worst . . . It can only help Mataafa's cause. No one in Apia will know anything about it. It will be such an exhilarating adventure ... I will meet Lady Jersey tomorrow at dawn at the last ford of the Papase'ea River. Belle, Lloyd, and Graham are coming with me ... And you are very welcome to come along as well!"

"Exhilarating, you say! You're playing at war, Louis, the way you used to play toy soldiers with Lloyd, the way you do now with Austin. And now with that vain and vulgar Lady Jersey!"

"You don't understand, Fanny," he said more gently. "I want to die with my boots on—to drown, fall off a horse, be shot by a rifle. Anything would be better than that slow disintegration at Bourne-mouth ..."

"Oh yes, I do understand! And your egotism is revolting. You are just like Cusack-Smith ... like all the Whites in Apia. You all think only of your own pleasure ... With them it's self-interest and money, with you it's adventure. But it's all the same! You're incapa-ble of renouncing your games, even if it costs the lives of the very people you claim to defend ... The natives are going to suffer for this *exhilarating adventure*. But you don't give a damn, as long as *your* heart is beating and *you* feel alive." She shot him a fierce look, full of contempt and menace: "If you take Lady Jersey to Mataafa, Robert Louis Stevenson is not the man I thought he was!"

"If I bow to the tyranny of a hysterical peasant," he answered in the same tone of voice, "I am not Robert Louis Stevenson!"

He slammed the door and left her alone.

*

"How I would love for Louis and his artistic nature to get a comeuppance, and the aristocratic Scottish pretensions of this fam-ily to get a good slap in the face," she was thinking angrily, listening to them laugh as they planned their expedition for the following day.

At the end of the table, Fanny kept her jaws clenched tight. Her face was severe and concentrated, her gestures slow and circum-spect. She would say nothing to them about the disaster she could foresee. Yes, she was making every effort to hold herself in check, she was rallying all her forces to guard that crafty prisoner, her mind. She was clinging to the table for fear of letting slip the thoughts that were devouring her soul. If she were not careful, she would shout at them all her forebodings and scorn. She gripped the tablecloth, digging her nails into the damask.

Suddenly her muscles relaxed and her will collapsed. Something seemed to have snapped inside her head and engulfed her with the din and heat of a flash fire. Belle had to leave Vailima. Aunt Maggy, Lloyd, and Graham had to go as well. She would be left alone with Louis, just the two of them, like in the good old days. Unless . . . unless she went too.

She jumped from her seat, crossed the room, and, rushing down the two steps of the veranda, found herself standing on the lawn. Talolo and Lafaele, who were arguing in low voices at the entrance to the kitchen, a shed built a little apart from the big house, raised their heads. They were surprised to see Tamaitai's distorted features. She disappeared into the shadow and reappeared not far from them but seemingly unaware of their presence. Back and forth she strode across the grass between the kitchen and Mount Vaea, murmuring and gesticulating. They finally dozed off as they continued to watch their odd mistress. They thought that Tusitala would call her back to the house and tell her to go to bed. But Tusitala did not call.

At sunrise the band of conspirators, Louis, Belle, Graham, and Lloyd, headed for the stables. They saddled the horses and rode off toward town in a mysterious procession.

The house was empty. Aunt Maggy was polishing the leatherbound books on the first floor, preserving the bindings from the destructive dampness. Or perhaps she had gone down to the paddock. In a straw hat and gardening gloves, with a little basket on her arm, she was hunting for the *lantau*, a kind of grain she accused of poisoning her horse. If by chance a visitor were to appear on the path, Aunt Maggy would quickly retreat to the house, go to her room by the back door, and reappear some moments later in a fluted bonnet and black taffeta dress. Gracious and smiling, she would happily play the hostess, especially if the visitor were the Rev. Mr. Clarke or one of the missionaries.

Crouching on the warm, rugged rocks of the waterfall, where the stream was no longer running, where the basin was dry now in August, Fanny searched the landscape above her, Mount Vaea . . . She hated this mountain with its forest and eternal shade.

This enormous swell looked like a mountain in a child's drawing and could be seen from any vantage point: from the sea, from Apia, from the entrance to Vailima, from the veranda, from Louis's room. By day it rustled and hummed with birdsong, at night with the shrill sounds of bats. Even its silence was audible. Everyone talked about Mount Vaea. Lafaele, terrified by spirits, refused to set foot there. Talolo, Sosimo, and Faamua told how they had met the *aitu* Fafine there, a female vampire who lured you into the woods to suck your blood. Even the Rev. Mr. Clarke brought up the battles that had been unleashed here less than twenty years ago. Last May the boys had found the remains of a skeleton, one body with two heads. They had figured out that it must have been a soldier carrying the head of his enemy, bringing it back as a customary trophy. And Louis, who spent every morning looking out his window at the top of the mountain, mentioned it only when speaking of his death: "I want to be buried up there. The top of Mount Vaea will be my grave."

Above her the mountain was a living, breathing presence, mingling with Fanny's fear and oppressive solitude. When she looked around she saw big black lizards wriggling on the ground and disappearing between the stones. Little fruits were falling from the trees, one after another, with the dry sound of a grenade being pulled, and exploding at her feet. Was some clumsy hand taking aim at her? On the edge of the woods, the grass was still trembling, a shudder running from the waterfall to the mass of dark trees. Not a breath of air stirred. Had someone just passed by? Was the *aitu* Fafine looking for her to lead her into the bushes? She got up and went through the narrow passage, that dark muddy path that wound between the trees and led nowhere. She was going forward, disconcerted, unnerved by the violence of this tropical life. Everything here needed sun to better ferment in the shadows. The forest, like Vailima, seemed full of colorful flowers, but this was only the flowering of death. The earth of Vailima, promising joy and beauty, contained only rot and poison . . . the sky above, with its trellis of enormous lianas, hid a vast emptiness.

The terror of an unknown force that had taken possession of her made her stumble. She fell to the ground and lay there sleepily in the sun that filtered through the leaves, rolled among the tree trunks, and was absorbed in the grass. She lay face up, losing herself in this warm and pungent mirage, relinquishing the last of her strength.

She suddenly felt soothed. She forgot her anger and despair.

The memory of her love for Louis, of her struggle to keep him alive, of her ambition and her failure slowly dissolved in this humidity that liquified both regret and hope.

*
**

The little band had stayed away for two days and nights. They would surely return this evening. She would go to meet them! All of Fanny's thoughts were henceforth concentrated on this great reunion scene. She would ask Louis's pardon for no longer being indispensable to him, and everything would be just as before. Yes, she would tell Louis how much it hurt her that he no longer needed her, how she had been afraid that he was casting her out. She would tell him. And everything would be fine. They would be newly united, the two of them standing alone to fight the world together.

Leaving the road to Vailima behind her, she went on foot toward the village. At the fork in the road, along the path to Apia, she heard a man laughing heartily and joyously. It was Louis's voice. Fanny stopped to listen, but the horses suddenly surged in front of her and the riders passed by at a gallop without seeing her.

When Louis and Lloyd, Belle and Graham returned from their expedition, they did not find her. Dog-tired, their heads full of images and dreams, they went to bed. By common agreement they had decided not to boast of their exploits to Fanny. They would tell her nothing.

Three days after their return, in the big hall where the family was gathered, Fanny shot Louis a ferocious look. The visit to Mataafa had provoked a diplomatic incident, just as she had foreseen. Lady Jersey had returned crestfallen to her husband, who had probably choked with rage. Sir John Thurston, the High Commissioner of the Western Pacific in Fiji, was planning to sign his deportation order for the Stevenson clan. The three powers had armed for war, and Great Britain was primarily responsible for outfitting Laupepa's troops with additional men and arms.

Stevenson was smoking in silence, mentally preparing the chapters he would dictate to Belle the following day. His wife construed this calm as an insult. Why wasn't this unconscious and indifferent egotist talking to her tonight? Was he exhausting all his pleasure in conversation with Belle? Did the chatterings of that insipid, flighty woman flatter his jaded pride? Was he trying to torture his wife with his silence? No doubt he thought she wasn't worthy of holding a pen and understanding his artistic pronouncements! He preferred that preening Belle, who wouldn't touch a rake for fear of spoiling her little white hands. Fanny Stevenson had nothing in common with those people. She had to go back outside to the grass, to the water, to the earth . . . Yes, of course, that was it. The forest was calling her. She rose and ran toward the door. In the passage, she knocked over a little table with a decanter and glasses. In the confusion that followed, no one reacted. Only Belle cried: "She's gone completely mad!"

For the first time, someone had expressed what Louis had dared not say for months, even to himself. He rushed after Fanny.

She was plunging deep into the bush, with the hallucinated movement of someone pursued by a ghost. When she reached the waterfall, she stopped, holding her head as if she were listening to a voice. The sweat was running down her forehead. Above her stood Mount Vaea, black against an even blacker sky. Silence. This stillness seemed a reproach, an accusation. There was no safety anywhere. Not even in the arms of Louis and Lloyd, who had joined her and were trying to take her back. The traitors! Spies, hypocrites. They were only trying to get rid of her . . . Why were they pretending to pull her away from the earth that was claiming her? She was struggling against this sense of defeat and lost her footing. She fell in the darkness. They were bringing her back to Vailima. She resisted them with all her strength. Suddenly, from one moment to the next, she gave up the fight.

Lying in her room, she was shaken by a powerful shudder. Brutally pushing her daughter's hand from her forehead, as though it were an object of disgust, Fanny jumped out of bed and ran to the door.

"Louis!" Belle screamed.

This name echoed through the night, riveting Fanny to the floor.

She stood a moment, immobilized. She was gasping, trying to catch her breath. Stevenson appeared in the doorway.

"She cannot stand me," Belle explained in tears. "She won't let me near her . . . She hates me."

"Go to bed. I will sit with her tonight. I will sit with her every night."

Belle went out. He came gently toward Fanny, took her by the shoulders, and turned her toward him as he had done for the first time in the canoe in Grez.

"What are you trying to tell me?" he asked in a tender, pleading voice. "What do I need to understand, Fanny?"

She rested her forehead against Louis's thin torso. Her head was bursting. "You talk," she whispered, "you're always talking, but you don't say anything!"

"Oh, my dear," he murmured, holding her against him, "talking is such a difficult thing. One talks and it is never what one means . . . So silence is better. Kindness, consideration, and indulgence are better . . ."

"But," she cried, suddenly pushing him away, "you are killing me with your indulgence!"

"All right," he said cheerfully. "From now on I won't let you get away with a thing, I'll be pitiless . . . And tomorrow you'll tell me everything you wanted to shout about tonight. Now, go back to bed."

Fanny obeyed. She fell immediately into a heavy dreamless sleep. She could rest only when Louis sat by her bed.

"Is she going to die, Doctor?"

It was Louis turn to pronounce this sentence, which Fanny had repeated for eleven years. Full of anguish, suffering, and compassion, he gazed, pained and bewildered, toward his wife.

"I do not believe that her life is in danger," murmured the doctor, closing his bag.

Whatever happened on the island, Dr. Bernard Funk, with his goatee, his long, drooping mustache, and his cropped gray hair, affected the most benign optimism. His dress, his cigars, and his cane had become part of the Apia landscape. He had come twelve years earlier, in February 1880, to work for Ets Godefroy and Son, the biggest German company trading in copra. A former Prussian army surgeon during the Franco-Prussian war, he had studied medicine in Berlin and Tübingen. But his hobby was meteorology. He loudly proclaimed that studying the clouds interested him more than studying his patients.

"Rest assured, it is nothing life threatening."

"What about her mind?"

Until that moment Belle had never realized how much her step-father loved this woman. The measure of Stevenson's love for Fanny could be read in the inflection of his voice, his trembling hands, his days and nights at her bedside. Everything in him spoke of his passion and his fear of losing her.

"Her mind . . . yes, she may lose it."

"For good?"

Dr. Funk made a sweeping gesture with his hand. Was this ac-quiescence? Ignorance? The German rose to leave.

Belle's intuition in coming to Vailima had not been wrong, and Joe was just a fool. Because Robert Louis Stevenson did not flirt with Fanny in corners or call her "sweetheart" and embrace her in public, they had thought his former ardor had cooled . . . Fanny's constant concern for her husband was obvious. And no one doubted that he still admired her and felt sincerely grateful to her. But why hadn't they seen the signs of this carnal attachment that had been staring them in the face?

Last month during a game of "truth," Louis had given ten out of ten to Fanny for beauty. Belle had understood this compliment as an act of kindness but she was wrong. At fifty-three, Fanny Vandegrift was still Stevenson's ideal of femininity: strange, unpre-dictable, elusive. She had a feline strength and mystery.

Like Lloyd, Louis loved women with dark skin. He liked rounded shoulders, small brown sinewy hands, and bare feet. During all these years Belle had missed the basic fact of life at Vailima.

She escorted Dr. Funk down the hall, as she had done in Sydney when Fanny, after the doctor's visit, had remained for a moment alone at Louis's bedside.

"Do you think, Doctor," the young woman asked with difficulty, "do you think that my mother is going mad?"

"What is madness?" Funk asked philosophically, "What is madness?"

"She refuses to eat. She refuses to speak. She is always turned to the wall. We cannot seem to interest her in anything. It's as if she didn't hear us . . ."

"Earlier you mentioned delirium . . ."

"She suddenly has something like hallucinations. She sees things."

"What does she say?"

"It doesn't make any sense."

"But what does she say?" insisted the doctor.

"I have the feeling she's confusing the past and the present . . . that she thinks she's someone else . . ."

"Who?"

"I think she is reliving the death of my little brother . . . That she's enduring his suffering again." Belle paused: "Sometimes she murmurs words I don't understand."

"For example?"

Embarrassed, Belle hesitated: "She says . . . that Louis is building a cowshed for milking her, that . . ." The young woman sadly shook her head.

"That . . . ?" the German repeated.

"That he treats her like a milk cow."

The vivacious Dr. Funk gave a little laugh: "In her delirium your mother still has a sense of humor . . ."

"You think so?" grumbled Belle.

"Mrs. Stevenson is using literal expressions that would translate her grief . . ."

"What grief?"

"That I don't know . . . If I knew, your mother would already be cured," he pronounced. "For twenty years she has lived with great stress . . . And these past two years have not been easy. But life is never easy, eh?"

The little doctor paused, as if he were weighing the extraordinary aptness of this reflection. Then, removing his pince-nez he looked around him: "This residence, for example, Vailima—what an accomplishment! Built in six months . . . Do you have any idea? Six months to build such a house in a place like this? A miracle! When I came in I saw that they have finished the roof of the new building. Are you doubling in size?"

Belle evaded his question: "This . . . this illness . . . could it be menopause?"

"Why not?" Funk acquiesced. "In your mother, the most benign symptoms are multiplied ten times over . . . Everything that touches her seems magnified, larger than life . . . Perhaps she is only suffering from the change of life, a very natural thing ... Unless ... unless she has contracted Bright's disease."

"What's that?"

"It's a new illness. We've known its symptoms for barely twenty years ..." Funk gave a deep sigh. "And our dear Upolu is so far from hospitals, universities, and professional meetings ... If memory serves, Bright's disease destroys the kidneys and leads to mental troubles ... It can modify behavior. I have been treating your mother for kidney stones for two years now ... It could be that the stones have shattered the whole system. And on the other hand, as you suggest, her illness could simply be mental."

"Do you mean madness?"

"Dementia praecox," corrected Funk. "Hadn't she already suffered from dizziness, memory loss ... when your brother died?"

"Yes, but her earlier difficulties weren't like this! You can't imagine how she is when ... when she loses her head," Belle gasped, remembering certain dreadful scenes. "Sometimes I think she ..." Belle did not finish her sentence. Leaning on the rail of the veranda, she looked out over the plantation: "I dreamed that she set fire to Vailima ..." she went on, "that she was feeding the fire with my stepfather's books."

"My child, you are the one who is overworked."

"It's as if my mother were incapable of joining in his happiness, so she is trying to drag him into death ... I sometimes have the feeling that she wants to kill him!"

"If there is one thing I am absolutely certain of," Funk cut in cheerfully, "it is your mother's absolute devotion to Mr. Stevenson."

"Precisely ... Love and hate are two sides of the same coin, aren't they?"

"Popular psychology!"

The boisterous little Dr. Funk shook his reprimanding finger at her. "You," he scolded in a familiar tone, "You have read *Dr. Jekyll and Mr. Hyde* once too often. Get some fresh air and forget these morbid notions!"

They crossed the lawn, walking slowly toward Lafaele, who was leading the doctor's horse by the bridle. Delicious scents rose from the shrubbery, from the fruit and flowers.

"There—look at your pineapples, how splendid they are!" the little man exclaimed. "So juicy I would bet they weigh more than five pounds ... Enjoy Vailima! Enjoy it, Mrs. Osbourne! Your garden is so abundant . . . the light is so beautiful, so rare! With that leaden sky, that gray sea, those tall phosphorescent trees, one would think this was Scotland after the rain . . . And the little red drops of your coffee plants flaming in the last rays of the sun. It's getting dark. You know how quickly night comes here . . ."

The doctor interrupted his lyrical flight to slip his cane into his saddle bags and mount his horse.

"Keep me informed," he said as he went off at a trot.

Belle hugged her arms to her chest to keep warm. She could not decide whether to go back inside. She remained standing on the grassy slope, like a large flower between the round tops of the mango trees, the glistening fans of the banana palms. "Enjoy it, Mrs. Osbourne!" When Funk had called her by her maiden name, she'd had the painful impression that he was not addressing her. "Mrs. Osbourne"—that was her mother. "Get some fresh air, Mrs. Osbourne": that was also what Hervey's doctor had said the day after the boy had died. From now on Belle was Mrs. Osbourne. How long would she have to take over her mother's role? She gave a sad sigh. She knew one thing for certain: Graham Balfour would not play the part of Louis Stevenson, he would not fall in love with an older woman . . . At least not with a Mrs. Osbourne. Yet she was attractive, full of charm and life. But Graham Balfour didn't seem to notice. Why? Perhaps she didn't have her mother's gift for attracting a young man. Perhaps Belle Osbourne was too healthy. Too easy, she thought bitterly. Her face was an open book, there was no secret, no mystery.

Slowly, Belle turned toward Vailima. Joined to the big house, a little behind it, she could see the construction on the new building. "Vailima, Fanny's work," Belle concluded with a melancholy thought. Fanny's work: incomparable, exotic . . . and violent. *Vailima* was the story of a man at the height of his fame; of a palace on an island served by a bottle imp; and of a woman who was fighting against madness in secret corners—a fantastic tale worthy of a Vandegrift daydream, a fable born of the maternal imagination, *Wuthering Heights* reviewed and rewritten by Fanny Stevenson.

Belle climbed the two steps of the porch. She walked in her bare feet silently toward the door. She delayed her return to the green room and leaned on the door frame. As it happened, Austin was with Aunt Nellie in Monterey. They had sent him off in September for the entire academic year. This separation, which had cost Belle dear, was some consolation to her this evening. Austin at twelve years old was going to school and playing with boys his own age. Aunt Maggy was spending the winter in Scotland. She had gone back to visit her sister and to sell the house at 17 Heriot Row. Next summer she would bring back the furniture, the remaining pictures, crystal, knickknacks, all the objects of the Stevenson tradition that would take their place in the second wing of the house. The central stairway, twelve feet across, led to the many rooms planned for a very large family . . . My God! How had Belle forgotten this detail? Why hadn't she mentioned this to the doctor? In her delirium, Fanny thought she was expecting ten of Louis's children—ten children she thought she was carrying inside her! She saw herself with such an enormous belly that she couldn't move . . . It was this heaviness, she had explained, that had forced her to wear the *holoku* all these years. She was pregnant! When Belle had shown her the insanity of this illusion, Fanny had burst into tears. She wanted to beg Louis's pardon. Yes, he absolutely had to forgive her for not having given him all the children he wanted. During this scene she had stopped her ears when Louis had sworn that she was mistaken, that he had not wanted any children, that he had never wanted them, that he would not have wanted to bequeath his poor health to anyone.

Belle breathed deeply in the evening air. She still had a few moments before she had to go in. She knew. She knew that Louis was lying. In the letters to Edmund Gosse he had dictated to her, he had confided to his friend the sorrow of a man who knows he will die without leaving any heirs. Fanny's formidable instinct had not been wrong. Tomorrow Belle would tell the doctor the story of this suffering.

"Old Funk did better than I could have hoped . . . Louis wrote to his mother on April 17, 1893. *In the midst of all this, Belle kind of bust up—I think it was only worry and overwork, both Talolo and Sosimo went upon the sick list with abscesses; and it was a jolly old household. I was mortal glad you weren't here. Now we are all recovered or recovering—Belle protests against this and says to tell the truth that Fanny is not recovering. But though it is true she seems to have taken a cast back, she is far indeed from being so dreadfully ill as she was before.*

(She lies in bed, his amanuensis intervenes, *does not smoke, doesn't want to eat, or speak; Louis does not want to alarm you but I think you should know what a really anxious time we are going through . . . I would like to see her take an interest in something. Belle)*

Well, perhaps Belle is right, but I indulge myself in a little better hope . . .

In the interval we have had lunch, and I personally, as totally distinguished from the amanuensis, think Fanny emphatically better than yesterday. (She ate no lunch and she ate no breakfast, if you call that better. B.)

Last night the cats woke us up around ten o'clock. Belle had not yet come to bed. As we are all three settled in my room, we drank a grog and smoked a cigarette. We were almost as gay as boys on an outing. It was marvelous. Fanny was as kind as possible and she did not seem at all ill. Yesterday for the first time she went out in her garden with an umbrella and I was exhausted trying to follow her everywhere.

One month later, in May 1893, Louis writes triumphantly: *Fanny seems to be in the right way now. I must say she is very very well for her, and complains scarce at all.*

What he does not say in this last letter is that the drums were beating in the mountains; that armed bands of guerrilla fighters were descending on Apia, their faces blackened to frighten their enemies; that the women had shaved their heads and used their hair to ornament the clothing of their fathers or husbands. He does not say that the men of Vailima were doing war dances on the lawn, uttering strange cries.

Vailima IV—July 1893–December 1894

At Vailima, in Apia, in Malinuu, in all the villages throughout the countryside people spoke of nothing but war.

The young men of Vailima, Louis, Lloyd, and Palema (as Louis's cousin Graham Balfour had been dubbed), childish with excitement, ventured out among the armed factions and returned to the plantation with their heads full of strategies, plans for alliances, and combat techniques. Fanny listened anxiously to their talk and wondered how she would ever keep Louis out of danger.

In town, the worries of the white traders seemed of a different sort. The same men who had formerly treated the Samoans like "niggers" and forced them to walk three steps behind, hurried to form new alliances with the roving bands of warriors marching beneath their windows.

"Very suggestive," Fanny noted contemptuously. The Whites had wanted war, and now they trembled. How could she and Louis disarm this bomb contrived by the three consuls to reduce and destroy all the native factions?

Once more the facts would confirm Fanny's worst fears.

Mataafa, the old chief supported by the Stevenson clan, was defeated in the first round of fighting. He was crushed by Laupepa's troops—or rather by the forces of the Whites, and betrayed, in the end, by the consuls themselves. In exchange for total submission, the three powers had promised to protect Mataafa's partisans, their families and houses from attacks by rival factions. Now, despite his word, the captain of the British warship allowed the old chief's villages to be reduced to ashes before his very eyes.

Fanny was apalled; she openly accused the white authorities of dishonorable behavior. The American consul retorted that they had not burned houses, only native huts.

"The fool!" she exploded. "I know exactly what a 'native hut' means. I have built three and would feel it a serious loss if one were burned. It's as if the Queen should say of his house: 'Burned? So what! It's not Balmoral, only a consul's house.' I would like to see that idiot's face!"

But Fanny could not forgive herself—and everyone at Vailima— for having played a role in Samoa's internal affairs that only hastened its demise. If Louis had not held Mataafa back these last years, she thought, if Mataafa had fallen on Apia when he had wanted, he would have won the war. Without the Stevensons' advice, the high chief whom Louis and Fanny had claimed to support would be safe and happy today surrounded by his loved ones, and this at the sole expense of a few worthless lives. The only profit Mataafa could show for his friendship with the people of Vailima, for the role Fanny and Louis had played in his life, was the ruin of all he held dear, and his people's death. How could she absolve herself of such a crime?

Thinking they were acting in Mataafa's interest and avoiding a bloodbath, Louis and Fanny had counseled peace. But the white cowards had taken advantage of this peace to arm Mataafa's rivals. How could she deny their responsibility for Mataafa's fate: He was to be exiled for life, while his warriors were imprisoned in Apia for God knew how long.

Fanny's journal of her years in Samoa closes with these painful reflections. But she did not lay down her arms. On November 22, 1893, the idle gawkers of Apia would witness a curious spectacle, an extraordinary parade by the Vailima clan.

That day, the first rays of dawn had scarcely touched the ocher roofs of the *fales* grouped behind the big house when Louis, Fanny, Belle, and Lloyd mounted their horses. Faint smoke from the fires was rising toward Mount Vaea, a dark mass in the early morning mist. Between the posts of four of the native huts, men were raising the shades. Half-naked women were already sweeping the black gravel of the oval room. A bird called from the top of the breadfruit tree spared by the last storm. A baby whimpered. The children related to the twelve Vailima servants ran out to the horses, crying gaily "Talofa! Talofa!" Belle answered, turning in her saddle.

The left side of the path was lined with barbed wire marking the property's boundary line, the right side was furrowed with ruts. The animals slipped and stumbled.

At daybreak, leaving the forest, the riders came into a clearing dotted with small huts among the banana groves. Famished little white dogs ran toward them, barking.

They broke into a trot on the straight track through the acres of coconut trees in the heart of the Weber plantation.

At the Tivoli Hotel they dismounted and left their horses. Then, walking abreast down Beach Road, they went to the largest grocery store in Apia, Herr Berger's Trading Post, which served the German colony. There they rented an enormous cart, the kind the black boys heaped with copra. In single file they carried coconuts, kava roots, bananas, breadfruit, boxes of smoking and chewing tobacco, and slowly loaded up so that all the residents might enjoy the details of their purchase. Fanny took the horse on the right by the bridle, Louis took the one on the left. Belle and Lloyd brought up the rear.

Walking along beside the palm trees lining the shore, slowing

down in front of the consuls' bungalows, the municipal office buildings and the court, they crossed through every part of the small
town. The carcass of the *Adler*, one of the warships wrecked by
the hurricane, surged up blackened in the bay, like a sea monster
rotting in the sun. A small group of natives murmured in low voices
as they trailed after the strange crew. They had rarely seen Whites
laden this way with such a heap of kava roots and taro.

Together Fanny and Louis crossed the narrow causeway strad-
dling the mangrove swamps. The prison stood behind the gray barrier
of corrugated metal at the end of the path. It was a single building,
a wooden barracks divided by a corridor opening onto six cells. The
eighteen chiefs, former followers of Mataafa, had gathered in the
courtyard. In *lava lavas*, their bare torsos covered with tattoos but
shorn of their necklaces of flowers and strings of seeds, their fly swat-
ters and walking sticks, looking thin and anxious, they surrounded the
visitors. Some of the most aged of the chiefs seemed at the end of
their strength. "Old Poe," Talolo's father-in-law whom Fanny knew
quite well, could hardly stand on his swollen feet. And yet this visit
brought them a breath of hope. In the presence of the whole town,
risking deportation, Tusitala had brought these betrayed and defeated
warriors the assurance of his friendship.

The following December, the eighteen imprisoned chiefs would
return the favor. The Stevensons would spend their Christmas of
1893 in prison. This time it would be their turn for a surprise. The
families, villages, and clans of the chiefs sent hundreds of pigs, fish,
and fowl, a heap of provisions and baskets for a Polynesian feast.
No celebration, Louis wrote to Colvin, *was ever given in honor of
a single family, none of these many gifts offered to a white man.
Belle sat at the right hand of the most important of the chiefs, and
Fanny was called up first to drink the kava. Never has a woman,
or a white woman, had this honor.* Then, in accordance with tradition, Louis was presented with each object, gift by gift. The speaker
greeted Tusitala as their only friend, apologizing for not having the
money to offer him things of value, such as salt beef and boxes of
biscuits. "These," he concluded, "are only poor prisoner's gifts to
the Rich Man." This was the requisite speech in which native rheto-
ric worked by understatement. The offerings included sumptuous
tapas, dozens of fans and baskets, and, the crowning gift, several
ulas, those strands of red seeds, which the chiefs took from their
own necks and placed on the shoulders of their guests. Fanny and

Louis protested, claiming that they could not accept such a sacrifice. They understood the purely political meaning of this gesture when they were told that King Laupepa had much admired these *ulas*; that he had even asked to borrow them; that Louis and Fanny, Belle and Lloyd should wear them as they passed slowly before the royal palace. They did as they were told.

Before the exasperated white authorities, Tusitala's clan paraded on foot, wending their way back along the peninsula to Malinuu, to the royal *fale*, wearing their purple *ulas* around their necks, their piles of gifts in their arms. The crowd took it upon themselves to comment on their elegance and the generosity of the gifts, which everyone was able to admire. Only the Samoans appreciated the courage it took to engage in this exhibition. The party of the third pretender to the throne, Tamasese, fomented a new war at the end of the year 1893. Tusitala and his family would make excellent hostages whose capture would embarrass the government of the three reigning powers, as well as the defeated faction of Mataafa. Louis and Fanny knew it. Their attempts to cope with their fear took all their grace and all their joy.

And this was not the full extent of Fanny's loyalty. Fifteen days later she managed to bring the jovial Dr. Funk to the prison. She wanted him to examine the legs of Old Poe, whom she had found so ill on their last visit. The doctor declared that the old man could not be cared for in the depths of a swamp. He had to be transported into town, or to Vailima. Fanny got the director of the prison, an Austrian count whom she had charmed, to look the other way while she took the prisoner with her. She gave her word that she would bring him back when he was cured. She kept her promise. Old Poe returned to his cell. The Austrian count lost his job, but she welcomed him at Vailima.

*
**

Mataafa would remain in exile in the Marshall Islands for several years. But on the first Monday in September 1894, the eighteen chiefs held in the prison at Apia were freed. After twelve months' detention, they could finally go home. They preferred to go up to

Vailima. At their head walked Old Poe. On the lawn, to the entire household assembled to celebrate their liberation, they announced that in gratitude for the generosity of the Teller of Tales, for his wife's compassion, and for their loyalty during the bad days, the chiefs had decided to make them a gift. After many deliberations, they had chosen to build them a road that would lead from Vailima to the Weber Road. They would recruit the young men of their villages, feed their crews themselves, and ask the Stevensons only to provide them with tools.

The magnitude of this gesture can only be gauged if we remember how the Samoans detest manual labor. The young men consider it an insult, the chiefs scorn it, and the absence of a network of roads remains one of the great shackles on the Samoan economy today.

This road would nonetheless be completed. The chiefs would call it the "Road of Gratitude," or, as it was called more often, the "Road of the Loving Heart."

Overwhelmed, Louis and Fanny Stevenson would accept this priceless gift at a celebration for the families of the chiefs, and all the members of the Tusitala clan.

That dawn on October 20, 1894, seemed to them the world's most beautiful morning. The air was so pure that the sky shimmered. Clouds of blue and bright rose surged up from the sea onto the roof at Vailima, and dissipated in purple waves on the flanks of Mount Vaea. The clusters of trees, vines, and flowers, the whole forest exuded a heady sense of peace. Miraculously, there was a cool breeze. Only the chirping of a bird in the tall pine tree on the lawn broke the silence. In the distance, the coral reef sparkled like a small swell, and it was impossible to tell where the sea ended and the sky began. The eternal roar of the Pacific, which never abated, belonged to life at Vailima like blood coursing through the veins of sleepers.

The celebration had begun with a *siva* offered by the young women of the house. Draped in their Scottish *lava lavas*, bare-breasted beneath the necklaces of flowers, they lined up on the lawn, serious and silent. They sat down cross-legged. Behind them, everyone could glimpse the purple posts of Vailima, the large bay windows, the pile of taro, fish, and piglets, a feast awaiting the guests on the leaf-strewn veranda.

Louis, Fanny, and the eighteen chiefs were seated on ancient mats that symbolized the power of each house. These mats had the meaning and value of a family jewel, a signet ring, or an armored crest passed along from generation to generation. The men stood behind them. Their powerful, glistening brown torsos, hung with necklaces, gave off the sweet odor of coconut oil and pandanus seed. They regrouped, advancing onto the lawn with that splendid bearing, that slow swinging of the hips, neck, and head, in a posture of indifference and self-possession. The meticulous arrangement of their *lava lavas* knotted around their waists or thrown over their shoulders, designating sex, age, and social rank, were reminiscent of the grooming of Ajax before the battle.

In front of them, like Indian idols, the young girls unfolded their long legs, their ankles ornamented with red bracelets. Faamua began to chant, and the others followed. They moved their arms rhythmically, undulating their shoulders, waists, and hips without moving a single vertebra. Holding themselves erect, they rose up a little using their thighs and their feet, their toes vibrating like waves continually lapping on the shore. Their bellies quivered, their fingers curved back, their shoulders pressed together, they waved their extended hands to the right, to the left, over the mats, stretching their torsos, while only the shuddering muscles of their still thighs followed the comings and goings of their undulations.

After the *siva*, the chiefs gathered under the veranda, standing according to rank. On the ground, with their backs to the house, Fanny and Louis listened to the interminable speeches of the orators and the translations of the interpreters. Lloyd, who spoke Samoan, whispered to them some of the details they might have missed. Then it was Louis's turn. Getting to his feet, his warm brown eyes took in the long line of men and women sitting along the veranda. There were few Whites. Few English, Americans, or Germans would agree to attend a celebration in honor of Mataafa's defeated rebels. Only the natives and the half-breeds were not afraid to compromise themselves.

The road is now done, he said. *You have trod it today in coming hither. It has been made for me by chiefs; some of them old, some sick, all newly delivered from a harassing confinement, and in spite of weather unusually hot and insalubrious. I have seen these chiefs labour valiantly with their own hands upon the work, and I have sat up over it, now that it is finished, the name of "The Road of Gratitude."* . . .

I will tell you Chiefs, that, when I saw you working on that road, my heart grew warm; not with gratitude only, but with hope. It seemed to me that I read the promise of something good for Samoa; it seemed to me, as I looked at you, that you were a company of warriors in a battle, fighting for the defence of our common country against all aggression. For there is a time to fight, and a time to dig. You Samoans may fight, you may conquer twenty times, and thirty times, and all will be in vain. There is but one way to defend Samoa. Hear it before it is too late. It is to make roads, and gardens, and care for your trees, and sell their produce wisely, and, in one word, to occupy and use your country. If you do not others will.

Two hours after sunset, the last guests went home. They left in procession on the Road of the Loving Heart. Louis and Fanny accompanied their guests to the fork in the road. There, all together, they erected a sign. The name and titles of the builders can still be read in the same place today. Then the clans went their separate ways, some toward the land, others toward the sea. Tusitala and Tamaitai walked slowly back toward Vailima. It was the first time that their ankles sank softly into the rich earth of this path, that they didn't stumble in the ruts. The torrents of mud in the rainy season, the gaping holes that caught horses and carts were smoothed and straightened now, the Road of the Loving Heart led directly to the large lighted house. The air smelled damp, the forest rustled with strange murmurings. Evening was falling, the birds were quiet. In the bower made by the trees, the figures of a man and woman could be seen quite clearly, walking close together. She was wearing a dress of black velvet, and the large gold hoops in her ears danced in the gray night of her hair. Louis, in shirtsleeves, his white trousers tucked into his boots, a wide purple belt around his waist, seemed too lanky and thin beside her. With his almond shaped eyes and the sibylline smile beneath his mustache, he still had the charm of a very young man. He would pass quickly from adolescence to old age.

Behind them the psalms that preceded evening prayers rose from the village of Tanugi-Manono, sweet, throbbing women's voices that mingled tribal chanting with the hymns of Christianity. In the depths of the forest, like a torch in the tropical night, glittered Vailima. Returning from Apia in the evening, Louis liked nothing better than to glimpse these lights in the heart of the bush. Custom dictated that a candle burn in each window. His life rested on the contrast, the balance, between "civilization" and "barbarism." He was intoxicated with the idea that his salon combined Piranese's *Prisons* with tribal drums from the Marquesas, the latest works of Paul Bourget with the shark's tooth necklaces of Tuamotu, Bob Stevenson's gouaches with Samoan mats of geometric design, Aunt Maggy's silk dresses together with Faamua's pointed breasts. These paradoxes enthralled him. In his view, Fanny's charm, her timid and savage grace, depended on such contradictions, on all that was inaccessible and mysterious in this little woman with her feet firmly planted on the ground.

Even after Louis had clearly understood and appreciated Fanny's strength and weaknesses, after he had plunged into the depths of her terrible illness, penetrated her despair, plumbed her soul and its secrets, even when he had seen and understood everything about her, this woman in her absolute nakedness still escaped him. Like a fleeting thought that vanishes before it can be fixed in words.

Lifting their faces toward the lights of the house, they slowly made their way back. In harmony with each other, Louis turned toward Fanny. Since her illness, she had seemed smaller, more fragile. Without stopping, he put his arm around her neck and drew her close. She let herself lean against the thin body that held her tight. A sphinxlike smile played on her lips when she looked up at that emaciated face whose mysteries she, too, had come to know.

"Your speech on Samoa," she whispered intently, "what you said to the chiefs was right."

He laughed with pleasure: "That's the first time you've given me a compliment in months."

She did not answer and leaned on his arm. They were both swept by a great wave of tenderness. The mysterious song of the rivers at Vailima coursed around them in the cluster of strange trees, of hibiscus bushes that looked black against the gray of the large leaves. As they climbed up toward the house Fanny's limbs felt increasingly heavy.

"Are you tired?" he asked.

Louis had worried very little about his wife's comfort during these years. And since they had moved to Vailima he had not backed her up in her quarrels with Belle, or in her constant sulkiness. But now he would do anything to help her find peace of mind.

He enveloped her with care and worried about her constantly. He was afraid that she would do too much, that she would exhaust herself. The organization of today's celebration, the heaps of chickens, piglets, marinades of fish, the preparation of the kava, were certainly Fanny's work.

"No, I'm not," she answered. "Are you?"

"I am getting old . . ."

She laughed: "We'll see about that!"

"I have written too many books," he sighed. "And the best are behind me!"

Disengaging herself violently, she jumped in: "What nonsense are you talking? I've never heard anything as fine as what you read us yesterday! . . . *Weir of Hermiston* is your masterpiece!"

"If I could begin all over again, I would redo all my women protagonists . . . You see, the worst thing about our education is that Christian morality condemns and denies sexuality. I suppose I couldn't have been freer than my generation . . . But I'm sorry that my female characters have been so uninteresting, if only—"

"But that's not true! Your two Kristies in *Weir* couldn't be more complex . . . various . . . alive!"

An expression of happiness relaxed Robert Louis Stevenson's features: They had signed a peace treaty. She had finally reconciled herself to the idea that Belle could work with him . . . This evening, they both knew how much Louis needed Fanny's approval and criticism.

"One question haunts me and won't go away," he went on. "I wonder if I have done anything at all good, and who could tell me? And why should I wish to know? In so little time, I and my books will have ceased to exist. My writing will be as dead as I am. And yet . . . and yet, one would like to leave an image for a few years upon men's minds . . ."

They crossed the grass and sat down on the cold, damp steps of the porch. Where was this new fatigue coming from? Should she distract him from this sadness he mistook for serenity? How could she shake him from this strange torpor? Sadness, illness—these things were not new to him. But until now his respiratory problems, his fear of dying, all his sufferings had belonged to him. They required less imagination, less effort, less compassion than this struggle he had waged in the past year to release his beloved wife from the despair to which he had perhaps contributed. Had he reached the limits of himself, had he touched the bottom of his own pain by plunging into the depths of Fanny's despair? Certainly he seemed in full possession of his faculties. And yet . . .

"You have worked too hard these past years," she concluded solicitously.

"But what talent I had, Fanny, was for work! My success has been due to my really remarkable industry—to developing the little I had in me to the extreme limit . . . How many volumes have I written in all? Twenty-two? Twenty-five?"

"Baxter will tell us that when he brings the first volumes of your complete works," she commented. "He must be sailing from Liverpool now."

"It was at his wedding that I first dreamed of having you by my side . . . Poor Charles . . . That day, I understood how much I wanted you to be my wife."

They were both thinking of the lawyer who had just lost his wife in Edinburgh. Rumor had it that Baxter had taken to drink.

"Of all my friends, he is the only one I still feel close to, the only one I would never have imagined coming here! As I get older, things lose much of their meaning . . . Like Baxter's wife, I should have died young."

"You still might," she said ironically.

She brushed off a mosquito, and leaning over the lamp, she blew out the candles lighting the stairway. Their faceless silhouettes were cut in half like two Balinese shadow puppets against the golden windows of the house. Louis sighed and looked at the black mass of Mount Vaea. Not a sound. Even the bats had stopped beating their wings between the leaves of the trees. Only the waterfall was murmuring, and the eternal surf breaking against the coral reef.

"Do you remember your doubts when Mataafa was exiled?" he asked. "You reproached me for interferring in Samoa's affairs? You said we were salving our conscience at the natives' expense. You were angry at me for taking responsibilities I couldn't assume, for playing a part I couldn't fulfill . . . The more time goes by, the more I think you were right. But what should I have done? Left the consuls to wreak their havoc? Left them to pillage Samoa with their mindless greed? What should I have done?" he repeated. "Sat still and watched the natives blown into the Upolu sky when the consuls dynamited their prisons? I thought I had acted well . . . Yet you were right . . . Our weaknesses are invincible, and our virtues sterile . . . The efforts we insist on making to behave decently are doomed to failure. Whatever we do, at sunset the battle turns strongly to our disadvantage . . . Ultimately, existence is splendid because it is desperate . . ."

She hated these words that did not belong to Louis, whose joy of life and optimism she had admired for twenty years. When he spoke these terrible words on the human condition, she refused to hear.

Was that what Louis thought when he closed his lips on the blood filling his mouth? Was that what he thought when he frantically cleared the bush at Vailima?

"*We* are not the ones in pursuit of an unattainable ideal, Fanny, it comes stalking us. The desire for the good pursues us, we cannot escape it . . ."

"Quiet," she murmured. "When you start philosophizing, I lose you. And without you, I do not exist . . . Without you, Louis, I am nothing."

"That, Fanny," he said gaily, "that is only a hypothesis . . . The sure thing, the only sure thing, is that without you I would not have lived long enough to publish a single book. You are responsible for the very air I breathe. I owe you my life."

She leaned against him, he took her in his arms. They sat quietly like this, the two of them, in the sweetness and peace that enveloped Vailima.

Monday, December 3, 1894

5 A.M.—It was raining. Sosimo, carrying a tray, knocked at the door to the study. This was the routine. He brought a cup of tea and two pieces of toast. Lying in bed beneath the lamp light, Robert Louis Stevenson was making notes for the work he would soon dictate to Belle.

6 A.M.—Daybreak. Breakfast in the big hall. Austin had come from his school in New Zealand for the summer vacation.

7 A.M.—Everyone went off to work.

Lloyd typed up the memos he would post on the bulletin board. On the big table in the hall Belle was supervising the polishing of the lamps, all fifty of them, which had to be taken apart piece by piece. At the bottom of the garden, Fanny shut herself up in her laboratory. She was distilling perfumes.

9 A.M.—Belle went up to Louis's room to take dictation. He was working on a big Scottish novel that took him far from exile and the Pacific. He considered *Weir of Hermiston* to be his masterpiece.

11 A.M.—Louis interrupted the writing of Chapter 9 in order to answer the letters delivered on Sunday by the monthly mail boat. Fanny entered the study. She wore the febrile expression she had on her bad days. Louis feared a relapse of her illness. He tried to distract her. She said that she could not work, that for two days now she'd had a terrible presentiment that something was about to happen. She did not know what. She did not know to whom. She dreaded some danger to Graham Balfour, who had just gone to sea on a shabby trading ship. He wanted to visit the islands, as the Stevensons had done earlier. She withdrew. She said that she would send Sosimo for news at the port.

12 NOON—The conch shell blew announcing lunch. Fanny was silent. She did not touch her food. At dessert, Sosimo appeared in the hall. He announced that there was no talk of shipwreck in Apia. Louis teased Fanny. He gently mocked her childishness. He hoped to shake her fear. He only managed to push her deeper into her dark mood. At coffee, she slipped off.

2 P.M.—Louis crossed the grass. He found her at the bottom of the garden. Side by side they walked back together toward the house. "I can't help it," she apologized in a small voice, "I know, I sense that something terrible is threatening someone we love. Where, who? One of us is in danger. My heart is so heavy and my head . . . Let me brood by myself. If we find out that I'm wrong, we'll laugh about it together. And I will take a good dose of calomel to sweeten the bile!" They smiled at each other and went their separate ways.

3 P.M.—Louis went back up to his study. Fanny returned to her perfumes.

6 P.M.—Louis whistled softly as he descended the stairs. He found Fanny sitting at a table under the veranda, making something for the evening meal. She had set out a dozen ingredients, the bottles and bowls necessary for the preparation of her "Vailima mayonnaise." This was the specialty of the house and Louis's delight.

6:30 P.M.—Lloyd came back up from Apia. He stopped to chat with them, and then repaired to his bungalow to wash up and change. Standing behind Fanny's chair, Louis murmured in her ear: "Would Madam like a tall, handsome man to give her a hand?" The two of them leaned over the salad bowl. One beat the mayonnaise, while the other slowly poured in the oil and lemon juice. Their heads touched. They did not speak. Louis suddenly banged the bottle of oil down on the table. "What pain!" He was holding his forehead. He tried to stand up. "Do I seem strange?" "No!" she shouted, lying. She had dropped the spoon and rushed to him. He fell to his knees. Sosimo caught him. Together they carried him into the shade. They brought his grandfather's big armchair. "My head," he murmured, "my head!" She sat him down. He lost consciousness. She slapped him, she called to him. She opened his shirt. She rubbed his arms, his chest. In a nearly inaudible voice she ordered brandy, hot water, and cold linen. His eyes were popping. His breath was coming in ragged gasps. She fanned him, she called to him over and over: "Louis!" Her cry attracted Belle and Aunt Maggy. She moistened his lips. She wiped his forehead. She unlaced his boots. "Go fetch Lloyd," she ordered.

Lloyd ran across the grass. He had seen Louis fall into the armchair. Fanny was on her knees, Belle and Aunt Maggy were standing, very pale.

"Funk!" she murmured. "Quickly!"

Lloyd saddled up the fastest mare. He galloped full speed down the Road of the Loving Heart between the coconut trees along the Weber Road. He rode across town.

"I have no mount," the doctor apologized.

"Take mine."

Funk went off at a trot. Lloyd ran behind. At the Tivoli Hotel he stole a horse right in front of its owner and set off at a gallop.

Fanny had a camp bed brought down to the hall. Louis was stretched out on it. He was breathing painfully. His face was red and congested, with only the whites of his eyes showing. The servants were seated in a half-circle around him. Talolo and Sosimo kept one knee on the ground, ready to obey the slightest order. "A stroke"—the news spread by word of mouth. The Rev. Mr. Clarke came up from the mission. He had been the first to see Louis and Fanny disembark at the port of Apia. He had taken them for wandering players.

Fanny, leaning over Louis, held his hand and took his pulse.

Second by second the rhythm slowed. Funk entered. Fanny drew back. Funk listened to his chest. Fanny came forward. Funk stood up: "A blood clot in the brain . . . There is nothing more to do."

At 8:10 P.M. on the evening of December 3, 1894, Robert Louis Stevenson died.

Fanny was standing in the great hall, at the foot of the big stairway, a small, upright figure cold as marble. She did not shed a single tear. "Without you," she had said, "I am nothing."

"He must be buried tomorrow before 3 P.M.," Dr. Funk murmured in Lloyd's ear as he was leaving.

Lloyd, staring at the summit of Mount Vaea, did not react. The doctor insisted: "Before 3 P.M. . . . because of the humidity . . . it would be a disaster . . ."

"Impossible!" Lloyd said. "I need at least three days. How can I have a trail cleared through that jungle in one night? It's a superhuman task!" 'I want to be buried up there,' Louis used to say. But out of superstition I had always refused to have the path made. And now . . ."

"Before 3 P.M. tomorrow," Funk repeated.

Again it was Fanny who summoned the energy needed to honor the final wishes of the man she loved. She sent messengers to the eighteen chiefs, her friends, the natives who had built the Road of the Loving Heart.

"But it will take at least two hundred men!" Lloyd exclaimed.

"You'll get them."

"But what about tools? Even if the chiefs gather all the *matais* together, all the able-bodied men, all the young people from their villages, even if they come before dawn, where would we find the hachets, the machetes, the knives, the levers, the picks and axes?"

"Louis's last wish must be respected . . . Go down to Apia, make them open all the stores. Let Moors and the others turn out their warehouses. Take Talolo and Sosimo with you. Knock on the doors of all the Whites and come back here with the tools the chiefs will need."

"But no one has ever gone to the top of this mountain. What are we going to find there?"

"Louis has gone there . . . The Samoans will follow him."

"But it's so steep, someone could fall forty feet in a straight line. The rains must have made the slopes muddy. And it's so dark . . ."

The only sounds we heard through the night, Belle remembered, *were the chopping of trees on the hillside, the low murmur of native voices responding.*

Dawn came heavy and hot. The air was stagnant. Hundreds of natives were still at work. Each chief had a team, each man had a little piece of the mountain. The mist descended slowly from the treetops to settle on the small trench of earth. Breathing became difficult. They carried on.

The lamps went out in the great hall. There was not a tear, not a cry, not a wail of lamentation. Sosimo murmured a prayer mingling Latin with the Samoan language. Fanny slowly wiped Louis's body with a scented oil. She gently rubbed that hollow chest, those thin arms, the long delicate legs. "To die with my boots on," he had said. She dressed him as he would have dressed for dinner that evening: a white shirt, brown trousers, a wide indigo belt. She also put on his black velvet jacket so familiar to her over the years in Grez, Paris, Hyères, and Bournemouth.

She placed his hands together on his chest. The simple silver wedding ring he had bought the morning of their marriage shone on his finger. Over this dormant body she slowly draped the Union Jack to which he had been so attached since his exile.

The chiefs came from everywhere. They brought necklaces of flowers and precious mats. One by one they placed the garlands and mats on the bed. Exhausted by the night, they sank into prayer. Men and women, members of Tusitala's clan, softly intoned the psalms and canticles. These hymns washed over the silent crowd gathered beneath the veranda.

At one o'clock in the afternoon, six Samoans lifted the coffin onto their shoulders. They crossed the wide lawn and threaded their way through the narrow passage. Sixty natives and nineteen Whites fell into step single file. The ascent would be so rough that many would have to stop on the trail. Groups of young men, six at a time, took turns carrying the coffin from hillock to hillock along the entire climb.

The procession would take more than two hours to reach the platform at the summit where Lloyd had dug the grave. His Samoan friends had fulfilled Tusitala's last wish. And no one who hasn't scaled this impenetrable mountain can appreciate the magnitude of that task.

Beneath the funeral cloths, sand, and flowers, facing the Pacific, Robert Louis Stevenson was laid to rest.

A few days later, Austin recalled, *I surprised my grandmother standing still in a ray of moonlight beneath the veranda. Her small face was lifted toward Mount Vaea.*

The suddenness, the betrayal of this death threatened Fanny with annihilation. For nineteen years she had fought against the threat of hemorrhage. For nineteen years she had protected Louis from the slightest draft, she had hunted down germs and microbes . . . She thought she had won the battle in Samoa and triumphed over illness and poverty. But fate had betrayed her. It was not her old enemy, tuberculosis, that had killed Stevenson, but something new and entirely unpredictable: an anuerism. *After all these years of preparation*, she wrote to Colvin, . . . *I was not ready when the time came. That very day, I had said to him, "I am not a coward; for a woman I am brave." Vain words; where is my courage now?*

Vailima V—January 1895–September 1897

Slouched in her big leather armchair, she had her eyes fixed on the hearth. The fire was dying. The chimney, the only chimney in the Pacific, was smoking. A candle shed its murky light on the long mahogany table. On this very table the silver of Heriot Row had glowed, and the four glasses of the Stevenson crystal sparkled at each place. God knows why the image of those glasses danced before her eyes. Less than three months earlier, at the last party at Vailima, the table had sparkled with golden sherry, purple madeira, violet port, crimson Bordeaux. What sweetness, what peace . . . Thanksgiving evening, Louis had received all of Fanny's fellow citizens, the American colony of Samoa. They had shared the traditional turkey in honor of the first immigrants to the New World. She could still see him standing there as he raised his glass, turning toward Austin's radiant little face; she could hear his warm, lilting voice proclaim: "Vailima is blessed—there is a child in the house!"

The downpour had stopped. The fire was dead. She did not move. Should she stay to welcome him when he came home? Should she go up to sleep? Go out? A feeling of infinite isolation enclosed her in this hall where everything spoke of him. Why should she open her eyes? She knew that behind her, in the wavering candle flame, stood the Sargent portrait of Louis walking and stroking his mustache. He was about to speak to her. He would tell her what he had kept repeating when she was ill, that doubts and conflicts were not pathological states, on the contrary, they were the essence of a human life. She was trying to be reasonable. Was his death the result of their truce in these last months, the absence of conflict between them? Was it because they had found peace at Vailima that Louis had left her? Fanny felt as though her head was full of cotton wool, and the skein of her thoughts kept unraveling. Finally she got up. She crossed the great hall and opened the sliding door. The current of air snuffed out the flame. She looked at the mountain. The night was very dark. Behind the veil of mist, the stars twinkled, pale and moist. With a peevish vigilance, a relentless curiosity, she scrutinized the peak. She felt she was floating like a ghost over the lawn, crossing the garden, and taking the trail up the mountain. Other solitary women hurried after her. A long line of identical women appeared in the bush . . . then disappeared. Their absence disturbed her. She was swept by a wave of anguish. She left the great hall, passed along the veranda and climbed the stairs leading to the study. Every step spoke to her of Louis. She heard him, she felt him near her. She wanted him so badly she was nearly sick. When she reached the landing, she stopped to catch her breath. His long hands had closed around the railing; his familiar voice had described this landscape, the resemblance between these phosphorescent hills and the valleys of Scotland. She passed Belle's room. She glimpsed her daughter in her nightgown, brushing her hair with that unflagging gesture. Belle was so proud of her wavy black hair, so long it reached her knees. But since December, she had been losing it by the handful. Between the trees, at the foot of the mountain, Lloyd's window shone brightly in the night. Charles Baxter, who had been in Suez when he learned of Louis's death, was keeping the young man sad company. Lloyd spoke very little. He had begun to cough, and Dr. Funk feared for his lungs. This was an old story: shortly after Hervey's death, Lloyd's pulmonary weakness had sent them to Grez.

Now, in two months he had lost over twenty pounds. Baxter and Graham Balfour would take him along when they went back through San Francisco. On the ground floor, Aunt Maggy's pretty green room, which Fanny had decorated with such care, stood dark and empty. The old lady had gone back to her sister's in Scotland. In the family Bible, Margaret Stevenson had written, beneath the dates of her son's birth and marriage: . . . *Died suddenly of apoplexy at Vailima, Samoa . . . and I am left alone and desolate.*

Fanny walked carefully along the balcony of the upper floor. From the *fales* below drifted the sounds of evening prayers. How would she manage at Vailima with all those mouths to feed? Without Louis and Louis's talent, how would she pay for the services of a dozen native house servants? Ten days after the burial, Fanny had been forced to lay off the plantation workers . . . How long had the Stevensons been living in Samoa? Four years? It seemed a century, and yet what was four years in the life of a cocoa tree?

She let herself into Louis's study by the outer door. The humidity had swollen the bookshelves, the wood was cracking. The familiar odor of books, the two red hibiscus that Sosimo continued to place each morning on his writing table, everything seemed to await his presence. He was going to come home. And she, she was going to wake up . . . She stretched out on the couch where he used to make his notes; she leaned against the wall where he used to lean, and closed her eyes. To sleep! When she awoke, Louis would have joined her once more, and Fanny would again belong to the proud world of Vailima. But she could not manage to sleep, she would not wake from this nightmare.

At first Belle was afraid. Through the glass of the closed door she thought she saw Louis lying on his bed, the way she used to find him when she came to take dictation. He would jump to his feet, and while he walked and gestured, his actor's voice taking the parts of all the characters in his books, the ideas would flow and the work would come to life.

But the figure did not move when Belle opened the door. Raising her lamp, she recognized Fanny. Her eyes were closed, her face pinched by suffering, her features and mouth a deadly pallor. She was an old woman. For the first time Belle was struck by the idea that her mother could die. That dry, huddled little body, those ravaged features belonged to a woman at the end of her days. It was heart-wrenching. Fanny's prodigious energy after Louis's death, the dizzying silence of her anguish, had all fed the idea of her immortality. Now Belle recognized that she was going to lose her mother. Soon Fanny would die as well.

As the young woman stood transfixed before the small, still form, Fanny opened her eyes and stared at her with that absent expression she had worn since that terrible Monday in December.

"I didn't hear you," she murmured with difficulty. "Aren't you asleep?"

Standing in her long nightgown, Belle shook her head and placed the lamp on the dresser. The room was huge and all the walls were lined with books. They both sensed Louis's presence, his thin figure walking back and forth from wall to wall.

Fanny raised herself up on her elbows and said: "Come here."

Belle stepped forward. She remained standing, leaning over that stunted body defeated by life.

"I would like to ask you something . . ." Fanny began. Her dark gaze wandered through the window and was lost in the shadow of the tall pine tree standing unencumbered on the grass.

"I would like to ask you . . . if you could forgive me."

Surprised, Belle straightened up. "Me?"

"You."

"Good Lord, for what?"

Their words seemed to take an endless amount of time to assemble themselves in Fanny's mind. But suddenly she gathered her thoughts and murmured: ". . . to forgive me for . . . my jealousy. I made your life hell here. All the trouble I gave you, you and Louis . . ."

She curled up in the corner. She was assailed by a thousand regrets, a thousand moments of remorse. Like a child traumatized by fear and shame, she seemed to anticipate the slightest sound. "Perhaps my quarreling and my attacks brought on his death . . ." She opened her eyes wide at the thought, and recoiled again: "Did I end up killing him?"

"Oh Mama, never think that!"

The two women held each other, and for the first time, together, they wept.

*
**

In the large empty house in the heart of the bush, two women remained alone together. One divorced, the other widowed, they would not leave each other again. They spoke very little and worked hard, carrying on the task they had begun. They tried to maintain the plantation Louis had loved. They avoided speaking of the deceased. They also avoided any mention of the future. They planted, they sewed, they cooked.

Until April 1895, Fanny and Belle would battle storms and weeds, silence and solitude. In the spring Belle cut her hair, which had continued to fall out. Fanny suffered from paralyzing gall stones. Dr. Funk strongly advised a change of air. So they left for a rest in Honolulu, where Belle had been so happy. But in Honolulu, too, everything they had known was gone.

The missionary party had overthrown the party of the king. Kalakaua was dead. His sister, Queen Liliuokalani, was living as a recluse under the surveillance of American officers. The United States was going to annex Hawaii. Fanny wandered on the beach at Waikiki.

Everything is different, everything is the same. Everything here reminds me of Louis, and I do not think there is one moment that I am not thinking of him. People say: "What a comfort his great name must be to you!" It is a pride to me, but not a comfort; I would rather have my Louis here with me, poor and unknown. And I do not like to have my friends offer me their sympathy . . . It gives me a sharp shock when I hear him spoken of as dead. He is not dead to me—I cannot think it nor feel it. He is only waiting, I seem to feel, somewhere near at hand.

They went on to San Francisco. Judge Timothy Rearden had just died. The banker John Lloyd had married a woman from Boston who refused to receive Fanny. He took her business affairs in hand nonetheless. She stayed with her old friend, Dora Williams, who had taken up spiritualism and participated in seances to communicate with her dead husband, Virgil. Fanny, too, became enthralled with levitating tables and speaking with the dead.

And yet this time she was not in danger of losing her mind. There was no attack, no relapse during this terrible period of mourning. Her mental equilibrium seemed more solid than ever. And she was no longer suffering physically. In San Francisco, her health even seemed to return. If she had no taste for anything and felt mired in boredom, she had stopped being afraid. The disaster she had dreaded for twenty years had finally happened. And her unbearable fear of losing Robert Louis Stevenson had died with him.

In her misery, Fanny relaxed. In some obscure way, the loss of Louis seemed to reassure her. Immutable in death, he finally belonged to her.

I want to talk with you of those people, Henry James wrote to Mrs. Sitwell, *who are very touching and interesting to me: Fanny S. so fine, in her way . . . She is like an old grizzled lioness—or resigned captive South-sea Chieftainess.*

Fanny only appeared to be resigned.

In California, Lloyd fell in love. He had suffered a nervous breakdown and almost died of sorrow the previous spring. One year after the loss of the man who had been his father, brother, and partner, he was caught by a young twenty-five-year-old teacher. Bold and well read, she taught in the mission schools of New Mexico. Her name was Katharine Durham.

Like all the Katharines she met, this one would not make Fanny's life easy. Beneath her solidity and genteel manners, Katharine hid a lust for power even more frenzied than her mother-in-law's, and a need to attract attention. More intellectual than Fanny, she lacked Fanny's generosity, charm, and finesse. Lloyd married in Honolulu on April 9, 1896.

At the end of a year's absence, Mrs. Robert Louis Stevenson welcomed Belle and Austin, Lloyd and Katharine back to Samoa. Fanny was exultant: With all these young people in the house, Vailima would be revived! This time, her famous intuition did not warn her that she was taking in a rival who would poison her relations with the white community of Apia, sow discord with her neighbors, and make life on the plantation pure hell.

When Katharine Durham Osbourne plunged into meditation on the top of Mount Vaea, she was struck by a revelation: No one here really understood Robert Louis Stevenson! Fanny, Belle, and Lloyd were betraying his memory and his work. *"Louis's favourite flower was the carnation"* [said Fanny] . . . *but if she said it was the carnation I knew it was some other flower.* Katharine had not known Stevenson—but never mind! She, the last Mrs. Osbourne, was the sole repository of the great author's literary testament.

Imbued with this certainty, she would publish articles, write books, and give lectures whose pathologically obstinate purpose was to discredit Fanny's influence on her hero. *Of course the "Vandegrifter" fascinated Louis in the first place,* Katharine wrote. ... *Fanny—I admit—had the very powerful fascination of the gypsy for the opposite sex. And her willfulness, daring, and love of sensation attracted by contrast some devoted, duty-ridden civilized people ... But looking back on my own life, why, Fanny Vandegrift's experiences couldn't hold a candle to all the adventure and romance of an order that could shame no one, which my life had given me. And as Stevenson said, "I am not dead yet." ... Ultimately Mrs. Stevenson never outgrew childhood ... and it seemed to me that she belonged to the childhood of the race ... in some dark-skinned peoples ... I do not think she was mad, but of the year 10,000 B.C.*

Katharine Durham's ill-natured gossip would spawn literary echoes for the next thirty years. Her relentlessness and her neurosis would project the image of Mrs. Robert Louis Stevenson as a wife both vulgar and prudish.

Fanny would not breathe a word of their conflicts. She maintained a lofty silence. With her customary efficiency, she took her revenge by seizing her daughter-in-law's books from the publishers and humiliating her in a paragraph of her will, which was reprinted in the *Pall Mall* magazine in London and in *The New York Times* after her death: *To Katharine Durham Osbourne, of incredible ferocity, who lived on my bounty for many years, at the same time pursuing me with malicious slander, I leave five dollars.*

The mordant humor of these few lines is beautifully characteristic. *A violent friend,* Louis had written of Fanny, *a brimstone enemy* ... And clever as well. This will, in which Katharine figures, could not be contested by Lloyd's wife since she had not been forgotten.

Waiting for posthumous vengeance, however, Fanny was living once again under terrible pressure; and without Louis, life at Vailima was anarchy. It was also a financial sinkhole. As a widow, Mrs. Stevenson no longer had the means to support Lloyd and his family, Belle, Austin, and the twenty natives she needed to employ to fight against the forest, the trees, the lianas and roots that invaded all their crops.

And then, her heart was no longer in it.

In Edinburgh, Aunt Maggy had just died. She had been only ten years older than Fanny, who now remained the sole heir to the Stevenson legacy. Colvin was engaged in the task of writing his friend's biography, but left to his own devices, he did not work. Charles Baxter, on the other hand, had taken it upon himself to publish a posthumous work of Louis's that Fanny judged unworthy of his talent. Readers were at risk of forgetting or misjudging Robert Louis Stevenson, unless "the Vandegrifter" stepped in.

In order to protect his work, to celebrate his genius so that Louis might continue to live beyond death, Fanny would again take up arms. She would return to England and meet those people she had sworn never to see again, *the fiends disguised as friends*. She would fight with Baxter to get him to cut *The Fables* out of the Complete Works. And she would fight with Colvin, pushing him to write the *Life of Stevenson. One thing always in my mind is the* Life *... and you are the only one fit for the work, and as you say it will be a great work. Aside from all else, there have been so few lives of such absorbing interest as Louis's. Even leaving literature out of the question ...*

She would breathe down Colvin's neck for two years until their final break. Ultimately, she would relieve him of the project and entrust it to Graham Balfour, whom Belle had in been love with, and whom Louis had charged with sorting his letters and papers.

Fanny's choice, she thought, respected Stevenson's wishes. Balfour was the only person who had an intimate knowledge of his cousin's family history, the only person who had shared his life at Vailima. He knew all its secrets ... And his vision corresponded to Fanny's. He told the story the way she wanted to hear it. There is no mention of the quarrel with Henley or of Mrs. Stevenson's serious mental illness; but Louis's courage, his generosity, and his genius elevate him to the rank of hero. Graham Balfour portrays the poet who had compelled Fanny Osbourne's respect at Grez, and won her love.

This version, Mrs. Stevenson's version, incurred Henley's wrath. In November 1901, in *Pall Mall* magazine, he lashes out at the biography, at Balfour, and at Stevenson. Clearly, Fanny was his real target: *Here we find ourselves*, he writes spitefully, *with the last letters of the great man and the judgment of Mr. Balfour: Stevenson an angel come from heaven. For my part, I refuse to recognize him in this nauseating portrait ... If my objections give the reader the impression that my vision of Robert Louis Stevenson is strictly personal, I apologize to him for not taking more interest in a seraph in chocolate, this barley-sugar of a real man. His best role, the most interesting part of Stevenson's life, will never be written—not even by me ... I hear his inexhaustible generosity vaunted everywhere, and I myself remember a few examples of quite different behavior ... A final word: I read on every page that we must admire "R.L.S." because he was a condemned man, and yet despite his illness he chose to live his life. Are we not all condemned and do we not all live our lives? That a man writes some fine pages at death's door does not make him a hero.*

For the first time, Fanny shrugged her shoulders: *Henley must have been drunk when he wrote those pages.* She refused to let this stop her. But she never forgot, and she never forgave Henley for declining Louis's most precious memento, the Union Jack that had flown over the *Casco* and covered his remains on the morning of December 4, 1894. Overcoming her own bitterness, Fanny had sent it to Henley as Louis would have wished. Henley remained unmoved. Well, she thought, it couldn't be helped. Never mind. Impatient to pursue her quest, untiring in her efforts, Mrs. Robert Louis Stevenson had recovered her reason to live.

She was about to leave Samoa forever. She had sold Vailima for a pittance, a fifth of what the plantation had cost them, to a German merchant, a former furrier from Vladivostok. But she had kept the summit of a mountain and the long, winding path that led to it. These and a tombstone would remain in her possession.

On that morning of September 7, 1897, seven years to the day after her arrival, Fanny inhaled for the last time that scent of vanilla, wood smoke, and lemon balm—the perfume of Samoa. One last time she went down the Road of the Loving Heart. All her native friends accompanied her. From the steamer she would continue to watch their narrow canoes laden with flowers dancing in the port of Apia. She would also see, behind the sleepy little town, the red roofs of Vailima and the wooded peak of Mount Vaea.

She has such extraordinary recuperative power, Louis had written, *that I do hope for the best.*

Epilogue

Fanny

SAN FRANCISCO—1903–1914

"Scandalous . . . shocking . . . sick . . . I don't dare go out anymore . . . How can my sons show their faces in town?"

This was how Mrs. Lloyd Osbourne expressed herself crossing the rooms of the vast house she shared with her mother-in-law. The south wing overlooked all of San Francisco. The view from the northeast wing, Fanny's rooms, plummeted into the Pacific.

Mrs. R. L. Stevenson's citadel still exists at the corner of Hyde and Lombard streets. Do the tourists who climb to the top of the hill each day to lean over the steep, picturesquely crooked street notice this fortress of rose-colored stucco with its flat roof, its wrought-iron porches, and its terraced garden? No guidebook announces that at the turn of the century, behind its thick walls, it housed all the treasures of the man who had made literature synonymous with adventure: the first editions of his works, the souvenirs of his travels, objects from his childhood home in Edinburgh, from Bournemouth, from Vailima. Where do we find the history of this house that withstood both the earthquake and the fire that destroyed San Francisco in 1906? It had a romantic destiny. Eventually it would shelter a Carmelite convent. But while awaiting the eternal silence of the nuns, the rooms echoed with the cries of an outraged daughter-in-law: "Disgusting! He's even younger than my husband . . . He's Austin's age .. the same age as her grandson! Twenty-three. And she is—how old? She admits to sixty, but who knows? How dare she move him in here under her roof, under my

491

roof, that . . . 'secretary,' that free-loader who's going to live off poor Louis's royalties and my sons' inheritance . . . How dare she? This . . . this protégé, this Field isn't even the first!"

The "first" to whom Lloyd's wife was alluding was not called Field, indeed, but Burgess. A young artist, a designer, a man of letters rather well known in San Francisco avant-garde circles for writing nonsense verse, Gelett Burgess had only one fault according to his friends: He was too much of an imitator of the literary tics of his favorite author. He copied all of Robert Louis Stevenson's mannerisms. And when his hero's widow had returned briefly to California from Samoa for the first time, Burgess had moved mountains to be introduced to her. He was thirty, she was fifty-eight. Fascinated by the *curve of her mouth made firm by courage, softened by generosity, by the line of her lips, by her determined chin*, Burgess had courted her. He had been bold enough to propose his own design for the gravestone of his literary master. And Mrs. Stevenson had allowed herself to be seduced by the sobriety of this project. She had it cast in bronze. The two tablets imagined by Gelett Burgess were henceforth sealed into the white tombstone on top of Mount Vaea.

Upon her final return to San Francisco, they had seen each other again. He already considered himself her protégé. She liked to play the patron. Burgess's gaiety, his spirit, his verve, did the rest. He became her lover, the third man in her life.

Their liaison, which I had long doubted, was confirmed by a packet of letters in the collection of the Bancroft Library at the University of California, Berkeley. Fanny's words convey a passionate acknowledgment of pleasure given and received. These are words of love calculated to make the most sceptical reader blush with surprise—or pleasure—at the passion of a man for a woman thirty years his senior.

The adventure was nonetheless short-lived. Gelett Burgess committed the blunder of using his intimacy with Stevenson's widow to sell several articles. She dismissed him. Five years later, her meeting with Edward Salisbury Field, known as Ned, would inaugurate a new era.

Ned Field was twenty-three years old and worked as a journalist for the Hearst newspapers. He was five foot eight inches tall and handsome. His conversation was so full of charm and wit that his famous employer used to have "this bright young man" to dinner.

Like Burgess, Field had a childhood passion for the life and work of Robert Louis Stevenson. Unlike Burgess, his only ambition was to be happy. And contrary to Katharine Durham's innuendos, Field needed neither Mrs. Stevenson's fortune nor her renown. His father was the founder of the Indiana publishing house that would one day become the celebrated Bobbs-Merrill. Field Senior now played a successful role in the Los Angeles real estate market. Two years earlier, he had sent his son to sow his wild oats in Paris. Ned, a pillar of the Bohemian Club, like Sam Osbourne and Timothy Rearden before him, was reputed to be a boon companion. In the Club archives he figures as an active member, popular and very athletic. He had three trump cards sure to please Fanny: a vagabond soul, a literary mind, and a "green thumb." And just the requisite personality to sustain the shock of meeting such a siren. *All who think of her in her last days, must have a picture in their minds of the dainty, lacy, silken prettiness in which she sat enshrined. She was pretty as a young woman, but as she grew older she was beautiful,* her sister Nellie writes. *She kept her spirit young to the last, so that no one could ever think of her as an old woman, and young people always enjoyed her company.*

With her barbarous jewelry, brocades, laces, and velvets, Fanny had indeed rediscovered her former flair. Her amber profile, now deepened by her white curls, her piercing black eyes, her tiny feet shod in red ballerina slippers made her a surprising and seductive sight. She knew it. *Now remember what I tell you,* she advised Belle, *always strike a personal note in your dress, and the way you do your hair; don't look like other people. If you succeed in that you are nowhere; only a plain, little pudgy dark woman. Keep to the slightly oriental, the rather unusual, and you are a houri.*

With a detachment that concealed her abiding timidity, Fanny gathered up all the threads of her existence. Her silence as Sam's lover, her impetuous vitality as Rearden's friend, her passionate devotion as Stevenson's wife. She listened, smiling, to Ned's conversation and presided like a sphinx over the San Francisco avantgarde.

Together, this young man and this shameless old lady built a ranch house in the Santa Cruz mountains, a little hacienda in Mexico, a house—her last—set in a splendid garden a few miles from Santa Barbara. *Building,* she said, *is so exciting.* As for Ned, he enjoyed himself. Every moment with her seemed to him full of charm, whimsy, surprise. So much so that he would not leave her for a single day—unless he could be more help to her elsewhere. For ten years Ned's pleasure would be to share every hour with Mrs. Robert Louis Stevenson. Until the end.

Ned's parents, like Louis's parents a generation before, could not help feeling unsettled by this arrangement. They were sorry to see their son wasting his youth with an aging bohemian lady—distant echoes of an old story. Fanny was well aware of the problem. *I wonder if you have forgotten that I once asked you to send me a photograph of a pretty girl for reasons of state?* she writes to Belle. *Please do so; no one will see it outside of a small circle. It doesn't make any difference whose likeness it is. You could buy one in a shop, and I would send you the money for it. A blonde is preferred. I really think the young man ought to have it. He will only show it once to his family, and then it will be locked up in his trunk. If you send it just direct it to Ned F. and I will understand.*

From rue Ravignan to rue de Douai, in an early Ford which she had imported from New York, Fanny Stevenson sped along the gray pavement of Montmartre. Her scarf floating in the wind, her little hands resting on the tartan traveling rug, she swept past the passage des Panoramas and the Academie Julian. In good company. Her son Lloyd drove, her companion Ned read the map. In their "motoring" costumes—gloves, hats, and goggles on their handsome faces—they crossed France as far as Hyères and Marseille, and came back up through the Cevennes, stopping at Puy, at Monastier where the donkey Modestine, thirty years earlier, had reminded a very young man of "a certain lady." Among the poplars, on the return trip toward Paris, they glimpsed the bridge at Grez, the tower of La Reine Blanche, the little twelfth-century church. But Fanny could not visit the village again, she could not look at the green river.

My plans are vague, she had written to Belle when she left Samoa. *The years ahead of me seem like large empty rooms, with high ceilings and echoes. Not gay, say you, but I was never one for gaiety much—and I may discover a certain grandeur in the emptiness.*

At seventy, Fanny Vandegrift had found something more than grandeur, she had found lightness at last. Compared to her middle years, the end of her life seemed pleasant indeed. But not for a single moment did Fanny give up. In Saint Jean-de-Mer, in Madeira, in Mexico, in London, in Paris she still pursued the same quest, the same dream: to keep Louis alive, to make sure that he continued to exist beyond death, that posterity should acknowledge and celebrate his genius. Now her aim was a new edition of the works of Robert Louis Stevenson. In collaboration with Edward Salisbury Field she was writing a preface, collating, correcting proofs, and supervising the publicity campaign. Together they were working for the immortality of the "Teller of Tales."

On March 25, 1911, she wrote again to Scribner's, her deceased husband's publishers: *With this note I send the introduction of Father Damien . . . I know this thing is about as bad as anything can be. I will try once again. Louis's work was so mixed up with his home life that it is hard to see just where to draw the line between telling enough and yet not too much. I dislike extremely drawing aside the veil to let the public gaze intimately where they have no right to look at all . . .*

She pursued the task tirelessly. Several days before her death, she finished organizing her journal of the voyage aboard the *Janet Nichol*, all her impressions intended to back up Stevenson's work on his great book on the South Seas.

In the middle of February 1914, twenty years after the death of Tusitala, six months before the beginning of the Great War, a strong wind blew through her Santa Barbara garden. The rain swept down in gusts, hammering on the tiles and terraces. The curtain was about to fall on a stage illuminated by the sudden flash of lightning. Dramatic to the end, Fanny died on a dark and storm-lashed day. The last word goes to those who had always loved her passionately, her servants. Her maid wrote to Belle:

Dear Mrs. Strong,
We are all heart broken, it is just too awful to think that our Dear little Madam is gone never to return . . . it really seems cruel that it should happen and you not here, for you devoted all your life and all your time to her, but . . . you can console yourself by thinking that she was surrounded by love and devotion. She was not sick and did not suffer . . .
You know Mr. Field came soon after you left and he has been the sweetest thing to her ever since. It seemed to me he was doubly

sweet just to make up for your being away, and O such a happy time we all had at Palm Springs, the days and evenings seemed too short for all we wanted to do . . .

. . . Sunday afternoon . . . Mr. and Mrs. Walcott and Mr. Gillespie came and spent the afternoon to hear Mr. Field read his new play, and Mrs. Stevenson looked so sweet that afternoon, she wore her long tailed blue satin gown . . and an airy black and white veiling on her head . . . Tuesday . . . evening she read her magazines till about nine o'clock and then Mr. Field played cards with her till 10:30. It . . . rained hard all night. The next morning I went to her room to tend to her as usual and there lay my Dear little Madam unconscious in her bed. I thought at first she had fainted and quickly ran for Mr. Field. He jumped up and put on his Bath robe and went to her while I called Dr. Hurst. It took Dr. Hurst about seven minutes to get here and as soon as he saw her he said it was a stroke, but he seemed to be hopeful, he thought he could pull her through . . . Mr. Field never left the room or either did I only to bring him a cup of coffee that was all the breakfast he would have. He sent a telegram to you and one to Mr. Osbourne. Mrs. Stevenson seemed to be breathing quite natural but she never regained consciousness and at 2 o'clock she just stopped breathing so you see she did not suffer. But O Mrs. Strong we all seemed so helpless, we all loved her so and yet could do nothing. Dr. Hurst worked hard from 8:30 to 2 o'clock and when the end came he cried like a little child, for he loved Mrs. Stevenson very much. It was an awful blow to us all—it was so sudden. This place will never seem the same to William and me, for we loved our little Madam dearly, and it was a pleasure to do anything for her—she was always so gentle and sweet. I adored her from the first time I ever saw her, and will always consider it the greatest pleasure of my life to have had the privilege of waiting upon her.

I remain very affectionately,
Agnes Crowley

And the rain kept falling for days and nights. Lloyd, who arrived from New York, had to spend long hours in trains rerouted by the flood, on roads made impassable by the storm before he could join his mother. Fanny's body would be cremated according to her instructions.

But had she foreseen the sensation that would provide the hottest gossip in San Francisco, make Colvin and his circle livid, and Henry James smile? On August 29, 1914, Belle Strong married Ned Field. She was fifty-six, he was thirty-four.

Were they having an affair while Fanny was still alive? Or had this death sparked new feelings between them? Did they marry out of affection, habit, solitude, or interest? If Belle had impulsively eloped in her first marriage, she'd had ten years to reflect on the second. Was she aware that Ned was seeking to bind himself as closely as possible to the woman he had loved so much, to the woman he had just lost, by marrying her daughter, her double? Forty years younger than Fanny, twenty years younger than Belle, Edward Salisbury Field would find happiness with both generations.

Before they could give themselves over to their newfound happiness, the Fields were haunted by the desire, by the need, to fulfill a last obligation. Namely, to honor Fanny's final wish, something they were prevented from doing by the intrigues of international politics.

Fifteen years earlier, just after Mrs. R. L. Stevenson had left Samoa, the three powers had abrogated the Berlin Treaty to divide up the pie. The United States retreated to Pago Pago on the island of Tutuila. England withdrew from the archipelago in exchange for Germany's renunciation of its claim to Tonga, the Solomon Islands and Niue. Germany had annexed Upolu, Savaii, Manono, and Aponina, henceforth called Western Samoa. The crowning irony was that the Germans had installed Mataafa in place of Laupepa as their puppet. At Fanny's death, World War I had closed the borders of the German colonies to the Anglo-Saxon world.

Another sensational turn of events: As part of Britain's empire, New Zealand took over Western Samoa without much resistance from Germany, which was busy with more serious battles.

The British flag again flew over Vailima. The governor, a Scotsman, put the property at the Fields' disposal. On May 12, 1915, Belle left San Francisco. With her mother's last companion, she was returning to Samoa.

Samoa—June 1915

On the evening of Wednesday, June 23, 1915, it had rained continuously at Vailima, and this downpour had caused Mrs. Ned

Field a good deal of distress. Late in the night Belle had listened
to the winds and she had remembered the past. The morning
dawned cool and sunny, just as she might have wished, more comfortable than the morning December 4, 1894, twenty years earlier.

The funeral ceremony of Mrs. R. L. Stevenson had been organized by her native friends and former servants who had been
spared by war and time. Belle had seen to it that the guests included the chiefs who had built the Road of the Loving Heart, the
200 men who had cleared the path up Mount Vaea in a single
night. From the stone ovens behind the house wafted the sugared
aromas of banana, pineapple, and pork in preparation for the great
feast that the chiefs would give after the funeral.

The bronze urn holding Fanny's ashes sat in the great hall opening onto the veranda overlooking the ocean. Belle, in a long mourning dress, a white tunic in the Samoan style, stood with her arms
open between the two sliding doors. She was watching the coral
reef that glittered beyond the treetops, and the groups of old Samoans who were walking up the lawn, black bands on their left arms,
garlands of red flowers around their necks. From a distance she
could no longer make out whether it was the great chief Tamasese
and Vaaaga, his wife, or the son of the former king Laupepa, or
children of their cook Talolo. "Everything is the same. Everything
is different. I don't recognize anything," she thought. The hibiscus
bushes had disappeared, the tennis courts, her mother's kitchen
garden, her flowers, her precious cocoa plants. The waterfall had
become a dam, and there was now a swimming pool with changing
rooms. "Yet I have returned to Vailima," she repeated to herself.
"I am at Vailima." She didn't believe it. "At Vailima." Her emotions, whose violence she had so dreaded, were muddled and
muted.

Nine o'clock had just struck. The sun was climbing in the sky.
It was time. Ned went to the table still laden with Samoan fabrics
and wreaths of flowers covering the urn, as they had covered the
remains of Tusitala. The procession set off toward the mountain.
The bush closed behind them. They advanced by easy stages. Belle
knew from previous experience that the path was steeper at the
summit, more twisting, more slippery. They would not see the sky
for two hours. But the light filtering through the leaves was hot on
their heads.

The procession zigzagged through lianas, palm trees, and giant roots. They crossed dark clearings and emerald pools. Sudden splashes of light blinded them, bringing them to a halt.

In tropical whites, with his head bare and his face tense, Ned Field, the youngest of the party, walked at its head. Her last companion, he was bringing Fanny Vandegrift to the man she had never stopped loving, carrying her bronze urn with her ashes wrapped in a precious tapa. Immediately behind him came Belle. She carried an unfolded funeral cloth that had once covered Louis's body. Then came the two chiefs of Laupepa's and Tamasese's lineage. Finally, lost from sight between the trees, their torsos wound with garlands of flowers, their hips covered with white *lava lavas*, came the survivors of the Road of the Loving Heart and all of Fanny Stevenson's friends.

After many stops along the way, the procession reached the top of Mount Vaea. There was a flat area, as big as a bedroom, nearly enclosed by the dense, humid bush. In the middle, facing the Pacific, in the constant roar of the coral reef, stood a large white tombstone: HERE RESTS THE TELLER OF TALES.

On the sides of the tomb were inserted the two funeral tablets the young Gelett Burgess had designed: WITHER THOU GOEST, I WILL GO; AND WHERE THOU LODGEST, I WILL LODGE: THY PEOPLE SHALL BE MY PEOPLE, AND THY GOD MY GOD. This was the verse from the Book of Ruth that Margaret Stevenson had chosen for her child's epitaph, which was engraved in the native language on the west side of the tomb, along with the symbol of Samoa, a flowering hibiscus, cast in bronze. To the east, on the side overlooking the luxurious mountains of Tamaaga, the rains, the wind, and time had polished a second inscription: the thistle of Scotland, a name, and the epitaph that Robert Louis Stevenson had written for himself when he thought he was going to die of his first hemorrhage in San Francisco: GLAD DID I LIVE AND GLADLY DIE.

They placed the coffer on the white pedestal among the fabrics and flowers.

The governor of the island read the Anglican service. The native pastor pronounced his funeral oration. And the stonemason who had built the tomb got ready to seal the ashes.

Then, stepping out of the semicircle of praying friends, an old chief came forward and turned toward Belle: "The occasion is too sweet for sadness," he said in Samoan. "They are finally reunited in the earth of their friends, who will cherish their memory. You can depart in peace. Tamaitai is happy: she has found her great love again."

Mrs. Field bowed her head. She felt as though she had lost her mother for the second time. This tomb enclosing the two lovers was pushing her away and rejecting her. For fifty-seven years Belle had accompanied Fanny. They had swept each other along, been parted, and reconciled. They had shared everything, art, adventure, love. They still shared Ned. How could Belle leave her now? How could she go in peace? Belle had lived her entire life through Fanny, but Fanny had lived only through her love for Robert Louis Stevenson. And Belle had not fathomed that secret, despite all her efforts.

The men of Malietoa Laupepa had hoisted onto the summit a third tablet, on which Belle and Ned had engraved the poem Robert Louis Stevenson had composed to the glory of the woman who had never left him and who was about to join him:

> *Teacher, tender comrade, wife*
> *A fellow-farer true through life,*
> *heart-whole and soul-free . . .*

Engraved in bronze, two flowers, the tiger lily and the hibiscus, framed those six anonymous letters, F.V. DE G.S., the initials of the woman who had been Fanny Van de Grift, Fanny Stevenson. Fanny.

What Became of Them

WESTERN SAMOA would remain part of New Zealand until 1961, when it won its independence. Vailima would serve as the official residence of all the heads of government until the cyclone of December 1992, which seriously damaged the house. Three American businessmen, two of whom had been Mormon missionaries on Upolu, obtained a twenty-year lease from the Samoan government on the property for the symbolic price of one coconut per year. They have restored the plantation and turned Vailima into the Robert Louis Stevenson Museum Preservation, which opened on December 5, 1994.

BELLE would delight in the New York theatrical world for nearly a quarter of a century. In the same week she could attend plays written by her brother, her son, and her husband. They would all live comfortably for the rest of their lives. Upon their mother's death, Lloyd would inherit the copyright to Stevenson's work, and his royalties. Belle inherited all of Fanny's houses and possessions, as well as the real estate investments Ned Field had brokered for Mrs. Stevenson through his father. Oil would be discovered on his Los Angeles property in 1920. Belle, the little girl who had grown up among gold seekers and played in the tunnels and on the slag heaps of a mining camp, would become a millionaire at the age of sixty-two. As for her young husband, screenwriter for Mary Pickford and George Cukor, he died as he had lived, partying. The day after Belle's seventy-sixth birthday, Ned died of indigestion at the age of fifty-six. But faithful to his legendary gaiety, he had asked to be buried in colored clothing so as not to depress anyone.

Belle would bury them all: her young husband, her brother, and her son. She did not die until 1953, in full possession of her faculties, at the age of ninety-three.

501

LLOYD OSBOURNE would have two sons from his marriage to Katharine Durham. Despite a childhood torn between mother and grandmother, their loyalty to the two women was unflagging. At the end of a long separation, Lloyd would divorce Katharine in 1914 and marry Ethel Head, a protégée of Fanny. The marriage would last twenty years and end in another divorce.

The wealth he inherited from his mother perhaps explains why Lloyd did not make much of a name for himself in literature. Despite his modest success as a playwright and several charming books, he would not live up to the promise of his literary collaborations with his stepfather.

The First World War surprised him in Grez, the Second in Nice. He was seventy-two. He was living with a twenty-six-year-old French woman, who had just borne him a third son. Lloyd recognized this child, whom he baptized with his father's name: Sam Osbourne. Fleeing the German invasion, he hurried back to the United States. He then brought over his companion and young Sam, who reached New York a few days before Lloyd's death on May 22, 1943. He was seventy-nine years old.

AUSTIN STRONG, his nephew, cosigned with him the first dramatic adaptation of *Treasure Island.* Of all Fanny's descendants, Austin would be the most successful. His grandmother had bequeathed him a taste for the land, and he became a landscape architect, designing Cornwall Park in Auckland, New Zealand. From his "Uncle Louis," a very young grandfather, he inherited a passion for sailboats, eventually becoming commodore of the celebrated Sailing Club of Nantucket. At the age of twenty-five, he abandoned horticulture for literature and threw himself into the theater. His plays were the toast of Broadway until the 1930's. *The Toymaker of Nuremberg* and *Seventh Heaven* would both be made into films several times over. *He has become a splendid young man,* Fanny had written proudly, *quite the opposite in every way of his poor father.*

JOE STRONG returned to San Francisco in 1892. Like his father-in-law Sam Osbourne before him, he remarried, this time happily; again like Sam, he died at the age of forty-six, seven years after his divorce from Belle.

ROBERT ALAN MOWBRAY STEVENSON, "Bob," the first Stevenson to catch Fanny's eye and win her heart, would survive Louis by only six years. He died in April 1900, at the end of an obscure life as a professor of art history at the University of Liverpool. His essays on Velasquez opened the way to modern art criticism. He left a wife and two children in relative poverty. William Ernest Henley organized a collection for their support.

WILLIAM ERNEST HENLEY would survive his article of November 1901 by only two years. The baseness of this attack on the memory of the writer who had been his dearest friend earned him a great deal of criticism. His former cronies, Colvin, Baxter, and Gosse all loudly proclaimed their indignation. His literary analysis of Stevenson's work, however, affected subsequent generations. For many years Robert Louis Stevenson would be relegated to the rank of minor master, a children's author, a *seraph in chocolate, this barley-sugar of a real man.* Until the 1950s he would embody the image of the timorous Victorian writer, though he had vehemently and constantly denounced fear and hypocrisy.

SIDNEY COLVIN, mistreated by Lloyd and Fanny during their battle over the Stevenson biography, wrangled with them for several years. In 1903 he would finally marry Mrs. Sitwell. They lived happily until the 1920's. Just before the publication of Graham Balfour's book, Colvin had published Stevenson's *Letters to his Friends and Family.* Taking care not to hurt anyone, he had suppressed long passages without indicating his cuts. He had glossed over Fanny's breakdown in Samoa. Colvin was the only man in whom Louis had ever confided. Colvin's arbitrary splicing would come to light only in April 1967, in an article that would not hesitate to suggest that Louis's anxiety during his wife's illness and the tension of those terrible months had contributed to his attack on December 3, 1894.

MRS. THOMAS STEVENSON, "Aunt Maggy," moved back to Scotland a few months after Louis's death. She left at Vailima all the furniture and objects from the house on Heriot Row, which she had sold. With her usual discretion, she attended incognito the ceremonies celebrating her son and his work. She died of pneumonia in 1897: *There is Louis . . . I must go,* were her last words.

NOTES
AND
BIBLIOGRAPHY

Notes

Prologue—Ned Field

See the obituary of Edward Salisbury Field, in *The New York Times* and *The Herald Tribune,* September 22, 1936. See The National Encyclopedia of American Biography. Also the Archives of the Lambs Club, the Players Club, and the Bohemian Club. And the list of his works in the general bibliography.

Edward Salisbury Field, twenty-three years old, native of Indianapolis, Indiana, had indeed met "Fanny Stevenson," an old friend of his mother's, in San Francisco in 1903. She was forty years older than he. They spent the next eleven years together. They would live under the same roof, travel, and work together without being apart for a single day. It was Ned Field who would close Mrs. Stevenson's eyes in their house in Santa Barbara, California, on February 18, 1914, at 2:00 P.M. Was he her lover? People said so, and it is likely. But unlike another young admirer of Fanny's, with whom she had exchanged letters that leave no doubt about their relations (see Epilogue), I have not found any letter to prove their sexual intimacy. Ned would marry Belle, and they would both live with the passionate memory of the woman they had both loved.

I
Jacob's Daughter

Indianapolis 1864

On Fanny's youth, see the biography written by her youngest

sister, *The Life of Mrs. Robert Louis Stevenson,* by Nellie Sanchez (Charles Scribner's, New York, 1920).

See also Fanny's unpublished writings on her father, *A Backwoods Childhood* (Centers' Collection, Indianapolis) and the highly detailed account of the Vandegrifts' country house in Hendricks County, *A Tiger Lily Transplanted,* by Lannes McPhetrige, unpublished (Danville Public Library, May 1926).

Letter from New York

What remains of the correspondence between Fanny and her family is preserved in Indianapolis by one of the descendants of Josephine Vandegrift. Twenty or so of these letters were recopied by Mrs. Betty Lane when she was curator of the municipal library of Plainfield, Indiana. Unfortunately, many other letters have been destroyed. I have quoted from two long letters Fanny wrote describing her train trip across the United States during the Civil War.

On life in Indiana during the Civil War, see Meredith Nicholson, *The Hoosiers* (London, Macmillan, 1916).

The Route Through Panama

See Doris Muscatine, *Old San Francisco, Biography of a City* (New York, Putnam, 1975); Dee E. Brown, *Gentle Tamers, Women in the Old West* (New York, Bantam Books, 1974).

I was also aided by the correspondence of Timothy Rearden. In order to reach California, Rearden had also passed through Aspinwall and had to wait a week for the steamer to come to the port of Panama City. Like Fanny, he had embarked on the *Moses Taylor,* but one year earlier, in 1863. Timothy Rearden's letters to his family are preserved in the Bancroft Library, University of California, Berkeley, in the Baeck Collection.

In her marvelous biography, *This Life I've Loved* (New York, Longmans, Green and Co., 1937), Fanny's daughter evokes their crossing of the Isthmus by train and their arrival in San Francisco. Belle Osbourne was only six years old at the time, and her memoirs sometimes contradict what Fanny says in her few letters to her family. I found no trace of Mr. Hill after he had been mentioned several times in the correspondence. Fanny would, however, remain in touch with other passengers, Miss Annie McAlpine and Art and Jenny Hyatt, who would visit her in the spring of 1867 in San Francisco.

Arrival in San Francisco

See Isobel Field, *This Life I've Loved* (*op. cit.*); Nellie Sanchez, *The Life of Mrs. Robert Louis Stevenson* (*op. cit.*). In their books, Fanny's daughter and sister differ on one point: One writes that Sam Osbourne met his family at the boat in San Francisco, the other that he was waiting for them 400 miles away on the Reese River, in Austin camp. I do not think either of these versions is very accurate. On June 17, 1864, Sam was in Austin where he filed a claim, again borrowing $300 to share a concession with two partners, Moses Kirkpatrick and Mr. H. Kurge. But on July 5, his name figures on a list of passengers arriving in Austin by stagecoach from San Francisco, a list published daily by the local paper, *The Reese River Reveille*. So between June 17 and July 5, he had left Austin and returned, both times without Fanny. The date of his return to Austin precedes by several days the landing of the *Moses Taylor* in San Francisco from Panama. I assume that he and Fanny missed each other.

Nevada—1864

I have found nothing on Fanny's first impressions of Nevada. I have therefore recorded my own reactions as I followed in Fanny's footsteps along the Pony Express route, nicknamed even today "The Loneliest Road in America." It certainly deserves its name: 1,966 miles in a straight line across the Great Plains, Wyoming, the Great Salt Desert, and the Sierra Nevada.

There is abundant documentation on the history of Nevada, the gold rushes and silver mines, which can be found in the general bibliography.

II
Sam's Wife

Austin

On Austin, there are two particularly noteworthy books: *The Town that Died Laughing* by Oscar Lewis (Boston, Little, Brown, 1955), and *Austin and the Reese River Mining District,* by Donald Abbe (Reno, University of Nevada Press, 1981).

I have also relied heavily on the *Journals of Alf Doten* (Reno, University of Nevada Press, 1973). Doten was a newspaper reporter who would become editor-in-chief of the *Reese River Reveille* of Austin, which is still published today. I found a stack of copies, unchanged, in the bar of Austin's International Hotel.

The archives of the *Reese River Reveille,* preserved at the Nevada Historical Society in Reno, are an invaluable source of information on the state of the mines, arrivals from the East or from San Francisco, departures, deaths, and marriages. Everything is registered there. Similarly, the census data preserved in Carson City, Nevada, provide a rather precise idea of the state of the population between 1862 and 1864. In the census of 1863, out of 1,168 inhabitants, I counted 44 women. Of these 44 women, 18 were less than 14 years old. Thus, there were 26 grown women for the whole region. A walk through the cemeteries also tells us that the average age of most of those who died there was below twenty-five.

In the *Reese River Reveille* of April 4, 1865, I found an account of the suicide of a certain Benton Van de Grift, employed at the telegraph office in Austin, formerly a postal employee in Indianapolis. I know that he was a cousin of Fanny's on her father's side and that Belle mentions his death in *This Life I've Loved (op. cit.).* She seemed to imply that Benton Van de Grift left Indiana at the same time as Fanny. Despite my research, I could find nothing on him and, for want of information, I had to choose to disregard him altogether. The only thing I'm certain of is that he did not leave Indiana with Sam. In a letter to Jacob Vandegrift, Sam assures him that he will find Benton work in Nevada, manual labor if need be.

He even encourages his father-in-law to embark with Benton, swearing that even if they do not make a fortune, they will not lose anything. In all his letters, Sam tries to convince his wife's family to leave the farm and join him in the West.

The obituary of Benton Van de Grift mentions that he suffered from an *inflammation of the brain* that drove him crazy and pushed him to suicide. An inflammation of the brain—encephalitis—is the illness Fanny would continually complain about in her correspondence.

We also note that the *Reese River Reveille* of April 4, 1865, records Virgil Williams's departure from Austin to San Francisco; he would one day become Fanny's teacher. Had they met in Nevada? Is this simply a coincidence? There is nothing to suggest that their friendship dated from the days in Austin.

For the daily life of women in the West, refer to the general bibliography. See in particular *Gentle Tamers, Women in the Old West,* by Dee Brown (*op. cit.*) and *Women in the West* (Antelope Island Press, 1982). The private journals of Flora Bender, preserved in the National State Historical Society, and of Claire Hewes (library of the University of Nevada) were particularly helpful, as were the autobiographies of E. J. Oulrin, *Mountain Charley* (University of Oklahoma Press, 1968), Melinda Jenkins, *Gambler's Wife* (Huston, Bufflin Co., 1933), and Sarah Royce, *A Frontier Lady* (New Haven, Yale University Press, 1932). Finally, I drew from the article published in the *Overland Monthly* (May 1869), "How we Live in Nevada," by Louise M. Palmer.

See as well *Ten Years in Nevada,* by Mrs. McNair Mathews (Bakers and John, 1880). This Mrs. Mathews is very representative of the mentality of the "respectable women" in the towns of the Far West. Many times her voice is indistinguishable from Fanny's. Reading the autobiographies, letters, and private journals of these pioneer women, I was tremendously impressed by the similarity of their views to Fanny's. Robert Louis Stevenson was not wrong: She remained part of this very distinct social group, the pioneer women of the Old West.

Virginia City

On the history of Virginia City and the Comstock Lode, I relied on the remarkable work of Carl Burgers Glasscock, *The Big Bo-*

nanza (Indianapolis, The Bobbs Merrill Co., 1931). See also *The Comstock Commotion,* by Lucius Beebe (Stanford, Stanford University Press, 1945); *Silver Kings,* by Oscar Lewis (New York, David McKay Co.); *Mark Twain, his Life in Virginia City,* by George William III (Riverside, CA, Three by the River, 1984); *Mark Twain in Virginia City,* by Paul Fatout (Indiana University Press, 1964). *Gold Digger and Silverminers,* by Marion S. Golman (University of Michigan Press, 1981) provides very useful information on the condition of "respectable" women and prostitutes, and their relations with the male population of Virginia City.

For the daily life of Virginia City, see *Ten Years in Nevada,* by Mrs. McNair Mathews (*op. cit.*); *This Life I've Loved,* by Isobel Field, (*op. cit.*).

Three masterpieces by reporters from Virginia City were extraordinarily valuable to me: *The Big Bonanza,* by William Wright (pseudonym Dan de Quille) (New York, Apollo Editions, 1969); *The Journals of Alf Doten* (*op. cit.*); and *Roughing It,* by Mark Twain (Hartford, American Publishing Company, 1872). Their writings share the same sense of humor and energy, a taste for the macabre, and a tendency to exaggeration that feed a sharp sense of realism. Despite its inaccuracies, or rather because of them, *Roughing It* offers a superb rendering of the spirit of the gold miners of the 1860's.

On work in the mines: *The Miners* (New York, Time Life Books, 1975).

I have compared data on the depth of the mine tunnels. As far as I could determine, they did not approach the depth of 300 feet until the 1870's, and not the year that Fanny was living in Virginia City, 1865–1866.

Sam's letter to his father-in-law is preserved in the Silverado Museum in St. Helena, California. For the year 1864–1865, he figures in the Virginia City almanac as Deputy City Clerk, Office #2, Roe Building.

It is true that Fanny left Virginia City for Sacramento after Belle's illness (Dan Centers collection, Indiana). It is also true that during her absence, Sam Osbourne loaned his furniture to one of his mistresses. When she returned, Fanny found the house empty. *If she doesn't give me back my belongings, I will call the police and act on my own. The good woman is half Turk, but even if she were all Turk, she should not have my belongings!* Letter to Jo, Dan Centers collection. (Fanny never dated her letters. Sometimes the correspondent kept the envelope and the postmark is still there.)

On Sam Osbourne's departure, see *This Life I've Loved,* by Isobel Field (*op. cit.*), and *The Life of Mrs. Robert Louis Stevenson* (*op. cit.*).

In March 1866, on the 26th to be precise, a convoy of prospectors left for Montana. Alf Doten notes in his journal: "A convoy of eight wagons left this city this morning for Montana. With 40 to 50 people. Many left on Horseback. This is the largest exodus this city has seen." Sam also left Virginia City for Montana at the end of March 1866. I have deduced that he took part in this convoy, but I cannot be absolutely certain.

Nor can I be certain of the exact date of Fanny's departure for San Francisco. Her letters are dated from Virginia City until November. After that, silence. I only know that during the winter of 1866, the mines in Virginia City were in *borrasca*—had a run of bad luck. In the two preceding years, many refineries had closed. They were systematically repurchased in the name of the Bank of California, by the man who would become the king of the Comstock Lode, William Sharon. The small bankrupt owners fled to San Francisco along with John Lloyd, former miner from Austin, who would one day become president of the bank in which Fanny would later deposit Stevenson's royalties.

San Francisco—1866–1875

Refer to the general bibliography. But four books were particularly helpful to me in describing the San Francisco of Fanny's day: *Americans and the California Dream, 1850–1915* by Kevin Starr (New York, Oxford University Press, 1973); *This Was San Francisco,* by Oscar Lewis (New York, David McKay Co., 1962); *Old San Francisco, Biography of a City,* by Doris Muscatine (*op. cit.*); and *Spectacular San Franciscans* by Julia Cooley Altrocchi (New York, E. P. Dutton, 1944).

Sam's disappearance is discussed in Belle's memoirs, *This Life I've Loved,* and in the biography by Nellie Sanchez, *The Life of Mrs. Robert Louis Stevenson.*

I have found several later allusions to it in a letter from Fanny to her sister Cora, who on December 24, 1874, married Sam Orr, Osbourne's best friend and companion on his Montana escapades.

The length of time they were absent varies, depending on the version, from eight months to two years. Eight months seems more likely, probably between March 1866 and November 1866. At the library in Plainfield, I found a letter from Fanny to Jo, posted from San Francisco and dated May 1867. She writes: *Sam is determined to go back to the East when he can. I am sure we will come back soon.* He must therefore have rejoined his family, and his return, from the tone of the letter, does not seem to have been very recent. *Do you know that Sam will be thirty in a month or two? He is just the same great romping noisy boy that he always was.*

Clayton (Indiana)

This Life I've Loved, by Isobel Field (*op. cit.*), provides a very good description of the Vandegrift house.

I have also relied on the impressive genealogy established by Frederick A. Thomas (son of Jo Vandegrift and her second husband, Benjamin F. Thomas), preserved in the Genealogy Department of the Indiana State University Library (Indianapolis). See also *The People's Guide,* by Hendricks County (Indianapolis Printing Pub., 1874), preserved in the city library of Danville. Last but not least, *A Tiger Lily Transplanted,* by Lannes McPhetrige (*op. cit.*), in which the photos of the house taken in 1926 show us what it was still like eleven years after Fanny's death. Today it remains nearly unchanged. It seemed rather smaller to me than I had imagined it, but very nicely proportioned. The house is still brick, its wooden porch painted white. It is the residence of farmers who cultivate the tree-lined fields.

III
Rearden's Friend

East Oakland

In the beginning of the 1870's, this part of East Oakland was still called Brooklyn. I opted for East Oakland in order to avoid any confusion with New York's Brooklyn.

In the almanac preserved in the Historical Room of the Oakland Public Library, Fanny is mentioned as the wife of Sam Osbourne esq., court reporter in San Francisco. In 1878 she is mentioned at the same address but this time as an artist. Sam is no longer mentioned.

There are numerous descriptions of the East Oakland property. Some are written by Belle, others by Nellie Vandegrift, who lived there with Fanny from 1878 to 1880. Belle's drawings are preserved in the Silverado Museum of St. Helena, California (Album Isobel Field #1), along with several photographs taken by Fanny.

San Francisco School of Design

There is abundant literature on the emergence of an artistic community in the Far West. See in particular *Inventing the Dream: California through the Progressive Era* (New York, Oxford University Press, 1985), a remarkable work by Professor Kevin Starr, who was kind enough to direct me in my research on the San Francisco bohemia of the 1870's and 1880's.

Kevin Starr also introduced me to the Bohemian Club, where he is a member. In the club archives, I found a good amount of information on the personalities of Virgil Williams and Ned Field, Fanny's secretary and last companion.

The works of Virgil Williams and his most talented students are preserved in the Oakland Museum. A nearly complete catalogue of these works can be found in Marjorie Arkelian's book *The Khan Collection of Nineteenth Century Paintings by Artists in California*

515

(The Oakland Museum Art Department, Oakland, 1975). Virgil Williams, Dora Norton Williams, Fanny Osbourne, and Belle Osbourne are mentioned in the book by Edan Milton Hughes, *Artists in California 1786–19540* (San Francisco, Hughes Publishing Co., 1986). I have also relied on the *San Francisco Art Association, Constitution Bylaws, List of Members, and Rules of the School of Design of the San Francisco Art Association* (San Francisco, B. F. Sterett, 1878); Jeanne Van Nostrand, *San Francisco (1866–1906) in Contemporary Paintings, Drawings and Watercolours* (San Francisco Book Club of California, 1975); Edmund Swingelhurst, *The First Hundred Years of Painting in California 1775–1875* (San Francisco, J. Howell Books, 1980); Oscar Lewis, *Bay Window Bohemia,* An Account of the Brilliant Artistic World of Gaslit California (Garden City, NY, Doubleday, 1956).

The Bancroft Library of the University of California, Berkeley, houses Fanny Osbourne's letters to the lawyer Timothy Rearden written between 1875 and 1892. Timothy Rearden would become a judge on the California Supreme Court in 1885. These letters were bequeathed to the library by Timothy Rearden's daughter, Mrs. Baeck. The Baeck Collection contains, among other things, two excellent photographs of Rearden, one of which dates from 1875, the beginning of his correspondence with Fanny Osbourne.

The Bancroft Library also preserves the papers bequeathed by Mrs. Anne Roller Issler, who was curator of the Stevenson Museum in Monterey. Miss Roller Issler wrote her splendid articles in *Robert Louis Stevenson in Monterey* (Pacific Coast Branch of the American Historical Association, University of California Press, Berkeley and Los Angeles, 1965) when she corresponded with Mrs. Baeck about her father, Timothy Rearden.

Mrs. Baeck's letter's are full of specific and touching details concerning Timothy Rearden's personality. She has no great fondness for Fanny and insists that there can be no question of anything romantic in the friendship between her father and "that woman". She is particularly critical of *A Violent Friend* (Garden City, Doubleday, 1968), the excellent book by the second biographer of Mrs. Stevenson, Margaret MacKay. Mrs. Baeck reproaches her for having portrayed Timothy Rearden as a frivolous character. Mrs. Issler tactfully defends Mrs. MacKay's version.

IV
Against the Odds

In order to describe the trip from San Francisco to Antwerp, I have relied on the book by Dee Brown, *Hear That Lonesome Whistle Blow* (New York, Holt, Rinehart and Winston, 1977), which provides an excellent idea of the state of American transportation in 1875.

It is amusing to observe, as well, that in this period France was quite interested in what daily life was like in the United States. In the spring of 1876 Sarah Bernhardt was playing in *L'Americaine*, at the Comedie-Française. From April to August of the same year, *L'Illustration* contains a series, "Notes sur les Etats-Unis," an exhaustive reportage on travel conditions in America. The drawings are full of details on the occupations of the passengers, the furnishings of the compartments and cars for the three classes of travelers.

Antwerp—Paris—Fanny Osbourne's Correspondence

Only the last letter, dated April 1876, in which Fanny tells Timothy Rearden about her son's death, is entirely in her hand. This heartbreaking letter was the reason why I chose to use the direct testimony of her correspondence for the entire first period in Belgium and France. I wanted the reader to discover the art studios for ladies, their Parisian poverty, and Hervey's illness through Fanny Osbourne's eyes and voice. I thought no one could tell the horror of that death better than the mother herself. In order to evoke this period in the life of the Osbournes, I relied on two groups of letters: The first, addressed to Dora Williams, is preserved in archives of the Beinecke Rare Book and Manuscript Library at Yale University; the other group, to Timothy Rearden (Baeck Collection), in the Bancroft Library, University of California, Berkeley. This last group of letters, totaling more than two hundred pages, was an extremely valuable resource. Fanny appears here with all her faults, all her weaknesses, all her humanity. It was a first reading of these letters that prompted me to write this book.

In some cases the letters addressed to the two correspondents were written on the same dates and tell of the same events. To have transcribed them unedited, with all their repetitions and digressions, would have considerably slowed down the narrative. Therefore I chose the paragraph in each letter that seemed to me most revealing, and spliced it together with the liveliest paragraph of the letter addressed to the other correspondent. Thus, the beginning of a letter to Dora is sometimes tacked onto the end of a letter to Rearden on the same subject. If the words do not always belong to Fanny, the vision is hers, and I have tried to render her way of thinking and her voice. I hope by this montage to have come closer to the truth.

Sam's telegrams and Fanny's answers are authentic. They are preserved in the Silverado Museum in St. Helena, California, where I found them in Belle's album. Fanny's daughter had even saved her father's train and ship tickets, as well as the ticket to an opera they saw together in Paris on April 9, 1876, the first performance at the Palais Garnier, *Jeanne d'Arc,* by Mermet.

Despite my efforts, I did not find the letters of Timothy Rearden. From Fanny's reactions in the letters she wrote back to him, sometimes quoting certain lines from her correspondent word for word in the process of defending herself, I imagined what Rearden must have written to her.

To fill in the last gaps in the puzzle, I relied on *This Life I've Loved* (*op. cit.*), by Isobel Field, as well as on the childhood memories of her brother, and the prefaces by Mrs. Robert Louis Stevenson and Lloyd Osbourne to the *Complete Works of Robert Louis Stevenson (London, Tusitala Edition, Heinemann, 1923–24).*

And for the information on little Hervey's grave, see Robert Louis Stevenson's letters to his lawyer and friend, *Stevenson's Letters to Charles Baxter,* edited by Ferguson and Waingrow (New Haven, Yale University Press, 1956).

Grez-sur-Loing

The Hotel Chevillon with its terraced garden still exists on the banks of the Loing. In 1988, the year when I began my research, it was up for sale. It was bought in the summer of 1989 by a Swedish industrialist and turned into a foundation. The Foundation Grez-sur-Loing has been working for months to restore the old building, which is now divided up into single rooms, apartments, ateliers, a library, and a large work room. The Hotel Chevillon will soon welcome a new generation of Swedish artists. To support the foundation's work and make it known to the public, the Swedish Cultural Center in Paris mounted, in 1991, a first exhibition on *L'Ecole de Grez-sur-Loing, une colonie d'artistes nordiques dans l'année 1880*. The paintings, though postdating Fanny's stay by ten years, evoked the gentleness of the Grez landscape, the cosmopolitan atmosphere of the inn, and the gaiety of the young painters. The exhibition catalogue, *L'Art suedois à Grez,* was particularly useful to me.

The reader will find a list of all the artists who stayed at the Hotel Chevillon in the fine monograph by Mme Fernande Sadler, *L'Hotel Chevillon et les artistes de Grez-sur-Loing* (contribution to regional history published by the *Informateur de Seine-et-Marne,* s.d.).

Some paintings are exhibited at the town hall of Grez-sur-Loing, or preserved in its storerooms.

In addition to the Goncourt brothers, who mention Grez and the Hotel Chevillon several times in their *Journal* (Flammarion-Fasquelle, Paris, vol. 2), the painter Will Low, in *A Chronicle of Friendship* (Hodder and Staughton, London, 1908), and the landscape painter Birge Harrison in his long article "Stevenson at Grez" (*The Century Magazine,* December 1916), recall the gaiety that prevailed at Grez. Birge Harrison liked it so much that he bought a house and moved there.

Grez-sur-Loing remained a mythic place in the imagination of all the protagonists. Belle Osbourne, who fell in love there for the first time, continually returns to this period of her life in *This Life I've Loved* (*op. cit.*). Lloyd Osbourne often repeats the story of his first meeting with the man who would become his stepfather. He comes back to it in his preface to the *Complete Works of Robert Louis Stevenson* (*op. cit.*), and in his book *An Intimate Portrait of Robert Louis Stevenson* (Scribner's, New York, 1924). Lloyd Osbourne was once again in Grez, at the home of Birge Harrison, when the First World War was declared.

Robert Louis Stevenson drew much of his inspiration from the forest of Fontainebleau, from Barbizon, and Grez. I have depended on his descriptions to evoke the charm of the artists' colonies he loved so much. Two were particularly helpful to me: "Forest

Notes," first published in *Cornhill* magazine, in May 1876, two months after his meeting with Fanny Osbourne; and a letter to his mother, dated August 1876, in which he describes Grez without being especially charmed by it that day, in *The Letters of Robert Louis Stevenson to his Family and Friends* (edited by Sidney Colvin, Methuen, London, 1901, vol. 1). And of course I drew on his wonderful novel *The Wrecker* (Tusitala edition, *op. cit.*).

For my portrait of Bob Stevenson, whom I felt to be particularly sympathetic, I relied on the letters of W. E. Henley, published in the noteworthy biography by John Connel, *William Ernest Henley* (Constable and Co., London, 1949).

If I had been at all skeptical at the beginning of my research about Bob Stevenson's love for Belle Osbourne, this doubt was dispelled by a letter from Bob to Louis that I discovered preserved in the archives of the Beinecke Library at Yale.

Cernay le Ville, Jan, 11, 1879
. . . As for getting more and more wretched that is true if one has no hope and gets more and more in love every day as I do . . . Belle has broken off with O'Meara. She wrote me . . . in a letter, but that is long ago, and she said how unhappy she had been and that she longed to see me as now she had nobody to love; but what good does that do me. If I had L500–1000 a year I dare say Belle would marry me, but then I haven't . . . I would go through my career moderately content if I saw Belle for 3 hours once a fortnight, even if she lived away in another house with other people . . . If Mrs. Osbourne ever says anything about Belle however uninteresting it may seem . . . let me know at once all about it, will you.

For the first love between Fanny and Louis, I relied on letters from Fanny to Rearden (in the collection cited); letters from Louis to Charles Baxter (*op. cit.*); Louis's letters to Mrs. Sitwell and to Sidney Colvin, *Letters of Robert Louis Stevenson* (*op. cit.*); and especially on two articles published by Robert Louis Stevenson, "On Falling in Love" (*Cornhill* magazines, 1876), and "Truth in Intercourse" (*Cornhill* magazine, 1879), essays informed by a similar philosophy in which Stevenson gives a romantic account of his own experience.

V

A Passionate Kindness

Paris—Second Winter—October 1876–April 1877

For the description of a ladies' art studio during the period of the Impressionists, I relied on the humorous article by Fanny Stevenson's flatmate at 5, rue de Douai, preserved among Timothy Rearden's papers in the Bancroft Library, "A Lady's Studio," by Margaret Wright. See also the two articles by Robert Louis Stevenson published in the *London Magazine* of February 10 and 17, 1877, "In the Latin Quarter: a Ball at Mr. Elsinaire's," and "A Studio of Ladies."

In the first article, Robert Louis Stevenson explicitly describes Belle, whom he calls Belle Bird. Fanny and Belle refer to this article in a letter to Rearden dated April 1877. Rearden had accused them, after reading the article, of superficiality and shallowness.

The wonderful series of caricatures Belle sent to her father, preserved in the archives of the Silverado Museum (St. Helena, California) captures perfectly the atmosphere of the Julian atelier.

I have also relied on the *Journal de Marie Bashkirtseff* (Edition Mazarine, Paris, 1980), in which she describes the Julian studio during just these years.

See also *L'Atelier Julian, 100 ans d'histoire de la peinture*.

For the developing love between Robert Louis Stevenson and Fanny Osbourne, see two superb biographies, one devoted to Robert Louis Stevenson, *Voyage to Windward*, by Mr. J. C. Furnas (Faber and Faber, London, 1952), the other to his wife, *The Violent Friend*, by Mrs. Margaret MacKay (Doubleday, New York, 1968).

To my mind, these books are models of intelligence and scrupulous scholarship. Mr. J. C. Furnas remains to this day the best biographer of Robert Louis Stevenson, with the finest sense of the man and his work. But he does not like Fanny Osbourne. It was to some extent the antipathy of this formidable scholar and splendid writer that made me want to rehabilitate Fanny Osbourne in his eyes.

For the love affair between Frank O'Meara and Belle Osbourne, see *This Life I've Loved* (*op. cit.*). See also Fanny Osbourne's letters to Timothy Rearden (Bancroft Library, Baeck Collection).

On the students at the Atelier Carolus Durand, among them Frank O'Meara, John Singer Sargent, and Robert Alan Mowbray Stevenson, see *A Chronicle of Friendship*, by Will Low (*op. cit.*). On their friends in Grez, and Theodore Robinson in particular, see also the excellent catalogue of the American Museum of Giverny, *Lasting Impressions, American Painters in France 1865–1915* (Terra Foundation of the Arts, 1992).

William Ernest Henley's poem, "A California Girl," belonged to a series entitled *A Gallery of Fair Women* published in the very conservative journal for which he was editor-in-chief, *The London Magazine*. The poem inspired by Fanny appeared in the May issue, 1877. The journal was always in need of articles, and Stevenson was obliged to produce copy for Henley. The two of them once provided enough material for an entire issue singlehandedly. The journal was about to fold by the spring of 1879.

Grez—Second Summer—June–September 1877

The biographers usually indicate that Sam Osbourne came to Paris only upon the death of his son (April 1876). I found evidence of a second trip Sam made to France in the album of photographs and mementos preserved in the Silverado Museum (St. Helena, California). Belle saved the boat ticket and notes the date of her father's arrival in Paris (May 20, 1877), as well as his return passage via Montreal (June 20, 1877). He spent only the first week of June in Grez: Fanny alludes to the message that called him back to San Francisco in two letters written from Grez to Timothy Rearden.

In the Baeck collection, the first of these letters is dated July 1876. I think this must be a mistake. In it, Fanny tells the episode of the strolling players Stevenson invited to stay at the Hotel Chevillon; and there is no question that this episode dates from July 1877. In addition, she tells Rearden that she has been staying with the artists in Grez for *two years*. This confirms my idea that Sam's stay in Grez dated from his second trip.

Louis's correspondence (*Letters to His Family and Friends, op. cit.*) establishes his presence in Edinburgh during the period when Sam was staying in France. I do not believe the two men met at this time. On the other hand, Bob and Sam shared meals at the Chevillon dining table.

I can hear Belle, also, flirting with six Scotchmen at once, all of whose names end in "son," two pairs of brothers and one pair of cousins . . . Fanny writes in this letter which I believe is from July 1877. *One of the Scotchmen, I am sorry to say, has quite lost his head from a story told him by my husband, and we had dreadful times with him; he will go to bed and stay there.* I imagine this is a case of one of Bob's extreme reactions.

For the dialogue between Louis and Fanny, I have quoted in full from some of Stevenson's reflections on love in "Falling in Love" (*op. cit.*) and on truth in human relationships in "Truth in Intercourse" (*op. cit.*).

After Fanny's death, her daughter and her sister, who was also her first biographer, went to great lengths to deny that there was any physical intimacy with Stevenson before their marriage. This was a lost cause. At the same time, many "Stevensonians" claim that they were mutually smitten as early as the summer of 1876, and immediately began an affair. I think both versions are improbable.

It may be difficult to date precisely the moment when Fanny succumbed, but she certainly became Louis's mistress before the spring of 1878. Stevenson, separated from her, shut up in Edinburgh with his parents, wrote at the time to Henley: . . . *I'm a miserable widower, but . . . I keep cheerful . . . And do I not love? and am I not loved? and have I not friends who are the pride of my heart? O, no, I'll have none of your blues; I'll be lonely, dead lonely, for I can't help it; and I'll hate to go to bed where there is no dear head on the pillow, for I can't help that either, God help me; but I'll make no mountain out of my little molehill and pull no damnable faces at the derisive stars.*

This very explicit passage, for the ordinarily discreet Stevenson, dates from April 1878, when Louis's intimacy with Fanny was established, accepted, and known to all their friends. I infer, therefore, that the liaison began at the end of the summer of 1877, and was consolidated during the winter.

Paris—Third Winter—September 1877–April 1878

A letter from Fanny to Rearden, dated November 1877, telling of her trip to London, her first impressions of English intellectual life, and her meeting with Sidney Colvin, William E. Henley, Leslie Stephen, and Mrs. Sitwell, is preserved in the Bancroft Library, Baeck Collection.

For Louis's father Mr. Thomas Stevenson's visit to Paris in February 1878, see two letters addressed by Louis, one to Sidney Colvin: *Don't be surprised . . . but admire my courage and Fanny's. We want as much as we can to be above board with everyone . . .* (Beinecke Library, Yale University, Stevenson Collection); the other to his father: *While I am writing gravely, let me say one word more. I have taken a step towards more intimate relations with you. But don't expect too much of me . . . Try to take me as I am. This is a rare moment, and I have profited by it; but take it as a rare moment.* (*Letters to his Family and Friends*, op. cit.).

Grez-sur-Loing—Third Summer—June–July 1878

The torments, hesitations, and anguish over imminent separation are openly expressed in all his letters to his friends, from February 1878 to July. The letter to Charles Baxter, asking him about the legal possibility of a marriage between a Scottish subject and an American citizen, dates from July 1878 (*Letter to Charles Baxter, op. cit.*). Baxter would be Louis's lawyer and see to all his business affairs, public or private. He would even take on the responsibility of looking after his royalties and negotiating the edition of his complete works.

No Man's Land—July–August 1878

Fanny left Paris for London at the end of July 1878. It was Bob who came to fetch her from Dover as Louis was retained in Paris by his job as secretary to one of his former teachers, the engineer Fleeming Jenkin, a member of the jury for the World's Fair. He settled the whole Osbourne family in Chelsea, in Radnor Street, where Stevenson came to join them at the beginning of August.

Officially, he was living with Henley in Shepherd's Bush. On August 12, 1878, he drove Fanny to the station, where she took the boat-train to Liverpool. From Liverpool, she embarked on the *City of Richmond* for New York, with a detour by way of Ireland. She spent the end of the month in Indiana, and then took the Transcontinental to Sacramento, where she arrived in September 1878, three years to the day after the beginning of her great European adventure.

All these dates are recorded by Belle in her album (Silverado Museum, St. Helena, California).

Frank O'Meara died in 1888 and remained her great tragic love. From Samoa on May 22, 1893, fifteen years after they broke off their relationship, Belle wrote to her friend Charles Warren Stoddard that she would give anything for "a week with Frank." But was it the same Frank? She had another affair with a "Frank" in Hawaii. Whatever the case, an impressive retrospective was mounted in Dublin in 1989 to draw the public's attention to Frank O'Meara's neglected work.

VI
A Romance of Destiny

San Francisco—Winter 1878–1879

For Belle's return and her feelings toward her father, see *This Life I've Loved* (*op. cit.*). See also the first biography of Fanny by her sister Nellie Vandegrift Sanchez, *The Life of Mrs. Robert Louis Stevenson* (*op. cit.*).

Nellie was the youngest of the Vandegrift sisters. Her eldest sister, Fanny, took her with her to California when she traveled back to San Francisco from Indiana. Ten years earlier she had taken another sister, Cora, with her out West.

On Nellie's character and her relations with Fanny, see her future brother-in-law's remarks to Sidney Colvin in a letter of October 1879. Louis alludes to Nellie's selfish fear that Fanny's liaison would compromise her own marriage. Relations between Nellie and Louis would improve and become quite close when Stevenson came to live in East Oakland. He would eventually dedicate *Prince Otto* to her (Stevenson Tusitala Editions, *op. cit.*). On Nellie's literary career, see the article on her by her son, Louis Adulfo Sanchez, in the *Academy Scrapbook* (Academy of California Church History, 1959).

On Fanny's behavior and her nervous depression in Oakland during the winter of 1878–1879, see her correspondence with Rearden (Beinecke, collection cited), Louis's letters to Colvin (Beinecke Library, Yale University), and his *Letters to His Family and Friends (op. cit.)*. See also the letters to Henley (National Library of Scotland, Edinburgh) and *Letters to Charles Baxter (op. cit.)*.

On Sam's infidelities, his income, his spending, and the stability of his character, see the interview given by Dora Williams to the *Indianapolis Star* of January 6, 1889 (p. 2, column 6), preserved in the Indianapolis State Library.

Monterey—February–October 1879

No one has described the Monterey Peninsula better than Robert Louis Stevenson in *The Old Pacific Capital* (Scribners, New York, 1897).

I used my own impressions and plunged into the collection of old photographs preserved by Mr. Pat Hathaway of Monterey. See also the plans for the old town and the paintings in the Colton Hall Museum of the City of Monterey.

An article signed F. M. O. (Fanny Matilda Osbourne) describes the pleasures of the peninsula. Entitled "An Old Spanish Rodeo on Catel Rancho in Carmel Valley," it appeared in January 1880—the approximate date of her divorce—in the *Lippincott Magazine of Popular Literature and Science*. The numerous illustrations are by Belle Osbourne and Joe Strong.

See also the Monterey Public Library, the *Monterey Californian* of the summer of 1879, with its advertisements for Jules Simoneau's inn (situated next to the former prison); Adulfo Sanchez's Bohemia Saloon; and daily life in the town. Read especially the issues of

October 7, 14, 21; November 4, 11, 18, 25; and December 9, 1879, for several unsigned articles Stevenson probably wrote, especially the story of a treasure hunt, in the December 16 and 23 issues.

Joseph Dwight Strong was certainly one of the founders of the first artists' colony in Monterey. The son of a former missionary to Hawaii now residing in East Oakland and its municipal treasurer, Joe Strong had been sent to Munich to pursue his artistic studies. The Bancroft Library in Berkeley preserves a copy of the short autobiography by Miss Elizabeth Strong, Joe's sister, who lived in Monterey with him, then moved to Paris to study painting, following in the footsteps of her sister-in-law, Belle Osbourne. She became an animal painter of some repute and figures with her brother in the list of California artists, *Artists in California 1746–1940* (*op. cit.*).

On Joe Strong, see the archives of the Bohemian Club (*op. cit.*).

The rooms of the Bohemian Club today contain a little known portrait of Robert Louis Stevenson signed by Strong. Some of his paintings of the Pacific Islands are exhibited at the Silverado Museum in St. Helena. His murals decorating the walls of the Sans Souci Hotel on the beach at Waikiki in Hawaii disappeared when the building was destroyed. The few works I saw seemed to me to be very interesting.

Swanston Cottage, Scotland—June 1879

On Stevenson's relationship with his parents and their feelings about his involvement with Mrs. Osbourne, I have relied on the correspondence of Robert Louis Stevenson found in the Beinecke Library (collection cited). For the description of Swanston Cottage I drew on my impressions during a visit in the summer of 1989. I was also inspired by the descriptions of Lord Guthrie, who leased it in 1908, in *Robert Louis Stevenson* (W. Green and Son, Edinburgh, 1924).

The jewelry worn by Mrs. Thomas Stevenson in this scene still exists, notably the bracelet of braided hair with a large medallion holding a picture of Louis as a child. This jewelry is part of the collection of Mr. Roger E. Van Dyke, of Hawaii.

Swanston Cottage, Edinburgh, London, Glasgow, New York, San Francisco—August 1879

Robert Louis Stevenson's odyssey is reported in his own works, masterpieces of travel writing: *The Amateur Emigrant* (Scribners, New York, 1897); *Crossing the Plains* (Scribners, New York, 1897); and *The Silverado Squatters* (Scribners, New York, 1897).

It is true that Thomas Stevenson did not think much of *The Amateur Emigrant*. It was therefore withdrawn from circulation. Mr. J. C. Furnas, in *Voyage to Windward* (*op. cit.*), explains this gesture as the result of Thomas Stevenson's conviction that the book was not worthy of his son's talent, as well as his refusal to hear anything about the hardships Louis explicitly relates; even if those hardships were freely chosen, they brought shame to the family.

Monterey—August 1879

In her autobiography, *This Life I've Loved,* Belle is vague about the exact date of her marriage, but she suggests to the reader that this event occurred *after* Stevenson's arrival in Monterey on August 30, 1879. Her marriage, however, is recorded on August 9, 1879, in the register of a pastor in Pacific Grove.

Seen from young Sammy's viewpoint, the story of Robert Louis Stevenson's arrival in Monterey and all the child's impressions during this summer's end in 1879, are gathered together in a little book, *An Intimate Portrait of R. L. S.,* which he signed with the name his mother gave him in 1887, when Samuel Osbourne Sr. disappeared. It was under this name, Lloyd Osbourne, that Fanny's son would be known to posterity. Lloyd Osbourne wrote several novels in collaboration with Stevenson, notably *The Wrecker* and *Ebb Tide* (*op. cit.*). He wrote many articles on his illustrious stepfather, collections of short stories, and plays.

Fanny's hesitation and distress at Louis's arrival are painfully described in Stevenson's correspondence (Beinecke Library, collection cited) and suggested in the biography by Nellie Sanchez (*op. cit.*).

Fanny's first marriage. The Osbourne family.

FANNY OSBOURNE

She turned twenty years old during the Civil War. She would soon leave the family farm in Indiana to join her husband on the other side of the country in a primitive Nevada mining camp. They were deeply in love.
(*Robert E. Van Dyke collection*)

SAM OSBOURNE

He studied law but preferred adventure. Fanny would bear him three children.
(*Robert E. Van Dyke collection*)

BELLE

She would share all her mother's passions.
(*Robert E. Van Dyke collection*)

SAMUEL LLOYD

To entertain him, his stepfather would one day write *Treasure Island.*

HERVEY

The child Fanny could never forget.
(*Silverado Museum, St. Helena, California*)

If not specifically credited, photos are from the R.L.S. Collection, Lady Stair's House, Edinburgh.

THE JULIAN ACADEMY AS SEEN BY THE YOUNG BELLE OSBOURNE

Situated in the Passage des Panoramas in Paris, this was the only academy in Europe open to women who did not have the money to study with a private teacher. Women from all over the world came here, and the competition was fierce. *(Silverado Museum, St. Helena, California)*

IN GREZ-SUR-LOING

In this little village near Barbizon, on the other side of the Fontainebleau Forest, the Anglo-Saxon bohemians of the Latin Quarter settled in for the summer. The painters took up residence in the inns along the river, and refused to tolerate "respectable women," whose presence might spoil the atmosphere. Two artists, however, would allow themselves to take this risk: Frank O'Meara *(left)* would fall in love with Belle Osbourne *(center)*, and Robert Louis Stevenson *(right)* with Fanny *(seated)*. *(Silverado Museum, St. Helena, California)*

DRAWING OF ROBERT LOUIS STEVENSON BY FANNY OSBOURNE

This drawing was done during the period when she was studying
at the Julian Academy. He had not yet written any of his great novels.
(*Photo taken from* The Life of Robert Louis Stevenson *by Graham Balfour*)

FANNY OSBOURNE IN 1875

(Photo from Beinecke Rare Book and Manuscript Library, Yale University)

ROBERT LOUIS STEVENSON IN 1879

He was almost eleven years younger than she.
(The Albert E. Norman Collection, California Historical Society, San Francisco)

LOUIS'S FATHER AND MOTHER (bottom right)

The austere Scottish engineer Thomas Stevenson. Margaret Stevenson, whom Fanny and her children would fondly call "Aunt Maggy."
(National Portrait Gallery, Edinburgh, and R. L. S. Collection, Lady Stair's House, Edinburgh)

TIMOTHY REARDEN

A San Francisco lawyer, he was Fanny's mentor and self-appointed conscience. In the end, despite his own objections, Rearden would handle Fanny's divorce from Sam Osbourne.

THE GREAT FEAST LOUIS AND FANNY
GAVE IN HONOLULU IN HONOR OF KING KALAKAUA

The king can be seen seated at the far end of the table. On his left, Margaret Stevenson; on his right, his sister, princess Liliuokalani, who would become the last queen of Hawaii. Robert Louis Stevenson is seated to the right of the princess. Lloyd Osbourne and Belle Osbourne-Strong are looking at the camera in the foreground.

KING TEMBINOK

He reigned over an empire of atolls, and the Whites, who feared him, called him "the Napoleon of the Gilberts." He used dozens of sewing machines as anchors for his canoes.

VILLA VAILIMA, first building, 1891–1893 (SAMOA)

Louis often said that he wanted to be buried on the summit.
of Mount Vaea, which no one had ever explored.

THE STEVENSON CLAN AT VAILIMA

From left to right, last row: Joe Strong, his
parrot on his shoulder; Margaret Stevenson
(Aunt Maggy); Lloyd Osbourne, Robert Louis
Stevenson; Fanny Stevenson, Simi.
Second row, seated and dressed in white:
Mary, Aunt Maggy's personal maid; Talolo the
cook; Belle Strong with young Austin; and
standing, with the axe in his hand, Lafaele.

The meals at Vailima
had the reputation
for being well-provided
with drink.

LOUIS AND FANNY AT VAILIMA

This photograph was taken a short while before Louis's death.
Behind them, Graham Balfour, with whom Belle, on the extreme
left, was smitten.

AFTER LOUIS'S DEATH

The Vailima clan regrouped around Fanny and Belle, who tried to maintain the plantation against the odds. Fanny is seated, looking very small, in the first row. Belle is
kneeling at the extreme left.
(*Roger-Viollet Collection*)

WEDNESDAY, JUNE 23, 1915. FANNY STEVENSON'S FUNERAL

Twenty-one years after the death of the man she had loved so much, Fanny joined him on the summit of Mount Vaea. At the head of the procession is young Edward Salisbury Field, "Ned," her last companion and posthumous son-in-law, who carries the funeral urn. On his right, immediately behind him, Belle carries one of the cloths that had covered the remains of Robert Louis Stevenson.

FACING THE PACIFIC, ON MOUNT VAEA, THE GRAVE OF THE
REUNITED LOVERS

East Oakland—mid-September 1879

Relations between Fanny and Belle would continue to deterio-
rate until Sam Osbourne's disappearance. Even after her marriage
to Robert Louis Stevenson, Fanny's letters to Dora Williams (Bancroft Library, collection cited) contain disagreeable remarks about
Belle, Joe, and even little Austin Strong. The two women would
be reconciled only in San Francisco in 1888.

London—The Savile Club—Winter 1879

For the dialogues of William Ernest Henley, Sidney Colvin, and
Edmund Gosse, I relied on letters they exchanged about their mu-
tual friend, and on their correspondence with Robert Louis Steven-
son. See Henley's letters, preserved in the National Library of
Scotland and at the Beinecke Library (Yale University). See also
The Colvins and their Friends (op. cit.). I have practically tran-
scribed their comments word for word, notably Gosse's letter to
Louis of February 27, 1879: *I betted sixpence with myself that we
should never see his face again,* and Henley's letter to Colvin of
February 1880: *Don't defer expostulation because he is ill.*

On the personality of Sidney Colvin, see E. V. Lucas, *The Colvins
and their Friends* (op. cit.). For the character and appearance of
Edmund Gosse, I relied on *The Life and Letters of Sir Edmund
Gosse,* by the Honorable Charteris Evans (Heinemann, London,
1931). Finally, for William Ernest Henley, read the biography by
John Connel (*op. cit.*) and the book by Jerome Hamilton Duckley:
*William Ernest Henley. A Study in the Counter Decadence of the
Nineties* (Princeton University Press, 1945).

Monterey—East Oakland—December 1879–March 1880

For the life of Robert Louis Stevenson in Monterey, see the
article by Anne Roller Issler, "Robert Louis Stevenson in Monterey" (Pacific Historical Review, vol. 34, n. 3, University of California,
1965). See also the book by Anne B. Fischer, *No More a Stranger*
(Stanford University Press) and the book by Fanny's daughter-in-
law, Lloyd Osbourne's first wife, Katharine Durham, *Robert Louis*

Stevenson in California (McClurg, Chicago, 1911). Finally, the very impressive chronology established by Mr. Roger Swearingen, *Robert Louis Stevenson in California—Chronology 1879–1880* (in manuscript).

The resemblance between Sam Osbourne and Robert Louis Stevenson has been commented upon by numerous biographers. Notably by George S. Hellmann, *The True Story, A Study in Clarification* (Little, Brown, Boston, 1925), a book that is also full of mistakes.

The comments on racism and tolerance that I cite were indeed written by Sam Osbourne and Robert Louis Stevenson. I have taken *Chinatown was burned last night . . .* from Sam's letter to his son, dated September 1881, preserved in the Silverado Museum;

Of all stupid ill-feelings . . . belongs to *The Amateur Emigrant* (op. cit.).

That it is only the half-baked who are extremists . . . appears in a letter from Osbourne to Sammy of November 29, 1882 (collection cited);

It is well for you to cherish a pride in the scenery of your own country . . . again comes from a letter from Osbourne, August 28, 1883.

Robert Louis Stevenson's confused feelings for Sam Osbourne led him to ask himself many questions about his own conduct; see *Letters to His Friends and Family (op. cit.).*

San Francisco—End of December 1879–March 1880

For Robert Louis Stevenson's life in San Francisco and the description of this period of penury and struggle, see the exhaustive work of Mrs. Anne Roller Issler, *Happier for his Presence (op. cit.).*

I invented the reports of Mrs. Carson, Robert Louis Stevenson's landlady, who did not like Fanny, and of Dora Williams, drawing inspiration from portions of interviews by Mrs. Issler and the lecture given by Dora Williams on November 13, 1897 at the Century Club of San Francisco, whose manuscript is preserved in the Silverado Museum. I have put together these testimonies in order to make two complementary and coherent narratives. But the way Stevenson spent his time, the cost of his meals, places, dates and events are quite accurate. As for Mrs. Carson's husband, he served as the model for "Speedy" in *The Wrecker*. Returning to San Francisco in 1888, Stevenson would pay a visit to Mrs. Carson. She would be one of the guests of honor at the inauguration of the first monument to the memory of Robert Louis Stevenson, which is still standing in San Francisco's Portsmouth Square.

The exact date of Fanny's divorce remains subject to dispute. I think, with Mr. Furnas, that it took place in January 1880 (see letter from January and February to Colvin and Baxter, *op. cit.*). But James Pope Hennessy, in his biography *Robert Louis Stevenson* (Simon and Schuster, New York, 1974) situates it quite precisely on December 18, 1879; while Anne Roller Issler speaks of March–April 1880. The first date is supported by oral tradition in East Oakland.

East Oakland—April–May 1880

Robert Louis Stevenson's first hemorrhage certainly took place in Tubb's Hotel in East Oakland, in April 1880. Tuberculosis was diagnosed by Dr. William A. Bamford.

But was it really tuberculosis, as they believed for the next fifteen years? One thing is certain: If Stevenson's illness seemed to entail all the symptoms of consumption, he did not die of it. He was killed by a cerebral hemorrhage in December 1894.

There are people in this century who have even claimed that Robert Louis Stevenson was never tubercular. He probably suffered from a disease of the pleura, the lining of the lungs, as painful as consumption but unrelated to the Koch bacillus. In his *Voyage to Windward* (*op. cit.*), Mr. Furnas speculates at length on the possibility of a mistaken diagnosis. A letter from the Head of the Department of Tuberculosis and Lung Disease at San Francisco General Hospital, received after the publication of his book, would tend to confirm this hypothesis.

Whatever the case, Stevenson nearly died, and the details of his convalescence are reported in the biography by Nellie Sanchez, who clearly has a tendency to idealize her sister.

Some of the letters of Margaret Stevenson to her son are preserved in the Beinecke Library at Yale; I found no proof that Fanny had written to Louis's parents *before* their marriage, though most of the Stevenson biographers suspect her of secretly corresponding with Edinburgh. Nor have I found the letter she might have written to Sidney Colvin, who would have communicated it to the family. That Fanny had notified Colvin of the seriousness of Stevenson's state seems quite likely. She knew Colvin, having met him and Mrs. Sitwell in London in March 1877.

The letter of April 19, 1880 from Nellie Vandegrift to her sister Betty is preserved in the library of Plainfield, Indiana. Betty had been very ill. It was feared she would go mad, and this fear of aggravating her sister's mental state induced Fanny to suppress the news of her divorce and delay her remarriage as long as possible. Robert Louis Stevenson alludes to this in his letter to Baxter of February 22, 1880. But it is also true that the doctor's pessimistic prognosis on Louis's condition would serve to hasten their wedding.

Wednesday, May 19, 1880

A painting of the *Casco* was indeed on exhibit in the waiting room of the embarcadero in East Oakland. But there are several paintings of Dr. Merritt's yacht, all preserved today in the Oakland Museum. Which version hung in the waiting room? In doubt, I chose the most evocative one.

A thousand scandalous rumors made the rounds about Robert Louis Stevenson's marriage to Fanny Osbourne. Thanks for the most part to Katharine Durham, Lloyd Osbourne's first wife, who despised her mother-in-law, they were taken up by various magazines.

In order to set the record straight, Fanny herself would describe the scene for Stevenson's first biographer, Graham Balfour, whose papers are preserved in the National Library of Scotland, Edinburgh. In a letter from 1901, she tells him that only Dora, the minister, his wife, and a cat witnessed the ceremony. Dora's version in her lecture to the Century Club of San Francisco on November 13, 1897, confirms this.

In the letters of Fanny's daughter-in-law, preserved in the Hamilton Library of Honolulu (in the Catton Papers Collection), Katharine Durham asserts that Fanny was not younger than her first husband, Sam Osbourne, as legend would have it, but his elder by six years. If this was the case, Robert Louis Stevenson would have been sixteen years younger than Fanny, not eleven. This version, contradicted by Miss Vandegrift's birth certificate in Indianapolis, continues to circulate among Stevensonians.

The day after the marriage, May 20, 1880, Robert Louis Stevenson would ask Dora to take his father's book, *In Defense of Christianity*, to the Rev. Mr. Scott. This little work was bequeathed by the minister, with all his books and papers, to the library of the Franciscan Theological Seminary of San Anselmo. On the minister who married Robert Louis Stevenson, read Clifford Merril Drury, *Biography of William Anderson Scott* (Arthur H. Clark Co., Glendale, California, 1967).

After the ceremony, Louis and Fanny invited Dora to eat at a Viennese bakery. They never returned to the cottage in East Oakland. They spent two nights at the Palace Hotel in San Francisco. See the articles in the *San Francisco Chronicle* of January 10 and 19, 1989. They collected their baggage from the port and left directly for the mountains of St. Helena, where they intended to spend their honeymoon. They spent it under the stars, in a defunct mine in the ghost town of Silverado. See *The Silverado Squatters* (*op. cit.*).

VII
Mrs. Robert Louis Stevenson

London—Savile Club—August 1880

For the discussion between Edmund Gosse and Sidney Colvin, I relied on some long letters written by Sidney Colvin in August 1889, particularly the one to William Ernest Henley. See *The Colvins and their Friends*, by E. V. Lucas (*op. cit.*, pp. 127–128). I used parts of this letter nearly word for word in the dialogues.

Liverpool—Northwestern Hotel

For Mr. and Mrs. Stevenson's first impressions, I used the *Journal of Margaret Stevenson*, preserved in the Beinecke Library at Yale.

For Sammy and Fanny's relationship with the Stevenson parents, see their letters to Belle Strong in the Silverado Museum (collection cited), as well as Fanny's letters to Dora Williams in the Bancroft Library (collection cited).

Edinburgh—17 Heriot Row

For Louis's surprise at the way Fanny adapted herself to his world, see *I Can Remember Robert Louis Stevenson,* by Rosaline Masson (Chambers, London, 1922), and the letter he writes upon his arrival in Scotland to James Cunningham, whom he had met on the ship from New York to Liverpool.

For the dinner party scene in which Fanny dares to stand up to her father-in-law, see the stories of her biographers, Nellie Sanchez, *The Life of Mrs. Robert Louis Stevenson (op. cit.),* and Margaret MacKay, *The Violent Friend (op. cit.).*

See also Fanny's letters to Belle (Silverado Museum) and to Dora Williams (Bancroft Library).

For the description of the house, I relied on my visit to 17 Heriot Row, where the present owners were kind enough to welcome me. I have also used the inventory of furniture and objects that belonged to the Stevenson family preserved at the Stevenson House in Monterey.

The verses from the Book of Job that Thomas Stevenson mentions in this scene were indeed recopied in his will and read at his funeral. Thomas Stevenson's will is preserved in the Beinecke Library, Yale University.

London—October 1880

For the description of Fanny by Sidney Colvin, see *The Colvins and their Friends (op. cit.),* and all the prefatory material Colvin wrote to the *Letters of Robert Louis Stevenson (op. cit.).*

Margaret Stevenson's letters are preserved in the Bancroft Library (collection cited), Fanny's letters to Margaret in the Silverado Museum (collection cited). Fanny's letter which I reproduce here dates from October 1880. It is the first of an important series running to about a hundred pages, which relates Mrs. Robert Louis Stevenson's state of mind during her seven European years.

I have taken the raw material for Louis's discussions of art with his friends from a letter written after this scene took place. It amounts to an aesthetic profession of faith, which Louis would send from Hyères to Bob Stevenson in October 1883. This letter is preserved at the Pierpont Morgan Library in New York.

Davos—Saint Marcel—Hyères—Bournemouth

See Fanny's letters to Margaret Stevenson (Silverado Museum); Fanny's letters to Dora Williams (Bancroft Library); Fanny's letters to Belle Strong (Silverado Museum). See also Robert Louis Stevenson's correspondence with Henry James. Refer as well to Lloyd Osbourne's book, *An Intimate Portrait of Robert Louis Stevenson by His Stepson* (*op. cit.*), and above all *Voyage to Windward*, by J. C. Furnas (*op. cit.*).

New York—Saranac

See Margaret Stevenson's book, *From Saranac to the Marquesas* (Methuen, London, 1903).

For the quarrel between Henley and Stevenson, read all the letters written by Louis and Fanny to Charles Baxter between March and June 1888. Some of Henley's answers will be found there as well. *Letters to Charles Baxter* (*op. cit.*). Read also Henley and Sidney Colvin's correspondence in *The Colvins and their Friends* (*op. cit.*). And especially Henley's letters, preserved in the National Library of Scotland, in Edinburgh, as well as the two biographies devoted to him: *William Ernest Henley*, by John Connel (*op. cit.*), and *William Ernest Henley, A Study in the Counter Decadence of the Nineties*, by Jerome Hamilton Duckley (*op. cit.*).

Fanny had already reached San Francisco in March 1888, when Robert Louis Stevenson received Henley's letter at Saranac accusing his wife of plagiarism. Stevenson, on his side, informed Fanny of the accusation in a letter she received on the evening before she was to undergo an operation for a lump in her neck which she thought was a cancerous tumor. I have deleted this episode, which even further complicated their relationship. I kept only what seemed to me essential for the understanding of "The Nixie" incident; a version of this story is preserved in the Silverado Museum (collection cited).

For the telegram announcing the possibility of leasing the *Casco*, see *A Chronicle of Friendship*, by Will Low (*op. cit.*), and *Stevenson at Manasquan*, by Charlotte Eaton (Bookfellows, Chicago, 1921).

VIII
The Sirens' Song

The epigraph is taken from a letter by Stevenson to James Payne in *The Letters of Robert Louis Stevenson* (*op. cit.*, vol. 3).

San Francisco—The Marquesas—The Taumotus—Tahiti—Hawaii—Aboard the *Casco*

Robert Louis Stevenson has written all about the adventure that began in the month of June 1888 in his travel writing, stories, novels, pamphlets, private journals, and letters. This constitutes a considerable work. Telling this story on the basis of his writings runs the risk of paraphrase. I would therefore invite the reader to return to the sources. The character of Nares in *The Wrecker* was directly inspired by Captain Otis of the *Casco;* and Stevenson's stories *The Bottle Imp* and *The Beach of Falesa*, as well as *The Isle of Voices*, are among the finest short stories I know.

I naturally drew for this chapter on the third volume of the *Letters to his Family and Friends* (*op. cit.*), which records the violence of Stevenson's feelings and those of his travel companions. Otherwise, I used my own reactions as I set out, a century later, to follow in Fanny's footsteps.

Hawaii

The description of Iolani Palace is based on my visit to Honolulu in August 1992. I also relied very much on *This Life I've Loved* by Isobel Field (*op. cit.*).

For the history of Hawaii, refer to the general bibliography. The book by Edward Joesting, *Hawaii* (Robert Hale, London, 1978) was invaluable in helping me to understand the economic and political situation of the archipelago, along with the book by J. C. Furnas, *Anatomy of Paradise* (Gollancz, 1950).

See as well, of course, James Michner's *Hawaii* and *Rascals in the Pacific* (Secker and Warberg, London, 1957). See also *Hawaii's Story,* by Liliuokalani, Kalakaua's sister and the last queen of Hawaii (Mutual Publishing, 1990).

The ten letters from Louis and Fanny that I have excerpted here are published in *Travel in Hawaii—Robert Louis Stevenson,* edited with a preface by A. Groveday (University of Hawaii Press, 1973). I have cited these excerpts in chronological order, but the second letter addressed to Charles Baxter is a composite of this letter to Charles, referring to the financial risk that Stevenson was taking with the *Casco* and a letter of the same period to Bob.

There is also an astonishing collection of photographs, a virtual chornicle of the Stevenson's daily life in the South Seas. Some of these photographs have been published in *R. L. S. in the South Seas, An Intimate Photographic Record,* edited with a preface by Alanna Knight (Mainstream Publishing, 1986). A hundred or so other unpublished photographs taken by Lloyd Osbourne, but also by Fanny and Louis, are preserved in Edinburgh, in the archives of the Lady Stair House Museum. Unfortunately, part of this collection had been burned during the Stevensons' third cruise in April 1890. Fanny tells about the accident in the only book she ever signed alone, *The Cruise of the* Janet Nichol—*A Diary by Mrs. Robert Louis Stevenson* (Scribner's, New York, 1914), which was published after her death.

The Gilbert Islands, Samoa—Aboard the *Equator*

See *In the South Seas,* by Robert Louis Stevenson (Complete Works, *op. cit.*). On the history of Samoa, the extremely complicated political situation, the conflicts between the three governing powers, the most complete and passionate account is still the one written by Robert Louis Stevenson: *A Footnote to History* (Complete Works).

See also the very good guide published by Lonely Planet, *Samoa Travel Survival Kit,* by Deanna Swaney. See also *Le Voyage a Samoa,* by Marcel Schwob (Ombres, Toulouse, 1990); the many short stories of Somerset Maugham on the South Pacific; the impressive stories of the trader Louis Beck, *Pacific Tales* (K. P. I. Ltd., 1987); and the travel notes of a man who met Stevenson in Samoa, the painter John La Farge, *An American Artist in the South Seas (op. cit).*

Apia—Samoa—December 1889–February 1890

The colonial politics of Germany, Great Britain, and the United States between 1880 and 1900 are extremely complex. Their tripartite government in Samoa, with its sudden reversals, its intrigues, and inconsistencies reached the height of confusion. Keeping in mind the need to clarify, even simplify, matters for the reader, I chose to tell some of the story from Fanny's point of view. But Fanny's letter to Aunt Maggy is entirely my invention. I used her impressions dating from just this period (Silverado Museum, collection cited); my own notes, my notes upon my arrival in Samoa a century later; the book by Robert Louis Stevenson recounting the history of this archipelago *(A Footnote to History)*; the book by the trader Henry J. Moors, *With Stevenson in Samoa* (Small Maynard, Boston, 1910); and the travel book by the painter John La Farge, *An American Artist in the South Seas (op. cit.).*

Sydney—February 5, 1890

This letter from Belle and Lloyd is a composite of two letters from February 5, and 6, 1890, which they sent to Aunt Maggy to inform her of the purchase of Vailima (Silverado Museum, collection cited).

For the way that Fanny managed to book passage on the *Janet Nichol,* see Belle's original account in *This Life I've Loved (op. cit.).*

The description of Vailima, of the clearing, of the first cottage, and of the two Stevensons comes from the acerbic pen of John La Farge's travel companion, the man of letters Henry Adams, in *Letters* (Constable, London, 1930).

IX
Stevenson's Folly: Villa Vailima

The epigraph is taken from a letter written by Robert Louis Stevenson to James Barrie. This letter, dated April 2, 1893, describes in detail every important person at Vailima. Robert Louis Stevenson puts himself in the picture with Belle, Lloyd, and Fanny. His analysis of Fanny's character reveals his deep understanding of his wife, and his fondness for her. It is the most lively and concise picture of Fanny's character that we have.

In order to write this chapter, I relied on many different sources, which are cited in detail in the general bibliography. *The Cyclopedia of Samoa,* (McCarron Stewart, Sydney, 1907) was particularly valuable to me in evoking Apia, its shops, its bungalows, and its inhabitants during the Stevensons' time there. I found in it photographs of Dr. Funk, the British consul Sir Thomas Cusack-Smith, the great chiefs Mataafa and Tamasese, as well as the curriculum vitae of the American trader Moors.

I was forced to reduce the profusion of government personnel, the chiefs and men of the three native factions, and the dozen servants of Vailima to a few human types. I chose the British consul Sir Thomas Cusack-Smith to embody the powerful Whites, the chief Mataafa to stand for the native factions, and to represent the servants I chose Lafaele, Fanny's right-hand man, Talolo, the cook trained by Belle, and Sosimo, Louis's valet. These are the only liberties I allowed myself to take in my concern for simplification. I did not discuss the various week or month-long trips Louis, Fanny, Belle, and Lloyd made during these years to Honolulu or Sydney, unless those trips contributed to moving the story along. Two documents were indispensable for reconstructing day by day the ordinary course of life at Vailima: the *Vailima Letters,* by Robert Louis Stevenson (Methuen, London, 1895); and *Our Samoan*

Adventure, by Fanny Stevenson, edited by Charles Neider (Harper Brothers, New York, 1953). These two documents had been previously censored, the first by Sidney Colvin, the second by Fanny's children. In order to fill in the passages in Louis's letters not included here, read the passionate article by Professor Bradford A. Booth in the *Harvard Library Bulletin,* vol. 15, April 1967: "The Vailima Letters of Robert Louis Stevenson." This article reveals the seriousness of Fanny Stevenson's psychosis in October 1892 and in the spring of 1893. He suggests that life at Vailima was far from being as idyllic as Belle and Lloyd would have it believed. Robert Louis Stevenson kept his wife's mental illness a secret. He confided it only to Sidney Colvin. Professor Booth suggests that Fanny's mental problems spoiled life at Vailima and hastened Louis's death.

Belle Strong and Lloyd Osbourne wrote at great length on Vailima. See especially their *Memories of Vailima* (Scribners, New York, 1902); *This Life I've Loved* (*op. cit.*); and *An Intimate Portrait of Robert Louis Stevenson* (*op. cit.*), in which Lloyd describes Louis's death. See also all of Margaret Stevenson's letters to her sister Jane Balfour, *Letters from Samoa* (Methuen, London, 1906), and all those written to her during her two trips to Scotland by Fanny, Belle, and Lloyd (Silverado Museum, collection cited).

For this entire section so rich in documentation I always returned to the two master works, one devoted to Louis, the other to Fanny: *Voyage to Windward,* by J. C. Furnas, and *A Violent Friend,* by Margaret MacKay. Margaret MacKay was the first biographer of Fanny Osbourne who dared to discuss her "secret illness." After reading the work of Scottish psychiatrists and psychologists, notably Dr. Harold Searls and Dr. Gregory Bateson, I have come to believe that Fanny did indeed present a number of symptoms of schizophrenia.

For twenty years Stevenson's biographers have mentioned the possibility that she was afflicted with Bright's disease, without ever expanding on the symptoms. It is quite likely that Fanny suffered from this kidney disorder, which she constantly complains about in her journal. She also suffered from gallstones, for which she underwent an operation in England in 1898.

A rumor still circulates that she might have been pregnant, that she may have had a miscarriage, and that the baby was buried in the cellar of Vailima. As dramatic and romantic as she was, this eventuality seems to me highly implausible. During Louis's life at

Vailima she was between fifty and fifty-four years old. I would therefore be tempted to conclude that along with all her other physical ailments she was dealing with the onset of menopause.

On Belle's feelings toward Fanny, Louis, and Graham Balfour, see her *Confidential Letters to the Poet Charles Warren Stoddard,* preserved at the Silverado Museum.

On the hatred of Lloyd's first wife for her mother-in-law and sister-in-law, see the abundant correspondence of Katharine Durham to Robert Catton, preserved in the Hamilton Library in Honolulu. Her letters are full of anecdotes about Fanny, Belle, and Lloyd. Always tendentious, they nonetheless clarify certain aspects of their personalities.

Fanny's letters to the same Catton family of Honolulu, also preserved in the Hamilton Library, give a good picture of the atmosphere at Vailima, of her efforts to save the plantation, of her failures after Louis's death. They also transmit the deep understanding she reached with her daughter after all those years of love and rivalry. Their fondness for each other is unflagging.

Epilogue

In her letters to the Catton family of Hawaii, Katharine Durham does not treat Edward Salisbury Field with any more indulgence than she does Lloyd and Belle. She would nonetheless acknowledge that her sister-in-law's marriage to the very young Ned was a success.

Fanny's letters to her young admirer Gelett Burgess preserved in the Bancroft Library of the University of California, Berkeley (Burgess Collection), leave no room for doubt about their relationship. The unpublished biography of Burgess by Joseph Backus, which I had the pleasure of reading at the Silverado Museum, describes clearly the young man's feelings for Stevenson's widow. Fanny would put Burgess in touch with Henry James, with whom he corresponded.

The letter by Agnes Crowley, Fanny's maid, telling Belle of her mother's death, is preserved in the Silverado Museum (collection cited). The same letter is reproduced nearly word for word in *The Life of Mrs. Robert Louis Stevenson* (*op. cit.*), but it is addressed to Nellie Sanchez.

To evoke the Fields's return to Samoa and Fanny's funeral, I relied on Belle's journal (May to September, 1915) in the Silverado Museum. She seemed very taken with her husband. There are some extraordinary photographs of the procession climbing through the bush to Mount Vaea, preserved in the Beinecke Library at Yale and in the Silverado Museum.

BIBLIOGRAPHY

Seven works have been especially valuable to me:

BALFOUR, Graham, *The Life of Robert Louis Stevenson,* 2 vol., Methuen, London, 1901.

FIELD, Isobel Osbourne Strong, *This Life I've Loved,* Michael Joseph London, 1937.

FURNAS, J.C., *Voyage to Windward,* Faber and Faber, London, 1952.

MACKAY, Margaret, *A Violent Friend,* Doubleday, New York, 1968.

OSBOURNE, Lloyd, *An Intimate Portrait of Robert Louis Stevenson,* Scribner's sons, New York, 1924.

SANCHEZ, Nellie van de Grift, *The Life of Mrs. Robert Louis Stevenson,* Scribner's Sons, New York, 1920.

STEVENSON, Robert Louis, *Works,* 35 vol., with prefaces by Mrs. R.L. Stevenson, Lloyd Osbourne and Sidney Colvin, Tusitala Edition, Heinemann, London, 1923–24.

—*Works,* 26 vol., Lloyd Osbourne ed. with Notes by Mrs. R.L. Stevenson, Vailima Edition, Heinemann, London, 1922–23.

ABBE, Donald R., *Austin and the Reese River Mining District,* University of Nevada Press, Reno, 1985.

ADAMS, Henry, *Henry Adams and His Friends,* Houghton Mifflin Co., Boston, 1947.

—*Letters,* Constable, London, 1930.

ADCOCK, A., St. J. ed., *Robert Louis Stevenson—His Work and His Personality,* Hoder and Stoughton, London, 1924.

ALDINGTON, Richard, *Portrait of a Rebel, Robert Louis Stevenson,* Evans, London, 1957.

ALLEN, Maryland, "South Seas Memories of Robert Louis Stevenson", *The Bookman,* New York, August 1916.

ANNAN, Noël, *Leslie Stephen, The Godless Victorian,* Weidenfeld and Nicolson, London, 1984.

BAILDON, H.B., *Robert Louis Stevenson,* Chatto and Windus, London, 1901.

BAKER, Ray Jerome, *Honolulu Then and Now,* Baker, Honolulu, 1941.

BALFOUR, Michael, "How the Biography of Robert Louis Stevenson Came to Be Written", The Times Literary Supplement, London, 15 and 22 January 1960.

BARNHART, Jacqueline Baker, *The Fair but Frail,* University of Nevada Press, Reno, 1986.

BAY, J.C.B., *Echoes of Robert Louis Stevenson,* Walter M. Hill, Chicago, 1920.

BECKE, Louis, *Pacific Tales,* K.P.I., New York, 1987.

BEEBE, Lucius Morris, *Legends of the Comstock Lode,* Stanford, Cal., 1956.

BEER, Thomas, *The Mauve Decade,* Alfred A. Knopf Inc., New York, 1926.

BENSON, E.F., *As We Were,* Longmans, London, 1930.

BERMANN, Richard A., *Home From the Sea,* The Bobbs-Merrill Co., Indianapolis, s.d.

—*Robert Louis Stevenson in Samoa,* Mutual Pub., Hawaii, 1967.

BETHKE, Frederick John, *Three Victorian Travel Writers,* G.K. Hall, Boston, 1977.

BILLY, André, *Les Beaux Jours de Barbizon,* Editions du Lavois, Paris, 1947.

BIRD, Isabella, *Six Months in Hawaii,* K.P.I., New York, 1987.

BLACK, Margaret Moyes, *Robert Louis Stevenson,* Famous Scots Series, Oliphant Anderson and Ferrier, London, 1899.

BLONDEL, Jacques, *Aspects du romantisme anglais,* Université de Clermont II, Clermont-Ferrand, 1980.

BONET-MAURY, Gaston, "R. L. Stevenson, voyageur et romancier", *Revue des Deux-Mondes,* september 1902.

BOODLE, Adelaide A., *R.L.S. and His Sine Qua Non,* Murray, London, 1926.

BOOTH, Prof. Bradford A., "The Vailima Letters of Robert Louis Stevenson", *Harvard Library Bulletin,* Cambridge, Mass., April 1967.
The Letters of Robert Louis Stevenson, Vols. 1 & 2 with Ernest Mehew, Yale University Press, New Haven, 1995.

BROWN, Dee A., *Gentle Tamers: Women of the Old West,* Putman I.W., New York, 1958.

BROWN, George, *Pioneer Missionary and Explorer,* Hodder and Stoughton, London, 1908.

BROWN, George E., *A Book of Robert Louis Stevenson,* Methuen, London, (no date).

BROWN, J. Ross, *A Peep at Washoe,* Lewis Osbone, Palo Alto, Cal., 1968.

BROWN, Mark II, and FELTON, W.R., *The Frontier Years,* 1955.

BUCKLEY, Jerome Hamilton, *William Ernest Henley,* N.J. Princeton University Press, 1945.

BUELL, Llewellyn M., "Eilean Earraid: the Beloved Isle of Robert Louis Stevenson", Scribners, New York, February 1922.

BURGESS, Gelett, "An Interview with Mrs. Robert Louis Stevenson", *The Bookman,* New York, September 1898.

—*Some Mad Americans in Dorking,* Illustrated London News CXIII, 17 september 1898.

BURLINGAME, Roger, *Of Making Many Books,* Scribner's, New York, 1946.

CALDER, Jenni, *R.L.S.: A Life Study*, Hamish Hamilton, London, 1980.

—*Stevenson and Victorian Scotland*, University Press, 1981.

CARRE, Jean-Marie, *Robert Louis Stevenson*, Gallimard, Paris, 1929.

CARRINGTON, James B., "Another Glimpse of R.L.S.", *Scribners*, New York, August 1927.

CHALMERS, Stephen, *The Penny Piper of Saranac*, Houghton Mifflin Co., Boston, 1896.

CHARTERIS, Evan, *John Singer Sargent*, Heinemann, London, 1927.

—*The Life and Letters of Sir Edmund Gosse*, Heinemann, London, 1931.

CHASTAINGS, Pierre, *Avec Stevenson dans les Cévennes en 1878*, Pensée universelle, Paris, 1979.

CHESTERTON, J.K., *Robert Louis Stevenson*, Hoddor and Stoughton, London, 1927.

CHURCHILL, William, "Stevenson in the South Sea", *McClure's*, December 1981.

CLARE, Maurice, *A Day with Robert Louis Stevenson*, Hodder and Stoughton, London, (no date).

CLARK, Harry Hayden, *American Litterature*, Appleton-Century-Crofts, New York, 1971.

CLARKE, W.E., "Robert Louis Stevenson in Samoa", *Yale Review*, January 1921.

CLIFFORD, Mrs. W.K., "The Sidney Colvins: Some Personal Recollections", *Bookman*, London, April 1928.

COHEN, Edward H., *The Henley-Stevenson Quarrel*, University Presses of Florida, Gainesville, 1974.

COLVIN, Sidney, *Memories and Notes of Persons and Places, 1852–1912*, Charles Scribner's Sons, New York, 1921.

—"Robert Louis Stevenson at Hampstead", *Hampstead Annual*, 1902.

—GOSSE, Edmund, et al, *Robert Louis Stevenson, His Work and Personality*, Hodder and Stoughton, London, 1924.

CONNELL, John, *W.E. Henley*, Constable, London, 1949.

CONRAD, Joseph, *La Folie Almayer*, Gallimard, Paris, no date.

COOPER, Lettice, *Robert Louis Stevenson*, English Novelists Series, Home and Van Thal, London, 1947.

COPELAND, Charles Townsend, "Robert Louis Stevenson", *Atlantic Monthly*, April 1895.

COULTER, E. Merton, *Auraria: The Story of a Georgia Gold-Mining Town*, 1956.

CUNLIFFE, J.W., *English Literature During the Last Half Century*, Macmillan Co., New York, 1923.

CUNNINGHAM, Alison, *Cummy's Diary*, Chatto and Windus, London, 1926.

DAICHES, David, *Robert Louis Stevenson*, Maclennan, Glasgow, 1947.

—*Robert Louis Stevenson and His World*, Thames and Hudson, London, 1973.

DALGLISH, Doris N., *Presbyterian Pirate*, Oxford University Press, London, 1937.

DANIELS, Zeke, *This Life and Death of Julia C. Bulette,* Lamp Post, Virginia City, Nev., 1958.

DAPLYN, A.J., "Robert Louis Stevenson at Barbizon", *Chambers's Journal,* Series 7, 1917.

DARK, Sidney, *Robert Louis Stevenson,* Hodder and Stoughton, London, (no date).

DAWS, Gavan, *A Dream of Islands,* Mutual Pub., Hawaii, 1989.

DELEBECQUE, Jacques, "A Propos du roman d'aventures: Notes sur quelques ouvrages de R. L. Stevenson", *Mercure de France,* Paris, January-February 1921.

DE QUILLE, Dan, *The Big Bonanza,* Alfred Knopf, 1947.

DE VOTO, Bernard, *Mark Twain's America,* Houghton Mifflin Co., 1932.

DICKIE, Francis, "The Tragic end of Stevenson's Yacht *Casco*", *World Magazine,* 4 January 1920.

DINNEAN, Lawrence, *Les Jeunes: An Account of Some Fin de Siècle San Francisco Authors and Artists,* University of California, Berkeley, 1980.

DOTEN, Alfred, *The Journals of Alfred Doten,* University of Nevada Press, Reno, 1973.

DOUGHTY, Leonard, "Answering R.L.S.", *Southwest Review,* Autumn 1928.

DOUGLAS, Ann, *The "Feminization" of American Culture,* Knopf, New York, 1977.

DROPPERS, Garrit, "Robert Louis Stevenson", *Harvard Monthly,* March 1887.

DRURY, Clifford M., *First White women over the Rockies,* 1966.

—*Biography of William Anderson Scott,* Arthur H. Clark C., Glendale, Cal., 1967.

DRURY, Wells, *An Editor of the Comstock Lode,* University of Nevada Press, Reno, 1984.

DUNCAN, William Henry Jr., "Stevenson's Second Visit to America", *Bookman,* New York, January 1900.

EATON, Charlotte, *A Last Memory of Robert Louis Stevenson,* Thomas Y. Crowell, New York, (no date).

EDEL, Leon, *Henry James, A Life,* Harper & Row, 1985.

EDINBURGH PUBLIC LIBRARY, *Catalogue of The Robert Louis Stevenson Collection,* Edinburgh, 1950.

ELLISON, Joseph W., *Tusitala of the South Seas: The Story of Robert Louis Stevenson's Life in the South Pacific,* Hastings House, New York, 1953.

ELWIN, Malcom, *Old Gods Falling,* Collins, London, 1939.

—*The Strange Case of Robert Louis Stevenson,* MacDonald, London, 1950.

ENO, Henry, *Letters from Californie and Nevada, 1848–1871,* W. Turrentine Jackson ed., 1965.

ESAREY, Logan, *Indiana Home,* K.P. (Rogers), 1953.

EWING, Sir Alfred, *An Engineer's Outlook,* Methuen and Co., London, s.d.

FABRE, Frédéric, "Un ami de France: Robert Louis Stevenson dans le Velay", Extract from the *Revue d'Auvergne,* 1932.

FATOUT, Paul, *Marc Twain in Virginia City,* Indiana University Press, 1964.

FENDER, Stephen, *Plotting the Solden West,* Cambridge University Press Cambridge, New York, 1981.

FERLINGHETTI, Lawrence and Peters, Nancy J., *Literary San Francisco,* City Lights Books, San Francisco, 1980.

FESTETICS de TOLNA, comte Rodolphe, *Chez les cannibales,* Librairie Plon Paris 1903.

FIELD, Edward Salisbury, *The Complete Optimist* by Child Harold, Ed. Dutton Co., New York, 1912.

—*Cupids Understudy,* Grosset and Dunlap Cop., New York, 1909.

—(in collaboration with FRANCES, Marion), *Happy Endings,* New York, 1930.

—*In Pursuit of Priscilla,* Philadelphia, 1906.

—*The Purple Stockings,* Grosset and Dunlap, New York, 1911.

—*The Quest and Other Poems,* R.G. Badger, Boston, 1904.

—*The Rented Earl,* W.J. Watt, New York, 1912.

—*The Saphire Bracelet,* W.J. Watt, New York, 1910.

—*A Six Cylinder Courtship,* Grosset and Dunlap, New York, 1907.

—*Twin Beds,* W.J. Watt, New York, 1913.

—*Twin Beds* (adaptation, with MAYO, Margaret), New York, 1915.

—*Wedding Bells,* Typed Script, NCOF, p.u. 467.

FIELD, Isobel OSBOURNE STRONG, *Robert Louis Stevenson, Saranac Lake,* Stevenson Society of America, New York, 1920.

—(with Lloyd OSBOURNE), *Memories of Vailima,* Charles Scribner's Sons, New York, 1902.

FIGARO (*Le*), 1875–1876.

FINCH, Philip, *Virginia City Fiction,* Birthright, New York, 1979.

FISHER, Vardis, and HOLMES, Opal L., *Gold Rushes and Mining Camps of Early American West,* 1968.

FLETCHER, C., Brundson, *Stevenson's Germany,* Heinemann, London, 1920.

FRADY, Steven R., *Red Shirts and Silver Helmets,* University of Nevada Press, 1984.

FRASER, Marie, *In Stevenson's Samoa,* Smith, Elder and Co., London, 1895.

FURNAS, J.C. *Anatomy of Paradise,* Curtis Pub., New York, 1947.

GAUGUIN, Paul, *Noa Noa; Séjour à Tahiti,* Complexe, Bruxelles, 1989.

GEDULD, Harry M., *The Definitive Dr. Jekyll and Mr. Hyde Companion,* Garland, New York, 1983.

GENUNG, John Franklin, *Stevenson's Attitude to Life,* Thomas Y. Crowell, New York, 1901.

GILDER, Jeannette L., *Stevenson—and After,* Review of Reviews (U.S.) February 1895.

GILDER, Richard Watson, *Letters,* Constable, London, 1916.

GOLDMAN, Marion S., *Gold Diggers and Silver Miners,* University of Michigan Press, Ann Arbor, 1981.

GORSKY, Bernard, *Trois tombes au soleil,* A. Michel, Paris, 1976.

GOSSE, Edmund, *Bibliographical Notes on the Writings of Robert Louis Stevenson,* Privately printed at the Chiswick Press, London, 1908.

—*Critical Kit-Kats,* Charles Scribner's Sons, New York, 1914.

—*Leaves and Fruit,* Charles Scribner's Sons, New York, 1927.

—*Questions at Issue,* William Heinemann, London, 1893.

—*Silhouettes,* Charles Scribner's Sons, New York, no date.

—*Some Diversions of a Man of Letters,* William Heinemann, London, 1919.

—"Stevenson's Relations with Children", *Youth's Companion,* 13 June 1899.

GREEN, Roger Lancelyn, *Stevenson in Search of a Madonna,* English Associates, Essays and Studies, Murray, London, 1950.

GREENE, Charles S., "California Artists. II. Joseph D. Strong, Jr.", *Overland Monthly,* May 1896.

GREEVER, William S., *Bonanza West: Western Mining Rushes, 1848–1900,* 1963.

GROFFIER, Jean, *Robert Louis Stevenson: la dualité incarnée,* H. Peladan, Uzès, France, 1977.

GUTHRIE, Lord C.J., *Robert Louis Stevenson,* Green and Son, Edinburgh, 1920.

—*"Cummy", the Nurse of Robert Louis Stevenson,* O. Schulze, Edinburgh, 1913.

GWYNN, Stephen, *Robert Louis Stevenson,* Macmillan, London, 1939.

HAMILTON, Clayton, *On the Trail of Stevenson,* Hodder and Stoughton, London, 1915.

HAMMERTON, J.A., *On the Track of Stevenson,* J.W. Arrowsmith, Bristol, s.d.

—*Stevensoniana,* J. Grant, Edinburgh, 1910.

HAMMOND, John R., *A Robert Louis Stevenson Companion,* Macmillan, London, 1984.

HARRISON, Birge, "With Stevenson at Grez", *Century,* December 1916.

HART, James D., *From Scotland to Silverado, Robert Louis Stevenson,* Harvard University Press, Cambridge, Mass., 1966.

HATTORI, Eugene Mitsuru, *Northern Paiutes on the Comstock,* Nevada State Museum, Carson City, 1975.

HELLMAN, Georges S., *Lanes of Memory,* Alfred A. Knopf Inc., New York, 1927.

—*The True Stevenson,* Little, Brown and Co., Boston, 1925.

—"R.L.S. and the Streetwalker", *American Mercury,* July 1936.

—"Stevenson and Henry James", *Century,* January 1926.

—"The Stevenson Myth", *Century,* December 1922.

—"Stevenson's Annotated Set of Wordsworth", *Colophon,* VII, 1931.

HENLEY, William Ernest, *Essays,* Macmillian and Co., London, 1921.

—"Obituary of R.A.M. Steenson", *Pall Mall Magazine,* July 1900.

—"R.L.S.," *Pall Mall Magazine,* December 1901.

HERVIER, Paul-Louis, "Stevenson jugé par son beau-fils", *La Nouvelle Revue,* May–June 1922.

HINCKLE, Warren, *The Richest Place on Earth,* Houghton Mifflin, Boston, 1978.

HINKLEY, Laura L., *The Stevenson: Louis and Fanny,* Hastings House, New York, 1950.

HINSDALE, Harriet, *Robert Louis Stevenson,* Caxton Printers, Caldwell, Idaho, 1947.

HOLLAND, Clive, "Robert Louis Stevenson at Bournemouth", *Chambers's Journal,* December 1934.

HUBBARD, Elbert, *Little Journeys to the Homes of English Authors*, Putnam, London, 1903.

HUGHES, Edan Milton, *Artists in California, 1786–1940*, Hughes Pub. Co., San Francisco, 1986.

ILLUSTRATION (L'), 1874, 1875, 1876, 1877, 1878.

ISSLER, Anne Roller, *Happier for His Presence*, Stanford University Press, 1949.

—"Robert Louis Stevenson in Monterey", *Pacific Historical Review*, Los Angeles, August 1965.

—*Stevenson at Silverado*, Caxton, Caldwell, Idaho, 1939.

JACQUETTE, Rodolphe, *Tusitala, ou la Vie aventureuse de Robert Louis Stevenson*, Seghers, Paris, 1980.

JAMES, Alice, *Diary*, Leon Edel, ed. Hart-Davis, London, 1965.

JAMES, Henry, *Letters*, 2 vol., Percy Lubbock, ed. Macmillan, London, 1920.

—*Partial Portraits*, Macmillan, London, 1888.

—and STEVENSON, Robert Louis, *Letters*, Janet Adam Smith, ed. Hart-Davis, London, 1948.

—*Selected Letters*, edited by Leon Edel, Belknap, Harvard University Press, 1987.

JAPP, Alexander H., *Robert Louis Stevenson*, Werner Laurie, London, 1905.

JERSEY, Countess of, *Fifty-One Years of Victorian Life*, Murray, London, 1922.

JOESTING, Edward, *Hawaii, an Uncommon History*, Robert Hale, London, 1974.

JOHNSON, Paul, *San Francisco: As it is, At it was*, Doubleday, New York, 1979.

JOHNSTONE, Arthur, *Recollections of Robert Louis Stevenson in the Pacific*, Chatto and Windus, London, 1905.

KELMAN, John Jr., *The Faith of Robert Louis Stevenson*, Edinburgh, 1903.

KENT, Harold Coinfield, *The Life of Rev. Dr. Charles Mc Ewen Hyde*, Charles E. Tuttle, Rutland, Vermont, 1973.

KNIGHT, Alanna, *The Passionate Kindness*, Hilton House Books, Aylesbury, 1974.

LAFARGE, John, *An American Artist in the South Seas*, K.P.I., New York, 1987.

LANG, Andrew, *Adventures Among Books*, Longmans, Green, London, 1905.

LAWSON, M.S., *On the Bat's Back*, The Story of Stevenson, Lutterworth, London, 1950.

LE BRIS, Michel, *La Porte d'or*, Grasset, Paris, 1986.

LE GALLIENNE, Richard, *The Romantic Nineties*, Putnam, London, 1925.

LESLIE, Mrs. Shane, *Girlhood in the Pacific*, Macdonald, London, s.d.

LEWIS, Marvin, *Martha and the Doctor*, University of Nevada Press, 1977.

LEWIS, Oscar, *The Autobiography of the West*, Holt, New York, 1958.

—*Bay Window Bohemia*, Doubleday, New York, 1956.

—*The Life and Times of The Virginia City Enterprise*, J.L. Osborne, Ashland, Co., 1971.

—*The Town that Died Laughing*, Little Brown, Boston, 1955.

—*Silver Kings*, Alfred Knopf, 1947.

—*The War in the Far West, 1861–1865,* Doubleday, New York, 1961.
LILUOKALANI, *Hawaii's Story,* Mutual Pub., Hawaii, 1990.
LOCKETT, W.G., *Robert Louis Stevenson at Davos,* Hurst and Blackett, London, s.d.
LORD, Eliot, *Comstock Mining and Miners,* David Myrick ed., 1959.
LOTI, Pierre, *Le Mariage de Loti,* Safrat, Paris, 1991.
LOW, Will H., *A Chronicle of Friendships, 1873–1900,* Hodder and Stoughton, London, 1908.
LUCAS, E.V., *The Colvins and Their Friends,* Methuen, London, 1928.
LYMAN, George D., *Ralston's Ring: California Plunders Comstock Lode,* 1934.
MacCALLUM, Thomas Murray, *Adrift in the South Seas,* Wetzel Publishing Co., Inc., Los Angeles, s.d.
McCLURE, Samuel S., *My Autobiography,* Murray, London, 1914.
MacCULLOCH, J.A., *R.L. Stevenson and the Bridge of Allan,* John Smith and Son, Glasgow, 1927.
McGAW, Siter Martha Mary, Stevenson in Hawaii, University of Hawaii Press, Honolulu, 1950.
MacKANESS, George, *Robert Louis Stevenson,* Privately printed, Sydney, 1935.
—*R.L.S., His Association with Australia,* Australian Historical Monographs, 1976.
McKAY, George L., *A Stevenson Library: Catalogue of the Edwin J. Beinecke Collection,* 6 vol., Yale University Press, 1951 on.
MacKENZIE, Copton, *International Profiles: R.L.S.,* Grampian Book Ltd., Morgan, 1968.
McLAREN, Moray, *Stevenson and Edinburgh,* Chapman and Hall, London, 1950.
McNAIR, Mathews, *Ten Years in Nevada,* Historical Society, F. 841, M 16, New York, 1880.
MAITLAND, Frederic William, *The Life and Letters of Leslie Stephen,* G.P. Putnam's Sons, New York, 1908.
MAIXNER, Paul, *Robert Louis Stevenson: The Critical Heritage,* Routledge and Kegan Paul, London, Boston, 1981.
MARDER, Daniel, *Exiles at Home,* University Press of America, Lanham, MD. 1984.
MARTIN, Michael Rheta, *Dictionary of American History,* Rowman and Littlefield, Totowa, N.J., 1978.
MASTER, Frederick E., *A Collector's View of Robert Louis Stevenson,* Philadelphia, 1970.
MASSON, Flora, *Victorians All,* Chambers, London at Edinburgh, 1931.
MASSON, Rosaline, *A Life of Robert Louis Stevenson,* Frederick A. Stokes C., New York, 1923.
—*I Can Remember Robert Louis Stevenson,* W. and R. Chambers, London and Edinburgh, 1922.
—*Poets, Patriots, and Lovers,* James Clarke and Co. Ltd. London, 1933.
—*Robert Louis Stevenson,* T.C. et E.C. Jack, London, s.d.
MAUGHAM, Somerset, *L'Archipel aux sirènes,* Hachette, Paris, 1961.

MEAD, Margaret, *Coming of Age in Samoa,* Morrow, New York, 1961.

MELVILLE, Herman, *Omoo,* K.P.I., New York, 1987.

—*Typee,* K.P.I., New York, 1987.

MIDDLETON-SAFRONI, A., "With R.L.S. in Old Samoa", *The Journal of the Robert Louis Stevenson Club,* London, May 1950.

MOODY, Eric, *Western Carpet Bagger,* University of Nevada Press, 1978.

MOORMAN, Lewis J., *Tuberculosis and Genius,* University of Chicago Press, Chicago, s.d.

MOORS, Harry Jay, *With Stevenson in Samoa,* Fisher Unwin, London, 1910.

MORRIS, David B., *Robert Louis Stevenson and the Scottish Highlanders,* Stirling, Eneas Mackay, s.d.

MORSE, Hiram G., *Robert Louis Stevenson as I Found Him in His Island Home,* N.P., 1902.

MOURE, Nancy Dustin Hall, *Dictionary of Art and Artists in Southern California before 1930,* Dustin Publications, Glendale, Cal., 1975.

MUIR, Edwin, "Robert Louis Stevenson", *Modern Scot,* autumn 1931.

—*Scott and Scotland,* George Routledge and Sons Ltd., London, 1936.

MUNRO, D.G. Macleod, *The Psychopathology of Tuberculosis,* Humphrey Milford Oxford University Press, London, s.d.

MUSCATINE, Doris, *Old San Francisco,* Putnam, New York, 1975.

NAKAJIMA, Atsushi, *Light Wind and Dreams,* The Hokoseido Press, 1962.

NICHOLSON, Meredith, *Hoosiers,* McMillan, London, 1916.

NICKERSON, Roy, *Robert Louis Stevenson in California*, Chroncile Books, San Francisco, 1982.

NOBLE, Andrew, *Robert Louis Stevenson,* Barnes and Noble, London, 1983.

NORRIS, Frank, *A Story of San Francisco,* Penguin Books, New York, 1982.

OAKLAND Museum, Art Dept., *The Kahn Collection of Nineteenth-Century Paintings,* by Marjorie Arkelian, Oakland Museum, 1975.

OSBOURNE, Alan, "A Letter to the Editor of The Times Literary Supplement" London, 25 March 1960.

OSBOURNE, Katharine Durham, *Robert Louis Stevenson in California,* A.C. McClurg and Co., Chicago, 1911.

OSBOURNE, Lloyd, *Somes Letters of Robert Louis Stevenson,* Methuen, London, 1914.

—and STRONG, Isobel, *Memories of Vailima,* Scribner, New York, 1902.

PINERO, Arthur Wing, *Robert Louis Stevenson as a Dramatist* N.P. printed for the Dramatic Museum of Columbia University, 1914.

POPE-HENNESSY, James, *Robert Louis Stevenson,* J. Cape, London, 1974.

PRIDEAUX, Col. W.F., C.S.I., *A Bibliography of the Works of Robert Louis Stevenson,* Rev. ed. Hollings, London, 1917.

—*Stevenson at Hyères,* Privately printed, 1912.

QUILLER-COUCH, Arthur Thomas, *Adventures in Criticsm,* G.P. Putnam's Sons, New York, 1925.

RALEIGH, Walter, *Robert Louis Stevenson,* Arnold, London, 1895.

RANKIN, Nicolas, *Dead Man's Chest,* Faber and Faber, London, Boston, 1987.

RATHER, Louis, *Stevenson's Silver Ship,* Rather Press, Oakland, 1973.

REARDEN, Timothy, "Favoring Female Conventionalism", Overland Monthly, vol. 1, no. 1, July 1868.

REINHARDT, Richard, *Treasure Island,* Scrimshaw Press, San Francisco, 1973.

RICE, Richard Ashley, *Robert Louis Stevenson,* Bobbs-Merrill Co., Indianapolis, 1916.

—*Journey to Upolu,* Dodd, Mead, New York, 1974.

RICKLEFS, Roger, *The Mind of Robert Louis Stevenson,* Thomas Yoseloff, New York, London, 1963.

RIVENBURGH, Eleanor, "Stevenson in Hawaii", *Bookman,* New York, October-November-December 1917.

—*Robert Louis Stevenson's Handwriting,* Edwin J. Beinecke Collection, Privately printed, New York, 1940.

ROSENBACH, A.S.W., *Catalogue of the Robert Louis Stevenson Collection in the Widener Library,* Harvard University, Privately printed, 1913.

ROSS, Nancy W., *Westward the Women,* 1945.

RUSSAILH, Albert Bernard de, *Journal de voyage en Californie à l'èpoque de la ruée vers l'or,* A. Montaigne, Paris, 1980.

RYAN, J. Tighe, "A Gossip about Robert Louis Stevenson", *The Antipodean,* Sydney, 1894.

SADLER, Fernande, *L'Hôtel Chevillon et les artistes de Grez-sur-Loing.* (Fontaine-bleau no date.)

SAFRONI-MIDDLETON, A., "A New View of R.L.S.", *John o' London's Weekly,* 20 January 1950.

—*Sailor and Beachcomber,* Grant Richards Ltd., London, 1915.

SANCHEZ, Nellie Van de Grift, "Some Stevensons Legends", *Overland Monthly,* January 1930.

SCHWOB, Marcel, "R.L.S.", *New Review* February 1895.

—*Voyage à Samoa,* Ombres, 1990.

SEGALEN, Victor, *Les Immémoriaux,* Le Seuil, Paris, 1979.

SHIPMAN, Louis Evan, "Stevenson's First Landing in New York", *Bookbuyer,* February 1896.

SILVERMAN, Ruth, *San Francisco Observed: A Photogrpahic Portfolio from 1850 to the Present,* Chroncile Books, San Francisco, 1986.

SIMPSON, Eve Blantyre, *Robert Louis Stevenson,* Luce, London, 1906.

—*The Robert Louis Stevenson Originals,* Foulis, Edinburgh, 1912.

—*Robert Louis Stevenson's Edinburgh Day,* Hodder and Stoughton, London, 1914.

SITWELL, Sir Osbert, *Great Morning,* Little, Brown and Co., Boston, 1947.

SLOCUM, Captain Joshua, *Sailing Alone Around the World,* Low, London, 1900.

Smith, George Horace, *History of Comstock Lode,* 1943.

SMITH, Helena Huntington, "Pioneers in Petticoats", *Am. Heritage,* 10, no. 2, 1959.

SMITH, Janet Adam, *Henry James and Robert Louis Stevenson,* Rupert Hart-Davis, London, s.d.

—*R.L. Stevenson,* Great Lives Series, Duckworth, London, 1937.

STARR, Kevin, *Americans and the California Dream, 1850–1915*, Oxford University Press, New York, 1973.

—*Inventing the Dream*, Oxford Univesity Press, New York, 1985.

—*Land's End*, McGraw Hill, New York, 1979.

STEPHEN, Leslie, *Studies of a Biographer*, Duckworth and Co., London, 1898.

STERN, G.B., *He Wrote Treasure Island*, Heinemann, London, 1954.

—*No Son of Mine*, Cassell, London, 1948.

STEUART, John A., *the Cap of Youth*, J.B. Lippincott Co., Philadelphia, 1927.

—*Letters to Living Authors*, Sampson, Low, Marston, Searle and Rivington, London, 1890.

—*Robert Louis Stevenson*, Little, Brown and Co., Boston, 1924.

—*Robert Louis Stevenson: Man and Writer*, 2 vol., Low, London, 1924.

STEVENSON, Fanny Van de Grift Osbourne, *The Cruise of the Janet Nichol Among the South Sea Islands*, Ghatto and Windus, London, 1915.

—"Too Many Birthdays", *St. Nicholas*, July 1878.

—"The Warlock's shadow", *Belgravia*, June 1881.

—"Miss Pringle's Neighbors", *Scribner's*, June 1887.

—"The Nixie", *Scribner's*, March 1888.

—"The Half-White", *Scribner's*, March 1891.

—"The Far West", *The Queen*, 31, March 5, April 1894.

—"A Backwoods Childwood", manuscript collection of Yale University.

—"Kept at the Undertaker", manuscript collection of Yale University.

—"Under Sentence of the Law", *McClure's*, June 1893.

—"Some Letters of Mrs. R.L. Stevenson and One from Henry James", *The Empire Review*, London, March-April 1924.

—"More Letters of Mrs. Robert Louis Stevenson", ed. *Scribner's Magazine*, New York, April 1924.

—et Robert Louis, *The Dynamiter*, Longmans Green, London, 1885.

—*Our Samoan Adventure*, Charles Neider, ed. Weidenfeld and Nicholson, London, 1956.

STEVENSON, Margaret Isabella Balfour, *From Saranac to the Marquesas and Beyond*, Methuen, London, 1903.

—*Letters from Samoa*, Methuen, London, 1906.

—*Stevenson's Baby Book*, John Henry Nash, San Francisco, 1922.

STEVENSON, Robert Louis, *Canaux et Rivières*, Encre, 1985.

—*The Complete Short Stories:* The Centenary Edition, Mainstream Publications, Edinburgh, 1993.

—*The Amateur Emigrant; Across the Plains; The Silverado Squatters*, Scribner's, New York, 1907.

—*An Inland Voyage, Travels with a Donkey*, and other stories, Collins, London, 1956.

—*The Black Arrow; The Misadventures of John Nicholson; The Body-Snatcher*, Scribner's, New York, 1907 (from The Novels and Tales of Robert Louis Stevenson, *Works*, vol. 8)

—*Catriona*, A sequel to *Kidnapped;* being the memoirs of the further adventures of David Balfour, Oxford University Press, London, 1947.

—A *Child's Garden of Verses*, with pictures by Tasha Tudor, Oxford University Press, New York, 1947.

—*Dr. Jekyll & Mr. Hyde*, with Other Great Tales of Mystery and Adventure, Platt & Munk, Publishers, New York, 1965. (Includes "Markheim," "The Bottle Imp," "A Lodging for the Night," "The Beach at Falesa," "The Isle of Voices.")

—*Fables*, Scribner's, New York, 1916.

—A *Footnote to History;* Eight Years of Troubles in Samoa, Scribner's, New York, 1895.

—*From Scotland to Silverado*, ed. James D. Hart, The Belknap Press of Harvard University Press, Cambridge, MA, 1966.

—*Henry James and Robert Louis Stevenson, a Record of Friendship and Criticism.* ed. Janet Adam Smith, Hart Davis, London, 1948.

—*Kidnapped*, Scribner's Sons, New York, (1913) 1982.

—*Island Landfalls: Reflections from the South Seas*, ed. Jenni Calder, Canongate, Edinburgh, 1987.

—*The Lantern-Bearers*, and Other Essays, ed. Jeremy Treglown, Farrar Straus Giroux, New York, 1988. (includes "In the Latin Quarter - I: A Ball at Mr. Eisinaire's; II A Studio of Ladies," "Forest Notes: Idle Hours," "On Falling in Love," "An Apology for Idlers," "Truth of Intercourse," "The Old Pacific Capital."

—*Some Letters*, ed. Lloyd Osbourne, Methuen, London, 1914.

—*The Master of Ballantrae*, Scribner's Sons, New York, 1922.

—Prince Otto; Island Nights' Entertainment; Father Damian

—*The Scottish Stories and Essays*, ed. Kenith Gelder, Edinburgh University Press, 1989.

—*New Arabian Nights*, Heinemann, London, 1924.

—*St. Ives:* Being the Adventures of a French Prisoner in England, Scribner's Sons, New York, 1914.

—*The Strange Case of Dr. Jekyll & Mr. Hyde* and other Stories, Penguin Books, Harmondsworth-New York, 1981. (Series: The Penguin English Library)

—*Treasure Island*, Grosset & Dunlap, New York, 1947.

—*Weir of Hermiston*, and Other Stories, ed. Paul Binding, Penguin Books, Harmondsworth-New York, 1979. (The Penguin English Library)

—*The Wrecker; The Wrong Box; The Ebb Tide*, with Lloyd Osbourne, Scribner's Sons, New York, 1923.

—*Collected Poems*, Janet Adam Smith, ed. Hart Davis, London, 1950.

—"In the Latin Quarter-I, A Ball at Mr. Elsinare's", from *London Magazine*, 10 February 1877.

—*Vailima Letters to Sidney Colvin*, ed. Methuen, London, 1895.

—*Letters to His Family and Friends*, Sidney Colvin, ed. Methuem, London, 1899.

—*Letters to Charles Baxter*, De Lancey Ferguson and Marshall Waingrow, eds. Oxford University Press, 1956.

—*Prayers Written at Vailima*, Chatto and Windus, London, 1895.

—*Some Letters*, Lloyd Osbourne, ed. Methuen, London, 1914.

—and Fanny, *The Hanging Juge, a play,* Privately printed, London, 1914.
—*Stevenson,* Edition by Francis Lacassin, Bouquins, Laffont, 1984.
—*Les Aventures de David Balfour,* Edition by Francis Lacassin, 10/18, 2 vol., 1976.
—*Le Creux de la vague,* Edition by Francis Lacassin, 10/18, 1977.
—*Dans les mers du Sud,* Edition by Francis Lacassin, Folio, 1983.
—*La Flèche noire,* Edition by Francis Lacassin, 10/18, 1983.
—*La France que j'aime,* Edition by Francis Lacassin, 10/18, 1978.
—*Le Trafiquant d'épaves,* Edition by Francis Lacassin, 10/18, 2 vol., 1976.
—*A Travers l'Ecosse,* Edition by Michel Le Bris, Complexe, Bruxelles, 1992.
—*Ceux de Falesa,* Edition by Michel Le Bris, La Table ronde, Paris, 1990.
—*Essai sur l'art de la fiction,* Edition by Michel Le Bris, La Table ronde, Paris, 1988.
—*Janet la revenante,* Edition by Michel Le Bris, Complexe, Bruxelles, 1992.
—*Les Nouvelles Mille et Une Nuits,* Edition by Michel Le Bris, Phoebus, 3 vol., Paris, 1992.
—*Robert Louis Stevenson—Henry James, une amitié littéraire,* Edition by Michel Le Bris, Verdier, 1987.
—*La Route de Silverado,* Edition by Michel Le Bris, Phoebus, Paris, 1987.
—*Charles d'Orléans,* Gallimard, Paris, 1992.
—*La Magicienne,* Rivages, Paris, 1991.
—*Olalla,* Rivages, Paris, 1991.
—*Will du Moulin,* Allia, Paris, 1992.
STEVENSON, Thomas, *Christianity Confirmed by Jewish and Heathen Testimony,* Adam and Charles Black, Edinburgh, 1884.
STEWART, George R., "The Real Teasure Island", *University of California Chronicle,* april 1926.
STODDARD, Charles Warren, *Exits and Entrances,* Lothrop Publishing Co., Boston, s.d.
—"Stevenson's Monterey", *National Magazine,* december 1906.
STRONG, Austin. "His Oceanic Majesety's Goldfish", *The Atlantic Monthly,* Boston, may 1944.
—"The Most Unforgettable Character I've Met", *The Reader's Digest,* Pleasantville, New York, March 1946.
STUBBS, Laura, *Stevenson's Shrine,* Alexander Mering, London, 1903.
SUTRO, Adolph, *Biography, 1830–1898.*
SWEARINGEN, Roger G., *The Early Literary Career of Robert Louis Stevenson,* Yale University, New Haven, 1970.
—*The Prose Writings of Robert Louis Stevenson,* Archon Books, Hamden, Conn., 1980.
SWINGLEHURST, Edmund, *San Francisco,* Mayflower Books, New York, 1979.
SWINNERTON, Frank, *Robert Louis Stevenson, Secker, London, 1914.*
—Jenni Calder, University Press, Edinburgh, 1981.
SYMONDS, John Addington, *John Addington Symonds,* John Murray, London, 1903.
—*Letters and Papers,* Murray, London, 1923
—*Our Life in the Swiss Highlands,* Black, London, 1907.

TAYLOR, Albert P., *Under Hawaian Skies*, Advertiser Publishing Co., Honolulu, 1926.

THEROUX, Paul, *The Happy Isles of Oceania*, Hamish Hamilton, London, 1992.

THOMPSON, Francis, *The Real Robert Louis Stevenson*, New York University Publishers, 1959.

TILDEN, Freeman, *Following the Frontier with F. Jay Haynes*, 1964.

TRIGGS, W.H., "R.L. Stevenson as a Samoan Chief", *Cassell's Family Magazine*, February 1895.

TRUDEAU, Edward Livingston, *An Autobiography*, Doubleday, Page and Co., New York, 1916.

TWAIN, Mark, *Mark Twain's Autobiography*, Harper and Brothers, New York, 1924.

VAN NOSTRAND, Jeanne Skinner, *The First Hundred Years of Paintings in California, 1775–1875*, J. Howell-Books, San Francisco, 1980.

—*San Francisco, 1806–1906, in Contemporary Paintings, Drawings, and Watercolors*, Books Club of California, San Francisco, 1976.

WALLACE, William, "The Life and Limitations of Stevenson", *Scottish Review*, January 1900.

—"Scotland, Stevenson, and Mr. Henly," New Liberal Review, February 1902.

WARD, Harriet S., *Prairie Schooner Lady: Journal, 1853*, Ward G. and Florence S. DeWitt, eds., 1959.

WEISBUCH, Robert, *American Literature and British Influence in the Age of Emerson*, University of Chicago Press, 1986.

WENDT, Albert, *Leaves of the Banyan Tree*, Penguin Books, New York, 1986.

—*The Birth and Death of the Miracle Man*, Penguin Books, New York, 1987.

WILLIAMS, George III, *The Redlight Ladies of Virginia City*, Tree by the River Pub., Riverside, Cal., 1984.

WILLIAMSON, Kennedy, *W.E. Henley*, Harold Shaylor, London, (no date).